CURRENT APPROACHES IN DRAMA THERAPY

CURRENT APPROACHES IN DRAMA THERAPY

Edited by

PENNY LEWIS, Ph.D., RDT-BCT

and

DAVID READ JOHNSON, Ph.D., RDT-BCT

Published and Distributed Throughout the World by

CHARLES C THOMAS • PUBLISHER, LTD.
2600 South First Street
Springfield, Illinois 62704

ISBN 0-398-07082-2 (cloth)
ISBN 0-398-07083-0 (paper)

Library of Congress Catalog Card Number: 00-032612

With THOMAS BOOKS *careful attention is given to all details of manufacturing and design. it is the Publisher's desire to present books that are satisfactory as to their physical qualities and artistic possibilities and appropriate for their particular use.* THOMAS BOOKS *will be true to those laws of quality that assure a good name and good will.*

Printed in the United States of America
SR-R-3

Library of Congress Cataloging-in-Publication Data

Current approaches in drama therapy / edited by Penny Lewis and David Read Johnson.
p. cm.
Includes bibliographical references and index.
ISBN 0-398-07082-2 (cloth) -- ISBN 0-398-07083-0 (pbk.)
1. Psychodrama. 2. Drama--Therapeutic use. I. Lewis, Penny. II. Johnson, David Read.
RC489.P7 C86 2000
616.89'1523--dc21

00-032612

The cover Alchemical Image comes from: Fontana, David. (1993). *The Secret Language of Symbols*. San Francisco: Chronicle Books.

The book is dedicated to our students and clients who continuously help reveal, deepen, and expand our understanding of drama therapy.

CONTRIBUTORS

Sherry Diamond, MA, RDT is Director of Resource Development, Clinical Programs/Training for STOP-GAP. She has extensive experience in drama therapy, curriculum development and administration including directing treatment, inpatient and community-based programs for special populations. A member of NADT since 1986, she has served as the Chair of the association's Membership Committee.

Pamela Barragar-Dunne, PhD, RDT-BCT is a board certified master teacher trainer in drama therapy and serves as the Director of The Drama Therapy Institute in L.A. She is a professor at California State University in Los Angeles and is a past president of the National Association for Drama Therapy. She has published several drama therapy activities workbooks. Her latest book is the *Double Stick Tape: Poetry, Drama and Narrative as Therapy for Adolescents.*

John Bergman, MA, RDT-MT is a master teacher in drama therapy and the director of Geese Theater Company. He has worked in prisons for 20 years both nationally and internationally. He currently has two Geese-linked companies in Romania and England.

Dale Richard Buchanan, PhD, TEP, CGP is a Trainer, Educator, and Practitioner certified by the American Board of Examiners in Psychodrama, Sociometry and Group Psychotherapy. He is the Director of Creative Arts Therapies for the Washington D.C. Commission on Mental Health Services (formerly St. Elizabeth's Hospital).

Renee Emunah, PhD, RDT-BCT is a board certified master teacher trainer in drama therapy and the Founder and Director of the Drama Therapy Graduate Program at CIIS in San Francisco. She is a past president of the National Association for Drama Therapy and the author of *Acting for Real: Drama Therapy Process, Techniques and Performance.* She is on the editorial board of the Arts in Psychotherapy and a recipient of the Gertrude Schattner award for Outstanding Contribution to the Field of Drama Therapy.

Diana Feldman, MA, RDT-MT is a registered drama therapist master teacher status who has developed a methodology for drama therapy. She also founded ENACT, a not-for-profit organization in New York City in 1987 which continues to use her methodology. Ms. Feldman teaches nationally and has published *The ENACT Workbook* and curriculum.

Antonina Garcia, EdD, TEP, RDT-BCT is a Trainer, Educator, and Practitioner certified by the American Board of Examiners in Psychodrama, Sociometry and Group Psychotherapy.

She is also a Registered Drama Therapist and Board Certified Trainer and Master Teacher. She is a full professor at Brookdale Community College and is Co-coordinator of the Creative Arts in Therapeutic Settings option to the A.A.S. Degree in Human Services.

Steve Harvey, PhD, RDT, ADTR, RPT/S is a licensed psychologist currently working with children and families at the Navy Hospital in Sigonella, Sicily. He is registered by the national dance, drama, and play therapy associations and is a frequent contributor to both national and international conferences. He has helped pioneer family play therapy and continues to present training in this work throughout the United States and Europe.

Eleanor Irwin, PhD, RDT is a founding member of the National Association for Drama Therapy and a graduate of the Child and Adult Program of the Pittsburgh Psychoanalytic Institute where she is on the faculty. She has a psychoanalytic private practice in Pittsburgh, Pennsylvania.

David Read Johnson, PhD, RDT-BCT is a board certified master teacher trainer, one of the founders of the National Association for Drama Therapy and a recipient of the Gertrude Schattner award for Outstanding Contribution to the Field of Drama Therapy. He is currently the Director of the Institutes for the Arts in Psychotherapy, New York, NY, the Director of the Institute for Developmental Transformations, and the Co- Director of Post Traumatic Stress Center, in New Haven, Connecticut. He is an Associate Clinical Professor at the Department of Psychiatry, Yale University School of Medicine. He is the former Editor-in -Chief of the *Arts in Psychotherapy,* the former Chairperson of the National Coalition for the Arts Therapy Associations and the former president of the National Association for Drama Therapy. He has authored *Essays on the Creative Arts Therapies: Imaging the Birth of a Profession* and is the co-editor of this text.

Fara Sussman Jones, MA, RDT is a registered drama therapist and the program coordinator at ENACT (Educational Network of Artists in Creative Theater). She works with at-risk children and adolescents, teachers, parents, and administrators in the New York City School System.

Don Laffoon, MA, RDT-BCT is the chair of the National Coalition of Arts Therapies Association and the past president of the National Association for Drama Therapy. He is a co-founder/Executive Director of STOP-GAP, dedicated to using the STOP-GAP method to promote personal growth and healing through drama therapy, interactive theatre and training at STOP-GAP Institute.

Robert Landy, PhD, RDT-BCT is a board certified master teacher trainer and the founder and Director of the Drama Therapy Program at New York University and an international trainer and educator of drama and play therapists. He is a recipient of the Gertrude Schattner award for Outstanding Contribution to the Field of Drama Therapy. He is a prolific researcher and author of scholarly books and articles as well as a theatre artist and musician. Among his books are *Drama Therapy Concepts, Theories and Practices, Persona and Performance,* and *Essays in Drama Therapy–The Double Life.* His latest book, *How We See God,* is a study of children's images of spirituality.

Penny Lewis, PhD, ADTR, RDT-BCT is a board certified master teacher trainer in drama therapy and Senior Faculty at Antioch University's Antioch New England Graduate School. She has authored several books, among them: *Creative Transformation: The Healing Power of the Arts.* The former Chair of Alternate Route Training, she authored and edited *The Alternate Route Training Handbook* for the National Association for Drama Therapy. A former Special Guest Editor for the *Arts in Psychotherapy,* she is the co-editor of this text and has lectured, presented, and published internationally since 1970. She is the Co-director of the Certificate Program in Transpersonal Drama Therapy for both local and distance learners and has a private practice in Amesbury, Massachusetts.

Saphira Linden, MA, RDT-BCT is a board certified master teacher trainer in drama therapy and the artistic director/drama therapist-trainer of Boston's Omega Theater since 1966. She founded the Omega Arts Network for Artist Healers. She is a management consultant and has been a meditation teacher/guide in The Sufi Order since 1971. She is the Co-director of the Certificate Program in Transpersonal Drama Therapy for both local and distance learners and has a private practice in Jamaica Plain, Massachusetts.

Jo Salas, MA CMT is a music therapist and the co-founder of Playback Theatre. She teaches the playback approach internationally. Her book, *Improvising Real-Life: Personal Story in Playback Theatre* has been translated into three languages. Her second book, *The Space Room: A Story of Children, Madness, and the Arts* is about using music and playback theatre with children in residential treatment.

Stephen Snow, PhD, RDT/BCT is associate professor of creative arts therapies, Coordinator of the new Graduate Drama Therapy Program and Director of the Center for the Arts in Human Development at Concordia University in Montreal. He is on the editorial board of the *Arts in Psychotherapy* and has published on drama therapy in that journal as well as in *Themes in Drama, Psychology and the Performing Arts* and *Dramatic Approaches to Brief Therapy.*

Patricia Sternberg, PhD, RDT-BCT is a recipient of the Gertrude Schattner award for her Outstanding Contribution to the Field of Drama Therapy. She is a full professor in the Theatre Department at Hunter College in New York City and heads their Developmental Drama Program. She is a playwright with over 25 plays produced and/or published and the author of eight books including *Sociodrama: Who's in Your Shoes?* with Antonina Garcia. Her latest book: *The Theatre for Conflict Resolution,* was recently published. She is a well-known trainer, presenter and workshop leader, having presented both nationally and internationally. Sternberg is a practicing drama therapist and has worked with a variety of populations in both psychiatric and educational facilities.

PREFACE

CURRENT APPROACHES IN DRAMA THERAPY attempts to fulfill a need for a comprehensive introduction to the various drama therapy theoretical models and techniques that are being utilized and taught in the United States and Canada. Although several volumes have been published describing the drama therapy approaches in England and the Netherlands, surprisingly, there has been no similar publication in the United States.

The purpose of this book is to begin to provide the field of drama therapy with a theoretical body of knowledge through the individual scrutiny of major frames of reference and through a comparative analysis in which the essence of each approach is gleaned and commonalities formulated into a fundamental conceptualization of drama therapy.

Senior professionals and board certified teacher-trainers have continued to ask for a researched integrated body of knowledge in the field of drama therapy. Although all concurred that there are core foundational concepts and postulates, no publication to date had brought all the approaches together in an organized manner.

The approaches were selected on the basis of the fact that they are taught in universities, institutes and mentorship relationships, have been presented at national conferences and published in professional publications. Each of the 16 approaches is authored either by their founders or key proponents of the method in the field of drama therapy. Each author accepted the discipline of working within a predetermined format; an outline addressing historical genesis, theoretical model and case example to allow the reader to compare, contrast and assess in an organized manner. Important to note is that these editors do not presume that this book includes all approaches extant in the field, nor were we able to include the work of many gifted clinicians who have yet to articulate a particular model or approach. Further editions will continue the process of expanding the body of knowledge in the field.

In the first section of the book, we begin with a chapter discussing the history of drama therapy in the United States and Canada, to provide a temporal context for this rapidly growing field. A second chapter discusses issues related to theory building in the health care professions, identifying important components of a theoretical model such as frame of reference and the establishment of validity.

Section II holds 16 specific approaches to drama therapy. Section III addresses the comparative analysis. The first chapter delineates the qualitative research method employed in this study, and the last chapter identifies the common fundamental conceptual structures of these major frames of reference in drama therapy and delineates the current consensual body of knowledge in the field.

A glossary of key concepts utilized by the approaches and subject index follows.

We are aware that this volume is the beginning of a continuous professional challenge: to articulate the similarities and differences among various approaches within one therapeutic discipline. It is our belief that this effort is long overdue, and required in order for the profession of drama therapy to mature.

Penny Lewis and David Read Johnson, Editors

ACKNOWLEDGMENTS

Several years ago Eleanor Irwin began the process of inviting contributors to a comprehensive drama therapy textbook. Her vision provided the foundation for this book. Additionally, the Board of Directors of the National Association for Drama Therapy, particularly Toddy Richmond, Linda Cook, Don Laffoon and Alice Forrester along with many Board Certified Trainers and Master Teachers paved the way for this book through their calls for a delineated body of knowledge in drama therapy and their support to back it up. Liann Marie provided immensely competent editorial support for which we are deeply grateful.

Finally and most importantly, we wish to thank the contributing authors who graciously and enthusiastically joined with us in the preparation of this volume.

CONTENTS

SECTION III: COMPARATIVE ANALYSIS

CURRENT APPROACHES
IN
DRAMA THERAPY

Section I

INTRODUCTION

Chapter 1

THE HISTORY AND DEVELOPMENT OF THE FIELD OF DRAMA THERAPY IN THE UNITED STATES AND CANADA

DAVID READ JOHNSON

THE CREATOR

IN THE BEGINNING, there was Moreno. This visionary single-handedly discovered drama therapy in the 1920s. His theatre of spontaneity, use of improvisation, and theatrical sensibility make him the original drama therapist (Moreno, 1946). Though there were others who used drama as therapy (including de Sade, Evreinov, Iljine–see an excellent review by Phil Jones, 1996), none had any substantial influence on the future of the field since there was no transmission of their work to others. Moreno, on the other hand, did nothing less than expand forever the boundaries of what was possible in psychotherapy.

Moreno trained as a psychiatrist, and emigrated to this country in the early 1930s. While he was at St. Elizabeth's Hospital in Washington, he influenced Marian Chace, the originator of dance therapy, as well as many art and music therapists. In New York during the 1950s, hundreds of therapists attended his workshops and presentations, many of whom later became leaders of the humanistic and encounter movement (e.g., Fritz Perls–Gestalt Therapy; Eric Berne–Transactional Analysis; Arthur Janov–Primal Scream).

Moreno's writings provide a strong foundation for drama therapy, and for some time it seemed that no more needed to be said: How could anyone imagine a drama therapy that was not Moreno's? However, in the late 1960s, a new group of theatre artists entered the mental health field–partly as a result of the cultural changes evoked by the Vietnam war, and partly due to the expansion of art, music, and dance therapies. As these "theatre people" encountered psychodrama, they found it wanting. Because Moreno had intended to influence his psychiatric colleagues, he had encapsulated his methods into a structured form, reminiscent of an enacted psychiatric interview. As a result, his method began to stray from the aesthetics of its theatrical roots. Increasingly, his audience had become mental health professionals rather than theatre people, so theatre training was not incorporated into the required training of a psychodramatist. A breach had developed between psychodrama's theatrical roots and its actual practice, a breach into which a number of drama therapy pioneers leapt.

THE TITANS

There were five of them. Each contributed in a special way to the creation of the field of drama therapy. Though by the 1960s there were many people practicing some form of drama therapy, these five had an influence that reached out beyond their immediate areas, inspiring others to move toward drama therapy. Each one embraced this new entity of drama therapy; without them, drama therapy as a profession would never have been born.

Eleanor Irwin received her degree in speech therapy, but found herself at the Pittsburgh Child Guidance Clinic under the tutelage and mentorship of Marvin Shapiro, a gifted psychiatrist who encouraged Ellie and other future creative arts therapists. Out of that clinic came Judith Rubin, Penny Lewis, as well as Ellie, all who have become leaders in their respective fields. Ellie Irwin published the first articles on drama therapy in the early 1970s, and soon they found their way into the hands of other drama therapists, inspiring us greatly (Irwin et al., 1972; Irwin, 1977). Her work was characterized by careful, rigorous clinical descriptions of cases, clear articulation of a theoretical base, and a delight in the play of children. Her psychoanalytic background (she later become a psychoanalyst) served her well in rooting her work in a widely accepted area of scholarship. As a link between drama therapists and the psychiatric community, Ellie Irwin was far ahead of everyone else in her integration of these perspectives. Her articles provided deep reassurance that we had the capacity to stand up to the scrutiny of psychiatrists.

Marian (Billy) Lindkvist founded the Sesame Institute in 1964 in London, which integrated psychiatric principles and research with movement, art, and drama (Wethered, 1973). She established a full-time course in drama therapy in 1976. She made several trips to the United States during which I and others were profoundly impacted. Marian was influenced by the British tradition of drama-in-education of Brian Way (1967) and Peter Slade (1954), in which guided play was used to explore topics of both social and personal importance. She extended their work with children to the elderly, adult psychiatric patients, people from other cultures, and even "normal" people (Pearson, 1996). Sesame had a serious research interest, and one of the first outcome studies in drama therapy was done with chronic schizophrenic adults with Sesame clinicians (Nitsun et al., 1974). Though Slade had written about drama therapy much earlier, he always had his feet planted on educational soil. Billy took a bold step over the line, committing herself entirely to the therapeutic arena.

Sue Jennings wrote *Remedial Drama* in 1973, one of the first books on drama therapy. She later started a course in drama therapy at St. Albans, and helped to create the British Association of Drama Therapy in 1977. Since then she has developed training programs throughout Europe, Greece, and Israel, written numerous books and journal articles. She has been the Johnny Appleseed of our profession, always traveling, sewing seeds of inspiration and wisdom on her way. Sue also emerged from the drama-in-education tradition in England, though she has preserved the influence of the professional stage and the literature of Shakespeare in her practice. She also did much work on shamanic ritual, particularly in African cultures, which drew her to Jungian concepts of archetypal expression. She has remained a powerful influence on the professional development of drama therapy internationally. United States and Canadian drama therapists were well aware of her work, which provided a strong impetus to us as we gave birth to a new profession.

Richard Courtney was steeped in the drama-in-education tradition of Britain, but was able to extend the field far into psychology and psychotherapy in his book, *Play, Drama, and Thought,* which was published in 1968 and spurred many of us on. This book established once and for all the links between drama and psychology. He later helped Gert finish editing her book on drama therapy. Richard was a man of immense breadth of knowledge and interest, who effortlessly wove intellectual themes among fields of great diversity. He became fascinated by the potential of drama for personal growth–at first from an educational point of view, and then later from a psychotherapeutic point of view. The essence of a British gentleman, mediated by years of living and teaching in Canada, he brought an air of gentility, perspective, and worldliness to the beginnings of the drama therapy movement.

Gertrude Schattner spent much of World War II in Switzerland with her psychoanalyst husband. After the war, she used drama with concentration camp survivors. She came to this country and trained in the Karen Horney Clinic in psychotherapy. For years she taught drama and then drama therapy workshops and courses, settling in at Bellevue Hospital and Turtle Bay Music School in the 1960s. Her life mission was drama therapy. Trained professionally as an actress in Europe, even working with Otto Preminger in prewar Austria, she became influenced by Viola Spolin (1963) and creative drama approaches including improvisation. Her work grew out of theatre games, movement exercises, and improvisational role-playing. After the war she had developed a clear vision of drama therapy which she embraced without an ounce of misgiving. Though she was not a writer, she initiated the project of an edited book that brought all of us together, and was instrumental in bringing the Association into being. Her fiery commitment to the field was the match that lit the smoldering doubts of others, igniting us into action.

These were our Titans. Though few of them were friends, each cast a large shadow, providing a protective shade for the developing profession.

OUT OF THE DESERT

By 1974, many people were experimenting with what we now know as drama therapy: Don Laffoon at Stop Gap in Los Angeles; Janet Goodrich with addicts in Washington, DC; Margaret Ladd and Imagination Workshop in New York; Roz Wilder, Toddy Richman, Naida Weisberg and Rose Pavlow with children and the elderly; Elaine Portner with families; Barbara Sandberg at William Paterson College; Ray Gordon with ex-prisoners at the Cell Block Theatre; John Bergman at Geese Theatre; and myself at the Yale Psychiatric Institute. Numerous psychodramatists such as Adam Blatner, Nina Garcia, and Jonathan Fox were rediscovering the theatrical roots in Moreno's teachings. Others, such as Lynn Temple, Pat Sternberg, Pam Dunne, and Bernie Warren, were also winding their way from creative drama to drama therapy.

In 1974, with some trepidation I presented a workshop on "drama therapy" at the Psychodrama Conference. Previously, drama therapists cloaked their presentations under the term, "sociodrama." After my talk, a short, older woman approached me, and without speaking, handed me a slip of paper. It read: "Hello, I am Gert Schattner. I am editing a book on drama therapy. Would you like to contribute a chapter?" In this way she had been collecting drama therapists all across the country. Even then she had a clear idea that we needed an association, though she thought that a book should come first. During the years 1974 to 1978, due to the need to develop the book, a network began to develop among nascent drama therapists. Finally, in 1977, Gert Schnatter and I decided it was time to begin the association, so we invited Eleanor Irwin, Barbara Sandberg, and Ray Gordon to join us for a weekend in February, 1978, in order to decide if drama therapy existed as a separate field. Not surprisingly, in about five minutes we had decided that it did exist, and spent the rest of the weekend planning the association. We wondered how psychodramatists might respond to the announcement of our existence. We recognized that each of us had gained much from our psychodrama training, and had always been welcomed into the psychodrama world. Ultimately, we realized the anxiety was ours, not theirs. We then jointly invited 17 drama therapists to join us as a Steering Committee to form the National Association for Drama Therapy.

ESTABLISHING BOUNDARIES

The Steering Committee met in Ray Gordon's Cell Block Theatre in New York City on April 9, 1978. The meeting was audiotaped and transcribed, and even now makes fascinating reading for anyone interested in the issues we struggled with then. The Steering Committee met three more times, elected a Board of Directors, and incorporated the Association in June, 1979.

The main issue was boundaries. If we were carving a new territory out of theatre, creative drama, psychodrama, psychotherapy, and play therapy, where were the lines? We needed to define ourselves specifically enough to have a meaningful identity, but if we drew the lines too narrowly, few present would qualify! As each person spoke, their definition of drama therapy inevitably left someone else out, who then became upset. At one point in the proceedings, someone said, "If you insist that to be a drama therapist you have to have two years of clinical practice, then that immediately excludes me and it excludes other things that I'm doing with the people I work with." Another countered, "Until there are qualifications, we don't know if any of us are qualified to be drama therapists." "Are we talking only about severely disturbed people in hospitals or does drama therapy also include the normal neurotic?" There were people with little clinical training, people who had been drama therapists and were no longer working, and people with little theatre training. Everyone understood what a real drama therapist should be, but no one matched the description entirely! It certainly would have been silly to form an association that no one would be allowed to join, but that is how we often made ourselves feel during those fretful meetings.

The Steering Committee was an effective transitional structure in which to begin the sorting out process. Fundamentally, people who were there for more peripheral reasons dropped out, while those who found themselves nearer the center of an emerging vision, remained. Though there was tremendous dissension and distress, we emerged without a major split in the organization at its birth. Gert became the first president, and I became the vice-president. Ironically, the book that had pulled us together was not published until two years after the association was incorporated (Schattner & Courtney, 1981).

ESTABLISHING LEADERSHIP

The next three years were a period of establishing the initial leadership and control of the organization among the different interests represented on the steering committee and in the field at large.

The view that the organization should be a formal one, with standards, in compliance with the structures of other arts therapy associations, versus a more entrepreneurial, albeit nonprofit, model was now played out within the Board. The need to remain open to new members and not be too exclusive was paramount in order to facilitate an energetic recruitment. How could this be done without inviting too much diversity that might fragment the organization? In the beginning, the more clinical, psychiatric values represented most by Ellie and myself came to dominate the Board. Later, as basic standards had been established, a need for recruitment of new members and integration of related people led to a need for finding ways of being more flexible.

The Board proceeded to establish standards of practice, registration, grandparenting, and ethical guidelines. As each standard was discussed, the fears that a new boundary was being erected that would eliminate people had to be dealt with. There were esteemed practitioners and authors who for one reason or another did not satisfy one or more of the requirements, or, alternatively, practitioners who did qualify but had not chosen to join us. Conflicts within the Board leadership were usually generated by these concerns. A great deal of elbow grease was used to navigate through these difficult personal and political waters during these early years. Fortunately, no major breaks occurred.

ESTABLISHING PROGRAMS

Meanwhile, two Masters Degree programs were being established by two leaders in the field, neither of whom was a part of the founding group: Robert Landy and Renee Emunah. Robert Landy began the drama therapy program in the Educational Theatre department at New York University in 1982. Renee founded a drama therapy program in the Psychology Department at Antioch University West in San Francisco in 1983 (the program has since moved to the California Institute of Integral Studies). Within a few years it became apparent that the future of the field was dependent upon these two programs, and others to be established. For the first time, in addition to independent pioneers each of whom had invented drama therapy, we now had students who were asking questions such as: what is our body of knowledge?

The very act of establishing a Masters Degree program raises the question: what are we teaching? We had barely begun to share our different perspectives on drama therapy; barely decided that it was not psychodrama, and we were supposed to have a curriculum based on a body of knowledge for our students! What proportion of courses should be psychology or psychotherapy-based? What drama therapy techniques should be taught, or could be taught? Should psychodrama be taught? How much previous theatre training should be required, and how much ongoing performance or theatre work should be integrated into the Masters? What about internships, and jobs beyond internships? Generally, neither program had enough money to hire many full-time drama therapy faculty, or invite many visiting drama therapists to teach, leaving their programs vulnerable to a lack of diversity. The Association's role was to develop standards of training, evaluate, and finally approve Masters programs without unnecessarily constraining them. Too vigorous an approach might strangle the very beginnings of our own profession! Despite these challenges, there was good communication and support among all involved to encourage the growth of these two programs. For example, with input from the two program directors, the standards for approval of graduate programs were implemented in 1986 with a strong consensus.

REACHING OUT

Development of professional standards and masters programs, as well as furthering our networking through national conferences, continued during the period 1982–1985. We became active in the efforts of the newly formed National Coalition of Arts Therapy Associations, becoming a member in 1983, and participating in the first National Coalition of Arts Therapy Associations Conference in New York City in 1985. We found ourselves thrust among larger, more established creative arts therapy associations. Our eyes were opened to legislative, legal, ethical, and professional dilemmas. We began to understand that we were part of a larger effort. We found ourselves on committees studying state licensure of creative arts therapists, regulatory agencies, and third party insurance reimbursement. We were represented in state coalitions of creative arts therapists. We learned how other associations were dealing with malpractice issues, sexual indiscretions, taxes, and lawsuits. These experiences were both exhilarating and intimidating, given our level of development.

The conference also gave us the opportunity to integrate another awkward split between American and British drama therapists. Many of us had trained in England, and some, like Renee Enumah, Lynn Temple, and others, had worked directly with Marian Lindkvist or Sue Jennings. Increasingly, students and faculty from the States visited England for training, and both Sue Jennings and Marian Lindkvist presented at our conferences. Currently, there remains strong impetus for international participation in our conferences and educational events, and links with the growing international drama therapy community continue to grow.

SCHOOLS OF THOUGHT

By 1985, however, there still were only beginning efforts to conceptualize approaches to drama therapy. Until that time, one could identify a psychoanalytic approach, represented by Eleanor Irwin and her Pittsburgh colleagues; a psychodramatic approach, in which drama therapists applied Moreno's theories; a performance approach, based on theatrical traditions but without a significant theoretical basis; and a somewhat generic improvisation or theatre game approach, based on Viola Spolin's work. The years 1985 to the present have seen the development of more sophisticated schools of thought emerge within the drama therapy field. Robert Landy developed distancing theory and in his book, *Drama Therapy: Theory and Practice* (1986) provided the most in-depth conceptual framework for drama therapy yet published. Now he has deepened this perspective further with role method, which he has elaborated in *Persona and Performance: The Use of Role in Therapy and Everyday Life* (1993). As the head of the New York University Program, he has been very influential in creating a group of students who are grounded in the same approach. Renee Emunah has developed her Integrative Five Phase approach based on humanistic and developmental principles. Her model is generally viewed as the most sophisticated integration of various drama therapy techniques available today (Emunah, 1994). I have worked on an approach called Developmental Transformations (Johnson et al., 1996), which is now taught through a three-year postgraduate institute training program. Pam Dunne has developed a narrative approach to drama therapy based on postmodern theories (Dunne, 1992), and Jonathan Fox has greatly refined and extended his Playback Theatre model and training program (Fox, 1994).

Other models, most of which are included in this book, have also emerged and are increasingly being recognized in publications and conferences.

As the number of discrete models grows, it is critical that metaanalyses be performed to compare and contrast them on fundamental principles relevant to drama therapy. Penny Lewis begins this task in the final two chapters of this book. It is also important to understand these approaches from an historical standpoint, to know from what roots we have sprung. As a step in that direction, I have outlined the general family tree of drama therapy approaches in Figure 1.1. Certainly it should be stressed that this diagram is greatly simplified in order to identify the major traditions that have influenced the development of drama therapy. In actuality, most approaches have been influenced by many factors.

The turn of the century produced three movements that made possible the creation of drama therapy: psychotherapy, occupational therapy, and the acting training of Stanislavski.

Psychotherapy

Freud's contribution to the development of drama therapy cannot be underestimated. The very possibility of psychotherapy exists due to his insights, and concepts such as the unconscious, projection, transference, and symbolism, now taken for granted, are psychoanalytic in origin. Carl Jung, Melanie Klein, Anna Freud, Erik Erikson and Jacob Moreno developed his ideas further, producing the methods of active imagination, play therapy, and psychodrama, from which many branches of drama therapy emerge, as indicated in Figure 1.1. Margaret Mahler's developmental perspective and Donald Winnicott's notion of transitional space have also been very influential among drama therapists. Jungian influence has brought an interest in myths, rituals, culture, and spirituality into the psychotherapeutic arena, offering a welcoming environment for many drama therapists.

Occupational Therapy

Occupational therapy began as a profession at the turn of the century because nursing had become professionalized to the point that nurses no longer cared for the recreational needs of psychiatric patients. Occupational therapists used the arts in their work, and indeed there are several articles published early in the century entitled drama therapy. By the 1940s however, occupational therapists had also turned to more specialized pursuits, opening up the way for the new profession of "activities therapies," which then divided in the 1970s into recreation therapy and the creative arts therapies (Mosey, 1973). Drama therapy as a professional identity was formed largely through the transformations in these disciplines, and many drama therapists today are hired in job lines that go back in history to activity therapists, occupational therapists, and even nurses. Nevertheless, when the drama therapy association formed, the field of creative arts therapies was ready to accept it, and our profession was modeled after those of art, music, and dance therapies. In terms of employment, this was our initial home. Many drama therapists working in this tradition of psychiatric care have naturally adopted integrated and eclectic models, and it is of no surprise that the most sophisticated of these (Emunah, 1994) was developed in this context.

Theatre

Stanislavski was pivotal in linking theories of acting to the personal, psychological realm of experience (Stanislavski, 1961). From this

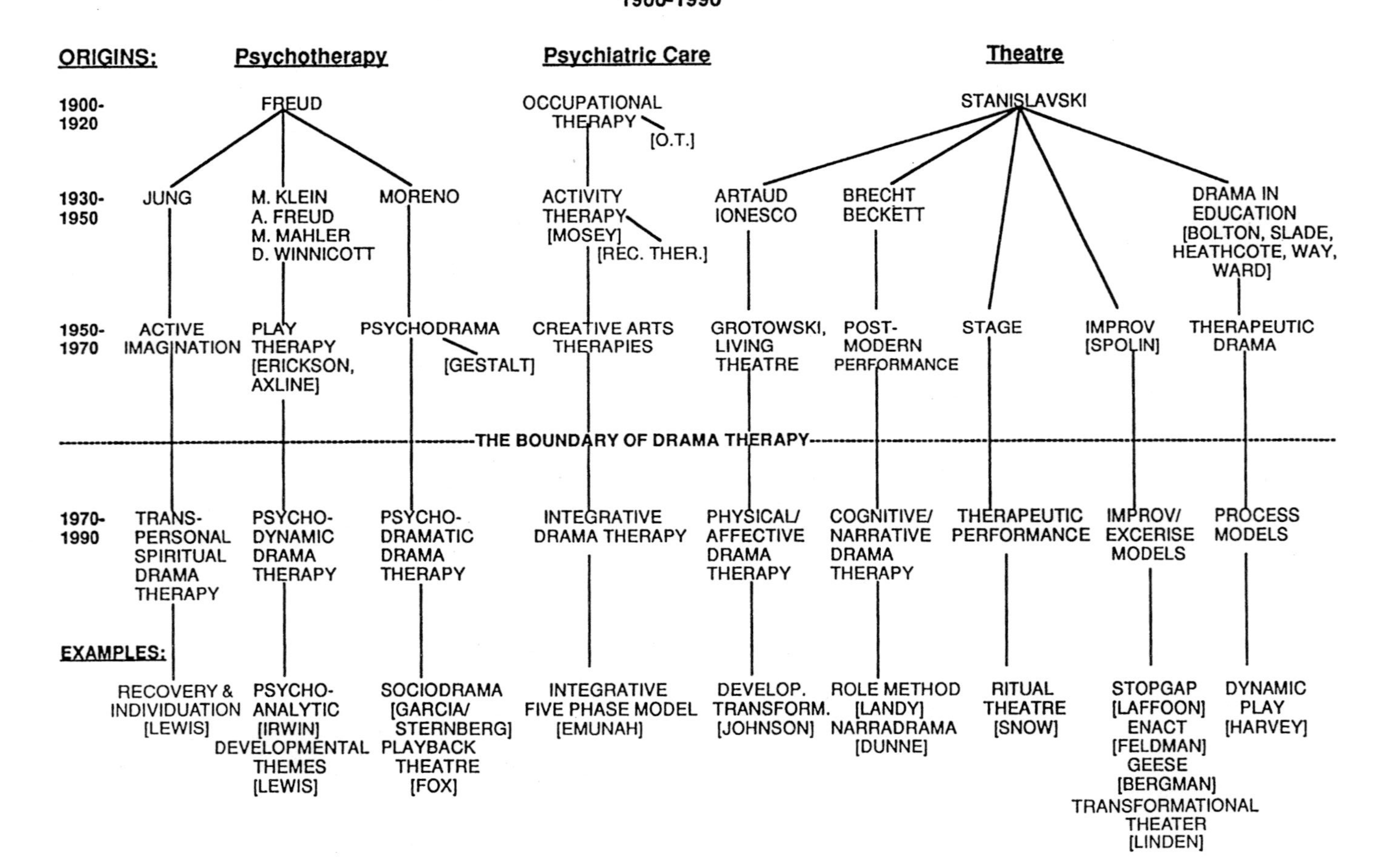

HISTORICAL ROOTS OF DRAMA THERAPY APPROACHES
1900-1990
ORIGINS:
Psychotherapy
Psychiatric Care
Theatre
1900-1920
FREUD
OCCUPATIONAL THERAPY
[O.T.]
STANISLAVSKI
1930-1950
JUNG
M. KLEIN
A. FREUD
M. MAHLER
D. WINNICOTT
MORENO
ACTIVITY THERAPY [MOSEY]
[REC. THER.]
ARTAUD IONESCO
BRECHT BECKETT
DRAMA IN EDUCATION [BOLTON, SLADE, HEATHCOTE, WAY, WARD]
1950-1970
ACTIVE IMAGINATION
PLAY THERAPY [ERICKSON, AXLINE]
PSYCHODRAMA
[GESTALT]
CREATIVE ARTS THERAPIES
GROTOWSKI, LIVING THEATRE
POST-MODERN PERFORMANCE
STAGE
IMPROV [SPOLIN]
THERAPEUTIC DRAMA
THE BOUNDARY OF DRAMA THERAPY
1970-1990
TRANS-PERSONAL SPIRITUAL DRAMA THERAPY
PSYCHO-DYNAMIC DRAMA THERAPY
PSYCHO-DRAMATIC DRAMA THERAPY
INTEGRATIVE DRAMA THERAPY
PHYSICAL/ AFFECTIVE DRAMA THERAPY
COGNITIVE/ NARRATIVE DRAMA THERAPY
THERAPEUTIC PERFORMANCE
IMPROV/ EXCERISE MODELS
PROCESS MODELS
EXAMPLES:
RECOVERY & INDIVIDUATION [LEWIS]
PSYCHO-ANALYTIC [IRWIN] DEVELOPMENTAL THEMES [LEWIS]
SOCIODRAMA [GARCIA/ STERNBERG] PLAYBACK THEATRE [FOX]
INTEGRATIVE FIVE PHASE MODEL [EMUNAH]
DEVELOP. TRANSFORM. [JOHNSON]
ROLE METHOD [LANDY] NARRADRAMA [DUNNE]
RITUAL THEATRE [SNOW]
STOPGAP [LAFFOON] ENACT [FELDMAN] GEESE [BERGMAN] TRANSFORMATIONAL THEATER [LINDEN]
DYNAMIC PLAY [HARVEY]

Figure 1.1

critical shift, Artaud later developed the ideas of suffering, emotion, and physicality, while Brecht explored the concepts of distance, cognition, and insight. Each of these orientations to theatre were developed further in the 1960s by Grotowski and Beckett, respectively, influencing many drama therapist's orientations (e.g., Brecht on the Role Method; Grotowski on Developmental Transformations). Separately, the emphases on stage performance and on improvisation continue to provide a methodological basis for many drama therapists, who may create therapeutic productions with clients, or who use improvisational theatre games and other exercises in their sessions. The relative absence of theoretical refinements in these areas is balanced by the well-established power of these primary theatrical experiences on participants. Finally, the drama-in-education movement in England produced a large number of practitioners who became interested in drama for personal growth, a tradition that has influenced many drama therapists. Today these models might be called play process models, since they retain much of the developmental qualities of the earlier work with children.

The Boundary of Drama Therapy

The 1960s gave the creative arts therapy movement a tremendous impetus, and practitioners in all areas: psychotherapy, theatre, and psychiatric care, were tiptoeing up to the idea of drama therapy, often without calling it by name. By the beginning of the 1970s, however, the time was apparently ripe for people to move over the line into drama therapy proper. Most practitioners were influenced by many of these approaches and have integrated them in their own ways. Some drama therapy methods, however, have retained their links to a particular tradition. I have listed some examples of these approaches in Figure 1.1.

Though there are only a few schools of thought in the field of drama therapy, we are now on the edge of a more sophisticated dialogue among them and within them. Until recently, the field has been characterized by a panoply of techniques, approaches, and personalities; a wonderful collection of creative and unique people. Now as different approaches are articulated, differences can be examined, preferences debated, and loyalties tested. The result will certainly be further clarification of approaches, deepening of the clinical work, and maturing of the profession.

STUDENTS AND MENTORS: A PROFESSION

We are now faced with our future. As a small profession we have both the capacity to make changes rapidly, as well as the vulnerability to influences from our environment. It is crucial that we continue to articulate our specific vision. Four challenges in particular loom large on our horizon. First, we need to develop new university programs, to expand beyond the two approved ones, and two developing ones (Concordia University, Canada, Stephen Snow, director; Kansas State University, Sally Bailey, director). We need to supply the field with a larger flow of students. The recent initiation of the Alternative Training program has allowed new institutes to form, providing more training opportunities to potential students. Second, we need to expand opportunities for advanced training beyond the internship and masters degree, to allow apprenticeships under caring mentors to help students internalize an identity as a drama therapist. Otherwise, we will be vulnerable to professional drift, where students move into other more established professions after training in ours. The establishment of PhD programs will eventually be necessary. This advanced training will also allow for the dialoguing and colleagueship necessary for each school of thought to deepen and become more sophisticated. Third, we need to write books. The production of excellent books will attract new students into our programs, as well as establish our field within academic circles. In this way we also contribute to the overall health care system. Finally, we need to participate with the other creative arts therapy organizations in legislative and regulatory arenas, both in order to protect our professional interests, and to protect the needs of our clients. Essential to that process will be the willingness to join with others in coalitions or a multidivisional National Creative Arts Therapy Association (Johnson, 1999).

Our field will be a temporary one unless we are able to manage the organizational demands of a maturing profession, and articulate our specific contributions to health care. This is not done through advertising or impression management. It is accomplished by attracting students of excellence, providing effective training, and creating an environment of exploration, depth, and focus. Through the efforts of many individuals over half a century, drama therapists have laid a foundation upon which we can build an enduring profession.

REFERENCES

Courtney, R. (1968). *Play, drama, and thought.* New York: Drama Book Specialists.

Dunne, P. (1992). *The narrative therapist and the arts.* Los Angeles: Possibilities Press.

Emunah, R. (1994). *Acting for real: Drama therapy process and technique.* New York: Brunner/Mazel.

Fox, J. (1994). *Acts of service: Spontaneity, commitment, tradition in the nonscripted theatre.* New Paltz, NY: Tusitala Publishing.

Irwin, E., Levy, P., & Shapiro, M. (1972). Assessment of drama therapy in a child guidance setting. *Group Psychotherapy & Psychodrama, 25,* 105–116.

Irwin, E. (1977). Play, fantasy, and symbols: Drama with emotionally disturbed children. *American Journal of Psychotherapy, 31,* 426–436.

Jennings, S. (1973). *Remedial drama.* London: Black Publishers.

Johnson, D., Forrester, A., Dintino, C., James, M., & Schnee, G. (1996). Towards a poor drama therapy. *Arts in Psychotherapy, 23,* 293–306.

Johnson, D. (1999). *Essays on the creative arts therapies: Imaging the birth of a profession.* Springfield, IL: Charles C Thomas.

Jones, P. (1996). *Drama as therapy: Theatre as living.* London: Routledge.

Landy, R. (1986). *Drama therapy: Concepts and practices.* Springfield, IL: Charles C Thomas.

Landy, R. (1993). *Persona and performance: The use of role in therapy and everyday life.* New York: Guilford.

Mahler, M. (1968). *On human symbiosis and vicissitudes of individuation.* New York: International Universities Press.

Moreno, J. (1946) *Psychodrama. Vols. I-III.* Beacon, NY: Beacon Press.

Mosey, A. (1973). *Activities therapy.* New York: Raven Press.

Nitsun, M., et al. (1974). Movement and drama therapy with long-stay schizophrenics. *British Journal of Medical Psychology, 47,* 101–119.

Pearson, J. (Ed.) (1996). *Discovering the self through drama and movement.* London: Jessica Kingsley.

Schattner, G., & Courtney, R. (Eds.). (1981). *Drama in therapy, Vols I & II.* New York: Drama Book Specialists.

Slade, P. (1954). *Child drama.* London: University of London.

Spolin, V. (1963). *Improvisation for the theater.* Evanston, IL: Northwestern University.

Stanislavski, S. (1961). *Creating a role.* London: Methuen.

Way, B. (1967). *Development through drama.* London: Longman.

Wethered, A. (1973). *Movement and drama in therapy.* London: MacDonald and Evans.

Winnicott, D.W. (1971). *Playing and reality.* New York: Penguin Books.

FOR FURTHER REFERENCE

National Association for Drama Therapy
5505 Connecticut Avenue, NW
Suite 280
Washington, DC 20015

Email: nadt@danielgrp.com

Tel.: 202-966-7409 Fax:202-966-2283

Chapter 2

THE DEVELOPMENT OF THEORY AND METHODS IN DRAMA THERAPY

David Read Johnson and Penny Lewis

The primary bond among drama therapists is a general sentiment that theatre processes have value; surprisingly, we are linked less by our theories and methods. Our profession has emerged out of direct clinical experience, and only now are we developing and articulating theories and methods that support this experience. This book intends to provide a detailed view of the state of our developing profession in the United States and Canada. (Similar reviews of models in the United Kingdom can be found in Jennings, 1987; 1992; 1997.) Each of the key approaches in drama therapy presented here has something of value to contribute to the understanding and practice of drama therapy. For the most part, these theories and methods are still closely linked to their originators, as training programs that will disseminate these knowledge bases have existed for a relatively short time.

Phil Jones (1996) has warned us about the early proliferation of "approaches," which tend to highlight their uniqueness, thereby overlooking the tremendous overlap among them. Indeed, as one reads the chapters in this book, one can readily see similar themes, concepts, and principles, often named differently, often justified by different psychological theories.

INDEPENDENCE VERSUS DEPENDENCE IN THEORY DEVELOPMENT

Most drama therapists began their careers as doers, as actors or clinicians, who discovered for themselves the exciting possibilities of drama therapy. Indeed, that is the nature of this field. Our convictions regarding our work have usually been founded on experience, not theory. As the field has developed, however, the need to ground our work firmly in theory has been increasingly appreciated. But theories of what? There are several conceptual levels at which theory can be directed: (1) a theory of the therapeutic effects of drama therapy, (2) a theory of psychotherapy in general, (3) a theory of theatre/drama, or (4) a theory of the self and human experience. Certainly at a minimum every approach needs to articulate a theoretical framework at the first level, the therapeutic basis of drama therapy. Beyond this, however, there is wide variation in level of theory development among the chapters in this book. For example, psychoanalytic drama therapy (Chapter 3) articulates a theory of drama therapy that is based on a theory of psychotherapy and a theory of human experience, namely psychoanalysis. Likewise, Role Method (Chapter 4) articulates theories at all four levels derived from sociological role theory. Other methods, however, may present theoretical material at only one or two levels. Most drama therapists must rely on theories from other fields (especially psychology, spirituality, or philosophy) for theories of the Self, such as developmental psychology, existentialism, psychoanalysis, or postmodernism. The only drama therapist to have created an independent theory of Self/Society is Moreno (see Chapters 9 and 10).

Because drama therapy is so interdisciplinary in nature, it is possible to trace the justification for our methods to basic concepts in psychotherapy, theatre, religion, and philosophy (Landy, 1985). Yet, our reliance upon other fields for our foundations has been of some concern to creative arts therapy scholars, who on the whole have expressed strong desire for independent theories for our disciplines. For example, Jones seeks a drama therapy "which can be understood within its own parameters, which does not need to look to models of analytic therapy or to psychodrama for the justification of how change and personal development occur. Too often in the past theorists and practitioners have had to look outside drama therapy itself to try to justify its relationship to change; to find clothing which is made up of items from others' wardrobes" (1996, p. 292). Robert Landy, in his book that describes in detail the interdisciplinary nature of drama therapy, also meditates on this question of the dependence/independence of our discipline: "if the drama therapist is conflicted as to which psychotherapeutic model to apply in formulating objectives, it is possible that he needs to discover a new or more comprehensive model which reflects the creative, expressive nature of drama therapy. Objectives which ignore this crucial reality will compromise the therapist's work in a modality that is inherently dramatic . . . . A therapist who works through the media of drama/theatre needs to formulate goals that are based in the art of drama/theatre" (1985, p. 44).

Shaun McNiff, in a similar vein, calls for "a theory indigenous to art. Art is the primary process of the profession and its power cannot be fully realized within theoretical systems and approaches to therapy that approach art as an adjunctive mode of operation" (1986, p. 7). He links theoretical independence to professional independence: "the creative arts therapy profession must realize that it has the ability to take on a primary role within the health field . . . If we perceive ourselves within adjunctive and secondary roles, we will create this destiny for the profession . . . In this respect, our conceptualization of the profession should become more empirical and primary rather than derivative" (1986, pp. 7–8).

In a previous article, one of the authors (Johnson, 1984) provides an alternate view of maturity as a profession, not as much in the development of entirely independent theories, but in the capacity through our discoveries to improve upon and contribute to the specific theories within which we work. Perhaps we unnecessarily place a burden upon ourselves and our students to suggest that we must create a "new and comprehensive model," dealing with issues others have worked on for centuries. Should not we be thankful that others have mapped out some of the terrain for us, to free us to focus on the drama therapy process itself? Certainly that seems an imposing enough project!

In any case, as one reads the chapters in this book, one will encounter an interesting dialectic between the unique and the dependent, the creative spark and the derivative, the apparently new and the very old.

PHASES IN PROFESSIONAL DEVELOPMENT

Fortunately many professions have traveled the journey we are on, and there is much information about how professions develop and the stages they traverse. Perhaps the most comprehensive source of information on professional development as it relates to the creative arts therapies is Shaun McNiff's book, *Educating the Creative Arts Therapist* (1986). Let us briefly outline the phases of development that typically characterize a profession such as ours.

First, in order for substantive progress to be made, it is critical that the originators of methods be steeped in direct experience, exploring the variations and nuances as they encounter their clients, populations, and settings. Theory and methods arising out of serious study and intense practical work are bound to last. Perhaps the best example of this is Jean Piaget, who revolutionized developmental psychology through the study of only about six children; but oh, what study! The direct, personal engagement with the relevant phenomena provides the immediacy, the concern, and the meaning required for any work of importance. Though this process initially links the method with the personality of the originator (Corsini & Wedding, 1989), subsequent development will extract what is generalizable from the initial birth.

The next phase is the publication and dissemination of detailed case studies using the particular method. The case study is a long-revered and very important phase in professional development. In England, for example, Steven Mitchell (1996) has contributed a whole volume on the case study in drama therapy; and in this country several of the authors in this book have produced case studies. More are needed, however, and in reviewing the publications of these authors there are not many true case studies in the literature; usually what are presented are modified case vignettes. The case study provides an opportunity for the step-by-step exposition of the therapeutic process, constrained as it must be by the particulars of the specific client, disorder, therapist, and setting. The phenomenological texture of the case study allows for a naturalistic testing of hypotheses, expansion of concepts, and discovery of new possibilities. The intrinsic complexity of real events curtails the impulse toward reduction implicit in most theory-building.

The next phase involves published case studies from a variety of clinical populations and different clinical settings; a theory or method designed in only one setting or with one population typically goes under radical transformation when tested in new areas. Some methods may, in fact, be found to be appropriate only for a particular client population.

The next phase involves publication of comprehensive descriptions of the theory and method by the originator, and again there is a wide discrepancy among the approaches in this volume on this score. Some approaches are supported by numerous articles and/or books; others only by a few. The act of writing often reveals new aspects or challenges to the author, who in the process of attempting to articulate the approach to a wider audience, discovers limitations or new directions. Publication provides organized feedback from a broader, more diverse audience than one's students or clients. Landy (Chapter 4), for example, gives an excellent example of how feedback from colleagues stimulated a significant revision in his theory.

The next phase involves training others in the approach. If the approach is only effective when used by its creator, its impact will be small. What is transferable to others with different personalities, sensibilities, and styles must be identified. Second, do others embrace the excitement and charm of the approach enough to desire to specialize in it, to further its development, and to contribute to its study? Thus, what is expected are publications about the method by people other than the creator. For the most part, the methods in this book have not achieved this level of development: publications are still written largely by their originators. The transmission and continued life of a method is directly dependent upon the degree to which students become committed to it, gain independent mastery, and then extend the method themselves.

The relative lack of transmission of models and methods in our field is of some concern. Certainly this is partly due to the youth of the profession. Many of the models presented here have only recently been articulated. On the other hand, perhaps our difficulties in mentoring, an expression of the artist's passion for autonomy, are also at work (Johnson, 1999). Clearly, without a continuous practice and study of an approach by a committed group of people, the method cannot deepen in sophistication. Paradoxically, our passion for autonomy casts its shadow in the reverence given by many of our methods to age-old traditions (i.e., Zen, shamanic ritual, Sufi practice, psychoanalysis) that require years of mentorship and apprenticeship in highly specific practices.

Finally, a profession arrives at a phase where publications about the method are produced by others not trained in the method. Here one enters the realm of commentary, analysis, and participation in the general scholarly debates within the larger intellectual and clinical community. Here one's world views are tested according to diverse criteria, stretched and linked to domains and processes not imagined by the originator, such as historical and cultural contexts. Only at this point can one say that a profession has matured; for in a mature profession, the various methods and theories are in some sense shared by all, through interactive discourse involving comparison and analysis among different approaches.

Significantly, with one exception, Snow, Chapter 12, the chapters in this book make almost no references to each other's work. Examination of references reveals recognition of major theories of psychology and psychotherapy, theatre traditions, and philosophy or spiritual works, not other drama therapists. This is interesting because these authors are members of the same small profession, are very familiar with each other, have attended each other's workshops, and read each other's publications. Without question they have influenced each other. Why is there no indication of this contact? Presumably a good way to identify the uniqueness of an approach is to differentiate it from other drama therapy approaches. Apparently this is being done indirectly and left for the reader to surmise. Penny Lewis addresses this lack in the last two chapters of this book by comparing the various approaches on a number of conceptual and theoretical dimensions. Such comparison offers a starting point for dialogue among these various practitioners.

There may be a number of reasons for this surprising lack of mutual referencing. First, it may reflect the early stage of work within which many of these authors are operating, where much attention must be placed on articulating self-consistent principles. It takes time to look outward. Second, because of the extremely small size of our field, concerns about competitive issues may govern the authors' reluctance to contrast their methods with each other. Third, if Jones is correct, then there may also be concerns that if one were to compare methods, one might discover how similar indeed one's method is with those of many others, undercutting the precious commodity of uniqueness that provides some of the impetus for the work.

The absence of noncompetitive dialogue in the literature among drama therapy practitioners and scholars remains a significant reminder of how early in development the profession is. This book is intended to support the beginnings of such dialogue, by providing in one venue a description of each approach and a comparative analysis of key concepts.

THE COMPONENTS OF A THEORETICAL MODEL

A theory of drama therapy will entail a set of interrelated, internally consistent concepts, definitions, and principles that provide a systematic description of, and a prescription for, a drama therapist's interaction with an identified population. Approaches in drama therapy, as with other systems of psychotherapy, organize a set of procedures for the purpose of influencing the behavior and/or self-perception of the individual (Rychlak, 1981). Though not all approaches presented in this book have developed a comprehensive, integrated theory, all have articulated a theoretical frame of reference and context.

Frame of Reference

A frame of reference "contains principles for guiding action which are deduced from postulates regarding change" (Mosey, 1970). For many of the approaches in this book, such a frame of reference is borrowed from other fields, usually psychology, psychotherapy, philosophy, or spiritual traditions. The concepts and postulates are then applied to the content domains of drama therapy.

Content Domains

All approaches should address the following essential areas:

- A definition of the drama therapy approach
- Concepts that form the theoretical base which are both general and specific to the field of drama therapy
- The goals of drama therapy
- Concepts regarding health
- Concepts regarding dysfunction
- Postulates regarding the method of identification and evaluation of the health dysfunction continuum
- Postulates regarding the various stages of the therapeutic process
- The drama therapy techniques employed
- The role of the drama therapist
- The populations served

Concepts

Concepts are the building blocks for theory. In the case of a human art/science such as drama therapy, these concepts are propositional in nature. A concept is defined as an abstraction that represents a particular class of situational events and/or behaviors (Ford & Urban, 1967). Concepts tend to be hierarchical in nature, varying in the level of conceptualization from the concrete to the abstract. For example, the exercise, mirroring, is concrete and directly observable, whereas the technique of doubling is a more complex concept requiring greater understanding of processes of empathy, timing, and aesthetic form in the dramatic process. Empathic attunement is an even more abstract, more complex concept. Generally good theories have both concrete and abstract concepts: the concrete concept is specific and close to the actual behavior observed in a session; the abstract may be less specific but more descriptive of the true aim of the approach. In the midst of the work, one needs to know both what to do, and why (Okum, 1990).

Important concepts include, at the macro level, concepts of human health and dysfunction, and the means by which healing takes place. Concepts of creativity, spontaneity, play, drama, theater, and imagination are also extremely relevant to the frame of drama therapy. Finally, at the level specific to the method may be concepts regarding role, theme or story, impulse, bodily expression, and/or dynamic aspects of dramatic process such as flow or structure.

Postulates

Postulates state the relationship between concepts. Postulates may spell out a cause-and-effect or correlational relationship between concepts. Postulates may be assumptions, which describe untestable relationships; hypotheses, which are concerned with observable and therefore potentially testable events, or propositions, that link concepts in an orderly system (Lewis, 1986). Important postulates for drama therapists might address developmental relationships along the health-dysfunction continuum, or means of identifying the various stages of the therapeutic process, or determining the timing of certain types of interventions.

EVALUATING INTERNAL AND EXTERNAL VALIDITY

Aristotle said that theories must be based on formulations that are "primary and true." Internal validity of an approach is based on the consistency of its concepts and postulates, its plausibility, comprehensiveness, and congruence with known facts and phenomena. One desires a theory to make implicit sense. External validity is based on the degree that what the theory predicts or claims to effect does indeed occur. Questions relevant to external validity include: How is the approach utilized and experienced in the actual process of drama therapy? How are the concepts actualized within the therapeutic process? How sensitive is this approach to diverse world views and cultures? How does the approach play out with different conditions, such as gender, ethnicity, socioeconomic status, location, and therapist personality?

Standards of Evidence

Once theories and techniques have been developed, it is generally viewed as important to establish whether their claims of effectiveness have any basis. Typically external validity has been determined by standards established by the scientific community. The basic principle of the scientific perspective is that judgment should be based on observations of phenomena, as opposed to earlier criteria such as the opinion of the authority (e.g., King, Pope), dogma (Bible, Koran), or opinion of the majority. In contrast to common belief, the scientific model does not subscribe only to controlled quantitative studies as means for establishing efficacy. The scientific spirit advocates that consistent observations from diverse sources are required before claims of efficacy by one practitioner should be deemed reliable, and that these observations should be made with great care and rigor. Quantitative, empirical studies are only one means by which these criteria can be satisfied.

In other health fields, criteria have been established for what are termed standards of evidence. The Agency of Health Care Policy and Research (1994) has developed a set of guidelines for classification of the level of evidence for particular therapeutic interventions. These are:

Level A: randomized controlled clinical studies
Level B: well-designed clinical studies without randomization or placebo comparison
Level C: naturalistic clinical studies and observations sufficiently compelling to warrant use of the technique

Level D: long-standing and widespread clinical practice
Level E: long-standing practice by circumscribed groups of clinicians
Level F: recently developed treatment not subjected to widespread clinical practice

Clearly many of our approaches satisfy the requirements of Level E, and some are still at Level F. However, given the publication of detailed and carefully observed case studies, some are at Level C. The field unfortunately has few rigorous empirical studies of treatment outcome. Nevertheless, it is important to note that a majority of clinical methods used in medicine are also at level C, as are many other methods of psychotherapy (AHCPR, 1994). This analysis therefore supports the importance of good, detailed case studies in establishing the validity of our approaches. Such practice is well within what can be considered a scientific paradigm.

Evaluation of Validity

The validity of an approach based on its consistency with self-evidence needs to be assessed. If it makes sense implicitly and cognitively, readers can then base their evidence on what appears to be plausible. Typically assessment of a theoretical proposition has been based on research within the scientific community. Systems of psychotherapy whether they be traditional or non-traditional, have struggled for years to be allowed into the hallowed halls of science. Scientific theories are based on a set of assumptions and observations that are then subject to rigorous empirical testing. Mendell may have limited the variables in exploring the genetic determinates of peas, but those involved in the human sciences realize that the variables which would affect an outcome within a human being in the world are far too complex and numerous. Quantitative empirical research methods, such as null hypothesis outcome studies rarely have significant enough sample populations nor capacity to effectively control and limit the variables to produce reliable valid outcomes. Thus the readers are encouraged to utilize their own "makes sense experience" while examining the chapters in Section II and to utilize the qualitative research method of the case study to assess the efficacy and usefulness of the approach presented.

Read these various approaches with a critical objective instinctual eye that is neither inclusive nor narrow-minded. Typically, major models of psychotherapy have had cult-like followers: Psychodynamic depth therapists admonish short-term solution focused behaviorists who return the same disdain. This form of turf competition and dichotomous thinking has led to theory-focused therapy rather than client-focused. Some assert that all good therapists are eclectic, manifesting a lack of allegiance to any single theoretical system (Okun, 1990, p. 5). Perhaps a synthetic approach acknowledging that there are many effective ways to view an individual's capacity to engage in the drama therapy relationship, as well as to work with a client or group is both desirable and effective.

Clearly, this suggests critical thinking in order to question the basic assumptions of these approaches as they relate to the populations they serve and the practice of drama therapy. Some questions to be asked are: Is the approach presented a technique or does it have constructs and postulates required for it to be a theory or theoretical frame of reference? Is the approach stated in an organized logical manner? Is the approach comprehensive and internally consistent? How are the approaches experienced, translated, and utilized in the actual process of drama therapy? Do the identifying concepts support the therapeutic process? Is there room for the clients to influence the approach? How sensitive is this approach to diverse worldviews and cultures; such as gender, ethnicity, socioeconomic status, geographical locus as well as the therapist's personality. All these paradigms can affect and be affected by the approach presented.

CONCLUSION

Hopefully in perusing the riches in this volume, the reader will find theories, methods, and styles that are compatible with their own personality and world view. Many have noted that the best theoretical model and method to adopt is often the one that resonates with one's own personality. Others may choose a model that reflects their shadow side, and pulls them toward the person they wish to be. Whatever the outcome, we hope that this book stimulates questions, discussions, and contact among all who believe in the therapeutic value of drama and theatre.

In this chapter, we have summarized the current state of development of theory and method in drama therapy. We have found trends both toward specialization into identified approaches, and toward exploration of common processes underlying all approaches. We have found a diversity in the degree of dependence upon theories from other disciplines, as well as a sentiment directed toward the discovery of independent artistic models. We have found that the field is still in the early stages of professional development, in which the need for intensive case studies is paramount. We have outlined the components of theory building, consisting of frame of reference, concepts, postulates, and validity.

The chapters following will reveal a dynamic, rich field deep in its process of becoming. Each one, in its own way, is challenged by the simultaneous demand for inner- and outer-directed reflection: in expressing its unique perspective on drama therapy and at the same time being able to communicate effectively with the broader community. Balancing these demands successfully will indeed be the path toward further maturity of the profession.

Nevertheless, despite these challenges, we firmly believe that as drama therapy continues to develop, a true professional community will emerge and mature. Such a community will be characterized by close contact and continuous dialogue, cross-fertilization, and feedback, where all of the theories and methods arising out of this creative medium will be experienced as belonging to the field as a whole. By writing and training and dialoguing, the originators will share their offspring with the wider field, a gift surely to be appreciated. We thank each one of them, as well as those who are to come.

REFERENCES

Agency of Health Care Policy and Research (1994). *Standards of evidence in the health care professions.* Washington, DC: AHCPR.

Barton, A. (1974). *Three worlds of therapy.* Palo Alto: National Books Press.

Corsini, R.J., & Wedding, D. (1989). *Current psychotherapies.* Itasca, IL: F.E. Peacock Publishers.

Ford, D., & Urban, H. (1967). *Systems of psychotherapy.* New York: John Wiley & Sons.

Jennings, S. (1987). *Dramatherapy: Theory and practice 1.* London: Jessica Kingsley.

Jennings, S. (1992). *Dramatherapy: Theory and practice 2.* London: Jessica Kingsley.

Jennings, S. (1997). *Dramatherapy: Theory and practice 3.* London: Jessica Kingsley.

Johnson, D. (1984). Establishing the creative arts therapies as an independent profession. *Arts in Psychotherapy, 11,* 209–212.

Johnson, D. (1999). The challenge of mentoring. In: *Essays in the creative arts therapies: Imaging the birth of a profession.* Springfield, IL: Charles C Thomas.

Jones, P. (1996). *Drama therapy: Theatre as living.* London: Routledge.

Landy, R. (1985). *Drama therapy: Concepts and practices.* Springfield, IL: Charles C Thomas.

Lewis, P. (1986). *Theoretical approaches in dance-movement therapy.* Vol. 1. Dubuque, IA: Kendall/Hunt Pub.

McNiff, S. (1986). *Educating the creative arts therapist: A profile of the profession.* Springfield, IL: Charles C Thomas.

Mitchell, S. (1996). *Dramatherapy: Clinical studies.* London: Jessica Kingsley.

Mosey, A. (1970). *Three frames of reference for mental health.* Thorofare, NJ: Charles B. Slack.

Okum, B. (1990). *Seeking connections in psychotherapy.* San Francisco: Jossey-Bass.

Rychlak, J. (1981). *Introduction to personality and psychotherapy: A theory construction approach.* Boston: Houghton Mifflin.

Section II

CURRENT APPROACHES

Chapter 3

PSYCHOANALYTIC APPROACH TO DRAMA THERAPY

DEFINING AND FINDING A THERAPEUTIC FRAMEWORK

ELEANOR IRWIN

GENESIS

A NUMBER OF YEARS AGO, I began to use drama with children who had emotional, physical and/or neurological problems. Although therapy took place in a variety of settings, the inclusion of drama seemed natural, given my long-standing interest and training in both drama and psychology. Two problems, however, hampered these early efforts at integrating drama and psychotherapy. First, since I knew no one who was doing similar work, I felt I was on my own. Second, I could find few references in the literature to this hybrid discipline I called "drama therapy." Much has been written about drama, especially spontaneous drama, which is of particular interest to me (e.g., creative drama, and theater games) and even more about therapy (e.g., play therapy, psychoanalytic child therapy, gestalt therapy and psychodrama). But while these fields have a great deal in common with what I began to call drama therapy, there were enough differences to make them seem more like relatives than siblings. Being on my own, therefore, trying to define and differentiate the term for myself was exhilarating and creative, but it was also perplexing. It was easy to see that drama was therapeutic, but what made it therapy? Sometimes I felt like a ship at sea, following the stars, hoping that my instincts would lead me in the right direction.

To my surprise, I found many professionals with different backgrounds who were interested in drama therapy. One supporter was Betty Jane McWilliams, Ph.D., Director of the Cleft Palate Research Center at the University of Pittsburgh who supported and funded many projects, including a research study that examined the effects of an intensive creative dramatics program on a group of preschool cleft palate children (Irwin & McWilliams, 1974). Another study focused on the mothers of this population (Irwin & McWilliams, 1973). Eventually our work resulted in several long-term follow-up psychoanalytic studies of these youngsters and their families (Tisza, Irwin, Zabarenko, 1968; Tisza, Irwin, Scheide, 1973).

Another institution that offered support and learning was the Pittsburgh Child Guidance Center. Marvin Shapiro, MD, an analyst, knew about the work at the Cleft Palate

Research Center and was interested in studying the effects of a spontaneous drama program on emotionally disturbed children. With a grant from the Maurice Falk Medical Fund, a research study was organized (Irwin, Shapiro & Levy, 1972), which ultimately led to the inclusion of drama therapy and other arts therapies at the Center. This stimulating experience with colleagues who were interested in the arts as therapy encouraged me to continue to learn about the diagnostic and therapeutic potential of drama with different populations.

Drama therapy, as used herein, refers to a therapeutic modality in which dramatic activities, within a therapeutic relationship, are used to help individuals or groups to make changes in personality and achieve a higher level of functioning. Dramatic activities can encompass a broad spectrum from spontaneous dramatic play (i.e., movement, puppetry, improvisation, theatre games, role-play, etc.) to formal drama. Depending on the age, population, and reasons for coming together, drama therapy goals might include: 1) fostering insight to lessen anxiety and conflict; 2) problem solving to gain control (not just relief) of the symptom; 3) recognizing and handling feelings; 4) improving social skills; 5) reducing social anxiety; 6) increasing self awareness; and 7) forging a stronger sense of self identity. The ultimate goal of drama therapy is to help individuals to develop more positive feelings about the self, bringing about changes in personality.

As I conceptualize it, drama therapy is a kind of marriage, a union, of both drama and therapy. Partaking of both, the process is an admixture of what each has to contribute, although at times one might seem to predominate over the other. There are broad overlaps between drama therapy and creative drama, but, in general, they strive for different goals (Irwin, 1979). The goal of drama therapy is to make changes in personality, which implies dealing with unconscious aspects of functions; while the aims of creative drama are educational and aesthetic. Obviously both can– and do– result in enhanced self-esteem and the acquisition of skills. Because of my past experience using creative drama with neurologically impaired children, I began to increasingly focus on the use of spontaneous drama, which seemed to allow rich opportunities for self-expression and self-growth.

Over time, my therapeutic orientation became a psychoanalytic one, largely because my first supervisor was an analyst and I worked in a clinic that had this orientation. When I discovered the child analytic literature, I became even more intrigued. I read, for example, Bornstein's account of her work with Frankie (1949); McDougall's (1969) account of an analysis with Sammy, a psychotic youngster; and of a French analyst, Rambert's, work with puppets (1949) and so on. Although we had never met, I felt a strong kinship with these individuals. We used different words, but I felt we were talking the same language. Here were descriptions of power affect, revealed through spontaneous play, fantasy, and symbolism.

Having worked extensively with troubled children and adults, I knew about the intense inner life they were writing about-a world that concealed, yet revealed, secrets obscured behind a screen of fantasy, the real/not-real, reality that masquerades as pretend. But these writers knew much more than I did. They were able to decipher what at times seemed indecipherable, and I wanted to be able to see, know, and understand in the way they did. What I did not know, and had yet to learn, was how to look beyond the surface to understand and use this wellspring of rich fantasy to bring about change. An example of work with an early group will illustrate how much I had yet to learn.

Case Example: Drama Therapy with Groups

In the second group session, I was perplexed when 8-year-old Tom, an anxious child, interrupted a drama about an exciting bank robbery, car chase. As though in the grip of a powerful daydream, Tom suddenly stopped driving the get-away vehicle and yelled, "Wait! We hit someone . . . I think she's dead! Git her to the hospital!" So mesmerized was he by his inner drama, that the group unhesitatingly followed his lead. "Call the doctor! Call the ambulance!"

When the patient (a female puppet) was put on the table, Tom took charge. "I'm the doctor. Where's the operating room?" The bank robbery forgotten, the group began to enact an operation, piling bandages everywhere. But after a few minutes, Dr. Tom announced, "Ah, too late. She's dead. . . . The baby's OK but she's dead." And with that, Tom unceremoniously tossed aside the now-dead woman puppet and signaled the end of the drama.

Debriefing, everyone agreed that the play was fun, especially the car chase and the operation. But when I wondered how we had gotten from a robbery to an operation, Tom, glum and silent, offered no help. I was perplexed; where to go from here?

In supervision, however, Dr. Shapiro reminded me of the obvious; in the initial interviews, Tom hinted at the topic of adoption, while his parents shifted uneasily and changed the subject. With that clue, the play suddenly made sense. In the next session, I encouraged the members, especially Tom, to go back to the story. What did they make of it–robberies, car chases, babies being born and mothers dying? Like hanging clothes out on a line, each action added to the previous one in a series of associations that eventually culminated in a personal story. It was a kind of free association in imagery and action. Encouraged, Tom opened up. About being robbed, he said, he sometimes felt that way. "See," he told the now-quiet group, "I was adopted. And it don't seem fair somehow, not to know, for sure, 'bout your mother." Warming to the subject, he went on to say that he had always had a "question in my head" about his birth mother. Adopted early on, he sometimes imagined that she was dead, maybe killed in a car wreck. Or, if she did not die that way, maybe she died when he was born. "Yeah . . . everyone tells me I'm wild, and my mom says I'm gonna' be the death of her!" Was he wild like that for his "other" mother, too, he wondered? "Like, did I . . . ummm, when I was born, did I kick too much or something? Can that kill someone?"

That was how it was in the early years. Intense dramas evolved, and I, along with the group members, was caught up by some powerful inchoate force. Pulled into the vortex, I, too, was swept along, and often felt at a loss. What was happening and why? With relief I turned to supervisors and colleagues for help in learning my role, so to speak. Having emotional distance outside the group, things made more sense. I saw clearly that the power of the drama was its strength in revealing the unconscious, but I could also see that this same power, unharnessed and unguided, might also be its weakness.

How to Account for Therapeutic Change?

In addition to trying to develop skills and learn my role, I kept trying to determine what, exactly, in this mix of drama and therapy brought about positive change. Was it the drama itself, the action of enactment, the process, the insight, the working through, the group experience–and/or was it the personality of the therapist? These questions, frequently asked by analysts, focus on the therapeutic action, the question of what works, and why (e.g., Strachey, 1934; Loewald, 1960; Panel, 1979; Abrams, 1980; Mayes & Cohen, 1993). Challenged, I found myself trying to answer the question that others had asked.

What intervention would have been appropriate following Tom's drama, when he was the playwright scripting the drama, the baby being born, and the doctor trying to save the mother's life? What direction, if any, would be best in helping him to manage his confusion, guilt, and grief? Was "uncovering" (i.e., altering defenses, lifting repression) the goal? For the experience to be meaningful, did Tom have to understand, then and there, how the drama was linked to his life (i.e., insight)? When, after playing many variations of this drama he suddenly said, "Hey, that's like ME!"–did that mean that the dramatic process was "curative" in and of itself? Was it curative because he had had a chance to work it through via repeated enactments? Or, did the therapeutic benefit come from the group experience? Was it the many opportunities to act out a powerfully felt fantasy with willing friends and "a new object" (the therapist), in a psychologically safe place where you could speak about unspeakable things, like adoption? Although Tom's progress over time was clearly evident (e.g., less anxiety, improved school performance, no longer called "wild" at home, etc.), the question was: why?

These concepts, which go to the core of the drama therapist's identity, have wide-ranging implications. These concerns have an impact on training and registration (and, soon, state licensure), and, perhaps more importantly, unconsciously guide all that we say and do, from the beginning hello to the last good-bye of our work with others. It helps to know that other arts therapists (and indeed therapists of all persuasions) have asked these same questions, and that they have found many different answers for themselves (e.g., see Ulman, *Art Therapy: Problems of Definition,* 1961). While initially it is natural to mimic one's teachers and mentors, over time, it is the ethical responsibility of each individual to work towards finding his/her own direction. That means becoming one's own unique, professional self, merging and blending drama and therapy in a way that feels intellectually and personally comfortable and right.

Just as there are many roads to Rome, there are many ways the fusion of drama and therapy can be achieved. Although for me the questions about the therapeutic action of the work were still to be answered, I gradually felt more secure about my therapeutic direction. The nature of my on-the-job training exposed me to a psychoanalytic way of thinking about development and clinical process, and I continued to find ways to use drama in the service of helping others, slowly learning to translate my views into language that my colleagues understood (Irwin & Rubin, 1976).

At first, psychoanalytic knowledge came in an informal and unstructured way–via close supervision and collaboration, the study group, and readings in the literature. Later, my understanding deepened as I undertook my own personal psychoanalysis, a vital and powerful learning experience. Psychoanalytic training at the Pittsburgh Psychoanalytic Institute followed, where I had rigorous course work, clinical and continuous case seminars, conducted analyses, and had weekly supervision on each case. In time, perseverance paid off, and led to completion of training as an adult and child psychoanalyst. Learning in this way, I felt that I had, indeed, found a congenial theoretical home. Behavior that once seemed strange no longer seemed so foreign. Having an analytic orientation helped me to see reflections and echoes of others in myself, and this understanding eventually led the way to an informed and empathic way of working. Psychoanalytic training was crucial in giving me a way of thinking about what I do and why. Often the guide was self-understanding; knowing myself in a deeper way helped me to better know others. Being aware of the vagaries of my unconscious behavior alerted me to the quirky patterns in others. Things began to make more sense. Knowing firsthand that the road is full of surprises–quick turns and pools of quicksand–makes one a better guide to another. In the material that follows, I hope to illustrate some of the key markers along the way that make the journey toward understanding easier. I will first talk about some broad psychoanalytic concepts, and then hope to illustrate these in the ongoing process of drama therapy.

DRAMA THERAPY FRAME OF REFERENCE

Psychoanalysis: A Brief Introduction

Perhaps a good way to begin is to say that there are many misunderstandings about psychoanalysis; in the jargon of the day, there are often a lot of "negative transferences" to this field. It is true that psychoanalysis began with Sigmund Freud, a "courageous explorer" as Oremland (1991) has written. It is also true that psychoanalysis as it is practiced today, is quite different from the theory and practice which Freud outlined 100 years ago; a fact that comes as a surprise to many. Just as we no longer drive Henry Ford's early prototype of the Tin Lizzie, so analysts today do not have the same theories, techniques, and practices that Freud promulgated during his lifetime. Diversity is the order of the day. Currently there are many forms of psychoanalysis, dozens of competing theories, schools, and forms of practice. Major tenets of Freud's theory have been challenged, resulting in radical revisions in theory and practice. Changes over the years have included the shift from hypnosis to free association; from id psychology to ego and postego psychology; and, in the last few decades, to self-psychology, object relations and relational psychoanalysis.

Classical analysis today is even different from what I learned 20 years ago. Freud thought that there were two major drives: libido and aggression, but many analysts no longer hold to his dual drive theory. Analysts even disagree about whether aggression is inborn (as Freud thought) or the outcome of frustration (as self-psychologists believe). Early analysts talked of "regression to the infantile neurosis," meaning that the precursors of adult neurosis can be found in childhood. While some still find this to be true, the emphasis is now on the importance of the early years of life. The focus is on preoedipal development (from birth to age three or four), rather than the oedipal period, which was once central in Freud's theorizing. Much of our current understanding comes from infant research and early childhood development, which helps us to see the early beginnings of interactional patterns. Even transference cannot be discussed without giving equal time to countertransference, because it is now understood that if two people are talking together, each influences the other. This has refocused attention on the process between the two parties, away from the misconception of the analyst as a "blank screen." Today one hears less about the ego and more about the concept of the self. Thanks to infant research, we now know a great deal about how "the self" is formed from infancy onward, and the role that caretakers play in the formation of personality. While many, if not most, still hold faith in the curative power of interpretation of intrapsychic conflict ("making the unconscious conscious"), this is not the be-all and end-all that it once was. Contemporary psychoanalysis puts more emphasis on the process, the dyadic mix, with the analyst as a "new object," not just a transference object. To highlight the importance of relationships, many analysts consider themselves to be "object relationists" or they prefer the designation of "relational analysis," a term made popular by Mitchell (1997, 1999; Mitchell & Black, 1995; Greenberg & Mitchell, 1983; Greenberg, 1995). These terms refer to a broad spectrum of theories, including object relations, self-psychology, constructivism, intersubjective and interpersonal psychoanalysis. Therefore, while classical psychoanalysis is by no means dead, there is new thinking, and lively debate on all sides.

The Impetus for Theoretical Change

The impetus for theoretical change in analysis came from many fronts: (1) from Attachment Theory, via the work of Bowlby, Ainsworth, Main and others (Cassidy & Sarver, 1999); (2) from research in infant and child analysis; (3) from analysts who, though they had many disagreements with each other as well as with Bowlby, slowly began to shift the focus away from Freud's drive theory to the mother-child relationship; and (4) from the pioneering work of Kohut and self-psychology which seems to have been the touchstone for "relational" analysis. A very quick overview of some of these many influences will be discussed.

ATTACHMENT THEORY. Although there is "bad blood" between attachment theory and psychoanalysis, as Fonagy (1999, p. 595) has said, this evolving field has been, and will continue to be, a rich resource for psychoanalysis and developmental psychology. Pioneering this work was John Bowlby, a psychoanalyst from the Independent School of British Psychoanalysis, where attachment theory had its roots. Bowlby, who was interested in ethnology and primate research, noticed the deleterious, often long-lasting effects of early mother-child disruptions. Joined by Ainsworth, a careful researcher, he soon became convinced that, for humans as well as primates, the mother is crucial for the offspring's early development, and that major disruptions in the parent-child bond is a precursor of later psychopathology. Attachment is a basic biological need, he felt, one fundamental to survival. The work of Bowlby, Ainsworth, and their followers has stimulated a rich outpouring of research that has broadened our knowledge of attachment and intimacy problems in childhood as well as adulthood. The relationship between attachment and psychopathology; and attachment and child abuse are just a few of the many crucial topics (e.g., for a comprehensive review, see Cassidy & Shaver, 1999).

INFANT RESEARCH. Another major contribution to psychoanalysis and developmental psychology has been the still-evolving field of infant research. The excitement of this area is illustrated by the work of many influential analysts who are examining aspects of developmental change between parent and child, attempting to learn more about possible parallels in psychotherapy and psychoanalysis (e.g., see the report of the "Process of Change Study Group," *Infant Mental Health Journal, Vol. 19,* 3, 1998). Daniel Stern, among many, has made significant contributions in this area. Stern sees the sense of self as being the organizing principle that is elaborated through Internal Working Models (IWM's), formed in interaction with caretakers. Unlike Freud, Stern sees the child as having a rudimentary sense of self from birth with more capacities than had been heretofore realized. Far from having an ego developing out of an id, or even being a blank slate, Stern posits that the child's sense of self is present from birth and continues to develop over time (i.e., an emergent self, a core self, a subjective self, and a verbal self develop in the first 18 months or so of life). This awareness of the infant's tremendous capacity for a relationship from birth has helped to shift the focus of attention to the early years of life and the mother-child interaction that forms the core of the personality.

OBJECT RELATIONS. A third impetus for change came from individuals who might be loosely categorized as being in the object relations camp. Although these analysts hold very different views about many aspects of psychoanalysis, they gradually helped shift the focus of analysis away from drive theory to the intrapsychic and interpersonal realm.

This group includes Anna Freud, a founder of child psychoanalysis and a major contributor to ego psychology. Interestingly, although they were far apart in their views of psychoanalysis, Freud's writings (with Burlingham) on the effects of separation on children during the WW II London bombings, were very similar to those of Bowlby. Also in this group are Melanie Klein, and W.R.D. Fairbairn, two individuals who are often credited with being the originators of object relations theory. Fairbairn stressed that the young child is "object seeking" from the beginning (meaning that the child's hunger is for mother, not just to be orally satisfied); and Klein's emphasis was on the child's intense, aggressive, and ambivalent fantasy life directed towards the objects (usually the mother) in his/her life. Strange as it seems to us now, this notion of a child's desire for a relationship with mother was novel for its day. In time, it was individuals like Benjamin Spock, author of the enormously popular book, *Child and Baby Care* in the 1950s, and television's *Mr. Rogers Neighborhood* who helped parents to think about children as something other than robots or miniature adults.

Interpersonal psychoanalysis stemmed mainly from the work of Harry Stack Sullivan, Freida Fromm-Reichmann, and Clara Thompson in the 1940s. These individuals emphasized actual interpersonal experiences in personality development and therapeutic process, and stressed that the analyst is a participant-observer in the process. Although not in the interpersonalist camp, per se, Erik Erikson's many contributions also stressed interpersonal and social influences, as the titles of some of his books suggest (Childhood and Society, 1950; Identity, Youth and Crisis, 1968). Erikson's theory of psychosocial concepts in his epigenetic scale stressed development over a lifetime, and (perhaps because of his own history) he was ahead of his time in being sensitive to and recognizing identity struggles.

Margaret Mahler's research illuminated the child's struggle for psychological birth in the process of separation-individuation; while Joseph Sandler and Edith Jacobson contributed conceptual clarity to the individual's subjective experience, via their seminal work on the representational world and self representation. In this camp, too, is pediatrician-psychoanalyst D.W. Winnicott, whose affect-filled writings seem to deliberately evoke in the reader the illusory feel of the real/not-real, me/not-me. Winnicott stresses the importance of the play space created by the mother for the child, a play space necessary for creativity, one that needs to be recreated in the therapeutic dyad. Hans Loewald writes beautifully of the interaction between mother and child, stressing that everything in the growing child is a product of interaction; and among Otto Kernberg's many contributions has been his integration of Freud's structural theory with object relations theory.

THE INFLUENCE OF SELF-PSYCHOLOGY. In another arena, Heinz Kohut, like Erikson, began to write about identity and the creation of a sense of self. In the 1970s, he published his theory of self-psychology, proposing a developmental line of narcissism. Kohut saw narcissistic patients as suffering not from conflicts derived from drives and defenses, but from deficiencies of the self. Like Winnicott, Kohut was preoccupied with the question of how a sense of self develops, and the role that the parents (as self-objects) play in this formation.

What do all these creative theorists have in common, and how have they begun to change psychoanalysis? All, in different words and at different times, began to speak of the child's attachment to mother, of the formation of an intrapsychic self, comingled with an interactional self that ultimately forms the core of the personality. Emphasizing the mix, Stroufe (1977) comments that it is not as though the child's "intrapsychic self" is carried in one suitcase, while the "interactional self" is carried in another. Rather, it is as though, in this dyadic, lively process, both intrapsychic and interpersonal selves become inextricably intertwined, and both are in the same suitcase. Each influences the other in the formation of the personality, making it impossible to speak of nature or nurture; both are involved.

The contemporary focus of psychoanalysis, therefore, is less on the id/ ego/superego, and the oral/ anal/ phallic phases than it is on the relationship between the two parties. But given that, there are still some core concepts that have been so smoothly assimilated into psychotherapy and the culture, that they have lost their once-shocking impact. We now take these concepts for granted. This includes a focus on the unconscious, resistances, transference-countertransference, and interpretation. After a brief definition of psychoanalysis, and a discussion of these core concepts, drama therapy cases will be presented to illustrate these ideas in ongoing work.

Core Concepts

Psychoanalysis

To step back into history for a moment, psychoanalysis, as defined by Freud and elaborated by legions after him, is, technically, (1) a *theory* of psychic functioning, of how and why human beings behave the way they do; (2) a *method* of therapy which might refer to three–five week "on the couch" analysis; or one–two week psychoanalytically-oriented psychotherapy. No matter which form of treatment is followed, however, the theory is the same, although the techniques differ; (3) a *theory* of human development; (4) a *theory* of the mind that offers understanding of emotional health as well as emotional illness, of normal as well as pathological functioning; and (5) a *research* tool.

The Unconscious and Resistances

Freud always considered the discovery of the unconscious and the unmasking of dreams to be among his most important discoveries. Through his work in hypnosis, Freud began to realize that there is mental content (ideas, feelings) that exist apart from conscious awareness. He began doing hypnosis after his friend, Josef Breuer, a highly respected physician, told him about a fascinating case he had treated through hypnosis in 1882. Breuer reported that when his young female patient was able to recall forgotten memories, along with their strong affect, her hysterical symptoms disappeared. In 1887 Freud, too, began to use hypnosis. In time, however, uncomfortable with this procedure, he substituted the cathartic or abreactive method: "I ostensibly dropped hypnosis, and only asked for 'concentration'; and I ordered the patient to lie down and shut his eyes as a means of achieving this 'concentration.'" (1893–95, p. 110). Like Breuer, Freud, too, found that when he was able to help the patient "abreact" forgotten, painful memories and their accompanying feelings, the patient's symptoms disappeared. Freud was convinced that painful experiences were accurately retained in the person's memory, even though they seem to have been forgotten. It was the task of the analyst to "unearth" them, along with the accompanying feeling, in order to free the patient of his symptoms. Initially, then, Freud likened analysis to archeological work, in that both involved unearthing the forgotten past.

In this way Freud discovered the unconscious, that part of the mind that is unknown to us. While unconscious affects and memories are not "consciously" available, Freud discovered that they could be reached via "free association" by encouraging the individual to say whatever came to mind. While conscious and preconscious thought can be brought to awareness via intention and attention, unconscious thought is at the deepest region of the mind, "repressed" and thus out of awareness.

Over time, however, Freud learned that analysis is not simply an intellectual activity of "telling" the individual what was forgotten or repressed. The patient, who prefers what is known to what is unknown, needs help in overcoming resistance in understanding. Freud at first used the term "repression" to refer to "defense" but in time he realized that his patients also used certain resistances (a kind of automatic defense) as psychological protection. Resistances are thought to be anything (words, thoughts, attitudes, actions) that interferes with the task of understanding, and prevents awareness of painful memories and feelings. Resistances are activated when individuals move toward greater awareness of their difficulties; it is a way to protect the self from what is unknown. Since defenses are ubiquitous to the human experience, the therapist needs to be alert to them because they are, at core, efforts that unconsciously block progress.

Not only are certain memories unconscious, but Freud soon learned that defenses can also be unconscious (defenses here referring to the mental mechanisms individuals use to protect themselves from psychological hurt). Defenses, which we all have and need, are thought to range from more primitive ones, such as splitting, projection, and denial, to more mature ones, such as rationalization, intellectualization, and humor. Since "making the unconscious conscious" did not always produce the wished-for cure, Freud soon learned that the factor of unconscious guilt was at work, meaning that the patient would/could find many ways to continue to punish himself, without knowing why.

The crucial significance of the unconscious is that it continues to make its presence known via its influence in the here and now. In this way, the unconscious, which is timeless, connects present reality to past reality (Modell, 1990). While this is most apparent in the dream, it can be seen in accidents, slips of the tongue, and, indeed, in all aspects of normal as well as abnormal behavior. Although operating out of awareness, the unconscious guides our thinking and shapes our lives. Psychic determinism, a tenet of psychoanalysis, thus holds that ideas and feelings (mental processes) are related in interconnecting and profound ways, linked by unconscious activity.

Tammy: A Vivid, Tragic Example of Unconscious Repression, Transference–Countertransference

Seven years old when her mother was suddenly killed, Tammy was silent, talking to no one about her mother's death. Referred because her eating, sleeping, and learning were disrupted, this sad, silent child played repetitively in the sandbox, her back to me. Scenes depicting natural disasters occurred suddenly, wiping out everything in sight. Constructing an elaborate village in the sandbox, for example, Tammy would, without warning, suddenly pour water over the construction, obliterating houses, people, dogs. All were killed. Or, if not a flood, then a hurricane, or a sandstorm, or a volcano; the plots changed, but the theme remained the same.

Questioning Tammy about these enacted disasters was not helpful. As though shell-shocked, she said the play was just "stuff I made up . . . I don't know why." In the face of such pain, I gave up all attempts to interpret. For many sessions, I joined her in her silence. An empty, painful feeling gripped me and I, too, felt unable to talk. It was some time before I could empathize with her, via my comments about the victims in the villages. How horrible to have everything wiped out so suddenly, to lose, without warning, the things you loved the most.

After months of such repetitive play, Tammy slowly emerged from her depressed state and began to talk about how things "used to be" when she was little. She remembered birthday parties, first communion, family picnics, the birth of a cousin, and the like. By the fourth month, disasters in play began to be replaced by dramatic play with quieter themes, but her beloved mother was always present in the drama. It was several more months before Tammy could enact a drama about a girl waking up to find that her mother had been killed. Tammy could not yet cry, but her story spoke of her own terrible sadness.

What constituted the therapeutic action for Tammy whose play reflects derivatives of unconscious thought. Symbolism, displacement, and other aspects of primary process thinking are evident in her play. So wholly absorbed in grief and mourning was she that I, too, almost felt dead. She seemed to completely block me out; I felt invisible. Yet her profound sadness affected me. I felt her despair so intensely that for several months I was uncommonly silent, as though we were both in mourning. Only after many months of painful play, could Tammy begin to come out of her protective shell, treat me as "real" and react to things going on between us. Although she was compelled to repetitively play out death scenes, for a long time Tammy showed no conscious awareness that her play was connected to her own overwhelming psychic disaster.

Symbolic Play

Through the lens of classical analysis, one can see the play as reflecting unconscious thought and resistance, transference and countertransference–the sine qua non of psychoanalysis. This vignette also illustrates the thinking of some contemporary analysts, however, that interpretation may not be as crucial as Freud once thought. Many relational analysts would say that the process of the therapy, the "realness" of the experience with an empathic other who shared the child's pain, is more important than the "exact" interpretation. Further, that the alive/dead sharing of palpable pain experienced by both parties through the symbolic play constitutes the therapeutic action that enabled Tammy to work through her depression.

Transference-Countertransference

The power of transference is astonishing, difficult to describe if one has not discovered it for oneself. Although transference is common in everyday life, Freud called attention to it and made it the object of study in the clinical situation. Many patients, he found, claimed their "love" for him, but he realized this could not be "real" love, only "transference love." Gradually coming to understand the power, ubiquity, and pervasiveness of transference, Freud saw that transference could be an ally in treatment, but could also be a powerful resistance to insight and change.

Giving the commonly accepted definition of transference, Freud (1912, p. 116) wrote: "Transferences. . . . are new editions or facsimiles of the impulses and fantasies which are aroused and made conscious during the progress of the analysis; but they have this peculiarity . . . . that they replace some earlier person by the person of the physician." So transference, seen initially as an impediment to treatment, eventually became one of the major ways of understanding how the patient was reenacting the past in the present.

While initially countertransference was seen as evidence of unresolved difficulty within the analyst, in time it became clear that countertransferences were an inevitable, helpful part of treatment (McLaughlin, 1981). Just as the individual has a transference to the therapist, so, too, does the latter have a transference to the former. For contemporary analysts, countertransference reactions become a crucial way of understanding the other. Normally, however, in once or twice/week therapy, the transference is not "analyzed," the adage being that one does not "mess with the transference unless the transference messes with you." (For exceptions with borderline and narcissistic patients, see Kernberg, 1984, 1985). But even if the transference is not normally talked about, transference phenomena can be helpful in better understanding the other and tracing the progress of treatment.

There is less controversy about transference in adults than in children. From the time of the acrimonious debate between Anna Freud and Melanie Klein (Irwin, 1998), there have been disputes about whether children do, in fact, develop transferences, and if so, whether these should be interpreted. My experiences lead me to believe that children have the same powerful transferences that adults have, and that I, in turn, reciprocate with feelings/fantasies about them. Sometimes this is talked about, sometimes not. Transference reactions can be invaluable in understanding what is being enacted clinically; i.e., seeing what "roles" the patient is taking, what is being projected/displaced onto the therapist in the drama that is (unconsciously) being enacted (Johnson, 1982a; Irwin & Curry, 1993; Landy, 1994).

Interpretation: A Method of Decoding, a Form of Translation

Interpretation, a core concept, simply defined, means "to explain the meaning of; to make understandable" or "to bring out the meaning of, especially to give one's conception of " (Webster, 1984, p. 737). Interpretation takes place when the therapist says in words what he/she has come to understand about the other. When an interpretation is accurate, it can be enormously helpful and clarifying.

While most, if not all, analysts believe in offering understanding, there is some disagreement about how much weight to give to interpretation in accounting for positive change. As is well known, one often knows the truth but is not helped by the knowing. Many analysts, therefore, say that the therapeutic process is of the greatest importance in therapy (as in the case of Tammy). Interventions that promote understanding or self-awareness, include the use of such techniques such as clarification, confrontation, catharsis and interpretation. Tact, timing, and humility are important, because, in truth, the drama therapist is only as good as his/her intelligence, empathy, and self-understanding. In the best of all worlds, both parties work together toward understanding, optimally experiencing a "therapeutic alliance."

In the following material, I hope to further illustrate these concepts.

CASE EXAMPLE

Carol, electively mute, was traumatized by operations and burdened by family conflicts. Outwardly docile, inwardly raging, Carol, almost five, is presented for several reasons. First, this anxious child was brought for help because she was not talking. Even though 60 percent or more of our communication is nonverbal, talk–putting ideas into words–is part of the drama therapist's stock in trade. While we hope that individuals will be able to verbally express themselves, we know that this is rarely possible at the beginning, especially with children. If people "talk" though gestures and nonverbal behavior (or through movement, dance, music, art or any other form of communication), we start where they are, looking for a way to connect, hoping to build a bridge that will allow a relationship to begin. Carol, silent, needed help in learning to talk out her feelings and ideas, rather than act them out, via her muteness.

The second reason Carol is presented is that she did not begin by using any of the dramatic play or fantasy-inducing materials offered to her. This is not unusual. Many times individuals have a preference for a particular art form, and, if possible, I try to facilitate their wish. Frightened as she was, Carol may have chosen to express herself through art because, at that moment, she needed the psychological distance and anonymity that this modality can afford (Rubin & Irwin, 1975). My task was to create an emotionally safe climate (Truax et al., 1966) which might help her to feel more comfortable and less anxious.

Social History

Carol was hospitalized four times because of ear problems and the need to surgically repair her cleft of the lip and palate. Except for surgery when she was about a year old, to be described later, she showed no outward distress about these medical interventions. Carol, I learned, had older brothers but mother wanted no more children, afraid there might be similar problems with a new baby. The early years were painful. Surgery at two months and again when she was about a year old repaired her cleft palate, but she was left with feeding problems, complicated by diarrhea, vomiting, and frequent earaches. Perhaps because she had taken aspirin for a cold, Carol had severe and unusual bleeding after her second operation. Placed in arm restraints after surgery, in pain from having had more stitches than usual, Carol was clearly traumatized. Thumb sucking, a favorite and vigorous activity, was forbidden, lest she tear off the bandages and undo the surgeon's careful work. Angry and scared, Carol refused foods for several days and cried, inconsolably. Nor was the situation better once she went home. Her depressed mother was overwhelmed. There were others to be cared for and no help available from her kind but withdrawn husband, or her bossy, critical mother.

Carol's difficulties and tension continued to increase. Two more operations followed, but a by-now-stoic Carol showed little reaction to them. Although bowel and bladder trained, she was intermittently incontinent, and had frequent accidents, especially when away from home. Separation anxiety was intense, making it difficult for her to go to school.

Although the marriage was solid and the parents had many strengths, there were palpable marital and financial tensions. Mother complained that her husband insisted on involving his mother in all activities–"It's always a threesome, never a twosome!" Father, a quiet and loving man, had a previous serious injury that curtailed his activities, and, over the years, he became more and more withdrawn. His job as an accountant, combined with his disability check, just barely paid the bills, and he worried a lot about money. This quiet inexpressive man seemed to identify with his "handicapped" daughter and formed a close (but mostly nonverbal) bond with her.

This family, like other families with elective mutism, showed marital strain and, like many others, had many secrets. One secret was that Carol's grandfather had a mistress with whom he had other children, unbeknownst to the rest of the family. When, through a quirk of fate, this secret was discovered, a wave of rage and shame swept through the family. The stress of this deception (which became known when Carol was three) took its toll on the family. Father, never talkative, became even quieter; mother, more depressed, struggled to express herself to her husband, but was hurt to see that he could not take the slightest hint of anger or criticism. "He won't talk; he won't fight; he just withdraws," she exclaimed, exasperated. Like a clone, Carol also withdrew, more and more.

This was the situation until kindergarten. There, Carol's "quiet, shy" behavior stood out because she spoke to no one; not even the teacher. If pressured to talk, she looked down, or walked away, just as father did at home. At the speech therapist's urging, Carol was referred for therapy.

Assessment Information

Before talking about Carol's first session, perhaps it will be helpful to talk about the information that can be gleaned from initial assessment interviews, and the social and developmental history. If it seems appropriate, I use a variety of semistructured techniques, depending on the age of the individual and the referral question. This might include, for example, Murphy's Miniature Toy Interview with young children; Lowenfeld's Sand World or a Diagnostic Puppet Interview with latency age children. With some preadolescents and adolescents, I use a "create a movie set" technique, or I invite the individual to enact an improvisation, using materials from a prop box (e.g., see Irwin, 1993).

In the assessment itself, I try to determine how individuals feel about themselves (i.e., self-esteem); the ability to recognize and handle feelings; the nature of internal and external difficulties (i.e., intrapsychic as well as interpersonal relationships); and the ways these concerns are generally handled (i.e., coping styles and defenses). When spontaneous dramatic material is elicited, it offers a rich opportunity to assess these aspects of an individual's personality, as well as creative and intellectual abilities. One can also observe the person's style of relating to someone new. The latter, of course, often has possible transference-countertransference implications. The way the individual "handles" the request for information during the diagnostic phase speaks to his/her usual style–that is, cooperative, competitive, controlling, combative, or submissive (Irwin & Rubin, 1976).

In a broad way, I look for that vague quality called "ego strength," which is a short hand, metaphoric way of talking about the individual's ability to handle problems and to deal with the realities of the inner and outer world. The term had its origins in Freud's discussion about a set of functions that pertain to the ego. Hypothetically, the ego's task is to mediate between the feelings (the id), the conscience (the superego), and reality. If appropriate compromises can be made between the demands of the inner and outer world, then the person is thought to have a "strong ego." The opposite, however is suggested if the person has a hard time recognizing and handling feelings; denies reality (as many borderlines or psychotics do); and/or has brittle defenses that render him/her helpless in dealing with conflict. Carol, for example, was unable to use her natural abilities to deal with the reality of her many painful operations as well as the tension in the household. I hoped, in the assessment, to learn more about her conflicts, defenses, and her ability to form a relationship that might enable her to change.

The Assessment Session

Given her intense separation anxiety, I was not surprised that Carol was afraid to come into the playroom with me. Calmly taking her by the hand, however, I led her to the playroom, telling her mother that we would be back in 50 minutes. (Although this outwardly docile child made no overt protest, had she done so, I would have had mother come with her into the session, as is sometimes necessary.) Once in the office, I showed a robot-like Carol an assortment of dolls, puppets, sandbox, miniature life toys and other materials. Although motionless while being shown the array of dramatic play materials, she nodded almost imperceptibly when I said she could also draw or paint if she wished. Delighted to find a spark of interest in something, I showed her an array of colors and sizes of paper, and then had her choose other drawing materials.

Still almost immobile, Carol began to make small marks on the paper, all the while surreptitiously watching me out of the corner of her eye. When I wondered if she was afraid to leave mother, she did not answer. I said that it was "safe, not dangerous" for her to come with me. I assured her that mom would be safe too. She remained expressionless.

As the fat red marker she had chosen made marks on the large white paper, however, Carol gradually loosened her fist-tight grasp and slowly began to make ever-larger lines. As she worked, I noticed an odd pattern. As one red mark "approached" another mark on the paper, she hesitated, as though afraid to make contact. What was this, I wondered? Was she afraid to "cross the boundary?" Was this a kind of nonverbal separation dance being played out on the paper, a kind of rough "crossing out" of the other? Noticing my gaze, Carol hesitated, then looked at me furtively. As we exchanged looks, she crossed over (or crossed out?) the other line with a fast gesture and great force, a smile creasing her face. Surprised, I laughed. Carol's behavior was a kind of "play signal" that suggests readiness to engage in play. As we made eye contact, the lines came quicker and quicker, each hesitating before the moment of contact, then zinging across the mark as a playful and interpersonal connection began to be established on the paper and between us.

With a few more "crossings," I began to say, "oh, oh!" as though to indicate that I knew what was to come. More lines were crossed, her body lost more of its rigidity, and gestures became freer as her red marks swept off the paper onto the table. Showing mock surprise, I taped another, larger, sheet to her original one, presumably to give her more room. This, too, she filled up quickly, showing increasing glee in the oppositional game being enacted. More lines broke through barriers and boundaries. Each time the (washable!) marker went off the paper, Carol "accidentally" made more of a "mess" on the table. Then the marks went from the table to the floor, and each time I expressed surprise at the "accident."

By the time the first session ended, Carol had not uttered a word but had communicated eloquently. Via her behavior, she showed her defiance of the "rules," so to speak. Carol also showed a high degree of ability to play in a representational, symbolic way. Through her willingness to engage me in her play, she showed trust in allowing an emotional connection to be forged between us. Although Carol began her session with art materials, it did not take long for an enactment to begin, a drama that I expected would move from "acting out" (id play) to "talking out" (ego play), as Ekstein (1966) has described. At the end of the session, I alluded to her oppositionality by saying that I was glad she could play the "crossing out" game with me. Seeing this symbolic play as a sign of her fear of her anger, I added that maybe she was afraid that she would cross ME out too, but I knew that would not happen. I added that as we got to know each other better, she could tell me about those lines and how MAD they were at being stopped when they sure did not want to be! Carol smiled, and for the first time looked at me directly. When I asked if she wanted to take the elevator or the stairs to return to her mom, she said, softly, "the stairs," thus breaking the code of silence.

First Phase of Therapy: Developing a Relationship

By the third session, Carol was chattering away without difficulty. In the first two months of therapy, variations and elaborations of the "NO!" game emerged. Continuing the marker game, Carol said "NO!" as the marker went off the paper, as though the marker was an errant child, defying the rules. The "NO's" got louder; the marker got spanked; and Carol threw "him" on the floor, saying, "He's bad!" It was as though she was expressing her own disapproval of her own (projected) messiness. In this way she was the playwright, as well as the one who defies and the one who is defied! Aggressor and victim rolled into one, she could play both parts of the drama–the oppositional, messy marker Carol; and the critical Carol who decries messiness and badness. The affect that ties both these roles together is anger, but one is passive-aggressively angry, while the other is openly, actively angry!

Often drama therapists want to intervene, but are unsure of just which side of the conflict to enter. Of course if one *does* enter the drama, one needs to be sensitively aware of the many meanings of the intervention. In this case, I entered the foray on the side of the "victim," the castigated marker. Speaking for the harshly-treated-but-messy-marker, I said, "But I think he WANTS TO DO THAT! He likes making a mess, going off the paper that way!" Carol laughed out loud, then became indignant. Grabbing the marker, she made him go off the paper, off the table, onto the floor, and then out the door. She slammed the door hard, leaving the marker outside, then, a minute later rescued him. Picking him up, she threw him across the room, saying, "BAD! SPANK!" It was quite a display of fireworks.

One can look at this enactment as role play demonstrating the conflict between Carol's "feeling" self (i.e., her id, in Freud's tripartite terminology) and her conscience (i.e., her superego). Freud conceptualized this kind of problem to be the core of neurotic conflict. One part of the self is in conflict with another part of the self. As a result, the person makes a compromise formulation that is partly gratifying, partly punitive. Carol's compromise formation? A symptom–she stopped talking, thus nonverbally expressing her feelings (in this case, oral aggressive rage), which unconsciously gives her some gratification and also punishes herself and her parents, making them feel impotent (as she often feels). The compromise reflects the ego's attempt to mediate between two "intrapsychic agencies"–that is, the id and the superego.

In object relations terminology, Kernberg (1976) might characterize this behavior as expressing the conflict between the internalized "self" representation and the "object" representation, with good/bad splitting. The "actors" in the drama are still the bad marker who wants to mess; and the "good" marker who insists on neatness and control. The role play with the "bad" (self-representation) marker is blocked by another part of the child (the "object" representation). And, as Kernberg suggests, they are tied together with affect, in this case, anger. In this enactment it seems clear that one MUST be good, clean, and nonaggressive in order to be accepted and loved. In this play, one can see the child's wish to regress, the guilt about such forbidden wishes, and the harsh (superego) condemnation for bad impulses.

In enactments such as these, it is necessary to remind oneself that the play is the child's creative product and only the child knows what it is about. We can have educated guesses, but we need to wait for the child's confirmation that our hypotheses are on the mark. In time, as Carol continued to enact and elaborate on the themes of badness and messiness, I suggested that she talk about the various parts of the drama, much as one does in analyzing a dream. I said, for example, "Poor magic marker! Thrown away . . . what happened?" Warming to the task, Carol cited chapter and verse of all the bad things the marker had done, projecting, personalizing, and displacing her own issues onto the marker. "He wet his bed, hit his brother, did not listen to his mother, etc."

More punishments followed, and in subsequent weeks, a variation of this "good/bad" game was enacted which became the yes/no game. Carol announced greater and greater punishments, to which I would protest, "NO! All that punishment?" and she would say "YES! He deserves it!" This eventually evolved into an elaborate hide-and-seek game, which, among other things, seemed to represent her fears of losing (the mother) and being lost. At first the marker was hidden and I was instructed to try to find it, and to CRY HARD because I did not know where it was. Then Carol said, in a mean voice, that I deserved to be sad, because I was so bad. When I asked what I had done that was so bad, she said, "Cause you're just bad, that's why."

In responding in this way, Carol seemed to reflect her confusion and her inability to articulate her sense of inner badness. When one represses "forbidden" wishes and anger, as Carol did, the final results often feels like a "core bad me" self (Gould, 1972). Several weeks later, Carol began to play hide and seek. After trying to find her for a period of time, she suddenly jumped out of her hiding place and propelled her body into mine. The meeting was a jolting, crashing one, much like the first sudden red collisions on the paper. She then roundly scolded me for being lost, threatening that the next time she wasn't going to find me (I wondered if this threat represented the child's fear of abandonment, as well as her anxiety about leaving mother. If she went away from her depressed mother, perhaps both would indeed be lost).

In the next few months, another variation of the magic marker game developed. When the marker went out of the lines, Carol told me to tape it down so he couldn't get away. I did so, only to have her violently pull the marker from its moorings, making it "escape" the masking tape. The taping and release game was repeated with all eight colored markers, and on several occasions, Carol taped my hands down, instructing me to make them escape also. After one escape, Carol put one of the markers into her mouth and began to suck on it, along with one finger. When I whispered, "What happens next?" she told me to tape the marker AND her hand to the table. As soon as I did so, she violently pulled away the marker and put it, along with three fingers in her mouth, sucking vigorously. She then offered her left hand for a repeat of the scenario, ending with furious sucking of all her fingers.

Because this "game" seemed to be an unconscious enactment of her hospital experience when she was put into restraints, I asked if this game reminded her of anything. She said, "Bad hands!" and smacked herself. Since the second hospitalization was basically a preverbal experience for Carol, she likely had much feeling, but no words to express this event. I asked if she remembered having an operation but she protested that she had NEVER been in a hospital (although she had had four surgeries!). Saying that I had a story to tell her, I recounted a tale of a little girl who was born with a hole in the roof of her mouth that had to be fixed through operations. After one operation, the little girl tried to help herself feel better by putting her thumb in her mouth, but people said "NO!" and taped her hands down. Carol looked sober and wide-eyed, and became uncharacteristically silent until the end of the session. At the beginning of the next session, however, I learned from mother that Carol had asked if she had been in the hospital. That same week Carol brought the family album and proudly showed me pictures of her being in the "hos-pittle."

Middle Phase of Therapy: Owning the Anger

Carol's next months were explosive ones. Aggressive themes tumbled out, one after another. In one session she made two mountains–a big one and a "baby" one. Telling me not to look, she hid a block under the "biggest mountain," saying I had lost it and needed to find it again. When I started to do so, she yelled at me, saying I was "bad" to "mess up the mountain" (i.e., mess with, be angry at mommy?). Because I was bad, she would have to punish me by locking me up behind 100 heavy steel doors. Besides, she added, the baby mountain would have to stay lost–and it was all my fault!

When I said it was scary to be yelled at by the big mountain, all because I was looking for something I lost, she said I DESERVED to be punished. When I asked, in a stage whisper, how I should answer, she whispered back, "Say you're mad too." This exchange helped us to trace the feelings from SAD (losing something) to MAD (being yelled at) to MEAN (because I was locked up "behind 100 steel doors").

Elaborations followed. In the following session, Carol told me to try to escape from my 100 steel-door prison. When I did so, she pretended to punch me in the stomach for my badness, saying that I was "bleeding all over–from your pee pee, to your stomach, and your mouth. And we won't give you ANY Kool Aid®!" (When Carol was in the hospital, she consented to drink only red Kool Aid.) After this punishment, she upped the amount of steel doors in my prison to 500, 550 and then to 2200 doors, apparently the largest number she could think of.

My role? My task was (1) to keep a narrative going that enabled us to construct a story about the events of her life that made sense to her (Spence, 1982); and (2) to keep an eye on the transference. At times when the intense anger seemed to scare her too much, I reminded her that while the story was pretend, the feelings were real. I said that in a way, by not talking, she had locked herself behind steel doors, just as we had played in the story, and those 2200 steel doors kept her from talking for a long time. In that way, no one knew just how SAD and MAD she was, and how MEAN she felt. She was so afraid of her feelings, that she had to make strong doors to keep the mad and sad inside.

These interventions helped Carol to clarify her feelings and aided the integration of the good/bad self and object representations. In this play, Carol saw that it made her feel bad to be angry with others, especially her mother. She also saw that it was not dangerous to be angry, and that there was a big difference in feeling angry (as in the story) and doing angry things, like hitting her brother. Developmentally this was a big step because it meant that Carol was beginning to give up some of her magical thinking. Young children, because of the immaturity of their cognitive abilities, frequently believe that if one thinks bad things, bad things will happen. This kind of concrete thinking and superstitious behavior may persist for some well into adulthood. Ergo: if Carol was angry at her mom, she might actually punch her mom in the stomach "and make her bleed all over." To protect the one she loved, Carol became mute.

Carol's rage was clearly seen in the transference. Her hold on reality was sometimes shaky in the midst of these intense dramas (what Gould, 1968, calls, "fluctuating certainty"). Getting impatient with me, she sometimes said with frustration that she really wanted to punch/kill/lock me up for real, and why couldn't she? But when I said that punching hurts and that we would not be playing if she was making it hurt for real, she stepped back and resumed an "as if" stance. A strong working alliance helped us to navigate these times which made it possible for the ambivalence to be expressed, faced, and worked through.

The Final Phase of Drama Therapy: Integration

But while Carol tried hard to express and contain her negative feelings in the sessions, she also began to show positive changes at home. Letting go of crippling fears helped her feel freer with family and friends. With less inhibition and anger, Carol went readily off to class; there were no more morning battles with mom about school. She talked to a few friends, participated in games, and formed a warm connection with her teachers. She showed a sharp sense of humor that often startled others, coming as it did from someone who was still a shy child. The surprise of the year was that she consented to sing a song at the kindergarten graduation, all by herself, showing no apparent stage fright or self-consciousness.

In the last phase of therapy, "the monster game," as it came to be known, helped focus Carol's feelings of disappointment and anger. This game developed as she was talking of locking me behind the 2200 steel doors. Making 2000 sand cakes and cookies for herself, she firmly announced that there would be none for me or my mother. Why not? "Because when I was sick you did not feed me and sent me to my room," she responded. (Like most young children, Carol held her mother responsible for all the bad things that happened to her, including her operations, the subsequent pain, and, at bottom, the cleft lip and palate.)

In the following sessions, Carol spoke to a bird who said I was a "monster" and could only be let out of prison if I were "nice." What did that mean? It meant "no hitting or biting." But what, I asked the bird, was I to do if I did not *feel* nice? What should I do if I felt mean or got mad? "Go tell your dad," was the bird's advice.

Following directions, I wrote a letter to Dad, zipping it along via a paper airplane to Carol/Dad, asking for advice. Carol's response, as Dad, offered no help. "Well, just don't get mad. Don't ever get mad! If you do, you'll go back to jail and we'll give you more steel doors." With this, Carol, with childhood wisdom, delivered the message she got from her father: repress your feelings, make nice. But of course, if Carol should follow father's advice, she would proceed directly to jail, back to the isolation and imprisonment of her elective mutism, undoing her therapeutic gains. In this struggle, father was no help because he, too, was a prisoner of his feelings, fearful of his own emotional life.

Finally, Carol decided that if she could not hit or kick me, she would like to make a "big mountain" and hit it instead, making sand-blood go everywhere. When asked what she thought this would do for her, she said it was better than hitting me and making me bleed, to which I readily agreed! But hitting the sand was actually not much fun, Carol found, nor was hitting "Mr. Bad Stuff"–a large stuffed male figure. Then Carol remembered her pleasure in mess-making (having by now forgotten about her initial superego stance on this topic). What she really wanted to do, she said, was make the biggest mess ever! So she set about with paints and water, mixing poisons from imaginary toxins, saying she was going to force me to drink the concoction. What might happen then? Well, she said, with a wicked gleam in her eye, then she would operate on me. How would I like that?

And mix a large vial of ugly looking anesthetic she did, but at the last minute she decided that I should be her helper, not her patient. In a complicated operation, she fixed a doll's mouth, "so now you can talk better." The reversal in fantasy seemed to be complete. Carol was now the doctor, fixing herself, as it were, repairing herself surgically and medically.

In her last sessions she turned once again to drawings. One set of drawings showed the members of her family, all with bumps on their heads. This drawing seemed to be an unconscious correction of the "hole" in her mouth. Rather than a "hole" that had to be surgically repaired, she gave herself and all members of her family a big bump. That, she said, showing some of her humor, was so that everyone would know they belonged to the "Bump" family, the smartest family in town. So smart, their brains sometimes stuck out with little bumps. This wonderful piece of humor showed that she was still conscious of her "hole," trying to deal with it through reversal and humor.

Another set of drawings showed a jack-in-the-box in the foreground while children were playing in the background. Carol enacted several stories wherein she was Jack-in-the-box, hiding, afraid of the children. But in time Jack felt lonely in his box, peeked out, and then decided that it would be more fun outside than inside. With a laugh Carol realized that she was talking about herself. Hiding in a box was not that different from trying to protect oneself from behind 2200 steel doors!

SUMMARY

Drama therapy with Carol was not that different from work with others, big or little, in group or individual work. Although the techniques may be adjusted to suit the age or reason for the referral, the theory is the same. In this chapter I tried to show how the core psychoanalytic concepts of the unconscious, resistance, transference-countertransference, and interpretation can illuminate the work and chart the path of therapy over time.

The drama therapist who is comfortable with fantasy play can help individuals express and elaborate on the inner life, symbolically moving toward change. Many factors contribute to the change, including skill and sensitivity, training, empathy and introspection. But in addition to those factors, two more stand out. The first is theory. As I have written elsewhere, it does not particularly matter what theory individuals follow, since it has been estimated that there are about 400 theories of therapy (Kazden, Siegel, & Bass, 1992) as Greenberg (1990, p. 134) points out, everyone holds a theory in mind, whether this can be articulated or not; and, further, he states that depriving technique of the influence of theory is harmful.

Ulman also talked of the goal of therapy as bringing about favorable changes in personality or living. Therefore, "specialized learning that leaves the core of the personality untouched is not part of therapy as we are here using the term" (1975, p. 12). Like Ulman, I agree that making favorable-changes in personality is an appropriate therapeutic goal. Having a theoretical framework that helps explain how and why individuals get sick, and how and why they get better is important. The therapist who has a view of illness/health can convey a sense of competence, hope and optimism to others, necessary ingredients for individuals to be able to make those "favorable changes." A final necessary ingredient is the drama therapist himself/herself. For while theory and skills are important, even crucial, these factors ultimately get filtered through the drama therapist who then is in a key position to help others find their way to a changed and an improved life.

REFERENCES

Abrams, S. (1980). Therapeutic action and ways of knowing. *Journal of the American Psychoanalytic Association, 28,* 291.

Bornstein, B. (1949). The analysis of a phobic child. Some problems of theory and technique in child analysis. *Psychoanalytic Study of the Child, 3-4:* 181–226. New York: International Universities Press.

Cassidy, J., & Shaver, P.R. (1999). *Handbook of attachment: theory, research, and clinical applications.* New York: The Guilford Press.

Ekstein, R. (1966). *Children of time and space, of action and impulse.* New York: Appleton-Century Crofts.

Erikson, E.H. (1963). *Childhood and society,* 2nd ed. New York: W.W. Norton.

Erikson, E.H. (1968). *Identity: youth and crisis.* New York: W.W. Norton.

Freud, S., & Breuer, J. (1953). Studies in hysteria. (1893–1895). *Standard edition: 2:* 3–17, London: Hogarth Press.

Freud, S. (1953). Fragment of an analysis of a case of hysteria. *Standard edition, 7:* 7–122, London: Hogarth Press.

Gould, R. (1972). *Child studies in fantasy.* New York: Quadrangle Books.

Fonagy, P. (1999). Psychoanalytic theory from the viewpoint of attachment theory and research. In J. Cassidy & P.R. Shaver. (1999). *Handbook of attachment: Theory research, and clinical application* (pp. 595–624). New York: Guilford Press.

Greenberg, J. Prescription or description: The therapeutic action of psychoanalysis. *Contemporary Psychoanalysis. 22:* 76–86.

Greenberg, J., & Mitchell, S. (1983). *Object relations in psychoanalytic theory.* Cambridge, MA: Harvard University Press.

Irwin, E. (1999). Child dramatic play as viewed from two perspectives: Ego psychology and object relations. *Journal of Clinical Psychoanalysis. 7* (4): 505–533.

Irwin, E. (1986). On being and becoming a therapist. *The Arts in Psychotherapy. 13:* 191–195.

Irwin, E., & Curry, N.E. (1993). Role Play. In C.E. Schaefer, K. Gitlin, & A. Sandgrund (Eds.), *Play Diagnosis and Assessment* (pp 617–635). Northvale, NJ: Jason Aronson.

Irwin, E., & McWilliams, B.J. (1974). Play therapy for children with cleft palate. *Children Today, 3,* 18–22.

Irwin, E., Shapiro, M., & Levy, P. (1972). Assessment of a drama therapy program in a child guidance setting. *Group Psychotherapy and Psychodrama, 25* (3), 105–116.

Johnson, D. (1982). Developmental approaches in drama therapy. *The Arts in Psychotherapy, 9:* 183–190.

Johnson, D. (1982a). Principles and techniques of drama therapy. *The Arts in Psychotherapy, 9:* 83–90.

Kazden, A.E., Siegel, T.C., & Bass, D. (1992). Cognitive problem-solving skills training and parent management training in the treatment of antisocial behavior in children. *Journal of Consulting Clinical Psychology. 60:* 733–747.

Kernberg, O.F. (1976). *Object relations theory and clinical psychoanalysis.* New York: Jason Aronson.

Kernberg, O.F. (1984). *Severe personality disorders: Psychotherapeutic strategies.* New Haven, CT: Yale University Press.

Kernberg, O.F. (1985). *Borderline conditions and pathological narcissism.* Northvale, NJ: Jason Aronson.

Landy, R. (1994). *Drama therapy.* Springfield, IL: Charles C Thomas.

Loewald, H. (1960). On the therapeutic action of psychoanalysis. *International Journal of Psychoanalysis. 41:* 16

Mayes, L.C., & Cohen, D.J. (1993). Playing and the therapeutic action in child analysis. *International Journal of Psychoanalysis. 74:* (6) 1235–1244.

McDougall, J. (1969). *Dialogue with Sammy.* London: Hogarth Press.

McLaughlin, J. (1981). Transference, psychic reality and countertransference. *Psychoanalytic Quarterly, 50:* 639.

Oremland, J.D. (1991) *Interpretation and interaction: Psychoanalysis or psychotherapy.* Hillsdale, NJ: Analytic Press.

Panel: Process of Change Study Group. (1999). *Infant Mental Health Journal 19:* 3.

Rambert, M. (1949). *Children in conflict.* New York: International Universities Press.

Strachey, J. The nature of the therapeutic action of psychoanalysis. *International Journal of Psychoanalysis. 15:* 137.

Sroufe, E.A., & Fleeson, J. (1986). Attachment and the construction of relationships. In W.W. Hartup & Z. Rubin (Eds.) *Relationships and development* (pp. 51–71). Hillsdale, NJ: Erlbaum.

Tisza, V., Irwin, E., & Scheide, E. Children with oral facial clefts: A contribution to the psychological development of handicapped children. *Journal of the American Academy of Child Psychiatry, 12* (2), 292–313.

Tisza, V., Irwin, E., & Zabarenko, L. (1969). A psychiatric interpretation of children's creative dramatic stories. *Cleft Palate Journal 6* (3), 228–234.

Traux, C.B., Wargo, D., Frank, F., Imber, S., Battle, C., Hoehn-Saric, R., Nash, E., & Stone, A. (1966). Therapeutic empathy, genuineness, and warmth and patient therapeutic outcome. *Journal of Consulting Psychology, 30,* 395–401.

Ulman, E. (1961). Art therapy: Problems of definition. *Bulletin of Art Therapy. 1:* (2) 10–20.

BIBLIOGRAPHY

Articles in Periodicals

Irwin, E.C. (1971). Why play? *The Publication: Children in Contemporary Society. 5* (2), 15–17.

Irwin, E.C., Levy, P., & Shapiro, M. (1972). Assessment of a drama therapy program in a child guidance setting. *Group Psychotherapy and Psychodrama. 25* (3), 105–116.

Irwin, E.C., & McWilliams, B.J. (1974). Play therapy for children with cleft palate. *Children Today, 3,* 18–22.

Irwin, E.C. (1975). Facilitating children's language development through play. *The Speech Teacher, 24* (1), 15–23.

Irwin, E.C., Rubin, J.A., & Shapiro, M. (1975). Art and drama: Partners in therapy. *American Journal of Psychotherapy, 24* (1), 107–116.

Irwin, E.C. (1975). Drama in education: Drama in therapy. *The Publication: Children in Contemporary Society, 8* (12) , 34–39.

Irwin, E.C., & Malloy, E.P. (1975). Family puppet interview. *Family Process, 14* (2), 179–191.

Irwin, E.C. (1975). Dramatic play and therapy. *Children's Theatre Review, 24* (3), 8–10.

Irwin, E.C., & Rubin, J.A. (1976). Understanding play interviews. *The Publication: Children in Contemporary Society, 9* (2) , 5–10.

Irwin, E.C., & Rubin, J.A. (1976). Art and drama interviews: Decoding the symbolic messages. *Art Psychotherapy, 3,* 169–175.

Irwin, E.C., Baker, N., & Bloom, L. (1976). Fantasy, play and language: Expressive therapy with communication handicapped children. *Journal of Childhood Communication Disorders, 1* (2), 99–115.

Irwin, E.C. (1976). Play in psychotherapy. *The Publication: Children in Contemporary Society, 9* (3), 75–79.

Irwin, E.C., & Frank, M. (1977): Facilitating the play process with learning disabled children. *Academic Therapy, 1* (4), 435–444.

Irwin, E.C. (1977). Play, drama and symbols: Drama with emotionally disturbed children. *American Journal of Psychotherapy, 31* (3), 426–436.

Irwin, E.C., & Kovacs, A. (1979). Analysis of children's drawings and stories. *Journal of the Association for the Care of Children in Hospitals, 8* (2), 39–45.

Irwin, E.C. (1984). The role of the arts in mental health. *Design for the Arts in Education, 86* (1), 43–47.

Irwin, E.C. (1985). Externalizing and improvising imagery through drama therapy: A psychoanalytic view. *Journal of Mental Imagery, 9* (4), 35–42.

Irwin, E.C. (1986). On being and becoming a therapist. *The Arts in Psychotherapy, 13,* 191–195.

Irwin, E.C. (1986). Drama therapy in diagnosis and treatment. Practice Forum. *Child Welfare, 65* (4), 347–357.

Irwin, E.C. (1987). Drama: The play's the thing. *Elementary School Guidance and Counseling, 21* (4), 276–283.

Irwin, E.C. (1988). Arts therapy and healing. *The Arts in Psychotherapy, 15,* 293–296.

Irwin E.C. (1988). Further thoughts on understandings. *The Arts in Psychotherapy, 15,* 307–308.

Irwin, E.C. (1999). Child dramatic play as viewed from two perspectives: Ego psychology and object relations. *Journal of Clinical Psychoanalysis. 7* (4), 505–533.

Tisza, V., Irwin, E.C., & Zabarenko, L. (1969). A psychiatric interpretation of children's creative dramatic stories. *Cleft Palate Journal, 6* (3), 228–234.

Tisza, V., Irwin, E.C., & Scheide, B. (1973). Children with oral-facial clefts: A contribution to the psychological development of handicapped children. *Journal of the American Academy of Child Psychiatry, 12* (2), 292–313.

Chapters in Books

Irwin, E.C., & Shapiro, M. (1975). Puppetry as a diagnostic and therapeutic tool. In I. Jakab (Ed.), *Transcultural aspects of Art: Art and psychiatry, Vol. 4* (pp. 86–94). Basel: Karger Press.

Irwin, E.C. (1978). Observation guide for drama activities. In J. Carlson (Ed.), *Counseling in the elementary and middle schools. A pragmatic approach.* William C. Brown Company.

Irwin, E.C., & Perla, R. (1978). Expressive therapy with a communicationally handicapped deaf adolescent. In *Arts for the handicapped: Why?* (pp. 23–29). Washington, DC: National Committee: Arts for the Handicapped.

Irwin, E.C. (1979). Drama therapy with the handicapped. In A. Shaw & C.S. Stevens (Eds.), *Drama, theatre and the handicapped.* (pp. 21–28). Washington, DC: American Theatre Association Publication.

Irwin, E.C., & Malloy, E.P. (1980). Family puppet interview. In J.G. Howells (Ed.), *Advances in family psychiatry, Vol. I* (pp. 191–203). New York: International Universities Press.

Irwin, E.C. (1980). The projective value of puppets. In R. Herink (Ed.), *Psychotherapy handbook.* New American Library.

Irwin, E.C., & Frank, M. (1980). Facilitating the play process with learning disabled children. In R. Strom (Ed.), *Child development: Growing through play.* New York: Brooks Cole Publishing Company.

Irwin, E.C., Rubin, J.A., & Shapiro, M. (1981). Art and drama: Parts of a puzzle. In G. Schattner and R. Courtney (Eds.), *Drama therapy, Vol. I* (pp. 197–209). Boston: Drama Book Publications.

Irwin, E.C. (1981). Play, drama and symbols: Drama with emotionally disturbed children. In G. Schattner & R. Courtney (Eds.), *Drama therapy, Vol. I* (pp. 111–124). Boston: Drama Book Publications.

Irwin, E.C. Learning to play: Playing to learn. In S. Stoner (Ed.), *Arts resources and training guide.* Washington, D.C.: National Committee, Arts for the Handicapped.

Irwin, E.C. (1982). Enlarging the psychodynamic picture through dramatic play techniques. In K. O'Laughlin & E. Nickerson (Eds.), *Helping through action: Readings on action-oriented therapies* (pp. 53–59). Amherst: Human Resource Development Press.

Irwin, E.C. (1983). The diagnostic and therapeutic use of pretend play. In C.E. Schaefer & K.J. O'Conner (Eds.), *Handbook of play therapy.* New York: John Wiley & Sons.

Irwin, E.C. (1991). The use of a puppet interview to understand children. In C.E. Schaefer, K. Gitlin, & A. Sandgrund (Eds.), *Play diagnosis and assessment* (pp. 617–635). New York: John Wiley & Sons.

Irwin, E.C., & Curry, N.E. (1993). Role play. In C. E. Schaefer (Ed.), *The therapeutic powers of play* (pp. 168–188). Northvale: Jason Aronson Inc.

Irwin, E.C. (2000). The use of a puppet interview to understand children. In C.E. Schaefer & K. Gitlin (Eds.), *Play diagnosis and assessment.* New York: John Wiley & Sons.

Rubin, J.A. & Irwin, E.C. (1975). Art and drama–Parts of a puzzle. In I. Jakab (Ed.), *Transcultural aspects of psychiatric art: Art and psychiatry, Vol. 4* (pp. 193–200). Basel: Karger Press.

Published Proceedings

Irwin, E.C. Art and drama in therapy: A multimodal approach to therapy. In E. Roth & J. Rubin (Eds.) *Perspectives in art therapy: Second Pittsburgh conference on art therapy.* Pittsburgh.

Irwin, E.C., Portner, E., Elmer, E., & Petti, T. (1982). Joyless children: A study of the effects of abuse over time. In I. Jakab (Ed.) *The personality of the therapist: Proceedings of the 1981 International Congress of the American Society of the Psychopathology of Expression.* Basel: Karger Press.

Irwin, E.C., & Portner, E. (Eds.) (1982). *The scope of drama therapy: Proceedings of the First National Association for Drama Therapy Conference.* Department of Psychiatry, University of Pittsburgh.

Rubin, J.A., Irwin, E.C., & Bernstein, P.L. (1975). Play, parenting and the arts: A therapeutic approach to primary prevention. *Therapeutic process: Movement as integration. American Dance Therapy Proceedings.*

Articles and Book Reviews

Irwin, E.C., & Malloy, E.P. (1976). Review of published article on family puppet therapy. *Human behavior. The news magazine of the social sciences, 35.*

Irwin, E.C. (1982). From trauma to mastery: A lesson in survival. Book review of *Reprieve, a memoir* by Agnes DeMille. *Theatre News*. Washington, DC.

Irwin, E.C. (1982). On re-learning old lessons. *Child Care in Practice, 8* (2), 2–3.

Irwin, E.C. (1983). On integrating theory and technique. Book review of *Clinical work with children* by Judith Mischne. *Journal of Art Therapy, l,* 56–58.

Irwin, E.C. (1996). Book review of *Drama therapy: Concepts, theories and practices* (2nd ed.) by Robert Landy. *The Arts in Psychotherapy, 23* (3), pp. 271–273.

Chapter 4

ROLE THEORY AND THE ROLE METHOD OF DRAMA THERAPY

ROBERT J. LANDY

GENESIS

ROLE THEORY HAS A HISTORY throughout the twentieth century in the fields of psychology, sociology and anthropology. It was developed by a number of theorists and practitioners who believed that the dramatic metaphor of life as theatre and people as actors could be applied to an analysis of social and cultural life and inner psychological processes. Those most associated with its early development include William James (1890, 1950), Charles Cooley (1922), George Herbert Mead (1934) and Ralph Linton (1936).

In the 1950s, two prominent role theorists, Theodore Sarbin and Erving Goffman, further developed the metaphor and offered complex social psychological views of life as performance. Goffman's book, *The Presentation of Self in Everyday Life,* became required reading for many psychology and sociology courses since its publication in 1959. The idea of life as performance influenced many social scientists throughout the 1960s and 1970s who analyzed everything from cab-drivers and their fares to gynecological examinations from the perspective of role theory (see Brissett and Edgley, 1975).

Somewhere on the fringe of scholarly acceptability lurked another theorist with a more direct and insistent message. The theorist was Jacob Moreno (1946, 1947, 1960) and his message was that life is not *like* theatre; life *is* theatre. Moreno was less patient and precise than his fellow role theorists. Rather than refining his theoretical speculation, he worked hard to apply his almost theological beliefs to the development of whole systems of therapy, social and cultural analysis and even means of dialoguing with God.

Moreno's work is significant to drama therapists and psychodramatists alike because it is practical. He created a role method of treatment even though his intention was to create both a theory and a practice. Although there have been attempts to glean psychodramatic role theory from Moreno's voluminous and redundant opus (see Fox, 1987), it seems clear that the theory remains in the shadow of the practice.

Drama therapy as a profession developed in a way similar to psychodrama although a number of individuals are responsible for pioneering the field. Since its inception, it has been a practical approach concerned more with the playing of roles than the thinking about roles. Although a number of methods have been developed in the past 30 years, many of which are represented in this book, little attention has been focused upon theory. Why is this?

It could be that drama therapists, like their counterparts in other applied forms of therapy, are oriented toward practice and less concerned with cognitive issues. Some with strong backgrounds in the arts and alternative modes of healing tend to value action more than reflection. Others might simply question the value of theory or ignore it altogether, trusting in the power of the spontaneous healing moment. Many of the leaders of the field have come of age during the cultural wars of the 1960s when stogy systems of academic thought were pushed aside to yield practical ways of solving profound and frivolous problems.

I was one of the fighters pushing my way beyond the old ideas. I still consider myself a fighter although I am aware that within this small field of drama therapy, I may have become a representative of a stogy system of academic thought. In reflecting back on the 60s I realize that my goal was not Maoist in nature–attempting to destroy all traditional cultural systems–but rather an attempt to integrate ideas that were worth conserving with those that needed to be changed. Although I thought that theory had to go and direct action had to be taken, I have come to change my view and to even understand that I misunderstood my metacognition at the time.

So I can unabashedly write that I believe in theory and in the traditions of role that have been established by my predecessors. As a 1960s radical suspicious of scientific thought, I believe that role theory is not just based upon recent trends in social science, but also in ancient traditions of performance that offer explanations of the meaning and purpose of entering into the guise of the other. I have certainly been influenced by the critics and philosophers writing about theatre like Aristotle and Cicero, Goethe and Nietzsche, Walter Benjaman and Northrup Frye, Martin Buber and Victor Turner. But more so I have turned to the thoughtful theatre directors and writers for a deeper understanding of the meaning and function of role. My theatre mentors include Stanislavsky and Brecht, Gordon Craig and Peter Brook. These have been theorists for me to emulate as they have been able to do the work and to reflect upon it with an equal measure of excellence.

From these and many other sources I have learned that the act of taking on and playing a role is mysterious and complex. I have learned that it occurs in many contexts–in everyday life, in artistic performance, in education, in therapy and in prayer, communing with one's god. In this chapter, I will try to clarify my understanding of role and to offer my version of role theory as it relates to drama therapy. Like my most respected theatre mentors, I will offer an application of my theoretical approach to drama therapy–the role method. The role method is not a theory, but a practical application of role theory. Like any other approach to drama therapy or any other healing practice, the method will be most effective if it can be understood and validated within the context of its theory. My aim in writing this chapter is to demonstrate the continuity of role theory and role method and to make a strong case for a sound intellectual foundation for the still nascent field of drama therapy.

When I speak of role theory in the following pages, I am referring to my version as it applies to drama therapy.

DRAMA THERAPY FRAME OF REFERENCE

Role Theory Assumptions

There are several assumptions that lie at the heart of role theory. The first is that human beings are role takers and role players by nature. That is, the abilities to imagine oneself as another and to act like the other are essentially unlearned and genetically programmed. Further, human behavior is highly complex and contradictory and any one thought or action in the world can be best understood in the context of its counterpart. Human beings strive toward balance and harmony and although they never fully arrive, they have the capacity to accept the consequences of living with ambivalence and paradox. It is not ultimately the need to resolve cognitive dissonance that motivates human behavior, but the need to live with ambivalence.

A further assumption is that the personality can be conceived as an interactive system of roles. This notion is close to other models that attempt to create a taxonomy to classify personality structures. Philosophically, role theory is more akin to archetypal systems, such as that offered by Jung (1964) than to more reductive behavioral systems, such as that offered by Bloom and his colleagues (1956).

When I published my book on role theory, *Persona and Performance* (1993), I stated emphatically that there was no room for the concept of self. I argued that the Self was a problematic, tired term too easily linked to modern, humanistic models and that role theory offered a more post-modern understanding of human existence as multidimensional. Many of my students and colleagues have challenged me on this point and accused me of creating a reductive system, flawed largely by my rejection of some form of observing ego and some essential core construct. As I have continued to work through role theory in practice and thought, I have been able to respond to that criticism by offering a new concept, that of the guide, which I will describe below. This part of the personality, a transitional figure that stands between contradictory tendencies and leads one on a journey toward awareness, is not quite the same as the self, although it serves some similar functions.

Basic Concepts in Role Theory

Role, Counterrole and Guide

Human experience, according to role theory, can be conceptualized in terms of discrete patterns of behavior that suggest a particular way of thinking, feeling or acting. Role is one name for these patterns. Each role, although related to other roles, is unique in terms of its qualities, function and style. Role is not necessarily a fixed entity, but one that is capable of change according to the changing life circumstances of the individual role player. However, like Jung's notion of archetype, each role is recognizable by virtue of its unique characteristics. For example, when one plays the role of mother, certain discernable qualities will be expressed, including a sense of nurturing and care taking of another. Although the archetypal nature of the role will remain constant over time, certain specific qualities may change as, for example, one in the mother role expresses the desire to be mothered herself or to abrogate her responsibilities toward her child. Even in the extreme, as a mother engages in fantasies of infanticide, Medea-like, she still maintains the essential qualities of mother. Each role can therefore be identified by its archetypal qualities and its degree of deviation from those qualities, as long as the deviance is understood in relation to the norm.

The primary source of role is the theatre where an actor takes on a role as a means of signifying a particular character with a particular set of qualities and motivations. The metaphor of life as theatre has been so powerful throughout history because so much of human existence concerns a struggle between opposing desires and opposing levels of consciousness. The dramatic structure of antagonist vs. protagonist is played out time and again in everyday life in social interactions and in the struggle with dissonant cognitions. In fact, one way of conceptualizing thought is as an inner dialogue among discrepant points of view (see Moffett, 1968).

When a client begins drama therapy, the drama therapist working from the point of view of role theory often assumes that at least one role the client needs to play in life is either unavailable, poorly developed or inappropriately aligned with other roles or other people in their roles. The initial task of therapy, then, is to help the client access that role and identify it.

In theatrical terms, the role is the protagonist in the client's drama, even though this figure might not yet be aware of the struggles it will undergo in its search for awareness and connection. The counterrole (CR) is the figure that lurks on the other side of the role, the antagonist. It is not the opposite of the role as evil is to good, but rather other sides of the role that may be denied or avoided or ignored in the ongoing attempt to discover effective ways to play a single role. CR is not necessarily a dark or negative figure. If one plays the social role of mother, the CR might be brother or daughter or father. Or it might be something more particular to a client's issues, like helper. For such a client, mother might represent a punitive or abusive figure.

The CR has no independent existence outside of the role. Role appears to have an independent existence and many clients hope to find a way to enact a given role with a degree of competence. Yet even role seeks connection to its counterparts. To be a truly moral person demands an ability to acknowledge and make peace with the immoral or amoral qualities that lurk on the other side.

Role and CR often shift, so that role reversals occur with some regularity. In struggling with moral issues, a client can choose to work with the role of saint or sinner and allow for a shift as one role moves from foreground to background.

The guide, as mentioned above, is the final part of the role trinity. The guide is a transitional figure that stands between role and CR and is used by either one as a bridge to the other. One primary function of the guide is integration. Another is to help clients find their own way. As such, the guide is a helmsman, pilot and pathfinder, a helper who leads individuals along the paths they need to follow. In its most basic form, the guide is the therapist. One comes to therapy because there is no effective guide figure available in one's social or intrapsychic world.

The following story illustrates the notion of therapist as guide. It was October and eight baseball teams were vying for a spot in the World Series. At the beginning of one session, Joe, a man in his mid-40s whom I had been treating in drama therapy for a number of years, asked me whether I had seen the Mets game the previous night. He told me that he watched the game intently so that he would be able to talk with me about it. He knew that I was an ardent Mets fan. The game had been particularly exciting and we chatted about it for a few minutes. Then he told me, with some sadness, that his father never took him to a baseball game.

During the session, we worked on a number of issues, one concerning his relationship with his adolescent nephew, whom he treated in a fatherly way on a recent visit. He worked very deeply with material concerning his relationship to present and absent family members, especially his father who had died 20 years earlier. At the end of the session, Joe quite spontaneously took my hand and said: "Thanks for taking me to the game." He embraced me, as if to say good-bye, a usual ritual for our closure. I held him for a moment and sang:

> Take me out to the ball game,
> Take me out to the crowd,
> Buy me some peanuts and cracker jacks,
> I don't care if I never get back...

When I reached the chorus he joined in:

> For it's one, two, three strikes you're out
> At the old ball game.

We looked at each other and laughed and then he left.

In that session, I became not only Joe's transferential father, but also his guide. Although his real father could not take him to a real ball game, his guide could take him to a virtual one. Our therapy session was a ball game in that we were able to share an intimacy painfully denied by his father. In the moment of intimacy, with the help of the guide, the past rejections of the father were corrected.

The guide figure is first visible as existing in the world outside the client. It takes many forms in everyday life including: parent, sibling, special relative or friend, teacher, coach, religious leader, media personality, criminal, demon and God. The guide can be moral, immoral or amoral.

Although drama therapy begins with the tacit understanding that the therapist will take on and play out the role of guide, the process moves toward a different aim–that clients will internalize the guide and discover, ultimately, a way to guide themselves.

Another way to look at the same internal understanding of guide is that clients enter therapy with all kinds of potential inner guide figures. For many, these figures are hard to access. Through the process of drama therapy, clients are challenged to recreate their inner guides which, once developed, can lead them through difficult territory.

Role and CR are more clearly properties of the client. They are revealed through behavior and thought. Like the guide they, too, will serve as internal figures that seek balance within the psyche. Joe seeks such a balance between the part of him that is a child, longing for a father's love, and the part of him that is a grown-up, capable of fathering others even as he fathers himself.

When the three parts of the psyche are intact, the inner guide will facilitate the connection between child and father. It will allow Joe to feel loved and loving at the same time. It will allow Joe to feel the pain of the missed moments of fathering without shame.

Role Types and the Taxonomy of Roles

For many years I asked the question–if it is true that the personality is a system of interactive roles, what are the specific roles within that system? In looking for answers, I turned to others systems. From Jung (1971) I learned about the attitudes of the extrovert and introvert and the four functions of thinking, feeling, sensing and intuiting. For a more archetypal understanding of role, I also looked toward Jung's notion of anima and animus, of shadow and persona and puer. From latter-day Jungians such as Campbell (1949) and Hillman (1983), I discovered a more contemporary way to understand role types.

I looked at less conventional systems such as the spiritual enneagram that proposes nine personality types: the reformer, the helper, the status seeker, the artist, the thinker, the loyalist, the generalist, the leader and the peacemaker (see Riso, 1987). And I also looked at a more literary system such as that offered by Carol Pearson (1989) who envisions personality structure as comprised of six types: innocent, orphan, magician, wanderer, martyr and warrior.

Although all these systems were valuable and revealing, none led me to the essential source of all work in drama therapy–the theatre. Having realized that the one unique feature of drama therapy, distinguishing it from all other healing forms, is its theatrical underpinnings, I paused for a long drink at the well of theatre.

It occurred to me that the one indivisible element in theatre is role. Many plays have neither plot nor spectacle nor even language. But all share the basic premise that actors take on roles to create a character. Starting with this premise, I began to look at the many roles available in theatrical plays since the beginning of recorded history. I limited myself to an exploration of Western dramatic literature as I was unfamiliar with the Eastern traditions. In recent years as I became more aware of such Eastern theatrical forms as Japanese Noh theatre, Peking Opera and Indian Kathakali, I have come to realize that these traditions, free from the modern Western influence of psychological realism, lend themselves more easily to classification according to character type. But this must remain the subject of another study.

As I searched the *dramatis personae* of many hundreds of Western plays, I became aware of a repeated pattern of character types that seemed to transcend time, genre and culture. They included heroes and villains, nobility and commoners, victims and survivors, wise fools and ignorant kings, deceivers and helpers and lovers of all kinds.

The repeated role of hero, for example, from the Greek Oedipus to the British Lear to the American Willy Loman, embodied certain archetypal qualities and I began to specify them. They included a willingness to confront the unknown and to journey forth on a spiritual search for a meaning just beyond their grasp (Landy, 1993, p. 230). I also noticed that all heroes serve a common function within the drama, which I noted as taking a risky psychological and spiritual journey toward understanding and transformation (Landy, 1993, p. 230).

Finally, I noticed that each role type, consistent with its aesthetic form and genre, tended to be enacted within a particular style. I noted two primary styles, the presentational, a more abstract form removed from the trappings of real-life speech and action, and the representational, a more reality-based form. Given my understanding of aesthetic distance, I postulated that presentational styles are linked to more cognitive modes of expression, and representational styles are linked to more affective modes. In playing a role, the actor achieves the desired aesthetic effect, whether comic or tragic, whether melodramatic or farcical, by playing with the level of distance. However, the role that an actor takes on is in itself determined by its aesthetically-based stylistic tradition. While it is true that the modern Willy Loman is a kind of anti-hero popular in mid-twentieth century literature, he still is typically measured against the classical tragic hero from which he derives. Although many actors play him in a realistic manner, attempting to discover the emotional depths of his suffering, he was written by Arthur Miller within a presentational style, consistent with the traditions of the role type, hero.

Parallel to the stage actor, the client in drama therapy is led through particular levels of cognition and affect as the drama therapist introduces more or less stylized roles and activities. The drama therapist facilitates the client's play with style in order to help her discover a balance of affect and cognition so that she might be able to work through a dilemma with the capacities to feel and to reflect intact. Style is the distancer in drama therapy, a way to move a client closer or further away from a role that she needs to play in order to discover balance.[1]

In completing the taxonomy of roles, I listed 84 role types and a number of subtypes. My main criterion for choosing a role type was its appearance in at least three historical periods, e.g., classical, renaissance and neo-classical, or repeated use throughout one

[1] For a full discussion of distancing in drama therapy, see Landy, 1983.

particular period and/or genre. In recent years I have refined the taxonomy, eliminating redundancy, especially for the purpose of developing an assessment instrument, to be discussed below.

It should be noted that all roles in the taxonomy work within the triadic system of role, counterrole and guide. Any one role type, such as the Child, can serve as protagonist (role), antagonist (CR) and/or guide within an individual's therapeutic drama.

Role System

In developing the taxonomy of roles, I made the assumption that all human beings have the potential to take on and play out all the identified roles plus others not specified. The quantity of roles available will be based upon many factors including biological predisposition, social modeling, psychological motivation, environmental circumstance, and moral judgment, as well as such secondary factors as readiness and will. The totality of roles available at any one moment is known as the role system. Role system is another way of thinking about personality structure. It is the container of all the intrapsychic roles. Within the role system are those roles that are available to consciousness and that can be played out competently. But there are also dormant roles within the role system that have faded from consciousness because of neglect or abuse or lack of need. Roles that are not called out will not be played out, even though they may exist within. They will be activated when given the proper social or environmental circumstance.

As an example, Jill was repeatedly told by her family that she was dull and unimaginative. She was discouraged from continuing her education beyond the age of 16. After her minimal schooling, she took on a series of menial and unfulfilling jobs. After a brief time in drama therapy, she enrolled in a continuing education course in art history. She recalled that her hand shook as she filled out the registration form. During the first class, when slides were shown of classical paintings, she was overcome with emotion and had to leave the room. She secluded herself in the bathroom and sobbed. The next class, for the first time in her life, she discovered that she had something to say about the paintings. She dared to speak up and was acknowledged for her insightful comments.

With my encouragement, Jill began to do her own drawings, very intimate images concerning her abusive past. Although the creation and dialogue with the images was very painful, she took great pride in discovering that a whole new role–that of artist–was suddenly available. During one session she exclaimed: "I think the artist has been there all the time. It was just asleep."

The structure of the role system is dynamic. When one role is called into the foreground, others fade into the background. One way of viewing the structure is as a staged scene in a play. When one actor speaks, the others on stage need to listen and react appropriately. Some remain silent and unseen, playing out their roles as extras.

Within the structure of the role system, roles tend to seek balance with their counterparts. This is especially true in a healthy, integrated personality. Such a personality is also one where a variety of roles from a variety of domains would be prepared to, if called, take a leading part in an individual's life drama.

View of Health and Illness

The healthy person, from the point of view of role theory, is noted by an ability to live with ambivalence, contradictory tendencies and paradox. In a previous book of essays (Landy, 1996a), I refer to this person as one who is effectively able to live a double life. The image does not refer to schizoid splits but to an acknowledgement that the human condition is in part one of living simultaneously within paradoxical realms of mind and body, thought and action, subject and object, actor and observer, a role and its counterpart. The healthy adult person who functions responsibly has found a way to live with her contradictory tendencies to act up like a child and to act out like an adolescent. The role and CR are in balance and when the need arises to play the child or adolescent, the individual can do so without the fear of losing all sense of maturity and judgment.

When out of balance, that is, when too much the child or too much the adolescent, the healthy person is able to draw upon the wisdom of a guide figure to help move back toward the center. The guide might be a friend or a therapist or it might be an inner figure that signals a time for reflection and a time for a shift of behavior.

The healthy person is also noted by her ability to take on many, if not most, of the roles in the taxonomy and to play them out in everyday life with some degree of proficiency. Very few people, the best character actors notwithstanding, are able to enact all 84 roles with a full measure of competency. Proficiency and competency are often hard to measure. However, these traits are generally present when one is able to behave in role and reflect upon that behavior in a balanced way, that is, with feeling and with understanding. The competent role player is also one who is able to articulate in words and/or action the appropriate qualities, function and style of any given role.

Health, then, is a measure of both the quantity of roles one internalizes and plays out and the quality of the role enactment.

The unhealthy person, from a role perspective, is one who has given up the struggle to live with ambivalence and has, instead, embraced one role or a cluster of related ones, at the exclusion of all others. Feeling overwhelmed by complexity, the unhealthy person finds ways to limit the quantity and quality of roles within his inner and outer world. This is the domain of the fundamentalist who worships one belief system as he rejects all other forms of belief or ways of seeing the world. This is the domain of the autistic whose world is limited to a very small private set of thoughts and behaviors. In most forms of extreme mental illness marked by obsessional or delusional thinking, the role system is severely limited.

From a social point of view, the unhealthy person is marked by an inability to take on the role of the other and thus to empathize with another. We find that narcissistic individuals, for example, live in a very narrow universe of roles. Each social encounter that offers a possible means of taking on a new role becomes a distorted mirror. Instead of looking at the other and seeing a reflection of what she might become, the narcissist looks at the other and sees a reflection of how she is. For the narcissist, the other cannot mediate or represent any new ways of being. In offering a fixed mirror, the other becomes the pool of water that ultimately drowns the mythological Narcissus.

The unhealthy person is also marked by his inability to internalize and enact a number of roles competently. In the extreme, this person finds many of the roles listed in the taxonomy foreign and distant. Further, he finds it difficult to attribute qualities, functions and styles to those roles with which he identifies.

Method of Assessment and Evaluation

In applying the taxonomy of roles to clinical work in drama therapy, I have developed two assessment instruments. The first, called Role Profiles, is a simple pencil and paper test that offers a modified list of the roles within the taxonomy and asks the subject to rate each one on a Likert-type scale from 0–4 according to two measures: how much one acts like the role in one's everyday life and how much one plays out the role in one's imagination. Role Profiles is currently undergoing revision. It is evolving into a card sort test and will soon be subjected to measures of reliability and validity. However, a number of studies have already been done (see Raz, 1997; Tangorra, 1997; Rosenberg, 1999) attempting to establish these and other benchmarks of research. Once the appropriate research and clinical protocols have been established, this instrument should serve as an effective means of viewing an individual's role system in terms of quantity and quality of roles taken and played. With further research, a clinical drama therapist should be able to apply this data directly toward treatment.

The second instrument developed from role theory is called Tell-A-Story. Its aim is to assess an individual's ability to invoke a role, CR and guide and to move toward some integration and connection among the roles. Through Tell-A-Story, the subject is given the following task: *I would like you to tell me a story. The story can be based upon something that happened to you or to somebody else in real life or it can be completely made-up. The story must have at least one character.*

The tester is instructed to provide any prompts necessary to help the subject tell the story. The tester encourages those who are not very verbal to tell the story through miniature objects or puppets. Following the story, the subject is asked to specify the characters in the story, limited to three, and answer a number of questions concerning their qualities, function and style of presentation. The subject is also asked to specify the theme of the story and comment on the connection between the fictional roles and their everyday life.

This assessment instrument is still in its formative stages and needs further research and refinement before it is applied to a broad clinical spectrum.

In evaluating change, the therapist looks for a shift in the quantity and quality of roles taken and enacted, as well as an ability of the client to identify and work through role, CR and guide figures. To determine the effectiveness of the treatment the therapist asks several questions:

1. Is the client able to identify a problematic role(s) and to take it on and enact it with a degree of competency? By competency I mean an awareness of the qualities, function and style of role presentation and an application of that awareness to effective social interactions in role.
2. Is the client able to identify a CR and take it on and enact it with a degree of competency?
3. Is the client able to identify a guide figure and use it as an aid in moving through a crisis?
4. Is the client able to live among contradictory roles?
5. Is the client able to take on and play out a range of roles throughout the six domains of the taxonomy of roles?

The therapist can evaluate a client's progress at the end of each session, at the conclusion of a given number of sessions or at the termination of the treatment. At any juncture, having made the evaluation, the therapist can share her observations and offer suggestions to the client. She can also help the client evaluate his own progress by sharpening his ability to identify roles, counterroles and guide figures.

The Therapeutic Process: Role Method

Role theory is applied to treatment by means of the role method (RM). In *Persona and Performance* (1993), I specified the method as proceeding through eight steps:

1. Invoking the role.
2. Naming the role.
3. Playing out/working through the role.
4. Exploring alternative qualities in subroles.
5. Reflecting upon the role play: discovering role qualities, functions and styles inherent in the role.
6. Relating the fictional role to everyday life.
7. Integrating roles to create a functional role system.
8. Social modeling: discovering ways that clients' behavior in role affects others in their social environments.

The model still holds although I have revised Step Four to accommodate my understanding of CR and guide. During the working-through stage, the client is presumably working with a single role that he has identified and named. For example, George, a visual artist in his late 50s, came to therapy because he felt like a professional failure. I pointed out that failure was more of a quality than a role and helped George discover that the failed role was that of artist. We worked with the artist role through stories and dreamwork and role play. Soon we discovered that it was not the artist part of George that felt like a failure, but its counterpart whom George first named the bank and then the businessman.

In identifying his problematic role as the businessman, George did not appear to me to be exploring a subrole of the artist but in fact discovering a counterrole. When George acknowledged his feelings of incompetence concerning the sale of art, he was able to reclaim the artist on the other side of the businessman and work toward ways of integrating the two with the help of several guide figures whom he identified and named.

There is an intermediary step between 3 and 4. This is the step of de-roling which generally applies to a shift in realities from the dramatic to that of everyday life. In this first instance of de-roling, however, the client distances himself from one role, enters for a moment into a neutral position associated with everyday life, and then prepares to take on the CR.

De-roling also occurs between Steps 4 and 5 as the client moves fully out of the imaginary realm, leaving the fictional roles behind, and prepares to reflect upon the fictions just created. De-roling signals the essential paradox of the dramatic experience–that of the continuity of the me and not-me, of the actor in relation to the role. In leaving the dramatic role, the actor resumes a life in a parallel universe that is less obviously masked and stylized. Because drama therapy treatment in role can become quite complex and confusing, the therapist needs to insure that the client de-roles each character and each object. While under the spell of the role, the client loses distance and has difficulty reflecting upon the drama.

There is no such rarified position as a fully de-roled human being. Behind all masks are more masks. The aim of de-roling is not to fully transcend one's personae, but to shift from one reality, that of the imagination, to another, that of the everyday, for the purpose of reflection. Another way of looking at de-roling is as a shift from a more affective, physically active mode to a more cognitive, reflective one.

The steps in the role method do not necessarily proceed in a linear fashion. As a client works with a problematic role, he might discover, as George did, that the problem really lies on the other side. The CR then becomes the role and needs to be clearly named and worked through in itself. At the place marked as Step Four, the client is encouraged to locate a guide figure. Many, however, begin therapy with a guide figure intact or temporarily lost, one that usually is based upon a nurturing or idealized parent.

Steps Five and Six of the role method are reflective and point to a cognitive component of the approach. Following some form of enactment clients are asked to reflect upon the roles they have played and then to link the roles to their everyday lives. Many drama therapists believe that enactment is healing in itself and that reflection is at best unnecessary and at worst counterproductive. I believe that reflection and verbal processing are potentially as important as enactment in leading to healing. However, I do recognize that verbal processing is inappropriate with certain populations with limited insight and verbal capacities such as autistic children and severely mentally ill or mentally retarded adults.

The final Step, that of social modeling, implies that once a role or configuration of role-CR-guide has been changed, the client becomes a model for others within his various social environments of home, work, and play. When George goes to an upscale cocktail party given by wealthy art dealers, many of whom he has encountered previously, feeling insecure each time, he is fearful that they will see him as a failed artist. But since therapy has helped him to revise his self-conception, he is able to go as a competent artist whose business and self-promotional acumen is a work in progress. The dealers react positively to his altered self-perception and engage him in conversation. At the same time, peers at the party who think of themselves as failed artists see George in a more relaxed state and wish they could be more like him. George then, in his transformed state, becomes a role model for them.

I begin both a group and an individual session in a variety of ways. Most often, I greet my clients and wait for them to verbalize or nonverbally indicate their present state of being. Sometimes, especially with a new group, I will lead them through a physical warm-up and help them locate a role. One exercise I use often is to ask the group to move through the room and let go of tension through breathing and stretching and extending. I ask them to focus upon one body part and allow a movement to extend from, for example, their belly. I ask them to play with the movement, adding a sound and letting a character emerge. Once the character is established, I help the group develop it further through improvisational interactions in role, brief monologues, and finally, a naming of the role.

Once individuals in the group are warmed up to their roles, we work through these roles by means of storymaking or sculpting or free play in small groups. Individuals can also work toward locating counterroles and guide roles and setting up improvisational scenes among the three.

The form of identifying the three roles is generally effective, especially in higher functioning groups. This approach can become more confusing with low functioning or highly medicated groups. In that case, I generally begin work with a single role. If and when there is an opportunity to move to the other side of the role, I will ask individuals or a full group to locate and take on the counterrole.

With this model in mind, I will utilize a range of techniques, generally staying within the scope of projective techniques (see Landy, 1994). With individuals as well as groups, I will use sand play and free play, mask and puppets, drawings and sculpts, storytelling and storymaking and playback theatre. Most recently, I have found that work with stories provides a clear structure within which clients can locate and work with their roles and subsequent counterroles and guides. If any of the three are missing, the story structure provides a frame in which to locate the missing pieces.

In treatment, I also make use of psychodramatic techniques including doubling, role reversal, mirroring and sharing during closure. I try to avoid the direct reality orientation and intense cathartic nature of psychodrama unless I sense that clients have distanced themselves too much from feeling and need to tell a direct story with a maximum of affect. In groups I also make use of sociometry in order to discover certain underlying dynamics and to encourage members to make more risky choices.

With some clients who have difficulty organizing their lives because of borderline tendencies or addictive dependencies, I will use a modification of cognitive-behavioral approaches. My aim will be to help them develop effective coping strategies. In terms of a role approach, I often ask them to identify a role that they need to play and to specify its behavioral qualities. I help them practice playing the role in therapy as a rehearsal for moments in everyday life. I model this kind of work on the approach of George Kelly (1955) who developed a form of treatment called fixed role therapy.

In working cognitively, my goal is to help individuals reconstruct their mental schemas and find appropriate roles and counterroles to structure their lives. Through this work, a conscious effort is made to locate an inner guide figure, a kind of reliable central intelligence that can effectively direct the show.

The Role of the Drama Therapist

The drama therapist working through the role method needs to be flexible and responsive. Generally speaking, the drama therapist serves as guide and model, standing over and above the client, encouraging him, finally, to find his own guide. It is inadvisable for the drama therapist to become too distanced as this may provoke too much transference on the part of the client. When moments of transference do occur, the drama therapist can take on the transferential role and engage with the client, encouraging him to take on an appropriate counterrole. In the example I offered above of Joe, both therapist and client enter the domain of father and son as they visit a metaphorical baseball game and sing the evocative song, *Take Me Out to the Ball game.*

In general, the drama therapist neither encourages nor discourages transference. When it appears, the drama therapist should be prepared to do one of two things. In the first instance, she takes it on in the form of a role and encourages the client to take on the counterrole. Then, in their respective roles, they enact a brief drama. Following the enactment, they de-role and discuss the experience. In the second instance, often in a group process, the therapist helps the group to shift the transference from the therapist to the group thus empowering the group to work through the drama of transference on its own. For a full discussion of this second approach, see Eliaz (1988).

The model of distancing very much guides the interaction of therapist and client (see Landy, 1983, 1994, 1996). The therapist will assess each moment and make instantaneous judgments as to how close and how distant to be with the client. The determination will be based upon two primary factors:

1. the client's diagnosis and ability to handle closeness and/or separation;
2. the therapist's ability to contain emotion and to deal effectively with his countertransferential reactions within a session.

Although the therapist must be willing to take on various counterroles to the client's roles and engage in a direct form of play, she will most of the time serve more as director and witness to the play of the client(s). One exception is when working with children through play therapy. In this case, the drama therapist will most often engage directly in the play unless the child clearly indicates her wish to play alone. In playing with the child, the therapist will work toward establishing open communication and trust, setting limits, containing emotion, and helping to clarify the theme of the play. The therapist will work through the structure of role-CR-guide to help the client find a way in and out of each.

When taking a more distanced stance, the therapist will guide the enactment and encourage the client to take on and play out the necessary roles. As an example, George comes into a session and tells me a dream. It is about a villain who sits in a room at the top of a tall tower. He has killed George's wife and George goes up to confront him. The villain transforms into many shapes. In one, he is driving George's car and George puts his hands over the villain's eyes so he will crash. In the front seat is a tough, sexy woman. In the end, George is with his wife who has come back to life. They are both descending the stairs of the tower. The villain is above and spits down at them. It is hard to avoid the spit. The villain is captured and sent to jail.

In working with the dream, I ask George to assume all the roles. He plays the villain, the wife, the sexy woman in the car, the car, the tower and the spit, giving a first person monologue for each role. He also identifies himself, George, as the protagonist. I watch George work. I am fully engaged in his drama, although I do not participate directly. I guide him from role to role, sometimes asking questions so that he will deepen his connection to a particular role or amplify a theme. After his enactment, I lead him through a discussion of the roles and their connection to one another. Finally, I ask him to link the roles in the dream to his everyday life.

Through our work together, George has learned to make the connections. Over time, George has learned to expand his repertory of roles, to deepen his commitment to several key roles and to find a way to guide himself without the fear of crashing. As therapist, I remain present as guide, reminding him to remove his hands from his eyes while he is driving, encouraging him to explore all the dark rooms at the tops of towers, urging him to look at ways to exist as a man among men and among women.

Populations Best Served through the Role Method

I began experimenting with drama therapy in the mid-1960s when I was a teacher of emotionally disturbed adolescents. My task was to teach English and drama, but many of my students were too disorganized and did not have the inner controls to learn how to scan poetry or to memorize lines in a play. Their pathologies ranged from learning disabilities and neurological impairments to severe mental illness and trauma. It took me several years of trial and error to begin to feel any sense of competence. I was learning the ropes, making up the work as I went along. For my students I was a guide of sorts, although very much a work in progress. I was not much older than some. Many had more life experience than I would ever have. Yet, I knew something about the theatre and had a great faith in its healing power. My years as an actor were more therapeutic than aesthetically gratifying as I found a form through which I could express and work through my pain. I was passionate about sharing my experience with others.

Twenty-five years passed before I developed role theory and the role method, and yet the seeds of my work as a drama therapist were planted at that time. I learned how to reach people who were unable to think and feel in a traditional way, who were unable to trust and to communicate and to empathize.

As I have developed drama therapy approaches over the years, I have kept my early experiences very much alive. The emotionally disturbed people I initially worked with remain my models, and when I speak of role-CR-guide or the taxonomy of roles or the role method, I still reflect upon my early work with them. It made sense that when I started to treat individual clients in drama therapy, the first population I worked with was learning disabled adolescents.

During the past 30 years I have worked with many people, including those from the following populations: attention deficit hyperactive disorder (ADHD), alcohol and heroin addiction, eating disorders, post-traumatic stress disorder (PTSD), bipolar disorder, sexual disorders, borderline and schizophrenic disorders, physical and developmental disabilities and normal neurotics, among others. My students trained in role method have applied the principles of role theory to the treatment of these and a range of other populations including conduct-disordered and incarcerated adolescents and adults, war veterans, sexually abused children, homeless mentally ill and frail elderly.

It is difficult to say which groups respond best to this treatment. On one level, it appears that the higher functioning normal neurotic population is most responsive in that this group can easily verbalize and reflect upon their enactments in role. Yet, there is growing evidence that the role method is also effective in treating lower functioning mentally ill individuals. One recent study (Sussman, 1998) offered evidence, primarily anecdotal, that a group of schizophrenics could effectively invoke and work through a number of roles, then relate these figures to their everyday lives.

It remains speculative as to which groups are best suited to role method as there is no hard research available. The evidence that abounds is largely anecdotal and based in process recordings and clinical observations. The exception is the development of systematic case studies that provide a view of the therapeutic process in terms of the role theory paradigm. Case studies include those of Michael (Landy, 1993), Hansel and Gretel (Landy, 1993), Sam (Landy, 1996), Kerry, Lena and Walt (Landy, 1997) and Fay (Landy, 1999).

Limitations and Challenges

There are a number of limitations to role theory. Like any other theory, it is limited by its own set of assumptions concerning epistemology and such psychological issues as personality structure, health and wellness, therapeutic goals and processes. It challenges the humanistic, existential, modernist assumptions that underlie much of drama therapy, moving drama therapy discourse into a cognitive, constructivist, post-modernist realm. Many practitioners find this particular orientation too theoretical and intellectual.

Role theory does not sufficiently address issues of human development. It relies on a model of the human personality–the taxonomy of roles–that is derived from an art form and has very little scientific basis. The taxonomy itself, no matter how flexible and fluid, remains a reductive system, not easily applicable to the fluid and spontaneous movement of individuals from role to role in everyday life and in therapy.

Role theory tends to have more of a literary than social scientific focus and thus does not lend itself to the development of a substantial research literature acceptable to social scientists. Even as modeled in dramatic literature, it relies almost entirely upon role and character at the expense of theme and plot, sound and sense.

The other side of this argument is that the part of role theory that is derived from sociology and symbolic interactionism has too much of a scientific focus as noted in the development of a substantial research literature (see Brissett and Edgley, 1975; Serifica, 1982). As such, it remains unacceptable to those who insist on an aesthetic perspective and minimize the importance of systematic research studies.

The role method is also limited in that it is based in a single theory that is limited in at least the ways mentioned above. If it were linked more clearly with other approaches it might allow the practitioner more leeway in treatment and analysis. Although role method practitioners do make use of techniques associated with play therapy, playback theatre, psychodrama, Gestalt therapy and related approaches, their primary means of treatment is through projective techniques. This can be a limitation, especially when clients need to work in a direct manner, unmediated by role.

There are two challenges to this and indeed to any method and/or theory of drama therapy. The first is to verify its efficacy through carefully designed research studies. Through research, the method/theory will assert its uniqueness among others. The second is to demonstrate its common bonds with other approaches to drama therapy which would, in a broad sense, further establish the credibility of the entire field of drama therapy.

CASE EXAMPLE

The experience I will describe took place during an intense two-day workshop in Israel. I think that it well represents both the philosophy of role theory and the practice of role method. The focus of the workshop was to explore the spiritual dimension of life. In the beginning, as the group was warming up, it became clear that many were uncomfortable with the topic. The group was comprised mainly of therapists and artists, who primarily considered themselves to be secular Jews. They harbored open resentment toward the ultraorthodox whom, they thought, tried to impose strict spiritual and moral guidelines upon their everyday lives.

After some heated debate, I helped the group identify several roles: the spiritual searcher, the doubter, the object of the search and the guide. Although I had intended to limit the role choice to three, I recognized the group's need to distance itself from associating God with the object of their search. The fourth role of guide was acceptable to the group because it felt more neutral than God and stood outside the object of the search.

As I reflected upon the choice of roles, I thought that the literal guide was redundant and that the object of the search would easily stand in for the guide. More than that, I imagined that any of the roles could be guide, although the searcher and doubter felt like a clear representation of the role and counter-role.

Following a complex process of storytelling, drawing and improvisational enactment, I asked the group to choose one story to dramatize. They chose Judah's story. Judah was an anomaly in the group–a businessman among therapists and artists. He had never attended a therapeutic or creative workshop of any kind. He remained quiet and withdrawn throughout the first several hours of the experience. On a number of occasions I wondered if he would be able to complete the tasks and enter fully into the process. Yet his story was extraordinary in some way. This is Judah's story:

> A man comes home from work early and lies down on the couch to take a nap. He wakes suddenly, as if from a dream, to find the light from the TV blinding him. He tries to turn it off, but he cannot. He is disoriented and in order to regain his balance, he must determine the time of day. He picks up the phone and calls an old girlfriend named Rona. He identifies himself as Robert. He asks her urgently: "Is it 6 o'clock in the morning or 6 o'clock in the evening? Please tell me. I must know!" There is no answer. The man cannot rest. He is desperate to know the answer to his question. The question remains unanswered.

The story baffled and intrigued me and probably the others in the group, for they chose it among many highly imaginative and poetic stories. I noticed that there did not seem to be a guide in the story. Although the man turns to Rona to answer his question, she is unable to answer. I wonder why Judah identified the man as Robert. Was this some form of transference? Did he think that I could help him answer his question or, better yet, understand what the question means? Was I supposed to be the guide for Judah who takes on my name in order to search for a sense of balance?

In terms of role theory, my speculation made sense. Judah, a man who has never experienced therapy or a creative arts experience, felt off balance in his life and his wife, a creative arts therapist, suggested that he attend this workshop. In search of a guide to help him find his balance, he takes on the role of the leader whom he imagines is powerful and wise. Judah hopes that the guide role will help him find the clarity and balance he so desperately seeks. In this example, the role and the guide are merged although, as we shall see, they soon become separate. The counterrole appears to be the ex-girlfriend, Rona, the one who cannot answer the question, the false hope, as many ex-lovers come to be.

After the group chose Judah's story, Judah read the story aloud. Unsure of how to proceed with the dramatization, I asked Judah: "Who is telling the story?" As the words came out of my mouth, I realized that I had no idea why I asked this question.

"Leonard is telling the story," Judah replied.

Something was happening that felt unexpected and exciting. Other presences were about to be revealed.

"Who is Leonard?" I asked.

"I am Leonard," said Judah.

Then Judah told the story behind the story. He was born Leonard in Poland. He immigrated to Israel when he was five years old. At the border, the immigration officer told him that Leonard, the Lion, was not a proper Jewish name. As he was about to enter his new land, he was given the name Judah, the Jew.

An important part of the role method concerns the naming of roles. I recognized that Judah's drama would be based upon discovering the right names for his roles and working them through. In discovering the twin names of Leonard/Judah, a significant role-CR relationship was present. On a whole other level, however, I recognized that Leonard would be Judah's guide, just like Robert. Judah seemed to need several guides. He was in foreign territory. By engaging in this workshop, he had stepped over another border.

I asked Judah to tell Leonard's story. He stumbled but managed to tell this:

> There is a little boy. He is not alone. He is with a group of human beings. I think they are grown-ups but they could be children. Or I think they are childlike. The human beings help Leonard to grow.

I ask Judah to choose three people as the human beings and one as Leonard. He chooses Avi, a very playful and dramatic member of the workshop, to be Leonard. Taking their cue from Judah, the group becomes light and playful. The human beings engulf Leonard, and Leonard loves the attention. They circle the room, arm in arm, singing and dancing. They are connected and happy. Judah stays by my side. He tells me that he is happy watching the drama.

I noticed that the human beings are easy guides for the little boy to follow. There does not appear to be a counterrole in the story. There is no tension, no strife. It appears to be a picture of the boy before he crosses the border, before the fall, before he was forced to change his identity and be a man.

I asked Judah if he was ready to enact Judah's story. He became more serious as he said "Yes." He chooses Dahlia to play himself. I ask him to help Dahlia enter into her role. But as he begins to instruct her, she stops: "Who am I supposed to be?" she asks. "Am I Judah or Leonard or Robert?"

Dahlia raises a very important question. In terms of role theory, is she to be the role, the CR or the guide? Judah, the spiritual searcher, seems to be the protagonist of the story, the central role figure. Leonard could be either a CR or guide. Robert would appear to be a guide figure.

Who is guiding whom, I wonder? Then I remember the four roles the group had specified at the beginning of the workshop. The first, the spiritual searcher, is well exemplified by Judah. The doubter could also be Judah in the guise of the storyteller or when he returns home from work, so weary that he falls asleep. The object of the search is unknown, but appears to be the one who can answer the man's question. It might be Rona. The guide appears to be Robert, the workshop leader whose name is taken on by Judah.

With all the potential role confusions it is no wonder that Dahlia is confused. Then she questions why Judah picked a woman to play a man. Dahlia is stuck and I ask Judah to choose someone else from the group to help her find her way. He immediately chooses Avi who again takes on the childish energy of Leonard and starts to wail: "I want my Mommy! I want my Mommy!"

Dahlia is energized and plays with Avi. They encircle each other as she tries to contain his energy, his mock expression of fear. Role and CR are finally present, the child in pain and the mother attempting to contain. They have transcended the story line, but something very important is happening and we all feel it. I bring Judah directly into the drama, having him reverse roles with Dahlia. Judah tries to calm the child. He pets Avi and says: "It's OK. You will be alright. You are such a good boy."

I tell Judah to try to reach Rona and ask her the question. He picks Roni from the group to play Rona. But as he moves toward her, Avi holds on to him tightly. Judah struggles to break free. He finally manages to pull away, but loses a shoe to Avi.

Judah asks the question: "What time is it? I have to know."

She replies: "It is six in the morning."

But I feel she is the wrong object of Judah's search, the wrong guide, and so I ask him: "Did you ask the right question?"

He replies: "No."

I invite others in the group to enter the drama as Judah/Robert and attempt to find the right question. No one is successful. Judah is not able to accept any of their questions.

Again, I am stumped. How do I end this enactment? What needs to happen? Then I realize that the role-CR tension needs some resolution. The drama now concerns Judah, the searcher, and Rona, the object of the search. I ask all in the group to touch the person with whom they most identify–the searcher or the object of the search. Most all choose Judah. They, too, are searchers who are not clear as to their spiritual questions. How different they are from the beginning of the workshop when most openly identified with the role of doubter.

Needing to integrate the two roles, I ask Avi and Roni to attempt to touch one another. When they do, the drama will end. I ask the group to ensure that the moment of touch does not happen too quickly. They take hold of Avi and Roni and pull them in different directions. I then ask Judah to stand in for Avi. Judah and Roni struggle to break free from the group.

Finally, exhausted, the group allows them to touch. The drama ends, and I work hard to de-role all the participants. Judah is in a heightened state and has trouble letting go of the extraordinary roles of the man who wakes up, of Robert and Leonard, of searcher, guide and child. This form of experience in role is all new to Judah. The full group helps him to breathe, to shake off the magic, to come back to the present moment in time. It is a hard journey back for all.

As we discuss this experience, many levels of role-CR-guide unfold. On the level of the dramatic reality, Robert and Rona become role and CR, the searcher and the object of the search. The question of time is never properly answered and doesn't even seem to matter since it might have been the wrong question to ask in the first place. What seems to matter most is the touch, the integration of the roles. Judah reports that this moment was the most satisfying of all. This might be so because of the integration of role and CR which, according to role theory, should have some relationship to Judah's everyday life.

That relationship is discovered when Judah explains that Roni, whom he chose to play Rona, the ex-girlfriend, is in reality his wife. On another level, then, this was a drama about Judah's connection to his wife. The figure of the ex-girlfriend becomes a kind of counterrole that leads Judah back to the strength of his current relationship. Incidentally, I recall that Roni led Judah to the workshop in the first place, hoping that it would move him out of his lethargy and imbalance.

On another level, Judah makes a conscious association of Robert as guide. He becomes aware that he took on this guide role as a means of searching for an answer to his burning question. I ask him to consider ways to hold on to this role as he reenters his everyday realms of love and work and play.

Finally we are left with the theme of the workshop, exploring the spiritual realm through drama therapy. At the beginning of the experience, I mentioned to the group that I was in the process of researching ways that children see God. It was at that moment that several group members expressed their uneasiness with the topic of spirituality in general, and the concept of God, in particular. I chose not to deal with God in any direct way, but here we were at the end of the workshop and I had a need to link our work with the central theme.

"Was Judah's story dramatization spiritual in any way?" I asked. Many nodded in the affirmative and tried to articulate the mysterious quality of Judah's story and the search for love as a spiritual theme. Some spoke about the question of time and related this to the timelessness of the divine. But the most striking comment was made, finally, by Avi, the one who was able to so easily take on the role of the child, Leonard, before and after the fall. He informed us that God is referred to in Hebrew as *Hashem,* literally, the name. There is a prohibition in the orthodox Jewish faith about speaking the name of God directly. Thus God is referred to as Hashem. Avi said that he saw the drama therapy experience as focused upon naming. Judah's search for the right name and Dahlia's confusion over the names was like the Jew's search for the right name of God. Then Judah recognized that the prohibition against speaking the holy name of God connects to his own prohibition against speaking the name of Leonard, the child that he was a long time ago.

Upon further reflection I became aware that Judah was a man very much in search of a guide, one who could help him integrate not only the name he lost as a child, but also the lost qualities of the child. In the end, he recognized that the playful qualities of the child could guide him in so many ways: to get him through his work, to allow him a restful night's sleep, to keep him focused in the present moment in time, to keep him connected to his wife. The implications of the name, Leonard, remained with Judah. Leonard is not only the child but also the lion, the king of beasts, the one in control of the jungle without and the jungle and playground within.

As the group was disbanding, we all also recognized a final political level. Judah's story is the story of a nation of immigrants who left behind their names, their original roles, to take on new identities and to build a nation in and among hostile forces. For many who have shut out the old roles, the counterroles they have taken on have seemed somehow incomplete. Although the state of Israel has had many powerful guides, no one has been universally accepted. Israel is a country of splits and it has been difficult for many to find integration and balance. Judah found his balance having rediscovered Leonard through the help of a guide, Robert. I should say, Judah had the help of several guides including Avi and Roni.

The final step of the role method concerns social modeling. As Judah takes his new awareness into the many realms of his everyday life, he has the opportunity to affect the lives of others. He has taken one large step toward assuming the qualities and function of the guide.

SUMMARY AND CONCLUSIONS

Role theory and role method in drama therapy are separate but intimately connected. Role theory concerns a way of understanding the origins and goals and processes of drama therapy. It is derived in part from the social sciences but primarily from the art form of theatre. As such it provides the field with its central and unique focus as first an art form and then a science. As a theory, it gives a framework in which to make sense of all other aspects of the clinical and research branches of drama therapy.

Role method is an extension of the theory to clinical practice. Although I have attempted to outline the approach in a sequential fashion, I feel that the actual process of therapy moves along a curve or circle rather than a straight line. In the example of Judah we see evidence of invoking roles, working them through, discovering counterroles and guides, reflecting upon the roles and connecting them with everyday life roles, integrating role-CR-guide and speculating among the possibilities of social modeling. Yet, I hope it is clear that the actual process is in many ways murky. In this case, the most important element, the actual turning point, seems to be the naming. In other cases, the key moment appears in the invocation or working through or reflection. Each case is unique.

Drama therapy is a very small field, a subset of psychotherapy or the art of drama/theatre or the creative arts therapies. Or perhaps drama therapy is a field in itself, derivative as much as all fields, yet indivisible. I think the field is too young to proclaim its independence. But then again, the same had been said about Israel and for that matter, about the United States of America.

If the field is to survive well into this new millennium and if it remains alive as more than a footnote in a textbook of psychotherapy or theatre or creative arts therapy, then it will need a solid foundation in theory and in clinical practice grounded in theory. Role theory and its concomitant role method is one attempt to do just that–to organize discrepant concepts, techniques and practices into a coherent system, one that has the weight and the lightness to travel through time.

REFERENCES

Bloom, B. et al. (1956). *Taxonomy of educational objectives, handbook I: Cognitive domain.* New York: David McKay.

Brissett, D., & Edgley, C. (Eds.). (1975). *Life as theatre: A dramaturgical sourcebook.* Chicago: Aldine.

Campbell, J. (1949). *The hero with a thousand faces.* New York: Pantheon Books.

Cooley, C. (1922). *Human nature and social order.* New York: Scribner's.

Eliaz, E. (1988). *Transference in drama therapy,* Ph.D. dissertation, New York University.

Fox, J. (Ed.). (1987). *The essential Moreno.* New York: Springer.

Goffman, E. (1959). *The presentation of self in everyday life.* Garden City, New York: Doubleday.

Hillman, J. (1983). *Healing fiction.* Barrytown, New York: Station Hill.

James, W. (1890, 1950). *The principles of psychology.* New York: Dover.

Jung, C.G. (1964). *Man and his symbols.* Garden City, New York: Doubleday.

Jung, C.G. (1971). *Psychological types.* Princeton: Princeton University Press.

Kelly, G.A. (1955). *The psychology of personal constructs,* Vol. I. New York: Norton.

Landy, R. (1983). The use of distancing in drama therapy. *The Arts in Psychotherapy, 10,* 175–185.

Landy, R. (1993). *Persona and performance.* New York: Guilford Press.

Landy, R. (1994). *Drama therapy: Concepts, theories and practices,* 2nd ed. Springfield, IL: Charles C Thomas.

Landy, R. (1996). Drama therapy and distancing: Reflections on theory and clinical application. *The Arts in Psychotherapy, 23,* 367–373.

Landy, R. (1996a). *Essays in drama therapy–The double life.* London: Jessica Kingsley.

Landy, R. (1999). Role model of drama therapy supervision. In Tselikas-Portmann, E. (Ed.), *Supervision and dramatherapy.* London: Jessica Kingsley.

Mead, G.H. (1934). *Mind, self and society.* Chicago: University of Chicago Press.

Moffett, J. (1968). *Teaching the universe of discourse.* New York: Houghton Mifflin.

Moreno, J.L. (1946). *Psychodrama, Vol. 1.* Beacon, New York: Beacon House.

Moreno, J.L. (1947). *The theatre of spontaneity.* Beacon, New York: Beacon House.

Moreno, J.L. (Ed.). (1960). *The sociometry reader.* Glencoe, IL: The Free Press.

Pearson, C. (1989). *The hero within.* New York: Harper Collins.

Raz, S. (1997). *Psychological type and changing acting personas–A hypothetical model of role theory in role acquisition among performing artists.* Ph.D. dissertation, Miami Institute of Psychology.

Riso, D. (1987). *Personality types.* Boston: Houghton Mifflin.

Rosenberg, Y. (1999). *Role theory and self concept.* MA thesis, Lesley College, Israel.

Sarbin, T. and V. Allen. (1968). Role theory, In G. Lindzey and E. Aronson (Eds.), *The handbook of social psychology,* 2nd ed. Reading, MA: Addison-Wesley.

Serafica, F. (1982). *Social-cognitive development in context.* New York: Guilford Press.

Sussman, F. (1998). *Application of role theory and myth to adult schizophrenics in a continuing day treatment program.* MA thesis, New York University.

Tangorra, J. (1997). *Many masks of pedophila: Drama therapeutic assessment of the pedophile role repetoire.* MA thesis, New York University.

FURTHER TRAINING

Masters in Drama Therapy
Approved by the National Association for Drama Therapy
New York University
School of Education
Dr. Robert Landy RDT-BCT, Director
35 West 4th Street
Suite 675B
New York City, New York 19912-1172

212-998-5258

Chapter 5

THE INTEGRATIVE FIVE PHASE MODEL OF DRAMA THERAPY

RENÉE EMUNAH

GENESIS

BOTH DRAMA AND THERAPY are richly layered, multitextured endeavors; both involve a process of gradual unfolding. Both entail risk-taking, which can evoke resistances and fears as well as instill trust. As a drama therapist, I am interested in creating a soft unfolding–promoting trust and minimizing fear, and creating a solid container–which can hold many layers of exploration and revelation. I am interested in the way an "aesthetic flow"–that is, a quality of seamless, organic progression of the work/play–furthers the therapeutic process. I am interested in the subtle interplay between leading and following, between creating an engaging structure and following the participant's cues.

I write this chapter during the first year of parenting my twin babies, and I wonder at the similarities between parenting and this approach to drama therapy. I am following my babies' leads–observing their modes of communication, sensing their needs, learning who they are, responding to their subtle cues. But I am also a facilitator, setting some kind of structure, offering particular realms of experiences to which they respond. We are in this mirroring dance, this melding of nature-nurture, and sometimes I lose track of who is leading whom. The same is true of my work as a drama therapist, especially in a group drama therapy context. The Integrative Five Phase model in itself is both a way of facilitating a drama therapy process and a way of understanding the clients' lead and identifying their cues.

As a parent too, I am drawn to creating soft transitions–from womb to life on the outside, from one stage to the next. The babies continued to sleep huddled together post-birth, the lights dimmed and sounds muffled. I wore them in a sling or carrier throughout the day, and played recordings of my voice or heartbeat when I couldn't be with them physically. I have enjoyed noting the subtle ways they indicate their readiness for the next stage–for example, the way they shifted from wanting to be held facing me, to wanting to look outward, a sign of their increasing desire to take in more of the world. Their focus now is on independent exploration, but they relish the moments of brief return to earlier phases.

DRAMA THERAPY FRAME OF REFERENCE

The integrative five phase model presents a developmental course of treatment, in which the therapeutic journey is paced and progressive, offering a sense of unfolding. Each stage paves the way for the next stage, spiraling a series of sessions toward deeper levels of play, intimacy, and self-revelation. The work progresses from interactive dramatic play, to developed theatre scenework, to role play dealing with personal situations, to culminating psychodramatic enactments exploring core themes, to dramatic ritual related to closure. The fictional mode provides a protective safeguard as well as a means of expanding one's capacities for (and range of) expression. But eventually the roles are shed, the masks unraveled, and the fictional scenerios give way to life scenes (Emunah, 1998).

The shift from the fictional to the personal is dictated by the clients; it is an organic process, in which the therapist is attentive to the point at which the clients naturally and spontaneously make personal connections to the fictional enactments. This point signals the end of Phase Two; the clients will soon be ready to explore their real lives more directly. The first two phases afford a sense of liberation and expansion, and also elicit the clients' most healthy selves, as their spontaneity, creativity, imagination, and resourcefulness are generated. The personal work that follows emerges from the fictional scenes and one's associations to these scenes, thereby circumventing the danger of having preconceived notions of one's "issues" as one embarks on psychodramatic work. The personal material is connected to the fictional material; indeed it is an outgrowth of it.

Based in humanistic psychology, the model elicits and expands the healthfulness of the person. The model is also guided by central concepts of existential, psychodynamic, and cognitive-behavioral approaches to psychotherapy. Emotional catharsis and mastery, cognitive insight and behavioral change are all essential and intertwining parts of the therapeutic process. The expansion of one's sense of self, role repertoire, freedom and possibility–along with an awareness of limitation–underlie this approach to drama therapy.

My approach is eclectic, encompassing the wide array of processes, techniques, healing properties and possibilities inherent in the medium of drama therapy–in a sequenced fashion, involving careful reflection and perception on the part of the drama therapist. The five phases are linked to the five conceptual sources that I find most primary to drama therapy. While elements of all five conceptual sources are evident in each phase, each source is most correspondent to a particular phase. Phase One is most influenced by dramatic play, Phase Two by theatre, Phase Three by role theory, Phase Four by psychodrama, and Phase Five by dramatic ritual. The phases are not separate blocks, but rather fluid and overlapping stages. The model is about fluidity, not rigidity; it is about facilitating a seamless flow and subtle progression, deepening both the aesthetic and therapeutic possibilities of our field.

The phases grow out of extensive observation of drama therapy groups rather than being a preimposed structure or design. Early videotapes of mine documenting long-term drama therapy treatment illustrate the phase-progression, even though I had not yet developed this model. In other words, the development of the model was a matter of articulating and conceptualizing what I was witnessing and instinctively facilitating. While the nature and course of the therapeutic journey are obviously dictated by each unique client and each unique group, the movement from one phase to the next tends to signify the positive development of the therapeutic process.

Every model, method and theory says a lot about the person who developed it. I know this model reflects many of my own sensibilities: I love the "hamams" (Muslim steam rooms) in Paris because you go from one steam room to next, each one slightly hotter–a gradual progression toward increasing intensity. I don't like the shock of plunging from steaming hot to freezing cold water. I like wading in shallow waters, frolicking in waist-high water, and then swimming in the very deep waters–and the journey through the levels of depth. I like the experience of complete immersion in an activity that happens when I have built up to it slowly. I like play of all kinds, including of course foreplay; I appreciate being-in-the-moment, anticipation, evolution, and readiness–all of which are key concepts in this model of drama therapy.

The initial playful stages of the Integrative Five Phase Model form a backbone for the later intensely personal stages of work. The early phases remain present even as a group progresses to later phases. Clients relish retasting the earlier work, and this creates a more continuous and cumulative experience, rather than one of loss. The process is thus not strictly linear: each stage encompasses and builds on elements of the prior stages; and the final phase is reminiscent of the first phase, bringing the journey full circle.

Basic Concepts

The model is based on the following premises (Emunah, 1997):

1. The therapeutic journey is eased and strengthened by a sense of gradual unfolding, in which the work is paced and progressive, creating in the clients a sense of readiness at all times for the next step/level.

2. Beginning the therapeutic process within the creative drama mode is liberating, enabling clients to experience a sense of freedom from the constraints of everyday life and from engrained patterns. The engagement in the fictional realm also circumvents the tendency to immediately rehash predictable, familiar life issues. Over time, the associations one has between the fictional scenes and one's real life lead to a more direct working through of real life issues, but from a fresh, often unexpected perspective.

3. The fictional realm is protective, at the same time that it enables self-revelation–in a safe and distanced manner. Over time, the need for a safeguard diminishes. But just as theatre director Chaikin (1984) poetically describes the way the wearing of a mask changes the actor's face, so too the process of taking on roles impacts the client's self image/perception/awareness. When the time comes to discard roles and unravel layers of masks, the person is not the same as s/he was prior to these acting processes.

4. The building of trust and interrelationships within the group provides a critical foundation to the later personal, emotional work. The therapeutic value of an individual's psychodramatic scenework is integrally linked to the depth with which other group members witness, support, empathize with, and thereby help contain that person's work (Emunah, 1994). Additionally, clients will play auxiliary roles in a fellow member's psychodramatic scene with greater commitment once they have established a caring relationship to that person.

5. Developing an ease with (and skills in) drama/acting leads the eventual psychodramatic scenes to be performed with greater authenticity. The more authentic the en/acting, the more deeply the client/actor is affected. A familiarity with dramatic processes also reduces self-consciousness and the cognitive distance/disruption that can occur when one is adjusting to various directions at the same time that one is dealing with emotional scenework.

6. Intense and varied emotions can be safely expressed in the context of fictional roles, scenerios, and acting processes. Through these drama therapeutic processes, the therapist comes to know the client's capacity and tolerance for emotional expression, and the degree of containment s/he needs–information that is

very useful in terms of guiding the client and making interventions, when the client later engages in the psychodramatic scenes.

7. In drama therapy, the client's creativity, expressiveness, spontaneity, playfulness, and imagination are accessed–qualities which enhance self-esteem and self-image. Experiencing, and having others witness, one's strengths enables a person to feel freer to later disclose and grapple with material/parts of the self that are frightening, shameful, or painful. The increased access to one's creativity also becomes an asset in the later stages, in terms of being able to master intensely emotional content.

The Therapeutic Process

Phase One: Dramatic Play

The first phase lays the groundwork, or foundation, that can support the work that is to follow. A nonthreatening, playful environment is established. Processes include adapted versions of creative dramatics, improvisation, playful, interactive exercises, and structured theatre games. In a group therapy context, many of the techniques are physically active, and most are socially interactive. Individual and group skills are developed. These skills, in turn, promote self-confidence and self-esteem, along with an awareness of and appreciation for the qualities of coparticipants. This phase is based on a health model. The strengths and healthy parts of the client are elicited; in keeping with the humanistic paradigm (Maslow, 1968; May, 1975; Rogers, 1961), qualities such as expressiveness, playfulness, creativity, spontaneity, humor and aliveness are nurtured. These qualities develop the clients' ego-strength, enabling them to tolerate the more regressive work, involving often painful self-examination, later in the treatment series.

Trust begins to develop–trust in one's own capacities, trust between group members, and trust in the therapist. Acceptance of self and others, a growing connectedness between group members, and group cohesion are central features of a successful group process. Although these features evolve naturally over a period of time, following an often slow and rocky course, drama offers particular means of accelerating and strengthening this course. Interaction between members, which can be so awkward and minimal in beginning phases of verbal groups, is facilitated via drama therapy. Drama is a collective, collaborative art form. This aspect of drama is central to the work in Phase One. The unifying capacity of drama is drawn upon; collective creativity is encouraged. In individual drama therapy, the interactive dramatic processes in Phase One facilitate the development of the relationship with, and trust in, the therapist.

Dramatic play, the most influential conceptual source of Phase One, generates spontaneity and facilitates relationship and interaction. The majority of dramatic processes used in Phase One are linked to dramatic play. Participants play out personally or socially significant themes symbolically, creatively, and collaboratively. Familiar themes and issues are also left behind, as participants enter the world of the imagination.

Phase One can be the most or the least structured part of the treatment series. It is the least structured when working in a mode of free-associative and nondirective play. By observing and participating in the client's dramatic play, the therapist gains a deeper understanding of underlying issues and themes. Informed therapeutic interventions can thus be made later in the treatment series. Phase One is the most structured part of a treatment series of sessions when the therapist takes the role of active facilitator, easing the clients into the drama therapy mode and treatment process, rather than prioritizing diagnosis and interpretation. Structured dramatic play and theatre games (both adapted for drama therapy) tend to diminish potential reluctance, fear, and self-consciousness, especially with adult clients who have lost touch with the dramatic play of childhood. In either case, unstructured or structured, the role of the therapist and the techniques s/he incorporates at this point significantly influence the process of treatment, whereas later in the treatment series the therapeutic interventions s/he makes are far more important than the choice of drama therapy techniques.

It is important that initial activities are simple, engaging, failure-proof, and *age-appropriate.* The use of unsuitable techniques at this early stage may increase the clients' inhibitions and resistances, which often results in wavering commitments and dropouts. In addition to the fears associated with beginning any therapy process and of joining a group, there are particular fears associated with *drama* therapy. These include the fear of appearing childish, of having to perform (and failing), and of being asked to be other than oneself (or other than how one actually feels). The therapist should avoid any techniques that might confirm these fears. The trust of the clients needs to be earned during Phase One; the establishment of a positive therapeutic relationship is paramount. Later in the series, the clients' commitment and connectedness to treatment is sustained also by peer relationships and the overall sense of group identity.

With sensitive leadership during Phase One, clients experience a sense of permission, freedom, and joy, reminiscent of the experience of dramatic play in childhood. This sense of permission expands into a sense of liberation in Phase Two, with the more developed dramatic acting and scenework.

Phase Two: Scenework

Phase Two progresses from the spontaneous improvised play and structured dramatic games in Phase One to sustained dramatic scenes, composed of developed roles and characters. The primary dramatic process in this phase is scenework, which is generally improvised (although some drama therapists use existing scripts). Though the link to dramatic play remains present, the conceptual source at the heart of Phase Two is theatre.

In contrast to psychodrama, in which protagonists play the roles of themselves in a variety of situations, the scenework of Phase Two involves playing roles other than those reflecting one's own life. This allows for greater role distance and less immediate self-disclosure, a useful step in the development of trust and spontaneity.

The aspect of drama central to Phase Two is the notion that acting gives permission to "be different." Diverse scenes and roles afford clients the opportunity to experience and exhibit new sides of themselves. Within the dramatic context, latent aspects of the self can emerge and suppressed emotions can be expressed. Wished-for qualities or characteristics can be tried on and embodied. The "shadow" part of the person can be tolerated and given voice via the sanctioned theatrical role.

The critical point of awareness for the therapist at this stage is to ensure the freedom that promotes self-expression and role-expansion. More specifically, the therapist should not insist on verbal "processing" or "ownership." Urging the person to own everything that emerges spontaneously or within the context of the role will be inhibiting; the beginning of Phase Two should be one of liberation, not inhibition. It is important not to destroy the very context that is enabling the "transformation" to take place.

By the middle of Phase Two, clients begin naturally to comment on or to discuss their enactments. Often there are manifestations of surprise at the emotion displayed in the scene or the type of character played. Typical remarks are: "I can't believe how much anger I expressed in that role," "I've never acted like that in my life" or "that's so different than the way I usually behave." Toward the latter part of Phase Two, clients relate yet more personally to their enacted roles. Comments here may be: "That's a pattern of mine, so it felt familiar to play that role" or "that part helped me to express the sadness I really feel." This is an exciting point in the series, for here clients make the connection between drama and therapy. This connection is often expressed as an "aha" experience. For the first time, they simultaneously apprehend this activity as both drama and therapy.

The end of Phase Two is marked not only by the responses of the "actors" but also by those of the "audience." Clients watching the scenes begin to express associations they had to the scene and feelings or memories that were evoked. An improvisation about a couple arguing might remind someone of his divorce; a scene about loss might elicit sadness and even tears, in much the same way that watching a movie or play affords cathartic release. Scenes also help people to recall positive moments in their lives and give occasion for these to be shared with the group. This verbal processing is not forced but spontaneous; clients manifest the desire to review and discuss the scenes.

Because of the personal disclosures and potentially intense emotional reactions arising at this point, it is important that Phase Two occur only after some degree of trust in the group and therapist has already been established.

To summarize, in the first two stages of drama therapy, the dramatic medium provides the safeguard, or disguise, which enables self-revelation. In this context, participants often seem to both expose more of themselves *and* to feel safer than in normal everyday encounters. Gradually though, as trust continues to develop between group members and toward the therapist, the need for safeguards dissolve, and what is exposed can be *consciously* tolerated and integrated. The verbal processing at the end of Phase Two steers the scenework in a more personal direction. In the latter stages of drama therapy, the dramatic medium is used to explore personal material more directly.

Phase Three: Role Play

Phase Three is marked by the shifting of the dramatizations from the imaginary to the actual: clients are now ready to use the dramatic medium to explore situations in their own lives. Current predicaments, conflicts, and relationships are presented and examined. The thin line separating drama and real life is particularly apparent at this point. The scenes, based on real life, seem *so real.* Yet the fact that they are fictional enactments rather than real life occurrences is of critical significance in terms of therapeutic possibilities. The stage becomes a laboratory setting in which real life can be explored and experimented with in safety. Central to Phase Three is the notion of drama as rehearsal for life.

The primary dramatic process in Phase Three is role play. Clients replay confusing or disturbing interactions with friends, express feelings to significant people in their lives, confront people with whom they are angry, practice job interviews. Common themes shared by a particular group are often explored. The dramatic examination of interpersonal issues within the group is also largely the domain of Phase Three, a phase which incorporates many aspects of psychodrama and sociodrama.

Role play and role theory are the most influential conceptual sources of this phase. Through dramatization and ensuing discussion, clients gain a clearer view of the roles they play in life and the patterns that emerge in their interactions. Moments from real life are magnified and elucidated under the illuminating lights of the theatrical stage. Clients simultaneously act and watch themselves in action, a feat difficult to accomplish on a regular basis in real life. The measure of distance from reality afforded by drama stimulates the functioning of the self-observing ego. This distance can be capitalized upon by pausing in the midst of a scene or just after the scene ends–at which point the players examine each person's role and behavior, how each interpreted and was affected by the other's role and behavior, and how effective each person was in his or her role. The drama therapist gradually makes interventions, under the auspices of theatrical directions, that facilitate awareness and change, rather than unending repetition.

Clients play not only themselves, but also other people in their lives. For example, adolescents may be interviewed *as* their parents, followed by enactments of relevant parent-teen conflicts. In playing the role of others, the client gains perspective; the responses and motivations of others are better understood. Taking on the role of another person in one's life relating to oneself (for example, if I play the role of my brother while someone else plays me) enables one to encompass and assimilate the multitude of roles and facets of self that are manifested in relation to others.

Work in Phase Three often occurs on a behavioral level; role play in assertiveness training, for example, is considered Phase Three material. However, through skillful intervention on the part of the drama therapist, insight into roles and behavioral patterns is also achieved. The drama therapist at this point needs to pay careful attention to the direction of the scenes, ensuring that the client is taken further–toward understanding or discovery of options, rather than simply repeating real life performances. Verbal processing is generally very integrated with dramatic work at this point. Dramatization and discussion help clients not only vent feelings and practice new behaviors, but understand and change underlying dynamics. Most importantly, at this stage clients experience themselves not only as actors, but as directors, playwrights, audiences, and critics of their own life dramas.

It is toward the end of this phase that clients often begin clearly to experience a sense of hope for change in their lives. The hope comes as a result of experiencing (as opposed to only imagining) themselves responding (via the dramatic mode) to personal situations differently from the nonconstructive patterns of response they fall prey to in actuality. The implication is that if they could act that way in scenes that are *almost real,* perhaps they could act that way *for real.* The importance of the development of acting skills in Phases One and Two must be reemphasized here. Without a certain level of dramatic proficiency, the scenes are not "real enough" for this dynamic to take place. It is at this point too that clients frequently report that they responded to a difficult real life situation in a new or uncharacteristic way. Many clients have told me that this was accomplished by pretending they were acting a scene. Put in other terms, these clients made use of the capacities they had manifested in drama to cope more effectively and healthfully with the trials of real life.

Phase Four: Culminating Enactment

The examination of roles, relationships, and conflicts in current life situations gradually leads clients to a deeper level of introspection. The increased level of consciousness regarding role and life patterns achieved in Phase Three facilitates entry into the unconscious. Phase Four is marked by the shift from concrete, present-day issues to more core issues in one's life. The past comes closer to the surface, and unconscious material becomes more accessible. Memories, dreams, associations, and images–some involving family constellations, childhood traumas, significant events–shed light onto unresolved issues, recurrent themes, ongoing struggles. Scenes frequently revolve around experiences that have affected or disturbed the person's present. Some scenes entail revelations about oneself that were until now kept hidden from the group, the therapist, or even from oneself.

The primary conceptual source of Phase Four is psychodrama and the primary dramatic processes are psychodramatic. There is an increased focus on the individual within the group, as the inner life of *protagonists* are dramatically explored and their stories relived. Many of Moreno's (1946) psychodramatic techniques, such as *doubling,* are vital early in Phase Four. By the middle of Phase Four, clients are enacting what I call *culminating scenes*. The culminating scenes are elaborations, deeper explorations of themes that have emerged or patterns that have been exposed during the preceding phases.

Though the culminating scenes resemble psychodramatic scenes, they have two unique features. First, the scenes are performed only at a point at which clients have already developed proficiency in drama, as well as a high level of trust in the group. Second, the content of the scenes is emergent, growing out of the process thus far. These features enable a degree of depth, subtlety and complexity that is often not possible when one begins a treatment series with psychodrama. The scenes are enacted with a particular sense of authenticity and possess intense power on a theatrical as well as a therapeutic level. In performance-oriented drama therapy groups, the *self-revelatory performances* (Emunah, 1994) are usually based on culminating scenes.

In my own work with clients, there is an evolution to this phase, largely because I believe it is critical that the degree of self-exposure and emotional intensity be matched by the level of group cohesion and support. (In psychodrama, the scenes often reach a level of power and profundity that far surpasses the level of connectedness between the group members; indeed intense scenes are not uncommon in one-time-only or "drop-in" sessions. One of the risks here is a postenactment feeling of alienation.) Also the gradual, paced process in drama therapy, in which significant issues (which cannot be predicted or prescribed in advance by the client or the therapist) emerge, facilitates a journey of surprise and discovery. The notion that to pretend or be disguised enables revelation and exposure, a notion capitalized upon in the early stages, is important to reemphasize here. In drama therapy one begins by *acting* rather than by *reenacting.* This process of acting steers the client away from initiating therapeutic work on predictable and familiar issues that often are unconsciously presented as a shield against dealing with more authentically significant issues. The gradual, paced process also enables the therapist both to gauge and to develop the client's tolerance for emotionality and self-exposure before embarking on the intense culminating scenes of Phase Four.

The culminating scenes are a climactic point in the group process. Revelation, disclosure, and sharing are heightened; insight is deepened. As buried emotions emerge and are given an outlet for expression, a powerful experience of catharsis occurs. The therapeutic intensity is matched by the theatrical power of the scenes; both are matched by the level of group support and cohesion. Inner resources, creative reserves, and untapped strengths are drawn upon in developing these scenes. There are often various stages and levels of exploration; one client's culminating scene may have several parts and take more than one session to unfold. The enactments result in a unique sense of both artistic achievement and mastery over often very painful content.

The immediacy and potency of this kind of dramatization tend to heighten the empathy of the other group members and the therapist. In this process of sharing and showing one's internal world, a burden is lifted, an inner weight removed. What was private is now witnessed. This often leads to an experience of intense acceptance and forgiveness, as clients expose what had previously been hidden, even from themselves. A sense of exoneration and of communion ensues–in individual therapy by and with the therapist, in group work within the group, and in performance-oriented drama therapy with the outside world–reminiscent of the ritual purging ceremonies of indigenous cultures, in which evil spirits were expelled in the presence of the entire tribe (Collomb, 1977, in Emunah & Johnson, 1983). The ritualistic aspects of drama pervading the end of Phase Four create a segue to the final stage of the drama therapy treatment series.

Phase Five: Dramatic Ritual

After the climactic, culminating scenes of Phase Four (the duration of which varies widely), the series begins to come to a close. This closure is in itself an important developmental process, facilitating the integration and assimilation of the therapeutic progress made in the preceding phases. The work of Phase Five assists clients in carrying the changes made within the context of drama therapy into the outside world. At the same time, the multiple and complex feelings regarding termination are explored. Phase Five is about transition and closure.

Phase Five is conceptually linked to ritual, and primary dramatic processes are dramatic rituals. In early societies, dramatic rituals were ways in which communities marked points of transition, shared fears, sorrows, wishes and successes, and celebrated events. The celebratory aspect of drama is central to Phase Five. Dramatic rituals (along with other dramatic processes) are incorporated to help clients review the series, evaluate progress, give each other feedback, experience the rewards of accomplishment, and express both the sadness and joy of completion. The processes also serve to reflect and intensify the sense of unity and kinship within the group. The unique *entity* formed by the group and the particular interrelationships within the group are acknowledged and honored.

The intense feelings evoked by the therapy process and its imminent conclusion, along with the deep level of intimacy that has been experienced within the group, can sometimes be best conveyed via dramatic ritual. Collectively developed and repeatable group creations, composed of powerful images, metaphor and story, rhythmic sounds, and poetry and movement, enable the expression of a seldomly mentioned dimension to the therapy process–the spiritual dimension. I am referring to the sense of awe one may encounter during a process that entails uncovering layers, discovering what was previously unknown, accessing the unconscious, transforming pain into art. In the course of treatment, there have been transformations–on small and large scales–witnessed in others, experienced in oneself, and shared with the group (or in individual therapy, with the therapist). These transformations can be perceived not only from psychological and aesthetic standpoints, but from the spiritual domain.

Much of the description of Phase Five applies too, to the final phase of each session within the series. Closure of the treatment series and of each individual session is not a matter of implying that there has been solution or even necessarily resolution. Rather, closure provides an arena for reviewing what has transpired, recognizing the steps that have been taken, and making the transition from the drama therapy session to one's outside reality. The drama therapist devises and utilizes creative techniques to facilitate this review of the process. Significant points in time, powerful scenes, trying periods, critical conflicts or challenges, and important insights are all recalled and further digested. This retrospection deepens the level of introspection, of awareness of all aspects of the process. The entire journey is, in a sense, encapsulated, helping the client to *grasp* and *own* the experience, with all its impact. The rituals in Phase Five provide a kind of *framing* of the treatment session and series.

By the end of Phase Five, clients tend to feel very validated for the process they have been through. The dramatic rituals help achieve this, for–like all rituals–they mark life events, rather than letting events fade into oblivion. In this way, there is a sense not only of loss for what is over, but of appreciation for what has been gained.

The intensive and carefully designed process of closure not only helps clients reflect on and integrate the past, but creates a sense of opening to the future–pointing to the steps that lie ahead, the possibilities, and the hope as one continues the journey. (See Figure 5.1 for a summary delineation of the elements.)

Practical Application of the Phases

The five phases are best viewed not as rigid entities, but as an analysis of the gradual unfolding of a therapeutic process. The phases are fluid and often overlapping. Phase One, for example, remains present on some level throughout the series; it is important not to drop the playful component, even as the clients enter more emotional terrain. Elements of several phases are often present within a single session.

The phases are not intended to be prescriptions for drama therapy, but rather helpful guidelines, which can assist the drama therapist in pacing, identifying needs, assessing progress, and determining appropriate techniques and interventions. Beginning drama therapists, in particular, may be confused about how to assess the degree of containment that is needed, how much and how far to develop therapeutic material, how much to encourage verbal processing after dramatic enactments, whether to interpret scenes or to encourage the client to make personal connections to fictional enactments, etc. Identifying the phase the group or client is in affords a context in which to make informed therapeutic decisions.

There is no set formula for the way in which a group progresses through these five phases. In some cases, the first two phases may be very brief; in others they may comprise the bulk of the series. The model is based on group work, but is also relevant to individual or family drama therapy. The model is suited to work with any population. However, some populations may be best served by an emphasis on a particular phase. For example, some groups of children or of people with a developmental disability may benefit most from Phase One work. Phase Three work, on the other hand, may be most appropriate for support groups (dealing with specific issues) composed of high functioning adults. A particular phase may also be most suitable with the therapeutic orientation of a facility or the length of treatment provided.

The model is based on work with a fixed group membership. With rolling group membership, there is an increased fluctuation in the phases (as the group dynamics and needs shift from session to session) rather than the more steady progression typical of fixed membership groups. With changing membership, Phases Four and Five are rarely apropos. My own preference is for fixed group membership, even in brief treatment, to allow for progression, and to foster the interrelationships and group cohesion that I believe play a most significant role in the journey toward health and well-being.

The phase-oriented model is based on work over a period of time, but this period of

	Phase One	Phase Two	Phase Three	Phase Four	Phase Five
Primary *conceptual sources*	Dramatic Play	Theatre (scenework)	Role Play	Psychodrama (culminating enactments)	Dramatic Ritual
Primary *dramatic processes*	Creative drama Improvised play Theatre games & D. T. techniques	Scenework (fictional)	Role Play role reversal replays [of lifescenes]	Exploratory reenactments Culminating scenes	Dramatic rituals
FOCUS	Humanistic/ health model	Experimentation/ liberation	Explore rehearse preview & review current issues	Core themes	Embracing the whole
OBJECTIVES	• Trust • Interaction & Relationship • Spontaneity & Creativity	• "selves" – expression • Role – expansion • Emotional expansion Make connection between drama & therapy	• Self / role – awareness (self-observing ego) • Role flexibility • Perspective	• Emotional catharsis • Insight • Empathy & Intimacy	• Integration • Review & Transition • Validation • Acknowledgment & Celebration spiritual dimension
	Dramatic Skills & Symbolic &	Ease Established Fictional	——— Actual	———	Symbolic, Actual & Spiritual
Therapeutic Progression	Spontaneity & Freedom	Liberation & Expansion	Behavioral change & Hope	Catharsis & Insight	Integration

Figure 5.1

time has a wide range–typically, from 16 sessions to several years. Brief drama therapy that entails at least 16 sessions can generally follow the evolutionary course from Phase One through Phase Five outlined in this chapter. The ascertainment of phases is especially important in brief drama therapy (Emunah, 1996) because the drama therapist often needs to be a more active facilitator, gently encouraging the group or client to move forward through the phases. In longer-term work the therapist is more of a witness to and follower of the group's pace and evolution.

In many forms of brief drama therapy each of the phases may not be lived out. Rather, the drama therapist determines which phase is most appropriate for and useful to the client or group, and focuses the limited work within that mode. Phase Three is typically the most applicable phase to brief drama therapy. Clients tend to enter brief therapy in order to deal with a particular problem, and are prepared to tackle specific issues, feelings, and conflicts related to this problem directly–all of which point to Phase Three work. The work of Phases One and Two are often too indirect and circuitous for brief drama therapy. While some of the playful and fictional components of these phases can be incorporated, lingering in these phases can lead clients to feel that their presenting problems are not being taken seriously enough. On the other hand, the work of Phase Four, revolving around unconscious and deep-seated material, is often also beyond the realm of brief therapy. Phase Four relies on preparedness and the gradual unfolding of layered therapeutic material; moving into this phase in either a premature or a superficial manner can be countertherapeutic. In that Phase Five represents a culmination and integration of the other four phases, it, too, is less applicable to brief therapy. [This is not to say that brief therapy does not entail closure, but rather that the inclusion of a complete phase revolving around the encapsulation of a treatment series is usually not necessary.] In general, Phases One and Five tend to be least incorporated phases in brief therapy. Phase Two is incorporated primarily as a prelude to Phase Three, and Phase Four is incorporated selectively and cautiously, in accordance with the emotional readiness of the particular client or group.

Despite the limitations of the use of all five phases in some forms of brief drama therapy, elements drawn from each phase are incorporated to enhance the Phase Three-oriented course of treatment, with the following primary objectives: Phase One for building interrelationships and individual strengths; Phase Two for expanding role repertoire and creating a sense of permission and possibility; Phase Four for deepening the level of catharsis, insight, and intimacy; and Phase Five for supporting integration and closure.

Different drama therapists, because of their own orientation and skills, may feel most affinity with a particular phase, and their work may incorporate little of the other phases. Those with a stronger creative drama background or belief in the importance of play and spontaneity, for example, may lean toward Phase One work, and an entire series with such a therapist may remain in this phase. Drama therapists with a stronger background in psychodrama and a preference for in-depth psychotherapeutic work may focus on Phase Four. Those who are more comfortable with "here-and-now," concrete approaches to psychotherapy will probably make most use of Phase Three. Theatre-oriented drama therapists may find Phase Two work the most natural and interesting. Thus the phases can be viewed not only as stages of group development, but as models of practice. In my own practice, however, I have made surprisingly equal use of all phases, with different phases being emphasized with particular groups and clinical population.

Populations Served

My groups with emotionally disturbed and acting-out adolescents (Emunah, 1985, 1990, 1995) tend to center on Phases Two and Three. With high-functioning adult clients the emphasis leans toward Phase Four. In my individual work with children, Phase One is the most primary and extended phase, but Phase Two becomes developed, and with older children the latter phases are also a significant part of the overall treatment process. Of course, it is not only population that determines emphasis, but the unique configuration of clients within a given group, or the dynamics of an individual in one-to-one therapy. In the majority of cases, I find in retrospect that all five phases have been present to a surprisingly equal degree.

CASE EXAMPLE*

I worked with Shawn twice a week for a year, in four three-month series. Shawn was among the more socially interactive, verbally sophisticated, and creative members of the adult psychiatric day treatment center. At 32, she was an exceptionally bright, sensitive, and attractive Australian woman. Long, wavy red hair framed her strikingly beautiful and expressive face. Shawn was divorced; she had been married for four years during her mid-twenties to an artist who was 15 years her senior. She had a seven-year-old son, who lived with his father during the week and with her over the weekends.

Shawn lived in her own apartment, had an advanced degree in Art History, and had achieved some success as the assistant curator of a small museum. She also had undergone two brief psychiatric hospitalizations for suicide attempts. At times she was anorectic, and even more frequently gave in to impulses of self-mutilation in the form of cutting herself. Her psychiatric diagnosis was Borderline Personality Disorder. Shawn came from a wealthy, professional family. Both of her parents had been alcoholic and incapable of providing her with sustained care. Her mother, now deceased, had been neglectful and emotionally unavailable, and her father, a radiologist, had been emotionally abusive as well as seductive with her. (There had not been explicit sexual molestation.) She had an older sister who was a talented musician and also a drug abuser, and two younger brothers–one an alcoholic and the other a successful attorney. One set of grandparents was still alive and seemingly supportive, but lived in Australia, where Shawn had spent the first ten years of her life.

In our early work, Shawn was depressed, but the sessions brought out her natural though rather buried playfulness and spontaneity. For the duration of the session, at least, the depression lifted. Her skits during Phase One (Dramatic Play) were wonderfully imaginative and creative, and she was surprised by the validation she got from others for her skills. She was drawn especially to dramatic play that allowed her to express anger safely and playfully, such as *Gibberish* (using sounds or made-up language instead of actual words), and this expression of anger further reduced her depression.

But as the group moved into the more developed improvisational scenes of Phase Two (Scenework), associations and feelings related to Shawn's childhood were easily triggered, and she quickly became overwhelmed. For example, after another client played an alcoholic stepmother in a fairy-tale scene, Shawn grew silent, and later I found out that that night she cut her arm with a razor. Her cutting seemed to be a way of inducing physical pain to distract her from emotional pain, and also to make the emotional pain more tangible and palpable. At

* Excerpted from Emunah, R. Acting for real.

this point in treatment (after approximately eight sessions over a month period), I began encouraging her to identify feelings as they came up in the session. This was difficult for her because she tended to have a delayed reaction; she put feelings aside and later felt devastated. In childhood, Shawn had never been allowed to express feelings, nor had she witnessed her family express feelings directly. Rather, her parents had used drinking as a way of avoiding and denying feelings. I tried to "check in" with Shawn frequently during the session and to give her extra support at the end of the session. Any feelings she acknowledged were validated. This process also served to develop her trust in me and in treatment.

But as her trust in me increased, so did her fear of abandonment. Her transference toward me was manifested by the degree of her upset and the feelings of abandonment she expressed when there was a change in schedule. For example, when I announced that I needed to end one session 15 minutes early in order to catch a plane or when, a month in advance, I announced that we would not meet the Friday after Thanksgiving, Shawn accused me of not caring about her or the group. Rather than interpreting the transference, I chose to reassure her, in an attempt to provide some consistent support and care.

Much of the work as the group moved into Phase Three (Role Play) revolved around helping Shawn to predict the situations that would precipitate overwhelming emotion and thus the cutting. She either had little sense of when this might happen, or did not care enough about herself to try to protect herself. For example, she had been planning a trip at Christmas to see her father, whom she had not visited in several years. I had her direct other members of the group in an enactment of what the visit might be like. As she watched the playing out of her father's drinking and seductiveness, two things gradually became clear to her. First, dealing with the feelings evoked by the enactment was difficult enough and she was far from ready to cope with this visit in reality. Second, she realized that her anorexia and self-punishing behavior were linked to guilt over her father's stated preference for her over her mother, and specifically his sexual comments about her body.

At this stage, I followed any scene evoking past feelings with a scene about how she could deal with these feelings. After the scene about the visit with her father, we enacted a scene about how she would feel alone that very evening and what she could do to cope, without resorting to the cutting. This served to help her anticipate her reactions, as well as practice new ways of responding to her pain.

Insight into the cutting deepened in an exercise entailing the creation of a sculpture depicting parts of oneself. The dominant role in Shawn's sculpture was the punishing part of herself. I had her enter the sculpture and assume this part. While playing the role, she surprised herself and the group by spontaneously exclaiming, "I'm your mother!" At the following session, she made a dramatic phone call to her deceased mother, whom she contacted in hell. Using some humor as a distancing device, she confronted her mother's negative and punitive attitude toward her. She also addressed her mother's self-destructiveness and the feeling she had that her mother wanted her (Shawn) to emotionally die with her. Shawn reported at the next session that as the impulse to cut herself had arisen a stronger impulse had taken over, which she had succumbed to: to buy herself a doll. It was to be her first doll. As a child, she said, she had never wanted dolls; she hadn't known what to do with them.

By the end of our fourth month, the self-mutilating and self-destructive behavior had ceased. The work from this point on centered largely on the theme of nurturing herself. Her rejection of her inner sad and wounded child was linked to the self-mutilation; she had wanted to get rid of this child. As she started to understand and accept this part of herself, and to experience the empathy that others had for this part of her, she began, via scenework, to find ways of taking care of herself. A great deal of sadness was expressed for the way she had been abandoned and the way she had abandoned herself. Now she struggled to reach this child inside her. There was a scene in which she desperately tried to place a long-distance phone call to her inner child, insisting on getting through despite the difficulty or cost. There was a scene in which she used her creativity and imagination to devise a planet in which people cared for themselves, or as she put it, there were no self-child abusers. There were many scenes in which she played the role of a child needing care. She was increasingly able to play a nurturing parent, albeit in scenes of other members of the group.

There were still days of hopelessness, or times in which emotions overwhelmed her. Any pain of the present triggered tremendous pain from the past. On one occasion, she had just found out that a neighbor had been diagnosed with AIDS. At this time, as at other times of increased emotional stress, she was asked to identify and direct others to play out all the feelings she had. She watched and conducted, which helped her to develop an observing self and to acknowledge and contain all of her emotions. This process also helped her to make the distinction between present stress and feelings leftover from her past. I gradually encouraged Shawn to make modifications in the scene, for example, to direct the anger outwardly, instead of inwardly toward herself, or to introduce a nurturing part that could tend to the sad child part of herself. One day I had Shawn enter the scene and assume the role of this sad child part of herself. I, along with two members of the group, sat next to her. "Doubling" for her, we repeated and added to the feelings she was expressing. Our presence enabled her to relive some of the desolateness she experienced in her childhood, but this time with supportive, understanding people at her side.

As the contact with her neglected inner child developed, Shawn was also drawn to examine her relationship with her son. Through role play, she reviewed challenging interactions with him and practiced communicating more openly and expressing her love more fully. Her skills at mothering her son clearly surpassed her skills at mothering herself, but Shawn was as motivated to enhance the former as she was to discover the latter.

The more playful work also continued and she manifested an increasing zest for improvisation. She seemed to be using this aspect of the group process to experience a childhood she had never really had. Shawn proved to be remarkably expressive. The roles and characters she improvised became increasingly strong and assertive. I directed her in scenes to apply the qualities displayed in character roles, such as assertiveness, toward situations in her own life that were difficult for her. Dramas were enacted in which she had to turn down requests for help by her peers at times in which she really needed all her energy to take care of herself, or in which she had to politely refuse men's invitations that did not interest her.

By the end of our seventh month Shawn was able to perceive her own strengths. She was also able to trust me and her peers without an excessive fear of abandonment. Despite anxieties, especially about separations and endings, she experienced more hope and optimism for the future. She began enacting in scenes (and thereby visualizing and emotionally preparing for) some of the future work and life situations for which she yearned.

In emotionally-laden scenes, Shawn no longer needed to stay in the role of director. The observing part of herself was internalized enough so that she could now be the actor. She could handle emotionality, without the need for distancing, though she still needed some help taking hold of her pain. For so long she had had a punitive attitude toward her inner child. Now she needed to embrace this child, with all the gentleness and compassion that she was so able to manifest toward other people in the group.

One of Shawn's *culminating scenes* in Phase Four was about saying good-bye to her mother, and not saying good-bye to herself. In the scene, she played herself expressing a multitude of intense feelings toward her mother, including rage and love and disappointment, all of which she could now tolerate. Her capacity to be in touch with and express emotion was matched by her capacity to contain emotion.

"I don't understand why you never lived," Shawn says, gazing toward the empty chair. "You've been dying for as long as I knew you. With the smoking and the drinking and the running and everything. And now when you're dying you don't want to die. It's a little late, don't you think? I don't want to be here watching you die. I've spent my life watching you die."

The tone of sadness is transforming to anger. "Why couldn't you ever live, damn it? And why couldn't you ever see me? Why did you leave me in a car because you couldn't remember I was there? And leave me in a store, and do all the other shit you did."

Now the sadness again, embedded in rage and hurt. "Was I that bad?"

There is a long pause, and I can see that an inner turn is being made. My directions are minimal because by this point in treatment Shawn is remarkably self-directed; the self-actualizing impulse within her, which Maslow describes as an innate force (that is often inhibited by fear), is clearly manifested–Shawn wants to get well. "But the fact that you're going to die doesn't mean I have to die. The fact that you spent your life dying doesn't mean I have to make the same choice." I ask her to repeat this last line. She does, and then thoughtfully adds: "I've sort of done that in the last two years, but I don't have to keep doing it. I'm learning to have my feelings now. Something you never did. That's what everyone in the family was afraid of–all the drinking, all the suicide–running from feelings. But now I'm having mine, and it's not easy. But it doesn't have to kill me to have my feelings."

I now ask Joanne, a very sensitive member of the group with whom Shawn is close, to assume the role of Shawn's neglected inner child. This is the part that Shawn has tried in the past to destroy. Gently, I direct Shawn to take hold of this part of herself. She does so physically, holding Joanne in her arms. Soon she does so with her tone and her words. "You're very special and you're very loveable. Sometimes I have trouble seeing that, but it's getting easier. When I have trouble it isn't because of anything you've done. It's just that I learned things a whole lot differently, and it's hard doing them the new way. But you're an important and special part of me. And you deserve to be held. And you deserve to be loved. And you deserve to have all the feelings you have."

Without interrupting the scene, I softly suggest to Shawn that she assure her child that she will never say good-bye to her again. There is a very long silent pause as Shawn struggles with this direction. This is by far the most difficult challenge yet: to promise never to abandon herself again. But slowly she reaches inside, until she finds the words. "I know we had to say good-bye to a lot of people in our life, and there will be a lot more. But there is one good-bye I don't ever have to say. And that's to you."

In the closing rituals of Phase Five of her final series of drama therapy, Shawn was able to say good-bye to me and to the group without the sense of abandonment she had experienced in previous endings of our group series. At this ending, what she expressed was gain rather than loss, because this time she was taking herself with her.

REFERENCES

Collomb, H. (1977). Psychosis in an African society. In C. Chailand (Ed.), *Long-term treatment of psychotic states.* New York: Human Sciences.

Emunah, R. (1985). Drama therapy and adolescent resistance. *The Arts in Psychotherapy, 12,* 77–84.

Emunah, R. (1990). Expression and expansion in adolescence: The significance of creative arts therapy. *The Arts in Psychotherapy, 17,* 101–107.

Emunah, R. (1994). *Acting for real: Drama therapy process, technique, and performance.* New York: Brunner/Mazel.

Emunah, R. (1995). From adolescent trauma to adolescent drama: Group drama therapy with emotionally disturbed youth. In S. Jennings (Ed.), *Dramatherapy with children and adolescents.* (pp. 150–168). New York and London: Routledge.

Emunah, R. (1996). Five progressive phases in dramatherapy and their implications for brief therapy. In A. Gersie (Ed.), *Dramatic approaches to brief therapy.* (pp. 29–44). London: Jessica Kingsley.

Emunah, R. (1997). Drama therapy and psychodrama: An integrated model. *International Journal of Action Methods,* 108–134.

Emunah, R. (1998). Drama therapy in action. In D. Wiener (Ed.), *Beyond talk therapy.* Washington, DC: APA Publications.

Emunah, R. & Johnson, D.R. (1983). The impact of theatrical performance on the self-images of psychiatric patients. *The Arts in Psychotherapy 10,* 233–239.

Maslow, A. (1968). *Toward a psychology of being.* Princeton, NJ: Van Nostrand Reinhold.

May, R. (1961). *The courage to create.* New York: Norton.

Moreno, J. (1946). *Psychodrama: Vol. 1.* Beacon, NY: Beacon House.

Rogers, C. (1961). *On becoming a person: A therapist's view of psychotherapy.* Boston: Houghton Mifflin.

BIBLIOGRAPHY

Emunah, R. (1994). *Acting for real: Drama therapy process, technique, and performance.* New York: Brunner/Mazel.

Emunah, R. (1996). Five progressive phases in dramatherapy and their implications for brief therapy. In Gersie, A. (Ed.), *Dramatic approaches to brief therapy.* (pp. 29–44). London: Jessica Kingsley.

Emunah, R. (1998). Drama therapy in action. In D. Wiener (Ed.), *Beyond talk therapy.* Washington, DC: APA Publications.

Emunah, R. (1997). Drama therapy and psychodrama: An integrated model. *International Journal of Action Methods,* 108–134.

FURTHER STUDY

The California Institute of Integral Studies in San Francisco offers one of two NADT approved graduate training programs in Drama Therapy, and incorporates specific training and experience in the Integrative Five Phase model.

Two documentary videotapes (available only for the purposes of training and education in drama therapy) of Emunah's clinical work illustrate the model.

A list of student theses, some of which are based on the model, is available from the drama therapy program at the California Institute of Integral Studies, 1453 Mission Street, San Francisco, CA 94103. Telephone: 415-575-6230. Web: www. ciis.edu.

Chapter 6

DEVELOPMENTAL TRANSFORMATIONS: TOWARD THE BODY AS PRESENCE

David Read Johnson

INTRODUCTION

Developmental Transformations is a form of drama psychotherapy that is based on an understanding of the process and dynamics of free play. The essence of Developmental Transformations is an *embodied encounter in the playspace*. These three components: embodiment, encounter, and playspace, will be described in detail later. Important aspects of this approach include: (1) the sessions consist entirely of dramatic, improvisational interaction between the therapist and client(s), (2) the therapist is an active participant in the play and intervenes through his/her own immersion in the client's playspace, (3) the process of play is used to loosen or remove (i.e., deconstruct) psychic structures that inhibit the client(s) from accessing primary experiences of Being (i.e., Presence), and (4) the client's progress in treatment is believed to follow natural, developmental processes that in themselves will lead to greater emotional health. Technically, Developmental Transformations is a treatment for disorders of embodiment, encounter, and play.

GENESIS

Developmental Transformations is based on the theatrical ideas of Jerzy Grotowski (Grotowski, 1968; Johnson, Forrester, Dintino, James, & Schnee, 1996) and Viola Spolin (Johnson, 1980; Spolin, 1963). Over the course of development of this approach, numerous theoretical perspectives have been incorporated to understand the processes involved. These have included the psychological perspectives of cognitive development (Piaget, 1951; Werner & Kaplan, 1963), psychotherapeutic perspectives of psychoanalysis, particularly free association (Freud, 1920; Kris, 1982), object relations theory (Jacobson, 1964; Klein, 1932), client-centered therapy (Rogers, 1951; Gendlin, 1978), authentic movement (Whitehouse, 1979), and dance therapy (Sandel, Chaiklin, & Lohn, 1993); philosophical perspectives of existentialism (Sartre, 1943) and deconstruction (Derrida, 1978); and the spiritual perspective of Buddhism. These widely divergent sources have been used to understand aspects of the therapeutic method, concepts of the Self-structure, and images of Being. Though therapists trained in this method are familiar with these ideas, paradoxically in practice the therapist is required to act on the basis of an atheoretical model, attempting to become the recipient of the client's theories, ideas, and perspectives. Thus, though it can be stated that this approach does have a theoretical basis, one of its theoretical tenets is for the therapist not to act on the basis of any theoretical tenets! Perhaps one function of theory in Developmental Transformations is to give the therapist support in letting go of the need for any framework or position, so as to be available to experience the encounter with the client.

DRAMA THERAPY FRAME OF REFERENCE

Basic Concepts

Emanation Theory

Developmental Transformations is based on an emanation theory of human experience, as opposed to a constructivist or role model. In emanation theory, which has had a long history within philosophy (Armstrong, 1993), the world is understood to be emanating (i.e., flowing out) from a fundamental Source of existence that remains beyond comprehension. Emanation theory is a developmental or evolutionary theory that suggests the world is naturally given, rather than willed. A tree, for example, has the natural impetus to blossom; similarly, a human being has the natural impetus to give rise to consciousness, and to expand its consciousness. Yet not only is there an outflow from the Source, but with the development of sensation and consciousness, Being turns back toward the Source through contemplation (Plotinus, 1996). Just as the flower departs from the branch and falls back toward the root, consciousness naturally separates itself from immediacy and seeks its Source, a process that we believe underlies the essence of psychotherapy. Emanation theory therefore diverges from the implications of a constructivist model, that through an act of will we can reconstruct (or "restory") our lives. In parallel fashion, Developmental Transformations is more interested in the process through which roles and images arise and then transform in the client, rather than what these roles are or how they are structured. Thus, we believe the best way to produce a large array of flower (i.e., expand the role repertoire) is to feed the root (i.e., connect to the embodied impulse)!

In order to better understand the nature of emanation theory, let me provide a metaphor that compares the structure of human experience to the Earth. Let us assume that we have emerged from the Earth, and that the Earth has emerged from the Sun. If so, then everything that is necessary for current human experience, including consciousness, must be present in the Sun. What has occurred is a natural developmental process of tremendous complexity; a miracle, surely. At its center, the Earth remains a boiling hot piece of the Sun, without form, in turmoil. The surface of the Earth has cooled, forming a crust, which has the appearance of "solid ground" but in fact is built out of huge tectonic plates that slowly rise up from and fall back into the depths. The crust has cooled because the Universe is cold, yet there remains strong pressure from the center to push material up from below.

It can be imagined that the Self has a similar structure: its surface has the appearance of solidity, but is in fact constantly changing; its crust, made up of large tectonic "narratives," is used to locate oneself in the cool social world within which we live; our identity is constructed of these "roles" which form what we call our persona. Yet underneath there remains the pressure of Desire, and at our center, let us call it the Source, is a turbulent, heated core, without form. To some, the absence of form at our center is a reason to proclaim that we have no core. But if we have no core, what then is *this* which rises up? The pathway through which the Source emerges within us is our Body. By Body we mean both our physical and energetic presence. Just as the Sun has both a physical and energetic presence, so do we. We refer to Consciousness as the energetic limb of the Body. Thus, as the Source is expressed, it "cools" and forms into desires and impulses, thoughts and perceptions, images of self and other, roles and identities. Health is understood to be the continued natural unfolding of this developmental process. Ill health is understood to be the stifling of this process when already-created forms block the emergence of new forms. This is often due to protective responses to painful encounters with other human beings. The result is a division among Other, Self, and Source.

Goals

Developmental Transformations intends to facilitate a renewed flow or link between Source, Self, and Other (not a withdrawal from others or attainment of a selfless state). It does so through the use of free play as a tool for continuous transformation. As one experiences embodiment, opens oneself to the encounter with others, and embraces continuous change (i.e., play), one finds oneself reconnected to one's Source. This is what we mean by Presence.

Embodiment

The Body is the source of thought and feeling, of physicality and energy. It is how we are present in existence. Of course, the Body is also how we feel pain; it can be struck, invaded, humiliated. Because the Body is our Location, it is the reason we can be found. States of disembodiment are natural responses to negative experiences: the desire to be hidden, to be immune to pain, to pretend to be another's possession. When disembodiment becomes engrained, however, strangling life, it becomes the source of ill health. In contrast, Developmental Transformations is an embodied process, in which whenever possible the Body is kept in motion, through movement, sound, gesturing, or speaking. The demand for action from the Body reveals the client's state of disembodiment, which then can be worked on. Eventually, the doors to embodiment can be opened and passed through.

Through our clinical experience with this method, four arenas of embodiment have been identified. Though we are always operating in all four arenas simultaneously, our experience of our bodies in a particular moment tends to fall into one or the other. The first arena to present itself in treatment is usually *Body as Other.* When the client enters the therapy space to find nothing other than a few pillows, and the therapist looking at him/her, the time is especially ripe for disembodiment! At the level of Body as Other, the person experiences their body as an object for the Other to perceive. I am a thing in the Other's social landscape: so and so tall, white or black, male or female, higher or lower status, a certain kind of person, dressed well or poorly, ugly or beautiful, commanding or shy. Many of us experience our bodies in this fashion in public settings, or on first encounters.

The next arena is *Body as Persona,* in which I experience my body not as a member of some larger social category, but as an individual. My body is me, David Johnson, with a particular history, character, talents, deficits, and relationships. My body reflects something personal about myself, the way I move, or speak, the way my hair is cut, which parts of my body I am proud of, which parts I hide from view. In my encounter with the therapist, I, too, view their body as a reflection of their personality, and I look carefully for signs that reveal their individuality, their intentions, their story. I am no longer interested in *whether* he is a man, but what *kind* of man he is.

As the therapist and client become more familiar, they often enter the arena of *Body as Desire.* I experience my own body less as a personality or Self, than as a pathway for impulses and sensations, pleasurable and unpleasurable. I notice what I like and dislike, the smells and sights of the body or parts of the body. I become aware of physical sensations, of sexuality, disgust, envy, tension. I wish to get away, or to get closer. I wish to be entered, or to invade or destroy. The other person's body becomes a source of tremendous danger, or relief.

The next arena is *Body as Presence* and here I experience my body and the other's body, not as social objects, not as personas, not as desires, but as simply present, perhaps like it would feel to be tall grass in a field. At this level there is appreciation for breath, amazement at the substantiality of the body, and awe at being with another consciousness. Here I can tolerate being intimate with the other, for the connection does not seem to constrain my freedom. In Buddhist terminology, I will have come close to Emptiness, by which is meant absence of form. I prefer to use the term Presence.

The capacity for these bodily states presumably develops from birth, first as *Body as Presence,* then as *Body as Desire,* then as *Body as Persona,* and finally as *Body as Other;* each layer adding on to the previous states. In Developmental Transformations therapy, the interactions between the client and the therapist also move through these arenas, though in reverse, from Body as Other towards the Body as Presence. At each level, fears and anxieties arise from memory or present circumstances; they stand guard at the gates, challenging us to enter.

Encounter

Developmental Transformations is a relational approach, and the intersubjective encounter between client and therapist is a central component. Following Grotowski's *poor theatre* notions, all obstacles to encounter are removed from the session room, including projective objects and preset exercises (Grotowski, 1968). The client has nothing to play with except the therapist. The therapist's job is to attend to the client, and to become their playobject in the playspace. In so doing, the therapist attempts to reveal the client. The therapist does so largely through a process called Faithful Rendering, in which he/she plays out what the client's play "calls for." It is the equivalent of Rogers' empathic technique, of placing oneself in the frame of reference of the client, only now in dramatic form (Rogers, 1951). The therapist may also utilize the Witnessing Circle, a small circular carpet on which the therapist sits to witness the client's play. The client is thus provided the opportunity to experience the therapist in two modes of encounter.

Encountering another person is an awesome event. Perceiving the gaze of the Other, we can feel our freedom constrained, invaded (Sartre, 1943). We can respond by becoming silenced, shamed, or disempowered. It seems almost impossible for such a meeting to be neutral, something always appears to be at stake. If object relations theorists are correct when they claim that the Self is built up out of others' perceptions of us, then each encounter risks shaking that foundation (Klein, 1932). Perhaps Sartre is right, when he claims that we experience ourselves as an object in the Other's view, questioning our own sense of personal freedom (Sartre, 1951). In any case, to be seen, to be known, when it leads to being hurt, results in protective measures. These often include controlling or narrowing the experience of encounter with others, crippling our efforts at intimacy. Simply being in a room alone with another person, especially when they are not located in a chair or behind a desk and can move freely, can bring up intense memories of encounters with others, as well as the protective measures against them.

The only things available to cloak the encounter are the dramatic roles and actions of the play, and indeed these are initially quite well-developed, clear, and "story-bound." Plot keeps an order to time, character orders self, story gives predictability to the ending. All of these pass away during our therapeutic work, as client and therapist allow themselves to be with each other with fewer and fewer intermediary veils; they fill their dramatic playspace with references to their in-the-moment feelings and perceptions of each other, and thus time loses its linearity, roles become collages, and the next act cannot be predicted.

If Developmental Transformations sought just an embodied encounter, it would be similar to Gestalt Therapy, which is also based on these principles (Perls, 1969). Developmental Transformations however is an embodied encounter *in the playspace,* which provides an entirely different context for the therapeutic work.

Playspace

The playspace is the mutual agreement among all participants that what is occurring is in play, that is, pretend. The playspace is the container of the entire therapeutic action in Developmental Transformations. Verbal discussion or processing occurs within the playspace, not at the end of the session outside the state of play. The kind of play that takes place in the playspace is free improvisation, in which the client is asked to play out dramatic movements, sounds, images, and scenes based on thoughts and feelings they are having in the moment. Thus, as these thoughts and feelings change, the scenes, characters, and actions change. Similar to meditative practice, the client is asked to allow thoughts and feelings to arise, to contemplate them, and then to let them go as others arise. In Developmental Transformations, this process takes place in an embodied, interactional, and dramatic form, rather than sitting in silent meditation.

Inevitably, thoughts and feelings arise that do not seem playable to the client. The therapist's job is to help the client maintain the state of play through these moments, often by shifting away from them. Over time, the goal is for the client to be able to play with the unplayable, for it is the unplayable that blocks our way to the Source. This process is essentially what Grotowski referred to as the *via negativa,* the negative way, being a process of removal of blocks. The play process serves the via negativa, or if you will, the deconstructive process, largely through repetition. As difficult issues repeatedly arise, are then avoided, then addressed again, the client and therapist find ways of playing with different aspects of the issue, until, with time, the issue becomes like a cliché to them, and loosens its grip on the client, who eventually lets what is to come next arise. In this way, client and therapist descend together through increasingly intimate stages of play.

Therapeutic Process

The beginning phase of the work, which corresponds to the level of Body as Other, is *Surface Play,* in which the client and therapist play with the social stereotypes and issues that first come to mind. Soon, however, as their encounter shifts onto that of Body as Persona, the client(s) begins to play with images, characters, and stories from their life and history, as well as aspects of their personality. Scenes with their parents, children, friends, and lovers, parts of themselves, fantasies of all kinds, are played out over and over in increasingly varied ways during this *Persona Play.* Every possible action toward significant people in their lives and themselves are portrayed, including those secretly held for years as well as new ones, never before conceived.

As this work proceeds, client and therapist begin to open themselves to the experiences of Body as Desire, and the play shifts into *Intimate Play,* where the client's thoughts and feelings about the therapist begin to fuel the dramatic action. The play now becomes about the client's relationship to the therapist and again all possible and impossible situations are portrayed. At first the scenes consist of what might happen between them, or what did happen in the past between them. Increasingly, however, the play is about the here-and-now relationship between them and what is occurring at the moment. As always, the unplayable feelings remain one step ahead of the playspace.

Eventually, the playing out of their relationship gives way to greater ambiguity and even mystery. They become acutely aware of each other's presence in the room with the other person/body/consciousness. Scenes devolve into silent gestures or mutterings, long pauses and glances, or simple bodily contact. Both client and therapist are aware of all the various stories, scenes, and actions of past sessions, but a feeling of not needing to play them out again, only making passing reference to them, seems strongest. In these states of *Deep Play,* client and therapist are intensely aware of each other and their bodies, and are freed up enough to work on their feelings of being bound or restrained by each other in the play. This level of intimacy is not available if there are still strong desires for each other as individuals; what desire is present might best be described as passion, the passion that has thrust them out into this life, and which is shared between them with a certain sense of irony.

It is not necessary for all clients to reach Deep Play in order to be helped. The playing out in Surface Play of many possibilities of being is a powerful way of increasing one's role repertoire and spontaneity. Persona Play, in which personal issues are explored, is the arena of many forms of drama therapy, and can have significant effects on a person's self-understanding, flexibility, and adaptive functioning. Intimate Play can be immeasurably helpful in increasing a person's tolerance of interpersonal encounters, openness to intimacy, and lowering fearfulness of others.

Role of the Therapist

The Developmental Transformations therapist takes the role of the guide with the client, demonstrating comfort and confidence in entering the imaginal realm of the playspace (see my discussion of therapist roles in Johnson, 1992). The therapist does not act as a sidecoach or director, but as an actor from within the play. As the client's playobject, the therapist becomes an animated presence that the client must contain; the roles of container/contained are therefore partly reversed in this method of therapy. Important in this process is the healing charisma of the therapist, who by showing spontaneity, creativity, and humor, encourages the client to continue their journey.

The therapist's main task is to help the client enter and remain in the playspace. The therapist accomplishes this by demonstrating the containing power of the playspace, through interweaving the dramatic scenes with the client's personal material, here-and-now processing, and previously unimagined possibilities.

The therapist must keep his/her attention on the client(s), to be open to their communication on all levels, and then to faithfully render in dramatic form the feelings, images, and scenes that are evoked by the client. In many therapeutic forms, the therapist gives empathic feedback to the client, usually in verbal form. Developmental Transformations is in many ways a form of client-centered therapy in which the therapist gives empathic feedback in embodied, imaginal form.

Finally, the therapist attempts to establish non-linear norms, so as to be able to facilitate the via negativa/deconstruction process. Thus, typical dramatic structures such as plot, consistency of character, storyline, ending, moral, and climax-denouement, are intentionally disrupted through such methods as repetition, transformation of the scene, introduction of divergent elements, and shifting attention to discrepant elements within a scene. This work facilitates a tolerance for what we call *emergent elements,* as opposed to *existent elements,* which means that the client begins to place his/her attention on what feeling is emerging within, rather than what is currently being played out in action.

General Clinical Principles in Individual Therapy

Individual therapy is initiated with a series of verbal sessions in order for the client to inform the therapist of their problems, personal history, previous therapies, and goals, as well as for issues of touch and personal boundaries to be discussed. The Developmental Transformation sessions occur in an empty, carpeted room with a few pillows and a circular carpet called the Witnessing Circle. After stretching and warming up, the client and therapist begin to move, or make a sound, or create a scene, which soon transforms into other images and scenes. As noted above, the major intervention made by the therapist is Faithful Rendering. However, the therapist will utilize other interventions at times to facilitate the play or to strengthen the playspace. These are described in detail in Johnson (1991; 1992). They include, for example, the use of *repetition* and *intensification* to explore or extend the play. *Diverting* is a purposeful attempt by the therapist to introduce a discrepant, irrelevant element into the play to disrupt a "thickening" story line. *Transforming to the Here-and-Now* is a particularly powerful technique in which the therapist and client transform the scene into "reality" and discuss something going on between them while still in the playspace. The effect is to discuss something real, but not really! The therapist at times sits in the Witnessing Circle and watches the client continue the play, and then returns to the play. This gives the client an opportunity to explore being witnessed by, as well as being with, the therapist.

The session continues until the therapist remarks, "take a minute," and leaves the room, giving the client a few minutes to silently reflect on the session. There is no verbal discussion of the session at the end, unless the client asks for it. Often the client will spend a few minutes at the beginning of the session to inform the therapist of events of the past week, and of course if there is a crisis, the entire session may be devoted to a verbal discussion. The purpose of not including a set-aside time for de-roling or verbal commentary is consistent with the overall goals of this therapy, which are to become present, rather than to gain insight. An embodied presence, necessarily ambiguous, at the end of the session is viewed positively, just as it is after meditation.

Since each individual's unique personality and expressive inclinations spring forth in these sessions, it is impossible to describe patterns or stages. One person's Developmental Transformations sessions are completely different in appearance than another's: some lay on the floor face down, others run around and scream, some exercise or perform dances, others play children, others play with mimed body parts. The therapist will always attempt to respond to these "playthings" as if they were the client's "toys" and the room is the client's "playroom." Nevertheless, it does not take long for clients to open their "toy chest," find something that scares them, and not want to play with it. Eventually, with the help of the therapist, they do find a way to play with it.

Transcripts of individual therapy sessions can be found in Johnson (1991; 1992), Johnson et al. (1996), and later in this chapter.

General Clinical Principles in Group Therapy

Developmental Transformations group work follows the same principles as individual therapy, with the additional challenge of managing the greater complexity inherent in a group. For many populations, being in a group is especially unplayful, and the therapist must find ways of engaging the group members in the play. The therapist accomplishes this task through interventions within five dimensions of play behavior: ambiguity, complexity, media of expression, interpersonal demand, and affect expression (see Johnson, 1982). These are based on developmental principles described by Piaget (1951) and Werner and Kaplan (1963). *Ambiguity* is the degree to which the therapist has not determined the spatial configuration, tasks, or roles in the group at a given moment. *Complexity* is the degree to which these space, task, and role structures include multiple elements (such as numerous, different roles). *Media of expression* refers to whether the action is being expressed along the developmental continuum of movement, sound, image, role, or word. *Interpersonal Demand* is the level of interaction required among members, as well as whether the roles are expressed in inanimate, animal, or human form. *Affect Expression* is the degree to which the action and imagery is personal, and/or intense.

In general, the group session begins at the earliest developmental level, which means clearly-directed, unison sound and movement, with little interaction and impersonal, nonintense imagery. The therapist slowly makes interventions that increase the developmental level of one or more of these dimensions toward greater ambiguity, complexity, interpersonal demand, and intense, personal imagery. The therapist will use the group's involvement in the play, that is, its energy or flow, as a signal of whether to continue on or to linger at a particular level. It is important to understand that the therapist's attention is on these developmental dimensions, not on the content of the client's imagery or scenes, nor on introducing preset exercises or structures. This is because the Developmental Transformations therapist is managing the state of play, not the content of the play.

For many clinical populations, typical stages of the group session include Greeting, Unison Movement and Sound, Defining, Personification, Structured Role Playing, Unstructured Role Playing, and Closing. A more detailed description of these stages is included in Johnson (1986). Suffice it to say that group work usually begins by inviting the group members into the playspace (Greeting), and then engaging in unison movement in a circle (Unison Movement). Over a period of time images begin to arise (Defining), followed by more organized roles (Personification), which are then worked on through the play (Structured Role Playing), only to dissolve into more free-flowing improvisation (Unstructured Role Playing). A departure from the playspace occurs during the Closing ritual. We have found that as groups become more familiar with the method, and as the therapist becomes more seasoned, these stages become less distinct.

Transcripts of group sessions can be found in Johnson (1986), James and Johnson (1996), Dintino and Johnson (1996), Forrester and Johnson (1995), and Schnee (1995).

Populations Served

Developmental Transformations has been applied for the past 20 years in a wide variety of settings, including inpatient hospitals, outpatient clinics, substance abuse and rehabilitation programs, nursing homes, and a private practice clinic. Both group and individual work has been conducted over both extended and extremely short (even one session) time periods. Populations served include schizophrenia (Johnson, 1984), affective disorder and substance abuse (Forrester & Johnson, 1995), posttraumatic stress disorder (Dintino & Johnson, 1996; James & Johnson, 1996), homeless mentally ill (Schnee, 1996), elderly (Johnson, 1986; Sandel & Johnson, 1987), and the "normal neurotic" (Johnson, 1991; Johnson et al., 1996). The goals of each treatment need to be tailored to the specific population, time frame, and nature of the clinical setting, though the method remains essentially the same.

In contrast to cognitive-behavioral treatments, Developmental Transformations is not best suited for addressing highly specific symptoms or issues (e.g., obsessive-compulsive disorder, phobias, psychotic symptoms, achieving sobriety, decision-making around divorce). Being an indirect process approach, existential, relational, and personal issues tend to be revealed and reflected by the therapist. The therapist does not take a structuring or advice-giving stance.

Clients whose behavior is violent, out-of-control, or floridly psychotic are usually not able to engage in the playspace and thus are not recommended for this approach. Clients whose intense dislike for play, drama, or body movement prevent them from participating should also be considered for other forms of treatment.

CASE EXAMPLES

Persona Play

The following is a transcript of a drama therapy session from my private practice (adapted from Johnson, 1992) that illustrates Persona Play. Parts of the session have been revised to protect the client's identity. Elaine is a 32-year-old woman employed as a therapist, who had come to me because she felt depressed, had a problem with overeating, and had lost interest in sex with the man she had been living with for several years. She had been sexually abused once by her father when she was about ten. She had no children, but had had two abortions about which she felt very ambivalent. I had been meeting with her for several months, and she had become very comfortable with the transformations. She had made substantial progress and at the time of this session was feeling much less depressed. Our sessions had evolved in structure so that the transformations began as I opened the door to the office.

The Session

Knock on door. Therapist opens door.

Elaine: My word!

Therapist: My word!

Elaine: *My* word. (Entering room).

Therapist: (laughing to self) No, no, it's *my* word.

Elaine: No it's not, that's *my* word (pointing to a spot on the floor).

Therapist: That? Are you kidding? That word there, is *mine*. I put it there only yesterday.

Elaine: Then what about *that* word?
Therapist: No, mine.
Elaine: Or that? (going around the room frantically)
Therapist: Nope.
Elaine: Then where is my word?
Therapist: (shrugs shoulders)
Elaine: I can never find the right word.
Therapist: For what?
Elaine: For it (makes large, vague gesture).
Therapist: For *it?*
Elaine: Yes, for it. (look at each other mysteriously)
Therapist: Well, what *is* the word for *it?*
Elaine: (shrugs shoulders and opens mouth)
Therapist: (opens mouth, tries to talk. Nothing comes out.)
Elaine: (whispers) I'm speechless!
Therapist: Me, too.

(Therapist and Elaine try talking, showing distress that they cannot speak. They begin to signal each other with their hands in strange ways. Gradually, guttural sounds begin to emerge, gibberish that grows to sound like bubbling noises. Their hands move like they are swimming, then like they are treading water.)

Both: Ohhhhhhh!
Elaine: It's hot!
Therapist: It's boiling!
Elaine: Oh my god, we're being cooked!
Both: Help! help!
Therapist: What's this? (holds up something)
Elaine: It's a potato.
Therapist: You mean we're soup? . . . Whose soup?
Elaine: Hers. (pointing in corner)
Therapist: (transforming to witch) Ha, ha ha, my my my, aren't you going to spice up my brew, honey! [Elaine often played these masochistic, victimized roles.]
Elaine: Oh please Gertrude, please don't cook me!
Therapist: Why not, you little twirp?
Elaine: I haven't done anything.
Therapist: Oh yes you have! (Therapist puts spices into pot and stirs)
Elaine: Oh! Oh! (in different tone, more enjoyable, she wriggles comfortably) What have I done to deserve *this?* [This was an advance for Elaine, who had had difficulty turning negative, victimized images into positive ones. In this case, it even had a sexual connotation.]
Therapist: (changing tone) Why, honey, just being you.
Elaine: (smiling) This feels wonderful.
Therapist: I knew you'd like the jacuzzi, isn't it great?
Elaine: Can you put a little more bubble bath in, dear?
Therapist: Sure. (Goes to other side of room to put away bubble bath.)
Elaine: I'm done. What should I do with the bath water?
Therapist: Oh just throw it out.
Elaine: (picks it up and throws it in corner.) I hope I didn't throw the baby out with the bath water! (laughs)
Therapist: (turning, looking very serious) Honey, did you throw the baby out with the bath water?

[Elaine had worked on her feelings about the abortions many times, and had felt terribly guilty about them. Her humorous way of bringing them up was striking, so the therapist decided not to let it pass]

Elaine: Oh, I, oh, I . . .
Therapist: You didn't! (rushes over to corner with Elaine; both gasp.) You DID! [The therapist felt it was important to acknowledge the act, so that the

full intensity of the experience could be evoked]

Elaine: I'm so sorry!

Therapist: I can't believe this, this is the fifth time you've done this. Look at all of those dead babies. You should feel ashamed of yourself! (both now walk around the room in despair.) What are we going to do?

Elaine: I just had to do it.

Therapist: You had to do it. Really, and what do *they* think about *that?*

Elaine: I don't know.

Therapist: Well, then, why don't you go over to that dead baby corner and find out! (Elaine goes over, and therapist leaves to the witnessing circle)

[Having evoked the anxiety situation and the internal self-criticism, the therapist heightened the tension by leaving her alone with her "deed." He wondered what she would do.]

Elaine: (Turns around in middle of room, sighing.) Ohhhh (drops down onto floor) I'm dead. She killed me. (Silence.) I'm dead. She killed me. (Long silence. Turns on floor, sighing.) Please! Please. Take me back, mommy! (begins to reach out into space, her eyes are closed) Pleeaasee, take me back mommy! (Turns again toward therapist, and reaches out toward him.) Please, please, take me back, take me back. (She cries, while still reaching toward the therapist, the reaches now turning into grabbing motions, which she expands into a motion of grabbing food and stuffing it into her mouth. She continues this with great energy, stuffing herself more and more, grunting, acting as if she is growing fatter and fatter. She leans back and rubs her tummy as if it is huge, and lets out a monstrous growl, standing up with arms out, and begins to stomp around the room.

Elaine: Pow, pow, boom boom (laughs) I am a GIANT, take that (stomps on floor–clearly image of stomping on little people).

[The transformation from guilt over the abortion into reaching out for her mother, into filling herself up with food, to becoming a powerful mighty giant showed a great deal of flow, indicating minimal inhibition. This was the first time she had actually played the babies. The therapist decided to join her after the scene had transformed. He was particularly taken with her willingness to represent the issue of fatness/pregnancy/female power.]

Therapist: (enters also as giant) Pow, booom (Elaine: laughs) Hi Bertha!

Heh, this is fun . . . squish!

Elaine: Yeh, boom, boom.

Therapist: Boy, are you FAT! I've never seen you looking so good.

Elaine: Yeah, and aren't you FAT, god you look great.

Both: (laugh)

Therapist: Oh, we're FAT! (begins to sing, Elaine joins)

Both: Oh we're fat, oh we're fat, it's so great to be fat . . . if we weren't fat, we'd have to be *bad* . . . (they dance together in a ridiculous way, then begin to hum) mmmm, mmmm, bad!

(the tone begins to change into a lower pitch, which quickly becomes more ominous. As they keep moving back and forth, holding each other by one hand, they begin to look over their shoulders furtively) Mmmmmm, oooooohhhh, oh! (they look and see something horrible) Ahhhhh!

Therapist: Run for it!
Elaine: Hide, hide, it's going to get us!
Therapist: Where are we going to hide?
Elaine: I don't know, we can't hide from ourselves.
Therapist: (stops and motions Elaine over; whispers), you don't mean that this improvisation really represents our running away from the fat, ugly, or destructive parts of ourselves, do you?
Elaine: Could be.
Therapist: Oh, I don't think so. How can you hide from yourself?
Elaine: I've been doing it for years.
Therapist: (Turning outward to room) Ladies and gentlemen, I would like to introduce to you, the one the only, a spectacle beyond belief, yes, the woman who can hide from herself! (applauds)
Elaine: (Runs around, turns around quickly in place, puts hands over eyes, puts head under a pillow, crosses her arms over her genitals)
Therapist: Yes, ladies, and gentlemen, this woman has been hiding important parts of herself, from herself, things so obvious to you and me, things anyone should know, but no, she hides from them, yes, she hides them *from* . . . whom? but why? Why, ladies and gentlemen? Well, let's ask her . . . (he turns and pretends he doesn't see her, she moves around room as if to avoid him. He begins to stalk her) Where is she? Where are you? You, who, Where are you? (Elaine now sits in a corner of room, fiddling with the carpet.) Where are you, Suzy? (pretends to knock on door) Suzy, let me in so we can play.

[The imagery of hiding developed a sinister quality that evoked in the therapist a feeling that he was the evil one she was hiding from. He realized this might be related to the father-image and the sexual abuse.]

Elaine: I don't want to, Daddy.
Therapist: Come on, Suzy, let Daddy in, he wants to play with you.
Elaine: (Both as Suzy and herself) We always get back to this.
Therapist: (Both as Daddy and therapist) Yes, that's true. This is what is called an "early childhood trauma," Suzy. [This interpenetration of dramatic role and real self is characteristic of a successful creation of a transitional space, in which the drama is sustained and at the same time the therapist and client are talking directly to each other]
Elaine: I know, Daddy, but do I have to go through it again?
Therapist: Don't worry, Suzy, you will be able to work it through in your therapy years from now. You'll want to have enough material for the sessions won't you? [Through this somewhat provocative humor, the therapist communicates that trauma are part of any human life. He also makes reference to an earlier concern of hers, that she wouldn't have enough to say in their sessions]
Elaine: That's outrageous! (comes to the pretend door, opens it) Listen, you daddy-therapist you, you think I make these things up just to entertain you? Well, leave me alone with my own traumas, I can deal with them myself!
Therapist: (leaves to the witnessing circle)
Elaine: Good riddance. (Wipes hands, looks down at them.) Blood. Blood on my hands. (looks over at therapist) Blood everywhere. A blood-

bath. Hum. Maybe it's my blood. (Goes over to wall and rubs hands on wall, then rubs both hands at once, then begins to hug the wall softly, places her cheek against wall. Silence.) I want to go back in. I am going back in. (Turns and crawls under a big pile of pillows. Silence. Then peeks out at therapist, then extends a hand through the hole like a tentacle, then retracts it. Long silence. Therapist enters quietly and sits near the pillow pile.)

[Elaine again shows a remarkable ability to stay with her associations, and again the image of a retreat to a mothering presence emerges. The therapist sensed her wish to have him come to her rescue, an often repeated pattern.]

Therapist: Hmmm (sternly). My client has gone back to the womb. As a result of my work, she has regressed terribly. I therefore have failed.

Elaine: (begins humming to herself, obviously trying to drown out the therapist.) Hmmmmm, hmmm!

Therapist: It must be safer in there than out here with me, can you believe that? Where did I go wrong? How have I frightened her? Answer me, someone, give me some advice!

Elaine: I want you to take care of me, but you are my therapist, so I have to take care of myself.

Therapist: Hmmm. That's probably good judgment. I have another interesting clinical case to present to you today, of a therapy that's reached an impasse. This is a woman who takes complete care of herself because she can't get what she wants from her therapist. Every time she wants him, he reminds her of terrible people.

Elaine: That's right! (Elaine gets up holding several pillows around her "for protection" and walks around the room)

Therapist: You can see, for example, that she carries her nurturance around with her. (Elaine has trouble holding all of the pillows, and drops several, picks them up) With difficulty. Let's see what happens when someone offers to help her. Maam, may I help you with your nurturance?

Elaine: No thank you, I'll keep my nurturance to myself, if you please.

Therapist: I beg your pardon. Where did you get all this self-nurturance?

Elaine: Why, at mother mountain.

Therapist: Really, can you take me there?

Elaine: Sure, follow me. (They walk around and then go to the pillow pile, Elaine puts rest of pillows together and sits on top.)

Therapist: Can I join you?

Elaine: Sure, come up here.

Therapist: Wow, you can see a lot from here. It's nice to know that there is a solid place like this around. How long has this been here?

Elaine: For generations. My grandmother lived here for many years, and I came to her when I was frightened or worried, and she comforted me. She was like a mountain!

[This was new information for the therapist, who had not known of the positive influence of her grandmother.]

Therapist: What's that place (pointing to the corner where she had hidden)?

Elaine: Oh, that's the hideaway, that's a great place, where I can go to get away from it all. Works like a dream.

Therapist: And that?

Elaine: Oh, that's the dead baby corner.

Therapist: It's so dark there.

Elaine: Yeah, not as dark as it used to be. A sad place, for sure, but I realize it's a part of me.

Therapist: What do you mean?

Elaine: Well, these are all parts of me (gestures to the room).

Therapist: Noo! You mean mother mountain, the hideaway, and the dead baby corner are parts of you? Forget it. They are out there, not in here! (pointing to her).

Elaine: I wish you were right, but it is an inescapable conclusion.

Therapist: I thought we just made it up . . . Well, then how are they related to each other?

Elaine: I'm not sure exactly, that's why I came to see you. (laughs)

Therapist: Okay, hmm, we could measure them.

Elaine: Great idea. (leaps off pillows and goes over to hideaway and pretends to measure it with a tape measure. Therapist follows, and they both scurry around taking measurements, mumbling numbers to themselves, and then both begin to write numbers and strange symbols on the blackboard, until there is a messy, complicated diagram).

[Jointly client and therapist are making fun of their own attempts to understand, and in so doing acknowledging the limitations of their profession, and more specifically, that Elaine is not ready to connect these parts of herself without intellectualizing]

Therapist: Well, there it is.

Elaine: Perfect understanding.

Therapist: It's amazing that we achieved so much after, literally, *minutes* of psychotherapy!

Elaine: Yeh. Really, you know, I'd like to hear you summarize it for me, you know, your *formulation* (sarcastic).

Therapist: No, I think that's something that *you* would gain a great deal from, since you're the client.

Elaine: But I'm paying *you,* and I want a report, *doctor.*

Therapist: Okay, after all, it shouldn't be much trouble. Hum (looks at diagram) well, let's see, I (laughs) can say that, uh (becomes silent, mouth opens but nothing comes out)

Elaine: My word, he's speechless (laughs)

Therapist: Nope, that's *my* word! (both laugh) . . . take a minute.

Discussion

Throughout this session the therapist acted as a guide who traveled with the client through her inner landscape, which consisted of memories of the past, current conflicts, and feelings about her therapist. The therapist tried to help her keep in touch with her stream of consciousness, at times underscoring and intensifying images, at times helping her to link different meanings between themes, and always trying to increase the depth and breadth of her experiencing–to allow the most enriched and variegated world to emerge. Maintaining a playful, humorous, and intimate environment sustained the "transitional space" in which inner and interpersonal worlds combine (Winnicott, 1971). Merely by allowing these processes to continue most freely, the healing message is given: you are all right, you are filled with many things, good and bad, and you can live with them all. The discovery of oneself and achieving forgiveness for being human is the intended result. Elaine used this and other sessions to acknowledge her feelings about not having children, about her fears that such a decision would be a rejection of her mother and grandmother, and about her doubts whether her career was the right one for her. In this session, the roles projected onto and played out by the therapist generally represented aspects of *her* persona. Later, as their work moved into Intimate Play, the client was able to play with her feelings and perceptions of the *therapist's* persona.

Deep Play

The following example is a complete Developmental Transformations session of a 36-year-old woman. I have disguised or altered parts of her history as well as sections of dialogue to preserve her privacy. I saw her weekly for three years in hour-long sessions. This is her 107th session, near the end of her treatment. She had come into treatment because she was concerned about her capacity for intimacy with a man. She was an elementary school teacher, unmarried and not in a relationship for several years, though she had dated numerous men through her twenties and early thirties. She had developed a very strong desire to have a child and to find a man to marry. She was the oldest of three children. Her father died of cancer when she was only seven years old (he was about her present age, 36) and she initially spoke about him in idealistic terms. Eventually she shared her concern that he may have abused her when she was three or four years old, though she had no specific memories. This concern was explicitly linked to her attempt to find an explanation for her difficulties with intimate relations with men. She reported no other traumatic events in her life. She had been in verbal therapy for several years with two separate therapists prior to working with me. In both cases she developed strong positive transferences to her (male and female) therapists. She was interested in drama therapy because she felt it might help "my body reveal what's holding me back."

In the following session, actions and speech of the therapist and client are followed by notations (made after the session) of the therapist's associations. As this is an example of Deep Play, the session is highly embodied and relational, and these associations are quite personal. Numerous double entendres occur between therapist and client, including references to her history, past sessions, and transference fantasies. Hopefully, by including them the reader may gain a better understanding of the material the therapist uses to motivate his/her actions in the session. In this sense, we say that the *actual* session consists of the co-occurring associations of client and therapist, not the actions or words that would be seen or heard by an outside witness. These expressions are the crystallizations of emergent, bodily impulses; as such, they are best understood as the *wake* of the session.

Session #107

They begin wandering around the room, looking down at the floor, moving their arms somewhat aimlessly.

T: ca, cann, canntt, can't believe, can't believe, can't be *leave* . . .
[can't believe that he is dead, can't believe she is staying in the therapy, can't believe a word we say, can't believe I'm not falling in love with you]

C: some, somer, summer, somerly, southerly. . . .
[some not all, sum it all up, its summer in the south and I am warm, there is a warm southerly breeze on my face]
movements slow down, turn to each other

T: caa . . .

C: ssss . . . **slowly collapses into ball in front of T**

[she is closing in, she is asking me to embrace her, to enclose her, the egg again, the egg and shell again]

T: **slowly descends over her so close but not touching**

[I am around you, I can hurt you or love you, hurt you with my love, but I won't, I won't touch you, so nothing will pierce your shell]

C: I . . . I . . . I am lost

[what's happening to us, come and find me, beauty and the beast, the darkened forest and the treasured gem, I will continue the search for you]

T: **hovering over her,** what if I find you?

[what if, what if, what if you let me in and we are together]

C: **long pause** . . . find me

[I am coming]

T: **slowly lowers body onto hers, touching softly**

C: **long long pause**

[I feel so close, I can stay here forever, will she turn toward me, what is there to discover, the egg again, so many sessions of this image, I am being allowed to make contact, what new form is being created, or will she kill us]

C: I thought you are dead

[I am dead, I am not making love to her, I am scared to go further, her father died and she feels abandoned, I am her father, she was never sure if her father abused her, am I abusing her? don't know, do know I am me and I am definitely alive]

T: **long pause,** I can be dead and I can be alive

[am I your dead abusing or nonabusing father or am I me?]

C: I think I want to be with you, not him

[so I am me, and you are with me, but what would your father say about this?]

T: Ewe, wood, lite, mee? (**a play on "you would let me?"**)

[who is she letting in, suddenly I feel something of a wood sprite, a hare, a skipping stone, I am a sprinkle!]

C: You can find me or you can lose me

[oh no she mentions losing, I am going to lose her, I have to prove it to her, like in so many past sessions, I have to prove my worth]

T: I don't want to lose you

[her father didn't want to for sure but he did, her lover to be won't want to for sure, I think I am going to]

C: Don't lose me (**both begin to sink**)

[we are together in sinking, the scene is slipping, like before, things slip away, we know it and it is so much fun to know it]

T: Slip away, slip away

[like oil, like skin, she is part of me, I feel her body as she leaves me]

C: **moving out, very slowly along his legs**

[we are leaving each other in a way that brings her close, the end of making love, the tingle on the skin]

T: Can't believe you are slipping away

[can't believe in you, your father's dying in the hospital, blind with pain and painkillers, your seven-year-old self's abandoning lover as he slips away]

C: **stops, leaning away on all fours**

[I want her, I can't stand this distance, this distance makes me ache for her]

T: **reaches out with hand toward her, she can't see but probably senses**

[I reach out as my desire, as her future lover will desire her, as her child will desire her, despite this terrible distance that defeats me, with her back to me my desire knows no bounds]

C: **long long pause**

[an aching, a reaching]

C: I want a baby

[she wants a baby wow, I am your baby, we will make love and I will give you a baby like we played out before, no,

I want you like I want my own baby, yes, she wants me, I am your baby]

T: I am your baby
[remember all the mother scenes you have played–now is the time to care for your child, here I am take care of me! forget the babies you have accidentally killed in our improvs, or stolen like Rumpelstiltzskin . . .]

C: Give me a baby
[yes she remembers, we are reading each other's minds, we are like one mind, it doesn't matter who is the baby]

T: You are my baby
[you are my baby, I have worked with you for nearly three years, you are my work, my labor, my love]

C: I am your baby
[I will protect you like my own, I own you, I can control you and destroy you, but I won't make love to you or eat you]

T: **long long pause, as both move slightly side to side, as if to play with the idea that they might be able to see one another**

C: I like this . . .
[I can't stop thinking or feeling and I feel proud of her that she is here so long with me, she likes this, what?, what is she doing?]

T: what is happening between us?
[look at me]

C: **They look at each other, she turns, both move ever so slightly towards each other**

T: **They get very close, half inch cheek by cheek, long long pause**
[I have no words for this, I smell her hair, I see the outlines of her face and eye, half a blur, and I imagine I am in a forest, the left side of my face is misshapen or removed, I am awaiting the arrival of another animal, I sense the slightest twitch, an eyelid blinks in the distance, an opening that I enter, willingly, filled with anticipation]

C: Maybe under everything there is love, not death
[is she saying she loves me, yes, me? not me, who am, I, rather this!]

T: Yes, love
long pause as they remain a half inch apart

C: Will it slip away
[the slope, the oil, the tension, the relief, the grief, her story of everything slipping through her fingers, yes it will slip away or we will imagine it slipping away]

T: It can slip away or not slip away
[play with me]

C: Seems inevitable
[she understands herself so well, she is joking, smiling to herself, to ourselves, about this Self that is wrapped around her and oh what it will do, but for the moment let us savor this weightless knowledge, here in this nameless place]

C: **Slowly lowers head onto T's shoulder, then slowly slips down his chest, T's arm wraps around her and she slowly slips through along his body. They pause, legs overlapping, facing away from each other**
[we play at missing each other and leaving each other while we play at making love which means mourning our not making love]

T: Who is dead and who will grieve?
[no one helped you grieve your father's death, no one helped you name what you lost]

C: I will grieve; you are dead
[don't mix her up I am the father and she is the daughter, "you keep switching roles on me!," she can do it]

T: I am dead; **he slowly turns and moves toward the witnessing circle but so slowly he will never make it**
[OK I am the role, you have expelled me, so I am going to pretend to go to the witnessing circle like I have so many times and upset you, only I don't need to

go there I just need to pretend to go there, and you will not get upset but you will remember getting upset and that is my little joke that I make, because I love you]

C: There will be no witnesses to my death

[she gets the joke and thanks me for not going into the witnessing circle but, guess what, her life is her own and we will not be together for ever and besides she can be the dead one and switch roles on me, so there!]

T: **holds still with arms up in air**

[you have caught me I am yours]

C: My baby

[you are mine I have you I love you can I come over and take you, will you the therapist allow it, of course you will, so now is the time for me to, now is the time for me to . . .]

long long pause

C: **She comes over and puts arms around him and he turns and lays on her lap**

[I am possessed, do with me as you wish, I feel like you are a mother, I wish my mother had been able to do this to me, she has not held me for years]

T: You hold me

C: You are holding me

[you me you me you me, how long will this last, what is this her inner space has become so wide and luminous, what warmth I feel]

long long pause

T: This time you will not sleep away

[you have let me in and I will carry this forever in my heart even though we will part. what time is it? probably the end of the session]

C: **smiles** Yes I will not slip/sleep away

[she smiles because she knows it is the end of the session and we both are keeping track, even though we now exist in a timeless place beyond reckoning]

long long pause

T: So near the end of the session and yet something is about to happen

[one of us might initiate a departure or entrance or embrace or kindness]

C: Yes something will happen

[yes to all of the above which we both know are possible, thus we have done them together anyway, even though her father did die and she has been sad for 16 years]

T: What's going to happen with us?

[us, us, uh, ssss, uh, ssssssss]

pause

C: Yes! **she silently strokes his hair**

T: Take a minute. **T departs the room**

Discussion

This is a good example of a Deep Play session between a therapist and client who have developed a high level of trust. This client also demonstrates a great deal of courage to stick with very upsetting issues. Viewed from the outside, this session appears to have little action and nearly meaningless dialogue. From within the session, I can say that it was an extremely powerful, tense, focused encounter with each other, and with ourselves. The session demonstrates how the Here-and-Now dialogue that had previously occurred out loud in the Persona and Intimate Play phases, has now descended underneath and between our vocalizations. The client, who has read this transcript, shares this view. The vocalizations and actions of the session of course were immensely meaningful and important, both as means of grounding our ongoing flow of associations and as markers of shifts in our imagery.

The issues of intimacy with men, concerns regarding her father's relationship with her, feelings of gratitude to me, and anxiety about termination, all were explored in the session. A feeling of tolerance for the complexity of life, of the ambiguity surrounding her childhood, and of joy for being with someone, mixed in this very large playspace we had created. The miracle of the transitional space occurred here, for we thoroughly enjoyed that I was pretending to be her father, pretending to be her lover, pretending to be her. Yes, only pretend, but *what* pretend! She had recaptured a child's eye on life: knowing the truck is not a real truck but feeling as though it is.

This client responded well to the treatment and had resumed dating during our work together. Two years after termination she married and I learned recently has had a child, fulfilling her longstanding dream.

Ethical Considerations

In a therapeutic method such as Developmental Transformations, which involves body movement, physical touch, intimate encounter, and play, ethical issues and professional boundaries are clearly paramount. The basis of any ethical practice is the therapist's intention to do no harm and that of course is essential in the training of our therapists. In addition, we attend to ethical principles in the following ways.

Informed Consent

Clients are clearly informed about the nature of the therapy and the possibility of both physical touch and playful rendering of upsetting issues. Previous experience in psychotherapy is elicited and direct inquiry is made about any improper behavior of previous therapists. Life history of psychological trauma and especially childhood sexual abuse is also taken and discussed with the client. An informed consent "contract" is then signed by the client, therapist, and supervisor, indicating the nature of the treatment, stating that the therapist will be following the American Psychological Association Ethical Guidelines at all times, that the therapist will have no outside social contact or relationship with the client and does not intend to engage in any behavior of an aggressive or sexual nature with the client. The client is instructed in what steps to take if he/she ever feels intimidated or concerned about the nature of the treatment on any issue.

Physical Touch

Developmental Transformations therapists are neutral regarding physical touch between therapist and client; there is nothing in our method that prescribes touching. Touching occurs because it is a natural human act. Complete absence of touch is unnatural. Inappropriate touching is unnatural. One of the crimes of incesting parents is that they cross the boundary between natural and unnatural touch, confusing the issue for the victim. In the early phases of Surface and Persona Play, physical touch is highly contextual, occurring as needed by the scene or role. The therapist only engages in "pretend" touch, that is, will never grab the client and really hold on, and will never kiss the client or touch any sensitive area of the body. In the later phases of treatment during Intimate and Deep Play, touch that occurs will often be decontextualized, that is, touch not derived from a role, but merely touch. Examples include leaning against each other, sitting on the client, pushing against each other on all fours, being pressed up against a wall by the client. Always, if there is a concern about the client's experience of touch, the therapist will address it, usually by Transforming to the Here-and-Now, and sometimes after the session.

Playing with the Unplayable

Some issues are so painful to the client that permission must be obtained, during the play, in order to proceed. Typically the therapist will Transform to the Here and Now and inquire if the issue emerging is something better left alone. Often this leads to a playful interaction about the decision itself rather than the issue, which may free the client to muster the courage needed to address it directly. If not, the therapist and client will move away from it, only to return at a later point.

Moral Dimension of the Playspace

At heart, we believe that the ethical basis of Developmental Transformations rests on the moral dimension of the playspace itself. The defining condition of play is the *restraint against harm* [see more detailed discussion of this critical concept in Dintino and Johnson (1996) and Johnson (1998)]. When playing with someone who pushes a little too hard or gets a little too angry, we say, "Hey, that was too hard, remember it's only pretend!" and thus articulate a boundary condition. Play ends when harm occurs; play deteriorates rapidly when harm is possible. Thus, in our work when the client fears harm, when the action is getting "too real," their energetic presence diminishes and their playspace shrinks. These are signals to the therapist. When the playspace is strong, more intense issues can be represented, including aggression, hate, sexuality, love, and intimacy. Representing love or horror is not equivalent to living love or horror.

In Developmental Transformations, the client and therapist progressively increase their capacity to represent extremely intimate states, as in other depth therapies. Having these states remain in the playspace paradoxically gives them their power to heal; confusion about whether they are real will disrupt the playspace and risk harming the client. Again, it is important to note that the therapist does not have an agenda to "get the client into Deep Play." Such an agenda will most certainly prevent any progress in earlier phases. Intimacy means vastly different things to each of us, and the therapist can never know ahead of time what form that will take for a specific client. The therapist will place trust in the natural process of emergence evoked by the play, and follow the client's lead. Due to the complexities of this method, a formal program has been developed to provide drama therapists supervised training and a community within which to share their experiences.

REFERENCES

Armstrong, K. (1993). *A history of God.* New York: Ballantine.

Derrida, J. (1978). *Writing and difference.* Chicago: University of Chicago Press.

Dintino, C., & Johnson, D. (1996). Playing with the perpetrator: Gender dynamics in developmental drama therapy. In S. Jennings (Ed.), *Drama therapy: Theory and practice, Vol. 3.* (pp. 205–220). London: Routledge.

Fink, S. (1990). Approaches to emotion in psychotherapy and theatre: Implications for drama therapy. *Arts in Psychotherapy, 17,* 5–18.

Forrester, A., & Johnson, D. (1995). Drama therapy on an extremely short term inpatient unit. In A. Gersie (Ed.), *Brief treatment approaches to drama therapy* (pp. 125–138). London: Routledge.

Freud, S. (1920/1966). *Introductory lectures on psychoanalysis.* New York: Norton.

Gendlin, E. (1978). *Focusing.* New York: Bantam.

Grotowski, J. (1968). *Towards a poor theatre.* New York: Simon & Schuster.

Jacobson, E. (1964). *The self and object world.* New York: International Universities Press.

James, M., & Johnson, D. (1996). Drama therapy in the treatment of combat-related PTSD. *Arts in Psychotherapy, 23,* 383–396.

Johnson, D. (1982). Developmental approaches in drama therapy. *Arts in Psychotherapy, 9,* 183–190.

Johnson, D. (1984). The representation of the internal world in catatonic schizophrenia. *Psychiatry, 47,* 299–314.

Johnson, D. (1986). The developmental method in drama therapy: Group treatment with the elderly. *Arts in Psychotherapy, 13,* 17–34.

Johnson, D. (1989). The theatrical dimensions of psychotherapy. In A. Robbins, *The psychoaesthetic experience* (pp. 77–92). New York: Human Sciences Press.
Johnson, D. (1991). The theory and technique of transformations in drama therapy. *Arts in Psychotherapy, 18,* 285–300.
Johnson, D. (1992). The drama therapist in role. In S. Jennings (Ed.), Drama therapy: *Theory and practice, Vol. 2.* (pp. 112–136). London: Routledge.
Johnson, D. (1993). Marian Chace's influence on drama therapy. In S. Sandel, S. Chaiklin, & A. Lohn (Eds.), *Foundations of dance/movement therapy* (pp. 176–192). Columbia, MD: American Dance Therapy Association.
Johnson, D. (1998). On the therapeutic action of the creative arts therapies: The psychodynamic model. *Arts in Psychotherapy, 25,* 85–100.
Johnson, D. (1999). Refining the developmental paradigm in the creative arts therapies. In D. Johnson, *Essays on the creative arts therapies* (pp. 161–181). Springfield, IL: Charles C Thomas.
Johnson, D., Forrester, A., Dintino, C., James, M., & Schnee, G. (1996). Towards a poor drama therapy. *Arts in Psychotherapy, 23,* 293–308.
Johnson, D., & Lubin, H. (1997). Treatment preferences of Vietnam veterans with posttraumatic stress disorder. *Journal of Traumatic Stress, 10,* 391–405.
Klein, M. (1932). *The psychoanalysis of children.* London: Hogarth.
Kris, A. (1982). *Free association: Method and process.* New Haven: Yale University Press.
Landy, R. (1986). *Drama therapy: Concepts and practices.* Springfield, IL: Charles C Thomas.
Landy, R. (1993). *Persona and performance.* New York: Guilford.
Perls, F. (1969). *Gestalt therapy verbatim.* Lafayette, CA: Real People Press.
Piaget, J. (1951). *Play, dreams, and imitation.* New York: Norton.
Plotinus (1996). *The Cambridge companion to Plotinus.* L. Gerson (Ed.). Cambridge: Cambridge University Press.
Rogers, C. (1951). *Client-centered therapy.* Boston: Houghton-Mifflin.
Sandel, S., & Johnson, D. (1987). *Waiting at the gate: Creativity and hope in the nursing home.* New York: Haworth.
Sandel, S., Chaiklin, S., & Lohn, A. (Eds.). (1993). *Foundations of dance/movement therapy.* Columbia, MD: American Dance Therapy Association.
Sartre, J.P. (1943). *Being and nothingness.* London: Methuen.
Schnee, G. (1996). Drama therapy with the homeless mentally ill: Treating interpersonal disengagement. *Arts in Psychotherapy, 23,* 53–60.
Spolin, V. (1963). *Improvisation for the theatre.* Chicago: Northwestern University Press.
Werner, H. & Kaplan, S. (1963). *Symbol formation.* New York: Wiley.
Whitehouse, M. (1979). C.G. Jung and dance therapy. In P. Lewis (Ed.), *Eight theoretical approaches in dance/movement therapies* (pp. 51–70). Dubuque, IA: Kendall/Hunt.
Winnicott, D.W. (1971). *Playing and reality.* New York: Basic Books.

BIBLIOGRAPHY

Articles and Chapters

Sandel, S., & Johnson, D. (1974). Indications and contraindications for dance therapy and sociodrama in a long-term psychiatric hospital. *American Dance Therapy Association Monograph, 3,* 47–65.
Johnson, D., & Munich, R. (1975). Increasing hospital-community contact through a theatre program in a psychiatric hospital. *Hospital and Community Psychiatry, 26,* 435–438.
Johnson, D., & Sandel, S. (1977). Structural analysis of group movement sessions: Preliminary research. *American Journal of Dance Therapy, 1,* 32–36.
Johnson, D. (1979). Drama therapy. In R. Herink (Ed.), *Psychotherapy handbook.* New York: Aronson.
Johnson, D., & Quinlan, D. (1980). Fluid and rigid boundaries of paranoid and nonparanoid schizophrenics on a role-playing task. *Journal of Personality Assessment, 44,* 523–531. Abstract reprinted in Yale Psychiatric Quarterly, 1982.
Johnson, D. (1980). Cognitive organization in paranoid and nonparanoid schizophrenia: A study of self-other representations. *Dissertation Abstracts International, 41,* No. 5.

Johnson, D. (1981). Effects of a theatre experience on hospitalized psychiatric patients. *International Journal of Arts in Psychotherapy, 7,* 265–272.

Johnson, D. (1981). Diagnostic implications of drama therapy. In G. Schattner & R. Courtney (Eds.), *Drama in therapy, Vol. 2,* pp. 13–34. New York: Drama Book Specialists.

Johnson, D. (1981). Drama therapy and the schizophrenic condition. In G. Schattner, & R. Courtney (Eds.), *Drama in therapy, Vol. 2,* pp. 47–66. New York: Drama Book Specialists.

Johnson, D. (1982). Principles and techniques of drama therapy. *International Journal of Arts in Psychotherapy, 9,* 83–90.

Johnson, D. (1982). Developmental approaches in drama therapy. *International Journal of Arts in Psychotherapy, 9,* 183–190.

Johnson, D., Sandel, S., & Margolis, M. (1982). Principles of group treatment in the nursing home. *Journal of Long-Term Care Administration, 10,* 3–11.

Ryan, E., & Johnson, D. (1983). Freedom and discovery within the therapeutic bond. *International Journal of Arts in Psychotherapy, 10,* 3–7.

Sandel, S., & Johnson, D. (1983). Structure and process of the nascent group: Dance therapy with chronic patients. *International Journal of Arts in Psychotherapy, 10,* 131–140.

Johnson, D., Sandel, S., & Eicher, V. (1983). Structural aspects of group leadership styles. *American Journal of Dance Therapy, 6,* 17–30.

Emunah, R., & Johnson, D. (1983). The impact of theatrical performance on the self-images of psychiatric patients. *International Journal of Arts in Psychotherapy, 10,* 233–240.

Johnson, D. (1984). Drama therapy. In T. Karascu (Ed.), *Manual of psychiatric therapies, Vol. 2,* pp. 767–775. Washington, D.C.: American Psychiatric Association.

Johnson, D. (1984). The arts and communitas. *Design, 86,* 36–39.

Johnson, D. (1984). Establishing the creative arts therapies as an independent profession. *International Journal of Arts in Psychotherapy, 11,* 209–212.

Johnson, D. (1984). The representation of the internal world in catatonic schizophrenia. *Psychiatry, 47,* 299–314.

Johnson, D., Sandel, S., & Bruno, C. (1984). Effectiveness of different group structures for schizophrenic, character-disordered, and normal groups. *International Journal of Group Psychotherapy, 34,* 413–429.

Johnson, D. (1984). The field of drama therapy. *Journal of Mental Imagery, 8,* 105–109.

Johnson, D. (1985). Expressive group psychotherapy with the elderly. *International Journal of Group Psychotherapy, 35,* 109–127.

Johnson, D. (1985). Envisioning the link among the creative arts therapies. *International Journal of Arts in Psychotherapy, 12,* 233–238.

Johnson, D., & Quinlan, D. (1985). Representational boundaries in role portrayals among paranoid and nonparanoid schizophrenic patients. *Journal of Abnormal Psychology, 94,* 498–506.

Johnson, D. (1986). The developmental method in drama therapy: Group treatment with the elderly. *International Journal of Arts in Psychotherapy, 13,* 17–34.

Johnson, D. (1987). The role of the creative arts therapies in the diagnosis and treatment of psychological trauma. *International Journal of Arts in Psychotherapy, 14,* 7–14.

Johnson, D. (1988). The diagnostic role-playing test. *International Journal of Arts in Psychotherapy, 15,* 23–36.

Johnson, D. (1989). Melody and rhythm of the creative arts therapies. *Music Therapy, 8,* 8–16.

Johnson, D. (1989). The theatrical dimensions of psychotherapy. In A. Robbins, *The psychoaesthetic experience,* pp. 77–92. New York: Human Sciences Press.

Johnson, D., & Eicher, V. (1990). The use of dramatic activities to facilitate dance therapy with adolescents. *International Journal of Arts in Psychotherapy, 17,* 157–164.

Johnson, D. (1990). How the arts are used in therapy. In *Health and medical horizons,* pp. 80–91. New York: MacMillan.

Johnson, D., Agresti, A., Nies, K., & Jacob, M. (1990). Building a therapeutic community in a nursing home through specialized groups. *Clinical Gerontologist, 9,* 203–217.

Johnson, D. (1991). On being one and many. *International Journal of Arts in Psychotherapy, 18,* 1–5.

Johnson, D. (1991). The theory and technique of transformations in drama therapy. *International Journal of Arts in Psychotherapy, 18,* 285–300.

Johnson, D. (1991). Taking the next step: Forming the National Creative Arts Therapies Association. *International Journal of Arts in Psychotherapy, 18,* 387–394.

Johnson, D. (1992). The drama therapist in role. In S. Jennings (Ed.), *Drama therapy: Theory and practice,* Vol. 2, pp. 112–136. London: Routledge.

Johnson, D. (1993). Marian Chace's influence on drama therapy. In: S. Sandel, S. Chaiklin, & A. Lohn (Eds.), *Foundations of dance/movement therapy,* pp. 176–192. Columbia, MD: American Dance Therapy Association.

Johnson, D., & Quinlan, D. (1993). Can the mental representations of paranoid schizophrenics be differentiated from those of normals? *Journal of Personality Assessment, 60,* 588–601.

Johnson, D., Feldman, S., Southwick, S., & Charney, D. (1994). The concept of the second generation program in the treatment of post-traumatic stress disorder among Vietnam veterans. *Journal of Traumatic Stress, 7,* 217–236.

Johnson, D. (1994). Shame dynamics among creative arts therapists. *Arts in Psychotherapy, 21,* 173–178.

Johnson, D., Feldman, S., Lubin, H., & Southwick, S. (1995). The use of ritual and ceremony in the treatment of post-traumatic stress disorder. *Journal of Traumatic Stress, 8,* 283–299.

Feldman, S., Johnson, D., & Ollayos, M. (1994). The use of writing in the treatment of PTSD. In J. Sommer and M. Williams (Eds.), *The handbook of post-traumatic therapy,* pp. 366–385. Westport, CT: Greenwood Publishers.

Sandel, S., & Johnson, D. Theoretical foundations of the Structural Analysis of Movement Sessions. *International Journal of Arts in Psychotherapy, 23,* 15–26.

Morgan, C.M., & Johnson, D. (1995). Use of a drawing task in the treatment of nightmares in combat-related PTSD. *Art Therapy, 12,* 244–247.

Forrester, A., & Johnson, D. (1995). Drama therapy on an extremely short term inpatient unit. In: A. Gersie (Ed.), *Brief treatment approaches to drama therapy,* pp. 125–138. London: Routledge.

James, M., & Johnson, D. (1996). Drama therapy for the treatment of affective expression in post-traumatic stress disorder. In D. Nathanson (Ed.), *Knowing feeling: Affect, script, and psychotherapy,* pp. 303–326. New York: Norton.

Dintino, C., & Johnson, D. (1996). Playing with the perpetrator: Gender dynamics in developmental drama therapy. In S. Jennings (Ed.), *Drama therapy: Theory and practice,* Vol. 3, pp. 205–220. London: Routledge.

Johnson, D., Forrester, A., Dintino, C., James, M., & Schnee, G. (1996). Towards a poor drama therapy. *Arts in Psychotherapy, 23,* 293–306.

Johnson, D. (1997). An existential model of group therapy for chronic mental conditions. *International Journal of Group Psychotherapy, 47,* 227–250.

Lubin, H., & Johnson, D. (1997). Group therapy for traumatized women. *International Journal of Group Psychotherapy, 47,* 271–290.

James, M., & Johnson, D. (1997). Drama therapy in the treatment of combat-related PTSD. *Arts in Psychotherapy, 23,* 383–395.

Johnson, D. Lubin, H., Hale, K., & James, M. (1997). Single session effects of treatment components of an intensive inpatient PTSD program. *Journal of Traumatic Stress, 10,* 377–390.

Lubin, H., & Johnson, D. (1998). Healing ceremonies. *Family Therapy Networker, 22,* 39–42.

Johnson, D. (1998). On the therapeutic action of the creative arts therapies: The psychodynamic model. *Arts in Psychotherapy, 25,* 85–100.

Books

Sandel, S., & Johnson, D. (1987). *Waiting at the gate: Creativity and hope in the nursing home.* New York: Haworth.

Johnson, D. (1999). *Essays on the creative arts therapies: Imaging the birth of a profession.* Springfield, IL: Charles C Thomas.

FURTHER TRAINING AND RESEARCH

Training in Developmental Transformations currently occurs within the Institute for Developmental Transformations, progressing through three levels. The first level involves a 400 hour internship under supervision, including individual and group work, seminar, and workshops. Level Two training includes a personal psychotherapy (minimum 80 hours) in Developmental Transformations, seminar, supervision of clinical work, assisting in teaching, and written papers. Level Three includes intense supervision of individual psychotherapy clients, seminars, teaching experience, and written work. Generally, full training takes three-four years after basic training and employment in drama therapy. Currently there are approximately 40 therapists in the Institute training program. All have at least a masters degree in drama therapy and most are registered drama therapists.

The Institute's research program has largely relied on intensive case study, and a volume of these case studies is in preparation. These case studies provide valuable data with which to examine the therapeutic process and therapist technique. In addition, clients in our psychotherapy clinic are periodically asked to rate their improvement anonymously, and results from these questionnaires indicate substantial satisfaction with the therapy method and with their therapists. On average, after six months of treatment, symptoms such as depression, anxiety, self-esteem have shown significant improvement (defined as greater than one standard deviation change). Finally, in a treatment outcome study with Vietnam veterans suffering from posttraumatic stress disorder, the Developmental Transformations group was rated by the veterans as one of the most beneficial treatments (out of 24) they received during a four month inpatient program (Johnson & Lubin, 1997). This data has been especially promising. More rigorous research studies are planned in the future.

Training in Developmental Transformations is available at:

The Institute for Developmental
Transformations
526 West 26th Street, Suite 309
New York, NY 10001

(212-352-1184)

Chapter 7

NARRADRAMA: A NARRATIVE APPROACH TO DRAMA THERAPY

PAMELA DUNNE

GENESIS

WHEN IT IS SAID AND DONE, it all comes down to stories. My passion, that is: a love for stories that has taken me down a long winding and wonderful road, from mesmerized rapture on my mother's lap (her "Back in the Day Tales," still give me a tingle) to writing this book chapter about Narradrama. Wherever that journey has taken me, from storyteller groupie to children's theatre regular to passionate drama therapist, my zest for stories, their drama, emotion, transformation and healing has continued to give me that inner smile. I'm having a lifelong love affair with stories.

DRAMA THERAPY FRAME OF REFERENCE

Narrative Therapy

Story or narrative provide the dominant frame for lived experience and for the organization and patterning of lived experience through which life is interpreted, according to narrative pioneers Michael White (1998), David Epston (1998) and Karl Tomm (1991). Stories show lives changing and determine which aspects of our lived experience get expressed. The self-narrative determines the shape of the expression of our lived experience. "We live by the stories that we have about our lives, these stories actually shape our lives, constitute our lives and they embrace our lives (White, 1998)." With every story and retelling of the story, persons reauthor their lives and relationships. "The evolution of lives and relationships of persons is akin to the process of reauthoring, the process of persons entering into stories with their experience and their imagination, and . . . taking these stories over and making them their own (Epston, 1998)."

Narrative thinking shows a profound respect for all people and a commitment to minorities such as ethnic groups, children and women and does not reinforce the dominant culture or system. Viewing a person in a pathological or dysfunctional way marginalizes the individual and leads to labeling. Narrative is culture and minority sensitive:

> There has been a general challenge to some of the practices of power that have incited persons to measure their lives, relationships, fam-

ilies, and others against some notion of how they should be and some challenges over the extent to which therapists have gone about trying to fashion persons and relationships to fit with the ideal frames that support these notions. I would like to reiterate that I don't believe that it is our mission to be wholly complicit in the reproduction of the dominant culture. (White, 1998)

Drama Therapy

Drama therapy offers possible ways to assist persons in integrating the emotional, physical and intellectual parts of themselves and in understanding and constructing solutions of personal, social and psychological problems. By encouraging creativity, imagination and role playing, persons reexamine or redefine their self descriptions. Drama assists persons to transform experiences through artistic expression and expansion of roles. By functioning in the mode of "as if," persons transcend immediate reality and transport themselves in time and space. The ability to participate in pretend or transcendent activities, "(Stanislavski's 'as if')" open doors to explore possibilities, alternative stories and move away from problem-saturated descriptions. Roles function psychologically to assert power over areas that human beings feel powerless. "By functioning in the 'as if,' persons start reverberations that transcend life circumstances, generating a sense of power and agency?" (Barragar-Dunne, 1992).

Shared Concepts

Narrative therapy maintains multiple perspectives. Truth is socially determined and negotiated. This field does not concern itself with truth and falsity. Drama therapy contains multiple voices. Drama throughout the ages embraces multiple perspectives/voices and no singular truth exists. Both drama therapy and narrative maintain an evolving, relational view of the self that is continuously being constructed. In drama therapy the self continues to be revealed through the different roles a person plays as well as the interrelationship between the roles. Through the narrative perspective the client tells different stories of her life and a self-view develops continuously and keeps evolving.

The drama therapist and narrative therapist both understand *restraints*. Individual, family and cultural *restraints* reveal the ways that clients become imprisoned by beliefs and cultural practices and the narrative therapist helps people to challenge these *restraints*. Traditionally drama therapists challenge political and social *restraints* as drama provides a viable form of protest. A drama therapist utilizes *physicalization* and *concretization* to free persons from *restraints*. *Physicalization* allows persons to communicate through their bodies and to open themselves to new meanings. *Concretization* provides a visual, enacted symbol of patterns that restrain persons. Both drama and narrative employ dramatic methods to draw contrasts between a person restrained by a particular belief or cultural tradition or externalized problem. Narrative therapists utilize *double descriptions* which allows them to compare the effect of problem stories with the effect of alternative stories. This sets up a way to look at the dominant problematic story versus the alternative resourceful story. Theatre offers the possibility of comparing stories through enactment and allows a range of possible roles to enhance the comparison such as observer, player and audience member.

Both drama therapy and narrative value the audience. The narrative therapist recruits an audience for the *performance of new meaning as* clients' make significant changes and decisions to follow new directions in their lives. Persons continuously serve as an audience to each other as they participate in each others' stories. For the drama therapist the audience plays a significant role in the theatre process. The audience participates in the dramatic action and provides feedback and sharing and a new story can be literally performed. Actors receive life and energy from an audience like clients receive sustenance and reassurance from friends and support systems.

One actor does not make theatre, rather it is a collaborative ensemble working together that make this event called theatre happen. Drama (informal, improvisation, person-based processes) also result from *collaboration*. Narrative therapy functions as a collaborative therapy between therapist and client. It is not a hierarchical therapy where an analysis of the situation by a therapist determines what will happen. Rather narrative therapy happens in a moment to moment way between a therapist and client with the therapist taking a collaborative posture, privileging the expertise of the client and allowing that expertise to come forth. True *collaboration* requires respect and a joint effort to make things happen. Drama therapy practiced from a collaborative perspective takes one of the already existing processes of theatre *(collaboration)* and extends it to the therapeutic environment. *Collaboration* engages all people to participate in meaning-making in which the therapist privileges the client, family or group as primary authors of alternative experience (experiences that contradict the problem-saturated description). The narrative metaphor challenges totalizing practices and encourages therapists to enter into a reflexive position in relation to the client.

> Alternative stories, generated collaboratively . . . cannot not be totally egalitarian, because the very structure of the context builds in what might be referred to as a power differential. To blur this distinction and to enter the belief that therapy can be totally egalitarian would make it possible for therapists to ignore the special moral and ethical responsibilities associated with their position. However, taking this into account, I do believe that we should do what we can to make it very difficult for that power differential to have a toxic or negative effect. (White, 1998)

Both drama therapy and narrative privilege the spontaneous moment. Two actors creating an improvisation respond to each other spontaneously, not preplanning how the scene will develop. Likewise in formal theatre actors perform a specific script over and over again but each time while the lines remain the same, the nuances are different. Each performer, if truly in the moment creates a moment to moment, event and no two performances are exactly alike. The narrative therapist comes to the therapy space without an agenda (an empty canvas) and allows this event called therapy to happen spontaneously. That moment to moment interaction and respect between client and therapist fosters collaboration and enlivens the therapeutic process. The drama therapist working in a moment to moment way privileges the expertise of the client which reflects itself through some form of enactment.

Narrative therapy comes from a nonexpert position which allows the client to explore the effects of the problem in her life and relationships. The therapist invites the client to compare the old story with the new to decide which direction suits better and to build on exceptions to problem behavior in constructing a new story. The drama therapist utilizing *narradrama* (drama therapy techniques from a narrative perspective) works in a nondirective way to offer the client opportunities through role playing to expand awareness, express emotions and discover alternative problem solutions. The drama therapist establishes a free, supportive, play environment and encourages the client's creativity in transforming problem situations through drama and theatre processes.

Techniques

Externalization

Drama therapy and narrative connect through the process of *externalization* which serves as a key to narrative thinking and summarized by the maxim, "the person isn't the problem; the problem is the problem." Taking a curious, open stance, the therapist invites the client to *externalize* through language with the idea of freeing the person from the grip of the problem. This externalizing process helps persons to separate themselves from the problem and offers new perspectives on the problem.

> In an *externalizing conversation,* I encourage persons to provide an account of how the problem has been affecting their lives and their relationships. Often in the early stages at least, for persons to enter this conversation necessitates something of a shift. (White, 1998)

Externalizing conversations allow persons to experience an identity that is distinct and separate from the problem. Through the *externalizing conversation* the problem becomes disempowered as it no longer speaks to the person of the truth about who the person is. As the *externalizing conversation* continues, persons revise their relationship with the problem. *Externalizing* encourages persons to objectify problems which helps to make the problem a separate entity and thus external to the person and therefore experienced as less fixed and restricting. This allows the person to separate from the dominant problem-saturated stories that have been shaping and effecting their lives and relationships and allows vital aspects of lived experiences to come forth.

Through *externalization* processes, the client begins to be aware of a crossroads made clearer by looking at the effect of continuing to privilege the problem-saturated story. Both drama therapists and narrative therapists look at the effects of problems on lives and relationships. The narrative therapist invites the client to look at what her life will look like in five years if she continues to remain in the problem-saturated story (i.e., affecting relationships with significant others, work and social contacts). The therapist invites the client to look at alternative life stories in which the client functioned in a more preferred way and did not give so much space for the problem. The effects of continuing to give the problem power become clearer leaving the client with striking choices such as: keep things the same; oppose the problem or strategize to bring the defeat of the problem or redefine one's relationship with the problem. A drama therapist utilizing *narradrama* might look at the effects of continuing to give the problem power by observing a PROBLEM EFFECTS SCENE (improvised scene showing effect of continuing to give into the problem) or LIVING SCULPTURE (body position by group or individual showing effect of the problem). Enacting PROBLEM EFFECTS SCENE allows the client to gain insights and draw distinctions between continuing in the grip of the problem or embarking on a different course. By emphasizing turning points, departures, embarkation and disembarkation, clients consider opportunities to dramatically announce their changed course.

> I'm really interested in what persons determine to be preferred ways of living and interacting with themselves and others... I'm interested in how I might assist persons to step more into those stories that are judged by them to be preferred, to perform the alternative understanding or meanings that these alternative stories make possible. (White, 1998)

Externalizing assists the client to separate herself from the problem, allowing her to identify problems, challenge the influence with the problem and discover ways not to accommodate to the problem (Epston, 1998).

A drama therapist using *narradrama* might *externalize*[1] by collaborating with the client to set up a PHOTO PROBLEM SCULPTURE where a client shows her relationship to the problem by placing herself in a physical position in relationship to the problem. Introducing a separation between the problem and the person opens space for persons to join in protest against the problem. The drama therapist creates a PREFERRED PROBLEM RELATIONSHIP SCULPTURE in which a client places herself in a preferred physical position in relationship to the problem.

Objects, puppets, masks, life size dolls, art work and other projective media may be used to assist in the process of *externalization*.[2] A teenage boy might create a SMALL OBJECTS PROBLEM SCULPTURE in the sandtray using a miniature lion to represent an externalized problem and a car with a broken wheel to represent himself. An adult might create an EXTERNALIZED PROBLEM MASK such as "Busy Frenzy," which assists the client to more clearly identify the problem and create separation from the problem. Creating a PERSONAL AGENCY MASK such as a "Spirit Guide," assists the client to discover personal resources. A UNIQUE OUTCOME SCENE from the past may become apparent (scene that shows an alternative to the problem-saturated story) and invite the awareness of another UNIQUE OUTCOME SCENE which leads to another. Sometimes these scenes may be real-life scenes and at other time hypothetical or imaginary scenes which help put the client in touch with some inner resources to utilize in relationship to the problem. Expanding personal resources through *narradrama* using the PERSONAL AGENCY MASK, PREFERRED PROBLEM RELATIONSHIP SCULPTURE and UNIQUE OUTCOME SCENE assists the client to embrace alternative narratives and become more familiar with strengths and possible resources to draw from when confronted with a problem.

Externalization for children happens easily through the use of objects, puppets, life-size dolls, masks and other creative materials (Barragar-Dunne, 1988, 1992, 1993). Inviting the exploration of the environment through objects becomes important for the child. These objects which are varied in texture, shape and weight and kind, become potential invitations for the child. Because the child is the author of the world created, this opens possibilities for change and other options. When a world is viewed in miniature, it becomes visible in a different way than previously experienced. Instruments, puppets, and dolls offer possibilities for exploring characters and stories. Young children often *externalize* by choosing or making puppet characters to communicate externalized problems (i.e., EXTERNALIZED PROBLEM PUPPET, i.e., "Mad Anger," "Soulful Sadness"). A child might pick up a tarantula puppet and begin taking the role of an externalized problem such as "mad anger." This helps the young child to create space between herself and the problem and to understand how the problem works.

The narrative therapist uses *externalizing language* rather than action techniques: (i.e., What is your relationship with anger?) and encourages the client to *externalize* through language which assists the client to separate herself from the problem. *Externalizing* the problem invites persons to actively discuss how they have been influenced by and on occasion able to overcome the influence of the problem.

[1] For more information on methods of externalizing with masks, puppets, dolls, art, video and objects refer to: The Media in Drama Therapy: An Exercise Handbook, Drama Therapy Activities with Parents and Children: Second Edition and The Creative Therapeutic Thinker: Second Edition

[2] Ibid

Curiosity, Reflection and Wondering Stances

Both drama therapy and narrative invite a posture of curiosity, wondering and reflecting. Many narrative therapists utilize a reflecting team to reflect on a client session. Dunne (1997) developed a *narradrama* technique to convey the posture of wondering and curiosity for younger children by introducing the WONDER SPACE. This is a special space designated by a fabric mat which allows a child to focus on wondering. When a child enters the WONDER SPACE she may draw, talk or create a scene with small objects about something the child wonders about. At any time in the therapy session, a child or therapist may go to the WONDER SPACE. Variations of the WONDER SPACE, may include a WONDER CHAIR, WONDER HAT or WONDER BOX. An older child may write down wondering question in a creative journal (Barragar-Dunne, 1995). In the WONDER SPACE children may draw a picture of their wondering, write about it or ask a question.

Transformational Circle and Transformational Ritual

Dunne (1997), took the concept of storying change and privileging preferences and made these accessible to young children through the technique of the TRANSFORMATIONAL CIRCLE. Young children enter the TRANSFORMATIONAL CIRCLE, an actual circle outlined on the floor designated with chalk or by a stretch rope or large circular mat. As children become aware that they have or want to hold onto a changed feeling, attitude or behavior or become aware that they want to change something, they enter the TRANSFORMATIONAL CIRCLE. A special TRANSFORMATION RITUAL, collaboratively developed in the moment helps to mark this change along with the taking of a photo to capture a key moment of the ritual. All of these *narradrama* techniques for young children assist children to become aware of alternative narratives and inner resources and strengths that they have.

Role-Playing and Improvisation

Role taking: " impersonation" remains at the core of the dramatic experience whether expressed in dramatic play, creative drama, improvisation or any other kind of theatre/drama activity. The ability of the person to take on a role, "I am me and not me" at the same time functions as a drama of engagement and separation (Landy, 1991). To take a role and separate from it opens up possibilities for viewing experiences from numerous perspectives. Life becomes a drama filled with countless stories that can be played out or reflected upon. The role serves as the single most significant feature that distinguishes drama therapy from other forms of psychotherapy and healing. Roles help players balance the emotional and intellectual parts of themselves. The actor strives for that same balance in playing a role (emotionally and physically) yet maintaining her own identity. In the ideal state of aesthetic distance the individual feels without fear of being overwhelmed by emotion and thinks without fear of losing the ability to respond passionately. Encouraging a client to take a role expands their world and their understanding of others. Taking roles allows the client to enact important stories from their lives and through the enactment the meaning and usefulness of the story becomes clearer.

Both drama therapy and narrative utilize role playing. The drama therapist uses *improvisational role playing* (Barragar-Dunne, 1992) which leads to empathic enactment and opens space for clients to understand each other and to discover new possibilities. When a person takes on a role she communicates that role physically and emotionally. A narrative therapist uses *internalized other interviewing* (Tomm, 1991) a form of interviewing which helps a person understand the role of a significant person in their life. Rather than becoming the role and communicating the role physically and emotionally, in *internalized other interviewing,* the person takes on the role of the other and responds to questions from the therapist. Often used with couples, one partner takes on the role of the other and the listener becomes extremely attentive. The partner seems curious to hear how the other answers the questions. The person playing the role looks inside themselves to find how the other would answer, thus the term *internalized other interviewing.*

Deconstruction and Reconstruction of Alternative Story

A narrative therapist utilizes *deconstruction* and *reconstruction* by taking a problem apart and exploring presuppositions. The therapist and client collaborate to reconstruct an alternative story by pointing out exceptions to the problem occurrence. The drama therapist utilizes these processes too by expanding dramatic possibilities. Playwrights break down stories to expand and refine characters and situations. A drama therapist uses *narradrama* techniques by breaking down or *deconstructing* a scene and putting it back together. As part of *reconstruction,* role retraining occurs based on an earlier presented problem scene in which the client replays this scene in a preferred way. Or the client may enact alternative stories that she considers reauthoring into her present life experience in meaningful ways.

Dramatization

Drama therapists use *narradrama* the technique of DRAMATIZATION. Persons continuously organize and give meaning to their lives through the "storying of experience." Dominant, problem-saturated stories restrict the roles and stories we perform, because they filter problem-free experiences from memories and perceptions. Significant people in a person's life tend to validate these dominant stories. In drama therapy, a person may be unable to see alternatives to a solution because their creativity and imagination seem overshadowed by the problem-saturated story. As experiences that do not fit with the dominant story are filtered out, so are areas of resourcefulness and abilities as well as hope in the future. These affirming descriptions are excluded from a persons' self view. DRAMATIZING alternative stories offers new input and expands the players repertory of roles. Actions and self-descriptions follow circular patterns. Actions influence our descriptions of who we are and our self descriptions shape what actions we feel capable of. By DRAMATIZING, a client begins to experience a shift.

A narrative therapist explores the alternative story through talking with the client, while the drama therapist encourages the client to DRAMATIZE the alternative story to facilitate opening space and finding alternative solutions. The narrative therapist works collaboratively with the client to invite the client to restory their life (choosing life stories) to highlight which invite preferred ways of being. The drama therapist utilizing the *narradrama* technique of DRAMATIZATION enacts a PREFERRED LIFE SCRIPTS and significant PREFERRED SCENES.

Therapeutic Process: Unique Outcomes

The drama therapist in generating *narradrama* techniques to act/dance/mime alternative stories expands possibilities and offers other options to the client. An actor takes a role that creates the story of a person's life according to the playwright. The actors show through a series of scenes, conflict and events, how the person's life gets lived out. Uncovering alternative stories assists the client to restory their life and choose experiences that she prefers. This working in the moment to create an emerging and continuing preferred life story helps the client to move forward. These aspects of experience that are uncovered are referred to as *unique outcomes*. Through these *unique outcomes*, persons can be encouraged to engage in performances of meaning in relation to these. According to White and Epston (1990), "success with this requires that the *unique outcome* be woven into an alternative story about the persons."

DRAMATIZING and enacting *unique outcome* stories opens space for more awareness and options. Incorporating a *unique outcome* in an alternative story may reveal itself in a PHOTO SCULPTURE, IMPROVISATION, MIME VIGNETTE or other dramatic form. By constructing alternative stories with *unique outcomes*, clients begin to become more familiar with alternative choices. By inviting personal creativity in the mapping and acting out of the alternative story, the client becomes more in touch with other possibilities and begins to experience a shift.

Role of the Therapist: Calling the Creative Spirit

The drama therapist and narrative therapist, through privileging the expertise of the client and acting spontaneously in the moment, encourage the creative spirit to come forth. The narrative therapist asks questions to open space and invite the personal agency and creativity of the client to come forth. Actors while trained in the craft of theatre (i.e., voice projection, movement) privilege the importance of inviting the creative spirit to express itself through enactment. It is this creative spirit that makes the difference between simple crafts and techniques and art. Creativity opens space for the alternative story to come forth as well as a push for the client to feel encouraged, less stuck and more hopeful about the future.

Challenges

Sometimes the lure of staying lost in the problem can trip up a session rather than opening space for alternative options, alternatives and ideas to come forth. Clients may also try to encourage the therapist to play the expert and this comes in many disguises. The other area is the challenge of not leading the session and allowing the lead to come from the client or a collaborative effort. The challenge is to refrain from being directive, letting curiosity carry the time as well as being gentle and invitational in approach.

CASE EXAMPLES

Amy, age 17 lives in a group home where she had been placed when she was a young child due to her mother's drug addiction problem. Amy's father continues in a prison due to drug involvement and physical abuse. Amy's three sisters and two brothers also reside in foster care. Amy feels betrayed, alone and speaks passionately about her past as well as her future-wish to graduate and go to college. As I connect with Amy's condition, I begin to appreciate and applaud her determination to change her life, graduate from college and open a home for runaway teenagers.

Amy passionately talks about her love for reading and photography. I inquire if she is interested in exploring writing and photography as part of her therapy. Amy's reluctance comes from years of negative vibes from other people; however she seems intrigued and decides to try.

This begins a therapeutic process utilizing *narradrama* technique that lasts over a year and results in Amy keeping a journal of poems, stories and photographs which she generates. Poetry and story become Amy's voice and each poem or story invites another one to come forth. Sometimes poems/stories burst forth with drawings or photos which further personify the images or characters contained in them. Other parts of the poem/stories that invite alternative stories Amy expands through *narradrama* techniques by acting out images, objects, dramatizing analogous improvisations, creating sculptures and inventing dialogues.

In our first meeting I invite Amy to talk about different kinds of words such as: adjectives, nouns, emotions words, significant words, scary words, favorite phrases, conflict words, action words, preferred words, funny words. Amy shouts out "rage, soul, heart, spirit, coldness, body, light, funny and God." She writes these words on 3 by 5 cards after *physicalizing* the word with her whole body through different movements, gestures and sounds that she prefers.

When working with a group, participants explore words in pairs or in small groups and make a WORD SCULPTURE by using different group members. WORD SCULPTURES may also be created in pairs or with objects or life-size dolls. Amy and I explore *spirit* by *physicalizing* together with outstretched arms, open gestures, body reaching outward movements. Amy shows *sadness* by closing up her body, clutching herself, dropping her head and sinking slowing to the floor. During the first month, Amy struggles with depression, anger and betrayal, but despite these problem-saturated stories, she persists in looking forward examining preferred moments, moments to keep, unfinished moments and conflictual moments. Discovering words empowers Amy to speak passionately through writing phrases and stanzas, and DRAMATIZING these through simple movement, mime, gesture, and story. Amy diligently writes in her journal and photographs important scenes, symbols and key moments.

During the second and third month of therapy, Amy creates a PICTORIAL HISTORY of her life from birth to the present. She draws and paints pictures or chooses photographs to capture important life moments ranging from traumatic events to problem stories to alternative stories. She keeps adding and changing her PICTORIAL HISTORY throughout the therapy to include picture/photos that represent what she wants to hold on to. Her PICTORIAL SUMMARY CHALLENGE immortalizes a range of strong emotions, attitudes, views and postures (Figure 7.1).

In a particular session, I notice that Amy seems to be acting in a despondent way and dulled in her spirit. I ask her if any of the picture/photos seem appropriate to describe her present experience. She creates a collage of her feelings in a toilet scene with red drops of blood all around her (Figure 7.2). Amy seems unable to talk about this picture verbally and with curiosity I inquire about the possibility of having her write me a story about it by personalizing some of the objects in the environment and letting the objects speak (similar to the technique of interviewing significant objects in a scene). Amy's story of, "The Invisible Girl," results from this process:

> Walking through the hallways of her high school with her hands sweaty and tears in her eyes wanting to tumble down her cheek like a river, says the paper thin walls. There she goes trying to hide her face from all of them, says them who pretend to really care. Of course they say things to make her feel better and tell

Figure 7.1. Summary Illustration of Pictoral History.

her that they all "care about her" and that she is not this or that says her mind that replays the comforting words of them in her head over and over. Of course they think she is trying to get attention, they whisper among themselves. She can't help it anymore, she starts to cry uncontrollably and runs into the bathroom stall and slams the door, says the toilet that she uses to flush out the noise of her tears. She sits on the floor, the closed door behind her the rest of the day, says her tears that are making a puddle around her. Nobody understands her. She doesn't understand herself either, reads her red blurred eyes that are swelling up more by the second. She cannot take it anymore. Slowly the clear puddle of tears becomes deluded. Dark red drops fall from her, as she wills her heart to stop taking a beat anymore.

Amy vividly remembers a scene from her PICTORIAL HISTORY a few weeks ago, based on a true incident from her life about two years ago, when she tried to cut herself as a death wish. She describes this time as one of the lowest in her life and calls it "Black Depression." She insists that "Black Depres-

Figure 7.2. Abstract Depiction of Red Drops of Blood.

sion" keeps trying to get her down. I am curious how she was able to pull herself away from "Black Depression" two years ago to claim a different life. "God helps me in the hardest moments. He takes my hand in his and I feel safe." She sculpts the moment of God holding her hand and warding off, "Black Depression," while I take photographs of the scene for her photo/poem journal. Amy impersonates herself by using a life-size doll and a mask to signify God (Figure 7.3). Surprised by the emotional impact of the scene, Amy traces her hand, filling it in with meaningful symbols, shapes and colors evoked from the scene. Later Amy demands in a dialogue with "Black Depression," a new future story. Amy role reverses with some of the meaningful symbols on the hand drawing like " the empty dish," "fire," "cross," "black blotches," and "wavy lines."

In another session later in the month Amy continues to find a way to change her relationship with "Black Depression" and "Rage Anger." Because of a breakup with her physically and verbally abusive boyfriend, I invite Amy to create a TISSUE PAPER COLLAGE (Figure 7.4) out of the emotions she feels, which leads to writing a poem in her journal called "Scared."

The soul is weak and so is the body
Not much more can it take
Looking into the low tide of the water
I imagine myself upon it
The legs move into the water
Led by the heart
Which cannot hold up any longer

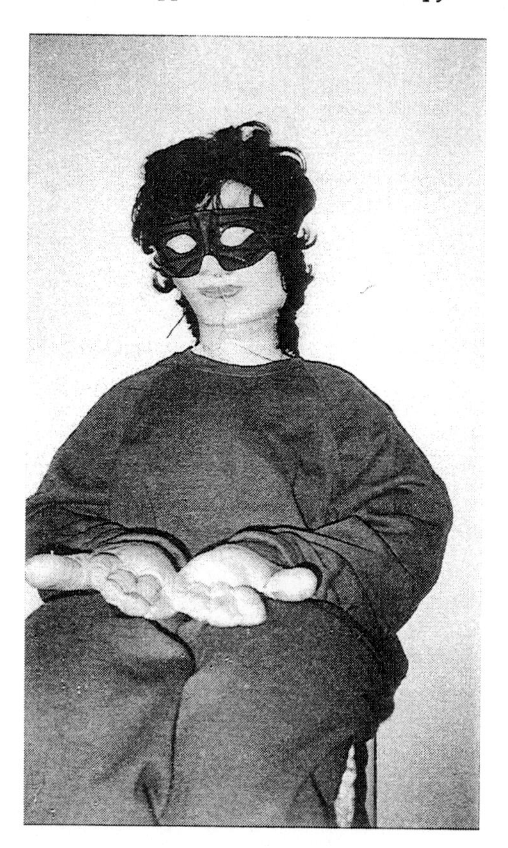

Figure 7.3. Showing God Using Life-Size Doll and Mask.

> The arms work with the legs to make the body move
> Across the silvery water
> Into the land without him and nobody.

Amy confesses suicidal thoughts triggered by the breakup of an abusive relationship with her boyfriend but assures me she will not act on these thoughts. I was curious about how Amy finds ways to restrict her suicide theme to only thought and how she continues in high school substance free. Amy insists that God and dancing give her strength in hard times and nurtures her. In ending the session, Amy draws a picture of herself dancing, with God's presence surrounding her (Figure 7.5). This exhilarating moment represents a UNIQUE OUTCOME SCENE and alternative narrative.

One month later, the building blocks of earlier sessions begin to become visible as Amy exercises more control with "Black Depression" and "Mad Rage." She joins a recreational drama class, continues passionately writing her own material which she performs in the class. In her journal she creates a collage of herself in a large rainy field surrounded by daisies, poppies and daffodils and writes a story which she calls, "Undone."

> I sit on the ground surrounded by lots and lots of flowers. Mostly roses but some daisies, poppies and daffodils, they scramble together to form zillions of subtle and vivid colors. I usually go there in the rain. When the drops glide through the flowers blending them all together I sit with the blanket over my head and body,

Figure 7.4. Tissue Paper Collage of Emotions.

the rain pouring down on me harder. I go there to think, scream, cry and just stare at the world surrounding me. I'm always alone although I dream of him there sometimes. Nobody can hurt me or blame me or yell at me for reasons I do not understand. The rain gives me answers to my questions where other times it makes the tears come down faster on my face. Everything around me is beautiful and nothing will ever change that. And when I come home, drenched

Figure 7.5. Abstract Cutouts Showing Dancing in God's Presence.

with water and tears, shivering from the coldness and returning to the realities surrounding me. I know...I just know.

Hearing this story touches me with feelings of hopefulness. It seems like some *unique outcomes* and alternative narratives different from the problem narrative of "Black Depression," and "Mad Rage," begin appearing. My curiosity prompts me to ask Amy about the "rain," a major *unique outcome* character as well as the "flowers." I invite Amy to expand this story further by creating it through

Figure 7.6. Unique Outcome Scene with Abstract Flowers and Cutouts.

dance. She uses long sheets of colored fabric to create the flowers and blue chiffon to show the rain that covers her body. A definiteness, strength and assuredness break forth and in the last moment of the dance ("when I come home, drenched with water and tears, shivering from the coldness and returning to the realities surrounding me, I know. I just know"), she covers herself with fabrics of all colors forming a cocoon-like shape like a peaceful refuge. Running around the room, I endeavor to capture these moments in photographs. This *unique outcome* scene, discovered through *narradrama* techniques of *journalizing,* further expanded through DRAMATIZATION and experienced more deeply in dance, open up some new pathways for Amy and encouragement for the future. Three art forms assist Amy to find and express this alternative self-narrative *(unique outcome),* namely writing, drama and art. Closing the session, Amy holds the photograph of the cocoon close to her self and writes in her poem/photo journal.

In the next session, Amy brings in a mask of her strong emotions (EMOTION MASK) and personifies the emotion of love in a poem called, "Love."

Anything I whisper you will not repeat
When I cry
You embrace me
And promise not to leave

When I scream you scream with me
Instead of covering your ears and walking away

You are always there when I need you
And protect me from the evil world
Surrounding us both

As I sit with the pills
Clutched in my hand
You hold the other
And eventually I drop them

You take off my mask
And see all of me
Hear all of me
And know all of me

But still you say
I'm beautiful

Curious about the meaning of the poem for Amy, I inquire about the most striking images in the poem. The *mask,* a strong image from the poem, holds multiple meanings like, " hiding parts of self that want to speak," hiding parts that want to be unknown," "monster parts," "hero parts," and "social and personal parts." In a creative mime vignette, Amy holds different masks to show character change throughout the scene, and enacts an encounter that reveals her vulnerability. Playing around creatively with the making of masks and various mask characters, helps Amy find characteristics in herself to appreciate which she feels comfortable sharing with others. *Narradrama* techniques emphasizing discovering of parts of yourself to appreciate, assist Amy to explore ways to function in the world and share her gifts with others.

Another client, Maggie, 14 years old, comes from a background of severe physical abuse, neglect and deprivation. Maggie hates her life, the staff, the therapists, the other girls at the group home and threatens to run away. At past placements she made several attempts at suicide, requiring hospitalization. Staff complain that they are unable to handle Maggie's uncontrollable moods. Her anger makes her dangerous to herself and others requiring her to take multiple medications that have become a part of her daily program. When Maggie comes for her first therapy meeting she carries her ghetto blaster with loud music playing. Instead of asking her to turn it off I encourage her to share some of her favorite songs as I explore ways to connect with her and know her better. Maggie's amazing energy and volatile emotions coupled with a quick mind and oppositional actions make for an interesting teen to get to know and appreciate. I conclude from her interactions with staff (who were suffering from burnout) that they didn't have the time or energy or time to deal with her. Because of the established negative interaction pattern, staff label Amy as a troublemaker and she defies all staff requests. Trying to work collaboratively in the moment prompts me to ask curiously, if Maggie was interested in creating a rap song that could tell me something about herself. No therapist every proposed that idea and Maggie gets on the therapy train down difficult but hopeful tracks.

Using *narradrama* techniques with clients like Maggie, makes it possible to find ways of connecting and collaborating that make sense and assist in uncovering strengths, *unique outcomes* and alternative narratives. In Maggie's case, allowing music to speak empowers Maggie to stick with therapy and rise above her past behavior of excusing all therapy as useless. By creating musical raps, life songs, musical dialogues with punctuating rap beats and rhythms to accompany scenes, *narradrama* enables Maggie to explore beyond problem-saturated narratives. She begins discovering engaging alternative narratives that challenge her. Confronting "High and Low Emotions," through musical rap dialogue and by making an EXTERNALIZED

PROBLEM MASK, assists Maggie to learn more about the role of emotions in her life. A PHOTO PROBLEM SCULPTURE confronts her with conflictual relationship with emotions. Constructing a PREFERRED PROBLEM RELATIONSHIP SCULPTURE reveals the relation between emotions and anger that Maggie wants. As the collaborative therapy train continues with Maggie, the journey contains many turns and challenges, but constructing a new PREFERRED LIFE HISTORY using autobiographical performance techniques and including remnants from her broken past help Maggie to face the challenging years ahead. Maggie takes pride in herself, something not experienced easily, as she wages war with "High and Low Emotions," "Mad Hate," and "Deviling Defiance." Maggie begins to applaud, "Creative Thinker," "Music Lover," "Rap Artist," and "Fun Spirit," as these alternative narratives provide preferred ways of thinking about herself and alternative possibilities for her future.

EPILOGUE

We build *narradrama,* layer by layer, and the building blocks of this deconstruction and construction are stories. As I travel daily through the complicated maze of drama in therapy, my heart stays open to the stories. Sometimes I get lost, but when I set my compass to the sound of a story, we usually find our way back to the building blocks. And I still love listening to my mother's Back in the Day Tales, even if she won't let me sit on her lap.

REFERENCES AND BIBLIOGRAPHY

Barragar-Dunne, P. (1995). *The creative journal.* Los Angeles: Possibilities Press, Imprint of the Drama Therapy Institute of Los Angeles.

Barragar-Dunne, P. (1993). *The creative therapeutic thinker (2nd ed.).* Los Angeles: Drama Therapy Institute of Los Angeles.

Barragar-Dunne, P. (1993). *Drama therapy activities for parents and children: An exercise handbook (2nd ed.).* Los Angeles: Drama Therapy Institute of Los Angeles.

Barragar-Dunne, P. (1992). *The narrative therapist and the arts.* Los Angeles: Possibilities Press, Imprint of the Drama Therapy Institute of Los Angeles.

Barragar-Dunne, P. (1988). *The media in drama therapy: An exercise handbook.* Los Angeles: Drama Therapy Institute of Los Angeles.

Bateson, G. (1997). *Mind and nature.* (1st ed.). New York: Bantam Books.

Dulwich Centre Publications. (1998). *Catching up with David Epston: A collection of narrative practice-based papers published between 1991 and 1996.* Adelaide, Australia: Dulwich Centre Publications.

Dunne, P. (1997). Catch the Little Fish in Smith and Nyland. *Narrative therapies with children and adolescents.* New York: Guilford Press.

Dunne, P. (1996). *Double stick tape: Drama, poetry and narrative as therapy for adolescents.* Los Angeles: Possibilities Press, Imprint of the Drama Therapy Institute of Los Angeles.

Landy, R. (1991). The Dramatic Basis of Role Theory. *The Arts in Psychotherapy. 18,* 29–41.

Morgan, A. (1999). *Once upon a time: Narrative therapy with children and their families.* Adelaide, Australia: Dulwich Centre Publications.

Smith, C., & Nyland, D. (1997). *Narrative therapies with children and adolescents.* New York: Guilford Press.

Tomm, K. (1991). *Internalized other.* Unpublished.

White, M. (1988/89). *The externalizing of the problem and the re-authoring of lives and relationships.* Dulwich Centre Newsletter, Summer. Adelaide, Australia: Dulwich Centre Publications.

White, M. (1989). *Selected papers (St Ed.).* Adelaide, Australia: Dulwich Centre Publications.

White, M., and Epson, D. (1990). *Narrative means to therapeutic ends* (1st ed.). New York: W.W. Norton.

White, M. (1998). *Papers by Michael White.* Adelaide, Australia: Dulwich Centre Publications.

White, M. (1995). *Re-authoring lives: Interviews and essays.* Adelaide, Australia: Dulwich Centre Publications.

FURTHER TRAINING

Drama Therapy Institute of Los Angeles
Pam Barragar-Dunne, PhD, RDT/BCT
Professor
Drama Therapy Institute of Los Angeles
1315 Westwood Boulevard
Los Angeles, CA 10024-4901

Tel: 310/478-7188
Fax: 310/589-0209
Web: www.dramatherapyinstitutela.com

Chapter 8

THE DEVELOPMENTAL THEMES APPROACH IN DRAMA THERAPY

PENNY LEWIS

FROM BIRTH TO THE FINAL RITE of passage we humans journey through life's metadramas. Unresolved childhood dramatic themes and their prescribed roles interweave and repeatedly overlap, recreating the past as if it were the present. The work of the drama therapist is to not only view the fabric of the drama as a momentary gestalt, but also to identify the repetitive phenomena. Once identified, their origins can be traced back etiologically where thematic scripts along with their associated roles and settings group themselves in developmentally based constellations. When these immature themes are cleared from unconscious habituation, mythelogems or archetypal life themes become available to healthy children, adolescents, and adults in their unfolding personal quests.

GENESIS

Conceptual Origins

Through the theories of ego psychologists (Erikson, 1963; A Freud, 1966), therapists have come to understand that with each stage of life there are specific themes that manifest and dominate an individual's way of viewing and interacting in the world, requiring defined roles for that person and significant others to enact. For example, the theme of the development of trust, self-nurturing, and a sense that the environment is need satisfying (Erikson's first stage, trust vs. mistrust) is very different than the drama to be played in Erikson's second stage of autonomy where themes of power and control dominate. Dysfunction and pathology emerge when these theme-based stages have been unsuccessfully integrated due to role deviation or inappropriate setting.

Greater sophistication in developmental theory emerged with the work of object relations therapists and neo-Jungians. Most therapists agree that the origins of their clients' dysfunctions began within the first three years of life. Ego psychologists covered these years but not with the specificity of object relations theorists such as Melanie Klein (1975), Margaret Mahler (1968), D.W. Winnicott (1971), and Ronald Fairbairn (1976), who held a magnifying glass up to the intrapsychic and interpersonal world of the infant. What they found were subtly changing themes within the mother-child drama which served with "good-enough mothering" to provide the child with a realistic sense of self and a constant internalized supportive and enabling object or inner mother.

Once object constancy has been achieved, life's drama expands. Here other theoretical constructs need to be introduced, as the dramas become far more complex and diverse given the gender and dominant characterological structures of the individual. The work of Jung (1977, C.W.) and post-Jungians (Neumann, 1973, 1976; Von Franz, 1978, 1982) have taken culture's externalizations of universal life themes and characters found in myths, fairy tales, religious rituals, and stories of gods and goddesses, and provided a rich view of the powerful archetypal mythelogems in the life quests and cycles of individuals. In addition more recent investigations have refined adult life stages (Sheehy, 1995; Moore & Gillette, 1990), expanding and enriching our understanding of mid-life phases.

Author's Genesis of the Model

In 1971, I began work at Pittsburgh Child Guidance as a dance therapist, joining Eleanor Irwin (one of the founders of the NADT) and Judith Rubin (renowned art therapist). We became the Creative Arts Therapy Team working collegially in consultation and education. My work with the children had an improvisational drama base in which I entered into the child's imaginal realm, costumed in a created setting, extending into a large group room. I followed the children's improvisational dramas, identifying the symbolic developmental themes and related dysfunction. I intervened in a dramatic role within the symbolic imaginal realm to transform dysfunction and foster healthy development.

I also had a private practice with adults and discovered that they, too, benefited from a developmental themes approach and were often struggling with the very stages that the children were with whom I worked. This resulted in the publication of my first book in 1972 *Theory and Methods in Dance-Movement Therapy* influenced by Anna Freud's concept of interconnecting developmental lines. Although titled "dance therapy," drama therapy was equally present.

DRAMA THERAPY FRAME OF REFERENCE: THE DEVELOPMENTAL THEMES APPROACH

Basic Concepts

Health

Health is seen as the successful integration of all previous developmental stages and the capacity to utilize all the themes and associated roles of those stages in an adaptive manner in service to oneself, respectful interaction with others, the environment, and other coexisting realms of reality. Additionally successful functioning requires the ability to experience current life themes toward further evolution and growth.

Dysfunction

Dysfunction occurs when healthy development is arrested due to trauma within the family system or externally or the inability of the primary caregivers to create the required ontogenetic setting and associated "role" relationship. No matter what the etiology, if the healthy integration of a particular developmental theme has not been fostered, the individual will be stuck in the developmental phase which was not successfully completed. The role that the individual plays as well those roles transferred or projected onto others and the way in which the surrounding setting is viewed will be based upon the developmental theme in which they have been arrested. They repeat the theme with the associated roles over and over again unable to utilize other themes or integrate new ones.

Techniques Within the Therapeutic Process

Awareness

Individuals' arrested developmental themes are played out in their lives through repetition compulsions or repetitive childhood patterns originally utilized either for aborted attempts at integrating the phase or for the recreation of the trauma in order to perpetuate the familiar. These thematic recreations keep them from responding adaptively to the moment. The threads of the themes and roles are gradually revealed to the client through etiologically based exploratory role playing. These enactments may entail the interviewing of childhood survival patterns as to their origin or the elucidating of developmental themes through such venues as improvisational drama, authentic drama, dreamwork as theater, and embodied sand play.

Encouragement to delve developmentally into the source of the theme and its associated role is made through redramatization of a typical formulating occurrence.[1] In this first state of awareness, the individual needs to get a fix on how these behaviors and interactions are internalized and projected onto their present life themes.

The Transformative Process

Drama therapists have long known that it is only through embodied enacted experience that change can occur. Many of our clients complain that they have talked about their problems with other therapists but to no avail.

These problem patterns would be simple to change if they only existed in the empirical left hemisphere cognitive realm. For example: "Oh, you have a behavior of running from empowered and assertive roles. Let me send you home with a chart to fill out all the times you feel this way along with your prior thoughts." To understand the notion of healing and developmentally-based transformation in psychotherapy, the elusive phenomena of transitional space (Winnicott, 1971) in object relations theory and the imaginal realm (Schwartz-Salant, 1983–1984, 1984a; Lewis 1985, 1993, 1998b; Turner, 1969) in Jungian theory need to be explored.

Winnicott's transitional space and the imaginal realm described by Jung in the *Mysterium Conunctionis* (Vol. XIV) have a common experiential link. In both cases the individual is experiencing the moment in a realm that lies between reality and the unconscious. It is akin to the world of "pretend" play in childhood. This is the realm where the internalized origin of the threads of repetitive dramas lie. Thus, in order to transform them, the client and/or group and therapist must enter into the bipersonal field of the imaginal realm in a fully embodied, enacted manner.

The Bipersonal Field and the Role of the Therapist

Individual depth work allows for the subtle dramatic nuances associated with early

[1] Since embodiment is perhaps the most powerful expressive arts technique, memories or flashbacks of severe physical abuse are clearly less appropriate for this method. In these cases I suggest individuals use drawing as a means to distance and contain their child selves. In addition I do not believe in individuals re-experiencing the trauma that caused their fixation in a particular developmental theme–rather only the relationship between the theme and the age-related child self.

object-related trauma to be monitored from moment to moment by the therapist and responded to through her subtle body and vocal responses, cocreating within the bipersonal field a transitional space of healing. The role of the therapist is paramount in healing early stages of development; for just as no infant can evolve a sense of self without the attentive ministerings of the attuned mother, no adult can do so either. Additionally, just as children know if their parents truly love and know them deeply, clients as well are not fooled by therapists "going though the motions" of acting like they care. Thus the role of the therapist is that of genuine care and concern seeking connection (relational model), contact (Gestalt model), and genuine intimacy.

This means that the therapy room can become a nursery for old pathological scenes to be reexperienced. Here classic psychodrama techniques and structures are exceedingly helpful, particularly in the re-creation of history, confrontation and protagonist transformation. Then redramatization of healthy development is possible between the client and myself or within a group.

Individuals' further development is, of course, also curtailed when early phases have been disrupted. In these situations it is not so much the "re" enacting but the providing the needed developmentally based setting for the client to integrate higher levels. This is not so much empirically provided as it is liminally and dramatically provided. Once childhood development is integrated, jungles are created for a hero to confront and individuate his or her inner instinctual beast. From a Jungian archetypal perspective, this means that numinous energy can enter the room through the embodied personification of a goddess or spontaneous enactment of a ritual or rite of passage. The therapist's repertoire of roles extends to all possible enabling and destructive characters in human development as described by the individual in their personal history or by individuals through culture's history in myths, fairy tales, literature, religious liturgy and other manifestations.

Being cognizant of adult stages of development allows the therapist to encourage and give meaning to archetypal life themes that emerge from the imaginal realm. For example, understanding the death, dismembering and putrefying cycle of the heroic quest can provide the needed support and encouragement for the client to undergo this sometimes frightening but necessary mid-life rite of passage.

Being in the Moment with the Creative Void

The third stage in the therapeutic process unfolds naturally. Clients observe, sometimes in retrospect, how their behavior has changed. They have choice as to whether or not they want to repeat an archaic dramatic theme and they no longer are fixed in an unconscious replay of a childhood role. They live in the moment and spontaneously respond to life's dramas.

Appropriate Populations for the Developmental Themes Approach

Because the approach is by definition developmental, all ages from infancy to aging and dying are appropriate. Those with functional diagnoses such as: personality disorders, PTSD, addictions including eating disorders, dissociative disorders, adjustment disorders, as well as nongenetic history-based mood and anxiety disorders; some forms of schizophrenia as well as many organic diagnoses such as: mental retardation, developmental delay, autism, and learning disabilities have worked within this model. This approach has been used with individuals, couples, mothers and children and groups of all ages.

Limitations, Challenges, and Growing Edge

Because this approach is developmental in nature, any problems that do not arise from unsuccessful development or do not influence development are less appropriate. Less relevancy is seen with those with paranoid schizophrenia, sleep disorders or some cognitive and medically related disorders. Families and organizations may be best helped with systemic approaches. The challenge and growing edge is to provide outcome studies and to see how easily this approach can comingle with other approaches such as role theory, psycho and sociodrama, playback theater, developmental transformations and ritual theater.

Drama Therapy Techniques in the Developmental Themes Approach

The Internal Drama

Reclaiming preverbal memories that lie in the body and bodily sensations allow both the client and therapist the ability to reconstruct early prelanguage experiences. Winnicott has stated that many memories are "pre-verbal, nonverbal and unverbalizable" (1971, p. 130). Since many memories of abuse occur prior to language, they are often held in unconscious somatic schemata that can only be recalled by imaginal embodied reconstruction. Asking clients to imagine journeying inside their body and personifying sensations, feelings, viscera and other body parts begins to create a dramatic communicational bridge from the clients' early history to the present.

Core to the formation of a sense of self is the suggestion for the client to journey to their solar plexus to find the core of who they are or the child within. Relating to the imagined child allows for the clearing of abusive history and the beginning of healthy reparenting or co-parenting with the therapist entering into the bipersonal imaginal realm.

The Use of the Somatic Countertransference

Another aspect of the internal drama is the technique of the somatic countertransference. Based upon phenomenological research (Lewis, 1981), I began to conceptualize this bipersonal dialogue between therapist and client. I was further encouraged when I began my analytic training in 1984 at the C.G. Jung Institute of New York. Jung (CW vol. XVI) in his *Psychology of the Transference* discussed an unconscious to unconscious connection between the client and therapist. Jung suggested that not only are client and therapist communicating on a conscious to conscious level or, as in psychoanalytic work, from the client's unconscious to the analyst's conscious level; but that there is also a direct unconscious to unconscious communication going on all the time. The therapist thus receives from the unconscious of the client into her somatic unconscious and can send back to the client's unconscious as well either through the conscious ego or the unconscious. In this realm, attending to the somatic countertransference it is possible, for example, to imaginally create dramas that transform projected split-off aspects of a person's psychology through remembering, and neutralize and detoxify transferred negative objects (Grotstein, 1981; Jung, 1977; Lewis, 1988a, 1988b, 1992, 1993; Racker, 1982; Schwartz-Salant, 1983–1984; Stein, 1984). The therapist may receive the client's negative judgmental or engulfing parent from the client's somatic unconscious and, may imaginally utilize themes from fairy tales or myths to heal and transform these feeling-charged personifications while still in the therapist's body vessel.

With others, their infant self may be imaginally received for love and healthy gestation to be retransferred when the client is ready. This form of projective identification has proven highly successful. Again, just as clients do not benefit from having a new role superimposed on them, it does not work for the therapist to conjure up what s/he *thinks* the character should act like. Nor am I suggesting something akin to Stanislavsky "method acting." I imagine I am playing the role of my client's symbiotic good mother; and based upon what the inner child needs that I receive from the client's unconscious, I imagine a corrective drama. Because this unconscious to unconscious connection travels both ways, this imagining can be received by the client's unconscious. This imagined enacted dialogue has a powerful effect and is always received by the client. I have had many confirmations of this through clients' dreams, poetry, drawings or statements, such as, "I know you've been holding me all along" or "my inner child feels your constant encouragement of her assertion" (Lewis, 1984, 1993, 1994).

Redramatization of Object Relations

Healthy infant and toddler care is conducted on a relational sensorimotor level. Mahler (1968); Kestenberg (1965); Stern (1985); and Winnicott (1971) discuss concepts such as attunement, rhythmic synchrony, holding and handling by the mother as conveying to the infant relatedness, appropriate boundaries and a sense of trust, safety, identity and internalized other. All of these are crucial in the foundation for healthy development. They are learned in vivo through the actual enacted experience and cannot be conveyed by "talking about them." Therefore the thematically based developmental redramatization of the mother/child embodied relationship by the client and therapist is often a *sine qua non* of transformation.

Dreamwork and Projective Techniques: Art and Sand Play

Dreamwork as theater, embodied art and sand play work are drama therapy techniques based upon the premise that the purpose of dreams and other art expressions are not only to inform but also transform the dreamer/artist (Lewis, 1993a, 1993b). For this reason, dream and art interpretation is found to curtail the full value of this unconscious expression. If a dream is interpreted, it serves to separate the dreamer from the dream. It has the same effect as interpreting a work of art does. In both cases the observer looks at and intellectually assesses the work rather than experiencing it.

With dreams that are symbolic in nature and emerge from the personal unconscious, the technique of dreamwork as theater can be used. This technique keeps the dream and the dreamer in the imaginal realm. The dreamer can then understand the dream though the experience of it and can frequently use the dreams as a vehicle of transformation.

In dreamwork as theater, the dreamer is asked to become different characters and symbols in the dream. The drama therapist interviews the dreamer in character and then, taking on roles, role reverses when needed in service to the client's integration of these parts of the self.

At times the dream appears to have a beginning and a middle but no ending. After interviewing the characters I suggest that the client imagine an ending. Since the responses and story endings emerge from the imagination, there is no "wrong" response as the dream has come from the same source (Lewis, 1993a, 1993c). Dreams invariably reflect history that needs to be revealed or new life themes and the associated shadow and animus/a aspects that seek recognition and integration.

Sand play, sometimes called "the world technique," is a Jungian technique in which an individual moves or shapes sand in a box or arranges small symbolic figures in the sand. Usually individuals allow their imagination to select from figures that range from animals (magical, domesticated or wild), human figures (all ages and character types), environmental objects (trees, containers, walls, stones, shells), dollhouse furniture, vehicles, sacred icons, and other small objects of symbolic significance. Often the result is a symbolic representation of their psyche or a map of their developmental psychological and spiritual journey. These figures are then given imaginal life and the small sand space is treated as a world in and of itself. The figures are interviewed and converse among themselves, with the client playing all the parts. Because the clients stay within the imaginal realm, they can experience the transformative power fostering healthy developmental growth as they come to understand the symbolic meaning through the experience of living in it (Lewis, 1993a).

The role of the drama therapist is to assist in the recreation of the art, dream or sand play world. On occasion I, too, enter into the dream, art or sand play world to further reveal the meaning and foster development. The experience of being in the bipersonal field can be expanded to include others in a group who can serve to continue to extend the drama of the developmental themes or related characters (Lewis, 1989, 1992, 1993a, 1993b).

In doing so, characters can transform for the purpose of integration or union. Developmental themes can unfold a map of a person's entire life journey or therapy process, and the archetypal life themes can propel the individual through adult life stage process.

Authentic Sound, Movement and Drama

Authentic Sound, Movement, and Drama is a technique of active imagination that was first identified by Mary Whitehouse (Lewis 1982, 1986, 1996). It is an experience of "being moved" by the imaginal metaphoric realm of the unconscious. The technique of authentic sound, movement and drama began its infancy in 1966 and reached full form in 1971. About this time I heard of Mary's technique of authentic movement and so decided to employ the name she had created. But the technique is slightly different than Whitehouse's classical approach as it is taught by those who trained with her. In the Whitehouse approach participants engage in the technique with the therapist acting as stationary observer. The therapist is identified as a "witness" who is not encouraged to interact on a movement level with the mover(s). Additionally, classical authentic movement is based upon a somewhat parallel process group style. Although interaction among the participants is not taboo, it is also not considered an integral part of the work. Authentic sound, movement and drama however encourages the interaction between therapist and individual mover when it supports relationally-oriented healing and developmentally-based growth. Additionally, it advocates group interaction in which individuals can coparticipate in each other's imaginal realm. Group members are encouraged to spontaneously transfer or project any role onto any member. Thus one member may transfer his engulfing space-invading parent onto another member and explore separating and maintaining healthy boundaries by finding and embodying the part of him that, although still in instinctual animal-like state, can growl and snarl. While the other person may project her distancing biting, snapping childhood survival pattern onto the man who is transferring onto her. In her case she may attempt to soothe him, telling him there is no reason to be so snappy and angry. While, he in turn, viewing her as attempting to cajole him back into enmeshed complacency, continues to growl. Thus each are reinforced positively: he in claiming his differentiating instinctual self, she in claiming her core self and desire for externalizing and attempting to transform her off-putting survival mechanism.

Authentic sound, movement, and drama is employed with individuals and with groups. Some movers prefer silence, others prefer white noise such as ocean or wind recordings, while others prefer the many New Age tapes available. With those individuals who are unfamiliar with authentic movement, I will offer an initial guided imagery to assist them into a deeper imaginal state.

Some individuals feel various sensations and are moved in response to them. Most however create imagistic environments and enact improvisationally within them. These can be recreations of the past that emerge from the unconscious realm to be consciously known or reclaimed by the enactor, or they may be new experiences that are unfolding for the individual to embody and integrate into their personality.

Developmental Theme-Based Improvisational Drama

Developmental theme-based improvisational drama is akin to authentic drama. The only difference is that a suggestion is made by the therapist, and then taken by the client into the imaginal realm.

For example, I have frequently offered the suggestion to explore a developmentally based thematic process that has emerged in a dream or in their life to increase the individual's experience of adaptive integration.

Ritual Drama

Ritual drama taps into the archetypal universal pool of transformational theater. The creation of sacred dramatic rites of passage, typically carried out in communities, help honor and support the transition from one developmental stage to another.

METHOD OF ASSESSMENT AND/OR INDIVIDUAL EDUCATION PLAN

Knowledge of the key themes that dominate each stage of development, or resulting maladaptive ontogenetically related themes, which are created due to unhealthy development, gives the drama therapist a built-in assessment tool that also serves as a natural treatment or education planning structure. It is vital to remember that each successful integration of a theme builds upon the themes from the former stages. The proceeding thus represents the metadrama of human developmental themes delineating within the various stages, examples of the optimum settings and roles that are needed to be played in order for a healthy and rich life tapestry to be woven. Culture's externalization of the unconscious via archetypal mythic stories of gods and goddesses, stories from the old and new testaments, as well as fairy tales are employed. Examples are also given of pathological dramas and developmentally based drama therapy processes that provide the needed roles and enacted dramatic themes for the individual to weave into their life.

Figure 8.1 delineates the healthy developmental life stage themes and corresponding-related dysfunctional themes:

Age/Stage	Healthy Developmental Themes	Dysfunctional Developmental Themes
Presymbiosis	Floating in life-giving fluid Being held Feeling at one with the All Being a part of the Light Being in heaven: endless love	Drowning Falling forever in endless space Overpowering ominous archetypal presence(s) due to size, power, or multiplicity Being chaotic within chaos Being in hell: endless torture
1. Symbiosis	Being able to care for oneself Allowing self to be appropriately cared for when needed Trusting others appropriately Retaining and digesting what is received that is positive and life enhancing Seeking & experiencing attuned mirroring Listening & responding to self needs Caring for self and others mutually	Needing others to care for self Filling an endless void through needing love, attention, food or other addictions Not wanting to leave a paradisiacal state Not trusting oneself, humans and/or a higher power Merging or enmeshing with others, their ideas or ways of being Being a baby or little animal looking for mommy or a caregiver Feeling or being wounded, abandoned and/or helpless Being wantless, needless or numb Feeling less than or better than (narcissistic)
2. Differentiation	Discriminating between self and others Discriminating between fantasy & reality Demonstrating healthy ego boundaries Demonstrating healthy body boundaries Allowing only healthy touch and being touched Separating mine and not mine Restraining from projection, displacement & transference Holding on & letting go appropriately Competing when appropriate Claiming and transforming imaged creatures with teeth who can protect "Spitting out" what is not one's own nor digestible	Lacking discrimination between self & others Confusing fantasy and reality Lacking or faulty ego boundaries: Possessing the ego by complexes Touching or being touched inappropriately Touching fear: wall-like body boundaries Confusing who is who through projecting, displacing & transferring Holding on or letting go inappropriately Envying and being rivalrous Seeking to destroy via out of control toothy monsters and creatures Swallowing everything without discrimination

Figure 8.1. Developmental Themes.

Age/Stage	Healthy Developmental Themes	Dysfunctional Developmental Themes
3. Practicing	Practicing going away and returning Refueling when empty Inspecting the mother Letting go pleasurably Messing and smearing playfully Pleasuring in one's products	Committing inability Leaving ambivalence Returning ambivalence Repeating approach/avoidance–come here/go away in relationships Fearing close inspection of the other Fearing letting go Devaluing one's own products
4. Rapproachment	Asserting of self Knowing who you are and what you want: independent thought & action Saying no when appropriate Presenting & representing self realistically Standing up for self Claiming power when appropriate Demonstrating healthy external boundaries Respecting one's & other's personal space	Asserting belief inability Being powerless or power & control obsessed Being unable to say no in some or all areas Being unable to realistically present self (either better or less than) Being unable to stand up for self Bulling & identification with aggressor Having wall-like, faulty, or boundaryless external boundaries Disrespecting self & other's personal space
5. Self & Object Constancy	Maintaining sense of self Sustaining a connection to the inner child Having realistic whole sense of self: "both good and bad" Carrying out tasks in timely fashion Demonstrating initiative Utilizing imagination to mediate instincts Maintaining healthy realistic constant inner parent Delaying gratification and sharing Demonstrating object constancy	Being unable to sustain sense of self Being unable to sustain a connection to the inner child Maintaining a split self: either is the good one or the angry two-year-old Being unable to carry out tasks Lacking impulse control Being caught in guilt; unable to move forward Presenting imaged themes of uncontrollable monsters Losing the significant other Searching for the other
6. Identification & Relationship with parents	Identifying with mother as creative Creating with pleasure Building, constructing, and making Penetrating & surprise themes	Blocking creativity Experiencing pain & ambivalence regarding creativity Being unable to be proactive

Figure 8.1. Continued

Age/Stage	Healthy Developmental Themes	Dysfunctional Developmental Themes
6. Identification & Relationship with parents *continued*	Killing the mother dragon for boys & animus Confronting the obstacle & gaining the treasure Presenting themes of three into four-chaos into organization	Sexualizing relationships Seeking to perpetuate triangular relationships Seeking to separate one from couple Being possessed by the power of the mother complex Being passively unable to confront and clear obstacles Being unable to compete
7. Latency & Peer Relationships	Focusing on rules & structure Forming chumship groups Creating themes of life at home Domesticating self or others Moving from wild or instinctual to more civilized in dramas Maintaining same-sex roles Reflecting industry themes	Being unable to relinquish adultified or parentified roles & associated themes Disregarding rules & structure Being unable to sustain membership in a group Sustaining wild, untamed, feral characters in dramas which require civilized behavior Being unclear on sexual identity Repeating themes of guilt
8. Puberty	Subduing wild beasts Mediating aggression of sexual or purely physical nature Letting go of childhood behavior toward adult behavior Experiencing body transformation toward adulthood Experiencing pubertal rites of passage Descending into the underworld for rebirthing Leaving what was, entering into a liminal realm Being initiated into a mystery Seeing the light from darkness Gaining power or special abilities Gaining courage, intuition, wisdom Heightening spiritual awareness or relationship to transpersonal	Having wild beasts being victorious Unmediating sexual or nonsexual acts of aggression Acting out behavior which is illegal Threatening life and freedom behaviors; such as, DWI & other addictions & behaviors which are illegal Experiencing nontransformative depression Being held in captivity Descending without meaning or possible transformation Being cast out of group without re entry Being unable to see the light Losing power or special abilities Experiencing fear which cripples courageous acts Lacking relation to the transpersonal
9. Adolescence	Trying on various adult roles and their associated life themes	Being stuck in childish roles and dependency themes

Figure 8.1. Continued

Age/Stage	Healthy Developmental Themes	Dysfunctional Developmental Themes
9. Adolescence *continued*	Trying on idealized role &life theme Searching for the beloved: Stories of romance Finding, rescuing & joining with the beloved Presenting themes of hostility to old authority Dethroning old rule Claiming the authority for self rule Striving to better oneself within socially acceptable venues	Maintaining projected idealized role on other Lacking in sexual exploration Blocking relation to inner feminine or inner masculine due to history Confusing or abstaining from sexual preference Repeating rapprochement issues with authorities Repeating need to dethrone realistic authority figures Being unable to claim one's locus of self rule Blaming others in authority for lack of success (given realities of minority societal discrimination)
10. Young Adulthood	Claiming of shadow (same sex) aspects of the self through role and associated archetypal life themes Claiming of contra sexual *animus/i* (inner masculine for women). and *anima/ae* (inner feminine for men) aspects of the psyche and their associated archetypal life themes Experiencing themes of the *hieros gamos* (the union of opposites)	Being unable to expand ego through shadow integration and relationship and the lack of claiming shadow aspects and archetypal life themes Being unable to claim and expand the integration of contra-sexual aspects of psyche and their archetypal life themes Projecting shadow and *animus/a* onto others continuously Lacking themes that join opposites of the psyche
11. Midlife	Experiencing aspects of love, work, and life as up for question Letting go of who one is Losing of self and life Revisiting history for healing and release Descending into death Being held in suspension Being impregnated symbolically Experiencing gestation Rebirthing and new birth Experiencing being more fully oneself Discovering who one truly is Serving the core of who one is–integrity	Fearing questioning who one is, unsuccessful relationships and/or work Holding onto unsuccessful aspects of who one is, relationships and work Repeating history: unable to let go of archaic unsuccessful roles and themes Experiencing being captive Escaping or flying: an inability to descend or enter uncharted settings Serving others without serving the core self

Figure 8.1. Continued

Age/Stage	Healthy Developmental Themes	Dysfunctional Developmental Themes
11. Midlife *continued*		Behaving in a way that supports a lack of connection to oneself and one's path
12.Middlesence	Letting go of young adult self image gracefully Mourning the loss of fertility (women during menopause) and physical competitive edge (men) Letting go of aspect of identity based upon work, power, and status Experiencing another "Great Round": letting go, death, descent, rebirth Experiencing deeper androgyny Shifting from "my will be done to Thy will be done" Expanding spiritual consciousness "I-Thou" or Mystical "Atonement" Being able to see and respond to the "bigger picture" Self-actualizing themes Experiencing ego-self axis & soul connectedness	Behaving in ways which inappropriately hold onto youth Being unable to accept and mourn loss of fertility or diminished virility Holding onto aspects of identity which have passed Worshiping at the alter of false gods: money, power, status, external beauty and youth Holding onto personal will and self needs over the greater good Blocking the expansion of consciousness Limiting view of existence Lacking capacity to evolve from being ruled by basic needs and their derivatives Lacking a relationship to self and one's eternal life force
13. Aging	Accepting aging process without losing inner eternal youth Entering another "Great Round": death–rebirth process Experiencing themes of "aging into saging" Becoming the wise wo/man Disidentifying with that which is not eternal Experiencing ego integrity Living in Love and Grace	Being unable to accept aging process Losing eternal youth and associated themes Being unable to surrender into another "Great Round" Experiencing themes of rigidity and death of capacity to grow and expand consciousness Holding onto worldly possessions and identities Living in bitterness, despair and/or fear of death
14.Dying	Going through the stages of dying: Denial, bargaining, anger, grief and acceptance in a responsible realistic manner Completing any unfinished business Saying good-bye Receiving Grace and spiritual transitional help Surrendering to death rite of passage	Being unable to move into the acceptance of death Being unable to complete unfinished business Being unable to say good-bye Being unable to receive Grace and spiritual transitional help Being unable to surrender to the death rite of passage

Figure 8.1. Continued

Pre-Symbiosis Themes

Described here are undifferentiated egoless themes of archetypal and mystical states of union. Dysfunctional themes are of psychotic proportions and may appear in dreams, collective or individual delusional or hallucinatory processes. With the former, individuals are encouraged to experience the "atonement" as it often heralds a rebirthing of a higher state of consciousness. With the latter, drama therapy that focuses on the development of the ego, ego boundaries and, in cases of psychoses, the capacity to reality test is in order. Here role playing reality-based activities of daily living and life skills and sociodramas which address differentiating what is from the unconscious from what is external and how to get help when the client is in a confused state is helpful.

Symbiosis Themes

Margaret Mahler (1968) describes the first stage of development of object relations as symbiosis in which there exists a dual unity between mother and child. The mother's role is to merge with her infant to attune to his/her body, to hold and fondle the baby, giving him or her a sense of entity and existence, personhood and uniqueness. The mother mirrors and reflects the child with love and acceptance and begins the process of filling the infant with a sense of self. Where this does not occur, pathology replaces a positive sense of self and a realistic trust in the environment as capable of being safe and need satisfying. Many oral associated addictions such as food, smoking, and alcohol develop as "false mothers" attempting to fill the endless void. This dysfunctional theme habitually replays as a result of a lack of early object-related ministerings.

One client had spent his whole life shut down. He was driven by the role of being a needless and wantless work-addicted perfectionist within the dysfunctional life theme of accumulating wealth, power and material goods in order to fill him with his missing inner substance. He came to see me because he felt something inside of him was beginning to sabotage his strategy. I suggested he imaginally journey into himself to find the origin of the saboteur. When he did, he discovered a screaming infant. He treated this infant with disdain, and stated he had no time for such antics. I suggested that this was perhaps how he had been treated as an infant by an overwhelmed mother. Since he had children I asked if he treated them in the same manner. He then began to sink into a deeper understanding. I suggested a role play dialogue between his adult self and infant who he eventually held and rocked tearfully.

There are some who are clueless about how to effectively parent because the parental experiences they had were so abusive there is no positive internalized object–no inner good parent. One woman in my authentic sound movement and drama group typified this phenomena. For months she found herself lying on my floor drifting back to her infancy. Here she found herself harnessed in a crib unable to move. She struggled to free herself. Since developmentally she could neither stand nor talk, she was often helpless to prevail over her bondage. There were times when I entered into her imaginal realm and assisted her. Finally over time the harness disappeared from her body memory as did the unemotionally attuned mother. Now she lay alone on the floor sounding weakened monosyllabic repetitive cries in an oral sucking rhythm (Lewis, 1986, 1990, 1993, 1999a, 1999b). Since her wounds were relational in origin they could only be healed relationally. She needed to experience healthy object relations. Since much of the mother-infant interaction is nonverbal, the redramatization of object relations was one that focused upon attunement to sound and movement, along with touch and proper holding.

I began by first mirroring her longing sounds from a distance. Then I gradually approached her, crawling to her on a diagonal. Now our synchronous repetitive sounds were more like coos. I touched her shoulder and moved slowly behind her. She was lying on her side in a semifetal position. I moved so that she could rest her back into my chest and nuzzle her head under mine. Now we were rocking and cooing in the same rhythm. I gently touched her graying hair. Two other members were alternatively singing and playing with words. Toward the end of the hour of this redramatization of object relations, she began to connect with these two participants responding to their sounds spontaneously–something she had never been able to do before. Indeed, it is difficult to feel free to spontaneously play if there was a lack of empathetic mirroring and reflection during symbiosis.

Separation and Individuation: Differentiation Sub-phase–Body and Ego Boundary Formation

Mahler describes the next phase in development as separation and individuation, beginning with the sub-phase of differentiation in which the infant experiences boundaries and the fundamental capacity to discriminate. This stage emerges with teething and is associated with the capacity to "chew over things and spit out what isn't digestible." A "me-not-me" body boundary paves the way for healthy touch and knowing the difference between one's own thoughts and feelings and those of others. Projection or the "ejecting out of what is part of the self onto or into another" demonstrates incomplete differentiation. Additionally, clients who fear sustained physical intimacy and who repeat themes of separating and pushing away in their interpersonal dramas did not have a mother and/or a developmental setting that allowed for them to successfully integrate the separation drama (Lewis, 1993).

On an intrapsychic level, this phase heralds the development of ego boundaries required to maintain the integrity of the ego's rationality against the onslaughts of invasive complexes such as addictions, inner critics, outmoded parental internalizations and "uncivilized" unconscious materials such as hallucinations and flashbacks which have the potential of flooding the ego if faulty boundaries exist.

One woman came to me complaining about just about everything in her life. A sharp derisive critic, she bit and chewed up anyone who approached her. Countertransferentially, I felt any suggestion to enact or embody the work was ripped apart and spit out. I became as helpless as I was sure her mother felt. She had come to me because I was a dance and drama therapist; she did not want to "talk about her problems," but when I suggested these techniques, she said she did not "trust me." She sat with her legs drawn up barring access and placed a pillow between her and me. Clearly, she was stuck in the "teething" oral aggressive differentiating phase (Lewis, 1990, 1993). Angered by what she did not get, she could not move on. But the clearest indication came when I gently began inquiring about the amount of boundaries she needed to put between her and me. It was then that she stated she felt she had been metaphorically dipped in an acid bath at birth. She had no skin boundaries. How could she feel safe? No wonder she had to fend people away with biting retorts.

It was in the second hour that she was able to embody her vulnerable child self. I suggested she or I could move a greater distance apart until she felt comfortable. She chose to move, and crawled behind my sand tray table peering out at me sheepishly. I asked if she wanted a blanket to put around her and extended my arm with it so as to not invade her space. She wrapped it around herself. Peeking into the sand she asked where the sand was from. I meanwhile sat very still so as not to scare her and answered her questions gently, simply and concretely. We were redramatizing object relations.

The development of healthy body boundaries cannot be done in one hour or in six hours; it takes time. Trust must be built through enacted relational experiences of "coming up against the other" and serve the purpose of establishing healthy skin boundaries rather than feeling that one is being violated.

One man in my authentic sound movement and drama group spent several months imaginally feeling enveloped by his enmeshed parents. "Get out of my room!" "Leave me alone!" was a constant refrain from his favorite side of the therapy space. At times I or others received the projection of the engulfing parent. One session I responded as his mother, "I need you. I need to devour your soul. I'm starving. Please let me breathe your air and consume what you do to make it mine." Repeatedly yelling, "No!" he shoved me along the floor until I was out of his space. The next series of sessions had him literally struggling to eject the object internalization from his body. Coughing and gagging over time brought forth a full baritone voice, one that had not been heard before. Now instead of remaining in his designated corner, he began to crawl around the room making instinctual animal-like sounds. Testing his new-found body boundaries, he bumped up against others, annoying them. They in turn either joined him in animal play or projected onto him their own violating objects.

A four-year-old boy is referred to me. He races into the room, immediately spits in my face and bites my knee. His mother had recently given birth and this little fellow, struggling with the shift in his mother's attention, had angrily regressed to the first stage of separation. A few sessions were spent with him "being the baby and me the mommy"; and then a gradual age appropriate improvisational shift developed in which we became "construction workers" like his dad, building tall edifices.

Separation and Individuation: Practicing and Rapprochement Sub-phases

Practicing and rapprochement are the final sub-phases in separation and individuation. Practicing entails the experience of spatially leaving and returning to the mother for refueling. Rapprochement involves asserting one's autonomy and joining the good and bad self and object. This final phase results in the experiencing of a realistic whole self and a caring, internalized mother. The capacity for a healthy external boundary denoting one's personal space and awareness of others is also organized in this phase.

This line between paradise and independence is a struggle many borderline clients face. A client redramatizes the practicing phase of separation by spatially moving toward me and farther away. In one session she asked me to go into the smaller sand tray room and close the door. In another she asked me to shut my eyes while she moved about. In another I was covered with material. At times she sat in my lap and at other times beside me. During rapprochement, she drew huge pictures of devouring dinosaurs, symbolic of her rage. Her rageful split-off self then began to appear and finally to be claimed and enacted. Claiming both sides of the self in relation to the other is vital in therapy with the rapprochement client as is healing the split in the transferred mother object.

Another client role plays a dialogue between her symbiotic needy self and her separating, wall-like boundaried rapprochement self. This split-self needed to be joined so that she could experience both her relationally-oriented vulnerability and her capacity for boundaries simultaneously. "I need a man; I'll do anything, be anything just to be with him" was followed by "who needs anyone. They're all just takers. Be alone." Finally she reached an agreement and moved to blend the two. Subsequently she began and sustained a relationship without the "come here- go away" practicing phase dramatic theme she would repeatedly enact.

Self and Object Constancy

In this final phase of Mahler's, the individual begins to internalize the mother so that full separation can occur without the fear of abandonment. If "good enough mothering" was present then the individual will experience a whole, full realistic sense of self. They will also experience being held, supported and loved for who they are. They will be internally encouraged to feel pride in their productions, confidence in their doings and interest in exploring their creativity.

All too often a negative parental object is introjected. A witch mother may want to smother the child, keeping them debilitated and infantile as in *Rapunzel.* She may demand that only part of the self be allowed to come out into the light of consciousness while the other "bad" parts must remain in shadow. They may be submerged in the oceanic unconscious as in *Cinderella,* or she may inflate the child self to a grandiose state of narcissism to feed off the child's accomplishments as in *Hansel and Gretel.*

When this cannibalism occurs, all products are rendered to the primary caregiver–not only the sense of self, but who one is and what one does. This creates tremendous ambivalence within their victims. I have had numerous clients, most of whom are males in their mid to late thirties, who have had one great aspiration crash after another. These men were adored by their mothers who told them early on that they were going to be great; and that, unlike others, they would never have to work for anything. Such was the case with one depressed man who was part of a men's group. He never seemed to be able to sustain any intimate relationship nor maintain any job stability. Enacting the mother-child drama, I as mother, say to him, "You are wonderful, my boy, no one can see how marvelous you are but me. Stay with me always, my little phallus." He moves toward me drawn to the mother-witch seduction. I clutch him. "You're mine and everything you do is mine. I'm hungry, you must do for me. So I can brag about my son and what he does."

The other men in the group are now getting agitated; "Get away from her!" "They're just jealous of our special relationship," I respond. The men are disgusted, but the man I am clutching appears deep in thought with furrowed brows as if he is struggling to get what appears so obvious to the other men.

I decide to "up the ante" and continue, "everything you think, say and do is mine. You're mine. Since everything you produce is mine, I want your balls." Now the men are yelling, "Get away from her!" Consciousness starts to dawn, and he shoves me away saying, "No, you can't have them! Get your own!" Feeling my power diminish I crouch to the floor, becoming an old beggar crone, "Please, I need you. Don't leave me." Now the men gather him into a huddle and then cover me with huge pillows for an early burial.

Mediation of the Instinctual and the Identification and Triangular Relationship with Parents: Magic Warlike and Magical Creative Phases

In the next stage delineated by Jungian, Eric Neumann (1973), the child must integrate much of his/her instinctual life in order to be civilized into the community of playmates. This instinctual realm is still viewed as related to the matriarchate. At this time, a child's dramatic skills naturally awaken to aid in this process within the *mundus imaginalis*. Nightmares begin around three and a half. Here the realm of the nightstalkers emerges from the earth and sea (mother realms); and bats, devils, witches, and zombies, manifest who seek to devour, smother or poison their prey. In this phase clients enact rageful, powerful creatures who have too long been repressed for fear of retaliation or envy from the parents. These creatures from the deep can be mirrored and engaged by the therapist.

One woman dreamt that a tiger leaps into her car. She wakes up screaming. Utilizing the technique of dreamwork as theater, I interview her as the tiger while I am the dream ego. "What are you doing in my car. You frighten me! Get out!" I exclaim in retreat. "Do you want to eat me?" I ask. "I should. You're a little wimp." She responds. "Well I had a rough childhood you know. If I stood up to my dad he would have clobbered me worse." I retort, "Well, I don't see him around here now. I'm tired of your wimping out." She as the tiger responds. As the dream ego I ask, "Well you're no wimp; maybe you could help me." "Yeah, I could help but you gotta let me speak up." "Then nobody will mess with me," I affirm. "Yeah," she reaffirms.

Giving her homework, I suggest she walk like and think like this tiger. She found this instinctual part of her became gradually civilized, but the "don't mess with me" core remained underneath.

During the fifth year the triangular relationship with the parents expands. In this magic warlike phase, it is vital for the male to kill off the inner mother no matter how wonderful she may appear to be in order for the Oedipal crisis to be resolved and for him to have access to his anima or inner feminine side. Without this act, a man will forever transfer his mother onto the women he is with resulting in his fearing commitment or symbolically clinging depending on whether his mother was controlling or abandoning.[2]

With women this phase, which I have called the magical creative stage, is much different. She does not kill the mother because they are of like sex, but she must learn to mediate the powerful feminine and to experience the father not as bestial under the power of the dark feminine as in *Beauty and the Beast* but as human and relatable.

One couple complains that they have drifted apart. We spend the first hour "identifying the players." The wife appears warm and loving with compassionate eyes, but her husband's response to her is clearly through a distorted lens. With some exploration he is found to have a mother (I name her the Ice Queen) who is emotionally and physically unavailable. His father, although more loving, is a harsh taskmaster and beat him with a paddle. Touching, caressing and feeling loved and safe did not come naturally to him. The wife had a more nurturing childhood, but inside her was a critical father judge who convinced her that her husband was unavailable because there was something wrong with her. Her critic protected her by asking the husband a myriad of questions devised to

[2] Eric Neumann (1973). was able to delineate male stages of development, but he decided that the ego was also masculine for the female as well. I disagree. I believe as did Jung that there are contrasexual aspects to both male and female psychologies, i.e., men have inner feminine complex(es). called animae and women inner masculine called animi. I feel that a woman's ego is feminine and that her quests and development are centrally different than that of the males. I do feel, however, that both men and women must undergo developmental stages for both their ego and animus/a with both moving toward the goal of androgyny in later life. I have, therefore, added female stages of development to Neumann's male ego stages. Thus the "magic warlike" is Neumann's and the "magical creative" is mine.

discover the "truth" i.e., that he did not really love her. Her husband, meanwhile, experienced "male relational dread" (Bergman, 1991) and felt unable to respond with the needed emotionally-laden relationally-oriented verbal processing of which most women are adept. Since he was raised without access to a communicating female and by a father who trained him to compete among males, he remained silent, ill-equipped to engage. She then was sure he was hiding something.

With the roles identified as ice queen mother and critical father, I began to roleplay their transferences. At times I physically put my body between them so they had to struggle to see and touch each other. Their goal in the drama was to connect; my task was to keep them from intimacy. "All women are cold and unavailable; don't touch her, she'll freeze your fingers off" I exclaimed as the husband's ice queen mother. As her critical father I said, "Don't listen to him, he's not safe. Only I can protect you."

Through the externalization of these intrapsychic phenomena, I was also able to "catch" the transferential and projective material thereby keeping it from contaminating their capacity to see each other. Intimacy was able to follow with a good deal of loving tenderness.

Latency, Peer Relationships and Puberty

With latency comes a shift in themes to those that reflect learning and living within the civilized realm of home and society. The industry of play and school become the precursors to adult work.

Pubertal rites of passage herald the next phase in the development of ego consciousness. Jung (CW VIII) felt that this was the time of psychic birth. For the boy as well as the animus in girls, this means being separated from the collective, undergoing pain or deprivation, and undertaking tasks which entail empowerment and mastery over masculine instinctual phallic energy. As boys develop, their bodies become stronger. Their brute force can kill; it thus needs to be mediated. Control over drives and fear is rewarded with spiritual consciousness.

For the maturing girl and the boy's anima, their rite of passage entails a descent and sacrifice of girlhood toward the search for embodied empowered feminine soulful wisdom.

One woman was in the process of reclaiming her inner children. Near terminating she reported a pubescent young girl who she had imaged on the way to the session. This girl had asked to be welcomed into her consciousness. She and I had previously discussed how her mother had felt shame and disdain for all aspects of female reproduction and sexuality. Her pubescent sensual self went underground, hidden under weight and layers of clothing to protect herself from the growing attention of the men around her. Menarche came and went in hidden shame. There was no pubertal rite of passage. Now in her forties, she and I enacted a pubertal rite for her embodied pubescent self. This woman then blossomed with creative ideas and ventures.

An eleven-year-old girl was referred to me for individual and group work. She lived with her stepmother without her salesman father much of the time. In the girl's improvisational drama group, she repeatedly took on angry male roles until the other girls encouraged her to enact female roles. As she began to claim her femaleness she came in one day with her beautiful hair butchered by her stepmother into a boyish cropped length. In individual work that day, she requested we dramatize *Snow White* with her as the heroine and myself playing the other roles. With much self-hate, she insisted I "cut her heart out" even though the story dictated otherwise. I suggested a pause, and had her interview me as the evil stepmother who, with

Wonder Woman's sash around her, had to "tell the truth" about her jealousy toward her stepdaughter.

Adolescence and Young Adulthood

Moving further in the transition between childhood into adulthood requires the exploration of new roles and the testing of familial and societal ruling principles. The striving for identity within one's peer group is carried out through costuming, roles and thematic enactments. Mythically, real identity can only emerge if one is willing to undergo a personal quest. If undertaken, the individual stands alone from the tribe and is identified as the hero or heroine. This journey frequently commences with a relationship to both the masculine and feminine sides. Thus, a man's male ego must join with his anima and a woman's female ego with her animus. Frequently, the contrasexual sides are projected into a lover for an embodied experience of the sexual union. However, the libido that belongs to the inner anima or animus must eventually be reowned and internalized or the individual will forever feel that s/he is only half a person without the other. Additionally, shadow aspects now emerge from the unconscious to be claimed. These same sex parts of the self often appear on more purely archetypal levels and can be readily dramatized and integrated into the psyche.

One client in her early forties brought in the following dreams. The first entailed her floating away from the reality she knew and becoming an instinctual Artemis figure. As she enacted her, she squatted on my green rug making gathering motions. She then brought her cupped hands upward through her body and extended them upward and outward from her heart–an ancient archetypal gesture (Lewis 1989, 1993). As Artemis, she spoke to the dreamer telling her to trust her instincts and profound intuitive ability and to continue to connect to nature to find a grounded energy source to fuel her busy day.

In the next dream a baby boy is born to her and placed in a bassinet which is too big for him. She is told his heart is broken. She wakes up crying. This newly emerging relationship to her masculine had been injured at infancy and not allowed to develop. I suggested she reenter the dream, hold and verbally soothe her baby and heal his heart through love and nurturance.

In the following session, it became apparent that her positive caretaking had paid off. The infant had grown to manhood. She dreamt that she says to a priest, "I really love you." This figure represented a highly developed inner masculine and an *agapé* experience of spiritual love. I encouraged her to return to the imaginal realm of the dream to continue the experience. This brought her to a higher conuinctio (Jung, CW XIV, XVI Lewis, 1993) or spiritual union. She reported feeling greater compassion and wisdom.

Mid-life Stage I: Heroic and Heronic Quest: Death and Rebirth and the Mid-life Crisis

Once both contrasexual natures have been differentiated out of parental complexes and joined together toward a united purpose, the quest begins its most treacherous phase. Because of this, many are unwilling to pursue it and stay frozen in the solar realm. But if the hero and heroine take on the quest, there are many myths of gods and goddesses that serve as guides; and through this relationship to the archetypal life themes, individuals can feel deeply connected to all of humanity–past, present and future–thus instilling meaning to their suffering.

This cycle of descent, death and ascent toward rebirth is typically undergone in midlife and is often identified as "mid-life crisis." It spans a period of time between 35 and 45 years of age. During this time beginning at the mid-point of life, individuals begin to be aware of their own mortality. During the next five years they slowly take stock in their lives: "Do I really want to spend the next half of my life with this person, job, or way of being?" Individuals often become preoccupied with aging signs. They may try to counteract the inevitable, by having affairs with younger individuals, buying youthful sports cars or clothing. They may attempt to stay the results of age on their body by getting into heightened physical exercise at health clubs. Others compete with their now adolescent children or younger colleagues at work only to find the inevitable, i.e., that their football player son beats them at arm wrestling or their daughter really does look much better in that dress than they do. Frequently behavioral patterns that began in childhood begin to be questioned. For example, one woman said, "I thought if I was nice to everyone, then they'd be nice to me. For 20 years I thought that if I just loved my husband more, he would stop undermining me." A man reflected, "I thought all I had to do was get this full professorship then I would have it all, but I'm still missing something. Status and money aren't 'it' like I thought."

This initial period is followed by an experience of breaking down or letting go of who one was. This occurs generally around 38–42. Described as "disassembling ourselves," (Sheehy, 1974), it is a dark time which is often precipitated by a crisis e.g., an affair being discovered, loss of a job or promotion, divorce, or the death of a parent. Some get into accidents or have their first experience with a life-threatening medical problem such as cancer or a heart attack. In any case, this is a time of letting go of who one was, and of suffering the insecurity of not knowing where one will end up. It is a time of grieving the years that were wasted not truly being oneself. At this time in therapy men and women are more willing to honestly recognize and feel the pain from their past and let go of repetitive developmental themes that have not been helpful to them in their life. This frees up energy for the final phase.

The final phase of the mid-life crisis is one of experiencing the development of a new, more authentic, expanded sense of self. Terms such as renewal and rebirth are employed here.

A 39-year-old man presented as the classic male in mid-life crisis reassessing his life. He was the oldest child of an alcoholic, physically abusive father and a narcissistic mother who adultified him at 6 at the time of their divorce. He remained shut down and dutiful throughout his childhood, graduate school and marriage.

In one session, he begins by dragging around a huge imagined excalibar sword–symbolic of his over-responsible ACOA behavior. He enters a forest and transverses a bridge. He sits down to rest and reports seeing a fox. Entering the imaginal realm I become him and he the fox. As the fox he says, "I'm free; you can live here too." Reversing roles repeatedly the drama continues. Darkness comes and he becomes afraid. The fox then attempts to teach him other ways to see.

He returns the next week and reenters the imaginal realm. He becomes possessed with despair. In the center of the despair is his inner 6-year-old. Over the course of several sessions I frequently portrayed the despair along with his survival mechanisms of cynic, Mr. Responsibility and "Shut down" while he as his adult/ ego and I battled for the possession of his soul/child. Finally he dreams and subsequently enacts a descent in which he rescues a submerged boy. In the following week, he brings in a dream of a laughing baby dropping from the sky into his arms. In one of the last sessions he and his inner child fend off all my/his strategies in a playful drama improv. At one point I dress in a witch cape and hat with a halo and pretend to be "only there for his best interests." I was perfunctorily dismissed.

Mid-Life Stage II: Middlessence

Working-class men identify middle age at 40; white-collar workers 50. This author takes the mean of these two. Thus the middle years span between 45 and 65. Menopause is considered a ten-year cycle from 45 to 55 years or the onset of climacteric (the cessation of menstruation).

This is a time when the new-found self from the resolution of the mid-life crisis manifests. Individuals in this phase are often free from their childhood history and from attempting to be like anyone else but themselves. They become far more outspoken about their own personal beliefs and care less about what other people think. Greer (1992) notes regarding women during "the change" that as they become less sexually attractive to men and many, after mourning the loss of being able to trade on their appearance, feel a new-found freedom. One woman in her latter 50s said in session, "I don't have to defer to men anymore and pretend I'm less than who I am to reinforce their fantasy that they're better than I."

Male menopause beginning around 45 is marked by decreased testosterone. They may have insomnia, chronic fatigue and headaches. Research also demonstrates the more anxious a man is the more his testosterone decreases (Sheehy, 1974). This can produce a downward spiral. Diminished sexual activity for males in Western culture is often equated with a decrease in power in general. This equation frequently makes a man more anxious which in turn decreases the hormone. Nervousness, irritability and depressive phases can be part of male climacteric.

Menopausal women, who have traded on their being pretty, experience what Greer (1992) identifies as a "free fall which brings with it panic" (p. 8). Until she can realize the freedom this gives her, she will feel she has been thrown into the scrap heap of a youth culture that is fearful of the aging process. Regardless, women in this phase mourn the loss of their fertility and capacity to give birth. One client remarked, "It's not that I want to have another child. Lord, no. I don't have the energy or the patience anymore. But it is the loss of being fertile. It's a feeling I've had ever since I was 13. It was so much a part of me that until it was gone I never knew it was so infused in me. It's in the way I walk, the dresses I wear. I did not realize it, but I was saying to all who could see, 'I am fertile.'"

In that final phase, a woman is able to let go of the childbearer and love goddess images, and claim her croneship. Clarissa Pinkola-Estes says about women that in their earlier years they shed blood to have children and now they hold blood to store wisdom (Geer, 1992). The postmenopausal woman has acquired deep serenity, power, wisdom, depth of love and spirituality.

In men, too, being able to let go of the burden of pretending to fit the male stereotype is freeing. Gone is the strength, gone the lithe body and tight stomach, gone the competitive edge. Contemplative, observant and knowing he has come through the retirement panic, i.e., that he was what he did. Now he is truly free. Men have no need for excuses anymore and women have no more apologies that have to be said.

Often clients have a series of spiritual dreams at this time in their life which when explored and experienced in an embodied way, can result in the client being deeply moved. A 58-year-old woman related the following dream four months into her depth therapy: "A Chinese man in a limousine hurls a plastique bomb into an old, dark fortress. One of my daughters dressed in a white clerical gown is pushing a woman on a hospital gurney toward a church."

Through dreamwork as theater she role played this Eastern figure symbolic of ancient wisdom and the rising sun of Consciousness. As I interviewed him, she learned he was bombing her rigid body and archaic defensive behavior (old fortress).

In the next scene with her daughter, she realized *she* was the body lying on the gurney. I then encouraged her to enact lying on the moving bed. A suggestion was also made that she imagine continuing the dream and experience what would happen next.

She then laid down on the couch and closed her eyes. "I am entering this church," she related, "and there is this dome with an opening at the center. There is light pouring down at the center point." "Allow your daughter to wheel you into the Light," I responded gently but firmly. Her breathing changed and became deeper. Her eyes teared. Her mouth opened with a sigh. No words could describe this feeling of the Holy Other. The therapy room and I were also transported into the sacred space of her dream. Both she and I felt surrounded by Grace. Deeply moved she left with an expanded vision of the many realms of existence.

This expanded vision is yet another byproduct of the mid-life aging process. Now the focus of a person's life can shift away from self in relation to one's immediate environment and attempts to attain what Western culture has deemed of value. Usually the more an individual has achieved these worldly plateaus, whether they be relationships, family, money, status and/or professional success, the easier it is to let go of what has been acquired. Many that failed, for whatever reason, to meet their ideals of the "good life," have difficulty letting go of their *sine qua non* place in their consciousness. These individuals often live out their lives in a quiet despair.

But for those who can shift their attention, their view expands. They see the "bigger pictures" of humanity, planetary existence and the possibility of Spiritual Consciousness.

Aging and Dying

Wisdom comes with the aging process. Those who live long enough see that trends in life among humans and in nature have a tendency to repeat themselves. The commonality of experience among all peoples becomes clearer. They come to know more deeply that all humans experience joy, anger and suffering. All share concerns over territory and survival. Thus greater consciousness concerning oneself provides a foundation for interpersonal consciousness which in turn provides a springboard for greater transpersonal or spiritual Consciousness.

The same man described in mid-life crisis returned years later for five months with a very different focus. He reported that he had not been depressed or cynical since our work, but something had happened. He was diagnosed with cancer and was scheduled for chemotherapy. He knew that chemotherapy not only kills any possible cancer cells, but just about everything else draining one's life force. He felt he wanted to know his path in life more clearly.

For the next several sessions, synchronistic phenomena occurred during his therapy hour in the form of animal appearances never before seen in my office. In his next session two seals appeared at river's edge in front of us. With a shamanic frame in mind, I suggested he enter into the imaginal realm with the seals and dialogue with them. "Be harmonious with nature, and joy and pleasure will be yours," was their response.

In the next hour, he looked up to find a magnificent eight-point stag in the meadow out front who appeared and stayed for his hour only. I knew from my research that the stag is one of the major power animals of shamans and is a symbol of Christ (Lewis,

1993). Through dramatic dialogue with the buck he received, "Get rid of fear. This is filling your mind with useless thoughts. Get off your butt. Don't waste time looking for outside guidance through books. Be open now."

In the following hour, he reported a dream, "I am in a medieval inner courtyard–like a circular paddock. The stag goes through a big dark wooden door. I feel I'm supposed to follow, but I don't want to. Then I'm aware there is a huge male figure dressed in white robes. He is laughing." I role played the white figure who is clearly a trickster psychopomp and he was the dream ego. I told him he must go through the door, and that if he does not all of his suffering from the chemotherapy will be meaningless.

He returned a month later racked with pain and nausea from the chemotherapy. He reported seeing two hawks facing in opposite directions on the same branch in the front of my office. He lay down, and I suggested he connect with the hawks. During this time I sensed something unusual occurring. He later reported that the hawks helped him leave his body. "Now I know I have a body; I am not a body." "Yes," I responded, "it is easier for people to be willing to have out-of-body experiences if they are in physical pain."

Three weeks later he returned with the following dream. He is in a monk's habit leading a group in the wilderness. He comes upon a rock impasse. Before him appear five angels. Each send him their names: Love, Compassion, Truth, Understanding, and Humility. He extends his hands and radiant beams of light emanate. He then tells me he is not religious and feels unworthy. I instructed him to ask the angels. He stretched out his arms and then began to laugh. "They say that is beside the point" he reported. I then instructed him to reenact his dream. During this drama he began to cry. "This may sound corny," he reported later, "but to touch people . . . we're all suffering . . . to touch with kindness . . ."

After a hiatus in which he was recovering from the chemotherapy, he returns. I suggested he imagine and reconnect through improvisational drama with the animals that had appeared to him. Moving about the room he reported "The hawk is circling above and the stag is entering a forest." "Follow him," I responded. He comes to a circular clearing with a 20-foot stone circle with a fire in the middle. He sees many faces in the fire. "Step into the fire." He stepped in and reported, "I'm looking out. Everything is dark. I sense there is something beyond, something green, but I'm afraid of the dark." My insistence for him to continue was to no avail. At this point all the electricity in my office went off and stayed off until he left.

In the next session, I returned him to his incomplete journey. He stepped into the flame and reported a dark hole in the middle. Reminding him to let go of his fear, he was able to descend down. The hole gets smaller and he crawls until he reports seeing large teeth in front of him that keep him from proceeding. He said finally, "You know this is funny but if I were a snake I could slither right through." "Be a snake" I responded. He proceeds and learns he can shape shift.

In his last session he reported that the president of his company wanted to place him in a managerial position, one in which he would be speaking nationally. But he told me he was afraid of what he would say. "They might ask questions that I don't know the answers to." I responded, "Ask the angels." The angels say, "It's not what you say. It is your being, your compassion and your love which is the message." He then said to me, "All my life I've always judged myself as being a 'jack of all trades master of none.' I've never reached the pinnacle of accomplishment in any field. Now I realize this is not the direction at all. It is not what you do; it is who you are." "Yes," I responded, "Manifesting your soul is truly the most important accomplishment."

CLINICAL CASE

Laura, a bright woman in her early thirties with a strong ego, was referred by a former client. She entered the room and quickly held me with intense riveting eyes. I felt immediately moved into a state of idealization. I then began to receive the full transference of a mother that needed to be pedestaled or there would be no chance of receiving any attention, let alone love. I pondered internally as to whether she unconsciously felt she needed to heal me, the mother-therapist, first i.e., to fill me with narcissistic supplies in hopes there would be enough to send back to her. I immediately began to send support, care, and valuing back to her through the imaginal realm of the somatic countertransference. I learned from her that her mother was empty and enmeshed and her father narcissistic. She was ignored or engulfed by the mother and spousified by the father. Neither parent instilled in her a sense of self. I wrote in my notes from this first hour, "must have very good boundaries with her. She needs to have her new sense of self encouraged and supported as she claims more of herself."

Developmental Themes of Symbiosis

The only one who noticed her was her father, but only in relation to what she looked like and what she did that he could use for his own aggrandizement. He had sexualized her and now her sexuality was split from her inner substance and used to seduce in order to be seen. As she role played her mother while I interviewed her, I began feeling as if I were in the presence of a mannequin who consisted solely of an outer shell. It became exceedingly difficult to make sure I did not get caught in her excellently trained ability to mirror what the other wanted and give it to them. Much of my response to her was on a nonverbal level. I sat in opened posturing and attuned to her breath and trace self-nurturing movements. In this type of transference, however, who is mirroring whom can be a very subtle, and at times, confusing pas de deux.

In five sessions her trust was sufficient enough to begin the work of self-formation. During this hour she realized that she had given up her soul's manifestation in return for the hopes of parental love. I asked her if she was willing to let me in i.e., for my soul to find her soul. Would she let me look inside her? She was intrigued; and looking into my eyes, she allowed me to look into hers. This suggestion brought us into the transpersonal. I connected to my soul and began looking inside her for a spark of "I"ness. Eventually she allowed me to find her. She said after, "I feel like we weren't the only beings in this room. I felt someone saying 'wake up.'" I responded, "Let those words be your mantra."

The next week she brought in a dream in which she was lead by a psychopomp figure into "seeing the light in the darkness, like the light that shines at the bottom of the sea." I encouraged her to enact this experience. She began by kneeling with her head downward. She then said, "I need to do this with someone." I then moved toward her, and I supported her as I mirrored her in this birthing. In this way we began the redramatization of object relations. We finished the sequence by her indulging in eye-to-eye contact. I felt her beginning to receive and digest my genuine care. She questioned, "Will you receive my anger too?" I smiled back and imagined her whole and sent the image back to her through the somatic countertransference.

In the next hour she reported dreaming that she was "deep in liquid–like a womb, and I feel my center." I suggested that she enact the dream. She lay on the floor. I sat next to her and supported her back with my hand gently following the flow of her breath. Role playing her fetal self, she began to speak, "I feel empty." I respond soothingly, "Yes little one, that is because there was no one to feed you, but we will fill you with love and care and you will feel full."

Developmental Themes of Differentiation

"I need to see myself" was Laura's first comment at the beginning of the next session. I brought her a mirror and encouraged her to look into her own eyes. "I am worried. I need space; I am empty." She continued to use the mirror and then became aware of her inner judge that we had explored in earlier sessions. I role played her judge to externalize it, and she was able tell it/me to leave her alone. Her inner mother then appeared in this imaginal process and her developmental themes changed from symbiotic to those of differentiation. She growled and snapped and clawed the rug as she struggled to claim the needed differentiation from her. In the next hour, her persona charming false self was personified by her telling her to stop expressing anger, that no one would like her, that it's not safe. Feeling that this survival mechanism needed to be externalized so that she could more fully claim her nascent self, I took over role playing it while she embodied her angry self.

Throughout the next few months she continued to enact the growing infant-toddler self. She often began the session connecting to the early infant. In one hour she said she imagined an egg that was between us; I then created a nest of pillows around her. She became concerned that the pillows barred access to me. So I moved next to her and extended my arm into the nest like an umbilical chord. In the nest she began to posit the concept of whole parents: "I have hated both my parents and stayed away to separate from them, but I now think that they are neither all good nor all bad."

The next session she crawled everywhere in the drama space. Embodying this differentiating self she related that she felt more energy, and that she wanted to "rip at the veils that keep me from being more here." She then related this to her mother and became angry once again at her mother's lack of connection. I elected to receive the negative transference and veiling myself in a parachute, I began to role play her mother, "If you become real, I will leave you; or make you go; or make you wrong or bad." Laura responded with more differentiating themes: demonstrating healthy body and ego boundaries serving to separate intrapsychically from her mother's toxicity.

With each session she continued to enact the differentiating toddler creeping and crawling while separating and discriminating her thoughts and feelings from her mother's. In one session she repeatedly reached out and grabbed. She then became contaminated by the negativity of her inner mother. "My mother is surrounding me with her disgust. I shouldn't grab or want or need!" I mirrored her sounds of exclamation while placing the parachute around her to externalize and objectify her experience of her invoked mother surrounding her with disgust. Additionally I placed a pillow between her and me. Laura continued to moan. As the shamed child she said, "I am yucky; my mother said I was disgusting." "It's a good thing," I responded using metaphors from this developmental stage; "because otherwise she would have devoured you." "Yeah," she returned; "It was safest to hide." Gradually she removed the parachute and risked being present in the room with me. For several minutes she looked into my eyes and received my good will toward her "a drop at a time" while I reassured her that her needs were not yucky but normal.

Developmental Themes of Practicing and Rapprochement

She began to crawl and roll about the room smearing the rug. Utilizing practicing developmental themes she stated, "I can be yucky and you won't push me away." I meanwhile sat some distance away honoring her entrance into the distancing aspect of this stage. In processing, I suggested she needed to sort her mother's and father's "yuckiness" from her own good shit, as the power to have pleasure in one's own bodily products paves the way for creativity.

It was four months before she moved developmentally from crawling to standing. She brought in a powerful dream. "I am at my mother's childhood home. The sky gets dark, ominous. The wind comes. The house collapses. It's snowing and icing. I only have time to grab one thing–my sturdy walking shoes. I leave and fall into the ice flows. I call for help, but a friend of mine (who has gone through a lot of recovery) says, 'You can stand,' and I do." I suggested that she dramatize the dream. She was able to stand but tried to walk prematurely. Her arms were unable to move in a reciprocal manner to her gait. In the next session she again moved to a standing position and this time asserted herself utilizing rapprochement themes as she invoked her mother in the room. "I hate you! You could not see me. I wasn't allowed to get angry or say you weren't mothering me. You told me I was mean. I felt I could not leave you because I would never get your love!" I again maintained a vertical position and imagined her whole with pride within the somatic countertransference. Following this session she arrived wearing a pair of red slacks and exclaimed, "My life has been about standing up."

About this time there was a hiatus in the work due to a vacation. Upon return she embodied her toddler self and yelled at me. "It was too long; I am angry. You know I do fine without you but inside it was too long." "Your adult self functions well; but this is about the child self inside you that is developing. You were just standing up and beginning to practice leaving, and I left you instead. It is you that should be leaving." "Yeah!" she affirmed. She continued, "I need the physical. It's physical how I feel. My body misses you. It's like I begin to feel empty again." "Yes," I responded, "It's like I am a part of you that creates a holding place for the you inside you so that you can fill with yourself." "It's like when you left, there was a hole, and I began to drain out of me," Laura replied.

During this conversation she was rocking on all fours. I was next to her with my hand on her back. Laura continued, "This mom stuff is so important to me. My life is really shifting." She then sat up to vertical, and I responded by giving her more spatial distance and shifting from the horizontal to the vertical. She then adjusted her body into the forward plane and began to describe a highly creative work in which she was engaging with another woman.

Developmental Themes of Self Formation and Identification and Relationship with Parents

Subsequently she had several dreams that she was pregnant. Her creativity began to expand at work as she was given new projects. Her sexuality that had been split off in service to gaining her father's and subsequent men of authority's value and approval, began to be reclaimed. In one session she gathered several figures from the sand play shelves and arranged them on the rug. Her libidinal needy self, her boundaried rapprochement self, her ego, and two Aphrodite statutes: one white, one brown. As the white goddess, she addressed her inner psyche's personifications, "I will seduce men and give them whatever they want." As the brown Aphrodite, "All men just want sex; they don't ever see me or want to. So I'll give it to them and have power over them." Her symbiotic child self responded to the split-off sexuality, "Oh take me with you; maybe I'll be loved too." But the new rapprochement self said to the needy child, "Wait! Just wait! I am the one to help and protect you, not the sex vamp. She can't take care of you; she can't take care of herself."

Developmental Themes of Puberty and Adolescence: Claiming her Sexuality and De-throning the Old Rule

The overlapping interrelationship between her rapprochement assertiveness and her awareness and experience of her pubertal sexuality continued for several sessions. Her capacity to claim her sexuality was contingent upon her integration of the rapprochement developmental themes of self assertion and independent thought and action as it is in this phase that healthy external boundaries are formed. Her sexual interiority had been perpetrated upon in early years by her mother's sexually competitive narcissism and her father's spousification of her. Later during puberty and early adolescence, her parents had violated her personal space through highly inappropriate interest in her desire, orgasmic performance, and intimate encounters with boys.

In one session she began via the improvisational technique of authentic sound, movement and drama. She writhed on the floor and discovered that she only felt comfortable moving from her shoulders upward. She had sheathed the rest of her body with an imaginal barrier in order to bar her parents access to her embodied sexuality. To get greater insight into her mother's abuse, I suggested she role play her mother while I interviewed her. With each response I encouraged her to remove a layer of her mother's false-self persona until her raw blood curdling competitive and provocative nature was revealed.

In the following week she reported a dream of waves or orgiastic energy moving through her body. She recalled saying in the dream, "I am preparing myself to be a virgin; this is what Penny meant."

She then arranged pillows around her external boundary and spendt 45 minutes shoving away the imaged holograph of her parents that existed in her personal energy field. Additionally she toned in differentiating and rapprochement sound reinforcing external and body boundaries.

She then formed a word, "Neeeeeed . . ." I added, "I need . . ." She responded, "I need floor, earth to be mothered. I need to be human." I responded, "You need to be fully in your body and out to your skin." "Yes!" she exclaimed and began to sob. I then brought a box of tissue over to her. She said, "Don't go." I sat next to her on the floor. She lay down with her head next to me on a pillow. I stroked her head. She said calmly, "I trust you."

Developmental Themes of Young Adulthood

Gradually she shifted her work from healing through the redramatization of earlier developmental themes to exploring adult life stage themes. She began to have dreams and do sand plays of shadow (same sex) and *animi* (inner masculine) aspects seeking to be claimed. Employing dreamwork as theater and embodied sand play she role played these complexes and integrated them through the experience of them. In one dream a woman "who has always been watching from a distance" pushed her into a pool. Enacting the punk styled woman with me interviewing her she, complained that the dreamer had always kept her away. Role playing the dreamer I responded, "well you would have gotten me into big trouble had I listened to you. Your 'nobody messes with me' attitude is just too 'uncivilized.'" "Well it's what you need, you've been a woose!" We made a deal: I encouraged her to embody her throughout the week and, with her shadow's influence, began to alter her responses to situations. Later she role-played and subsequently joined two other shadow aspects–one a blitheful *puella* (eternal youth) and another a responsible, maternal archetypal woman caught in tribal tradition.

In sand play, she placed an animus figure next to her inner mother. She then realized that, instead of supporting her, he had become her mother's henchman as in *Sleeping Beauty*. She role-played him and I her. I encouraged him to come and be in relation to me. As he shifted, his personality developed demonstrating strength, gentleness, thoughtful caring and responsibility. Soon she began dreaming of archetypal unions with her inner masculine.

SUMMARY

From birth to the final rite of passage we humans explore developmental themes that build upon preexisting stages. If unintegrated, these themes become dysfunctional and perpetuate themselves keeping the person from moving forward and responding spontaneously. The drama therapist identifies the repetitive phenomena and their developmentally associated roles; and through the techniques of inner drama, the redramatization of object relations, psychodrama dreamwork as theater, sand play embodiment, dramatic improvisation, and authentic sound, movement and drama; resolves and clears the habitual patterns. Then mythelogems or archetypal life themes become available to healthy children, adolescents, and adults in their unfolding personal quests.

A clients' recovery into wholeness means that they can fully experience the uniqueness of each moment. It means that the inner masculine and feminine are balanced and integrated. It also means they have potential to be in relationship to the archetypal Self, to that which can continuously provide the stage for involvement in developmentally stimulated archetypal life themes.

REFERENCES

Bergman, S. (1991). *Men's psychological development: A relational perspective, work in progress.* Wellesley: The Stone Center. No. 48.

Edinger, E. (1982). *Ego and archetype.* New York: Penguin Books.

Eliade, M. (1974). *Shamanism: Archaic techniques of ecstasy.* Princeton: Princeton University Press.

Erikson, E. (1963). *Childhood and society.* New York: W.W. Norton and Company.

Fairbairn, R. (1976). *Psychoanalytic studies of the personality: The object relation theory of personality.* London: Kegan Paul.

Freud, A. (1966). *Normality and pathology in childhood.* New York: International Universities Press.

Greer, G. (1992). *The change: Women, aging and menopause.* New York: Alfred Knopf.

Grotstein, J. (1981). *Splitting and projective identification.* New York: Jason Aronson.

Jung, C.G. *Collected works, Vols. XVI and XIV.* New York: Bollengin Foundation.

Klein, M. (1975). *Writings of Melanie Klein* (Vols. 1–3). London: Hogarth.

Kohut, H. (1997). *The analysis of the self.* New York: International Universities Press.

Lewis Bernstein, P., & Bernstein, L. (1973–1974). A conceptualization of group dance movement therapy as a ritual process. *Writings on body movement and communication, Vol. III.* Columbia: ADTA Pub.

Lewis Bernstein, P. (1980). The union of the gestalt concept of experiment and Jungian active imagination. *The Gestalt Journal, III:* 2, 36–45.

Lewis Bernstein, P. (1982). Authentic movement as active imagination. In J. Hariman (Ed.), *The compendium of psychotherapeutic techniques.* Springfield, IL: Charles C Thomas.

Lewis Bernstein, P., & Singer (Eds.). (1983). *The choreography of object relations.* Keene, NH: Antioch University Pub.

Lewis Bernstein, P. (1985). Embodied transformational images in dance-movement therapy. *Journal of Mental Imagery, 9* (4).

Lewis, P. (1986). *Theoretical approaches in dance-movement therapy, Vol. I.* Dubuque, IA: Kendall/Hunt Pub.

Lewis, P. (1987). The expressive arts therapies in the choreography of object relations. *The Arts in Psychotherapy Journal,* Vol. 14.

Lewis, P. (1988a). *Theoretical approaches in dance-movement therapy, Vol. II.* Dubuque, IA: Kendall/Hunt Pub.

Lewis, P. (1988b). The transformative process in the imaginal realm. *The Arts in Psychotherapy Journal.*

Lewis, P. (1989). The soul and spirit in the work: The transformative power of the archetypal. 2nd International Dance Therapy Conference. Toronto.

Lewis, P. (1992). The creative arts in transference-countertransference relationships. *Arts in Psychotherapy.* vol. 19, no 5.

Lewis, P. (1993). *Creative transformation: The healing power of the expressive arts.* Wilmette, IL: Chiron Publications.

Lewis, P., & Loman, S. (Eds.). (1990). *The Kestenberg movement profile–Its past, present and future applications.* Keene, NH: Antioch-New England Graduate School Pub.

Lewis, P. (1996). Authentic sound movement and drama. *A Moving Journal.* vol. 3, no. 1.

Lewis, P. (1999). The clinical interpretation of the kestenberg movement profile with adults. In Amaghi, J., Lewis, P., Loman, S., et al. (Eds.), *The meaning of movement: Developmental and clinical perspectives as seen through the Kestenberg movement profile.* New York: Gordon & Breach Pub.

Lewis, P. (1999). Healing early child abuse: The application of the kestenberg movement profile and its concepts. In Amaghi, J., Lewis, P., Loman, S., & Sossin, M. *The meaning of movement: Developmental and clinical perspectives as seen through the Kestenberg movement profile.* Newark: Gordon & Breach Pub.

Mahler, M. (1968). *On human symbiosis an the vicissitudes of individuation.* New York: International Universities Press.

Moore, R., & Gillete, D. (1990). *King, warrior, magician, lover: Rediscovering the archetypes of the mature masculine.* San Francisco: Harper San Francisco.

Newmann, E. (1973). *The origins and history of consciousness.* Princeton: Princeton University Press.

Newmann, E. (1976). *The child.* New York: Harper & Row.

Racker, H. (1982). *Transference and countertransference.* New York: International Universities Press.

Schwartz-Salant, N., & Stein, M. (Eds.). (1984). *Chiron: Transference/Countertransference.* Wilmette, IL: Chiron Publications.

Schwartz-Salant, N. (1982). *Narcissism and character transformation.* Toronto: Inner City Books.

Schwartz-Salant, N. (1983–1984). *Transference and countertransference.* New York: C.G. Jung Institute of New York, course, Oct. 1983–May 1984.

Searles, H. (1981). *Countertransference and related subjects.* New York: International Universities Press.

Sheehy, G. (1995). *New passages: Mapping your life across time.* New York: Random House.

Stein, M. (1984). *Power, shamanism, and maieutics in the countertransference.* In Chiron, Wilmette, IL: Chiron Publications.

The Jerusalem Bible (1968). New York: Doubleday & Co., Inc.

Turner, V. (1971). *The ritual process.* Chicago: Aldine Pub.

Von Franz, M.-L. (1982). *Individuation in fairytales.* Dallas: Spring Pub.

Von Franz, M.-L. (1978). *Interpretation of fairytales.* Dallas: Spring Pub.

Winnicott, D.W. (1971). *Playing and reality.* New York: Penguin Books.

BIBLIOGRAPHY

Books

Lewis Bernstein, P. (1975). Editor. *Therapeutic process movement as integration.* Columbia: ADTA Pub.

Lewis Bernstein, P., & Singer, D. (Eds.). (1982). *The choreography of object relations.* Keene: Antioch University.

Lewis, P. (1986). *Theoretical approaches in dance-movement therapy, Vol. I.* Dubuque, IA: W.C. Brown-Kendall/Hunt Pub.

Lewis, P. (1987). *Theoretical approaches in dance-movement therapy, Vol. II.* Dubuque, IA: W.C. Brown-Kendall/Hunt Pub Co.

Lewis, P., & Loman, S. (Eds.). (1990). *The Kestenberg movement profile: Its past, present and future applications.* Keene: Antioch University.

Lewis, P. (1993). *Creative transformation: The healing power of the expressive arts.* Willmette: Chiron Publishing.

Lewis, P. (1994). *The clinical interpretation of the Kestenberg movement profile.* Keene: Antioch New England Provost Fund.

Lewis, P. (1999). *Schopfennshe prozesse. Kunst in der therapeutis chen praxis.* Zurich/Dusseldorf: Verlag Pub.

Amaghi, J., Lewis, P., Loman, S., & Sossin, M. (Eds.). (1999). *The meaning of movement: Developmental and clinical perspectives in the Kestenberg movement profile.* Newark: NJ: Gordon & Breach Pub.

Articles and Chapters

Lewis Bernstein, P., & Cafarelli, E. (1972). An electromyographical validation of the effort system of notation. *Writings on body movement and Communication, Vol. II.* Columbia: ADTA Pub.

Lewis Bernstein, P. (1972). Range of response as seen through a developmental progression. *What is dance therapy really?* Govine, B. (Ed.), Columbia: ADTA Pub.

Lewis Bernstein, P., & Bernstein, L. (1973–1974). A conceptualization of group dance-movement therapy as a ritual process. *Writings on body movement and communication, Vol. III.* Columbia: ADTA Pub.

Lewis Bernstein, P., & Garson, B. (1975). Pilot study in the use of tension flow system of movement notation in an ongoing study of infants at risk for schizophrenic disorders. *Dance therapy–Depth and dimension.* Delores Plunk (Ed.), Columbia: ADTA Pub.

Lewis Bernstein, P. (1975). Tension flow rhythms: As a developmental diagnostic tool within the theory of the recapitulation of ontogeny. *Dance therapy–Depth and dimension.* Columbia: ADTA.

Lewis Bernstein, P., Rubin, J., & Irwin, E. (1975). Play, parenting, and the arts. *Therapeutic process movement as integration.* Penny Lewis Bernstein (Ed.), Columbia: ADTA.

Lewis Bernstein, P. (1980). Dance-movement therapy. *Psychotherapy handbook.* Richard Herink (Ed.), New York: The New American Library Press.

Lewis Bernstein, P. (1980). A mythic quest: Jungian movement therapy with the psychosomatic client. *American Journal of Dance Therapy.* Spring, vol. 3, no. 2, pp. 44–55.

Lewis Bernstein, P. (1980). The union of the Gestalt concept of experiment and Jungian active imagination within a woman's mythic quest. *The Gestalt Journal,* Fall, vol. 3, no. 2, pp. 36–46.

Lewis Bernstein, P. (1981). Moon goddess, medium, and earth mother: A phenomenological study of the guiding archetypes of the dance movement therapist. *Research as creative process.* Columbia: ADTA Pub.

Lewis Bernstein, P. (1982). Authentic movement as active imagination. *The compendium of psychotherapeutic techniques.* J. Hariman (Ed.), Springfield, IL: Charles C Thomas.

Lewis Bernstein, P. (1986). Embodied transformational images in dance-movement therapy. *Journal of Mental Imagery,* vol. 9, no. 4, pp. 1–9.

Lewis, P. (1987). The expressive therapies in the choreography of object relations. *The Arts in Psychotherapy Journal,* Vol. 14, No. 4, pp. 321–332.

Lewis, P. (1987). The unconscious as choreographer: The use of tension flow rhythms in the transference relationship. *A.D.T.A. conference monograph.* Columbia: ADTA Pub.

Lewis, P. (1988). The transformative process within the imaginal realm. *The Arts in Psychotherapy Journal,* Vol. 15, No. 3, Fall, pp. 309–316.

Lewis, P. (1988). The dance between the conscious and unconscious: Transformation in the embodied imaginal realm. *The moving dialogue.* Columbia: ADTA Pub.

Lewis, P. (1988). The marriage of our art with science: The Kestenberg profile and the choreography of object relations. *Monograph 5.* Columbia: ADTA Pub.

Lewis, P. (1990). The Kestenberg movement profile in the psychotherapeutic process with borderline disorder. *The KMP: Its past, present application and future directions,* Lewis & Loman (Eds.), Keene: Antioch University Pub.

Lewis, P., & Brownell, A. (1990). The Kestenberg movement profile in assessment of vocalization. *The KMP: Its past, present application and future directions,* Lewis & Loman (Eds.), Keene: Antioch University Pub.

Lewis, P. (1991). Creative transformation: The alchemy of healing, individuation and spiritual consciousness. *Shadow and light: Moving toward wholeness.* Columbia: ADTA Pub.

Lewis, P. (1993).The use of reflection, reciprocity, rhythmic body action, and the imaginal in the depth dance therapy process of recovery, healing and spiritual consciousness. *Marian Chace, her papers, 2nd edition,* Sandel, S., Chaiklin, S., & Lohn, A. (Eds.), Columbia: ADTA Pub.

Lewis, P. (1993). Michael Jackson, analysiert mit hilfe des Kestenberg-bewegungsprofils in Tanztherapie, Hormann, K. (Ed.), *The application of the Kestenberg movement profile and its concepts.* Zurich: Beitrage zur Augewandten Hogrefe.

Lewis, P. (1992). The creative arts in transference-countertransference relationships. *Arts in Psychotherapy Journal,* vol. 19, no. 5, pp. 317–324.

Lewis, P. (1993). Kestenberg movement profile interpretation: Clinical, cultural and organizational application in *American dance therapy association proceedings.* Columbia: ADTA Pub.

Lewis, P. (1993). Following our dreams: Dance therapy as transformation in *American dance therapy association proceedings.* Columbia: ADTA Pub.

Lewis, P. (1994). Die tiefenpsychologisch orientierte tanztherapie in *Sprache der bewegung,* Berlin: Nervenklinik Spandau Publication.

Lewis, P. (1996). Depth psychotherapy and dance-movement therapy in *American Journal of Dance Therapy,* vol. 18, no. 2.

Lewis, P. (1996). Authentic sound movement and drama: An interview with Penny Lewis, Annie Geissinger interviewer, in *A Moving Journal,* vol. 3, no. 1. Providence.

Lewis, P. (1996).The Gestalt movement therapy approach. In Tsung-Chin, L. (Ed.), *Dance therapy.* Taipei, Taiwan: Publisher identified in Chinese Characters. In Chinese.

Lewis, P. (1996). Authentic sound, movement, and drama: An interactional approach. In Robbins, M. (Ed.) *Body oriented psychotherapy, Vol. I.* Somerville, MA: Inter. Scientific Community for Psycho-Corporal Therapies Pub.

Lewis, P. (1996). The Kestenberg movement profile. In Robbins, M. (Ed.), *Body oriented psychotherapy, Vol. I.* Somerville, MA: Inter. Scientific Community for Psycho-Corporal Therapies Pub.

Lewis, P. (1997).Multiculturalism and globalism in the arts in psychotherapy. In *The Arts in Psychotherapy Journal.* vol. 24, no. 2, pp. 123–128.

Lewis, P. (1997) Appreciating diversity, commonality, and the transcendent. In *Arts in Psychotherapy Journal.* vol. 24, no. 3.

Lewis, P. (1997).Transpersonal arts psychotherapy: Toward an ecumenical worldview. In *Arts in Psychotherapy Journal.* vol. 24, no. 3.

Lewis, P. (In process). An embodied relational model: The use of the somatic countertransference and inter subjectivity within the affective-imaginal realm. In Robbins, M. *Body oriented psychotherapy, vol. II.* Somerville: Inter. Scientific Community for Psycho-Corporal Therapies.

Lewis, P. (1999). Healing early child abuse: The application of the Kestenberg movement profile. In Amaghi, J., Loman, S., Lewis, P., et al. *The meaning of movement: Developmental and clinical perspectives of the Kestenberg movement profile.* Newark: Gordon & Breach Pub.

Lewis, P. (1999). The embodied feminine: Dance and drama therapy in women's holistic health. In Olshansky, E. (Ed.), *Woman's holistic health care.* Gaithersburg, MD: Aspen Publishers, Inc.

FURTHER TRAINING

For those who are getting or who have already received their masters or doctoral degree and are interested in a sequentially based alternate route program or for those who are looking for courses, intensives or supervision in this approach to add to their clinical work:

The Institute for Healing and Wellness, Inc.
and Omega Theater, Inc.
Penny Lewis, PhD, LMHC, NCC, ADTR, RDT-BCT and
Saphira Linden, MA, RDT-BCT
Co-directors: Graduate Certificate in Transpersonal Drama Therapy
The Institute for Healing and Wellness, Inc.
Eaglepoint
27 Merrill St.
Amesbury, MA 01913

Tel: 978/388-3035
Fax: 978/388-5757

Email: drplewis@seacoast.com

FOR ONGOING INFORMATION ON UPCOMING TRAINING SEE THE WEB AT:

www.dramatherapy.com

For those who are interested in a masters graduate program in counseling psychology or dance-movement therapy with a focus in drama therapy:

Antioch New England Graduate School
Penny Lewis PhD., LMHC, NCC, ADTR, RDT-BCT
Phone:978-388-3035
Department of Applied Psychology
40 Avon Street
Keene, NH 03431-3516

Tel: 603/357-3122

Chapter 9

PSYCHODRAMA

ANTONINA GARCIA AND DALE RICHARD BUCHANAN

PSYCHODRAMA IS A DEEP ACTION method developed by Jacob Levy Moreno (1889–1974), in which people enact scenes from their lives, dreams or fantasies in an effort to express unexpressed feelings, gain new insights and understandings, and practice new and more satisfying behaviors. A variety of intervention strategies have been developed to help accomplish these aims. Moreno (1953) said that the only true goal of therapy is nothing less than all of humankind.

GENESIS

The history of psychodrama to a great extent is also the history of its founder, Jacob Levy Moreno, M.D. This chapter could not possibly document all of Moreno's contributions. An in-depth review of his work can be found in two fascinating and well-documented biographies (Marineau, 1989; Hare & Hare, 1996).

While Moreno is best remembered for his creation of psychodrama, sociodrama and sociometry, his legacy lives on as a pioneer and innovator in other fields as well. Corsini (1955) credits Moreno with being one of the founders of group psychotherapy, and Thomas and Biddle (1966) credit Moreno as one of the founders of role theory. Compernole (1981) credits Moreno with being the first family therapist and Abraham Maslow (1968) attributes many of the Human Potential Movement exercises to Moreno.

While Moreno's professional training was as a medical doctor and psychiatrist he was a man of many interests. He invented a magnetic sound recording device; he founded an Impromptu Theatre Company at Carnegie Hall; he taught fencing to actors and human relation skills to Macy's employees and became a prize fight prognosticator, successfully predicting the outcome of many fights including Joe Louis' win over Max Baer.

Rather than focusing exclusively on psychopathology and treatment as so many of the other great psychotherapists have done, Moreno was interested in all areas of human behavior. William Wellman said, "The really distinguishing fact is that he broke all conventional stereotypes in order to live and deal with the universal in man–the ordinary man in all places and states. " (Hare & Hare, 1966, p. 120).

Rene Marineau (1989) describes Moreno as a prophet, scientist and a revolutionary. Moreno's life span can be divided into three parts: The European Years (1989–1925), The Early American Years (1925–1941), and The Later American Years (1942–1974).

The European Years (1989–1925)

Moreno was born and educated in Europe and received his medical degree from the University of Vienna. During the years 1908–1925 he formulated his theories of psychodrama, sociometry and group psychotherapy. From 1908–1911 he played spontaneous theatre games with children in the parks of Vienna and discovered the importance of spontaneity and creativity.

In 1913, he organized and did group work with prostitutes. He dates this as the beginning of group psychotherapy. This experience revealed the power of the group and he discovered that each member of a group is a therapeutic agent for the other.

Sociometry, the measurement of groups, had its beginnings when Moreno was Superintendent of a World War I resettlement camp at Mittendorf. Observing the unrest in the refuge camp, he petitioned his superiors to reorganize the camp along the lines of choice. He wanted to empower the refuges, torn from the comfort of their homeland, to make here and now choices of the people they worked and lived with, thus maximizing their chances for positive human interaction in an already difficult situation.

Between the years of 1921–1923, Moreno returned to Vienna and developed his Theatre of Spontaneity. Moreno dated the first psychodrama session as occurring on April 01, 1921.

Moreno trained a group of professional actors in spontaneity work and as social researchers. Audiences suggested topics from the current events and the troupe spontaneously enacted them to explore and resolve the underlying social issues.

During this period, the husband of one of the actresses complained to Moreno about a marital problem. One of the interventions he made was to have the couple enact onstage a scene that had occurred before they arrived at the theatre. The two set up the stage as if it were their apartment and recreated the scene in an effort to resolve their difficulties. In this way psychodrama was born.

The Early American Years (1925–1941)

Finding Europe to be too conservative for his revolutionary ideas, Moreno immigrated to the United States where he hoped his ideas would be better received. During his early years in the United States he coined the term group psychotherapy, conducted sociometric studies at the Hudson School for Girls and in Sing Sing Prison, opened a private sanatorium and founded and published several journals. He also wrote his magnum opus *Who Shall Survive?* and continued to develop psychodrama as a therapeutic modality.

The Later American Years (1942–1974)

In 1942 he met Zerka Toeman, who became his wife, his muse and his equal partner. She organized and edited his writings and maintained and nurtured his professional connections. She also encouraged Moreno and accompanied him as he traveled extensively promoting the uses of psychodrama, sociometry and group psychotherapy.

While Moreno was a visionary thinker and prolific writer of great breadth, Zerka made an enormous contribution to the theory and practice by expanding upon his ideas and deepening them as well as developing practical applications for everyday use.

After a prolonged illness, Moreno chose to die by abstaining from all food and water. At his request, his epitaph was "the man who brought laughter to psychiatry."

After Moreno

Since Moreno's death the field of psychodrama has continued to thrive. Zerka T. Moreno continues to be actively involved in the training of the next generation of psychodramatists. While most of Moreno's books were published through his private publishing company, Beacon House, and were difficult to obtain; today there are scores of books on psychodrama and sociodrama published by major publishing companies and available on the shelf of any major bookstore.

PSYCHODRAMA FRAME OF REFERENCE

Underlying the practice of psychodrama is a strong theoretical foundation that informs the work. Moreno developed four cornerstones of psychodrama: (1) role theory; (2) sociometry; (3) the theory of spontaneity/creativity; and (4) psychodrama intervention constructs. Each of these interlaces and interfaces with the other. While each can be used independently, and often is, Moreno created and envisioned them as interdependent parts of an organic whole.

Basic Concepts

Role Theory

Moreno believed that each person is a composite of the roles he/she plays. Human beings are known and evaluated by self and others through the roles they play. When we say someone is a nice person, what do we mean? We mean that we have observed the person acting in a positive way toward someone else or toward ourselves. The father picked up the fallen child, comforted her, cleaned up the cut on her knee, and put a bandage on it. We notice he is a father (role), she is a daughter (role), and from his behavior in the role, he appears to be a "good father."

In Psychodrama: First Volume, Moreno (1946) said, "Role can be defined as the actual and tangible forms which the self takes." (p. 153) He also considered role as a cluster of behaviors that is culturally recognized and labeled. A particular behavior may be utilized in a variety of roles, but isolated behaviors do not make up roles. For example, the behavior of reading may be present in scores of roles: student, teacher, researcher, or secretary. The specific joining together of behaviors is what makes one role different from another.

The cultural aspect is important as well, since all cultural groups do not have the same roles. Nor do all cultural groups have the same expectations for how roles should be played. The roles of husband and wife, for example, may carry different cultural expectations among different ethnic groups. Clinically, it is essential to treatment to understand the role expectations members of a couple have of each other, particularly if they are from different ethnic groups.

Attitudes and emotions also add personal descriptors to role enactment. Although there are collective components to every role we play (and it is through these that we recognize a particular role), each of us has our own unique way of playing a role.

For every role that we play we have expectations of how we "should" play the role. Our expectations come from how we have seen the role modeled by others, by our own personal dynamics, and the demands of our culture. Functionality exists when a person has a wide range of roles available to him or her and flexibility in playing those roles. One measure of dysfunction is a limited role repertoire. This can occur when individuals become locked in a particular role, thereby excluding other roles from their repertoire. Burnout is an example of role-lock. Other examples of dysfunction include role fatigue, role confusion, role conflict, role tension, role crisis, and role stripping.

Moreno said that there are three types of roles: the psychosomatic, the social and the psychodramatic. These are hierarchical in nature in that our psychosomatic role needs must be satisfied before we can warm up to our social and psychodramatic roles. Our **psychosomatic roles** are those which manifest physically, e.g., roles like eater, runner, sleeper. These roles may or may not have a psychological component. For example, in the role of eater, I may have a larger breakfast than usual because I've just come back from a seven-mile hike (physiological) or I may have a larger breakfast because I'm nervous about the interview I'm to attend in an hour, and I'm eating from anxiety (psychological).

The **social roles** are those that we enact in relation to other people, e.g., mother, friend, lover. They exist in the social sphere. These roles are always reciprocal, requiring others to take roles in relation to us: husbands need wives in order to enact their roles, and vice versa. One of the reasons that people seek psychotherapy is that they are in unsatisfying role relationships or are mourning from the loss or lack of a reciprocal role partner.

The **psychodramatic roles** are those that are enacted inside our heads. They are the interior or intrapsychic roles of imaginer, problem solver, and creative thinker. They also comprise wished-for roles that exist in our minds until they become externalized in social reality. They are a manifestation of the imaginative process of who we think we are and who we would like to become.

For example, if I want to enact the role of ice skater, I may imagine myself in the role long before I actually take ice skating lessons. On the other hand, if I imagine myself a Rock star and neither sing well nor have any intention of working to become a Rock star, I am also engaging in a psychodramatic role when I play out in my mind and take pleasure from a scenario of myself singing before thousands.

Role Dysfunction

Dysfunction occurs when a person has a lack of either social roles or psychodramatic roles, and function is seen as having a balance of both. One of the aims of psychodrama is to activate the birth of psychodramatic roles by stimulating the imaginative processes through play and fantasy. Another aim is to assist individuals to give birth to social roles through behavioral rehearsal and therapeutic role assignment.

Another type of dysfunction comes from inaccurate role perception. For example, a husband buys his partner a vacuum cleaner for a special birthday and is shocked that she does not seem to appreciate it and wants to know why he couldn't give her something more personal. He has perceived her in her role as housekeeper, but has ignored her role as romantic partner. Functionality comes when one accurately perceives the role of the other as well as one's own role.

Dysfunction comes also when a person accurately perceives a role but is unwilling or unable to enact it. For example, take the worker whose boss tells her to complete certain tasks by a particular deadline. She has the time to complete the tasks but she would rather do something else. She does not like to be told to do things so she balks and does not adequately enact her role.

Moreno believed that the self emerges from the roles we play. Moreno postulated that when people learn a new role, they follow a particular pattern of role development. The arc of the learning curve begins with role taking and proceeds to role playing and role creating.

Role taking refers to an enactment of the role in a routinized, somewhat stilted way. When a person is just learning to play tennis, for example, he is likely to appear awkward as he tries to coordinate his stance with his arms and both of these with the racket and the ball. He may have to practice long hours simply to get the ball over the net, or to serve to one spot on the court.

As he progresses with his experience, he will gain ease and will be able to move around the court freely and feel comfortable making choices spontaneously as the ball comes his way. He will not have to think every minute about the basics of the game. They will have become second nature. He has entered the phase of **role playing** in which a person enacts a role with comfort, flexibility and spontaneity. Literally, he infuses the role with a playfulness that is lacking in role taking.

Finally, when he has mastered the rudiments of the role and has become comfortable enacting the role, he is ready to move into the phase of **role creating.** When one role creates he is able to add new and sometimes unique elements to the enactment of the role and to think beyond the confines of the role to develop unexpected solutions for difficulties that emerge in the enactment of the role. At this point, the tennis player may devise a new method for serving the ball, and his method of role enactment becomes a model for others.

Sociometry

As was said earlier, each of us is a composite of the roles we play. Many of those roles are social roles, and social roles have reciprocal partners. This aspect of reciprocity brings us to another of Moreno's basic contributions: sociometry. Put simply, sociometry is the assessment of social choices and a set of intervention tools designed to facilitate social change.

In life, each of us is engaged in making many choices every day. When we make a choice that places us in proximity to others, in avoidance of others or in a neutral relationship to others, we are making a sociometric choice. Moreno was very interested in the choices we make and the criteria upon which we base our choices.

Clearly, families and communities function or dysfunction in part as a result of the choices individuals in the system make in relation to each other. Moreno believed that the more options a person has available to him or her, the more opportunity for satisfaction for the individual and the collective.

All choices that we make are related to our perception of the role of the other. If someone were to say to you, "Whom do you choose?" you would ask, "For what?" Choice of a person is always connected with at least one role related criterion: "Whom would you choose to accompany you to the movies to see a romantic comedy?" Based upon specific criteria, we have reasons for our selections. For example, a functional person may choose to invite one friend to accompany her to a romantic comedy film and another to accompany her on a backpacking trip in Appalachia. She may make these choices because the first friend considers camping out to be staying at a motel and ordering in a pizza and the second talks incessantly during movies.

A colloquial meaning of sociometry is the invisible and visible network of connections in any group. Although the connections among the individuals may not necessarily be observable to us if we step into a room, the connections are there nevertheless. Two people with whom you are chatting at a party may have been in the same geometry class in high school, but you will not know about that connection unless one of them tells you. Moreno referred to this aspect of sociometry as social reality.

A successful group leader understands that there are invisible connections among group members and facilitates the rising to the surface of these connections so that the group may work together to accomplish its goals. This is one of the functions of the warm-up in a psychodrama session.

The instruments of sociometry make visible some of the invisible aspects of social reality. One of these instruments is the sociogram. A **sociogram** is a map of the connections that people have with one another. The sociogram can be completed in action or on paper when working with groups. One example of an action sociogram in a group is to ask the group members to place their hands upon the shoulder of the person with whom they'd like to have lunch at the end of the session. Another is to ask group members to place their hand on the shoulder of the person whose issue is most closely related to their own. Conducting sociometric explorations often stimulates strong feelings in participants and, therefore, should be used with caution.

There are a variety of sociometric instruments and exercises that have been devised for promoting social change. Among these are the social atom, role diagram, spectrogram, social barometer, and diamond of opposites (Buchanan, 1984; Carlson-Sabelli and Sabelli et al., 1992; Edwards, 1996; Hale, 1986; Sternberg & Garcia, 2000).

Moreno believed that the smallest unit of study of a human being is the social atom, since all of us in the human community are in relationship with others. The **social atom** consists of the person and all those who are significant to the individual at any given time. In functioning people the social atom is dynamic and changes over time as people wax and wane in their importance to us. Each of us is the center of our own social atom, with those who are significant to us vibrating in orbit around us. Clearly, though a person is at the nucleus of his own social atom, he is merely a satellite in the social atom of his significant others. In this way, all social atoms across the globe are joined through the interconnections of significant people and none of us are more than six degrees of separation away from any other person on the planet.

This having been said, when a person walks into the therapy room, he in a sense does not enter the room alone, but brings with him all the relationships (real or fantasy, dead or alive) he has with others outside the room. In this way, psychodrama treats the social atom, not the individual and seeks to heal the relationships. When asked what he did for a living, Moreno was fond of saying that he was a "social atom repairman." Psychodramatists conduct social atom explorations with clients to gather information, assess functioning level, set treatment goals with the client, and make interventions.

Moreno also developed an instrument called the **role diagram** in which a person inventories the roles he or she plays. This can be particularly helpful in working with couples as the pair explores reciprocal role partnerships and which roles each enacts separately from the other.

Both spectrograms and social barometers are based on the continuum between 0% and 100%. They reflect how a person feels in relation to activities and social issues, e.g., going to see horror films in the case of a spectrogram, or, in the case of the social barometer, gun control.

The limitation of traditional sociometry is that it is unsuccessful in melding intensity of feeling with choice of a person. While one can make a choice in a sociogram, that choice does not indicate the intensity of feeling that the person has in making that choice. For example, if Joe chooses to ask Marlene to go out to lunch, we do not know from the sociogram if he is excited about that choice or if he just figured, "Well, why not?" Nor does the sociogram, which is linear, provide the opportunity to chart ambivalence. Sabelli and Sabelli et al. (1992) developed a new instrument, the diamond of opposites that can chart both ambivalence and intensity of feeling and is three-dimensional. It also charts neutrality.

Sociometry can be used descriptively to describe intra- or intergroup relations at any given time. It can also be used prescriptively to make changes in the system. For example, during World War II a study was conducted in which fighter pilots chose their copilots. A significant number of those who chose returned alive as opposed to others who were randomly assigned copilots.

Moreno and other social psychologists researched sociometry extensively and found that left to their own devices a group tends to overchoose some individuals and underchoose others. This is called the sociodynamic law. Moreno felt that the psychodramatist's work is to assist groups in sharing the sociometric wealth. Moreno also noted that just as individuals without intervention revert to homeostasis, or the status quo, so does a group seek to return to sociostasis, even if the status quo is dysfunctional. In one way the psychodramatist is always a revolutionary, in that he seeks to facilitate change in the status quo in assisting a group to more spontaneous functioning.

When looking at sociometry, one can view it from the perspective of the group or the individual. When using sociometry in a group, there are four basic positions that individuals occupy: positive star, rejection star, isolate and star of incongruity. All of these positions have benefits and liabilities. The functioning individual and group rotates through all these positions over time. The psychodramatist assists the group in shifting sociometry in positive ways.

Those who receive the largest number of choices based on a particular criterion are called stars. A positive star receives the most positive choices, and a rejection star receives the most negative choices. On the surface it may seem that it is far better to be a positive star than a rejection star. However, as wonderful as it is to be regarded highly for some gift, quality or competence, to be consistently overchosen is a burden. If a star is incapable of saying no to the role demands of others, both the individual and the group become stuck. If taken too far, sometimes a star who cannot say no becomes physically ill as a way of removing himself from overresponsibility.

At the same time, while it may seem unpleasant to be rejected, the rejection star is freed from the responsibilities the positive star carries. She is also freed from the norms, rules and expectations of the group. It has been said that the positive star belongs to the group and the rejection star belongs to him or herself. If taken too far, the rejection star becomes an outcast whom the group engages in scapegoating.

A person may also be an isolate when he or she neither chooses, nor is chosen based upon a particular criterion. An example of functional isolation would be a group where Joe is undergoing a chronic fatigue episode. He may choose not to participate in a particular sociometric exercise, and other group members may respect his decision and, not choosing him, select another member of the group.

On the other hand, if for every exercise in nearly every group, Joe, whether sick or well, neither seeks anyone out nor does anyone seek him out, his isolation will be dysfunctional for him and the group. Those who persistently choose isolation and who are persistently not chosen are true isolates. These people are found among the homeless, the mentally ill and in prisons.

Incongruous choices are those that lack reciprocity. This may occur if there is inaccurate perception of the choice of the other, for example, if Betty chooses Brent, thinking he reciprocates her choice, but he does not. This may also occur if Betty chooses Brent even though she knows he does not reciprocate her choice. The star of incongruity is the person who receives the greatest number of incongruous choices.

What we seek is mutuality. In groups when there are high levels of incongruity, group members will express dissatisfaction, feel disconnected, and the group may fall apart if interventions are not made to increase mutuality.

Even grammar school children are aware of sociometric stars, rejection stars, and isolates. The work of the psychodramatist is to provide opportunities to share the sociometric wealth of the group in a group setting and to assist individuals in shifting their personal sociometry in positive ways in individual psychotherapy.

Regarding tenor of feeling between people, Freud talked of transference and empathy. Moreno said that there is another phenomenological experience between two people. This he termed tele. **Tele** is a deep, accurate knowing of the self and the other. Tele is present between two people when each sees the other as the other truly is and accepts the other as the other is. One does not try to change the other even though he or she knows the other is not perfect. Moreno wrote a poem in 1915, part of which describes tele:

> A meeting of two: eye to eye; face to face;
> And when you are near I will tear your eyes out and place them in place of mine,
> And you will tear my eyes out and place them in place of yours,
> And I will look at you with your eyes and you will look at me with mine.
> (*Invitation to an Encounter, Part 2,* 1915:2)

Moreno believed that each relationship has some degree of tele and some degree of transference. There are some people whom we meet with whom we have very high tele: we are comfortable with them almost immediately, and feel we have known them forever. As we get to know them better and have more concrete information about them, we feel reinforced in our original feelings. Even though they have just as many faults and foibles as the next person does, we accept them and they accept us. We feel at home when we are with them and can pick up where we left off when we see them after a long time apart. They are the people about whom we are thinking when we go to the phone and they are at the other end of the line. Or we call them or email them and they say, "I was just thinking of you."

Many of our relationships may have more transference than tele at the outset. Ideally, over time we can diminish transference and increase tele. Moreno felt that through sociometric, sociodramatic, and psychodramatic interventions one could help people to remove the veils of transference and reveal the tele and the true person underneath.

Moreno had a tremendous interest in the concept of the Encounter. He believed that each of us is at our best when we live in the "here and now," a term he coined. Further, if we live in the moment, not in our past or future, we can fully relate to those whom we meet and they to us. The encounter occurs when two people meet in as honest a way as they are able.

The Encounter Movement of the 60s was based on this concept but went awry as people confused confrontation and attack with encounter. In psychodramatic encounter, both people make room for each other and respect the other, while taking responsibility for one's own feelings and actions. Good will is a necessary ingredient as are speaking from an "I" position and accepting that what the other person says is his/her personal truth.

Moreno said that we are wounded in relationship and can be healed in relationship.

He devised psychodrama and sociodrama as modalities for accomplishing that healing.

Spontaneity/Creativity Theory

The third and key cornerstone of psychodrama is spontaneity/creativity theory. It is based on Moreno's belief that all humans are fallen gods.

The Godhead

While other methods of psychotherapy have either been silent or shunned the very concept of God, Moreno was deeply interested in spiritual issues. Of course, readers should be clear that there is distinction between organized religious practice and spirituality as a base of human behavior. Moreno focused on the spiritual aspects of behavior.

As Kraus (1984) has noted, the psychodramatic process attempts to bridge the paradoxical relationship between humanity and divinity. Moreno said that the central paradox for humans is the wish to be God and the reality that we are not: the fantasy of omnipotence and the need to face reality.

Moreno coined the term "Meglomania Normalis" for that human state of wanting to be at the center of our universe and wanting the rest of the human race to be our auxiliaries. In other words, our desire to create the perfect world for ourselves from our perspective.

As infants we all begin with the experience of being at one with the world and in perfect harmony with all that is. We do not know where we leave off and the other begins. We are boundaryless. He called this the "First Universe," and it is a state to which we often wish to return. When we are old enough to realize a separation between the self and the other, between illusion and reality, we enter what Moreno called the Second Universe.

In Morenean philosophy anxiety is caused by the breach between the First and Second Universe. Moreno referred to anxiety as a cosmic hunger to maintain identity with the entire universe. One of the objectives of psychodramatic treatment is to help individuals become less anxious and more fearful. This means replacing an individual's generalized anxiety about separation/connection with specific fears about people, places and things. For example instead of an overwhelming anxiety about a job interview, it is far better to be fearful of being asked your employment history. Spontaneity training and role playing can be used as rehearsals for life to lessen our cosmic anxiety and increase our mastery of our everyday fears.

Moreno's philosophical solution to bridge the breach is to live in the here and now. Unlike man other schools of psychotherapy, Moreno believed that enlightenment can only be found in community.

The Canon of Creativity

Moreno developed the Canon of Creativity to describe how spontaneity and creativity work. The Canon of Creativity (see Figure 9.1) shows the interrelationship and interaction of spontaneity and creativity with the cultural conserve (e.g., status quo). It also demonstrates that it is necessary to warm up to our spontaneity and creativity.

According to Moreno (1953) spontaneity-creativity is the most important problem in psychology. In the midst of the great depression, Moreno hypothesized that only the creative and spontaneous would survive and that the rest would be relegated to the dustbin of history.

Moreno viewed spontaneity and creativity as an open system with limitless potential that cannot be stored for future use. He further postulated that spontaneity and creativity are available to everyone and that all our success

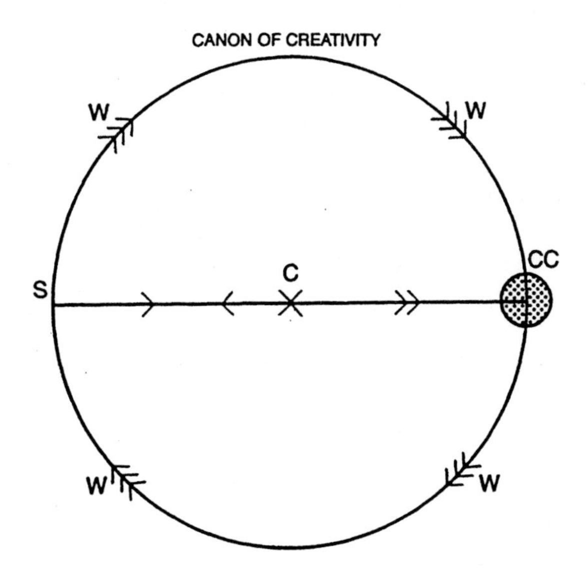

Figure 9.1. Spontaneity–Creativity–Cultural Conserve.

Field of Rotating Operations Between Spontaneity–Creativity–Cultural Conserve (S-C-CC)

S–Spontaneity, C–Creativity, CC–Cultural (or any) Conserve (for instance, a biological conserve, i.e., an animal organism, or a cultural conserve, i.e., a book, a motion picture, or a robot, i.e., a calculating machine); W–Warming up is the "operational" expression of spontaneity. The circle represents the field of operations: "operational" expression of spontaneity. The circle represents the field of operations between S, C, and CC.

Operation I: Spontaneity arouses Creativity, C. S –>C.
Operation II: Creativity is receptive to Spontaneity. S<–C.
Operation III: From their interaction Cultural Conserves, CC, result. S–>C–>>CC.
Operation IV: Conserves (CC) would accumulate indefinitely and remain "in cold storage." They need to be reborn, the catalyzer Spontaneity revitalizes them. CC–>>>S–>>>CC.

S does not operate in a vacuum, it moves either toward Creativity or toward Conserves

Total Operation

actor
Spontaneity-creativity-warming up act <
conserve

Source: Moreno, J.L. (1953).

is directly connected with our ability to be spontaneous.

Spontaneity

Spontaneity can be thought of as the readiness for an action and creativity as the idea. The twin concepts of spontaneity and creativity are responsible for the formation of our cultural conserves. Cultural conserves are the given patterns, relationships, or products of our society. Cultural conserves define the norms, mores, and folkways of our culture and help transmit these normative patterns to future generations.

God is spontaneity. Hence the commandment is: "Be Spontaneous!" (Moreno, 1920).

Moreno (1953) stated that "spontaneity propels the individual toward an adequate response to a new situation or a new response to an old situation." Adequacy encompasses the concerns of appropriateness, competency, and skill in interacting within any given situation.

Our spontaneity is highest when we are infants and decreases with age. As noted earlier in the history section The Theatre of Spontaneity was designed to increase the spontaneity of the actors and the audience.

Moreno called those times when we are most spontaneous as being in the "moment." The moment may last for a few seconds or it can last hours or days. The moment is the experience of living in complete harmony and unity while staying connected to the social realities of the here and now. Csikszentmihalyi (1991) has called this concept "flow." According to Csikszentmihalyi, this moment of peak spontaneity is the point when the ego disappears, the time space continuum evaporates and there is a sense of connection and flow with the entire universe.

Spontaneity Dysfunction

Moreno viewed life as a series of spontaneity tests. All dysfunction is caused by a lack of spontaneity and/or creativity; while all functionality can be attributed to an adequate amount of both. The reason that people come into treatment is that they either do not know what to do about a given situation or they cannot spur themselves into action in the situation, or both. There are three threats to our spontaneity: paralysis, impulsivity and reactivity.

Paralysis occurs when we are faced with a new situation and we become frozen and are unable to act. The situation passes us by and we feel disappointed in ourselves that we were unable to find an adequate response for the situation.

Another threat is impulsivity. Impulsivity is simply action without reflection. Our act hunger is so great that we act without contemplation or reflection about the act's appropriateness or its consequences.

The third threat to spontaneity is reactivity. Reactivity is reflection without here and now action. In reactivity we are so mired in the past that our actions today are based upon our experiences of the past. When we are reactive we are unable to be proactive and simply react to the world and the situations around us.

The litmus tests for spontaneity and creativity are novelty and adequacy. Many of us are stopped dead in our tracks because we cannot bear to engage in an activity in which our behavior will merely be adequate. In striving to be brilliant, we sometimes do not even begin an activity for fear of being average or of failing. The Morenean way is to strive for adequacy rather than brilliance. If we strive for brilliance we are often inadequate, and if we dare to be adequate we are often brilliant.

Creativity

Creativity is the spark from whence the novel comes. Creativity is the ability to think beyond our own personal limitations and see the world in a new way. To be creative means to risk, to see people and things different than as we might normally view them and to experiment with the new and different. Not all of us are up to the challenges posed by this endless quest for creativity and some of us retreat to pathological creativity, violence and destruction, or passive ascription.

Dysfunctional Creativity

One retreat from creativity is pathological creativity. Pathological creativity is a compulsive drive for creativity that becomes so great that the quest of the new overwhelms the need for adequacy. Pathological creativity is caused by the lack of tangible and challenging creativity in our everyday life; this lack of usable creativity festers into a compulsion for novelty regardless of its adequacy to the task.

Another retreat from creativity happens when we become frustrated at our inability to create new roles and role relationships. Blocked creativity can lead to violence or destruction as the last resort for the impotent creator. In the Morenean philosophy, all rage is viewed as crushed creativity. All intrapersonal and interpersonal violence is correlated with an increase in frustration that stems from failing to produce a creative and spontaneous response.

A third threat to our creativity is in becoming overwhelmed by the sheer number and complexity of choices in our everyday life and looking for someone or something external to make those choices for us. The responsibility involved in assuming the role of creator and engaging with spontaneity and creativity is too frightening for some. So instead of embracing the role of creator, they retreat to a passive role and vest their creative power to some authoritarian figure. Erich Fromm (1941) brilliantly discusses this concept in his seminal work *Escape From Freedom.*

Cultural Conserves

A cultural conserve is any finished product of the creative process. Cultural conserves operate on both the individual and collective levels. Whether created by an individual or a group the cultural conserve preserves the values of its creators.

As individuals each of us creates our own cultural conserves of affect, cognitive, behavioral and spiritual states. We have habits and routines and particular ways of doing things or interacting with others. These interactions become our cultural conserves. When others say that we are not being ourselves today, what is really being said is that we are not enacting our "usual" cultural conserves.

As collectives whether in families, small groups or societies there are also cultural conserves of how we as a collective should interact with one another and our environment. When individuals say that is how we should act, they are saying that is what the cultural conserve prescribes.

In the beginning what is now called a conserve was a spontaneous/creative act that met the needs of the situation. The repetition of the act is what institutionalizes the conserve. Cultural conserves are the springboard for new spontaneity and creativity and inherently are neither good nor bad. Cultural conserves are good when they contribute to our creativity and spontaneity and bad when they stifle or repress any individual or group. As individuals we can thrive through change or thrive by changing.

Spontaneity Theory of Child Development

Moreno, based on scientific observation, created a complex theory of child development. A complete discussion of the theory can be found in *Psychodrama: First Volume.*

According to the spontaneity theory of child development, Moreno points out that when we are born, each of us needs others in order to stay alive and to flourish. He termed these people auxiliaries and noted that their method of relating to us and us to them warms us up to our first social roles.

As was said before, humans are most spontaneous in infancy. The reason for this is that all of the situations that the infant encounters are new and require new responses. Our auxiliaries help us to develop roles by their interaction with us. Auxiliaries also help us to put names to what we experience.

In order to develop functionally, Moreno believed that each of us must first be doubled when we are newborns. By doubling is meant that our caregiver joins with us and accurately interprets our cries and body language and responds to those cues.

Later, we are mirrored by our caregivers when we make a face or a sound and they make that same face or sound, not to mimic us but to reflect our experience back to us. The final stage is role reversal in which the child in a rudimentary way role reverses with the caregiver and the caregiver takes the reciprocal role, as when a child initiates a peek-a-boo game that she has seen her caregiver initiate.

Psychodramatists believe that if a person has not been adequately doubled or mirrored, he will be unable to role reverse with others. Treatment may consist in part of doubling and mirroring for the client so that he may learn to role reverse.

Theoretical Constructs of Psychodrama Methodology

The theoretical constructs form the fourth cornerstone of the practice of psychodrama. Moreno began to write about his philosophy in the 1920s. In 1966, he discussed the nub of his theory. He said, ". . . The objective of psychodrama was, from its inception, to construct a therapeutic setting which uses life as a model, to integrate into it all the modalities of living, beginning with the universals–time, space, reality, and cosmos–down to all the details and nuances of life" (Fox, 1987, p. 3).

Time

As was said earlier, Moreno was a great proponent of living in the moment and participating in the ever-evolving present. As a result, in psychodrama all time is present. It is as if all time were liquid in a large bowl. Although you may float a little boat sending it from one point to another, the boat is still in the liquid, all of which exists simultaneously and which has no start or finish.

As with all other events, when a traumatic event occurs in a person's life, the information about that event is stored in the body, mind, emotions, and spirit. Moreno believed that when we get trapped in our past, it is because our spontaneity and creativity were insufficient to help us at the time, so that a piece of us is snagged on the past as a sweater would be snagged on a bramble bush.

In psychodrama the protagonist has the opportunity to recreate the past, and correct the scene, changing history so that he disentangles the snag from the bramble and moves more freely in his present-day life. He may correct the scene by expressing emotions unexpressed until now; he may gain a new insight into the experience; and he may find another, more satisfying way to end the scene than the way it occurred in his literal past. One might say, "How can you change what actually happened?" The fact is that in reexperiencing the situation in a new way kinesthetically through the body in action, the protagonist is implanting new information about the prior experience in the neural pathways. The aspect of changing history is profound as it neutralizes traumatic incidents and builds a new frame of reference.

One may ask how psychodrama is about the present, if a protagonist is dealing with a scene from the past. The answer is that the protagonist is asked to recreate and step into that past as if it were now the time the event is happening. For example, if a protagonist reenacts a scene from when he was five years old in 1989, he is asked to imagine that it is now 1989 and he is five years old. He is asked to describe what is *happening* in 1989, not what *happened.*

In the same way that the past becomes present in psychodrama, so, too, does the future. Through future projection the protagonist steps into a wished-for or feared future, as if it were here today, to explore its possibilities, to role rehearse for future situations and to find advice in dealing with current concerns.

One of the most powerful aspects of psychodrama is the collapsing of time. In one psychodrama, the person from today can receive advice, support and encouragement from her future self and then go back to care for her younger self and help her heal an early trauma.

Space

Moreno was acutely aware of the evocative nature of place in therapeutic work. Not only is what happened to the client important but where it happened. While it would be painful and difficult for a child to endure being slapped in the face by his parent, it would be even more humiliating if this happened in front of his friends at school. Further, we experience some places as safe while others feel less safe. If we want to have a private, intimate conversation with someone, we might not choose the local diner to initiate it.

When setting up a psychodrama, the client and director decide where the scene will take place and set it carefully, using props and furniture in the therapy room to set the scene. Scene-setting warms the protagonist up to the work and anchors the action in space. Further, it quickens the imagination of the audience and warms them up as well. It is not uncommon to hear someone a month or two later say something like this, "You know, whenever I'm feeling stressed, I think of that tree by the stream from your psychodrama. In my mind's eye, I imagine I'm sitting under the tree, and listening to the water flow over the stones. It's so restful."

Reality

Moreno believed that reality was larger than that which is observable via the five senses. He discussed three levels of reality: infrareality which is our own subjective experience of the world, e.g., *megalomania normalis;* reality, which is the group's consensus map of the world; and surplus reality, which incorporates a perspective beyond our collective and ourselves (Moreno, Z., Blomkvist, & Rutzel, 2000).

One of the aims of psychodrama is to make our personal world bigger by helping us to integrate other's perceptions into our own world. Every time we have a conversation with a friend and imagine ourselves in their position, we are engaging in surplus reality. Our daydreams and night dreams are also forms of surplus reality as are the fruits of our imagination. In fact, all theatre games, plays, and most play activities are vehicles for creating surplus reality.

In some ways all of psychodrama exists in the realm of surplus reality. Someone reenacts a segment of his life experience onstage. He chooses people from the group to play the roles of others who were present at the time, and the role players assist him successfully even though they were not present when the event occurred originally. While the original father or mother is not onstage, the protagonist steps into the scene and experiences the reality of the portrayals nevertheless, and is thereby able to suspend disbelief and experience the reality of the moment. It is through the use of surplus reality that the client is healed.

If the client is unsatisfied with the manner in which he plays a role in life, he may through simulation and role rehearsal train himself to play the role differently. He can in this way utilize surplus reality to expand his everyday reality.

One of the most powerful surplus reality techniques is role reversal. Clearly, we cannot literally step into another person's shoes and become the other. However, we can come to a close approximation and expand our view of reality by changing places and changing roles with another. The perspective shift is enlightening.

Cosmos

Moreno believed that, while each of us is an individual and a social being, we are also all cosmic beings, connected to the universe and seeking to find our purpose in relation to all that exists. He felt that a psychotherapy that does not address man's teleological and cosmological concerns is incomplete.

As a result, gods and heroes appear on the psychodrama stage. Reality is expanded and we connect beyond the flesh with others as men portray women and women portray men. An older person may play a younger and vice versa. People can play animals. The unborn and the dead are alive on the psychodrama stage.

Psychodrama explores the cosmos within us and the cosmos outside us; the visible world and the invisible. It helps us to find our place in the universe and restores soul and spirit to those who have misplaced those vital entities.

Psychodramatic Goals

All of us are physical beings with bodies, minds, emotions and transpersonal longings. Moreno believed that psychotherapy should be broad enough so that its interventions can touch all of these factors that make us human. Therefore, there are four primary goals that cover the ABCS, Affect, Behavior, Cognition, and Spirituality.

A for Affect

In the realm of affect the goal is catharsis, a deep expression of feelings. There are two primary types of catharsis–the catharsis of abreaction and the catharsis of integration. Catharsis of abreaction occurs when the client regresses to a difficult experience and reexperiences an expression of emotion that is associated with that time. The catharsis of integration is not simply the expression of deep emotions, but also contains a simultaneous action insight. Catharsis of integration occurs when the client is able to gain a new understanding of the situation and imprints a new experience of the situation through the expression of emotion as well as the finding of a new way to deal with the situation. Thus, the catharsis of integration is a vital part of the working through process.

In psychodrama, a person may experience a catharsis of laughter as well as of tears. These are equally valuable in promoting healing and lasting change. If clients are embarrassed at or fearful of their tears, the authors remind them that tears water the seeds of the soul.

B for Behavior

Behavioral rehearsal allows people to practice new and more satisfying ways of handling situations. Sometimes in life it feels unsafe or frightening to experiment with new behavior. Psychodrama provides a safe setting where people can role train, adjusting their behavior as they learn through trial and error. They can learn to restore spontaneity and creativity to areas of their lives where they feel blocked.

C for Cognition

The goal of insight occurs when the client achieves an epiphany, or enlightenment, regarding the situation at hand. Because it happens kinesthetically, it is thorough going, rather than just in the mind. When one gains insight in a psychodrama, the person will often look startled, or the mouth will drop open or the person literally steps back as if taken aback. One can almost see the light bulb lighting up over the person's head as in a cartoon. There is a reorganization of perceptions that takes place as a result of action insight.

S for Spirituality

The process of psychodrama is a transpersonal one. Whether in groups or in individual therapy, the whole is greater than the sum of the parts. In a group, when a member plays a significant other of the protagonist, the auxiliary ego also learns and grows from the experience. The audience, as active observers of the drama, step into the protagonist's life and step into their own as well. They are healed through the work of the other. The protagonist encounters the group both through means of the story of the drama and through the help of group members in cocreating his world in the enactment. Many times the goal of spiritual connection is overtly a part of the contract as when a protagonist says, "I feel so alone. I've lost my faith in people and in a Power greater than myself. I want to stop feeling so empty. I want to feel full again."

It's rare that clients have deficits in all four areas–ABCS. An overarching goal is to help clients to integrate these four areas in their lives. When behavior and affect are at variance, for example, the goal is to bring both to consciousness and develop a new solution that encompasses both.

Act Hungers and Open Tension Systems

Moreno said that the body remembers what the mind forgets. Act hungers are connected with Moreno's theory of human development. The act hungers are strong urges or desires for expression, for understanding, for mastery in a situation or for connection. Open tension systems are the context within which we have an act hunger. Open tension systems are the unresolved issues that are emergent in a group at any given time. They may be intrapsychic or interpersonal dealing with people inside or outside the group.

For example, Elise had a terrible argument with a friend the night before the group meets. She is still upset about it when she comes to the psychodrama session. She feels that her friend didn't listen to her and cut her off and walked away. Because of the argument, Elise has an open tension system about abandonment. The act hungers are what we want to do about the open tension systems. Elise is tense and upset and seeks resolution of her problem and relief from her fears. Her act hunger may be to tell her friend off, to reconcile with her friend, to understand her better, or to practice other ways to relate to the friend.

The psychodrama director works to help a group to close at least one of its open tension systems and satiate its act hungers through interventions made in the psychodrama enactment. This is done so that the protagonist can restore spontaneity and begin again to live in the here and now. In fact, the contract which the director makes with the protagonist is essentially an agreement to do just that. The ABCS are accomplished by facilitating the fulfilling of the protagonist's act hungers.

Instruments of Psychodrama

Moreno adapted many of the psychodramatic techniques and methods from the theatre. In a speech to the American Psychiatric Association Moreno (1946) said, "Drama is a translation of the Greek word which means action, or thing done. Psychodrama can be defined, therefore, as the science which explores the "truth" by dramatic methods." He went on to elaborate the five instruments of the psychodramatic process–the stage, the protagonist, the director, the auxiliary egos and the audience (i.e., group).

The Stage

Moreno (1969) envisioned and created a therapeutic theatre where men can play women and women can play men; where a black person can play a white person and the white person can play a black person; and where an old person can play a child's role and a child can play an older person's role. Moreno concluded by saying that as a result of psychodrama a healthy person may live more effectively, a sick person may learn to bear his misery, and the dead may continue to play a part in our lives. On the therapeutic stage people can act out not only their ordinary everyday lives, but also their dreams and desires.

Moreno knew that each space evokes memories and expectations. He created the classical psychodrama theatre with its three-tiered stage and balcony to warm-up the participants to the magic and mystery of psychodrama. Unfortunately most of us do not have a classic psychodramatic theatre so the psychodrama meeting space is often an ordinary room used for other events (e.g., treatment team meetings, birthday party, downsizing seminar). The residual warm-up from these other events can permeate and contaminate the healing space. Psychodramatists can transform the ordinary space into the scared space of the therapeutic theatre through rituals such as the forming of a circle of chairs, the placements of a few colored scarves, music, or incense.

Whether one is working on a classic stage, within a circle of chairs, or at one end of a room, it is necessary to assign part of the room to the stage. This defines the area where the drama will be enacted and separates the stage from the everyday reality of group interactions. When the protagonist, director and auxiliaries step into the space they are leaving ordinary reality and entering the world of surplus reality.

The Protagonist

The protagonist is the term given to the person who is the focus of the psychodrama. The protagonist is encouraged to be as spontaneous as possible. Rather than being an actor in a play who must follow a script, be guided by a director and whose movements are choreographed by another, the protagonist in a psychodrama is encouraged to write his own script, cast his own characters, direct his own life and choreograph his own movements. The protagonist must begin with the affirmation of his own "subjective" truth before the director can ask the protagonist to expand his perceptions of that experience.

The protagonist is encouraged not to tell his story in the third person but to enact the story in the here and now. The goal is for the protagonist to enact his story, not merely be the spectator or teller of his story. The protagonist is also given the freedom to undo the past, redo the present and create a different future for himself.

While the protagonist is encouraged to have maximum involvement and to enact his story with vitality and passion, psychodrama is just as much a method of restraint as it is of expression. For example, a protagonist will not only learn new behaviors, but will also learn to contain feelings or thoughts so as to be more spontaneous in the here and now. The protagonist encounters not only others that are familiar to him, but he is also encouraged to expand his perceptions and encounter the unknown or rejected parts of himself and others.

There is an ancient Eastern belief that just prior to dying we review all the actions in our own life from the perspective of how they have impacted upon others. This is also the way of psychodrama where a protagonist is encouraged and supported in assuming all other roles so that he can experience his life from the outside as well as the inside.

The Director

The preferred term for the group leader is the director rather than the therapist. Moreno said that the director was a member of the group with directorial responsibilities and that all members of the group are therapeutic agents for each other. The director must be the most spontaneous member of the group. Kellerman (1992) has discussed the four main roles of the director: analyst, producer, therapist, and group leader.

Analyst

As an action analyst (Haskell, 1975) the director analyzes not only the intrapsychic and interpersonal issues of the group but also the transpersonal issues. The critical function of this role is the empathizer who brings understanding and affirmation to the protagonist and group members.

Producer

As a producer the psychodramatist is responsible for the dramatic action that unfolds during the course of the group session. There are many sub-roles to the producer role including: scene-setter, choreographer, coach, dramaturge, and timekeeper.

Therapist

The director must be the therapist both for the protagonist and all the other group members. In the role of therapist it is essential to distinguish good therapy from adequate drama. The director as therapist observes, monitors and guides the protagonist's production. Kipper (1986) states that the two major vehicles of change in psychodrama are catharsis and role training.

While the drama is unfolding the director must also assume the role of the family therapist and mentally role reverses with each person from the protagonist's social network. The therapist structures the drama in such a way that all the characters in the drama become real, complex human beings rather than stereotypical projections of the protagonist.

Group Leader

As the group leader, the psychodramatist is the manager and facilitator of the group process who helps to cocreate a supportive sociometry that maximizes freedom in choice of roles and people. Since sociometry is the base of all the work a psychodramatist does, in a group session the director notes the currents of feeling that flow between participants and in relation to the director. He is noting what issues emerge as the group members interact and how the members feel in relation to those issues. He makes interventions to include silent members and to encourage participation from everyone. He helps the group to warm up enough that a protagonist will emerge. He makes interventions based on his observations.

The Auxiliary Ego

Auxiliary ego is the term given to other group members who play roles for the protagonist in the psychodrama. The auxiliary ego brings life to the protagonist's world. Auxiliary egos may play parts of the protagonist's self (e.g., double, shy and afraid me, the loud and abusive me) and/or interpersonal and transpersonal roles. The auxiliary egos may play wished-for, dead or absent others in the protagonist's social network.

The auxiliary, in service to the protagonist, is called upon to connect on a deep inner personal level with the role assigned and to communicate the experience of that role to the protagonist, director and group members. The auxiliary ego serves as a bridge between the protagonist and the director, the protagonist and the group and the protagonist and his drama.

The auxiliary must match the spontaneity and creativity of the protagonist and gently encourages the protagonist to embrace deeper levels of connection and experience. An auxiliary who assumes the role too quickly and too strongly can extinguish production from the protagonist, while an auxiliary who takes the role too cautiously and too slowly can deaden the protagonist's production.

As a general rule it is easier to contain an auxiliary who is too creative rather than to expand an auxiliary who is too cautious. The auxiliary ego has the greatest freedom to challenge, promote, extend and expand the protagonist's perceptions.

The group member also personally benefits from the playing of an auxiliary role. Playing the auxiliary role provides an access and opportunity to become connected to another dimension of the self and the other. As an auxiliary we may be called upon to play a role that is foreign, unknown or disclaimed by our self. If the individual makes a total commitment to the role, that very role will transform the auxiliary's life as he connects with and incorporates new information gleaned from playing the role.

There are several tips for being an auxiliary ego:

1. *Trust your intuition:* Trust that you will do a good enough job for the protagonist and embrace the role.
2. *Bring everything you have to the role:* A good auxiliary learns to go inward and pull forth experiences, expectations, behaviors and verbal responses that are congruent with the role assignment.
3. *Maximize production:* Use both verbal and nonverbal communication to embody the role.
4. *Stay in role.* Once assigned a role the auxiliary should respond to all situations from that role. If you are chosen to play the father in a drama do not look to the director and say, "What I am supposed to do?" but use those feelings and speak directly to the protagonist and say "I do not know what I'm supposed to do with you."
5. *Role Reversal.* In the role-reversed position, assume the body posture, voice and gesture of the protagonist and repeat the last few lines of dialogue from before the role reversal. This will anchor you in your new role and provide continuity to the drama for the protagonist.
6. *Maximize the creativity of the protagonist.* Do not be too clever or too smart, but rather encourage and support the protagonist in the production of new affect, thoughts, behaviors and spirituality.

The Group

The group serves as a microcosm for the larger community. The group members serve as both social lubricants and social irritants. They are the witnesses and provide existential validation and objective confirmation for the protagonist. The group functions in both individual and collective roles.

On an individual level the group can represent the struggles within the protagonist. It is one of the major tasks of the director to establish connections between group members (see sociometry). When the protagonist is a mirror for the individual members of the group, there is an experience of awareness and connection with the protagonist's story. The individual group members discover parts of themselves and their relationships within the protagonist's drama.

As a collective, the group is a microcosm of society and serves as a stand-in for the world at large. The group acts as a mirror for the protagonist. The roles that are present in the protagonist's life are reflected back to him through the group members: the critical parent; the annoyed sibling; the supportive friend, the loving partner, etc.

Therapeutic Process

While the time for a psychodrama group may range from 30 minutes to three hours, all psychodrama session are divided into three parts: warm-up, enactment and sharing. Generally 50 percent of the allotted time is used for the enactment phase. The warm-up and sharing phases equally share the remaining time.

Warm-up

The warm-up is an essential component of every psychodrama session. It would be highly unlikely for group members to enter the therapy room and be instantaneously ready to leap into a psychodrama. The warm-up provides them with a gradual readying for the enactment. In psychodrama, the concept of resistance does not exist. Instead, a client's reluctance is perceived as being connected to an incomplete warm-up. Rather than trying to force the client to go where he does not want to go, the psychodramatist meets and joins the client where he is and assists him in the warming up process.

The warm-up is the time when group members begin focusing on the issues that they may wish to explore during the session. The warm-up may be either structured or unstructured. With a structured warm-up the director leads the group in an exercise designed to facilitate the emergence of issues of importance to group members. The warm-up may be cognitive, as with a brief didactic about relapse prevention to a substance abuse recovery group. Or the warm-up may be affective as with putting an empty chair in the center of the room, telling the group that alcoholism is in the chair and asking members to tell the disease what it has done to them.

There are literally thousands of structured warm-ups (Dayton, 1990; Schutz, 1967; Sternberg & Garcia, 2000; Weiner & Sacks, 1969). Prior to selecting a structured warm-up the director should review the history of the group, the overall goals for the group and the developmental stage of group process.

An unstructured warm-up occurs when group members discuss their issues and the director focuses the group on themes that spontaneously emerge from their discussion. The Central Concern model (Buchanan, 1980) is one way of looking at a group's warm-up and providing a structure and method for selecting a protagonist when the group is unwilling or unable to select a protagonist.

Selection of the Protagonist

The four ways a protagonist is selected are: (1) system, (2) director, (3) group, and (4) self-selection. Prior to the session the director should have already developed a plan about the method of protagonist selection. If the protagonist is identified prior to the session (system's or director choice) other group members should be informed early so that they do not become too warmed up to their own issues and so that they do warm up to the preselected protagonist.

System Selects the Protagonist

The system selects approach usually occurs when the psychodrama group is sponsored by an agency. The selection can be an institutionalized process such as providing an opportunity for each new patient in an acute care psychiatric program to enact a psychodrama as a method of assessing the strengths and weakness of that client. The system selects approach may also be used when a case manager requests that a client be chosen (e.g., The case manager of a substance abuse program requests that Mr. Jones do a psychodrama to see if he is ready to go for a home visit).

Director Selects the Protagonist

The director selects the protagonist approach occurs when the director of the group chooses a protagonist. The director can routinely choose the protagonist or this approach can be used on an as needed basis. An example of an as needed basis is when there is a crisis in the group or a group member and the director wants to ensure that the person(s) and issue will be dealt with e.g., Ms. Smith, who is a quiet and underchosen member of the group, just learned that her mother passed away. Ms. Smith wishes to attend the funeral service, but her brother, who was her sexual perpetrator, has already announced that he plans to attend the funeral. She does not know what to do and the funeral is tomorrow.

The director selects approach can also be used routinely in the group when the group members are either unwilling (nonvoluntary clients such as prisoners and juvenile delinquents) or are unable (psychotic or schizophrenic patients and abuse victims) to participate in a voluntary process. Psychiatric clients and people in crisis may simply not have the ego strength to risk volunteering to be chosen and deal with the consequences of not being chosen.

As noted in the warm-up section, The Central Concern Model was developed for use at Saint Elizabeths Hospital precisely because group members were incapable of making choices and withstanding the rejection of the group selection process.

The director selects approach is also useful in groups that have become fixed and stagnant in their sociometric processes. The director can select a rejection star or isolate to facilitate greater spontaneity and creativity among the group members. For example, the director may choose an underchosen emotionally expressive person to be the protagonist in a group that is stuck in intellectuality and avoids dealing with emotions.

A Group Member Volunteers to Be the Protagonist

Usually a volunteer protagonist is used for short enactments or demonstrations. The director asks for a volunteer who highlights the training issue or the group's issue (e.g., "Who would like to enact a ten-minute drama with a significant other to demonstrate how to use a double" or "Who would like to do a ten-minute drama where you practice some new behavior you'd like to introduce into your life"). The first person who volunteers is the protagonist.

Group Selects the Protagonist

This is the most common technique for selecting a protagonist in ongoing personal growth and therapy groups. Following the group warm-up (see above) the director informs the group members of the time limit for the drama and opens the process to volunteers. Group members who wish to be the protagonist come forward and gather in a circle. One at a time the potential protagonists briefly speak about the issues they would like to explore in the drama.

The director instructs the audience members to place a hand on the shoulder of the potential protagonist whose issue is closest to their own issue. The person who receives the most choices is the protagonist. Following the selection of the protagonist, some of those who chose the other potential protagonists tell these volunteers why they chose them–what in their own lives is similar.

It is helpful for the director to commend the volunteers on their courage and encourage them to be persistent in continuing to offer themselves as protagonists in future sessions. The director may state, "Each story has a time to be told. We need to be ready to tell our story, and we need others to be ready to witness it and participate in the telling of it."

The authors have observed that virtually all groups have the innate wisdom to know in what order stories should be told in order to provide maximum benefit to the group and to the protagonist. Telling our story before someone is willing to listen is as bad as not telling our story at all.

Action Phase

After the protagonist is selected the action phase begins. This, too, has a kind of warm-up with the Walk and Talk, Casting and Role Training the Auxiliary Egos, and Scene-Setting. These activities further warm up the protagonist and the group to the specific issues and relationships that will be explored in the drama.

Walk and Talk

After the protagonist is selected, the director and the protagonist walk side by side in a circle and discuss the contract for the drama. The walk and talk serves to deepen empathy between the director and the protagonist, to clear up any distorted expectations, to warm-up the protagonist and group to the drama, and to establish a contract for the drama. The director and protagonist will negotiate appropriate boundaries for the enactment. For example, the director might say, "In the time we have available, I do not feel comfortable directing a four person exercise with two scenes. Is there a way to do your drama with one character in one scene?"

The director also focuses the protagonist on his own work rather than on changing others. The director might say, "No, I can't get your father to understand you, but you could tell your father your side of the story and your feelings about his lack of support for you."

At the end of the walk and talk, the director should clearly and succinctly restate to the protagonist and the group the contract for the work. If the protagonist concurs, the scene setting and auxiliary training begins.

Casting and Role Training the Auxiliary Egos

The first order of business after the establishment of the contract is to cast the characters for the drama. Usually the protagonist is asked to choose group members whom they would like to play the roles.

It is imperative that group members have the right to decline any role. Also, the director encourages spontaneity in the choice of auxiliaries so that group members are not role locked into playing the same types of roles every time they are auxiliaries, e.g., Tashika always plays the mom roles. Occasionally, directors will suggest a therapeutic role assignment, by recommending a specific group member to play a role because they feel it will be particularly useful for the person.

If a protagonist has difficulty casting a role because she believes it is a role no group member wants to play, the director may ask the group who is willing to play the role. This is done so that the protagonist will know that these people are not afraid to play the role and are willing to assist in the drama. If several people raise their hands, the director will ask the protagonist to choose from among them. Sometimes what happens is that once someone raises a hand, the protagonist feels freer to make a choice and will request that someone who didn't raise a hand be the auxiliary.

One by one the characters are chosen and the formal role training of the auxiliaries begins. There is a basic assumption that the protagonist casts the roles for both overt (you look like my mother) and covert (undiscovered sociometric connections) reasons.

Role training can be done "Hollywood Style" with all the roles being cast simultaneously and role training for one role at a time, or each role being selected one at time with role training prior to the selection of the next character.

The protagonist begins with a physiological description (height, weight, age, posture, etc.) and moves on to include qualitative issues such as personality characteristics or how the protagonist feels treated by the person.

After the verbal description by the protagonist, the protagonist is role reversed and assumes the role of the other through posture, movement and comments. The director may ask, "What are some things you generally say to the protagonist? Use the tone of voice you tend to use with her." The auxiliary ego is asked if she has sufficient information to play the role or if she has any questions for the protagonist. To summarize, the protagonist first describes the role of the significant other then assumes the role. After the auxiliary egos are assigned and role trained, the first scene is set.

Scene Setting

The scene setting begins with the director asking the protagonist where the action occurs. The first question generally will be, "Where does this scene take place?" When the protagonist is unsure or uncertain of where the scene takes place the scene may be set in the "mists" (i.e., the unknown, the area between heaven and earth).

Setting the scene for the drama is important in that it anchors the protagonist in time and space. If the scene is set in the protagonist's family home, is it occurring when the protagonist was ten years old or in the home as it is today? The setting may be much the same or quite different.

One of the first tasks of the director is to decide on the time limits that will be allocated to the scene setting and each particular scene. Although it is possible and sometimes desirable to use an entire thirty-minute enactment solely for the purpose of exploring in depth the details of the scene and that scene's relationship to the protagonist, it is an exception to general practice to do so.

When a scene is being set within an overall psychodrama, the director should be judicious with the use of time and set broad parameters and descriptions for the scene. The scene gives form, function and direction to the protagonist.

After the place of the scene has been chosen, the protagonist is asked to set the scene. In setting the objects within the scene it is important to allow the protagonist time to create their own space. Unless the protagonist is physically challenged, the protagonist is responsible for moving all the objects in the scene. Neither the director nor the auxiliaries should, unless asked, participate in moving objects or creating the space. The actual physical creation of the space is the protagonist's warm-up to the scene and the warm-up to the creation of his own world.

Whatever objects are available in the group room are transformed by surplus reality into the objects in the scene. The protagonist speaks aloud in the present tense and says, "This chair is my father's armchair." The protagonist is encouraged to provide texture and flavor to the object. "My father's armchair is big and well worn. The cushions are faded brown corduroy, and they sag. You can see the rings from my father's beer can on the right arm of the chair and the cigarette burns from when he falls asleep in front of the television."

Although it should be used sparingly, a director may request that the protagonist reverse roles with an object. Nonverbal cues from the protagonist and cultural sensitivities may indicate a role reversal with an object could be useful. If the protagonist states that her mother was a devout Catholic, a role reversal with a statue of the Virgin Mary may yield significant results.

After the scene is over, the protagonist is asked to strike the scene. Again, neither the director nor any of the group members, participate in the dismantling of the scene, unless directly asked by the protagonist. The speed and order with which the protagonist clears the scene are additional cues to the protagonist's psychological state.

In these days of managed care and shorter sessions most psychodrama sessions are from 60 to 90 minutes and thus the number of scenes during the action phase are reduced.

Common Production Techniques

Zerka T. Moreno (1978) provides a full description of basic and advanced psychodramatic production techniques that are designed to increase the protagonist's creativity and spontaneity in the here and now. The five basic and most frequently used production techniques are the soliloquy, double, aside, role reversal, and mirror.

SOLILOQUY. Hamlet's soliloquy is among the most famous in the world when he says, "To be or not to be; that is the question." The soliloquy is a moment between reflection and action. It brings the protagonist out of his head and into the moment so that the covert is made overt and we can all hear the running commentary in his mind. The soliloquy is most often used as a bridge in beginning or in ending a scene.

The protagonist is asked to perform a soliloquy by walking in a circle and speaking aloud the thoughts and feelings in his head. A protagonist may also be asked to leave the scene for a moment and soliloquize on her experiences within that scene. The soliloquy is analogous to the free association technique in psychoanalysis except that the individual is asked to move while speaking. The soliloquy is done in action so that the protagonist's movement patterns and gestures are visible.

ASIDE. The aside is another term that comes from theatrical tradition. This technique is used when the protagonist is acting within a scene, but appears to be someplace else. The protagonist is instructed to turn his head to the side (an aside) and speak the thoughts he is thinking but not saying. During the aside, the action continues but the other characters are instructed that they cannot hear the aside.

The aside technique is most commonly used when the protagonist is disassociating from the enactment and is engaged in a residual warm-up. The aside gives voice to the residual warm-up so that the residual warm-up can be incorporated into the scene. A visible indication for the need for the aside occurs when the protagonist's body language is significantly different from his words, or when the protagonist is distant from the scene and appears to be lost in his own thoughts.

It is also used when the person's affect seems incongruent with his words and the protagonist seems constrained from speaking by social mores of the situation. An example of this is a person not wanting to admit feeling rejected in a situation where the auxiliary is ending a relationship with the protagonist.

DOUBLE. The double is the most frequently used technique in psychodrama. The primary purpose of doubling is to provide the protagonist with an awareness and integration of a domain of self that has previously been underdeveloped (e.g., emotion, mind, body and spirit).

Classical doubling occurs when an individual, chosen by the protagonist, literally reflects the protagonist's physical posture and brings a voice to the underdeveloped domain. There are many kinds of doubles: Affective, cognitive, somatic and amplifying (speaks louder for a quiet protagonist), and containing doubles are the most common. Paradoxical and antagonist doubling is less often used.

The double begins by assuming the same posture and gestures as the protagonist. He stands beside and slightly behind the protagonist in a place where he can see the protagonist's affect, yet not be upstaging the protagonist. The double first establishes rapport with the protagonist by stating the obvious and giving expression to the unexpressed manifest content. After establishing rapport, the double slowly and gently begins making statements that deepen the protagonist's awareness of these unexpressed thoughts and feelings. The best doubling statements are direct, pithy and evoke a response from the protagonist. Sentence stem doubling statements are often useful as well, e.g., "I'm feeling...." or "What I would like to tell you is . . . ."

The protagonist and other group members are informed that only the protagonist can hear the double. All other auxiliaries respond only to words and actions initiated by the protagonist. It is a disservice to the protagonist, and reinforces "magical thinking" that an individual can be heard without speaking. The protagonist must incorporate, change or disavow the words of the double so that the protagonist deepens his internal experience. During the doubling, the director must be vigilant in monitoring the protagonist and directing the protagonist either to repeat aloud, clarify or disavow the double's statements.

In spontaneous doubling, rather than having a particular double assigned to the protagonist for the entire drama, group members are encouraged to rise, stand in the double position, make one doubling statement, wait for the protagonist's response and then sit back down in the group. Spontaneous doubling is excellent for developing emotional intelligence in other group members and providing the protagonist with a deep feeling of connection with the group.

Doubling can also be used as a method of restraint. Clients with impulse control disorders often benefit from cognitive doubling. A cognitive double builds introspection, reflection, and future projection within the protagonist. For example, a cognitive double of an impulsive, aggressive client might say "I'd like to hit this person but hitting others results in my going to seclusion and losing my phone privileges. I want to call my girlfriend tonight, so I'd better not hit him."

An assignment of a double is contraindicated when the protagonist is fully experiencing the drama.

ROLE REVERSAL. Zerka T. Moreno has called role reversal the *sine qua non* of psychodramatic techniques. A role reversal occurs when the protagonist reverses with another and becomes the other (when A becomes B and B becomes A). The protagonist and the auxiliary literally change places in the room and switch roles.

When directing multiple role players it is essential that the protagonist is role reversed back to home base before assuming another role reversal (if the protagonist (A) is in the role of B, the protagonist is reversed back to his own role (A) before being reversed with C).

A role reversal is indicated under any of the following conditions:

1. when the protagonist has information that the auxiliary does not have.
2. to provide an opportunity for the protagonist to see himself from the role of the other.
3. when the protagonist lacks empathy or understanding of the role of the other.
4. to avoid physical harm to the auxiliary.
5. when the protagonist lacks spontaneity and role reversing will increase his affect, cognition or performance.
6. to verify the accuracy of the statements from the other.
7. when the protagonist asks a question. The idea here is that all that we need to know is within.

Role reversal is contraindicated when the protagonist is highly codependent and routinely and automatically assumes the role of the other and abandons the role of the Self. Role reversal with abusers is contraindicted for abuse survivors until the final stage of treatment.

MIRROR. The protagonist is asked to "step out" of the scene and choose someone to take his role. The protagonist then observes his "mirror" enact the scene. The mirror technique allows the protagonist to see himself as others see him.

Mirroring was created before audiovisual feedback and can be an excellent way for a group member to gain a perspective on his own actions. This technique is useful when the protagonist becomes overheated or overwhelmed and a cool down is indicated so that the enactment does not get too chaotic. A mirror is also useful in unblocking protagonists who have distorted images of themselves. For example, from the mirror position the protagonist might note that rather than being assertive, he is instead being docile.

This technique is contraindicated when it would be used to shame or embarrass the protagonist or in situations when the protagonist might feel ridiculed rather than supported.

Other Specialized Production Techniques

In addition to the five most commonly used psychodramatic production techniques, a variety of specialized techniques have been developed.

EMPTY CHAIR. The empty chair technique while coined and first used by Moreno was popularized by Fritz Perls, who borrowed and adapted the empty chair as a Gestalt Therapy technique.

The protagonist is asked to place a person or object in an empty chair and to begin a dialogue with that person or object. This technique is often used as a warm-up for a group. The director can also suggest who should occupy the empty chair. The subject in the empty chair can be someone from the past, present or future, or it can be a part of the Self or someone transpersonal (e.g., St. Peter, Buddha, Hercules).

In general the dialogue begins with the protagonist speaking to the empty chair. The director can prompt the protagonist by asking the protagonist to make a statement, ask a question or speak a feeling. When appropriate, role reversal is used with the protagonist becoming the person in the chair and speaking back to herself.

FUTURE PROJECTION. As noted earlier in the theoretical constructs section, time collapses in psychodrama. Instead of enacting a scene from the past, the drama can include a scene from the future. According to Moreno (1946) the future is a better motivator for the present than is the past. The future projection technique can be used as one scene within a psychodrama, as a warm-up technique and for separate one-scene enactments.

In the future projection the protagonist is asked to imagine what a specific future might look like. Auxiliary egos are chosen to play the main characters (real or fantasy) and are trained by the protagonist to take the roles. A person is chosen to play the present self while the protagonist plays the future self. At the conclusion of the future projection, the director instructs the future self to role train the present self to identify concrete behavioral actions that will create the wished for future.

The future projection technique is best used to instill hope, provide motivation, and to assist the protagonist in creating a plan to solve a current dilemma. The future projection technique is contraindicated when it may break through a protagonist's denial and cause trauma to the client (e.g., a client who is in denial over a terminal illness).

Psychodrama a Deux. Psychodrama a deux is psychodrama for two (Stein & Callahan, 1982). *Psychodrama a deux* is often the focus of individual therapy when provided by a psychodramatist.

Psychodrama a deux is accomplished through use of as many empty chairs as there are auxiliaries in the drama. The protagonist places them in the room as she would set the scene in a group session and is asked to imagine that the chairs are filled with her auxiliaries. The director reverses the protagonist into each role to learn more about the role. When the protagonist is sufficiently warmed up, she begins the drama. If one does not want to use chairs, scarves or props may be used to mark the spots held by the auxiliary roles. It is best for the director to refrain from playing roles, but to be an active double for the protagonist.

The director can also interview and coach the protagonist in the role of the other at various moments in the drama. For example, if the protagonist is in the role of her usually critical mother, the director may say, "I know that you do not like Mary to be overconfident, yet she's feeling that you do not love her and you think she's seldom competent. Do you love her? Do you want to help her? Would you be willing to tell her that you love her? Can you tell her one thing about her that you admire?"

There are some pitfalls to avoid when using psychodrama production techniques in individual therapy. One of the great benefits to the psychodramatic group process is that more of the transference is projected onto other group members and less is projected onto the director. However, in a one on one setting all the transference will be placed upon the director. The danger in *psychodrama a deux* is in the director assuming roles within the process. Assuming the role of an antagonistic other in *psychodrama a deux* heightens the negative transference towards the director and often results in a client's premature termination.

Another danger in *psychodrama a deux* is that experiential methods can too quickly cut through defense systems and can lead to premature breakthroughs or breakdowns of natural defense systems. In using *psychodrama a deux* on a regular basis, the director should spend considerable time working with supportive relationships and supportive parts of the self rather than focusing mainly on dysfunctional role relationships (internal or external).

Sharing

The final phase of a psychodrama session is the sharing. The sharing is a vital and integral part of the session. The sharing phase incorporates the protagonist back into the group and offers the group members an opportunity to connect, on a personal level, with the issues and concerns explored in the drama. It is a time for closure and integration. It is a time for group members to acknowledge how the drama has affected them personally and what they have learned about their own lives through the protagonist's journey.

Prior to the sharing the auxiliary egos are de-roled from their assigned roles and resume their membership in the group. Just as it is important to warm-up the auxiliary egos to play a role so, too, is it essential for the auxiliary egos to formally discard the assigned roles and return to themselves. After the de-roling is concluded, the sharing portion begins.

Sharing is unique in that the verbal statements by the other group members to the protagonist are based on identification and connection rather than evaluation or interpretation. Group members are encouraged to identify with rather than critique or interpret the protagonist. To facilitate this process group members are encouraged to begin their sharing statements with an "I" statement: "When watching your drama, I thought about my own rocky relationship with my partner, and I felt a sense of hope that we could work something out too." The depth and level of sharing from the group members can also serve as an assessment of how adequately the drama met the needs of the group members.

If a group member becomes critical, judgmental or advice giving rather than sharing, it may be because that group member has identified with the role of the other rather than the role of the protagonist. For example, "You know, you are very sensitive and as your partner I would have a hell of a time putting up with you." It is best for the director to nip these statements in the bud and refocus the group member to share with the protagonist. The director might say something to the group member, such as, "It would be helpful to the protagonist and to you to share from your own experience and say what the drama brings up from your life." After the group member responds, the director might say, "You noted you feel the protagonist is sensitive. How does sensitivity play out in your own life?"

The director monitors the group members and establishes sociometric connections among the protagonist and other group members. The director can ask for clarification or elaboration from group members who are finding it difficult to make a bridge between themselves and the protagonist. If a group member is having difficulty in finding something to share, the director can gently guide her to a similar issue (e.g., The group member might say, "I've never been married, so I do not have anything to share." The director could respond, "I know you have never been married, but have you ever had a relationship with someone you loved and feared losing that relationship?").

Depending on the time allotted for sharing and the number of people in the group, there are several ways to conduct the sharing. If the group is small and there is sufficient time, the group can share as a whole, with each group member sharing with the protagonist. If there is limited time or if there is a large group sharing can be done in small groups with the auxiliary egos sharing with the protagonist and other group members forming small groups for sharing. After the small groups have shared, the director asks a few group members who have not already shared with the protagonist to share with the protagonist in the larger group.

It is important that the auxiliary egos have time to share with the protagonist both their experience in playing the role (e.g., "As your father I felt . . .") and from their own personal life. Sharing from the role often provides invaluable feedback to the protagonist.

In an ongoing group the sharing illuminates the next phase of the group and highlights the issues that will be on the agenda at the next meeting. It is to be remembered that sharing is an absolutely essential part of a psychodrama session. It helps a group to cool down from the action, to reach closure, to deepen connections with one another and the self, and provides time for introspection and reflection on the drama.

Populations and Settings

Psychodrama has been used with a broad range of people in a variety of settings, including but not limited to: the severely and chronically mentally ill (Buchanan, 1984); alcohol and substance abusers (Fuhlrodt, 1990); both normal and emotionally challenged children and adolescents (Hoey, 1996); eating disordered clients (Hornyak and Baker, 1989); clients and staff of the criminal justice system (Buchanan, 1981); and individual and group counseling and psychotherapy clients (Blatner, 1996; Garcia, 1984; Holmes & Karp, 1991; Holmes, Karp, & Watson, 1994; Williams, 1991).

There are also several recent adaptations of Moreno's work including Jonathan Fox's (1994) Playback Theatre and Peter Pitzele's (1998) Bibliodrama.

Clinical Indications and Limitations

Psychodrama can be used successfully with virtually every population, provided that the psychodramatist is skilled enough to modify treatment to suit the population. Psychodrama can be preventive. With psychodrama, one can help clients cope with stressful situations and learn how to enact alternative solutions to repetitive problems. Psychodrama can also treat specific symptoms. For example, psychodrama is highly effective in the treatment of phobias. It can also be used for personal growth, such as improving relationships and restoring a sense of joy in life.

Psychodrama treatment can be brief (1–6 sessions) or of longer duration. Psychodrama is the original brief therapy. Goals and interventions are specific and behaviorally oriented and tested.

While practically any client can benefit from psychodrama, careful screening must be done so that the person can be placed within the appropriate psychodramatic treatment setting. A client with a substance abuse problem, for example, is best treated in a homogeneous substance abusers group rather than a generic group. Clients with fragile ego boundaries are best placed in groups where the treatment focus is on behavior and interpersonal skills development rather than in a group dealing with strong emotions and regressive early childhood dramas.

Psychodrama is a powerful treatment modality, and it has a unique ability to heal or to harm. Moreno cautioned against the use of psychodrama to rehearse homicidal and suicidal fantasies. Psychodrama should also be used judiciously with individuals with severe impulse and acting-out disorders so that they do not rehearse destructive actions. While van der Kolk (1987) has stated that psychodrama may be helpful in working with abuse survivors, Hudgins and Drucker (1998) caution that psychodramatists working with abuse survivors need specialized training in the application of psychodrama techniques with this population.

The trained psychodramatist will have the knowledge, skills, and abilities to design the right treatment for each specific client rather than rely upon a cookbook of structured techniques. A skilled practitioner understands dramas can range from the behavioral (role rehearsal) to the affective (catharsis for release of tension) to the cognitive (reorganization of perceptual patterns) to the spiritual (establishing and deepening transpersonal connections).

For issues regarding competency, the American Board of Examiners in Psychodrama, Sociometry and Group Psychotherapy has set standards of professional practice and certifies individuals based upon these standards with a written and an onsite examination. The minimum requirements for certification are a Masters Degree in a related field of practice; 780 hours of training from certified trainers and one year of supervised clinical practice. While it is not essential that all individuals who use psychodrama are certified, it is essential that they have received proper training, education and supervision for its use.

CASE EXAMPLES

Case Example One: Psychodrama in a Group Setting

Joan had been dating a wonderful man who had asked her to marry him. She had also been dating another man off and on over a period of years. She felt that this man, too, was finally ready for marriage. Tom, the first suitor, was a civil servant, a sweet and loving man with a wonderful sense of humor. Andre, the second suitor, was handsome, exciting, and charming. Joan and Tom loved the same kinds of activities and shared basic values. Joan and Andre went to chic nightspots and had differing views on life.

Joan was in a quandary. What to do? Which man to marry? In the walk and talk it seemed clear that she was in love with Tom, but the lure of excitement with Andre was compelling, especially since she felt that her deceased mother would have wanted her to marry Andre. Her mother had known Andre and liked him and would be disappointed if Joan didn't marry him since he was so handsome and charming, apparently a mover and shaker. The contract made in the walk and talk was to help Joan move closer to a decision. She decided that she wanted to encounter both men in the drama as a way of clarifying her feelings about both. As she brought them in she continued to talk about what her mother wanted her to do. We decided to bring her mother in too and give her a chance to encounter Mother about choice of mate. Joan placed the men in a tableau and in a surplus reality scene talked to her dead mother about both men. As Joan spoke to her mother she began to realize that Tom was very much like her father, whom she deeply loved and admired. It became clear in the scene through role reversal that Mother did not share Joan's love and respect for Father. Joan's mother would far rather have married a debonair and handsome man like Andre.

The director reversed Joan back into her own role to hear her mother's statement and respond to it. Then the director doubled, "Well, if you think he's so great, you marry him." Joan said, "Yeah, you marry him" and began laughing at the thought of her mother marrying Andre. The director asked her if she would like to see that happen. Joan's mouth dropped open at the prospect of such an odd event but she quickly decided she would love to see her mother walk down the aisle with Andre since they seemed "perfect for each other."

The scene was quickly set up and Joan watched gleefully as her mother greeted churchgoers and asked them if they were impressed that she had finally landed such a great catch. Joan stood at the side with Tom. In a soliloquy she noted her relief at seeing her mother happy.

She recognized that she had been hanging onto her unsatisfying relationship with Andre as a way of making up for her mother's unhappy relationship with her father. Up to that moment she had been a bit ashamed that she was in love with Tom, a sweet, ordinary guy like her dad, rather than the exciting Andre.

The truth was she couldn't make herself love Andre as she loved Tom. "I do not really trust Andre. He does not have much substance. And I do not think he's as financially stable as he implies. I think it's all flash. And– I think he'd spend the rest of our life together running after other women."

When she saw her mother as Andre's happy bride, she felt so relieved of the burden of her mother's wishes and unmet needs. She ended by telling her mother how much she loved her and how delighted she was that Mother was now happy. She asked Mother for her blessing with Tom. Reversing Joan into the mother role, she told her daughter that now that she was so happy, she wanted Joan to be happy too and gave her blessing for the marriage to Tom. Joan reversed back to her own role to receive her mother's blessing. She ended the drama by telling Tom how much she loved him and why she did. Within a couple of months after the session, Joan and Tom were married. When the director saw her some years later, she said how happy she was that she had married him and that they were still very much in love. She had found a soul mate.

Case Example Two: Psychodrama in an Individual Setting

Moreno felt that each of us needs to spend as much time as possible in the present moment, not fretting over the past or obsessing about the future. As a result, he designed psychodrama so that all scenes are placed in the here and now. Because all of the work is done in the present, we are able to collapse time and change history, as it were.

Bob's father had died of a heart attack at work when Bob was only seven. His mother was distraught, depressed and unavailable to him for nearly a year afterward. During that time he had no one to comfort him in his grief and he devoted himself to cheering up his mother and taking care of her in any way his child's mind could imagine. He grew up to be a very responsible but emotionally remote young man.

He married and when his wife became ill during a pregnancy, he became angry with her and depressed. Since his emotions and responses to the current situation seemed confusing to him, Bob began to explore his past. He noted that because of the suddenness of his father's death, he had had no opportunity to say good-bye. Because of his mother's state after the death he had never explored either his own grief or his feelings about being emotionally abandoned by her, a woman who loved him very much.

In a psychodrama, using an empty chair, with a scene set in the mists, Bob encountered his dead father and told him what life had been like in the family after his death. He told his father how deserted he had felt when he died and how hard it had been to take care of his mother. He noted that he still felt overly responsible for her and how angry it sometimes made him feel.

The director role reversed Bob into the role of his father. As Father, he tearfully told Bob how sorry he was to have left him so abruptly. The director doubled and coached the father in telling Bob other things he wanted to tell Bob and that he felt Bob needed to know. His "father" then told Bob how much he loved him and how proud he was of him. Reversing back to his own position, the director repeated the father's last words and Bob sobbed with tears of joy and relief. The director returned to the double position behind Bob as Bob told Father how much he loved him. He also said the good-bye he had not been able to say as a seven-year-old.

In another session, Bob spoke to his mother, telling her what he had not felt comfortable saying to her in life, for fear of wounding her. Without blaming her, he expressed his childhood worries and feelings of loneliness and responsibility. As he spoke to his mother, he realized that his wife's sudden illness (which necessitated his taking care of her for a brief time) had triggered his worries and angers from the past.

This realization helped him to acknowledge that his wife's illness was temporary and that there were many ways in which she was available to him. Also, he saw that he had been fearful that he would somehow lose her and that she, like his father, would die and abandon him.

At this point, another empty chair was used to represent his wife. Bob had been contaminating her role by confusing his wife with both his mother and father. He spoke to his wife and acknowledged both how she is different from his parents and that the situation was different as well. In a role-training moment, Bob also tearfully acknowledged her importance to him and his deep love for her, something he had been unable to tell her in the past.

When reversed into his wife's role, Bob-as-wife noted that in fact her sickness wasn't life-threatening, that he had been overreacting to her illness, that she loved him deeply too and that he wasn't getting rid of her so easily. Bob reversed roles and chuckling at "her" final comment, contracted with the psychodramatist to tell his wife directly that he loves her and is beginning to trust that she will not leave.

Bob continued with treatment for another six weeks, deepening his relationship with his wife, and beginning a new and more openly affectionate and supportive relationship with his mother.

REFERENCES

Blatner, A. (1996). *Acting-in: Practical applications of psychodramatic methods* (3rd ed.) New York: Springer Publishing.

Buchanan, D.R. (1984). Moreno's social atom: A diagnostic and treatment tool for exploring interpersonal relationships. *The Arts in Psychotherapy, 27,* 173–183.

Buchanan, D.R. (1984). Psychodrama. In T.B. Karasu (Ed.), *The Psychiatric therapies.* Washington, DC: The American Psychiatric Association.

Buchanan, D.R. (1981). Action methods for the criminal justice system. *Federal Probation, 45,* 17–25.

Buchanan, D.R. (1980). The central concern model: A framework for structuring psychodramatic production. *Journal of Group Psychotherapy, Psychodrama and Sociometry, 33,* 47–62.

Carlson-Sabelli, L.C., Sabelli, H.C., Patel, M., & Holm, K. (1992). The union of opposites. *Journal of Group Psychotherapy, Psychodrama and Sociometry, 45,* 147–171.

Compernole, T. (1981). J. L. Moreno: An unrecognized pioneer of family therapy. *Family Process, 20,* 331–335.

Corsini, R.J. (1955). Historic background of group psychotherapy: A critique. *Journal of Group Psychotherapy, Psychodrama and Sociometry, 8,* 219–225.

Csikszentmihalyi, M. (1991). *Flow: The psychology of optimal experience.* New York: Harper Collins.

Dayton, T. (1990). *Drama games: Techniques for self-development.* Deerfield Beach: Health Communications, Inc.

Edwards, J. (1996). Examining the clinical utility of the Moreno Social Atom Projective test. *Journal of Group Psychotherapy, Psychodrama and Sociometry, 49,* 51–75.

Fox, J. (1987). *The essential Moreno: Writings on psychodrama, group method, and spontaneity* by J.L. Moreno, M.D. New York: Springer Publishing.

Fox, J. (1994). *Acts of service: Spontaneity, commitment, tradition in the nonscripted theatre.* New Paltz, NY: Tusitala Publishing.

Fromm, E. (1941). *Escape from freedom.* New York: Harper Collins.

Fuhlrodt, R.B. (Ed.). (1990). *Psychodrama: Its application to ACOA and substance abuse treatment.* Caldwell, NJ: Promises Books.

Garcia, A. (1984). Psychodrama: Creative approaches to human growth. *Design for Arts in Education, 86,* 40–42.

Hale, A.E. (1986). *Conducting clinical sociometric explorations: A manual for psychodramatists and sociometrists.* Roanoke, VA: Blue Ridge Human Relations Institute.

Hare, A.P., & Hare, J.R. (1996). *J.L. Moreno.* London: Sage Publications.

Haskell, M.R. (1975). *Socioanalysis: Self-direction via sociometry and psychodrama.* Long Beach, CA: Role Training Associates, Inc.

Hoey, B. (1996). *Who calls the tune? A psychodramatic approach to child therapy.* London: Routlege.

Holmes, P.H., & Karp, M. (Eds.). (1991). *Psychodrama: Inspiration and technique.* London: Routledge.

Holmes, P.H., & Karp, M. (Eds.). (1991). *The inner world outside: Object relations and psychodrama.* London: Routledge.

Holmes, P.H., Karp, M., & Watson, M. (Eds.). (1994). *Psychodrama since Moreno: Innovation in theory and practice.* London: Routledge.

Hornyak, L.M., & Baker, E.K. (Eds.). (1989). *Experiential therapies for eating disorders.* New York: The Guilford Press.

Hudgins, M.K., & Drucker, K. (1998). The containing double as part of the therapeutic spiral model for treating trauma survivors. *International Journal for Action Methods, 51,* 63–74.

Karp, M., Holmes, P., & Tauvon, K. (1998). *The handbook of psychodrama.* London: Routledge.

Kellerman, P.F. (1992). *Focus on psychodrama: The therapeutic aspects of psychodrama.* London: Kingsley Publishers.

Kipper, D.A. (1986). *Psychotherapy through clinical role playing.* New York: Brunner/Mazel.

Kraus, C. (1984). Psychodrama for fallen gods: A review of Morenian theology. *Journal of Group Psychotherapy, Psychodrama and Sociometry, 37,* 47–65.

Maslow, A. (1968). Letter to the editor. *Life Magazine,* August 02, 1968, 15.

Marineau, R.F. (1989). *Jacob Levy Moreno 1889–1974, father of psychodrama, sociometry and group psychotherapy.* London: Tavistock/Routledge.

(Moreno) Levy, J. (1915). *Einladung zu einer begegnung heft 2 (Invitation to an encounter, Part 2).* Vienna/Leipzig: Anzengruber/Verlag Bruder Suschitzky.

Moreno (published anonymously), J.L. (1920). *Das testament des vaters (The words of the father, in Die Gefahrten, 3,* 1-33. Berlin/Potsdam: Kiepenheuer Verlag.

Moreno, J.L. (1946). *Psychodrama and group psychotherapy.* Paper presented at American Psychiatric Association Meeting May 30, 1946 in Chicago.

Moreno, J.L. (1946). *Psychodrama first volume.* Beacon, New York: Beacon House.

Moreno, J.L. (1947). *The psychodrama of God: A new hypothesis of the self* (revised edition). Beacon, New York: Beacon House.

Moreno, J.L. (1953). *Who shall survive?* Beacon, New York: Beacon House.

Moreno, J.L. (1966). Psychiatry of the 20th century: Function of the universalis: Time, space, reality and cosmos. *Journal of Group Psychotherapy, Psychodrama and Sociometry, 19,* 146–158.

Moreno, J.L. (1969). *The magic charter of psychodrama.* Beacon, New York: Beacon House.

Moreno, Z.T. (1965). Psychodramatic rules, techniques, and adjunctive methods. *Group Psychotherapy, 18,* 73–86.

Moreno, Z.T., Blomkvist, L.D., & Rutzel, T. (2000). *Psychodrama, surplus reality, and the art of healing.* New York: Routledge.

Pitzele, P. (1998). *Scripture window's toward a practice of bibliodrama.* Los Angles: Torah Aura Productions.

Schutz, W. (1967). *Joy, expanding human awareness.* New York: Grove Press, Inc.

Stein, M.B., & Callahan, M.L. (1982). *Journal of Group Psychotherapy, Psychodrama and Sociometry, 35,* 118–129.

Sternberg, P., & Garcia, A. (2000). *Sociodrama: Who's in your shoes?* 2nd ed. Westport: Praeger.

Thomas, E.J., & Biddle, B.J. (Eds.). *Role theory: Concepts and research.* New York: John Wiley & Sons.

Van der Kolk, B. (1987). *Psychological trauma.* Washington, DC: American Psychiatric Press.

Weiner, H.B., & Sacks, J.M. (1969). Warm-up and sum-up. *Journal of Group Psychotherapy, Psychodrama and Sociometry, 22,* 85–102.

Williams, A. (1991). *The passionate technique: Strategic psychodrama with individuals.* London: Tavistock/Routledge.

FURTHER STUDY

For further information on psychodrama, individuals are encouraged to contact:

The American Society of Group
Psychotherapy and Psychodrama
301 N. Harrison Street, Suite 508
Princeton, NJ 08540

Phone: (609) 452-1339
email: asgpp@ASGPP.org

Or one can contact

The American Board of Examiners in
Psychodrama, Sociometry, and
Group Psychotherapy
PO Box 15572
Washington, DC 20003

Phone: (202) 483-0514.

The Society has been the general membership organization for over 50 years and publishes a newsletter, sponsors an annual conference and several regional meetings. The official journal of the Society is *The International Journal of Action Methods,* which is published quarterly.

The Board of Examiners publishes an annual directory, which includes the standards for certification and names and addresses of those who are certified. The directory is available free of charge to individuals who request it. The Board also maintains an ethics committee to oversee the professional conduct of all certified psychodramatists.

Chapter 10

SOCIODRAMA

PATRICIA STERNBERG AND ANTONINA GARCIA

SOCIODRAMA CONCERNS ITSELF with the role aspects that people share. For example, all students are expected to study; most nurses encounter dying patients in the course of their careers; most police officers handle traffic violations at one time or another; all employees have bosses with whom they must deal. Jacob Levy Moreno, M.D., originated sociodrama between 1921 and 1923. One of the reasons that sociodrama works so well is that Moreno was able to tap into the truth about humanity, that we are each more alike than we are different.

In *Who Shall Survive?* Moreno said, "The true subject of sociodrama is the group. . . . Sociodrama is based upon the tacit assumption that the group formed by the audience is already organized by the social and cultural roles which in some degree all the carriers of the culture share. . . . The sociodramatic approach deals with social problems and aims at social catharsis." (59–60)

Basing itself on the premise of shared experience a sociodrama group might seek to define a problem that the members would like to solve. If they are social workers for example, they might want to be better able to deal with a situation in which family members disown a child's misbehavior at school. If they are police trainees, they may want to enhance their understanding of a rape victim's feelings. The members of a sociodrama group will work with a situation in which they would like to gain greater understanding. The members may also define and work with a decision that they would like to be able to make; for example, high school students wanting to decide whether or not to go away to college rather than live at home and commute.

Members may seek to train themselves in certain role aspects about which they may feel uncomfortable. Thus, if they are a group of the hard-core unemployed, the members may want to role-train interview decorum.

Sociodrama is an action method in which individuals enact an agreed upon social situation spontaneously. The participants volunteer or are assigned roles by the director of the sociodrama. After every enactment there is a sharing in which group members discuss the enactment; the solutions or ideas it presented, and sometimes generate new material for future sociodramatic clarifications. The sharing is a time to begin the process of cooling down and integrating what has taken place moments before in action.

Sociodrama, with its action/reflection components, speaks to both sides of the brain. It is a kinesthetic, intuitive, and cognitive modality. Unlike simple role playing, sociodrama employs many specific techniques to deepen the action of the enactment. Some of these techniques are: the aside, doubling, role reversal, soliloquy, and mirroring. It is important to mention that theatrical training and/or interest in theatre are unnecessary for sociodrama. The modality is not meant to train actors but rather to draw upon a person's innate need and ability to learn with his whole body, mind, and intuition.

GENESIS

Moreno was born in Bucharest, Romania in 1889. His parents moved their family to Vienna while he was a small child. As a young man, Moreno took a degree in philosophy, then received his MD from the University of Vienna. Throughout the time when he was a student, he was developing the ideas that ultimately blossomed into sociodrama.

Between the years of 1908 and 1911, Moreno experimented with dramatic play in the parks of Vienna. He gathered children around him, told them stories from fairy tales and theatre, and then enacted the tales with the children. After a while, he encouraged the children to enact stories from their own imaginations. As he watched children take on and practice roles from the culture and work through their issues via play, Moreno hypothesized about roles and the educational and therapeutic benefits of role playing.

In 1913, while he was a medical student, Moreno began to explore the sociodynamics of groups. One day, Moreno met a prostitute on the Praeterstrasse. Because she was away from the red light district and wearing gaily-colored clothing rather than the more sedate apparel of a proper lady, a policeman carted her off to jail. Moreno, rather stunned by this occurrence, searched out the woman when she was released. He discovered from her that prostitutes had no rights under the law and were further not entitled to public medical care. Ever the social activist, Moreno interested a newspaper editor in the women's plight, got them medical care and organized the women into a kind of guild of prostitutes. The ladies met weekly to discuss their concerns. Moreno dates these groups as the inception of group psychotherapy.

As he observed the women and what they discussed, he began to realize what makes groups work: that we are more alike than we are different. He noticed that for every role a person plays there are both collective and private aspects. The prostitutes were able to communicate with each other so well because they shared difficulties and joys that were role-related. They all had to worry about aging, pregnancy, and venereal disease. These are some of the collective role aspects. At the same time, each prostitute had her own personality, personal concerns, and way of playing the role. These are the private aspects of the role.

Between the years of 1921 and 1923, Moreno developed and ran the Theater of Spontaneity. He loved theatre but was put off by the theatre of his day because he felt it had become sterile. He felt the actors and plays did not reach the community the way the theatre of the ancient Greeks did. Moreno believed that there should be interaction between audience and actors. Further, he believed that the theatre was lifeless because it did not explore issues that were of vital importance to the general public.

Moreno gathered together a group of professional actors and trained them both in spontaneity work and as sociological researchers. He wanted them to be actively aware of the current issues of their culture so that the audience members could mention a current event and the actors and audience could explore that issue onstage. As enactors and audience joined together spontaneously to examine social problems and discover possible solutions to them, sociodrama was born.

Moreno came to the United States in 1925. He had been invited to come to the States to develop a prototype of the tape recorder that he and a friend had invented. Once in the United States, Moreno worked using threads of sociodrama with children in New York schools and with racial issues in Harlem.

In the years from 1929–1931, Moreno again created a theater company called the Impromptu Theater and began experiments with his actors in developing the Living Newspaper format. They performed in New York City at Carnegie Hall. Audience members were encouraged to come up on stage and interact with the actors. Moreno abandoned the Impromptu Theater when, as part of WPA, the company expanded to include playwrights. Moreno felt that playwriting was an anathema to spontaneity and interaction between audience and actor.

Since Moreno's initial creation of sociodrama, role play has developed as an offshoot and is a standard part of many forms of training in business and education. Role play enjoys wide usage because it is quite easy to do and does not require much training. It differs from sociodrama in that it does not utilize the many techniques of sociodrama, which widen and deepen the scope of the action, providing for a more profound learning experience. Simulation games also have their roots in sociodrama.

Sociodrama has developed primarily in terms of specific techniques and varied populations to fulfill Moreno's idea of healing all of mankind. At present, sociodrama is utilized in education, business, industry, psychotherapy, religion, spirituality, and theatre.

Author's Genesis

Antonina Garcia

In 1972, Nina, a theatre professor, was invited to train county and state police using role play. She enlisted college students to interact with police trainees in a variety of situations: family crisis intervention; sex crime investigation; dealing with suicidal people; managing those under the influence of drugs or alcohol; and safely handling motor vehicle stops.

The method used to train the police cadets was that they first heard lectures and read on the topics for the role plays. Then cadets were chosen to enter a scene (enacted by college students and police academy faculty). Their task was to appropriately intervene in the situation, calming the crisis, discovering what was occurring, making referrals if required by the circumstances, and making arrests if necessary. Afterwards, they discussed the experience and their behavior.

During the twelve years that Nina provided action training at the academies, the police consistently rated the role rehearsals as the most useful part of their training. As valuable as the role plays were, over time Nina began to feel that they could be doing so much more than they were doing, although she was not sure what that would look like.

Finally, in 1976, Nina began to study psychodrama and sociodrama and learned that sociodrama could offer far more enriching training opportunities and began to introduce some sociodramatic techniques into the police training provided. In 1978, she started offering a course in Sociodrama at Brookdale Community College. Since then her students have brought sociodrama to schools, mental health treatment centers, workshops for the developmentally disabled, the local youth detention center, their churches and synagogues and to department stores to train salespeople in customer relations.

After being certified as a Trainer, Educator and Practitioner by the American Board of Examiners in Psychodrama, Sociometry and Group Psychotherapy, Nina began to train professionals and students in sociodrama. These trainees have brought sociodrama to the settings mentioned above and have additionally used sociodrama in corporations, in psychotherapy, in the community to increase interracial tolerance, in senior centers, and in the training of rabbis.

In addition to training police, Nina has utilized sociodrama in a hospital for the chronically physically ill; with psychiatric patients in day treatment programs; with developmentally disabled children; with clients in psychotherapy; with youthful offenders in youth detention centers; and with members of the community wishing to explore racial intolerance. She has also used sociodrama to train teachers, juvenile justice workers, daycare workers, census interviewers, social workers, psychotherapists, and theatre practitioners. Sociodrama has applications for widely diverse populations and in practically any setting.

Patricia Sternberg

Pat Sternberg has been involved in drama and theatre for as long as she can remember. She began in a children's theatre herself when she was 11 years old and has been working in the field ever since. Like many of us, her career in drama therapy began long before there was an NADT.

She recalls her early years in New York directing a children's theatre with children ages 7 to 14. Local teachers began sending her children with reading problems. Pleased with those results, they sent her children with emotional problems. During those years she also founded and directed a community theatre. At that time Jacob L. Moreno was conducting psychodrama and sociodrama sessions at Town Hall. Some of the members of the troupe attended those sessions and shared many of the techniques with the group.

When she arrived in Philadelphia, she again taught drama but this time on a university level. At the same time, she continued her own academic studies. Her career as a drama therapist began seriously when she was hired at a psychiatric hospital to do drama therapy. There she worked under the supervision of two psychiatrists and a psychologist to create a program in the hospital for drama therapy. She continued her work there with adolescents at risk and further added to her experience in other venues by being brought in to train police officers dealing with domestic disputes and health care personnel dealing with dying patients and their families. She feels that sociodrama has provided a way to deal with all types of groups dealing with most every situation in the metaphorical sense.

Returning to New York in the mid-seventies as a professor of Theatre at Hunter College, she saw a demonstration of sociodrama led by Linda and Michael Gregoric dealing with their work in prisons. Pat recognized many of the techniques that she was using, not even knowing they were sociodrama techniques–role reversal, soliloquy, and future projection.

At that point she knew she wanted to know all there was to know about sociodrama and continued to study and learn all she could about the modality. At the same time she expanded her clinical work and research with psychiatric patients and substance abuse groups, doing drama therapy. Her clinical work continued and she added more techniques of sociodrama in dealing with adolescents-at-risk and with physically and emotionally-challenged groups.

DRAMA THERAPY FRAME OF REFERENCE

Basic Concepts

Spontaneity

Moreno believed that each of us is potentially a spontaneous, creative genius. He said that rather than focus on the worst aspects of human behavior, we should instead study the geniuses, artists, inventors and saints, those who achieve the highest of what it means to be human. Through this examination, social scientists can discover what the rest of us can do to develop ourselves as fully as possible. Thus, Moreno did not follow the medical model in relation to human growth, development, function and dysfunction. He believed that each of us is a work in progress and that psychotherapy and sociotherapy are methods for assisting people in their personal evolution.

In *The Future of Man's World,* he said, "Man must take his own fate and the fate of the universe in hand, on the level of creativity, as a creator. It is not sufficient if he tries to meet the situation by technical control–defense weapons–nor by political controls–world government–he should face himself and his society in statu nascendi and learn how to control the robot not after it is delivered, but before it is conceived (creatocracy) . . . . The future of man depends upon counter weapons developed by sociometry and sociatry." (21)

Moreno believed that functionality had to do with the degree of spontaneity and creativity the person engages in the playing of life roles in relation to both the self and others.

Moreno's Role Theory

Moreno began looking at roles and role relationships as early as 1913 in his work with prostitutes in Vienna.

He developed his role theory, which serves as the basis for using sociodrama. He defined role this way:

> Role can be defined as the actual and tangible forms which the self takes. We thus define the role as the functioning form the individual assumes in the specific moment he reacts to a specific situation in which other persons or objects are involved. The symbolic representation of this functioning form, perceived by the individual and others, is called the role. The form is created by past experiences and the cultural patterns of the society in which the individual lives, and may be satisfied by the specific type of his productivity. Every role is a fusion of private and collective elements. Every role has two sides, a private and a collective side. (as quoted in Fox, *The Essential Moreno,* p. 62)

Role is a unit of behavior that reflects socially agreed upon boundaries. These behaviors clustered together create the broader category called role. Roles are important to us as a society, since we often identify people by the roles they play. For example if a person says, "Jack is a police officer," we have a pretty clear idea of that role. We may ask for more details as to what Jack's specific job is as a police officer, but his role is clearly understood.

When we identify the people we know it is difficult to obtain any meaningful description of the person without considering his or her behavior. If I say, "Linda is a workaholic," what do I mean? Did that label come out of the blue? No, every time I see Linda, she is busy with at least two or three projects going at once. She is frequently called upon by others and is always willing to take on another task to help someone else. Her actions tell a lot about her personality. Looking at the roles others play, as well as those we ourselves play, goes a long way to help us understand ourselves.

Each of us plays many roles in our lives. Moreno pointed out that each role a person plays has two parts to it: a collective component and a private component. The collective component of the role is the common denominator or aspects of the role that are similar to all who play it. For example, Jack, Tom, and Barry are all police officers. All of them arrest suspects; all are proficient in the use of firearms; and all have concerns about being injured on duty. It is easy for them to converse with each other because they have the same frame of reference in role.

However, sooner or later they will probably begin discussing their own experiences. When that happens, they are moving from the collective to the private role components. It is the private component that distinguishes us in our own personal way. For example, Tom may work out of the 18th precinct and work on the beat, while the others work at the 20th precinct and ride in a patrol car. Jack especially likes lecturing kids in grammar schools on safety, while Barry feels he has a gift for intervening in domestic disputes.

Moreno felt, as the authors do, that as individuals we have much more in common than we have different. Beginning with those commonalities, or collective role components, group members can find a common ground on which to interact. In fact, communication, identification, and empathy are impossible in a group without people's recognition of collective role elements and, therefore, shared experience. Sociodrama emerges from that focus and explores in action aspects of our collective components. The focus of sociodrama is the group and the common threads of members' concerns.

Role Types: The Psychosomatic, The Social, and The Psychodramatic

Moreno further categorized roles into three types: the psychosomatic, the social, and the psychodramatic, or intrapsychic roles. The psychosomatic roles come first. Those are the physical roles that we see in newborn infants and continue in us throughout life, e.g., the eater, the crier, the eliminator. Moreno used the term psychosomatic to indicate a psychological connection with bodily functions. If a lightning flash frightens a child, he may cry out in fear. The crying out is a physical manifestation, while the response of fear is an emotional one.

Moreno noted that newborns are unable to differentiate between themselves and others. He felt that infants do not know where mother or father begin and they themselves end. The newborn is the center of his universe, experiencing himself as one with everything else in existence. In fact, Moreno termed this state the First Universe.

As the child interacts with those around him, he begins to develop social roles and an imaginary life that are independent of reality. At about two and a half, the child becomes aware of himself as a separate being. Moreno called this phase the Second Universe. The I and Thou are totally separate, and illusion and reality are recognized as two different phenomena.

Social roles come from our interaction with others: mother, father, doctor. The first social roles emerge slowly: the baby cries and the mother feeds him. The toddler smiles and the father plays with him. This action and response continues as we develop a sense of role reciprocity.

Psychodramatic roles are interior roles, such as the imaginer, the planner, the humorist. Among our psychodramatic roles are those which we play in our fantasy lives: the super hero, the prima ballerina, the baker, the novelist, the ruler of a new nation. These roles are important in our lives. We can imagine those roles and some perhaps are roles we would like to perform in the future.

Moreno noted that we are warmed up to different types of roles at different times in our lives. That realization can be important to the sociodrama leader. At times people may be more warmed up to psychodramatic roles rather than social roles. For example, the planner may be deeply involved with his next project, listening to his own inner dialogue and not listening to what his fellow group member is saying. At these times the leader can address those psychodramatic roles and bring the members back to group interaction by asking them to discuss what happens when distractions prevent them from focusing on what is occurring in the here and now. From this discussion a drama may emerge on managing distractions or scheduling time to devote to planning.

Role Taking, Role Playing and Role Creating

According to Moreno there are three ways of assuming roles: role taking, role playing, and role creating. *Role taking* is the most rigid or routine form. When someone role takes, he follows the parameters of a role exactly as the culture established it with little or no deviation. *Role playing* offers a greater degree of freedom and responsibility and implies comfort in role enactment. Finally, *Role creating* offers the highest degree of spontaneity and creativity. When a person role creates, she adds something new to that role or creates a totally different version of the role. For example, if one were to take the role of a substitute teacher, that teacher would follow the syllabus given to him verbatim (role taking). If he were role playing, he might switch the first topic on the syllabus to the third or add an item for discussion that was not included on the syllabus (role playing). However, if he were role creating, he might decide to forget the syllabus entirely and take the class in an entirely new direction with the material (role creating).

Every role that we play proficiently has aspects of all three: role taking, role playing and role creating. When we learn a new role we usually begin with role taking. As we learn the role more thoroughly and become comfortable in it, we move to role playing, and finally when we see a new way to perform that role, we move to role creating. The understanding of how we engage in various stages of role development can help us find satisfaction in what we do well and spark us to try new ways to play the role (role creation). Through sociodrama we can explore the various roles we play and experiment with new roles, thus increasing our role repertoire. We can examine and practice ways to play our life roles with greater flexibility and tap into our inner creativity in dealing with our own lives.

Sociometry

Sociometry is the measurement of social choices. Throughout our lives we constantly make choices, choices that join us with one person or group and choices that separate us. Some of our choices are visible to others, such as which social club or community action group we belong to, or with what group of friends we spend time. Other choices may be invisible to other people, such as who our favorite co-worker is or what political party we vote for.

Moreno was fascinated by this constant choice-making that goes on around us all the time. He was even more intrigued by visible and invisible networks of choice, connection and rejection. He noticed that a person has his own individual criteria for choosing, rejecting or remaining neutral to another person. Moreno developed the science of sociometry to study the circumstances and reasoning that motivate social choice. He further saw sociometry as an opportunity for providing direction in making positive changes in the future based upon what was uncovered through sociometric examination. In *Who Shall Survive?* Moreno says, "Sociometry deals with the mathematical study of psychological properties of populations, the experimental technique of and the results obtained by application of quantitative methods. This is undertaken through methods that inquire into the evolution and organization of groups and the position of individuals within them." (p. 51)

Sociometric Instruments: Sociogram and Spectrogram

Moreno developed several measuring instruments to map social choices and interrelationships among people, including the sociogram, the social barometer, the spectrogram and the social atom. The sociogram is a graphic representation of the social choices a group has made based upon a particular criterion. For example, a group may be asked, "With whom in the group do you have the most in common?" The sociogram can be written down or offered as an action sociogram. The director asks the group questions such as, "Who would you like to accompany you mountain climbing? Who would you ask to help you pick out a wedding present for your fiancée? Whom would you seek out to assist you in setting up a cooperative day care center?"

The action *spectrogram* is a sociometric device that measures what people "like most" and "like least." It gives the leader and the group a reading of the group's tenor of feeling at a given time. When administering it in action, one end of the room represents "like most" and the other end represents "like least." One is to imagine there is a line on the floor that goes from one end of the continuum to the other. The area in between represents gradations of the feelings between the two poles. In a group devoted to exploring the ramifications of technology in everyday life, the director might ask the group questions like, "How do you feel about using cellphones in restaurants or while driving?"

A variation of the spectrogram is the *social barometer*. This technique focuses on the group's feelings regarding social issues. Once again the continuum line is used, but this time one end represents, "Pro or Yes" while the other end represents "Con or No." Again, the director calls out questions but this time the questions are about social issues. For example, "How do you feel about prayer in the schools? Or welfare rights for noncitizens?"

In observing the interaction in the group and listening for the issues, the sociodrama director routinely employs sociometry. She encourages participation from all members of the group and values all contributions to the discussion. Group members see where others stand on certain issues, and lively discussions begin. Each of these sociometric devices mentioned above can serve as an excellent warm-up for a group. From there it becomes obvious which issues the group is warmed up to and what it is they want to explore in a sociodrama. Sociometric connections build through the enactment and continue to strengthen in the sharing segment of the group experience.

Theory of Spontaneity and Creativity

Moreno developed a theory of spontaneity and creativity that underlies the practice of sociodrama, the spontaneous enactment of group concerns. Creativity is the seed of the idea, and spontaneity is the get up and go that impels us to actualize the idea and give it life outside the mind. In *Who Shall Survive?* Moreno postulated that, "There were many more Beethovens born than the one who created the sonatas. However, although they may have had the ideas for a symphony, they did not have the spontaneity to actualize the idea." (p. 39) Thus, spontaneity and creativity are partners in moving us through life. When only one of them is operating, we become stuck. We either have the idea with no push to bring it to action or we are ready to move but cannot think what to do. Sociodrama helps people to gather the forces of spontaneity and creativity to utilize those partners in solving problems and finding new ways to play roles and view situations.

Moreno hypothesized that warm-up and cool down were necessary functions in life. In the morning, the alarm clock rings. As we wake up, we warm up to getting out of bed and begin a longer warm-up to our day by performing our daily wake-up routines. Many of us do not like it when our warm-up is broken by outside circumstances, as when we reach for the coffee in the cupboard, there is none left, and we need that coffee to wake up fully.

Throughout the day we warm up to various activities and cool down from those activities when they are ended. Moreno found the warming-up process to be integral to the spontaneity-creativity cycle. If either our spontaneity or creativity is blocked, we need to warm up to it. For example, say that a group is questioning how to manage anger. If they have had difficulties with anger management and have become explosive when angry, they may need to warm up to the desire (spontaneity) to handle the situation differently or they may need to generate ideas (creativity) for how to manage their anger differently.

People's reluctance in a group is viewed as connected with the warming up process rather than "resistance" to doing the work. In sociodrama the concept of resistance has no place. Moreno instead said that the person's warm-up is inadequate. This view takes away the pejorative aspects inherent in the concept of resistance that implies a certain willfulness that may in fact be absent.

The sociodramatist evaluates function or dysfunction in individuals and groups through testing the sociometry of the group and individual. How does a person play the roles he plays? What degree of spontaneity and creativity does he display? How warmed up is he to the roles he plays? If he states he wants to make shifts in his behavior, how warmed up is he to doing this? What is the nature of his role relationships with others in the group? How do group members relate to each other in particular circumstances? What interferes with their warm-up if their warm up is blocked? How warmed up are they to fulfilling the goals of the group?

The Sociodrama/Drama Therapy Interface

As the authors think about the similarities and differences between classic drama therapy and sociodrama, the similarities far outweigh the differences. In both, there is enactment of metaphorical, nonprivate materials. People are telling their personal stories through metaphor or role rather than directly playing out scenes from their lives. The enactments are issue-focused. The sessions are structured to provide a warming up to action and a cooling down segment with feedback, processing and/or sharing from group members.

The primary differences, as far as we can tell, are the following: In sociodrama, many action intervention techniques have been developed to facilitate the goals of the group, particularly in the warm-up and enactment phases of the session. These intervention strategies and techniques come primarily from Moreno and his followers and grow out of Moreno's theories. In drama therapy, the enactments employ more theatre-based interventions developed by many practitioners from a variety of theoretical frameworks. For example, one aspect of classic drama therapy is the creation of scripted works and their theatrical production, whereas, in sociodrama, enactments are wholly spontaneous and not scripted. Over the years there has been much cross-fertilization between drama therapists, psychodramatists and sociodramatists, so that many drama therapists integrate sociodrama and psychodrama techniques into their work routinely.

The Sociodramatic Process

Every sociodrama session has three components: the *warm-up,* the *enactment,* and the *sharing.*

Warm-up

The warm-up is the time when group members leave behind their extraneous concerns and focus on what is happening in the group at the time. During the warm up, issues emerge that the group wishes to explore.

In *Psychodrama: First Volume,* Moreno says, "This 'warming up' process of an entire group to a re-experience of a perennial social problem unsolvable by conventional means, as newspaper reporting, books, pamphlets, social casework, interviews, religious sermons, and so forth, is opening new roads for social therapeusis. It is inherent in the method that all phases of the sociodrama, even the most technical preparatory steps are initiated *within* the group situation and not outside of it. As nothing whatsoever is left out from observation and action, everything which happens is available to research and analysis." (p. 361)

During the warm-up the director (leader of the session) is observing connections among group members and is facilitating the building of connections where they are absent. She is also making interventions to bring in isolated or underactive members. She is listening for issues to which the group is warming up so that she may facilitate the group's exploring these issues later in action. She may help the group to move toward action by creating a structured warm-up or may facilitate group discussion of a topic brought up by a participant (unstructured warm-up).

In the course of the warm-up, group members will decide what issue they wish to explore and will decide upon a situation that illuminates that issue. Members volunteer to play roles in the enactment and choose a setting for the first scene. Once this occurs, the session moves to the enactment stage.

The Enactment

The enactment is characterized by the action of the sociodrama. The director readies participants to play their roles by interviewing them in role. She may also ask group members to contribute suggestions as to how the role should be played. After the enactors have received this warm-up to the specific situation of the drama, they spontaneously interact.

During the enactment the director utilizes various techniques to assist the group in accomplishing its goals. If, for example, she feels the characters need to develop empathy, she may call for a role reversal. Or if she sees that several members of the group have suggestions for the enactors regarding how to solve a problem, she may freeze the action, ask the enactors if they would be open to suggestions, and facilitate the interaction between audience and enactors. If group members wish to rehearse behavior, they may take turns, practicing in action, making corrections as they go along. Some examples of this are a group of patients from a day treatment center practicing job interview skills, or a lower functioning population practicing how to give a compliment or make a request for service.

The Sharing

After the enactment is complete, the sharing begins. The director asks the enactors what they were feeling in the role and/or what they learned from playing the role. This serves as an opportunity for the enactors to de-role as well to integrate back into the group. During the sharing, group members may express what they felt watching the enactment. Then the director asks them to relate what they learned from the enactment, to make suggestions for further enactments or the testing of alternate solutions, and to share their own experiences regarding the issue.

The sharing is not a time for criticizing the acting of the enactors in any way, nor is it a time for claiming that the portrayal was not true to life. If the latter occurs, the director may first point out that there are many ways to deal with a situation. Perhaps the dissenting person has a different way of doing so and would like to share it. This makes room for both the enactor's style of relating as well as that of the person criticizing his behavior.

Role of Director

Throughout the session the director's role is to assist in the group's warm up to each other and the issues emerging in the group. He must ensure a safe, nonjudgmental environment where people can express their thoughts and feelings with impunity, and where they feel comfortable enough to risk new learning. It is up to him to facilitate conflict resolution if it emerges in the group and to help build positive connections among members.

As the session draws to a close, he facilitates the cool-down of the group by helping members to share feelings. Then he helps them to share thoughts so that they may leave the room in a cognitive place rather than a raw, affective place. (For a lengthier discussion of application of techniques and how to conduct a sociodrama session and master skills, see Sternberg and Garcia's *Sociodrama: Who's in Your Shoes?* second edition)

Goals

Every sociodrama has three goals: catharsis, insight and role training. One or all three of these goals may be achieved through the enactment and/or sharing.

Catharsis

The term catharsis comes from the ancient Greek theatre. Aristotle defined the term in his book, Poetics, as the purging of the emotions of fear and pity. He used the term to describe the emotions the audience feels when they watch Oedipus Rex blind himself for the sin of marrying his mother and murdering his father. In sociodrama catharsis can occur both with the enactors participating in the session as well as with the audience observing.

Everyone has felt the relief from releasing pent up emotions after a good cry. That feeling is catharsis in one of its most common forms. Another familiar form of catharsis is the belly laugh.

Sometimes catharsis comes as a surprise to the participants who are unaware of their feelings, or who are holding a tight rein on those emotions dealing with a certain issue. The opportunity to express these feelings spontaneously offers an immediate relief to those involved. It also provides an opportunity for a better understanding of the specific emotions brought into play. Therefore, when an enactor expresses his emotions fully and achieves catharsis, he is freed to explore alternative solutions to the situation he faces.

Insight

Everyone has had that feeling of "Oh, now I understand!" That is the experience we call insight. It is that "Aha!" moment, when you understand the full meaning behind what you said or what someone else said to you. This new understanding usually gives us a different way of viewing or comprehending a problem. In sociodrama, however, because insight occurs with the whole body in action, it tends to be profound and thoroughgoing.

For example, a student comes to the director after a sociodrama in which he played the role of someone who was unheard by a co-worker and would not hear the requests of his co-worker. He says, "Now, I know how my wife feels when I say I have to go out with the guys. We're not really communicating with each other." Prior to this, they had simply tried to convince each other that each was right in his or her request, but they were not really listening to what the other was saying and meaning. As a result of his insight he later reported that he was able to have a full conversation with his wife and tell her how he felt about spending time with the old gang who goes out on Friday nights. It had nothing to do with her or with looking for women. "It's a thing with the guys," he said. When he went on to explain, she understood his need to spend time with his old friends, and he came to understand her need for companionship. They compromised. Now, he takes her out to dinner one Friday every month.

Role Training

Role training is a rehearsal for future life situations. We all practice role training in our heads. We say to ourselves, I'll say this, then he'll answer with . . . Then I'll say . . . We all feel a need to try out new behaviors and practice our actions before we encounter new or unfamiliar situations. But many of us do not have the option of practicing before stepping into a new environment. Moreno felt we should have that chance.

He advocated role training as a way of providing an opportunity for people to try on new roles and situations in a safe environment. Since sociodrama recreates those feelings and emotional reactions that occur in real life situations, role training offers a way to practice a variety of behaviors to meet any given situation. With the help of other group members, trainees can receive feedback on which areas of their behavior are most effective, or which action solves the problem most effectively. They can replay their actions until they feel comfortable in their role and confident that they are ready to meet whatever challenges come their way. Simply put, role training offers a rehearsal for life situations, for the desired behavior or action one chooses.

Role training in sociodrama serves many purposes, from rehearsing job interview techniques to dealing with a bomb threat in crisis intervention training. Most employee orientation classes use role training especially in those areas of the job where an employee has to deal with the public. Recognizing potential problems, difficult situations, and typical client questions can go a long way in creating confidence in the new employees as well as preparing them for possible problems that they may encounter.

While sociodrama can be and is used in psychotherapy, it can also be utilized in many other venues as was stated above. Moreno considered sociodrama to be more of a sociotherapeutic than a psychotherapeutic modality because sociodrama helps to heal the rifts between and among people not merely in the psychotherapy office but in other settings in the community as well. He felt that as sociodrama focuses on group issues rather than personal ones, it can go just about anywhere with positive results.

Sociodrama Techniques

Sociodrama and psychodrama share techniques although there are some differences in their uses.

Role Reversal

The concept of role reversal derives from perhaps the most brilliant of Moreno's observations. He recognized that most humans over the age of seven are capable of figuratively putting themselves in someone else's shoes and imagining what the other feels like in a given situation. People do this inside their heads all the time and request that others do it too: "Put yourself in my place. How do you think I feel?" What is especially noteworthy is that it occurred to Moreno that if one could reverse roles in one's mind and gain new understanding and empathy, much more could be gained by asking people to actually change physical places and their roles with each other.

As it turns out, the result of external role reversal (as opposed to that done in the mind) is profound. When an enactor reverses roles, he sees the world from the perspective of the other person. He can develop empathy and understanding. He can see himself as others see him. Routinely, after a sociodrama in which enactors have experienced role reversal, they report that they have gained new realizations, a broadening of understanding of others, a new compassion for others' behaviors and a new tolerance for others' viewpoints. They also say they were able to see a problem in a new light and, from the perspective of the other role, could generate new solutions.

When the director calls for a role reversal, two enactors switch places and exchange roles. This shift in space is essential to achieve the full benefits of the technique.

Enactor A says, "You never listen to me." The director says, "Reverse roles." After enactors A and B have reversed, the director instructs B to repeat the last line before the reversal. Enactor B (in A's role) says, "You never listen to me." This repetition of the last line is important because it picks up the action where it left off. It also offers an anchoring to the enactor who is speaking in the new role. Further, it reanchors, the audience and reminds them that Enactor A is playing B's role and vice versa.

Some of the reasons a director will use role reversal are:

- To increase understanding
- To develop empathy
- To facilitate insight
- To shift perspective
- To help the enactor see self in role as others see him or her
- To facilitate cool-down if the enactor is over-heated in role
- To increase spontaneity

A director may call for role reversal many times in a sociodrama. It should be mentioned that at the end of an enactment, enactors must be back in their original roles.

The Double

The concept of the double also derives from Moreno's observation of the way the human mind works. There are many times in life when we are conversing with someone and saying one thing while feeling another. We tell our boss, "Sure I do not mind staying late at work tonight," when we feel, "I'm exhausted! This is the third time in two weeks he asked me to stay late. How annoying!" Or we may say to our steady, "I really like you," when we feel, "I love you and want a more committed relationship."

Everyone has an inner voice. Moreno chose to invent a technique, the double, that is designed to externalize that voice so that everyone can hear it in a sociodrama. The double expresses the unexpressed thoughts and feelings of an enactor. The director or any member of the group can act as a double, for an enactor. In order to double, the person doubling stands to the side of and slightly behind the enactor in the drama. The double speaks the unspoken, and the enactor repeats what was said if it correctly reflects her feelings or corrects it if the expression is inaccurate. Although everyone in the drama can hear what is said by the double, it is a sociodramatic convention that one responds solely to the enactor who has repeated or corrected the double's statement. If you have several enactors and a few people doubling it becomes chaotic if everyone is responding to everyone else.

Sometimes a permanent double is assigned to an enactor as in a sociodrama about what a shy person experiences at a party where she does not know anyone. Sometimes there are several permanent doubles who interact with the main enactor as in a sociodrama in which a student is torn between one part of himself that wants to quit school and get a job; another part that wants to stay in college; and another part that wants to live in the wilderness. Each of the enactors playing the interior roles is a double.

The double has several functions. Here are some:

- To offer support
- To verbalize nonverbal gestures, movements, and sounds
- To maximize the feelings expressed by the enactor
- To question the self
- To make self-observations
- To provide sentence stems ("I feel -) that the enactor can complete as appropriate

Aside

This term comes directly from the theatre and is performed by an enactor in the same way that an actor in a play does it. When an enactor is thinking or feeling something that he wants to acknowledge but does not want to say directly to the other person in the enactment, he turns to the side and speaks, often starting with, "I would not tell her this, but . . ." The other enactor is to ignore the aside as if she never heard it being spoken.

Soliloquy

This term also comes from the theatre. The soliloquy is essentially a monologue in which an enactor speaks aloud his thoughts and feelings at some length. The soliloquy is sometimes used if the enactor seems confused, overwhelmed or stuck. The director may freeze the scene and ask him to step out of the scene for a moment and talk about how he is feeling and how he views what is happening in the drama. He may also ask the enactor to brainstorm aloud some solutions if the enactment is problem-focused. After the soliloquy the protagonist returns to the drama. In a drama about a family in denial about the mother's alcohol relapse, a teenager confronts the problem by challenging the mother about her drinking. An argument ensues with other family members supporting the mother and shouting down the teen. The director freezes the scene and takes each member of the family out of the drama one at a time to soliloquize about feelings and figure out what to do. After all soliloquies are complete, the action resumes.

Walk and Talk

In this technique, the director walks around the stage with the enactors one at a time and discusses with them the parameters of the roles they are to play. This helps the enactors to warm up to the roles, to develop the roles and to discuss the issues of the drama as the group wishes to explore them. For example, the director may ask the enactor playing the new employee how glad she is to be working for the company and how she likes her co-workers. If the group defined the issue as how to cope with sexual harassment, he may also ask how she felt when her supervisor asked her out for a drink after work.

The walk and talk most often occurs at the beginning of a drama, but it can also occur in the middle of the drama if the enactor loses spontaneity and gets stuck, overwhelmed or confused. The director takes the person out of the scene and walks and talks with him about the situation. If the enactor wants assistance from the group, the director may ask audience members to make suggestions for handling the problem in the scene. If the enactor playing the new employee cannot figure out how to deal with her supervisor's advances, she may walk and talk with the director, ask for and receive suggestions from the audience. When spontaneity is restored and she decides what she wants to do, she returns to the scene.

The walk and talk is also useful in conflict situations in which enactors are getting overheated. Freezing the action and taking the enactor out for a few minutes gives her a chance to cool down and think over the triggers for her highly-charged emotional reaction as well as to find new and more satisfactory approaches to the situation.

Empty Chair

A chair is put before the group or an enactor and they are to imagine that someone or some quality is in the chair. Group members are then instructed to speak to whomever or whatever is occupying the chair. For example, Benjamin Franklin is in the chair. The director may instruct the group to say something to him or to step in and occupy the chair for a moment and speak to the group from the role about what it was like to be a great inventor and great wit. One can also put an emotion in the chair (anger) or an abstraction (alcoholism).

Freeze Frame

This term comes from film vocabulary, meaning to stop the action on a single frame on the screen. In sociodrama there are times when we want to stop the action and view it as a tableau. The facilitator calls, "Freeze!" and the enactors do just that. This technique is used for a variety of situations. You may want to take an enactor out of the scene in order to use additional techniques such as soliloquy or walk and talk. Perhaps the structure of the action is lost because there are too many people in the scene all talking at once. You can freeze one area of the group and focus the action on another or you may call for a freeze and elicit audience reaction to the scene. "What do you see happening in this scene? What can they do to make things better?" Remind your audience that this is not a time to judge or analyze the acting of the participants but simply to observe and discuss the situation.

Concretization

A concretization is a literal portrayal of figurative or symbolic language or feelings. Often the director notices a physical response to something that is occurring in the sociodrama and asks the enactor to concretize the feelings she is experiencing. For example, if in a sociodrama Maria says, "I feel like I'm being pulled in two different directions," the director can ask two other enactors to take hold of Maria's arms and each pull her in opposite directions. Therefore, the statement of being pulled in two different directions becomes literally true and is made concrete by the action.

Sculpting

This term describes a living tableau scene. It is a kind of concretization of interrelationships. In a work-related sociodrama, Nick volunteers to be the manager, and Sally says she will play his overworked secretary. Jerry will be the desk clerk and Donna volunteers to be his assistant, who feels she is experiencing gender discrimination from the manager. Each takes a position in the tableau. As a further warm up for the enactors in their roles, the director asks each enactor to sculpt his co-workers in relation to themselves, placing each of the others in a position that symbolizes how they feel about the relationships. Donna places Nick very far away from her, while Nick places Donna on her knees next to Sally. Sally turns her back on them both, and Jerry places himself close to the manager.

Another use of sculpting is to stop the action when the enactors seem stuck or appear to have lost their spontaneity. The facilitator asks the enactor to sculpt the scene as it feels to him, or how he perceives the relationships or the emotional tone occurring in the scene. This technique works well for setting up the issue in a sociodrama.

Sculpting is also useful in setting up a sociodrama where internal voices are present: the studious self, the lazy self, the enthusiastic self, the stressed self. The enactors playing the internal roles can arrange themselves as they feel appropriate in relation to the role of the external person.

Mirror

The mirror is used to show the enactor how he looks and sounds to others. A player comes into the action and takes the enactor's place. He mirrors the enactor's verbal and nonverbal communication. The enactor steps out of the action and observes how the other player looks and sounds to others. This gives the enactor the opportunity to figure out what is going on in the situation and what he wants to do next.

Additionally, if the enactor displays an especially revealing body position, the director can take him out, and ask for a volunteer to assume that posture. The enactor is asked what she observes and how she interprets the body language. A word of caution when using this technique–direct the mirror to take the role of the enactor accurately and without stereotype, so that the enactor does not feel mocked or judged.

Future Projection

This technique takes the action to a future scene. This may be a scene in which the enactors play out their projection of what would happen if they were to continue on the same course in a conflictual situation or their fantasy of an ideal ending to the conflict. This gives them the opportunity to try out the scene the way they hope it will happen or wish for. It also offers the opportunity to play the scene in a way they fear it may happen, so they can respond in an appropriate manner.

For example, in a sociodrama regarding poor safety conditions in a work environment, Michael enacts a future projection in which he playfully approaches his boss about instituting new safety rules in the workplace. He then returns to the present scene, and practices other methods of encountering his boss about his concerns. Although the final action ends the way Michael hopes for, he had to overcome several obstacles put in his path by the enactor playing the boss in order to make a case for the value of the new rules. In this instance, future projection stimulated role training.

Role of the Drama Therapist in Sociodrama

The role of the drama therapist is to direct the sociodrama session, insuring the safety of all members. She is responsible for creating a comfortable, nonjudgmental environment in which members can feel free to express their thoughts and feelings openly. She needs to be cognizant of sociometry so that she can facilitate group process and move the group toward sociodramatic action that is group-centered and nonpersonal.

Frequently, deep feelings emerge in relation to issues enacted. It is important for the director to remember that all emotions are role related and that it is appropriate for feelings to arise if the chosen issue is affect-laden, as with euthanasia, abortion, and gun control. Ethically, she needs to uphold the contract and not switch over to psychodrama just because the group members are expressing strong feelings.

The director is also responsible for helping the group achieve its stated goals. In addition to facilitating the action segment of the session she assists the group in the process of integration of learned material after the drama has ended. When observing a skilled facilitator, the modality looks easy. The danger is that someone without training and sufficient knowledge of group dynamics and of her own limits may inflict harm unwittingly on others.

Populations Served

Because of the metaphorical nature of sociodrama, it is suitable for virtually any group. What is wonderful about sociodrama is that it can go just about anywhere since the focus is on group issues and common concerns rather than one person's story. It is appropriate as a modality for business, schools, churches and synagogues, psychotherapy, and for the community. It works well with both high and low functioning people, including the developmentally disabled, and people without vision or hearing, and those without speech or mobility (see the section on Case Examples).

Limitations, Challenges, and Growing Edge of This Approach

Sociodrama is by nature a group modality and is seldom done with individuals. At the other end of the spectrum it is challenging to find ways to manage extremely large groups in facilitating sociodrama. The logistics present a problem in mobilizing the entire group in an organized fashion.

It is our belief that the sociotherapeutic aspects of sociodrama will become particular areas of growth and study in the next decade. For example, the authors believe that sociodrama will become a staple intervention in conflict resolution programs. It will find greater usage in the training of trial lawyers, labor negotiators, managers and executives. More problem-solving skills groups will utilize sociodramatic techniques and more community-based groups will employ sociodrama to enhance positive connections among diverse elements of the population.

Sociodrama works in all kinds of milieus and with all kinds of people. The problem is that, like many other seemingly new things, people are often reluctant to try the unfamiliar, particularly if the word "drama" is part of the terminology. The question that arises is what practitioners will need to do to interest new populations in introducing sociodrama in their setting.

CASE EXAMPLES

Example One: Aphasia Group

Aphasia is a disorder in which a person is unable to understand and use the symbols that comprise language. It may occur as a result of a traumatic head injury, a cerebrovascular accident, or from some other brain disorder. Whether because of stroke, encephalitis, head injury, surgical accident, or whatever else, the patient who has lost his use of speech finds himself isolated. He is incapable of communicating in ways that were previously commonplace.

In addition to loss of speech, many aphasics experience other concomitant disabilities, such as paralysis of one side of the body or spasticity. Their inability to use both hands in addition to their difficulty in understanding language symbols makes it hard to teach them traditional sign language. Aphasics who are in long-term treatment facilities tend to interact primarily with staff. Interactions with other patients often seem to be minimal.

Adult aphasics, because of their communication problems, tend to be treated individually or allowed to passively participate in a group setting. While individual treatment is appropriate for redevelopment of speech skills and physical therapy, group-oriented approaches provide an opportunity to reduce feelings of isolation, helplessness, and withdrawal, while improving communication skills. The question is how to implement group sessions with people who cannot speak.

The Director of Occupational Therapy at a local hospital had some acquaintance with the value of sociodrama in improving communication skills and interpersonal competence. She approached the author (AG) to work with a group of aphasic patients who were long-term residents at this public hospital that housed people who were chronically physically ill. Most patients were elderly or confined to wheelchairs and had multiple disabilities.

The occupational therapy director and the author organized a group that was composed of aphasic patients, relatives of patients, and staff members. It was felt that staff members' presence was essential, since the entire patient population of the group was confined to wheelchairs, and except for one, the patients were incapable of moving their own chairs because of paralysis of a least one arm. The staff, in short, could move the chairs during exercises and enactments.

The OT director and the author (who led the group) also felt that staff members could provide verbal doubling and sharing, thus increasing the chances for group cohesion. Further, they could potentially take information about the aphasic patients' newly learned communication skills back to the rest of the staff. Two other members of the group were the mother of one patient and the daughter of another. The group members who were patients ranged in age from late 20s to 60s.

The author led two in-service sociodrama training sessions with hospital staff, doctors, nurses, occupational therapists, and medical technicians. These sessions were designed to acquaint the participants with basic sociodrama techniques so they could easily double for the patients and take roles if called upon to do so.

Goals of the Group

The goals of the group were to improve communications skills, promote patient interaction and venting, to train spontaneity, and to improve patient/patient and patient/staff relations.

Content of the Sessions

At the first session, everyone was given a 4" x 6" matte board name card and a choice of a colored felt tip pen. The leader asked the patients to choose a color that represented how they felt that day. Then she asked them to draw a picture or make lines or shapes that represented how they would like to be seen by the group. There was space on the cards for a drawing. After the drawings were completed, the leader walked around the circle, showing the first, which was a flower. Some members responded with sounds, gestures, and showing of cards to indicate that they, too, had drawn flowers. Someone suggested arranging the flowers on the floor in a circle. Next came abstracts; those were arranged as leaves. There were also human shapes, a tree and a butterfly to be fitted into the picture. Finally, the picture of a sun shining over all, and the group had begun the making of sociometric connections. To further feelings of connection, the leader asked the members to make gestures expressing how they felt. She asked the members to mirror the gestures. Later, members spontaneously added sounds to accompany the gestures and worked on changing the gestures and accompanying facial expressions to indicate various nuances of feeling.

In succeeding sessions patients continued to express, mirror, and double each other's feelings. As was mentioned earlier, chronic aphasics are thought to be unable to learn sign language because of their difficulty in symbolizing language. Also, most of the patients in the group had use of only one hand. Some also had impaired body image. Thus, if the leader said, "Put your hand on your chest," a patient might touch his leg. Nevertheless, since patients did seem to be able to be expressive through gesture, the leader sought to devise simple signs that the patients could accomplish and that could be understood and responded to in the closed system of the hospital.

After teaching the patients a sign for, "How do you feel?" the group divided into dyads to ask the question of a person whom they wanted to know better. They took in their partner's response, mirrored it and represented their partner's response to the whole group when the group reformed after the exercise. In later sessions, patients developed other signs to express feelings, I'm sad, I'm happy; make somatic statements I'm hungry; I'm sleepy, and finally developed a complete sign exchange: "Please give me a blanket which is over there. Thank you." Patients readily expressed negative as well as positive feelings and expressed relief at having an accepting forum for presenting themselves honestly in the moment.

Many of the sociodramas dealt with hospital issues. In every instance group members chose the subject for and parameters of the enactment: dealing with a noisy neighbor, making clear your need to use the lavatory and convincing staff to take you there; dealing with hospital administration relative to room changes; getting the love and support you need in a hospital. One, at holiday time, was a family meal sociodrama set in the past: patients enacted both a noisy family and a quiet family. One of the group's and the leader's favorite sociodramas took place when it was snowing outside. As everyone watched the ground grow whiter, people began to remember snowfalls of their childhood. The group decided to enact a drama about playing in the snow.

Sessions were held in a large space with large windows. All the patients were in wheelchairs. They designated one end of the room for the top of a hill. With wheelchairs as sleds and staff as wind to help push the sleds, the patients zoomed across the room, shouting, laughing, "talking" and holding on for dear life. They made snowballs and had a snowball fight and made a snowman. By the end of the sociodrama, their cheeks were as rosy as if they had actually been outside in the falling snow. What fun!

Throughout the group's life doubling was essential for adequate functioning. The leader and group members with any measure of speech doubled in all segments of the session. The members without words doubled nonverbally or through sound production. Those members who were doubled made very clear when they were doubled accurately and when they were not.

As the weeks went on, patients began to bring issues to the group that they wanted to work on. For example, the room change and family sociodramas were ones introduced by two patients who haltingly spoke and repeated, respectively, "Move me," and "Go home!"

During the last two of the seven weeks the group met, the members and dealt with termination issues. They reviewed signs they had learned, expressed their feelings regarding what the group meant to them, what they had learned, what sociometric connections they had made, what surprised them about belonging to the group, what expectations were met and unmet and how the members felt about the group's concluding.

Conclusions

It was the evaluation of the staff and patients alike that the group had been useful in decreasing feelings of isolation among the patients. This was further evidenced by patients going out of their way to greet each other and wait for a response, and by their gestures and sounds during sessions indicating that they felt the same as another patient in a given situation. This was in direct contrast to the beginning of the group life when patients related solely to staff one on one.

Staff and patients also noticed an increase in the repertoire of communication skills used by the patients. They also felt the sessions provided an opportunity for a safe and supportive environment in which to express feelings. This was further evidenced by both staff and patients, vocally and gesturally supporting the expression of each other's feelings.

Example Two: Health Care Professional Group

The following case study was conducted at a large metropolitan teaching hospital. There were 12 health care professionals who participated in the sociodrama group. However, the number at each session averaged between 8 and 10, since not all participants were able to leave their units during the time scheduled for the group.

Eight nurses, two male therapists, and two female administrators made up the group. Only six of the participants attended every session; eight attended three; ten attended two; and one only attended the initial session. The group met once a week for five weeks for two hours each session.

The sociodramatist (PS) met with the supervisor first for an initial meeting to discuss her needs and the needs of group before the sessions started and once again for an evaluation after the five sessions were completed. At that time there was an assessment of the value of this type of training.

The sessions scored exceptionally high and sociodrama was rated as one of the best instructional tools the hospital had ever employed. This assessment ranked sociodrama highly successful both from the attendees' point of view and the supervisor's. In the weeks that followed, feedback from the attending physicians further reinforced the positive value of the sociodrama experience for the participants. Doctors reported that nursing support to patients and their families had dramatically increased the comfort level on the unit.

Background and Brief Overview of the Sessions

The supervisor of nurses in a large metropolitan teaching hospital became concerned about the young nurses in training there. Those that worked on the oncology unit with young children were especially vulnerable to their own emotional reactions. Very often, talking to the parents or siblings of these young children was even harder than dealing with the patients. The times that were especially difficult for the student nurses were when the first cancer diagnosis was given or the estimated length of life left was first discussed with the families. That was the moment when everyone had to face the reality of a dying child.

The supervisor was pleased that her young charges were showing so much empathy for their patients and their families, but she was also fearful that they were becoming too emotionally involved with the situation to function as a source of strength in the situation. She knew from experience that one had to maintain a professional demeanor even when she felt like crying herself.

This balance between empathy and professionalism was vital for a nurse to be able to do her job on the unit adequately. Frequently, the nurse was the one who was in attendance after the doctor had broken the news to the family. She had to offer both sympathy and courage to the family members and frequently a shoulder to cry on. In order to do that, these nurses had to learn to put their own feelings on hold, while assisting others with their grief and/or denial. Nurses had to be strong enough to offer as much support as possible in the situation.

Although the main purpose was to help the young nurses deal with the feelings mentioned above, several of the other staff members, including some older nurses, chose to participate also. The first sociodrama the group chose to enact was set up primarily to offer role training, but a great deal of catharsis and insight occurred as well. During the sharing that first day, one question came up and was quickly echoed by several members of the group. "What do I say when a child asks me, 'Am I dying?' I know the old line that says, 'We're all dying,' but that's no answer. What do I say?" This question prompted a great deal of discussion among the group. Some answers given were: "No one can be sure of that;" "We're trying as hard as we can to keep you with us for as long as possible;" "The doctors and scientists are coming up with new drugs and treatments everyday. They may find one tomorrow for you too."

One insightful moment occurred during the next sociodrama session when one of the older male nurses played a young patient. "I do not want everyone walking around here like death warmed-over," he said. "I know I'm going to die, but let's do something with the days I have left?" In the sharing the nurse explained that he'd heard those lines or similar ones frequently over the years. "And they want to talk about it–about dying," he added. "They ask questions like, 'What happens when you go to heaven? How do you feel when you die?'"

One of the therapists agreed that he had heard those kinds of questions often from children on that unit. "Sometimes I think it's harder for us to talk about it than it is for them. They need to see we're not afraid to talk about it." Thanks to his comments, one of the young nurses had a new insight: "I never thought about it that way. I guess talking about the unknown makes it easier."

The third and fourth day's sociodramas moved in the direction of dealing with the families of the patients. One of the young nurses played a distraught mother. She adamantly denied that there was anything wrong with her child. "It's all a mistake," she said over and over again. When feelings were discussed later, everyone thought she was probably a mother herself. "I'm not yet," she said, "But I certainly felt like it in the sociodrama. It's amazing how you have all those real feelings when you are in a role."

Each succeeding day brought greater depth to the work and greater understanding among the participants. At the fifth and last session, in the sociodrama one of the young nurses volunteered to be the one to break the news to a young mother. She handled it with such compassion and strength, that after it was all over, during the sharing, one of the older nurses told her that she had handled the situation much more sensitively than many of those who had done it for years. "I really feel like I have gained tremendous insight into my own feelings and those of others," she said. "We are all so much alike and have so much in common."

REFERENCES

Boal, A. (1992). *Games for actors and non-actors.* Florence, KY: Routledge.
Boal, A. (1995). *The rainbow of desire: The Boal method of theatre and therapy.* Florence, KY: Routledge.
Boal, A. (1985). *Theatre of the oppressed.* New York: Theatre Communications Group.
Cossa, M., Fleischmann Ember, S., & Grover Hazelwood, L. (1996). *Acting out: The workbook: A guide to the development and presentation of issue-oriented, audience interactive, improvisational theatre.* Bristol, PA: Accelerated Development.
Fox, J. (Ed.). (1987). *The essential Moreno.* New York: Springer.
Gold, M. (1991). *The fictional family: In drama, education, and groupwork.* Springfield, IL: Charles C Thomas.
Moreno, J.L. (1985). *Psychodrama: First volume.* Ambler, PA: Beacon House, Inc.
Moreno, J.L. (1993). *Who shall survive?* (Student Edition). Roanoke, VA: Royal Publishing Co.
Moreno, J.L. (1947). *The future of man's world psychodrama, monograph 21.* New York: Beacon.
Rohd, M. (1998). *Theatre for community, conflict and dialogue: The hope is vital training manual.* Portsmouth, NH: Heinemann.
Sternberg, P., & Garcia, A. (2000). *Sociodrama: Who's in your shoes?* 2nd ed. Westport, CT: Praeger.
Sternberg, P. (1998). *Theatre for conflict resolution: In the classroom and beyond.* Portsmouth, NH: Heinemann.
Tomasulo, D. (1998). *Action methods in group psychotherapy: Practical aspects.* Bristol, PA: Accelerated Development.

Where to Go for Further Training in Sociodrama

For a complete list of certified Trainers, Educators, and Practitioners in Psychodrama, Sociometry and Group Psychotherapy, please write to:

American Board of Examiners in
Psychodrama, Sociometry, and
Group Psychotherapy
PO Box 15572
Washington, DC 20003-0572
or call (202) 483-0514

Training in Sociodrama is offered at Hunter College, New York City and at Brookdale Community College, Lincroft, New Jersey.

Chapter 11

RITUAL/THEATRE/THERAPY

THE HEALING POWER OF MYTH, RITUAL, SYMBOL AND ROLE IN THE PERFORMATIVE FRAME OF DRAMA THERAPY

STEPHEN SNOW

The therapeutic impact of performance is different from, and often greater than, process-oriented drama therapy. *Renée Emunah*

Persons in the psychotic episode tell us that they are participating in a ritual drama emerging spontaneously from the psychic depths. *John Weir Perry*

[creating the theatrical production gave the participants] opportunities to deconstruct the current disabling constructions and to reconstruct new and more powerful identities. *Amorim and Cavalcante*

GENESIS

The Ancestry of Therapeutic Ritual Drama

THEO WAS ONE OF THE MOST withdrawn patients I had ever observed on Ward 13. Then in his late twenties, he had been hospitalized, or in special schools, since the age of six. Very early on, he had been diagnosed as a paranoid schizophrenic of the chronic type. He was a dark, shadowy, sombre figure on the ward. During that period, he spent a large amount of time in the dayroom, sitting next to a table, with his head resting on his folded arms. In fact, when I first met him, he always had a mark on his forehead, which I assumed came from the impression made by holding his head on his folded arms for such a length of time. His eyes were deeply sunken in their sockets, and with his black shock of hair and goatee, he seemed like some kind of occult persona, with the look of someone like Edgar Allan Poe.

As might be expected, Theo was filled with fears and terrible hallucinations. He "saw" dead people hanging in trees, outside his window, on the hospital grounds. Once, he "saw" his father who died of cancer when Theo was five, standing in his closet, wearing a long cape, and peering out with the face of a cat. Theo believed the world was filled with vampires. He was very hypochondriacal, often making statements like "I have cancer in my chest" or "I have a tree in my brain." It was believed that he may have been molested by male staff in one of the special schools for emotionally disturbed children. In the least, he was highly homophobic. When he was 17, he tried to kill his mother by kicking and beating her, so he had been hospitalized on a chronic psychiatric unit since that time.

In April of 1988, after I had directed a ward play, entitled "New Faces of 1988," I first made contact with Theo. I cannot remember whether he first spoke to me or I to him, but I do recall he had a story or a "script" that he wanted to share with me. The more I listened to Theo's description of his tale, the more I became fascinated with it as an allegory of Theo's mental illness. We agreed to "make a movie" of this narrative, in which he would write the script and the songs, and also "star" as the central character.

I saw, right away, that this script represented a kind of ritual drama that came from Theo's psychopathology, but that it also contained his dream for a healthy life. So, I thought that it just might be therapeutic for Theo to embody this ritual drama through a video production, a "movie." Theo was extremely excited by this concept. I received the permission of the unit chief, who was also enthusiastic about the project, and we began the work on "Rocky Roads," also known as "Elvis Presley's 34th Film" (Theo was also very identified with Elvis, whom he considered a vampire–one of the "Undead"–and whom he had "incarnated" between 1954 and 1960). In brief, the script was framed as a dream, in which the hero, "Tom," (Theo) who leads a very normal life with his wife and child in their lovely country house with a white picket fence, falls into a dream state (Theo's psychotic world view). In his dream, Tom is captured by demons and taken to the "Kingdom of the Ancient Demon Worshipers of Rock 'N Roll." The "Demon god" asks Tom to sing for the multitudes in his kingdom. Tom does so and, then he awakens to find himself back in his '57 Chevy, with his dear wife, Beth, who tells him that he had fallen asleep for the past three hours. As the "movie" ends, they pull into the driveway of their pretty little house with the white picket fence.

The whole process of embodying, enacting and "catching" this ritual drama on film took well over a year. All the procedures involved with this production are much too complicated to go into here, but the effect on Theo was truly amazing. It was as if he suddenly came alive. He was always ready and prepared to play his role. His level of concentration was as good as many professional actors with whom I have worked. He constantly made very creative suggestions, many of which were incorporated into the work. He developed excellent connections with all the members of the production team; and this carried over into his forming some new relationships on the ward, for example, with the ward custodian whose "helper" he became. Theo was definitely no longer the withdrawn, seemingly fatigued figure, slumped over the table in the dayroom.

This was the beginning of my work in exploring the embodiment of ritual dramas, symbols and inner "mythology" of schizophrenic patients in drama therapy. I was, at that time, very influenced by David Read Johnson's work with schizophrenic patients at the Yale Psychiatric Institute and felt that my success with Theo was an exemplification of Johnson's perspective that:

> The nature of the drama, with its tolerance for the unreal and the imaginative, entices the inner self of the schizophrenic, which is occupied in fantasy, to reveal some part of itself. The patient finds he can explore with some freedom the various fragments of himself while, at the same time, actualizing them for others. In this way, the inner self makes contact with the world, and the individual's fantasies become part of objective existence. (Johnson in Schattner & Courtney, 1981, p. 60)

The process of this performance, this production, and how it related to the transformative power of the embodiment of symbols within ritual, seems linked to the historical background of ritual healing performances. For instance, one of the symbols that we actualized in the "movie" was the "Demon-god" or "Demon-king of Rock 'N Roll." Theo made a preliminary sketch of the face of this archetypal figure and then, the art therapist, who was part of the production team, collaborated with him on a design for a mask to be worn by the actor who played this role in the film (see Figure 11.1). All the talk about demons got us into a bit of hot water with other staff on the ward. One of the O.T.s took it all quite literally and perceived us as practicing some form of modern-day demonology. Although I truly regard my creative arts therapies work as taking place in what Penny Lewis calls the "transitional space of the imaginal realm" (1988, 1993), I have to admit my colleague on Ward 13, unawares, may have been pointing in the right direction.

Roots of Drama Therapy in Shamanism

After more than 20 years of studying the scholarship on and the traditions of shamanism, I am deeply convinced that drama therapy is based upon the essential structures of shamanic healing rituals, as they have evolved in human experience over the past 30,000 years or so. I will bypass the thorny questions in regards to cultural evolution and transmission of cultural knowledge and psychological structures that are implied in this point of view, and instead focus on the fundamental correlations between shamanism and drama therapy.

My first real insights into this relationship came with the reading of a cross-cultural study by Lucile Hoerr Charles, entitled *Drama in Shaman Exorcism,* in which the author clearly demonstrates that "the shaman's chief function in exorcism of the sick is psychotherapeutic; his method is dramatic" (1953, p. 97). The shaman's ritualized psychosomatic healing of the sick is, in fact, a performance that, according to Charles, includes:

> . . . impressive setting and lighting, costume and make-up, theatrical properties and sound effects . . . possession of or battle with the shaman by the spirits through ecstacy and frenzy which may be considered a supreme example of dramatic improvisation, often with elaborate use of voice, dialogue, and body pantomime . . . . (1953, p. 96)

I was, at that point in time, quite familiar with the literature that related shamanism to the origins of theatre and theatrical acting (Bates, 1987; Cole, 1975; Kirby, 1975; Schechner, 1973), but my real interest was the investigation into how and why the ritual performances of shamans were and are psychotherapeutic. Ellenberger's (1970) excellent essay on *The Ancestry of Dynamic Psychotherapy* was very helpful in this direction. Obviously, besides being a kind of protoactor, the shaman was also a protopsychotherapist. As I have written elsewhere (Snow, 1996b), roots of the use of dramatic means for psychotherapeutic purposes are very ancient. Another drama therapist, exploring similar territory, was able to articulate this concept quite succinctly: "Shamans seem to be aware of the fact that that which is performed in the imaginal world has a healing potential, while actors generally do not make much of this potential. In this regard, drama therapists may be more like shamans than actors" (Pendzik, 1988, p. 83). It seemed to me, also, that this realm of healing through dramatic ritual, which for *millenia* had been owned by shamanic practitioners, was being reclaimed, reconstructed and reconstituted by contemporary drama therapists.

Back to Demon Exorcism. I had been working therapeutically with the demon fantasies of a person with schizophrenia in a pre-

Figure 11.1. Mask Design for Ancient Demon-God of Rock 'n Roll. (Collaboration of Theo and Art Therapist, Samuel Sherrod)

sent-day psychiatric hospital. Meanwhile, the fundamental pattern that I was comprehending, from Charles and others, as the basis of shamanic healing was the exorcism of evil disease-causing spirits. "Exorcism" is, of course, an extraordinarily loaded term in our culture. Images of spinning heads and pea soup spray from horror films immediately come to mind. However, one only has to briefly peruse the ethnography of shamanism to realize how common the experiences of "possession" and "exorcism" are in tribal cultures.

According to Ellenberger's (1970) model of primitive disease theory, the two most common psychosomatic illnesses were "loss of soul" and "spirit intrusion." In regards to the first of these, he makes an intriguing comment:

> Could not the therapist who gives psychotherapy to a severely disoriented schizophrenic patient by trying to establish a contact with the remaining healthy parts of the personality and to reconstruct the ego be considered a modern successor to those shamans who set out to fol-

> low the tracks of a lost soul, trace it into the world of spirits, and fight against the malignant demons detaining it, and bring it back to the world of the living? (Ellenberger, 1970, p. 9)

"Spirit intrusion" is, of course, "possession." The entry of a disease-causing spirit into the soul of the sick person is a phenomenon reported on, worldwide, by shamans and ethnographers of shamanism (Halifax, 1982; Harner, 1980; Lommel, 1972; Shirokogoroff, 1935). However, in tribal societies, the two etiological concepts are often blurred; the quintessential idea is that a demon or malignant spirit has somehow "mastered" the spirit of the patient. Here is an eye-witness account of shamanism practiced amongst the Tungus in the early twentieth century:

> A man over forty is affected by an unknown spirit. He himself has made several attempts at shamanizing but . . . he cannot master the spirits, while the latter master him. The *performing* female shaman is a young but experienced shaman. The aim is to find what kind of spirit is doing harm. For the purpose, she introduces into herself spirits [she becomes possessed by her "helping spirits"]. By . . . *drumming* and *singing*–she brings herself into a state of ecstacy and the spirits enter her. Through her spirit the shaman wants to find the road to the spirit which affects the client. She goes [trance flight] to the yurt of the family . . . During the performance the shaman fell down several times at the moment when the spirit entered her [possession]. The people who were near her support her and lifted her up, just like a piece of wood . . . the body and limbs were rigid. Before the entry of the spirit, she increased the intensity of the *singing* and *drumming* and began to tremble; when she was travelling [her spirit], she jumped and beat the drum with great force. (*Mine,* Shirokogoroff, 1935, pp. 311–312)

Herein, we discover the image of the shaman as the *Master of Spirits* (Eliade, 1964) and the *Wounded Healer* (Halifax, 1982). But how can we locate this shamanic functioning in the practice of a modern drama therapist?

I have purposefully italicized words in order to emphasize that the shaman is utilizing a dramatic ritual performance to accomplish her therapeutic efficacy. I would like to point out a few key themes that begin to constitute a formula for shamanism as a precursor of drama therapy: (1) *The shaman is performing.* Kirby (1975) has clearly demonstrated how the shaman's therapeutic enactment is the beginning of theatrical role playing. Like the shaman, an actor can become possessed by his or her role (Bates, 1988); (2) *the healing ritual is a performance.* Drumming and singing are included in the example above; movement is also intimated. Charles (1953) also cites the use of puppets, masks, storytelling, ventriloquism and prestidigitation. Cole (1975) compares the "trance flight" of the shaman to a spiritual realm (an *illud tempus*) with the actor's entry into the mythological and symbolic work of the play script. In fact, Cole defines theatre by what he designates as the "rounding;" for the actor like the shaman must make a "trance flight" to a "spirit world," and allow him or herself to become possessed by the spirit of his or her role (1975, p. 15). The actor does this in service for the audience. In the example above, the shaman performs both functions ("trance flight" and "possession") in the service of healing her client, (3) *The shaman journeys in the imaginal realm,* (4) allows herself to become possessed without getting sick; and, ultimately (5) masters the disease-causing spirit through *a dramatic ritual performance.* All of this said, a pattern begins to emerge that directly correlates shamanic ritual performance with the performative frame of drama therapy (Figure 11.2). In this formulation, the structures and processes of ancient shamanism are paralleled with those of contemporary drama therapy, especially regarding the use of a ritual performance space.

SHAMANISM:

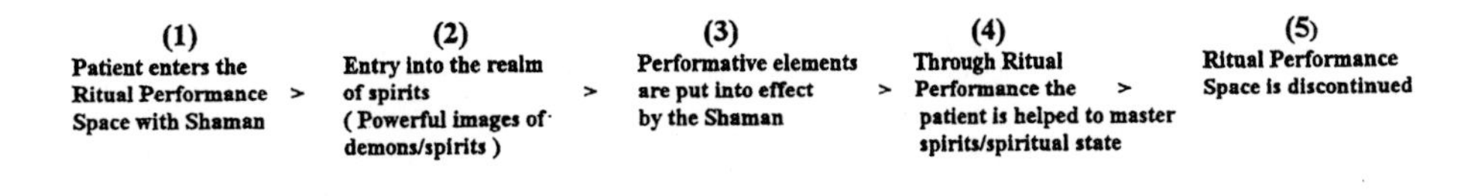

DRAMA THERAPY

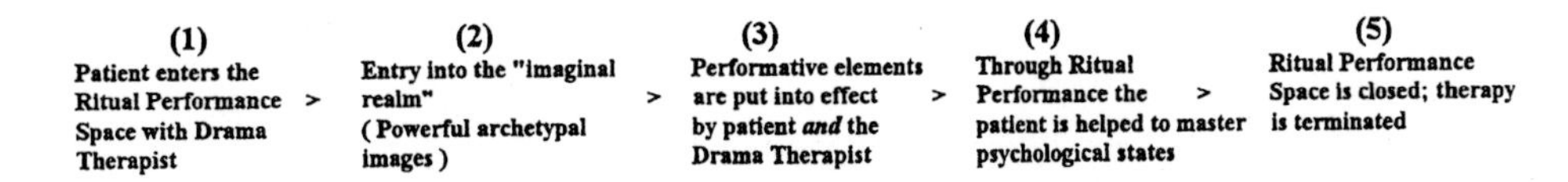

Figure 11.2. Ritual Performance in Shamanism and Drama Therapy.

The Theory of Archetypes

I would like to turn now to the contents that might be processed in such an imaginal realm. As R.D. Laing suggested many years ago, Jung certainly broke ground here in terms of the importance of myth and symbol in psychotherapy (1967, p. 168). As Jung himself wrote in *Symbols of transformation* (which, in fact, is a commentary on an analysis of a person in the "prodormal stages of schizophrenia")

> Modern psychology has the distinct advantage of having opened up a field of psychic phenomena which are themselves the matrix of all mythology–I mean dreams, visions fantasies, and delusional ideas. Here the psychologist not only finds numerous points of correspondence with myth motifs, but also has the invaluable opportunity to observe how such contents arise and to analyze their function in a living organism. (1959, p. 390)

Jung established his theory of the archetypal contents of the psyche, at least in part, based on observations he made early on in his career, of the psychotic ideation of schizophrenic patients ([1936] 1970). He postulated that in the depths of the human psyche there is a matrix of extraordinarily powerful symbols or symbol-engendering structures that have the potential to catalyze great transformations in the individual's experience of himself and the world. He states in *The Psychology of the Child Archetype:*

> Archetypes were, and still are, living psychic forces that demand to be taken seriously, and they have a strange way of making sure of their effect. Always they were the bringer of protection and salvation, and their violation has as its consequence the "perils of the soul" known to us from the psychology of primitives. Moreover, they are the infallible causes of neurotic and even psychotic disorders, behaving exactly like neglected or maltreated organs or organic functional systems. (In de Laszlo, 1958, p. 119)

In this same essay, Jung also describes the archetypes as "psychic organs"–I will pick up this theme, later–but, notice how the potentially "demonic" quality of the eruption of an archetype, like the shamanistic "disease-causing demon," might easily master the soul of the neurotic or psychotic individual. The course that an archetype imposes on an individual might well be described as a rite of passage and, for many Jungians, the process of psychotherapy is exactly that: a rite of passage that takes one into the depths of the unconscious and then out again; a death and rebirth, so well depicted in the famous mythological image of the "dark night sea journey." Barbara Sullivan, in her essay, *The Archetypal Foundation of the Therapeutic Process* equates the Jungian tradition with the "symbolic practices of primitive societies" and correlates these with Campbell's well-known model of the *Hero's Journey;* all three constituting ritual processes in which there is a psychological death and rebirth (in Schwartz-Salant & Stein, 1987).

John Weir Perry, a Jungian psychiatrist, has developed a formidable theory as to how and why ritual dramas are spontaneously played out in the psychotic episodes of persons with schizophrenia (1974, 1976, 1987). He discovered the parallels between the inner process of acute psychosis in his patients and the ancient Hebrew New Year's ritual (a basis for the messianic myth in the Judeo-Christian tradition). Perry designates this course as "the reconstitution process as deriving from the archaic ritual dramas of renewal" (Perry, 1974, p. 3). Through his research on this ritual tradition from the times of King David, Perry found this myth/ritual system to be filled with powerful archetypal symbols, including that of the "divine kingship" (later to become the image of "Christ the King"). He writes:

> These archetypal affect-images mobilized, governed, and directed the emotional energies of the people through their expression in dramatic form. As history moved on, however, the imagery changed and the role of the sacral king evolved into that of a particular kind of hero and savior. (Perry, 1974, p. 61)

Theatre Evolved From Dramatic Ritual

I was very fortunate during my graduate studies to have studied with Richard Schechner, and also for a brief time with Victor Turner. These two great scholar/writers helped me to gain an appreciation for the intricate ways in which ritual and the other performative modes in culture are interconnected. Schechner has written brilliantly about various kinds of cultural performances, including Asian and Native American ritual performances (1977, 1981, 1985). Schechner was, of course, very influenced by Turner (actually they mutually influenced each other up until the time of Turner's death in 1983). Both men were fascinated with the possibilities of "cultural transmission" and saw performance as a potential source for a "new transcultural communicative synthesis" (Turner, 1982, p. 19). Turner, of course, developed the concept of and coined the term for "liminality" (a term used, pervasively, today, by creative arts therapists, especially in relation to the concept of the therapeutic play space). Turner, himself, was very keen to identify ways in which the "liminal genres" of tribal societies were reflected in contemporary culture. As he wrote in From Ritual to Theatre:

> Just as when tribesmen make masks, disguise themselves as monsters, heap up disparate ritual symbols, invert and parody reality in myth and folk tale, so do the genres of industrial leisure, the theatre, poetry, novel . . . play with the factors of culture, sometimes assembling them in random, grotesque, improbable, surprising, shocking, usually experimental combinations. (1977, p. 40)

I see drama therapy as one of these "experimental combinations," deeply rooted in the healing traditions of ritual performance and shamanism. I have written elsewhere (Snow, 1996a) of my debt to

Schechner's development of what he calls "Turner's Talmud" on Van Gennep's conceptualization of the liminal phase of rites of passage and its connection to Bateson's "Play Frame" (Schechner, 1981, pp. 2–45). My own interest turned away from the analysis of cultural performances and, in the early 1980s, I began to focus on how ritual performance was used for healing. As in Perry's study, I was especially interested in how collective forms of ritual drama sometimes functioned as "community therapy" in certain cultures. I must have watched Bateson and Mead's *Trance and Dance in Bali,* their documentary film on a very special Balinese ritual dance drama, over 100 times! My essay, *Rangda: Archetype in Action in Balinese Dance-Drama* (1983) was an attempt to articulate how the archetype of the *Devouring Mother* (Rangda) operates psychologically in this ritual performance. It is clear from this documentary that, at least in the 1930s, this performance is still a very dynamic community ritual and, according to Bateson and Mead, the embodied archetype, the demonic Rangda, has the power to cause a large number of the ritual participants to fall into trance. This film made me very curious about how an embodied archetype in a ritual drama can affect both actors and audience in such a psychologically dynamic way. I became aware of psychologist Stephen Larsen's notion of the "mythic seizure," which is constituted by a deep emotional experience of what Perry has called the "archetypal-affect images." Larsen theorizes:

> The *mythic seizure,* sought in it terrifying immediacy as in shamanism, is still bound to forms of an orthodox mythological tradition. The relativity always accompanies contacts of the personal with the *numinous,* and produces those intensely private mythologies which are incomprehensible to others and are labeled as madness, is here constrained by the forms of the traditional mythology. (Larsen, 1976, p. 56)

Larsen is here speaking of Haitian Voudon, but he could just as easily be talking about the ritual performances of Rangda in Balinese culture, for the whole dance-drama is contextualized with traditional "Bali Hindu" mythology. Even from Bateson and Mead's film, it is possible to get a sense of how powerfully the dramatic embodiment of Rangda affects the participants–one might even say in a therapeutic way. For at the conclusion to this ritual enactment, audience and actors all appear to be relaxed and calm, as if they had been exorcised by their trance possession.

These were some of the experiences, some 15 years ago that began to point me in the direction of developing a form of ritual theatre therapy based on constructing and performing plays.

David Read Johnson and Renee Emunah have written about the therapeutic efficacy of theatrical performance (1983). These two pioneering drama therapists have investigated the significant effect that actually rehearsing and performing plays can have on the self-images of psychiatric patients. I was inspired by their work and in the mid to late '80s began to create therapeutic play productions in the psychiatric hospital where I was employed as a drama therapist (Snow, 1991, 1996b). Some of these were real explorations of *ritual dramas* that, in Perry's words, had emerged "spontaneously from the psychic depths" (1974, p. 54). I especially remember one performance that evolved out of a patient's story about an "Energy Creature." This central figure in the narrative was a kind of fairy tale archetypal image of an immortal being who could "appear and disappear anywhere in the universe at will . . .(with) no physical needs and . . . (who) will live as long as God" (Script A 1991). This being was locked and frozen (image of mental illness) in his own super high tech orbit, yet he yearned to become human (a metaphor for mental health). The Energy Creature, one day, lands in Central Park and a cast of characters (all played by psychiatric patients) debate the pros and cons in regards to living on planet Earth. In response to his request to do so, one of the characters responds "Are you crazy? Disease–Poverty–Homelessness–Drugs–Crime!" and goes on to enumerate all the undesirable qualities of life on Earth. Finally, after witnessing the gentle caring of two young lovers, the Energy Creature makes his decision. He decides to give it a try and, in that moment, he is transformed. Theatrically, in front of everyone, he was literally changed from his mechanical, computerized, robot-like suit to everyday normal street clothes. This moment was very moving to both the staff and patients in the audience, and they responded with a standing ovation for the patient/actors who created and performed this play, called "The Energy Creature and His Friends."

Here, an archetypal image was embodied and a metaphorical death and rebirth were enacted. The patient/actors had developed their performances out of improvisations on themes and images (some text was finally set for "raps" and "songs"), so, this experience fits within the model delineated by Emunah and Johnson:

> The self is the material of the creation, and the self is applauded. The impact on self-image is extraordinarily powerful. The fact that the achievement is shared with one's group of patient-actors strengthens and intensifies the impact. The reaction is one of exhilaration, pride and affirmation of identity. (1983, p. 236)

A shift in one's perception of one's self can be actualized through the performance, which almost always carries in its process the sense of a rite of passage. Fears must be overcome, obstacles surmounted and the threshold towards a new self-concept, potentially crossed. All of this can be enormously therapeutic for an individual who has been stigmatized with a mental health disability.

RITUAL/THEATRE/THERAPY FRAME OF REFERENCE

As Emunah states in her excellent textbook on drama therapy:

> . . . the other important dimension to drama therapy is public performance. Performance transforms notions about theatre and about therapy. The setting of the therapy scene changes from the closed room to the public stage; the cast changes from client and therapist to client/actor, therapist/director, and outside audience. The therapeutic impact of performance is different from, and often greater than, process-oriented drama therapy. (1994, p. 251)

Out of my own experiences producing therapeutic theatre over the past 15 years, and taking into consideration the therapeutic effects of the archetypal imagery evoked in the process of theatrical performance, I have delineated a model that demonstrates how and why the performative frame of drama therapy is "different from" and "often greater than" the process-oriented mode of drama therapy.

Basic Concepts

Health

The essential paradigm for mental health here is a Jungian one, based on the fundamental concept that health is wholeness or balance, especially in relationship to the archetypal components of the unconscious. Sullivan suggests that "the psyche rests on the archetypes" (in Schwartz-Salant & Stein, 1987, p. 27). The point of view taken is also in alignment with that of Neumann. "The archetypal structural elements of the psyche are psychic organs upon whose functioning the well-being of the individual depends, and whose injury has disastrous consequences" (Neumann, 1954, p. xv).

It is my belief that one of the reasons that the experience of theatrical performance is often innately healing is because it evokes the positive healing energies of the archetypes. This is congruent with Cole's theory concerning the actor's journey to and experience of the mythological realm of numinous symbols (Cole, 1975). Everything in performance-making is intensified because of this. Many of my former drama therapy students have told me how they intuited the healing function of theatre and how specific performances have served as therapy for them (a good number of them came to drama therapy from professional theatre). I believe that they are rediscovering what Bates calls the "Lost Tradition" in which "The shaman actor . . . in performance dips into the timeless ocean of human concerns, and intervenes in the conduct of life by incarnating the spirits and their wisdom" (1987, p. 23). Just making contact with this spiritual dimension can have a salubrious effect. However, many of the psychiatric patients with whom I have worked are extremely out of balance, sometimes being totally overwhelmed by such mythological content. In these cases, "the complexes take on in the unconscious an archaic-mythological character and an increasing numinosity through the enrichment of their contents, as can be easily observed in the case of schizophrenia (Jacobi, 1959, p. 11). Here there is the need to develop a very contained ritual drama of renewal in order to bring the client back into balance and help them to detach from the "mythic seizure" that possesses them. Thus, a great deal in this model depends upon the ego's relationship to the archetypes.

Another extremely important factor in mental well-being is the quality of the self-concept. Everyone who enters into the performative frame risks injury to their self-concept. This is especially true for individuals who have been highly stigmatized and marginalized by their society. As Emunah and Johnson (1983, p. 233) point out: "The negative self-images of psychiatric patients undermine the stability of every self-presentation, and make every interpersonal interaction a potentially dangerous event."

But in this very risk is also the potential for positive transformation of the self-concept.

Dysfunction and Spiritual Emergencies

In Jung's early writing on schizophrenia, he defines the grandiose delusions of his patients in terms of a compensatory function, related to profoundly wounded self-images ([1936] 1970, p. 136). Perry has further developed this perspective in his own work:

> From observing the behavior of the archetypal affect-images in schizophrenic episodes, the impression has grown on me that the syndrome revolves around the problem of self-image . . . the self-image of that of being faulty, undesirable, unworthy and unpromising . . . Close behind these feelings are the fantasy ones–from the compensatory archetypal affect-image–of being superlative, more than human, a genius, or a person of momentous importance in the world. Thus, when the personal self-image is severely debased–as it usually is in the pre-psychotic make-up–the archetypal image is in the same measure exalted. (1974, p. 26)

The patient who created the role of the Energy Creature saw himself as being omnipotent and immortal, having no limiting human needs and being able to live "as long as God." The great transforming symbol in the play was his de-roling from this grandiose state and accepting his human limitations.

Patients may present their fantasy material in very different styles, according to the nature of their psychopathology. Perry worked with first-onset psychotic episodes of persons with schizophrenia in their twenties or early thirties (1974, p. 25). I have worked with one schizo-affective patient (the same individual who created the Energy Creature) in a period of extreme decompensation (Snow, 1991, 1996a). In the case of Theo, his mythological fantasies were mostly long-term defenses, protecting him against any real contact with the world. Psychiatrist Stanislav Grof (1986) has discerned another type of psychotic state which he defines as a "spiritual emergency" or "transpersonal crisis." Often these are a kind of "shamanistic initiatory crisis." This is exactly how psychologist David Lukoff (1990, p. 26) describes his personal experience of a psychotic episode at the age of 23: "My shamanistic initiatory crisis awakened certain healing abilities in me that contribute to my work with psychotic patients." This type of intensive inner voyage is certainly not unlike that which Jung underwent, after his break with Freud, around 1912. It is why Laing points to Jung as having opened up the territory for exploring the organic healing process involved in contacting the archetypal domain of the psyche.

In terms of psychiatric rehabilitation, the drama therapist must work in consultation with the treatment team in order to determine a reliable assessment of the type of psychotic experience which a specific patient is undergoing. Many projective techniques, such as mask-making, puppets and scripting, can be utilized as assessment tools. Johnson has also developed an instrument based on improvisational role playing, which he calls the "Diagnostic Role-Playing Test" (1983).

In terms of developing performance as the therapeutic modality, understanding the nature of the damage to a client's self-concept is of paramount importance. This applies to all potential participants, not just those with severe psychopathologies. I borrow a very basic definition of self-concept from Ross (1992, p. 3): "the self-concept is no more than the concept a person has of him or herself. That concept represents how one thinks and feels about oneself–how one perceives oneself." This relates directly to the issue of self-esteem, for if one feels badly about oneself, then that individual has low self-esteem. This is especially true for persons who are members of a highly stigmatized group. As Fishman, Scott and Belof state in regards to individuals with intellectual and cognitive handicaps:

> . . . when someone is diagnosed as mentally retarded, he is thrust into a hall of mirrors. The label creates a special contact with other people: expectations are scaled down; people no longer call upon the retarded person to use daily skills that would ordinarily be expected were he not retarded. The way normal people assess and treat him affects his self-image. (Klepac, 1978, p. 343)

Another possible purpose for the performative frame in drama therapy is to improve the self-image of the patient/actor, through the construction and performance of a play, so at the end, like Emunah and Johnson's clients, they can say to the world: "See, I'm able!" (1983, p. 236).

The central notion here is to utilize the full force of a theatrical production as a vehicle for therapy. The intention of the performance is to help in the reconstruction of self-image through the various media of drama, including the final performance and cool down period. As Amorim and Cavalcante (1988, p. 154) describe in their process of developing a puppet play to be performed for the public by young adults with developmental disabilities, the whole procedure gave the participants "opportunities to deconstruct the current disabling constructions and to reconstruct new and more powerful identities."

Therapeutic Process

The essential formula for the use of the Ritual/Theatre/Therapy approach takes into consideration both the nature of the damage to self-concept and the dynamic of the relationship of ego to archetype (Figure 11.3). In the process of constructing the performance,

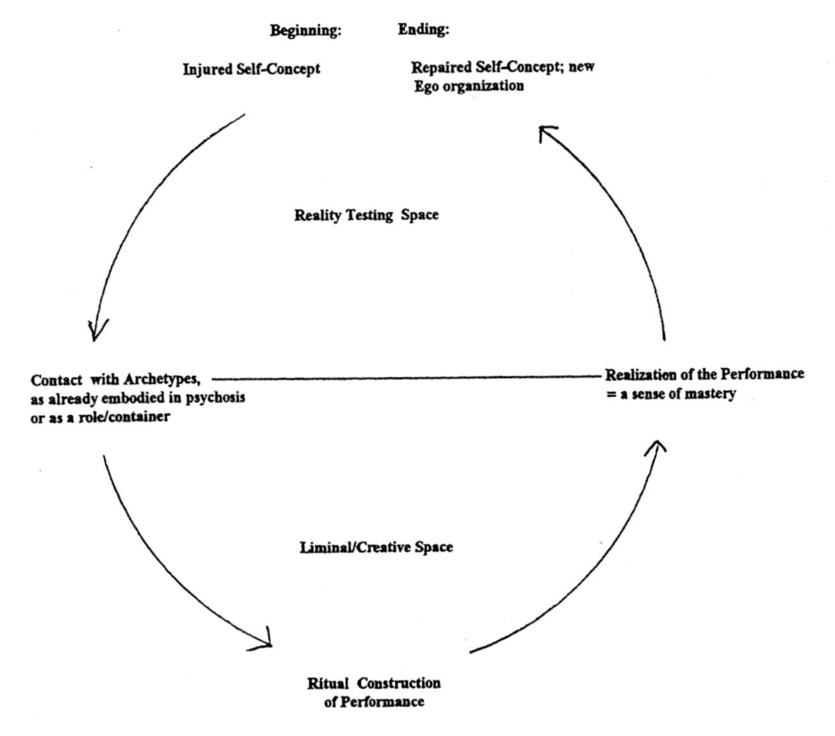

Figure 11.3. Therapeutic Formula for Ritual/Theatre/Therapy.

the injured self-image is put in contact with the archetypal image or story. There is an intention to help balance the relationship of ego and archetype, either by "working through" an embodied archetype (as in the case of persons in psychotic episodes) or by using an archetypal role as a catalyst to assist the client in developing a more positive self-image. Either way the ritual construction of the performance leads toward a sense of mastering, like the shamans who master the spirits, one's out-of-balance psychological state. The realization of the performance enhances this sense of mastery. As Emunah and Johnson comment: "Members usually sense the development of their self-images as a result of the group's work in rehearsal, but the brutal and exciting confrontation with the audience is seen as a confirmation of it" (1983, p. 236). Landy also helpfully points to the necessity of creating a support system for the patient/actors as they move through ritual performance process. He writes:

> . . . in order to facilitate the development of positive self-concept and social interaction through the theatre experience, the drama therapist must develop support groups both during and following the performance experience and must not lose sight of the therapeutic needs of the performers through focusing on the entertainment needs of the audience. (1986, p. 153)

Of course, having to focus on the "therapeutic needs of the performers" and other desideratum for the positive outcome of the performance (so that it will, in fact, have a beneficial effect on the actors' self-images) can put an inordinate degree of pressure on the therapist/director.

Reviewing the work of Emunah, Johnson, Landy and others, it seems that there are several prerequisites for performance to have maximum therapeutic effect:

- clients' therapeutic needs must be placed first and foremost *before* aesthetic or entertainment values
- all roles must be appropriate for the physical, psychological and emotional needs of the clients involved
- improvisationally-developed and self-revelatory performances hold the most therapeutic value
- support groups must be in place during and after the performance experience

Techniques

The whole spectrum of drama therapy techniques is available to the process of constructing a performance. The choice of methods, of course, depends on the intentions regarding the manipulation of "distance." Landy, who developed the theory of distancing for the field of drama therapy, writes: ". . . the drama therapist draws upon a wide range of psychodramatic and projective techniques that implies a variation of relationship between self and role, self and other" (1983, p. 175).

Mask Work, Scripting, and Puppets

I have used mask work to help embody a powerful archetype emerging from the patient's creative expression (Figure 11.1). I have guided the scripting process to help contain the overflow of psychotic ideation. With groups in geriatrics and psychiatric rehabilitation, and with developmentally disabled adults, I have employed puppets to establish contact or to set a frame of "aesthetic distance."

Psychodrama and Role Selection

I have utilized psychodramatic methods to help seniors process painful memories, and also to bring out blocked or repressed memories that might become the basis for scene work. Certainly, one of the major considerations is always the choice of role. When the right role is chosen really following the client's lead, its performance has the most likelihood of being a therapeutic experience. The right role helps to empower the client in a way that often brings balance to an otherwise chaotic, disorganized and conflicted personality.

Ritualization

Finally, a ritualization within the rehearsal-performance-closure process is another important issue. For persons with severe psychopathologies, ritualizing the time and space of the production helps gives structure and a sense of security. This can be as simple as using the same song to welcome everybody, each day, or to implement the same opening and closing exercises at every rehearsal. In a production with developmentally disabled adults, entitled "Oh! That Aladdin . . . ," the music therapist/musical director devised a wonderful, short welcoming song that always helped to promote the unity of the group. It became a kind of musically ritualized group identity. In the same production, the drama therapist/director instituted the same closure techniques at the end of each rehearsal. Participants will quickly show when they desire the repetition of such actions and when they prefer a change. For many, the repetition of activities in time and space is an important structure for them to experience the environment of the play production as safe and holding. I have written elsewhere of how the drama therapist needs to be a ritual specialist, especially in work with psychotic episodes, creating and sustaining a transitional space where clients can deconstruct and reconstruct themselves (Snow, 1996a).

Role of the Therapist

The role of the drama therapist in this performative frame is multifocal and multidimensional. The single most important function is integrating the therapeutic and the aesthetic, sacrificing neither for the other. The art product must become the context for an important experience of mastery for the client, and, at the same time, the "exquisite attention to the person"[1] must never be lost. The therapeutic process must constantly parallel the creative process, and sometimes be the same thing. To do this work effectively, it is to the advantage of the drama therapist to have a strong background in a number of areas: play directing, dramatic construction, and dramaturgy; comparative mythology and symbology, ritual theory and practice; psychodrama and sociodrama; videography; and, of course, improvisational role-playing.

Populations Served

This type of work is open to all populations. I have practiced therapeutic ritual performance, in different styles, with youth-at-risk, seniors, persons with mental health disabilities and persons with developmental disabilities. This is a very human process, with deep phylogenetic roots. As Joseph Campbell suggested, some years ago: "It has always been the prime function of mythology and rite to supply the symbols that carry the human spirit forward . . . In fact, it well may be that the very high incidence of neuroticism among ourselves follows from the decline among us of such an effective spiritual aid" (1949, p. 11).

Challenges

I have attempted to build a case for how Ritual/Theatre/Therapy can offer such a process, especially for persons with extremely wounded self-concepts. Perry has even suggested that such rituals of renewal will emerge spontaneously, when the psychic pressure is too great. In these situations, the drama therapist can serve as guide, facilitator and ritual specialist who helps the suffering individual to greater health through drama.

Probably, the greatest single challenge in doing therapy within the performative frame is the lack of time and focus to really allow for the working through process. In other words, it is important to not allow the client to get stuck in their defense mechanisms so that they use the ritual performance merely to recycle their repetition compulsion or the psychotic fantasies that form their psychotic prison. For instance, I thought I was making great progress–even incredible progress–with a psychiatric patient with a schizo-affective disorder. I had actually been his guide through a number of therapeutic performances. Without a doubt, he was replacing large areas of psychological disorganization and fragmentation with genuine creativity. He was out of the hospital, living on his own, and had even applied and been accepted to graduate school. Then, on his first day at his new graduate program, he completely decompensated. Recidivism is, of course, a kind of norm in psychiatric rehabilitation, but this really came as a shock to me, and I had to humbly admit that all my work with this patient had had only minimal effect. He

[1] A definition of therapeutic focus that was given by a member of a panel at the NADT Conference at Yale University, in 1995. I'm quite sure that this phrase was coined by Remi Barclay Bosseau, RDT.

could not seem to integrate and sustain new levels of balance and health.

Most of the work in the context of performative drama therapy is, by its very nature, brief therapy. How can it be expected to induce long-term structural changes in the personality? Perhaps all it can do is point the individual patient in the right direction. The short-term intensive work of creating a performance can be a boost to the individual's self-image, but an enduring restructuring of the personality takes a long period of working through (Epstein, 1995). However, there is some evidence to contradict this point of view. Mehl-Madronna clearly states his belief that short, intensive work, like three-day, all-day sessions, can produce more therapeutic results than a year of once or twice per week psychotherapy (1997). This model is closer to the kind of "crisis" intensity in the performative frame of drama therapy. At the Centre for the Arts in Human Development at Concordia University, in Montreal, where we conduct research on the effectiveness of the creative arts therapies in helping adults with developmental disabilities, it has been quantitatively demonstrated that, for some clients, the peak of therapeutic effectiveness during the year is when we produce our theatrical productions (D'Amico et al., 1999).

Summary

Why, then, is it possible for performative drama therapy to sometimes be more effective than process-oriented drama therapy? I believe it is because the intensity and concentration, which I just described as a possible weakness, can be also be a great strength, creating the frame for a very effective, focused rite of passage. The creative intensity of preparing and performing a piece of theatre offers a context for the kind of "liminality" that is conducive to the deconstruction and reconstruction of the personality; the performance offers a whole new role, and perhaps a whole new way of viewing life. Sometimes, that which is performed in the liminal, imaginal realm can get carried over into real life and be maintained as a new component of the personality. Such results of performances can definitely be described as the therapeutic consequences of this style of drama therapy.

CASE EXAMPLES

Psychotic Population

With the film production that actualized the mythic content of his fantasies, Theo became more energized and more socially interactive. His creativity and self-expression were enhanced, and he seemed to have less fear of the world. He co-wrote and acted in scenes; he wrote and sang seven original songs. His lyrics were plaintive, poignant, haunting. He seemed to be reaching out to the world, trying to make contact. The ritual performance of the film-making served as a bridge. The scenes were ritualistically enacted. For instance, in the role of the film's protagonist, "Tom," Theo was tied up by the demons, released, and then tied up again. Finally, sitting, bound with ropes on the top of a hill, he sang:

> I'm stuck on a mountain
> Dreaming of you . . .
> I'm stuck on a mountain
> Waiting for you . . .
> And if you ever dare
> You will see me there.
> Then, I'm stuck on the mountain
> Dreaming of you . . .
> (filmscript A)

A sense of Theo's inner landscape is embodied, exteriorized and frozen in time in this film. His performance has allowed him to objectify some small piece of his inner world. This contact, on the plane of fantasy, was repeated in the everyday reality of the ward, i.e., he made friends with the ward custodian. A little progress in a life that has been harshly isolated and profoundly defended by paranoid ideation.

Peter moved through a chaotic decompensation in which stereotypical images of grandiosity possessed his whole personality. He marched around the ward, proclaiming himself to be an Israeli fighter pilot, a cardiovascular surgeon and a Broadway producer. However, acting in the production of his own play script, he engaged in a ritual of renewal based on several of the archetypal motifs described by Perry. As the protagonist, he made a descent into hell to prove that the Devil (actually the Goddess of Love) was innocent. In the process of constructing this ritual performance, Peter became more organized, stopped the perpetual complaining about his symptoms and was able to activate some genuine talent as a writer. At the conclusion of the whole process of the play production, he was the most reality-oriented he had been in some time, and his delusions of grandeur had disappeared (Snow, 1996a).

Although these instances are only partial successes, they seem to suggest the potential efficacy of the performative drama therapy model defined in the previous section. The contact with and embodiment of the "archetypal affect-images" appear to guide these patients towards decreasing social isolation, better communication, increased reality testing and improvement of self-image through the completion of the task of performing what they have created. As Jacobi writes:

> The motifs of the archetypal images correspond to the part of man's make-up that is conditioned by phylogeny, and they are the same in all cultures. We find them recurring in all mythologies, fairy tales, religious traditions and mysteries . . . In every single individual psyche they can awaken new life, exert their magic power, and condense into a kind of 'individual mythology' . . . To open upon this store in one's own psyche, to awaken it to new life and integrate it with consciousness, means nothing less than to save the individual from his isolation and gather him into the eternal cosmic process . . . The archetype as the primal source of all human experience lies in the unconscious, whence it reaches into our lives. Thus it becomes imperative to resolve its projections, to raise it contents to consciousness. (1962, pp. 47–49)

For the individual possessed by the "mythic seizure," the embodiment of the archetype, framed in a ritual dramatic performance, can serve to structure and organize the psychotic experience that threatens to tear them apart. For the person who has had their self-image wounded by social stigmatization or neglect, the contact with the powerful archetypal symbols, especially when contained in the performance of a role, can lift them up and empower them.

Developmentally Disabled Population

Timothy had been an extremely abused child. Born with a developmental disability, he had been rejected by parents whom he had never known. He had been placed in a number of foster homes and, on several occasions, he was beaten by his supposed caretakers. By the time he was an adolescent, he was almost completely shutdown emotionally. When I first met him, he was terribly insecure, with a constant need to prove himself. However, I noticed he also had a genuine aesthetic sensibility and a real talent for dramatic improvisation. I cast him in the lead role in a production called "Oh! That Aladdin . . . ," the culmination of a drama workshop that was part of the "Drama Experiences for Special Populations" course at Concordia University. This course brought together 20 university students and 20 developmentally disabled adults.[2] I believe that Timothy's contact with the numinous symbols of the great Persian fairy tale, on which the play was based, had a truly transformative effect upon his self-image. This ancient story embodies the essential hero myth that is at the heart of so many of the classic fairy tales. As Bettelheim tells us, ". . . fairy stories represent in imaginative form what the process of healthy human development consists of . . ." (1977, p. 12). This story is particularly inspiring and hopeful. In the beginning, Aladdin is a selfish, little wretch, a "street rat," laughed at and scorned by his neighbors. However, through his own courage and hard work, he is elevated to the position of a prince. This story seems to be the perfect therapeutic vehicle for persons with developmental disabilities, who are often themselves the object of scorn and ridicule. Timothy was truly beautiful in this role. He paralleled Aladdin's bravery and industriousness with the enormous amount of hard work and commitment he put into developing his performance. This "subtext" played to the audience. In the first performance, in 1994, after Aladdin defeats the Evil Magician and wins back his princess, Timothy sang the following song:

I am someone
Can you see
I am someone
Special
I know someone
And its me
Someone very
Special
Maybe you
Know someone too
Someone who
Can say its true that
I am someone
And I see
You are special and I see
We are all so special
(Aladdin Script A 1994 lyrics by Roger Jay)

Although this was not the end of the play, the entire audience of about 400 people spontaneously stood up after the song was over, and gave Timothy and the cast a standing ovation. Five years later, Timothy reflected on this moment as a powerful validation of his personhood. He had been opened emotionally for singing through his work with the music therapist/musical director, in her role as vocal coach. The authenticity with which he sang this song was remarkable. The story of this hero, who begins in the gutter, perseveres and, finally, finds his true happiness showed Timothy that real change was possible in his own life. He states: "It shows that you're able to change the situation that you are in. You can actually reverse it, from being bad to being good. Show people you're actually capable of doing . . . by expressing yourself, telling or showing people" (Interview October 1999).

The standing ovation at the end of the song was a confirmation of the therapeutic exclamation: "See, I'm able!" Certainly, it imprinted that message in the consciousness of Timothy and the rest of the cast.

I would also suggest that this theatrical embodiment of the powerful archetypal symbols and meanings in Aladdin go far beyond the verification of capability, the "reality principle" which, in Bettelheim's view, stories like this make manifest: "fairy tales depict an ego integration which allows for appropriate satisfaction of id desires" (1977, p. 41). Genuine fairy tales can serve as powerful agents of healing. Well-known storyteller and author Clarissa Pinkola Estes made the claim that these stories are actually "medicine" (1992). In his essay on *The Phenomenology of the Spirit in Fairy Tales,* Jung describes

[2] Also known as the Aladdin Project (www.total.net/~aladdin/), this was the beginnings of the Centre for the Arts in Human Development at Concordia University (Montreal).

the "spiritual presence" of the archetypes of the Spirit in fairy tales and the life-enhancing power of these "affect-images" (in de Laszlo, 1958, pp. 61–112). This force is even more potent when the images are embodied through the drama. I think of Timothy in the "Cave of Wonders," that brilliant symbol for the unconscious, and how that symbol must have resonated with his own courageous adventure as a neophyte actor, his own exploration of himself as a hero. The experience of entering this role as the container for the archetypal motif of the hero's journey must have carried for Timothy a little of what Jung meant when he said, "Experience of the archetype is not only impressive, it seizes and possesses the whole personality, and is naturally productive of faith" (1959, p. 232). It surely provided Timothy with what Jacobi describes as ". . . awakening of new life," in experiencing a whole new sense of self.

Perhaps there is no more archetypal story among the modern-day fairy tales than L. Frank Baum's *The Wizard of Oz*. As Madonna Kolbenschlag writes in her wonderful book about the orphan archetype (1994): . . . "The Wizard of Oz is exceptionally endowed with an intuitive representation of both psychological and cultural myth–it has a power of metaphor and symbol that derives from unconscious rather than conscious design. Indeed, it is an extraordinary metaphor for transformation, and Dorothy is the classic archetype of the spiritual orphan." (p. 18)

The Oz books, especially the second, became the material for the first therapeutic theatre production at the Centre for the Arts in Human Development at Concordia University in Montreal. The image of the orphan swept up in a cyclone and carried on an incredible "hero's adventure" seemed to be another ideal vehicle for a therapeutic exploration via theatre. The orphan archetype has very great resonance for many of our developmentally disabled clients at the Centre.

We began our process with improvisations on images and themes in the story. I wanted to see what individuals would take to what characters and, also what kinds of imaginary additions might be made by the participants. I will report briefly on two successful examples of role-taking and how and why these roles were particularly therapeutically valuable for two individuals.

Autism

Jane was an extremely anxious person. Diagnosed with "autistic features" (there had been an earlier diagnosis of schizophrenia), she periodically had major panic attacks, even going so far as to strike herself in the face. She could become hysterical and scream and shout. Now she claims that her experience of participating in the play has made her a "calmer person." Interestingly, it was her creativity in improvisation that led us to discovering the central metaphor for our play production. Through improvisation, Jane created a new character, not found in the original stories of Oz. Her name was Winda, "Queen of the Wind." As director, I began to see how the image of the wind guided the whole story. Jane's contribution to the development of the production was essential and her invented character became a cornerstone of our new version, entitled "The Winds of Oz." Winda brought on the cyclone, blew the Wizard away in his hot air balloon and helped Dorothy return to Kansas. It was a very empowering role for Jane and she really enjoyed making a unique creative contribution to the ritual process of constructing the play. She reports in an interview (November 1997):

Q: Is there anything about the experience you think changed you?

A: It made me a calmer person . . . It made me happy, feel good, give a good performance, loving it so much, liking it.

Q: And that made you feel calm?

A: Yup.

Q: Would you like to do a play, again?

A: Yup. But not the Wind. I want to be Fire.

Jane has a wonderful sense of humor and this role gave her a chance to express herself (even to the point of improvising some very obscene puns concerning the wind). She felt very confirmed in her talents and uniqueness, and the experience of being in a symbolically empowered position.

Lack of Aggressive Impulse Control

Jacques was a person with a moderate degree of intellectual disability and some tendencies toward aggression. He had even been hospitalized for a brief time in a psychiatric institution because of this uncontrolled aggression. Jacques found the role of the Cowardly Lion, who, in our production, sang a Rock 'N Roll song about courage (all lyrics, music, dialogue is developed from scratch for these productions), to be an excellent vehicle for his personal development. The role served as a container for many of his strong feelings, and his rendition of "Courage" was genuinely one of the highlights of the show. In an interview (November 1997), he comments:

Q: Does it make you feel good after you've done all the hard work ?

A: Yeah. It makes me feel good.

Q: Would you like to do a play again?

A: Yeah. I'd like to do a play, again . . . A play is a lot of fun. You have to work very hard to be in a play. And I have to focus (points to his head) and say my lines. You have to focus on your Rock 'N Roll song and that's all.

So for Jacques and Jane, as well as Timothy, the role became a way to their own self-development, especially as it helped to ameliorate their negative self-images.

For those in our society who have been severely stigmatized, the applause at the end of a theatrical performance has a special meaning. As Emunah and Johnson (1983) have clearly demonstrated, performances can have a powerful positive impact on the self-images of performers. Emunah states elsewhere:

> For the actors, the sense of kinship and shared emotionality with the audience brings about a sense of connectedness. The connectedness is especially significant for those who have experienced themselves as different or alien, who have been institutionalized or segregated. The combination of the feelings of connectedness, accomplishment, and acceptance, in conjunction with the ensuing rush of love for one's fellow actors and director with whom one has shared the entire journey, is awesome. As the actors walk off stage, with the applause of the audience still flooding their ears, they experience a rare and sacred sensation: glory. (1994, p. 294)

This is the culmination of all the hard work and all the unique contributions that every individual has given to the production. It has been a journey, a rite of passage and the applause is a confirmation that it has all been worthwhile, and that the parts of oneself that one has shared with the world have been accepted.

CONCLUSION

The roots of the therapeutic uses of performance are ancient and go deep into the history of our collective human experience. Theatre has its origin in ritual, most especially in the shamanic dramatic rituals in which disease-causing spirits were embodied and exorcised. In many cultures, shamans were and are known as the "masters of spirits."

Actors who become possessed by the spirit of a character are also a kind of "master of spirits," but their function is aesthetic, educational or for the purpose of entertainment. As Pendzik (1988) has pointed out, drama therapists are more like shamans because we assist our clients to "master spirits" through the various media of drama and theatre. One approach is through performance, itself. I have defined this as the performative mode of drama therapy. Emunah (1994) has commented that the use of performance in drama therapy can at times be even more effective than "process-oriented drama therapy." This chapter has attempted to demonstrate a theoretical basis for why this is so, at least within a style of practice that I have developed over the past 15 years. One of my major themes has been to elucidate how the evocation and embodiment of archetypes in the construction and enactment of various kinds of performances can serve as healing ritual dramas for patient/actors. I believe that the spontaneous archetypal material that sometimes emerges in persons undergoing psychotic episodes can be contained and restructured through the process of performance-making. I also maintain that archetypically symbolic roles can serve as containers and assist to some degree in the reconstruction of wounded self-concepts. All of this, goes to show how performative drama therapy, within a Ritual/Theatre/Therapy context, is a viable means for effective therapy with many different populations.

Certainly, I am not the only drama therapist to use theatrical performance and theatrical methods to assist clients in developing themselves and to work through the pathological aspects of their personalities. The work of Emunah, Johnson and Landy has already been cited. I would also like to mention the important work of British drama therapist Steve Mitchell whose "Therapeutic Theatre" is modeled on the para-theatrical explorations of Grotowski (Mitchell in Jennings 1992; Mitchell, 1996, 1998). U.S. drama therapists Miller James and Cecilia Dintino have also effectively utilized theatre productions as therapy with veterans with posttraumatic stress disorder. Their essay, *Theatre and Trauma: An Object Relations Approach* is an excellent analysis of one performative style of drama therapy (James and Dintino, n.d.). Finally, my colleague and friend, the Canadian drama therapist Barbara Mackay has made use of ritual and performance in her work with different populations (Mackay, Gold, & Gold, 1987; Mackay in Gersice, 1996; Mackay, 1989).

As the field of drama therapy develops, increasingly refined perspectives and methodologies emerge in the use of drama as a therapeutic tool. I have attempted to articulate the context for and the application of my own particular approach to performative drama therapy. It is most surely still in a process of evolution. My hope is that my words will be both evocative and provocative for the reader: evoking the genuine powers of our ancient heritage in the human utilization of drama for healing, and provoking the reader to think deeply about how we can further develop the dramatic tools we have inherited for the future benefit of human beings in need of healing.

I am still very excited about the many ways in which performance and the development of theatre productions can be shaped as vehicles for therapy. I am presently very much looking forward to developing the next therapeutic theatre production for the Centre for the Arts in Human Development at Concordia University. I know that this work will be built on the Lewis Carroll material, *Alice in Wonderland* and *Through the Looking Glass,* and it will be related to both the Australian Aborigine concept of the "Dreamtime" and the real dreams, nighttime and daytime, of the clients of the Centre. I am looking forward to, once again, stepping into the theatrical "Cave of Wonders," to see what powerful symbols and characters may evolve as we create, together, a ritual of renewal via the construction of a dramatic performance.

REFERENCES

Amorim, A.C., & Cavalcante, F.G. (1992). Narrations of the self: Video production in a marginalized subculture. In S. McNamee, & K.J. Gergen (Eds.). *Therapy as social construction*. London: Sage Publications, Ltd.

Bates, B. (1988). *The way of the actor: A path to knowledge and power.* Boston: Shambhala.

Bettelheim, B. (1975). *The uses of enchantment: The meaning and importance of fairy tales.* New York: Vintage Books.

Campbell, J. (1949). *The hero with a thousand faces.* Princeton: Princeton University Press.

Charles, L.H. (1953). Drama in shaman exorcism. *Journal of American Folklore, 66,* 95–122.

Cole, D. (1975). *The theatrical event: A mythos, a vocabulary, a perspective.* Middletown, CT: Wesleyan University Press.

D'Amico, M., Barrafato, A., & Varga, S. (1998). The Centre for the Arts in Human Development. Unpublished progress report 1996–1998. Montreal: Concordia University.

Eliade, M. (1964). *Shamanism: Archaic techniques of ecstasy.* Princeton: Princeton University Press.

Ellenberger, H. (1970). *The discovery of the unconscious.* New York: Basic Books, Inc.

Emunah, R. (1994). *Acting for real: Drama therapy, process, technique and performance.* New York: Brunner/Mazel Publishers.

Emunah, R., & Johnson, D.R. (1983). The impact of theatrical performance on the self-images of psychiatric patients. *The Arts in Psychotherapy, 10,* 233–239.

Epstein, M. (1995). *Thoughts without a thinker: Psychotherapy from a Buddhist perspective.* New York: Basic Books.

Halifax, J. (1981). *Shaman: Wounded healer.* London: Thames and Hudson, Ltd.

Harner, M. (1980). *The way of the shaman: A guide to power and healing.* New York: Bantam Books.

Jacobi, J. (1962). *The psychology of C.G. Jung.* New Haven: Yale University Press.

Jacobi, J. (1959). *Complex/archetype/symbol in the psychology of C.G. Jung.* Princeton: Princeton University Press.

Johnson, D.R. (1988). The diagnostic role-playing test. *The Arts in Psychotherapy, 15,* 23–36.

Johnson, D.R. (1981). Drama therapy and the schizophrenic condition. In G. Schattner & R. Courtney (Eds). *Drama therapy, Vol. 2* (pp. 47–64). New York: Drama Book Specialists.

Jung, C.G. ([1936] 1970). *The psychology of dementia praecox.* New York: Johnson Reprint Corp.

Jung, C.G. ([1956] 1970). *Symbols of transformation.* Princeton: Princeton University Press.

Jung, C.G. (1958). The phenomenology of the spirit in fairy tales. In V. De Laszlo (Ed.). *Psyche & symbol.* (pp. 61–112). Garden City, NY: Doubleday Anchor Books.

Jung, C.G. (1958). The psychology of the child archetype. In V. De Laszlo (Ed.). *Psyche & symbol* (pp. 113–131).

Kirby, M. (1975). *The ur-drama: The origins of the theatre.* New York: New York University Press.

Klepac, R. (1978). Through the looking glass: Sociodrama and mentally retarded individuals. *Mental Retardation, 16* (5), 1343–345.

Kolbenschlag, M. (1994). *Lost in the land of Oz.* New York: Crossroad.

Landy, R. (1986). *Drama therapy: Concepts and practices.* Springfield, IL: Charles C Thomas.

Landy, R. (1983). The use of distancing in drama therapy. *The Arts in Psychotherapy, 10,* 175–185.

Laing, R.D. (1967). *The politics of experience.* New York: Ballantine Books.

Larsen, S. (1976). *The shaman's doorway: Opening the mythic imagination to contemporary consciousness.* New York: Harper Colophon Books.

Lewis, P. (1993). *Creative transformations: The healing power of the arts.* Wilmette, IL: Chiron Publications.

Lewis, P. (1988). Transformative process within the imaginal realm. *The Arts in Psychotherapy, 15* (4), 309–316.

Mackay, B. (1996). Brief drama therapy and the collective creation. In A. Gersie (Ed.) *Dramatic approaches to brief drama therapy* (pp. 161–174). London: Jessica Kingsley.

Mackay, B. (1989). Drama therapy with female victims of assault. *The Arts in Psychotherapy, 16,* 293–300.

Mackay, B. (1987). A pilot study in drama therapy with adolescent girls who have been sexually abused. *The Arts in Psychotherapy, 14,* 77–84.

Mehl-Madronna, L. (1997). *Coyote medicine.* New York: Scribner.

Mitchell, S. (1998). The theatre of self-expression. *Dramatherapy, 20* (1), Spring 1998.

Mitchell, S. (Ed.). (1996). *Dramatherapy clinical studies.* London: Jessica Kingsley.

Mitchell, S. (1992). Therapeutic theatre. In S. Jennings (Ed.) *Dramatherapy: Theory and practice, 2* (pp. 51–67). London: Routledge.

Neumann, E. (1954). *The origins and history of consciousness.* Princeton: Princeton University Press.

Pinkola Estes, C. (1992). *Women who run with the wolves: Myths and stories of the wild women archetype.* New York: Ballantine Books.

Pendzik, S. (1988). Drama therapy as a form of modern shamanism. *Journal of Transpersonal Psychology, 20* (1), 81–92.

Perry, J.W. ([1953] 1987). *The self in psychotic process: Its symbolization in schizophrenia.* Texas: Spring Publications, Inc.

Perry, J.W. (1976). *Roots of the renewal process in myth and madness.* San Francisco: Jossey-Bass.

Perry, J.W. (1974). *The far side of madness.* Englewood Cliffs, NJ: Prentice-Hall, Inc.

Ross, A. (1992). *The sense of self: Research and theory.* New York: Springer Publishing Company.

Schechner, R. (1985). *Between theatre and anthropology.* Philadelphia: University of Pennsylvania Press.

Schechner, R. (1981). Restoration of behavior. *Studies in Visual Communication, 7* (3), 2–45.

Schechner, R. (1977). *Essays in performance theory 1970–1976.* New York: Drama Book Specialists.

Sullivan, B. (1987). The archetypal foundation of the therapeutic process. In N. Schwartz-Salant & M. Stein (Eds.), *Archetypal processes in psychotherapy.* Wilmette, IL: Chiron Press.

Snow, S. (1996a). Focusing on mythic imagery in brief drama therapy with psychotic individuals. In A. Gersie (Ed.), *Dramatic approaches to brief therapy* (pp. 216–235). London: Jessica Kingsley.

Snow, S. (1996b). Fruit of the same tree: A response to Kedem-Tahar and Kellermann's comparison of psychodrama and drama therapy. *The Arts in Psychotherapy, 23* (3), 199–205.

Snow, S. (1991). Working creatively with the symbolic process of the schizophrenic patient in drama therapy. In G. Wilson (Ed.) *Psychology and the performing arts* (pp. 2161–268). Amsterdam: Swets & Zeitlinger.

Snow, S. (1983). Rangda: archetype in action in Balinese dance drama. In J. Redman (Ed.) *Themes in drama 5* (pp. 273–291). Cambridge: Cambridge University Press.

Turner, V. (1982). *From ritual to theatre: The human seriousness of play.* New York: Performing Arts Journal Publications.

BIBLIOGRAPHY

Scripts

Filmscript A. (1988). *Rocky Roads.* Bronx Psychiatric Centre. Bronx, New York.

Playscript A. (1990). *The Energy Creature and His Friends.* Bronx Psychiatric Centre, Bronx, New York.

Aladdin Script A. (1994). The Centre for the Arts in Human Development. Concordia University, Montreal. Lyrics by Roger Jay.

Videography

Documentary: The Centre for the Arts in Human Development at Concordia University. Producers: Frank Roop and Stephen Snow. Montreal, 1996.

Archival: *Oh! That Aladdin.* 1994, 1995. Concordia University, Montreal.

Archival: *The Winds of Oz.* 1997, 1998. Concordia University, Montreal.

Interviews

Audio taped interview with *Timothy,* October 30, 1999, Montreal.

Videotaped interview with *Jane,* November 8, 1997, Montreal.

Videotaped interview with *Jacques,* November 8, 1997, Montreal.

FURTHER TRAINING

Stephen Snow, Ph.D., RDT/BCT is Associate Professor of Creative Arts Therapies, Coordinator of Graduate Drama Therapy and Director of the Centre for the Arts in Human Development at Concordia University in Montreal:

Concordia University
1455 de Maisonnueve Blvd. West
Montreal, Quebec H3G 1M8

Phone: 514-848-4641 Fax: 514-848-8626
ssnow@alcor.concordia.ca

Chapter 12

HITTING THE BULL'S EYE: THE STOP-GAP METHOD

Don R. Laffoon and Sherry Diamond

The STOP-GAP Institute is a professional, community based nonprofit theatre company dedicated to the use of interactive theatre as an educational and therapeutic tool to positively impact individual lives. STOP-GAP's vision to help individuals explore their range of roles, choices and alternatives is realized through The STOP-GAP Institute's three primary program components:

- Drama Therapy Sessions serving a variety of special populations
- Interactive Touring Plays serving both youth and adults
- Institute Training Programs providing training

This chapter will focus on The STOP-GAP Method of Drama Therapy as applied in programs serving the needs of battered women and their children, children with life-threatening illness, youth sheltered due to abuse and neglect, people recovering from alcohol and chemical dependency, gay and lesbian homeless street youth and other client groups.

GENESIS

During the late 1970s, there was a great deal of discussion and debate about the pending graying of America. Veterans of World War II were becoming senior citizens and the baby boomers would soon follow resulting in unprecedented numbers of older adults. Clearly, there would be a need, not only to serve older adults, but to facilitate what would surely be difficult transitions for individuals, families and indeed, entire communities.

STOP-GAP co-founders Don R. Laffoon and Victoria Bryan believed that theatre had the power to change people's lives. Their vision was to create a theatre-based process utilizing professional actors and theatre artists that engaged seniors in a way that provided a means for them to communicate their concerns and express their feelings; an opportunity that would surely be lacking in a social structure so ill-equipped to serve them. In short: create a theatre company and a theatre process that was ultimately therapeutic.

The name STOP-GAP began as an acronym: Senior Theatre Outreach Program for Growth and Aging Problems. STOP-GAP's earliest programs took place in a wide variety of settings such as senior adult daycare centers, nutrition sites, convalescent hospitals, even bingo halls. The original ensemble of seven members reflected STOP-GAP's commitment to working across the life span with company member ages ranging from 24 to more than 70 years old. The combined expertise among company members included music, storytelling, acting, playwriting, directing, pantomime, design, photography and psychology. STOP-GAP's mission then was to use these theatre techniques to build bridges of communication between generations, to reintegrate families and communities and to explore the creative potential of all individuals regardless of age, circumstance or disability (Laffoon et al., 1985).

In its early days, STOP-GAP explored several different theatre-based formats including script-in-hand plays, set design through visual art, and formalized discussion. STOP-GAP also tried various forms of creative dramatics, improvisation, and performance, eventually devising a process called "thera-play," before solidifying and refining what today has become known as The STOP-GAP Method.

A precursor to The STOP-GAP Method, thera-play, was a brief issue-oriented play designed so that one or more of the clients could be involved as characters. Client participation generated tremendous investment from the rest of the group and gave clients an opportunity to rehearse real-life scenarios within the safe confines of dramatic distance (Laffoon et al., 1985). Because clients were often intimidated by the prospect of performance–and because of the astounding insights achieved when clients freely dialogued–improvisation became the natural foundation for STOP-GAP's quickly evolving process.

While the groups of older adults with whom STOP-GAP worked varied greatly in terms of their health, interests, socioeconomic status, ethnicity and age–there were far more shared concerns than there were differences. They were troubled by issues surrounding independence, identity and changing family roles. Whether or not they had children, there were mutual concerns about young people. They worried about the future, about economic conditions and their own vulnerability. They also shared a reluctance to talk about these issues and many confessed to feeling a kind of powerlessness.

They responded to STOP-GAP's techniques and processes with remarkable enthusiasm, interest and insight. The techniques STOP-GAP was developing and using provided an opportunity for increased clarity and objectivity, a chance to view situations similar to their own in a safe and nonthreatening manner. More importantly, STOP-GAP was providing these older adults a process through which to explore possibilities–a significant consideration for many who believed they were without choices (Laffoon et al., in press).

As STOP-GAP processed the work with the senior clients, their families and staff at the sites, it became apparent that the techniques being used with this client group would have similar benefit to other populations. STOP-GAP fined-tuned its process, and redefined its goals and its mission to include using theatre as a therapeutic tool to positively impact individual lives.

While STOP-GAP's techniques have evolved considerably since its inception in 1978, the work continues to be guided by the same fundamental principles and values. Today, STOP-GAP collaborates with a variety of community agencies serving special populations by designing customized one-time interactive theatre pieces to meet specific goals, offering a repertory of interactive plays exploring particular issues and providing ongoing drama therapy programs in day treatment settings, recovery programs, and shelters (Laffoon et al., in press).

The STOP-GAP Institute provides for the training of STOP-GAP's repertory company, the development of its interactive touring plays, special presentations and performances, customized training programs for schools, corporations and other organizations as well as responds to community needs in a comprehensive way. In addition, The STOP-GAP Institute offers alternate route training in drama therapy for qualified candidates interested in pursuing their registration as a drama therapist and provides continuing education units for licensed clinicians (MFT/LCSW).

DRAMA THERAPY FRAME OF REFERENCE

Basic Concepts

Person-Centered Philosophy

The STOP-GAP Method is guided by a philosophy that is rooted in person-centered therapy. Developed by Carl Rogers, the person-centered approach to therapy is experiential and relationship-oriented (Corey, 1991). Person-centered therapy is not a rigid construct. It is more of a belief system. It is an attitude that is revealed within the therapist-client relationship. Person-centered therapy values the subjective experience of the client and seeks to explore the client's perception and work from within it.

According to Corey, person-centered therapy aims to create an environment of safety for clients that encourages and supports self-exploration. This enables clients to identify obstacles to personal growth and experience aspects of self that were previously denied or unclear. Person-centered therapy encourages clients toward openness and an increased trust in the self, increased awareness and the experiencing and expressing of feelings.

The capacity for self-awareness–the ability to recognize a feeling as it is experienced–is a critical factor in achieving psychological insight. Those who are more in touch with their feelings are inclined toward greater self-assuredness in personal decision-making and are likely to be in greater control of their life direction (Goleman, 1995). To this end, STOP-GAP aims to facilitate clients' exploration of personal feelings.

The STOP-GAP Method and the philosophy on which it is based is client-centered, interactive and grounded in mutual respect. Many of the client groups with whom STOP-GAP works feel defeated, devalued and dehumanized (Laffoon et al., in press). Through a specific style of improvisation and a person-centered approach to therapy, the STOP-GAP team, consisting of two professional actors and the drama therapist all working from The STOP-GAP Method, offers these individuals a voice, an opportunity to be acknowledged, respected and empowered. The STOP-GAP Method of Drama Therapy provides the means to gain insight and understanding in a way that is safe, nonthreatening and *fun*. Through its interactive approach, it provides a platform to speak and be heard, a feature that is all too often lacking in the lives of individuals seeking therapy. Dignity, respect and personal empowerment is at the heart of the STOP-GAP philosophy (Laffoon et al., in press).

The STOP-GAP Method of Drama Therapy relies entirely upon the client group's input, their ideas, opinions and most importantly their feelings about the characters and situations developed for the improvisations. Every program is interactive, with each client involved up to the extent s/he is willing. Clients are never asked or required to do anything they do not want to do. This respect for the client's personal space and boundaries not only promote a sense of personal safety but lays the groundwork for client empowerment and choice-making.

Client involvement can mean stepping into a role play but can also include giving direction for what will happen next in a scene or identifying what was really going on in a scene, that is, what the characters were feeling and thinking. That the clients themselves build the scenes enables them to contribute to the fullest extent possible and comfortable for them. If the client, for whatever reason–physical or emotional–is unable to come to the "stage area" (STOP-GAP never uses an actual stage)–the role play will come to the client. It is the involvement of the clients that is key. This interactive quality is integral to the STOP-GAP philosophy and the Method (Laffoon et al., in press).

Another component of the STOP-GAP philosophy is to "Listen to the Experts." Central to the person-centered approach is the active listening, clarification and reflection of clients' feelings by the therapist. Also key to person-centered therapy is the contention that the therapist is not the final authority–the one with all the answers subjecting clients to their mandate. Rather, the person-centered approach to therapy holds clients as ultimately responsible for accomplishing and maintaining their therapeutic goals (Corey, 1991).

The STOP-GAP Method holds that the clients themselves are the experts. Only a battered woman fully grasps the terror inherent in domestic violence. Only a recovering addict can know the insidious nature of chemical dependency. STOP-GAP holds that it would be inappropriate, indeed disrespectful, to presume to understand and know how important issues affect other people's lives. STOP-GAP talks with the clients and more importantly, The STOP-GAP Method is to *listen* to what they have to say and reflect or incorporate those comments and feelings through the scenes.

The STOP-GAP philosophy does not impose value systems and ideas, but rather, the philosophy is to *expose* them. STOP-GAP does not judge. STOP-GAP is not there to "fix" anyone. The STOP-GAP philosophy contends that we cannot change others, we can only change ourselves. STOP-GAP believes there is power in choice and urges each client to consider his or her own choices rather than what choices s/he would like others to make. STOP-GAP's intent is to use theatre to stimulate dialogue about issues relevant to particular populations, clarify feelings and explore options (Laffoon et al., in press).

Many of the groups STOP-GAP works with feel victimized, powerless and without choices. In a climate of safety, clients come to realize there are other possibilities. The STOP-GAP Method identifies and explores just what those possibilities might be. The person-centered approach does not solve problems–it facilitates a process of personal growth enabling clients to better cope with current circumstances as well as effectively address future setbacks (Corey, 1991).

The strengths of the person-centered approach to therapy underscore the philosophy on which The STOP-GAP Method is founded. Person-centered therapy holds the client in the highest regard, respecting the client's values with warmth and sincerity. Person-centered therapy holds as integral components active listening, reflection of feelings, a nonjudgmental attitude, empathy and a willingness to allow the client to determine the issues to be explored. Person-centered therapy emphasizes safety and a noninterventionist style that facilitates and encourages personal growth (Rogers, 1961).

The STOP-GAP philosophy espouses mutual respect for both the client and the STOP-GAP team, an emphasis on client input and opinion, a fierce dedication to working toward the needs of the client and facilitating clients' capacity to assume personal responsibility, develop appropriate assertiveness skills and a heightened awareness of feelings.

Both person-centered therapy and The STOP-GAP Method provide clients the opportunity to be truly listened to without fear of being judged or shamed. Each provides a rare opportunity to experiment with new behaviors–a chance to *rehearse for life*.

Improvisation

The roots of improvisation are the roots of accessibility. The origin of improvisation involved the development of theatrical entertainment for the common man rather than the aristocracy. The improvised performances were played in venues open to large audiences such as festivals and fairs attended by the working class. Early improvisation involved the development of stock characters that were roles its street audience identified with (Tanner, 1982). Today, contemporary forms of improvisation continue to demonstrate the capacity of the genre to engage audiences from all walks of life with astonishing immediacy.

STOP-GAP's early experimentation with various theatre forms revealed a greater level of client involvement when provided the opportunity to dialogue freely and openly through improvisation. It can be a powerful experience to achieve catharsis in prewritten material, but STOP-GAP found the process and the insights more meaningful for clients when the subconscious revealed itself through the spontaneity of improvisation. STOP-GAP believes improvisation–making it up as we go along–is the best definition for life.

The Role of the Therapist

Consistent with the person-centered approach the role of the drama therapist is to set a tone that is supportive and noninvasive. The drama therapist creates a climate conducive to growth and free expression through a genuine show of caring, acceptance, understanding, and above all, mutual respect. The drama therapist serves as a conduit between the clients and the playing out of their perceptions, the concretizing of their views and feelings. As such, the drama therapist becomes an instrument for client validation, affirmation and empowerment.

The role of the drama therapist is to listen, clarify and reflect the feelings, ideas and opinions of the clients. The STOP-GAP Method, like person-centered therapy, does not utilize assessments or other diagnostic tools. There are no case histories, interviews or invasive questions. There very simply are the clients from whom the presenting issues are elicited, and the STOP-GAP team to reflect those issues through improvised scenes.

Therapeutic Process

Who-What-Where Cards

In STOP-GAP drama therapy sessions, the clients themselves identify the issues for the drama therapy session. STOP-GAP has developed a methodology for the drama therapist to draw these issues from the clients in a way that is anonymous and nonthreatening. This process involves the use of "WHO-WHAT-WHERE" cards, that allow clients to identify characters (significant persons in their lives) and situations occurring between them from their life experience–past, present or future–that they would like to see role-played. They may indicate any two characters (WHO) on their card. Examples include spouses/partners, friends, parents, children, employers, siblings, teachers, doctors, counselors, even God–anyone who may impact their lives. The situation (WHAT) described should briefly identify what's going on between the two characters. Is there some confusion, a disagreement? Does one of the characters need advice about something? Is there something the client wonders about, that keeps him/her awake at night? The card also asks for WHERE the situation is taking place. This could be someplace specific such as the kitchen or a bar, or someplace quite ambiguous such as the future or "inside my head."

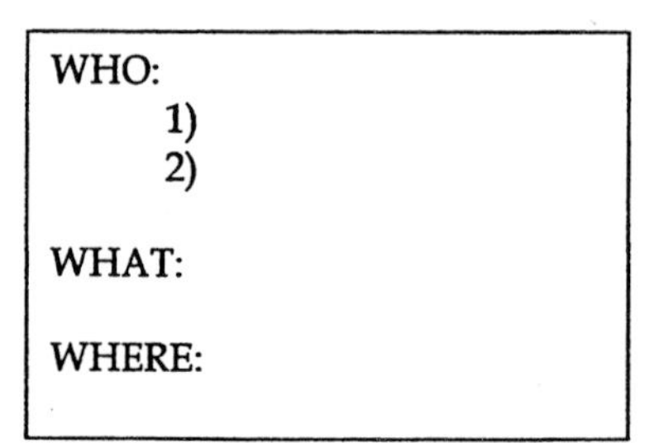
WHO:
1)
2)

WHAT:

WHERE:

Figure 12.1.

Using these cards as a springboard, the drama therapist guides the STOP-GAP actors in improvised scenes using input from the group to develop characters (including fictitious names and details) and identify their feelings. The facilitator stops the scene at crucial moments or key points to explore the feelings and behaviors of the characters and to stimulate dialogue among the participants about the characters' choices.

When a client chooses, he or she may step into a role and become part of the action. In this way clients may discover new perspectives and insights while receiving the support and encouragement from their peers as well as the STOP-GAP team as they role play situations that mirror their own lives. The STOP-GAP Method of Drama Therapy provides clients the chance to practice facing the issues and significant people in their lives in a safe and supportive atmosphere. Most importantly, clients have an opportunity to play and *experience* the role of VICTOR rather than the role of victim.

STOP-GAP Improvisational Method

The STOP-GAP Method of Drama Therapy consists of the use of a specific style of improvisation involving five distinct components. The five components of The STOP-GAP Method are:

- Make the Menu
- Focus on Feelings
- Cut to the Chase
- Swing the Pendulum
- Hit the Bull's Eye

A typical STOP-GAP drama therapy session, includes two professional actors (members of STOP-GAP's repertory company), who under the guidance of a registered drama therapist, role play scenes using these five components based on the clients' experiences as indicated on the cards (Laffoon et al., in press).

Make the Menu

Make the Menu consists of the drama therapist leading the clients in suggesting characters, lines, situations, reasons for the situation, how each of the characters are feeling (see Focus on Feelings) and a first line for a character to say. This process lays the foundation for client involvement. It is through Making the Menu that clients become actively involved in the development of the improvisations that will ultimately tell their story. The more invested in the process the clients are the more engaged they remain throughout the session and the more interested they are in the outcome. More importantly, Making the Menu introduces the concept of choice (expressing opinions and preferences) and empowerment (having those preferences heard and honored) for the clients (Laffoon et al., in press).

The process of Making the Menu also creates an opportunity for clients to interact and establish rapport with one another and with the drama therapist. This process also reveals for the drama therapist the group dynamics at work and roles the clients have already chosen or been habituated to playing.

Acting as a conduit between the clients' perceptions and what will ultimately be the concretizing of those perceptions, the drama therapist will be most active in guiding the clients through Making the Menu. The actors however must listen to, and act on the responses of the clients. The STOP-GAP Institute trains its actors to listen to the responses, the names, places and relationships and repeat them if they are unclear. If the drama therapist asks for a first line, the actor must repeat that line exactly as it was spoken. Hearing their thoughts, their views, indeed their exact words validates and affirms clients whose experience it has been to be ignored or patronized. Again, STOP-GAP is not there to judge or teach, but to stimulate thought-provoking dialogue that explores the complexities of relationships and feelings, and elicits alternatives for the effective communication of those feelings and the making of healthful choices (Laffoon et al., in press).

Focus on Feelings

According to Rogers (1961), experiencing feelings is a discovery of that which makes up the self. In *On Becoming a Person,* Rogers states, "In our daily lives there are a thousand and one reasons for not letting ourselves experience our attitudes fully, reasons from our past, and from the present, reasons that reside within the social situation. It seems too dangerous, too potentially damaging, to experience them freely and fully. But in the safety of the therapeutic relationship, they can be experienced fully, clear to the limit of what they are" (p. 111).

The STOP-GAP Method holds there is a universal language of feelings–joy, sadness, fear, loneliness, compassion, etc. The question is what do we do with those feelings; how do we sift through layer upon layer of conflicting and confusing feelings. By creating scenes that focus on characters that either mask or distort their feelings or behave ineffectively or inappropriately, clients are able to recognize their own feelings and gain insight into the feelings of others. Many of the clients with whom STOP-GAP works have become habituated to minimizing their feelings or discounting them altogether, often for the sake of others. This Focus on Feelings of the characters creates an opportunity for clients to consider their personal feelings (often for the first time) and express them safely through the characters (Laffoon et al., in press).

Battered women, for example, have been denied their feelings and have learned to reject them in order to survive. People recovering from substance abuse have made a fine art of hiding, avoiding and masking their feelings. Focus on Feelings creates an opportunity for clients to begin the journey toward honesty and self-discovery.

Cut to the Chase

Cut to the Chase refers to the use of shortcuts to explain what the clients already know about the situation being role played. For example, "You know the trouble I'm having with my husband," sums up what has been established by the group and gets immediately to the crux of the issue. In The STOP-GAP Method of improvisation, a lengthy build-up is not necessary–we know the characters, we know the situation–these were agreed upon during Making the Menu and Focus on Feelings. We want to explore the dynamic existing between the characters. We want to know where the scene is going.

If the actors need more information about their character or the situation, they find out before the scene begins by asking very direct questions such as "What is my character feeling?" or "Has this happened before?" Getting information from the clients can help to focus their attention; getting to the point quickly helps to maintain it (Laffoon et al., in press).

Besides promoting good theatre however, Cut to the Chase plays a much more critical role. It discourages avoidance behavior. It prevents clients from over intellectualizing an issue or from spinning off on tangents in an effort to steer the focus away from the uncomfortable, away from the feelings.

Swing the Pendulum

To take the opposing point of view best defines Swing the Pendulum. Strong conflict lies at the heart of drama. Indeed, strong conflict often lies at the heart of dysfunction. Two characters in agreement will never make a good dramatic scene. The best scene will come from two characters having strongly opposing or contradictory views, or between a character that is absolutely certain and one who is uncertain.

Provocative questions or statements such as "You are so stupid! You never do anything right!" establish conflict and move a scene forward quickly. The STOP-GAP Method requires the actors to Swing the Pendulum (take opposing positions) to get a strong response not only from the other character in the scene, but from the clients (Laffoon et al., in press). Observing through the objective eye of the spectator, clients often gain tremendous insight into another point of view as well as their own as a result of this technique.

Hit the Bull's Eye

Hit the Bull's Eye underpins the whole of The STOP-GAP Method. Sometimes referred to as the "It," the Bull's Eye is the point of the play or the scene. What is it really about? Is the scene about being inept and incapable or is it about feeling belittled, badgered and isolated? From inside dysfunction, it is difficult if not impossible to recognize the "It" in a relationship or situation. From the safe distance of The STOP-GAP Method, clients are better able to sift through the thick layers of confusion, anger or guilt and understand more clearly what their behaviors and attitudes and those of others are really about.

In STOP-GAP's scripted plays, the Bull's Eye is predetermined and known to the actors and drama therapist. Scenes improvised within the drama therapy sessions on the other hand, involve a Bull's Eye that is determined by the STOP-GAP drama therapist working from the needs of the clients and input from the staff. It is imperative that Hit the Bull's Eye remains the focus of every drama therapy session. Otherwise, clients may view the session as entertainment and be less likely to become involved in the process or invested in the outcome.

The responsibility for hitting the Bull's Eye is held by both the drama therapist and the actors. The process involves the actors and drama therapist working closely together, listening and responding to the input of the clients. Each improvisation should help to make the Bull's Eye of the piece much clearer. By the end of the session, the clients should have a clear understanding of what the Bull's Eye of the scene is (Laffoon et al., in press).

STOP-GAP Rules and Tools

Supplementary to the components of The STOP-GAP Method are certain devices employed to further engage the clients in the active processing of the issues raised in the scenes and to facilitate the hitting of the Bull's Eye. The most significant of these devices is the Pause.

Pause

At key moments or critical junctures in an improvisation, the drama therapist will say, "Pause." This stops all action and dialogue immediately. The drama therapist then engages the clients in a dialogue about the feelings of the characters at this point and asks for input as to what the options for a particular character might be. Strong phrases such as, "Well, what can I do?" or "It's all my fault isn't it?" give the drama therapist prime opportunities to stimulate dialogue and gather input from the clients, turning to them for their input, e.g., "What can he do?" or "Is it her fault?" Also, if an actor is uncertain about what to say in an improvisation, "I don't know what to say to you" is a perfect line. The drama therapist will Pause the scene and turn to the clients for their ideas–"What *can* he say?"

The dialogue that takes place among clients and the drama therapist (and often between the actors responding in-role to the clients) during the paused scenes is sometimes lively, sometimes somber, and always insightful. During the Pause, clients have an opportunity to explore and relate to the feelings of the characters. The actors glean even more information for their characters by listening carefully to the clients' responses and perceptions. Choices for the characters, and ultimately for the clients, begin to emerge through this dialogue, choices involving effective communication, safe and healthful living and increased understanding of roles, behaviors and emotions. The Pause is a powerful tool for gaining perspective, objectivity and clarity on issues and feelings that were previously too overwhelming and confusing to cope with (Laffoon et al., in press).

This dialoguing among clients during a Pause also creates opportunities for new roles to emerge through mutual peer support and encouragement, a sharing of personal knowledge, experience, and a kind of intimacy with an impact much more meaningful, poignant and cathartic for a client than a counselor's most empathic admonitions.

Clarity and Directness

Other tools inherent in The STOP-GAP Method include being clear and direct with actions and speech. For some clients, cognition may be somewhat compromised and rapid rates of speech will cause much of the scene to be lost. Also, many elders have hearing impairments making it extremely important to speak loud enough to be heard. The STOP-GAP Method discourages the use of inappropriate language, such as slang and profanity unless it is integral to the scene as it is more likely to defocus the attention from the scene than to add to it.

Body Language

Body language, of course, helps to establish the character but The STOP-GAP Method does not play stereotyped mannerisms or behaviors. For example, the STOP-GAP actor playing a frail elderly person will not slow his/her gait or change his/her pattern of speech. The STOP-GAP Method involves playing feelings and emotions, not the stereotype. This allows clients to remain focused on the content of the scene rather than the look of it.

Empathic Embodiment

Unlike contemporary improvisation, getting laughs is never the point of any scene. Although humor can be valuable in helping clients become more comfortable, especially with a subject that is difficult to talk about, The STOP-GAP Method requires that actors embody the voice and the feelings of the clients and essentially, act at their direction.

Client Enrollment

Client involvement lies at the crux of The STOP-GAP Method. Clearly, the more we can dialogue with clients about the issues most affecting them, the more true the improvisations will ring and the more real and meaningful they will be. But never is The STOP-GAP Method more effective than when a client is enrolled in an improvisation. Here clients have an opportunity to speak their mind, have their say and experience the sense of validation and empowerment that is inherent in the role of the assertive, effective communicator or advisor, helpful friend or family member while enjoying the support of their peers and the STOP-GAP team (Laffoon et al., in press).

The STOP-GAP Method requires that any client enrolling in a scene take on a role that is empowered, confident and wise. It is the intent of The STOP-GAP Method to remove the sense of victimization by eliminating victim as a role option. The actors will *always* play the character that is behaving inappropriately, being taken advantage of, or in need of advice. It is the responsibility of the drama therapist to keep the enrolled client as well as the rest of the group safe. The drama therapist must guide the scene, instructing the actors carefully, always working in the best interest of the client to provide a role-playing experience that is positive and successful.

The STOP-GAP Method works diligently to remain within the framework of a person-centered therapy-based drama therapy and not to blur the distinction between drama therapy and psychodrama. The STOP-GAP Method involves creating scenes based on a personal experience without being the actual experience of a particular client. The cards are anonymous and the identities of the card writers remain unknown to the drama therapist, the actors and the rest of the clients. If the writer reveals him/herself, the drama therapist must guide the group to keep the focus of the scene on the characters the group developed. Further, it is often more appropriate for that particular client to refrain from taking a role in the scene. In this way, clients are able to maintain as much distance and subsequently, perspective and clarity, as possible.

STOP-GAP Safety Net

The client-driven quality of a person-centered approach combined with its disinterest in pursuing radical personality changes in clients provides an inherent safety net. Insisting on genuine positive regard for the client on the part of the therapist and encouraging the client to set his/her own pace assures that clients are not harmed emotionally by addressing issues too deeply, too abruptly (Corey, 1991).

Because STOP-GAP works with transient populations in community-based agencies, the need for a safety net-oriented approach is clear. STOP-GAP cannot predict the make-up of the group from week to week nor can it control for the level of follow-up counseling and care available to clients after each session. Some facilities are staffed with licensed clinicians and mandate regular personal counseling for the residents. Others offer only minimal therapeutic support. STOP-GAP establishes and diligently maintains active communication and supportive working relationships with the sites in which it works in order to remain apprised of the needs of the clients. Guided by the supports in place within each site and working within the structure of The STOP-GAP Method and a person-centered therapeutic style, the drama therapist can carefully see the clients safely through the therapeutic process without leaving clients feeling exposed, vulnerable or threatened.

STOP-GAP Goals

According to Goleman (1995), an individual's ability to manage feelings effectively has a direct bearing on that individual's ability to cope effectively with life's setbacks. The clients with whom STOP-GAP works have, by and large, experienced tremendous, life-altering setbacks. Devastated by abuse, neglect, addiction, violence, poverty or catastrophic illness, the ability to face these challenges and cope with the barrage of associated feelings is severely compromised if not altogether destroyed. STOP-GAP's ultimate goal in its drama therapy programs is to increase clients' attunement to their own feelings; to facilitate the awareness of and the tools to cope with those feelings.

STOP-GAP's drama therapy programs pursue this goal overall as it works to achieve specific therapeutic goals and objectives identified by agency staff, families, or the clients themselves. These objectives may include self-awareness, awareness of others, social interaction, effective communication, personal responsibility, accountability, and self-reliance.

SUMMARY

In day treatment settings as well as longer term residential, recovery and hospital environments, STOP-GAP works in close partnership with the site to remain informed about ongoing issues faced by clients in their homes, the community or within the site itself. As discussed previously, these sessions are purely improvisational and are conducted by a registered drama therapist accompanied by two actors (one male and one female of differing ethnic backgrounds) from the repertory company.

After a brief introduction to the team, the clients are asked to complete WHO-WHAT-WHERE cards. The drama therapist selects a card to work from and guides the clients, as a group, to agree on names for the characters the actors will portray, their ages and necessary details about their relationship. Make the Menu names for the characters may not bear any personal meaning or association for anyone in the group so clients are encouraged to "veto" names or other details that make them uncomfortable. Again, the opportunity for assertiveness presents itself, often for the first time for clients whose spirits have been broken, along with the opportunity for validation and affirmation.

The situation or what the scene is about is set up (according to WHAT and WHERE information indicated on the card). The drama therapist then asks the group who in the scene will have the first line and what it will be. Once the actor has heard the line, s/he repeats it verbatim and the improvisation runs until Paused by the drama therapist.

STOP-GAP steers away from playing any one person's story as is intended in psychodrama or playback theatre, and in fact, discourages clients from "owning" their cards or concerning themselves with whose card the STOP-GAP team might be playing. Ultimately, STOP-GAP's goal is to create scenes that become a collective experience for the group–to explore issues and feelings that the whole group can identify with, relate to and contribute to in a way that feels safe and comfortable for everyone.

Situations role-played vary extensively according to the nature (presenting problems, short/long term program) and make-up (age range, gender balance) of the group. Some of the issues for which The STOP-GAP Method has proven an effective approach include: autonomy and independence, health concerns, parenting, social, familial and romantic relationships, trust, sober living, fear, control and guilt.

CASE EXAMPLES

As previously described, STOP-GAP works with extremely transient populations: homeless youth seeking shelter from the streets, women and children fleeing violence in their homes, young patients in and out of hospital for chronic conditions, and youth in and out of foster care are a few examples. As a result, STOP-GAP may see a client as few as one time in a county shelter or children's hospital or as many as six times in a 45-day emergency shelter. The substance abuse recovery programs visited by STOP-GAP house residents for anywhere from 28 days to 15 months, which results in a range of two to six sessions before the client has completed the program, graduated to an advanced level within the facility or perhaps gone on to seek employment.

Further, because The STOP-GAP Method does not utilize intake interviews or assessment tools, STOP-GAP has very little information about its clients other than their collective presenting problem. Indeed, STOP-GAP rarely even knows clients' first names. These factors–transience, variability in frequency of sessions and differing structures within facilities–combined with the anonymity of The STOP-GAP Method, makes tracking individual or group progress in any tangible way extremely difficult if not impossible.

Case examples illustrating the impact of The STOP-GAP Method of Drama Therapy, to the extent that they can be reasonably described, tracked and reported, follow.

Substance Abuse Recovery

Chemical dependency affects *everything*. It affects the user, the family, the friends, the employer, the co-workers, the neighbors, the community, politics, law enforcement, correctional systems, rehabilitation systems, the list goes on and on. It eats away at trust, honesty and the ability to communicate openly and effectively. Eventually, the substance abuser will stop growing emotionally altogether (Woititz, 1985).

There is general agreement among clinicians and recovering substance abusers alike that drugs and alcohol serve to soothe feelings of anxiety, anger, and depression in the user. Whatever the drug of choice, it seems to ease emotions that have plagued them for a long time (Goleman, 1995). Attributes common to chemically dependent individuals include an *inability* to express emotions, emotional immaturity, low self-esteem, low frustration tolerance and feelings of isolation and guilt (Beattie, 1987). There is pain, desperation and blame. As the insidious layers and layers of unexpressed, unresolved feelings grow deeper, feelings of isolation and hopelessness grow more profound. Confusion, anger and suspicion reign.

The STOP-GAP Method of Drama Therapy has been extremely effective in working through the issues surrounding chemical dependency. The very nature of The STOP-GAP Method gently challenges the recovering addict/alcoholic to face his feelings in a very concrete way–by writing them down on a card.

WHO are the significant others that have influenced your life?
WHAT is going on between you and this other?
WHERE does it take place?

The process of recovery involves feeling–something the substance abuser has never done before. For the duration of their using,

WHO:
1) Me (girl)
2) Mom or Dad

WHAT: I always felt abandoned. I could never do anything right. I never felt good enough for them.

WHERE: at home

WHO:
1) me (female)
2) Dad

WHAT: Dad beat me when I was little. He never has showed any remorse or apologized. I want to address it.

WHERE: Home, Living room

WHO:
1) Me
2)

WHAT: I am having a problem asking people for help

WHERE: go to a meeting and ask somebody

Figure 12.2.

their feelings have been numbed, masked, avoided, buried, suppressed, minimized and denied. Do not feel. Do not trust. Do not talk. This is the unwritten, unspoken, highly defended code of the alcoholic/addict (Black, 1981). The STOP-GAP Method of Drama Therapy serves to support the recovering substance abuser through the painstaking task of self-inventory and personal responsibility, revisit the past and the roots of addiction and explore the future for a glimpse of sober living and ways to avoid relapse. In other words, The STOP-GAP Method of Drama Therapy enables the recovering substance abuser to begin to feel, to trust and to talk.

Above and following are examples of cards from actual STOP-GAP Drama Therapy sessions in substance abuse recovery programs illustrating how clients use this technique to articulate their feelings as they revisit their pasts, focus on their presents and explore their futures:

The WHO-WHAT-WHERE Cards, integral to The STOP-GAP Method of Drama

WHO:
1) Self
2)

WHAT: I feel confused and scared.

WHERE: Present

WHO:
1) Me
2) Family

WHAT: I've been out of my son's life for so many years and want back in his life but my family isn't sure I am ready.
WHERE:

WHO:
1) Me
2) Low self esteem

WHAT: My self esteem trying to apply for an excellent job but feel very inadequate even though I can perform job well & have excellent skills.
WHERE:

Figure 12.3.

Therapy, concretizes that which has been masked, feared and avoided by those in substance abuse recovery for a lifetime. The opportunity to make feelings and life experiences real in both written and dramatic form serves other client groups equally effectively. For children whose emotional and maturational development is impeded by terminal illness, The STOP-GAP Method of Drama Therapy provides an opportunity to sort out overwhelming feelings and emotions. For battered women, whose feelings have been entirely disallowed and whose very perception of reality has been challenged and distorted by terror, the WHO-WHAT-WHERE cards are their first tangible source of validation and affirmation.

Children with Life-Threatening Illness

Since 1983, STOP-GAP Drama Therapy has been a weekly part of the treatment plan at a local children's hospital for young patients coping with chronic and often terminal illness. AIDS, cancer and Cystic Fibrosis are just a few of the conditions these young patients are facing. In 1990, STOP-GAP began working with Carlos, a 12-year-old South American boy with Cystic Fibrosis (CF) being raised solely by his mother who had already lost twin daughters to CF.

CF is the most common fatal hereditary disease in America, affecting 1 in every 2500 births. A disorder of the cells that line the lungs, pancreas, sweat glands and small intestines, CF causes the development of thick mucous that destroys lung tissue, interferes with breathing, and impedes the absorption of nutrients and the release of digestive enzymes. As a result, patients with CF are generally smaller than average in weight and height and suffer from secondary conditions such as diabetes, liver dysfunction, sinus and lung infections and digestive disorders for which they are frequently hospitalized (Cystic Fibrosis Research Institute, 1999).

According to Heather Sahargun, CTRS (Certified Therapeutic Recreation Specialist) and the head of the Recreation Therapy Department of the hospital, the standard protocol for CF patients in the late 1980s and early 1990s was for 2–3 hospitalizations per year for 3–4 week periods. These hospitalizations were so commonplace that it was not unusual for there to be several CF patients hospitalized at any given time. More often than not, the patients knew one another from both previous hospital stays and/or annual CF camp experiences. The result was a tremendous sense of fraternity among CF patients. As a group, they were reluctant to confide in others, establish new relationships or build trust with people who did not have CF. After all, they had each other.

A charismatic personality, Carlos quickly became the "leader of the pack" whenever hospitalized. His posture and body language presented a certain adult-like maturity while his effect revealed a quite animated boy. He often sat with one leg folded across the other, his hand stroking a nonexistent beard as he giggled and mimicked the other patients. This was his role–the man-boy. He often elected to play the role of responsive doctor or authoritative parent in STOP-GAP improvisations.

When he came to STOP-GAP, it was less out of personal need or desire than an to attempt to challenge the drama therapist (the perceived new leader of the pack) by undermining the focus and flow of the session. He skillfully used his relationships with the other kids, drawing on their inside knowledge of one another to control or derail the session. He was inclined to influence the responses of other patients, answering questions for them or cleverly twisting their words. But because The STOP-GAP Method is client-centered and client driven, Carlos' need to control the group went uncontested. Instead, The STOP-GAP Method worked from Carlos' point of reference and offered him opportunities to explore new roles–roles perhaps he had not allowed himself–all within the safe confines of the scenes.

Carlos had a natural affinity for improvisation and an admirable skill for switching roles on a theatrical level: from boy to man, from desperate to inspired, from infantile to individuated. Through The STOP-GAP Method of Drama Therapy, Carlos began to let go of his role as mature, philosophical, understanding and accepting. He experimented with an *experienced* infantile, embittered, uncooperative and difficult, Carlos was able to use The STOP-GAP Method to meet his own emotional, psychosocial and developmental needs. Over the course of Carlos' eight-year relationship with STOP-GAP, he became fully self-actualized, having integrated the lessons each of his many roles offered him.

Carlos fully grasped The STOP-GAP Method and began working *with* rather than against the drama therapist to Hit the Bull's Eye. In this way his role evolved from controller to role model. He made himself accessible not only to other CF patients but to all chronic patients. Carlos began to improvise scenes and take on roles for the benefit of younger patients. Having processed himself many issues, he personified younger patients' fears, their frustrations and their dreams in scene after scene taking care not to dominate the group. Through The STOP-GAP Method of Drama Therapy, Carlos became empowered. He discovered that he had something to give indeed, something to leave behind. He used the STOP-GAP Drama Therapy sessions as the vehicle for his legacy: his staggering insight for the benefit of other patients.

In 1994, the CF community suffered a devastating blow. A particularly resistant bacteria known as Pseudomonas Cepacia (or simply Cepacia) was making its way across the country. This most aggressive and lethal bacteria is transmitted to CF patients from other CF patients. Within two years, CF camps were discontinued and CF patients had to be kept in isolation from one another. This combined with the advent of managed care and subsequent reduced and abbreviated hospitalizations resulted in the near dissolution of a vital, self-supporting community. Ironically, just at a time when more therapeutic intervention was needed, far fewer opportunities were available.

Building on the tremendous trust established between Carlos and STOP-GAP during those first several years, Carlos requested STOP-GAP in his room whenever hospitalized and STOP-GAP accommodated that request, seeing Carlos one on one. During these one on one sessions, he sorted out his relationship with his mother and the roles he played in the family–son, only child, only male, head of household, protector, advisor and the one who would abandon his mother through death. "I can't die," he said in one session, "my mother won't let me." Carlos likened his fight against CF to a game of Tug o' War. CF had hold of one end of the rope and Carlos held on to the other. During a one on one session with STOP-GAP, Carlos wondered how he would ever let go of the rope, asking in desperation *"What if your hands are one with the rope?"*

As Carlos' one on one sessions continued, his capacity for insight deepened and his sense of empowerment strengthened. At no point was this more evident than when Carlos' best friend contracted Cepacia. When told if he continued to see his friend, he himself would contract Cepacia. Carlos replied, "I will not turn my back on my friend." He went to his friend, consciously exposing himself to the deadly bacteria, which would ultimately take his life. Carlos had finally found a way to let go of the rope.

Battered Women

Domestic violence is an insidious, tangled knot of deception, manipulation, power and control. It preys on love and trust and loyalty. It seeps into the workplace, into the lives of friends, family, neighbors and perfect strangers. Indeed, STOP-GAP contends that domestic violence isn't domestic at all. It is violence. It is battering. It affects each and every one of us. STOP-GAP is committed to working with survivors of battering relationships, helping them to rebuild their sense of self as they rebuild their lives.

According to the Western Institute for Therapeutic Studies based in Sacramento, California, domestic violence includes physical force, emotional force, verbal force and sexual force. Verbal and emotional abuse gradually increases and worsens, eventually escalating to horrific acts of physical violence that all too often ends in death. Many survivors report that emotional and psychological abuse is more difficult to recover from. Physical injuries heal but the hidden wounds and buried memories of betrayal, relentless badgering, humiliation and hateful remarks linger for a very long time (WITS, 1999). STOP-GAP witnesses first-hand this truth played out in scene after scene. Feelings of shame, defectiveness, ineptitude and lack of worth are the legacy of harsh criticism and attacks on one's character (Goleman, 1995). These women are damaged, as one battered woman, stated, "from the inside out."

Louisa, a native of Spain, is a graduate of a shelter program for battered women. Because of the positive impact the STOP-GAP Drama Therapy sessions had on her, Louisa returned to the shelter to volunteer as a Spanish language translator for the STOP-GAP sessions in order that monolingual Spanish-speaking women may benefit as she did. It is in this way that STOP-GAP came to know her identity.

This is her story.

> I was married for nearly eight years to a prominent and highly regarded scientist. Shortly after we married we relocated to the United States from Spain for his work. I came from a well-to-do, close-knit family and once relocated, I was discouraged and eventually forbidden to maintain family ties. I was made to stay at home and assigned daily tasks and projects that would further my husband's career. I could have no outside contact or stimulation and I was constantly put down, ridiculed and criticized. I became more and more isolated. The emotional and psychological abuse was very deep. I became very depressed and thought about killing myself. I don't have to live like this, I remember thinking. I either leave or die. So I left. I took two pairs of blue jeans and three sweaters. Nothing else. And I left.
>
> I was in the emergency shelter for six weeks and then I spent five more months in one of their apartments. I went to STOP-GAP every week that first month and a half and as often as I could after that. My card was chosen many times but many of the issues are a part of all of our lives. I remember very clearly when it was very definitely my card that was chosen. And it was STOP-GAP that shed light on what was happening to me.
>
> The card was about me and my brother. My brother, who had been like best friends with my husband in Spain, had dropped everything–his very successful business in Spain–when he found out I was in a shelter. I was afraid. I knew my brother's purpose was to take me back to Spain. A shelter was no place for his sister. I knew my family could be healing for me but it wasn't the kind of healing I was looking for. I also knew that my brother would contact my husband and try to bring us together again.
>
> Neither of those things happened because it was not what I...ME...wanted. STOP-GAP helped me to see that and helped me to know what I could do.
>
> By putting my case on stage, STOP-GAP gave me the reassurance I needed to face my brother with what I wanted and what I needed. The way STOP-GAP portrays our lives, the way the scenes carry the issues through, and the input of the other women helps us all to see that we are all a part of relationship and shows how we should be for each other. Giving respect, dignity and the encouragement to be who you are.
>
> STOP-GAP gave me light when I had no light at all.

Karen is another battered woman who returned to the shelter to volunteer for STOP-GAP. Karen survived 12 horrifying years of emotional, verbal and psychological abuse that eventually escalated into brutal beatings. She describes the impact The STOP-GAP Method of Drama Therapy had on her:

> When I finally made it to the shelter and to STOP-GAP, I felt like I was totally insane. I was physically sick–I hadn't been able to eat much of anything in a very long time–and I was suicidal. I couldn't talk. I could not articulate the emotional and psychological abuse I had suffered, the betrayal, the beatings...I could not begin to articulate the fear I had inside me. I had been so full of fear for so long that when I first got there I just cried and cried and cried. You know, I'm not unintelligent. I'm smart. I'm professional. But when your abuser

relentlessly chips away at you, you begin to doubt. You doubt your thoughts, your feelings–everything.

At STOP-GAP, there was no pressure. And I could identify with every card they did. They'd act out this snippet of your life and it helped so much. I could step back from it (my experience) and grow from it instead of allowing it to swallow me. The first thing I discovered by going to STOP-GAP was that our abusers were all the same but with different faces. They all used the same tactics to get the same things–but with different faces.

I remember STOP-GAP doing one of my cards. I was very angry that our abusers lives go on, that they are only mildly inconvenienced without us–their slaves–to fulfill their wants, needs and desires, without someone to relentlessly criticize–while our lives are completely taken away from us.

So the STOP-GAP actress played me and they asked for a volunteer to come up as a woman in the shelter and talk with her and I volunteered. So there I was–talking to myself! I told her Yes, but the reality is each of us makes up life as we go along. I had to stop and say Listen to yourself! That's a great bit of wisdom!

I could virtually feel the layers of gunk being lifted off me. For so long, I had stuffed my feelings down, but I needed to explore my feelings and connect them to myself. STOP-GAP allowed us to find the self that was deep inside. I had given myself up for him and I wasn't at all conscious of having done that. STOP-GAP taught us to go to that inside place of knowing. When you work through your feelings, you will come back to the loving person that is you.

STOP-GAP DRAMA THERAPY IN SUMMARY

Most of us will weather the uncertainty of change as we travel along life's journey. We will face conflict, difficulty, doubt and fear. We will know joy, exhilaration, confidence and security. How we perceive and react to our life circumstances is directly affected by how connected we are to our feelings (Goleman, 1995). For a battered woman, a chronically ill child or a person in recovery, there may be little opportunity for self-awareness and few coping skills. There is only hurt, confusion and fear.

People who experience such high level states of anxiety are generally unable to respond effectively. Their ability to process information accurately is severely compromised (Goleman, 1995). It is nearly impossible to communicate effectively, make healthy choices and take responsibility for one's own life. Having emotional control, according to Goleman, is a critical factor in one's personal effectiveness and in the successful meeting of personal goals. So when an individual enters a hospital, shelter or recovery program, they open a window of opportunity. They take the first step in assuming an active role in their personal well-being.

Working in tandem with the clients and the community agencies serving them, STOP-GAP joins these individuals on their quest to better understand where they have been and where they are going. The STOP-GAP Method of Drama Therapy seeks to be a catalyst for insight, personal growth and self-awareness. Clients in STOP-GAP's Drama Therapy programs come from all walks of life but often with an arrested or impaired emotional development. The STOP-GAP Method of Drama Therapy helps clients to develop self-awareness and attunement to feelings, enabling them to rebuild their sense of self as they rebuild their lives.

The STOP-GAP Method of Drama Therapy serves to awaken and reinforce competence and confidence in the client through an opportunity to "rehearse for life." Through this process, clients internalize very powerful, positive messages that they will take with them into their futures. As one battered woman so aptly stated, "We get taught that to think of ourselves is selfish. At STOP-GAP we learned that to think of ourselves is "self-full"–I love that! STOP-GAP helped me learn that I am worthy of my time–I am worthy of my attention–I am worthy of my love! I am going to stay in touch with my feelings and honor and respect myself."

REFERENCES

Beattie, M. (1987). *Codependent no more; How to stop controlling others and start caring for yourself.* New York: Harper & Row, Publishers Inc.

Black, C. (1981). *It will never happen to me.* New York: Ballantine Books.

Corey, G. (1991). *Theory and practice of counseling and psychotherapy.* Pacific Grove, CA: Brooks/Cole Publishing.

Goleman, D. (1995). *Emotional intelligence; Why it can matter more than IQ.* New York: Bantam Books.

Laffoon, D., Bryan, V., & Sinatra, C. (1985). STOP-GAP: Senior Theatre Outreach Program. *Creative arts with older adults: A sourcebook.* Weisberg, N. & Wilder, R. (Eds.), New York: Human Sciences Press, Inc.

Laffoon, D., Bryan, V., & Diamond, S. (in press). Life Journeys: The STOP-GAP Method with Elders. *Creative arts with older adults: A sourcebook* (2nd Ed). Weisberg, N. & Wilder, R., (Eds.), London, England: Jessica Kingsley Publishers.

Rogers, C. (1961). *On becoming a person: A therapist's view of psychotherapy.* Boston, MA: Houghton Mifflin Company.

Tanner, F. (1982). *Basic drama projects.* Caldwell, ID: Clark Publishing Company.

Woititz, J. (1983). *Adult children of alcoholics.* Deerfield Beach, FL: Health Communications, Inc.

Woititz, J. (1985). *Struggle for intimacy.* Deerfield Beach, FL: Health Communications, Inc.

FURTHER STUDY

At present, training in The STOP-GAP Method of Drama Therapy is available solely through The STOP-GAP Institute. The STOP-GAP Institute can be contacted in the following ways:

The STOP-GAP Institute
1570 Brookhollow Drive, Suite #114
Santa Ana, California 92705

Phone: 714-979-7061
Fax: 714-979-7065
http://www.stopgap.org

Chapter 13

RECOVERY AND INDIVIDUATION TWO STAGE MODEL IN TRANSPERSONAL DRAMA THERAPY

PENNY LEWIS

TRANSPERSONAL PSYCHOTHERAPY is the process through which individuals transform their identity from a limited history-based sense of self to an experience of their soul essence. From the experience of soul, individuals can access a relationship to the numinous and their unique life purpose.

Transpersonal drama therapy utilizes the embodied arts in the recovery from all forms of abuse, addictions, dysfunctional relationships, outmoded survival behaviors, and associated limitations acquired from personal history toward an experience of being fully present and whole, capable of intimacy with oneself, others, and the transpersonal. From this relational wholeness, the process of individuation supports an individual's continuing development of self, deepening connection to meaning of their soul's journey and their potential service to the transpersonal realm and the expansion of human Consciousness.

GENESIS OF TRANSPERSONAL THERAPY

C.G. Jung and Individuation

Carl Jung is considered the first of the European/American psychotherapists to bring the transpersonal into the field of psychotherapy. Jung expanded the psychoanalytic concept of the unconscious as receptacle of repressed drives, split-off parts of the self, and trauma to include an archetypal layer of the unconscious. It is through the inner journey that the analysand accesses the collective unconscious and taps into the universal pool of wisdom. This connection is seen outwardly through synchronistic phenomena such as astrology and the *I Ching* and events that cannot be explained by rational cause and effect logic, as well as through archetypal images, themes, sounds and movement for which art, drama, music, and dance provide the sacred containers. The connection also presents itself internally through dreams, visions, active imagination, and meditation practices (Jung, CW 9.1).

Jung, unlike the Eastern-influenced transpersonal therapists, saw the process of therapy as individuation, i.e., the process by which a person becomes a psychological "individual"; that is, a separate, indivisible unity or "whole" (Jung, CW 9.1, p. 275). Instead of disidentifying with duality, Jung felt it was vital to be in relation to the archetypal lest the individual gets too close, identifies with it and becomes inflated. Myths such as found in the motifs of Icarus, Medusa, and Prometheus point the way to the devastating results of attempting to liken oneself to the gods. The danger of inflation has also demonstrated itself with Hitler, Jim Jones, and the numerous priests, gurus and spiritual teachers who like Icarus, crashed because they felt they were "above" human limitations and ethics. Thus the concept of an ego-Self axis (Edinger, 1982) is viewed as the ideal relationship to the transpersonal. This highly Western view maintains that one should stay at a humble respectful distance or axis, as Edinger identified it. Yet Jung saw the self-actualizing power of the archetype of the Self, the transpersonal organizing principle of wholeness, as having a profound effect on the ego. Jung wrote:

> The Self in its self-realization reaches out beyond the ego personality on all sides; because of its all-encompassing nature it is brighter and darker than the ego, and accordingly confronts it with problems which it would like to avoid. Either one's moral courage fails, or one's insight, or both, until in the end fate decides.
>
> The ego never lacks moral and rational counter arguments which one cannot and should not set aside so long as it is possible to hold on to them. For you only feel yourself on the right road when the conflicts of duty seemed to have resolved themselves, and you have become the victim of a decision made over your head in defiance of the heart. From this we can see the numinous power of the Self, which can hardly be experienced in any other way. For this reason the experience of the Self is always a defeat for the ego. (Mysterium Coniunctionis, par. 778)

This so-called defeat can shake loose all of that which individuals have identified prior and move them into a liminal phase where they are no longer who they are and not yet who they will become (Lewis, 1993). This disidentification process reoccurs throughout adult life stages. Each time individuals let go of their egocentric needs; they gradually receive universal wisdom.

Assagioli and Psychosynthesis

Although Roberto Assagioli was a contemporary of Jung's, his work did not receive larger attention until the 1970s. Psychosynthesis "is a name for the conscious attempt to cooperate with the natural process of personal development . . . to perfect itself" (Carter-Haar, *Synthesis,* vol. 1, 1975, p. 116). This approach asserts that each individual has a "transpersonal essence" and that it is each individual's purpose to manifest this. Assagioli adopted Jung's concepts of the transpersonal Self and the collective unconscious and added the concept of the superconscious from which emerges impulses for "altruistic love and will, humanitarian action, artistic and scientific inspiration, philosophic and spiritual insight, and the drive for purpose and meaning in life" (Ibid. p. 116).

Dysfunction occurs, in addition to those identified in the psychodynamic, existential-humanistic, and cognitive-behavioral Western frames, when an individual is unconscious of or unable to manifest his or her sublime highest nature. Similar to the Jungian view, the transpersonal work of psychosynthesis can result in a person caring more about the community, the environment, and the transpersonal while living in a state of grace.

Maslow, Vaughan, Walsh, Groff and Tart and Transpersonal Psychotherapy

It is unclear just who coined the term transpersonal. It appeared in the fifties but really acquired a larger usage in the late sixties with the formation of the *Journal of Transpersonal Psychology* and with Tart's *Transpersonal Psychologies* in the mid-seventies. Out of the humanistic ideal of Maslow's self-actualizing person capable of so-called peak experiences evolved a foundational philosophy for an Association of Transpersonal Psychology. Influenced as well by Eastern traditions such as Taoism, Buddhism, Sufiism, Hinduism as well as Native American shamanic frames, a more culturally universal approach continued to develop. From this synthesis, transcendental dimensions of existence and experience, soul connected unfolding of what one is meant to do, the involvement in a spiritual path, and the dis-identification with thoughts and limited world views are seen as major concepts identifying health.

Regarding the need for dis-identification, Walsh and Vaughn identify dysfunction as occurring when individuals believe that they are what they think. Walsh and Vaughn (Boorstein, 1991) write, "When the individual identifies with mental content, this content is transformed into the context within which he or she interprets other content, determines reality, adopts a logic, and is motivated" (p. 17). No cognitive therapist would disagree with this assumption, but transpersonal psychotherapists do something very different with this premise. Rather than utilizing charts, rational discussions and behavioral techniques with the goal of having the individual "think something different," the transpersonal therapist supports the individual's transcendence from all identification; lifting them from their own world view to one in which the "individual would presumably identify with both everything and nothing" (Walsh and Vaughn in Boorstein, 1991).

Neo-Transpersonal Approaches to Psychotherapy

The first wave of "the human potential movement" of the sixties and seventies gave way to the second wave of "new age" in the eighties and nineties. The belief in Buddhist and Hindu systems in the first wave supported such approaches as mindfulness and past life regression and therapy. Additionally shamanic practices from a variety of native cultures around the world have rekindled spiritual channeling, soul retrieval and active imagination techniques, which, like those of psychosynthesis, draw the individual into contact with sentient beings.

Reincarnation and Therapy

Those who adhere to the existence of past lives believe that individuals may at times need to heal from abuse either they or others committed in former lifetimes, thus expanding the individual's consciousness and clearing their karma. Utilizing much of the same techniques that are employed in today's recovery models (Lewis, 1993, 1996), therapists support individuals' deeper discovery of the etiology of survival patterns and the repeated reexperiencing of the same karmic lessons. This healing is often at a soul level and must always be respectful of the fact that karmic clearing has its own time frame.

Shamanism and Therapy

Shamanism, explored in the *Arts in Psychotherapy Journal* (vol. 15, no. 4), views individuals as capable of existing both in ordinary and in nonordinary states of reality. Vital for well-being is the maintenance of one's personal power (Harner, 1982). Individuals with diminished power are seen as "dis-spirited" and often experience harmful intrusions, which can energetically reduce the individual's life force. (Eastern traditions refer to this as chi, ki, and kundalini.) Individuals are encouraged to employ active imagination to enter into "shamanic states of consciousness" and channel power animals or more human-like spiritual beings. Therapists such as those trained in the somatic countertransference (Lewis, 1986, 1988, 1992, 1993, 1996) can draw connections of this drama therapy technique to both psychoanalysis and shamans who receive the dis-ease of their patients and release them from their suffering or possession. Through projective identification and other forms of unconscious to unconscious connection the therapist can receive the toxic psychic material or split-off material of the client, detoxify or heal the split-off or wounded aspect and aid in its reidentification.

Psychic Intuition

Channeling, or the capacity to intuitively receive on behalf of the client through nonordinary means, is receiving greater acceptance and tolerance. Here therapists empty themselves similar to the preparation needed for meditation. Information can be received through synchronistic events or simply as thoughts that seem to intuitively emerge out of nowhere to be utilized as the therapist sees fit in service of the healing and expanded consciousness of the client.

GENESIS OF TRANSPERSONAL DRAMA THERAPY

The transpersonal drama therapy approach evolved from the joint collaboration of Saphira Linden and myself. My background emerged from my training in Jungian Analysis at the C.G. Jung Institute in New York reinforced by profound peek satori meditative experiences as well as an inexplicable miraculous happening that has left me and my "seeing is believing" inner rational mind totally convinced that we are not alone. I have repeatedly seen synchronous events and the sacred profoundly transform my drama therapy clients. I have come to know with greater clarity, that I am called to do this work. Ecumenical in transpersonal orientation, I let the client and their archetypal unconscious dictate what religious or spiritual frame we use.

Saphira Linden has been a Sufi spiritual leader for over 20 years. She has woven her work into her training with Moreno and her therapeutic theater technique called transformational theater. Additionally she has created community productions on issues such as world peace and ecumenical faith. (See Linden's chapter.) In 1998, we brought our institutes together to form an alternate route certificate program in Transpersonal Drama Therapy.

DRAMA THERAPY FRAME OF REFERENCE

The drama therapy process is viewed in two separate, but at times overlapping stages:

Stage I: Recovery

Health and Goal of Therapy

Health and thus the goal in the recovery process is to have the capacity for intimacy with oneself, others, and the transpersonal. Additionally health is seen as the capacity to be fully present in the moment. That means that individuals are no longer reacting to the present as if it were the past dramas and no longer allowing childhood survival patterns to keep them from experiencing their whole self in relation to the world in a spontaneous manner.

Dysfunction

Dysfunction occurs from abuse, less than good enough parenting, cultural oppression, and the repeated ineffectual use of survival patterns that were created in childhood in the place of healthy boundaries. Dysfunctional families are unable to instill in a child a healthy realistic sense of self with an intact functioning ego, body, and personal space boundaries. This results in fragmented or split-off parts of the self, faulty boundaries, and habitual survival mechanisms created in order to endure what could not be escaped. Addictions are seen as one category of survival patterns. These are called "false mothers" as they frequently try to convince the addict that they can take care of them: fill the inner emptiness or stop the pain and that the addict does not need anyone else. Addictions whether they are alcohol, drugs, food, retail shopping, sex, love, money, power, or work use the same strategy as other survival mechanisms such as isolation, shutting down, people-pleasing, or judging oneself and/or others. They all attack intimacy on three levels: with the inner core self or what recovery therapists call the inner child (ren), with other individuals and with the spiritual transpersonal realm.

Method of Identifying the Health-Dysfunction Continuum

Method of identifying and evaluating health and dysfunction is carried out by interviewing regarding their limiting behaviors and presenting problems through the use of the embodied psyche technique, sand play, dreamwork, art and other venues into the imagination that reveal the functioning of their psyche.

Stage II: Individuation

The second focus of the work is the process of individuation.

Health

Health is seen as the capacity for self-actualization. This ability supports the process of individuals to become freely and spontaneously more fully who they are. Shadow aspects that have been waiting in the wings can now enter the stage and be integrated into a person's life. Once this begins to occur, individuals have a better sense of what their personal myth is, i.e., what they are meant to do. This journey occurs after individuals have gone through recovery. Once freed from habitual patterns, everything is "up for grabs": relationships, livelihoods, old survival patterns. Everything must reflect and resonate with the goal of becoming who they truly are. Thus there is often an initial experience of a letting go of who they were, a transitional liminal phase akin to a metaphoric death, and a rebirthing of a greater experience of selfhood.

Once this occurs there are gradual shifts from self-focus to an ever-expanding one in which the community, the earth, and the many realms of spiritual reality engage their interest and investment. Thus the individuation process inevitably brings individuals toward an evolving spiritual consciousness.

Dysfunction

Dysfunction is viewed when individuals remain focused upon themselves and their problems and are not fully free to be present. Dysfunction is also seen with individuals who limit their view of existence to the empirical realm of physical reality. Thus the "bigger picture" is obstructed from their awareness and interest. Their capacity to expand their consciousness and be in relation to the sacred, either from a spiritual Judeo-Christian or Islamic I-Thou perspective or from a mystical "we are all one with the Light," is blocked.

Method of Identifying the Health-Dysfunction Continuum

The method of identifying and evaluating health and dysfunction is through tracking what genuinely gets individuals' attention. There are those who have utilized spiritual practices as a defense and escape from doing their own work. These individuals are often characterized as being *Puers* or *Puellae*–eternal youth, inspirational, charismatic, with high flying ideas without the groundedness that comes from claiming its polar opposite–the *senex* or wise woman. These individuals eventually crash, for they tend to soar too high and think they do not need to abide by human rules such as committing to a job or relationship or, if they have power, not abusing it through inappropriate monetary gains, status, fame or sexual acting out. The archetypal and its balance in the psyche both from the inner masculine and inner feminine perspectives can be assessed through the embodied archetype technique and other accesses to the transpersonal in sand play, dreams, guided shamanic and psychosynthesis journeys, and synchronistic events.

The Therapeutic Process

The Imaginal Realm

The means by which recovery and individuation can occur is through the use of the imaginal realm. The left hemisphere of the brain is typically thought of to provide rational analytic assessments. Time is seen as quantitative, linear. Most events have a cause and effect relationship to one another. This portion of the brain basically ascribes to two tenants: "what you see is what there is" and "if it can't fit into an existing logical scientific model, it does not exist." This is the realm of reductive thinking and interpretation.

Juxtaposed to the left hemisphere is the right hemisphere. This is the realm of imagination, creativity, the mysterious, the intuitive, synchronicity and qualitative time. The language of this realm is symbol and metaphor. In this realm is the threshold to the unconscious filled with unacceptable split-off parts of the self, horrible memories too painful to feel, and all the potential of who one could be waiting for the right time to come forward. These painful events along with childhood survival patterns and toxic aspects of significant others organize themselves into autonomous "feeling toned complexes." These so-called complexes become anthropromorphized or theriomorphized into human-like or animal-like symbolic entities in the psyche.

For example, an individual may have a judging survival mechanism that was created in childhood based upon the premise that if the child could judge his or herself more severely than the parent or other criticizing individual, then s/he would be protected from further shameful pain. This inner judge complex frequently becomes personified as a relentless voice criticizing the person. The left brain says that, of course, there is not a little nasty figure of a judge inside, but the right brain, where it resides knows very well that it exists.

Inner child(ren) complexes also exist and are frequently stuck imprisoned and disconnected from the adult ego self. They remain surrounded in the intolerable abusive event which resulted in their being sent into the unconscious often with the abuser remaining with them like some horrible scene frozen in time.

These complexes reside in what Jung called the personal unconscious, but he also wrote of a deeper layer or collective unconscious. In this realm, time is relative. Past, present, and future all reside in the now. Access to this archetypal unconscious allows individuals access to the transpersonal realm.

Because the abuse, inner core child selves, childhood survival patterns, shadow aspects as well as access to the spiritual realm all lie within the right hemisphere's imaginal realm, it makes sense that here is where the focus of the work should be. Although it may be possible to understand what happened and why a person is the way they are in the left relational hemisphere, this knowing often changes nothing. Only when both the drama therapist and client can access and enter into the imaginal realm where history and future potential lie, can recovery, healing, and transpersonal transformation occur.

Drama Therapy in Recovery and Individuation

Jung, as did Freud, understood that dreams came from the unconscious. But Jung realized that the arts, which utilize creativity and the imaginal realm, also came from the same source. Thus painting, drawing, storywriting, stream of consciousness journaling, poetry, improvisational sound, movement and drama all come from and access the imaginal realm. It is vital when employing the arts in the recovery and individuation process not to switch over to the left brain and interpret. Interpretation kills. Rather it is important to enter into the imaginal realm with the artist-client where healing and transformation can occur.

The "unconscious lies in the body," Jung proclaimed. The embodied art of drama is the most powerful as the person is experiencing the healing process as it is happening. But when childhood abuse violates physical boundaries, embodiment may be too powerful and literally send the individual out of their body, triggering the childhood survival pattern of dissociation. Thus arts media that externalize trauma-based complexes may be far more appropriate. Through art, poetry, storywriting, and journaling the individual can distance themselves from the events; then personifying different aspects, they can utilize drama therapy role playing to interview them and can begin to put the pieces together in a way that does not tear them apart in the process.

Recovery Stage Therapeutic Process

The therapeutic process of the phase of recovery entails the therapist identifying the presenting problems and goals of the client through initial client interview. The therapist then assesses ego strength and explores within the imaginal drama therapy process, the presence, accessibility and connection to the core self or inner child. Through the use of the embodied psyche technique, the personality and intrapsychic structure is revealed, including those survival mechanisms, addictions, trauma, and/or parental and societal introjects which conflict with health.

In the second phase, that which inhibits a connection to the self, others and the transpersonal is transformed utilizing drama therapy techniques such as the embodied psyche and recovery of the inner child(ren) from trauma. After each drama therapy process, client(s), the drama therapist and any drama therapy trainees de-role; and utilizing the symbolic language of the dramatic experience, gradually aid in transitioning the client back into the here and now. With groups, classic psychodrama sharing from the audience and alter egos occur.

Individuation Stage Therapeutic Process

The therapeutic process within the individuation phase entails interviewing of clients regarding what their goals are as well as gleaning any information regarding the outcome of any past recovery therapy. In the second phase, the unconscious is sourced for the direction of the work through such techniques as dreamwork as theater, authentic sound movement and drama, and embodied sand play. The transformative process occurs within these techniques. As clients become more of who they are and are impacted with the experience of transpersonal grace, their presence becomes more soul–directed and their relationship to what guides and influences them shifts profoundly.

Drama Therapist's Role

As part of my training in Jungian Analysis, I was taught that it was the patient's unconscious and not the analyst, who was the authority. Thus it is the unconscious with its access to the trauma held in the personal unconscious and the spiritual connection through the archetypal unconscious that provides the subject matter and the direction. My role is that of midwiving consciousness. I encourage the process but also make sure that the birth is not traumatic or too swift. I frequently use the metaphor of "having an appropriate amount on your plate." Too much material from the unconscious and the person can become overwhelmed, and the adult self or ego can metaphorically be flooded and lose consciousness, requiring hospitalization. On the opposite pole, overworked survival mechanisms can keep a person from having any access to the unconscious and result in the person living in a psychic desert without any ability to find the wellspring of potential awaiting them. With too little on their plate, they go through life starved for a connection to themselves and depth of meaning.

Thus the drama therapist must be facile at moving in and out of the imaginal transitional space of the drama, flowing with needed role reversals and interviewing strategies. The drama therapist is skilled at subtlely reframing, delivering important psychoeducational information within each character enactment, and cognizant of the direction and therapeutic process, asking the right questions of the protagonist in order to bring about awareness and transformation.

The Somatic Countertransference

The use of the doubling technique of the somatic countertransference (Lewis, 1993) allows for the therapist to receive the unconscious transferred objects or projected split-off affect, self and shadow aspects, sensations, and images from the client's personal unconscious and grace and numinosum from the transpersonal archetypal unconscious on his/her behalf. This informs the drama therapist in doubling, role playing, or in imaginally transforming projected split-off aspects of a person's psychology through remembering, as well as neutralizing and detoxifying transferred negative objects while still in the therapist's body vessel. With others, their infant self may be imagistically received for love and healthy gestation to be retransferred when the patient is ready.

Appropriate Populations and Limitations

Any child or adult who is in need of recovering from issues of abuse and addictions can benefit from this approach. Additionally adults who are undergoing adult life stage transition and seeking a deeper meaning to their life and/or greater transpersonal connection are appropriate for this model. The embodied psyche technique has been successful in short term as well as long term therapy and has proven effective with individuals, couples, and groups. Clearly individuals such as atheists, who do not have a belief system that embraces the possibility of the transpersonal, might appear to be less appropriate for this approach; but I have found that the unconscious and its manifestations often hold very different experiences and have a trickster way of jarring the disbeliever. Since this model does not proselytize any particular view, "a wait and see" attitude often brings forth the numinous when least expected.

DRAMA THERAPY TECHNIQUES IN ASSESSMENT AND HEALING IN THE TWO STAGE MODEL

In addition to psychodrama, sociodrama, playback theater, solution-focused role modeling and rehearsal, the following techniques are utilized in this two stage model: the embodied psyche technique, inner child recovery, the redramatization of object relations, arts and sand play, gestalt, dramatic personification, archetypal enactment, authentic sound, movement and drama, and dreamwork as theater. The embodied psyche, inner child recovery, dreamwork as theater, and archetypal enactment will be discussed here.

The Embodied Psyche Technique in Assessment and Treatment

Because self-formation and the internalization of the object is accomplished in and with the body, embodied techniques, which employ the imaginal-transitional play space, are utilized. Whether working individually, with groups, or couples therapy, it is vital to know "all the players." The first cast of characters is always in the head of each individual present. Within the initial interview the drama therapist can assess the level of health of the individual based upon the presence, relationship, and the amount of power or psychic energy distribution of the various inner voices. These inner characters are called complexes by Jungians, schemata by cognitive therapists or sub-personalities by those who utilize psychosynthesis. The following complexes are looked for and role played in a person's psyche.

Ego or Inner Adult: Chairperson of the Psyche

A healthy psyche has a functioning ego which acts as the "chairperson of a board of directors" listening to what different sub-personalities have to say. The ego, referred to as the inner adult (transactional analysis), is the mediator and reality tester. The ego deciphers inner reality from outer reality; it assesses what belongs to the person and what does not. If healthy, the ego will know what projections and transferences are being sent out by the psyche, or being received from another person. In order to execute this filtering process the ego needs healthy ego boundaries that differentiate what is part of the individual's psyche from what is someone else's.

The boundaries must also be secure so that toxic intrapsychic complexes do not invade the ego and possess it as Jungians claim. The person is often unaware when this happens and operates from a false belief that it is the inner adult that is speaking. This occurs, for example; when an addiction invades the ego and individuals "think" they should reabuse a substance, when a rage possesses the ego and individuals batter another, or when an inner critic complex enters and clients misperceive the voice to be their relational ego who is self-trashing.

Self or Inner Child: Source of Feelings, Needs and Wants

The ego is expected to have a good connection to the core self (object relations and self psychology) also referred to as the inner child (recovery theory and transactional analysis). This connection means that the chairperson of the psyche always knows what the person feels, needs and wants. Without access to the self, the person will not be able to give the self what it needs nor fill the self with realistic positive love and regard. Without this connection, self-esteem and an experience of being seen and understood is impossible. This disconnection begins in the first few years of life with a parent that does not provide the ego with a role model of a healthy parent-child relationship. The parent or primary caregiver either emotionally or physically abandons, attempts to control, or violates the developing child. The self, instead of feeling full of love and realistic positive regard, remains depleted and in pain and fear.

Childhood Survival Behaviors: Defenses against Inner Pain, Survival Fear, and External Others

The child then soon develops behaviors to disengage from the ongoing pain, loss, emptiness and survival fear. These survival behaviors are designed to disconnect the ego both from the inner core pained self and from external others. Initially they are needed in childhood as children cannot "fire" their parents and so must somehow endure growing up in the family. However, these survival patterns do not leave in adulthood, but stay, keeping the ego forever disconnected from the self and caring others. The following are some examples of these survival complexes:

- *The denier*–"I have no pain; no needs and wants; I had a happy childhood."
- *The insulator*–"It's not safe to be vulnerable, I'll hide the child self so no one not even you (the ego) can find it."
- *The inner critic*–"Do not say or do anything spontaneously, someone might find out that you are unacceptable and abandon you or judge you adversely."
- *The controller*–"Remember it was not safe having our parents be in control; and it was not safe having needs in that chaos. I'll just protect you by controlling others and by controlling your vulnerable feeling."
- *The abuser*–"You know what it felt like to be the victim; it's much better to be the one on top. Get that needy self away from me! I'm the bully now and I won't have that vulnerable-self messing this up. So let's find someone to project onto and attack."
- *The victim/martyr/ people pleaser*–"If we just focus on other peoples needs then sooner or later someone will focus on us and heal the child. Besides it's selfish to focus on your own needs."
- *The forgotten one/isolator*–"If we do not say anything then no one will notice us and no harm will come to us."
- *The "ambivalator"*–"If we never take a stand or never make a decision then we won't get anything wrong and end up alone, shamed or abused."
- *The scapegoat*–"If we agree to be the bad one then it will please the family and draw attention away from the real problem: mom and/or dad."
- *The perfect one*–"I can't control what is going on outside, but I can control myself." Or "Maybe if I am perfect; then I can fix my family."

Addictions: The Inner Compelling Voice of the Addiction

Like survival behaviors, addictions too, split the inner adult-ego off from the core child self and from the possibility for intimacy with others. These "false mothers" tell the ego that they'll take care of the child, stop the pain, or fill the void. They demand total obedience and control over the addict's life.

Inner Objects: Mother or Father Complexes: The Internalizations of the Child's Parents

Early in childhood, the many experiences with the person's mother, father, and any primary caregivers are internalized. If a parent was absent there will not be the constant inner parent who offers advice to the ego to support and care for the inner child or encourage the adult to develop. If any parent was verbally abusive, an individual will internalize an inner abusive judge and will feel "less than." If the parent lived off the greatness of the child, the person will internalize a complex that views the ego as "better than" and entitled to all his/her needs and wants being met. Negative parental complexes continue to treat the child self in the same unhealthy way and advise the adult ego to do the same. They, too, can disconnect the ego from a functioning connection to the core self.

Often when parents and other authority figures are toxic, individuals disconnect from access to a Higher Power especially if their parents acted like gods. Other individuals feel that if there were a higher consciousness then it would be like a human parent and hold their view on what an appropriate family of origin would be. Since their family was hurtful, they surmise that there is either no God or that they are being punished in some way. This can result in a disconnection from the transpersonal.

Devaluing Negative Collective: The Internalizations of Society's Distorted World Views

Dysfunctional families are not always the only source of disconnections of the ego from the core self or external others. Minorities, whether they be people of ethnic diversity, socioeconomic stigma, or do not fit the ideal stereotype due to physical appearance or intellectual ability, often internalize negative devaluations of themselves and so disconnect as a result of the painful assaults on the core self. Additionally, they feel ashamed and/or feel that God has punished them in some way and thus disconnect from external others and the transpersonal.

Figure 13.1 represents schematically how the transpersonal, the ego, the inner child self, and the external others can be disconnected.

Animus and Anima: Inner Masculine and Feminine Aspects

When an individual has successfully connected to the self and healed their pain, access to their contra-sexual inner masculine or animus in women or inner feminine or anima in men becomes more available. Frequently the same sex parent can occlude a relationship to this contra-sexual complex. For example, if a man has a controlling mother complex, he frequently sees all women as potentially controlling. His anima may render him moody and depressed, but if freed, she is often a beautifully wise hierophant. Likewise, if a woman had a judgmental or unprotective father, she may not trust men and have a piercing derisive inner animus that attacks her and castrates other men. There are an infinite variety of animi and animae that can organically emerge from the unconscious to be claimed. They often make excellent advisors to the ego particularly if

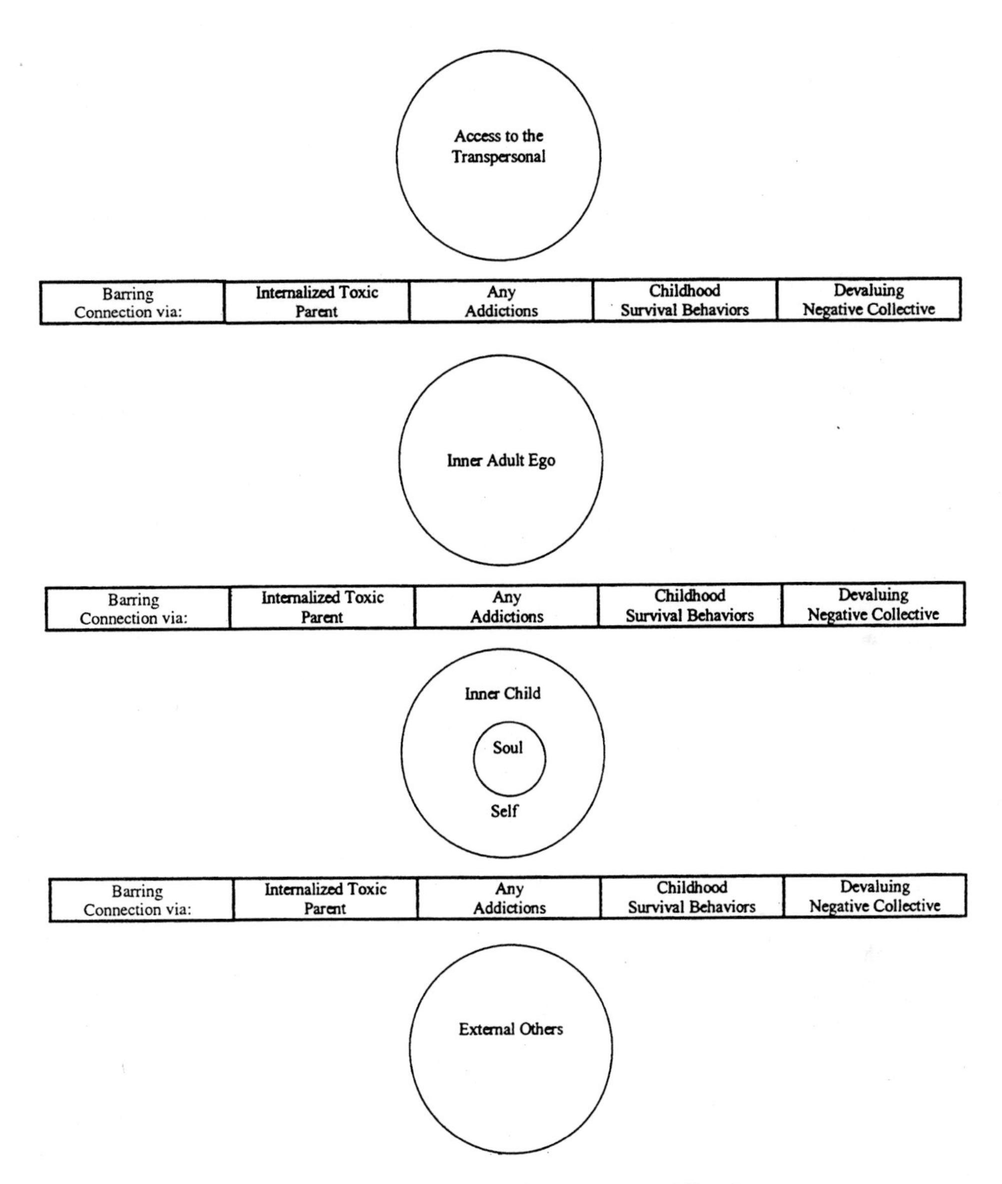

Figure 13.1. Dysfunctional Disconnected Psyche.

they are not projected out of the psyche and onto someone else.

The collective world view and family scripts often hinder a person from claiming their androgeny through a relationship to his anima or her animus. The collective voice might say, "Men shouldn't take care of the children" or "Women shouldn't be powerful."

Within these personal contra-sexual aspects, lie archetypal cores. A woman's animus might have an inner rational Apollo or protective Mars; a man's anima might have a wise Sophia or romantically loving Aphrodite.

Shadow Aspects: Inner Same Sex Aspects Waiting to be Claimed by the Ego

Likewise, same sex aspects or shadow complexes wait to emerge to be integrated into the ego or remain as advisors when the need arises. These aspects may initially appear as highly instinctual and uncivilized, but, with embodiment and intrapsychic dialogue with the ego, frequently become more civilized. They then are invited onto the inner board of directors.

Just as family roles and the collective can negatively influence the integration of animi/ae, so can they curtail the ego's relationship to the same sex shadow complexes. For example, a sibling may already have been identified as the smart one or the artist or athlete, leaving a younger sibling to be given another role.

As with *animi/ae,* shadow aspects also have archetypal cores to be discussed later in the chapter.

Soul: The Eternal Self

The soul, an individual's eternal being, lies within the core self or inner child. If individuals do not connect to the self, they will never be in relation to their soul. Thus they will never be able to connect to who they truly are and what it is they are meant to do in this life time. Figure 13.2 schematically represents a healthy inner psyche.

The Technique Itself: With Groups, Individuals, and Couples

Basically, the individual's psyche is role played. If they are part of a group, various group members take on the different roles and may be arranged in an initial tableau not unlike Satir's family sculpture. Each personified complex is given a characteristic phrase and movement. The antagonist can observe and is then asked, "Is this the way you want your psyche to be?" If the answer is no, then the drama therapy process commences with the person role playing parts of their psyche with whom they want more connection: the ego, child self, soul, animus/a or shadow aspect. Others play those complexes that need to be externalized and depotentiated: survival mechanisms, addictions, and toxic introjects. Role reversal by the protagonist is encouraged with complexes to be empowered and drawn into closer relationship to the ego.

For example, the embodied psyche technique was utilized in an ongoing drama therapy group at a men's long-term residential treatment center for addictions. Men were paroled to the site due to battering and drug-related crimes. Each group commenced with the premise and goal: "Recovery is the capacity to connect to oneself, others and the Higher Power. Addictions and outdated survival behaviors attack this connection. They need to be replaced with healthy boundaries." Making a case for drama therapy I add, "We believe that it is often more helpful to see what's happening and to experience change rather than just talking about it."

In the second group of a series of eight, 18 men were each asked to connect to his core self/ inner child and see what he feels, needs and wants. Matt, three months into the program, responded, "I want to be respected, to be loved, to be seen and missed." He then reported feeling confused. His inner confusor complex clearly did not want him to connect to himself. If that occurred, the "confusor" survival behavior would be out of a job. Matt picked one of the men who was particularly connected to himself to be his inner child; another man who knew his own inner confusor volunteered to portray Matt's complex. Another older man volunteered to be his addiction: the pill pusher. Interviewing Matt I came across another inner voice: his internal-

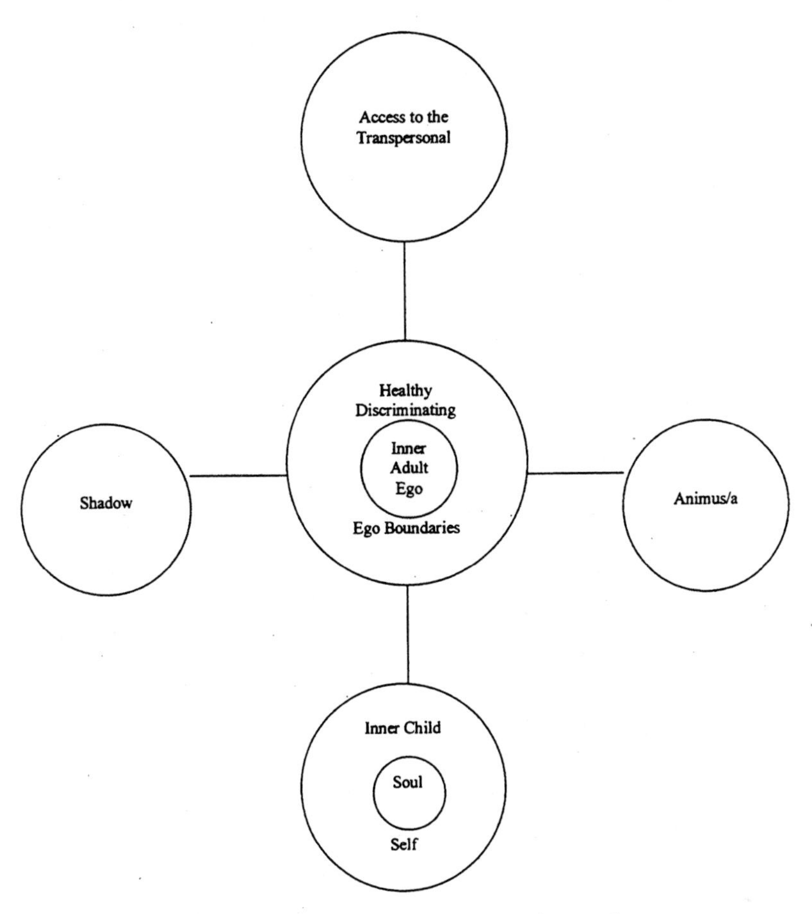

Figure 13.2. Healthy Interconnected Psyche.

ized father complex who repeatedly trashed him and told him that he was worthless. In short order, after interviewing Matt as his dad, another resident heard the familiar scenario and volunteered. Finally another resident was selected to be his ego/inner adult. Matt then told them what to say and with some more directing on his part, he sat back to watch.

His father began, "You're no good. You'll never be any good. You're a f...-up." Then his addiction began, "Who needs him. Who needs anybody. Let's take some of these pills and feel good." His inner child responded, "No please see me. I do not want those pills." His inner confusor, blocking access and interrupting his inner child and aligning himself with his addiction, said, "You're confused. It's just all too confusing. Do not feel anything; the feelings are way too confusing. Just take the pills."

"That's it!" he exclaimed with some amazement, "That's just what it sounds like in my head." "Is that how you would like your head to sound?" I asked. "No" was his emphatic response.

He was then instructed to take his ego's place and his complexes began their litany. Doubling his addiction, I exposed what I call the belly-side of this complex. "What do you mean you do not want me anymore? I have to have your attention. I live off you. I'll lose my power over you if you pay attention to your core self. You'll get stronger and I'll get weaker. I do not like that." "Tough!" was his response. Doubling his inner confusor, I say, "We'll go now, but we'll be back when you forget to connect to yourself or when things get tough." "Yeh," pipes up his addiction, "You can't get rid of us." With very little repetition he was able to shut his father, addiction, and survival behavior up. He then joined his child, and they gave each other an enthusiastic special handshake.

Other groups at this residential center had residents representing themselves encouraging the protagonist to come out from under his tough guy needless and wantless survival behavior to relate and feel their support. On occasion, an emissary from the Higher Power has been enacted (typically by one of my interns, as being in control is a larger than life issue for these men and generally not encouraged.)

In individual work, the drama therapist role plays the survival mechanisms, negative introjects and any addictions. The languaging is always the same. First the therapist attempts to sway the ego of the client into believing that it is a caring mother surrogate, then the devouring self-gratifying power hungry side is revealed.

One woman, having struggled with anorexia, began work with me. She reported that her throat felt blocked. I was not sure whether her throat was keeping others from entering or herself from expressing. Interviewing the block it appeared that it was both. It was neither safe to express herself nor had it been healthy to let in others. Since it is vital for a client to feel safe in the therapy container, I began shifting my distance from her in the room. She needed to feel her boundary and my respect of it. What became clear, however, was that present in her personal space subtle energy were imprints of individuals who had violated her space. Anyone who came within two feet of her body got contaminated by these energetic trauma memories of emotional and physical violators. I asked permission to enact these holographic energy forms which barred the possibility of interpersonal intimacy. "I still have you trapped. You are mine. No one else can be with you. I will contaminate them if they come near you, and cast a spell over you, so you cannot tell that they are safe. Do not trust Penny. Do not trust anyone."

I then de-roled and placed a large pillow between us, infusing it with the contaminated energy of the pervasive abusive objects. From this point we worked gradually, with her always in control, to clear the toxicity and create a safe bipersonal field between us (Lewis, 1987, 1993).

With couples, the projections and particularly the parental transferences are role played by the drama therapist. In one instance, a man's dark internalized mother complex was transferred onto his partner. He saw her as controlling and withheld from her. She, in turn, transferred onto him her unavailable internalized father whom she felt never really saw her. Role playing both transferences while placing my body between them allowed them to begin to see the other. In a witch-like tone I said to the man, "All women are controlling. They want to take you over and feed from your accomplishments. Stay away from her, you are mine. I will blind you to her gentleness and love for you." To the woman I say, "All men are cold, unavailable and care only about themselves. No man will ever want to see you and love who you are. Besides, this one is imprisoned in a witch's spell." Playfully they dip and sway to get to each other, finally shoving me out of the way.

Hence, drama focusing on enacted personifications of the inner child self, intrapsychic survival mechanisms, addictions, and other split-off aspects of the psyche as well as the internalized parents can be embodied by both client and therapist; and, if in group therapy, by group members in service to healing. This technique allows for externalized viewing by the client and the therapist as well as for the needed transformation of the psyche. Through dramatic process, needed shifts in psychic energy distribution and placement of the complexes can occur in relation to the ego.

Recovery of the Inner Child(ren)

With severe physical abuse the core self can become lost and fragmented into many inner children. This occurs when the abuse is so horrifying that the experience is thrown into the unconscious, typically with the child self still surrounded by the abuse and the perpetrators. The individual survives by casting the event(s) into the unconscious, but often at the expense of maintaining a connection to the child(ren) within. The split-off part of the self then remains in a freeze frame of the abuse until the individual reclaims the memory and separates the part of the self from the abusive event.

Rescuing the Inner Child(ren) from Abuse

The parts of the self that have been abused must be located and subsequently rescued by the adult ego in order for the person to feel safe enough to begin to talk about the event along with the many associated feelings. If the person does not first rescue the child, adolescent, or adult self who suffered the abuse, they will retraumatize themselves when they delve into the perpetration. If an individual was repeatedly abused throughout childhood, the inner children may be of different ages.

This rescue may be enacted in a group or imagined in an inner drama. The individual is asked to imagine the traumatic event just prior to the event happening. (Retraumatization through the reexperiencing of the event is unnecessary and abusive.) Then the individual is asked as an adult to enter into the scene and take the child out to a safe place such as their heart or a previously created sanctuary. This technique, first made popular by Bradshaw, allows the person to retrieve his or herself from each abusive event. In one group drama, the protagonist had one group member literally take the member who was playing her child-self out of the drama therapy space into my garden while she confronted the abuser.

Where the abuse is severe, resulting in dissociative responses, embodiment through drama may be initially too powerful. Arts media, such as art, sand play, storywriting, and journaling which externalize trauma-based phenomena can provide the needed distancing. These external symbols may be personified and interviewed by the therapist. With the needed healing and transformation carried out externally first, primitive survival behaviors and flashbacks are less apt to be triggered. The client can then internalize the drama therapy process when it is safe to do so.

Placing the Child(ren) in a Safe Place

Thus a safe place may be a picture or a physical representation of the child in a serene or loving setting. Externalized for a period of time, they can then be reinternalized after sufficient healing. Many clients have given me figures of mothers and children to be left in special "safe places" in my office while the transference heals their mother through my nurturing and supporting of their truth and healing. These figures are then reclaimed by the client when the healing of the inner mother, now capable of protecting them, is complete.

Rescuing the Child(ren) from Survival Behaviors

Primitive survival behaviors such as dissociation, when the soul leaves the body, deanimation, when the child is placed in suspended animation, and multiple personality dissociative states, when the ego complex is cast out of consciousness while inner children of different ages and personalities take over, are often present with severe repeated physical abuse. In these instances, the inner children must feel safe enough to be fully present in an embodied manner along with the attention of the inner adult ego. With multiple personality disorder, the therapist must be the appropriate parent to each alter and help to develop interrelationships among the inner children and the inner adult ego.

Everything stops when a person leaves his/her body. This typically only occurs when the individual is having a flashback early on in the recovery work. Often this disabling process is what brings them into treatment. Speaking and moving minimally, the therapist asks concrete safe questions. I once spent much of an hour talking about recipes; while, through the somatic countertransference, intuiting an imaginal drama that would coax the frightened self back into my client's body.

Deanimation may be enacted as a survival behavior. "I will keep your inner child frozen in numbness for eternity. Aren't I a caring protector? You do not ever have to pay attention to your core self. No need to ponder what you truly feel. I will make sure you sense that you feel, want or need nothing." Often the inner child(ren) feel a false sense of safety within this survival mechanism, but with unconditional love and care, they can be retrieved.

Healing and Reintegration of the Child(ren)

Through embodiment or giving voice to a picture, photo, dream, sand play figure or other external representation, the child(ren) begin to be healed. One woman dreamt that a child had been found wounded and starving in a comatose state with maggots crawling on her. I encouraged her to reenter the dream and pick her up. She wouldn't do it. She felt disgusted by the condition of the child. Asking permission to enter her dream, I moved over and cradled the dream image. The woman began to cry. I picked the maggots off her and began imaginally to give her liquid. Then I bathed her in healing waters. By this time the woman had moved closer. I said to her, "Look she is beautiful. She has your eyes." The woman was then able to receive her into her arms and heart.

Dreamwork as Theater

Dreams are one of the avenues into the unconscious that can be of invaluable help to someone engaged in recovery or individuation. Dreams can symbolically identify parts of the self that have remained unavailable to the ego. They can be "red flags" brought forth to tell the individual that they are in a toxic situation or relationship or generally going in the wrong direction in their sacred path. When an individual is in therapy or analysis, the unconscious often presents the dreamer with symbolic information pertinent to their process. Typically these dreams come from the personal unconscious. But occasionally they emerge from the transpersonal archetypal unconscious. These are what Jungians call "big dreams." Their purpose is to expedite the therapy process by providing profoundly compelling experiences often of a deeply spiritual nature.

In addition to symbolic dreams, individuals can also have flashbacks during the dream cycle. These are typically not symbolic but the reexperiencing of actual prior traumatic events. There are occasions when the individual will have nightmares that are partially symbolic and partially from a real recollection. The specific symbolism utilized is typically created at the time that the abuse was suppressed, and can be of archetypal proportions.

Because there are very different types of phenomena that can occur during dream cycles, it is very important to be able to distinguish among them. For example, many women upon first encountering their inner masculine, may dream that some strange man is chasing them. In the dream they fear for their life or that they might be raped. Interviewing the pursuer it is discovered that this inner male is angry with the dreamer for not paying any attention to him, so he decided to make his presence known. Communicating with this aspect in the imaginal realm results in his softening and becoming more compellingly attractive to the dreamer. A union frequently ensues that is filled with all the romance and loving pleasure that could be hoped for. Flashbacks, even if couched in a layer of symbolism, have a very different feel to them. Attending to the somatic countertransference, the drama therapist may pick up fear or have a dark foreboding sensation. Noticing any primitive survival mechanisms such as deanimation or dissociative responses exhibited by the client indicates the possibility that this may be a flashback contraindicating the technique of dreamwork as theater.

In the dreamwork technique, the individual is asked to become different characters, inanimate objects, or atmosphere in the dream. I then interview the dreamer as the personification. At times dialogues ensue between two characters or aspects of the dream. If the dream is too scary, I further distance the dreamer from the dream by having them pretend that the dream is a movie in the process of being filmed. I suggest that the actors and crew just took a break and that I am an entertainment newsperson interviewing the dreamer who is cast in the role of the dream/movie character or script writer.

Dreams can be altered through the imaginal realm to give the dreamer an experience of greater individuation. After interviewing the characters I suggest for the dreamer to imagine the dream in a way that supports the awareness that has occurred in the dramatization.

The role of the therapist is to assist in the enacted re-creation of the dream. Upon entering the dream, characters can be interviewed understood, claimed, transformed, and integrated in service to recovery and individuation. Themes and plots can unfold a map of a person's entire therapy process, and the archetypal can profoundly reconnect an individual to the many layers of Spiritual Consciousness.

One person, in the dark night journey of the soul, had a series of archetypal dreams. She fought not to let go of what she had known in the past. But in the end, as Jung said, the decision was made over her head and despite her ego. She let go of her life as she knew it and moved into the liminal realm. She dreamt that a bomb had exploded outside her home. When she went out, everything was in devastation. She knew she would be dead soon from radiation poisoning. In the next dream a male (not any one she knew, but clearly her animus) had been shrunk and lay in a small casket. She wanted to reanimate him but to no avail. Utilizing dreamwork as theater, she gestured as if she were disrobing, and climbed into the coffin. Lying down on the floor, she reported feeling at peace for this first time. The next week she dreamt she was in a church that had the reputation of being filled with the grace of God. She reported that the church was packed but that she was able to lie down on the pew.

Before she closed her eyes with the rest of the attendants, she saw a large black man enter the church carrying an automatic weapon. She feared for her life and the lives of others. She stayed frozen, afraid to attract attention to herself. With her eyes closed she heard him walking up the aisle and stop in front of her. The next thing she felt was his kissing her heart. She awoke with a start. She lay down in the therapy space and asked him, "Why did you do that?" "You are doing the right thing," he commented in a wise voice; but if you leave, I will have to shoot you." She commented, "God's grace comes in unexpected ways. I know I must stay in this gestating death. I do not know who I will become when I arise, but I know I am on my spiritual path."

Archetypal Enactment

At the center of each complex within the psyche is an archetypal core. Often the recovery and individuation process clears personal history allowing the archetypal energy to be accessible to the individual. The experience of the archetypal is a sacred event. All present are healed when the numinous enters the drama therapy space. Through art, sand play, dreams, authentic and improvisational drama, individuals can access and experience its power to shake loose any disconnection to the archetypal's transpersonal power to heal and bring consciousness.

The process of individuation fosters various inner masculine and inner feminine aspects previously waiting in the wings of a person's psyche to enter and be claimed. Often the negative qualities manifest if an individual keeps their personal relationship to the archetypal out of the civilizing influence of consciousness. Figure 13.3 represents pantheons of inner feminine archetypes; Figure 13.4 the inner masculine archetypes available to the individuating pilgrim. Each archetype has its positive and, if not balanced by its opposite, its negative aspects.

An example of the integration of these techniques can be seen in a workshop that brought individuals to an island in Greece for a spiritual journey of self exploration employing daily embodied sand play, dreamwork as theater, and archetypal enactment. Daily female archetypes were invoked through Greek goddesses for theme-based dramatic experiences.

One evening Persephone, the daughter of the Earth Mother Goddess, Demeter was invoked. An innocent girl (Kore), she was abducted by the god of the underworld and eventually transformed from being a victim to becoming the queen of the underworld. Through this process she moved from unconsciousness into being one who had psychic abilities and became a charismatic guide for those who journey into death.

Many women and men's *animae* have suffered victimization in their lives through their experience of being abused either by their family, perpetrators, and/or the culture. The capacity to let go of this view of being a victim and to claim the power of womanhood with all its wisdom and capacity to venture into the cyclic realms of death and rebirth is key for some. In the drama experience, men and women let go of who they were in service of claiming greater wholeness. A tenor, who had come from generations of African American Baptist ministers, began leading the group in a wail. All members joined in until the group became the wail, speaking-moaning of their suffering and loss as they dropped to the floor, surrendering to the pull of symbolic death. I shrouded each one as they ritually experienced their life force leave their bodies. They then floated into a gestating pregnant timelessness. After a period of time, they experienced reanimation and gradually arose renewed with a greater access to divine wisdom.

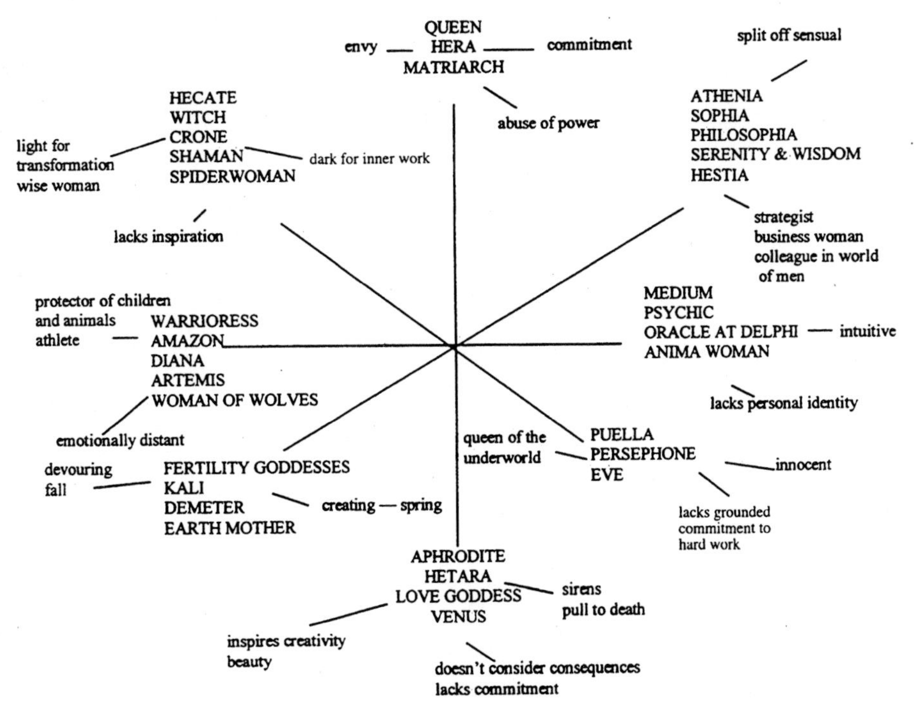

Figure 13.3. Archetypal Inner Feminine.

A man said of this experience, "I thought that Persephone was a goddess only for women; I realize I am a Persephone. My innocence was ravaged, I was forced to leave a deep connection to the safety of my mother, but I see now what I have received in the hellish place of my despair. I have my own power in my recovery." A single middle-aged woman said, "I have not wanted to let go of my innocent Kore (Persephone before she claimed her queenship). I felt that I would be thrown into the disposal heap of 'older women' when it comes to men. They do not want powerful women. But I finally see that unless I claim my wisdom and intuitive abilities; I might as well stay in suspended animation under this shroud you put on me. If a man only wants a Kore, I wouldn't want him!"

A couple came to me. The wife complained of volatile abusive outbursts from her husband. Working first with solution-focused role play, the behaviors were arrested. He then began individual recovery work with me in which he found his core inner child frightened and rageful at not being seen. Healing the relationship between his adult self and child also brought about a clearing of his mother complex. Through my involvement in co-parenting, his mother was transferred into me for healing. At one point I needed to switch his hours twice in a week. He responded to this break in the consistency of the holding environment by missing his next two appointments. When he finally came in, he experienced permission to be appropriately angry. I not only received his anger but reflected how this inconsistency affected him at a deep level. In the next hour, he came in and stretched out in an open posture. He reported feeling safe. He noticed two trees outside my window. I

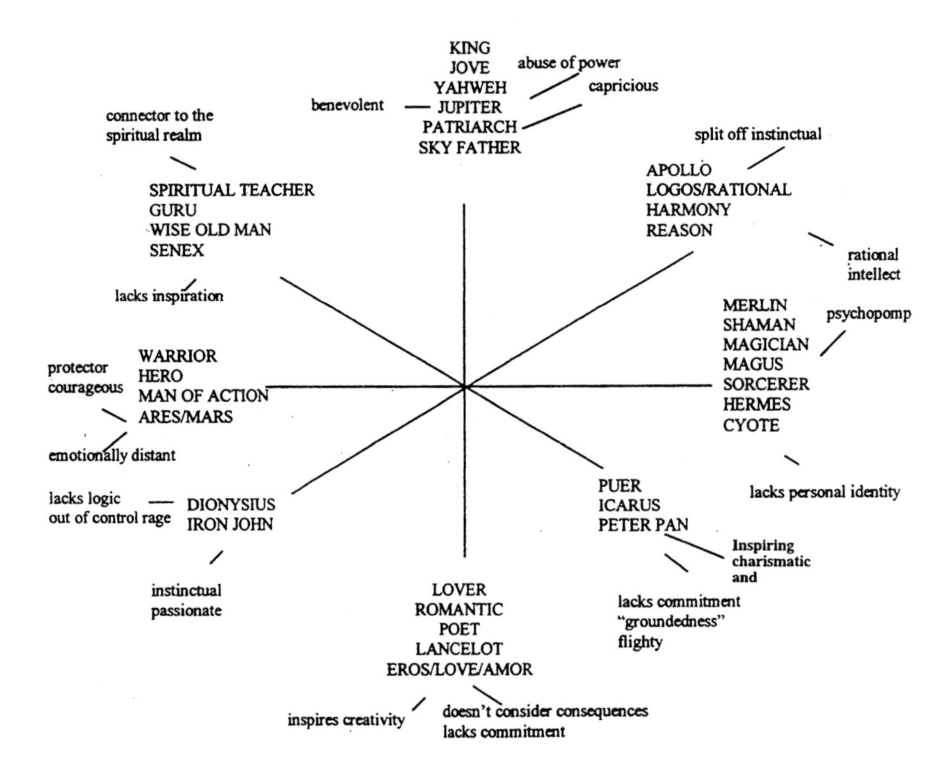

Figure 13.4. Archetypal Inner Masculine.

respond by saying, "Once upon a time, there were two trees. . . ." He continued this derivative story about relationship. At the end, he expressed love for me. I responded, "You have given a part of yourself to me. She is your inner feminine. I will hold her, but she is yours and belongs with you." I began feeling his anima. She was genteel, wise, loving and compassionate–goddess-like. I suggested he dialogue with her, which he did and left with her in his heart. The following week, he reported experiences of being at one, fully present with those around him, with nature and his involvement with it. He had been offered promotions that would bring him power and status. He declined as he served a different God. He called his inner feminine Grace.

CASE STUDY

A woman in her fifties was referred to me for recovery work. I had already heard of her, as she was a well-known psychic. I pondered what it would be like working with someone who reported such a connection to the transpersonal. Since her physical and emotional abuse occurred over many years, her core child self was fragmented into many children of different ages. All of these inner children needed to be rescued from the trauma within which they were frozen in her now emerging memories. This took several weeks of working within dream/flashback images, externalization through drawing, and much transpersonal assistance creating a safe place.

Sometime later she brought in a dream about a child that had no skin. The experience of being skinless is a frequent metaphor of individuals who have had their body boundaries violated. My client wrote in her journal: "I had a dream about a child with no skin. She was raw. Penny asked me to try to relate to the child. I took away the covers and surrounded the child with Light. I could not have a conversation with this child; I could only heal her. Penny asked me to be this child. The child was frozen with stark terror: stuck; iced up. I did not like doing this. I felt numb and then I felt the mothering part of me emerging wanting to help this baby. Drawing the healing process brought forth a picture of an angel holding the child."

Once her inner children were freed from the abuse memories, they needed further releasing from her childhood survival patterns that attempted to protect her. Individually each child self emerged from the wall (see Figure 13.5) and frozen numbness of her past. My client drew each released child. I would often put the drawing of the child on my lap as if I was holding the actual child; and with my client speaking for her, she would tell us what she wanted us to know. (See Figure 13.6.)

Once all children were reclaimed, the emergence of a new child came hidden in a cave-like surround who later came to be know as "The Butterfly Soul Child." Her soul, who frequently left her in dissociation, now felt safe enough to return. (See Figure 13.7.)

An excerpt from one of her many poems speaks to the powerful spiritual belief that began to grow in her.

> Tell all the pained ones
> About the POWER OF GOD
> That I am finding in ME.
> I give the children a mirror
> To show them their own Light.
> Do not be afraid, little ones.
> You are in 'the remembering.'
> Come away from the fires of pain
> to my garden where
> my feet are planted among the flowers.
> I am the butterfly
> Child soul
> There is fresh air-sunshine-loving
> transformation here.
> Come little ones,
> my arms are long and wide enough
> to hold you.

Throughout her work with me she channeled drawings and messages into her journal from her spiritual guides. Toward the end of the work, she accessed a transpersonal connection. Through embodiment she spoke the following message:

> Breathe with compassion. Compassion is the salve you seek to relieve your pain. It is the rock that you search for to hold you securely above the floods of time. Sometimes the winds may temporarily cool the surface and cause you to wonder where you are, but it is your understanding of the fire within and trust in its eternal Light that will keep you on your path, your rock of truth.
>
> Compassion is a very powerful soul voice that automatically seals boundaries and allows the soul voice to be heard. It is powerful medicine for accumulated pain and does not allow anger and fear to dwell for very long in anyone's life. Anger and hatred are defenses. Compassion is the way of the soul and the only way to spiritually respond to life. Life is not as complicated as it seems.
>
> If you dwell on sickness you will become it. This is the lesson that you have to learn, that beyond all of the physical and mental violence there is still the soul, and the soul cannot express itself if it is surrounded by hate and fear. The real work is the clearing the energy that surrounds your center of love. If your energy field is filled with your soul's compassion and the gentleness and strength of its love, you will have what you need to feel safe in your life. This is not a weakness. It is the power of God becoming your presence.

Figure 13.5. Childhood Survival Mechanism: The Wall.

In summary, when my client left her body, as many do during physical abuse, she reaffirmed a connection to the transpersonal. That connection maintained throughout her life has evolved into her life's vocation. What was a means of escape in childhood has become the foundation of her livelihood and the means through which she serves the transpersonal and her fellow humans.

SUMMARY

In summary, the two stage model focuses upon an individual's life work to recover from their past so that they may be fully present in the moment able to connect with themselves, other individuals, and transpersonally. Additionally individuals continue throughout their life in the process of indi-

Figure 13.6. An Inner Child.

viduation undergoing adult life stages, deepening their understanding of the meaning of life and their role in it, and expanding their spiritual consciousness.

REFERENCES

Arts in Psychotherapy Journal. (1992). vol. 15, no. 4.

Barber, T. (1976). *Advances in altered states of consciousness & human potential.* New York: Psychological Dimensions, Inc.

Boorstein, S. (1991). *Transpersonal psychotherapy.* Stanford, CA: JTP Books.

Carter-Haar, B. (1975). What is psychosynthesis? *Synthesis, 1,* 2, 115–118.

Edinger, E. (1982). *Ego and archetype.* New York: Penguin Books.

Harner, M. (1982). *The way of the shaman.* New York: Bantam Books.

Jung, C.G. (1969). *The archetypes and the collective unconscious.* CW, vol. 9, part. 1. Princeton, NJ: Princeton University Press.

Jung, C.G. (1963). *Mysterium coniunctionis.* CW. 14. Princeton, NJ: Princeton University Press.

Figure 13.7. The Butterfly Soul Child.

Jung, C.G. (1969). *Symbols of transformation*. CW vol. 5. Princeton, NJ: Princeton University Press.

Lewis, P. (1993). *Creative transformation: The healing power of the arts*. Willmette, IL: Chiron Pub.

Lewis, P. (1996). Depth psychotherapy in dance/movement therapy. *American Journal of Dance Therapy, 18,* 95–114.

Lewis , P., & Greene, C. (unpublished manuscript). *Soul healing through the arts*.

Lewis, P. (1986). *Theoretical approaches in dance-movement therapy. Vol. II.* Dubuque, IA: Kendall/Hunt.

Lewis, P. (1988). The transformative process in the imaginal realm. *Arts in Psychotherapy. Vol. 15.* pp. 309–316.

Lewis. P. (1992). The transference and counter-transference in arts psychotherapy. *Arts in Psychotherapy, 15.*

Smart, N., & Hecht, R. (1982). *Sacred texts of the world: A universal anthology*. New York: Crossroad Publishing Company.

Walsh, R., & Vaughan, F. (1993). *Paths beyond ego: The transpersonal vision*. Los Angeles: Jeremy P. Tarcher/Perigee Books.

BIBLIOGRAPHY

Books

Amaghi, J., Lewis, P., Loman, S., & Sossin, M., (Eds.). (1999). *The meaning of movement: Developmental and clinical perspectives in the Kestenberg movement profile.* Newark, NJ: Gordon & Breach.

Lewis-Bernstein, P. (Ed.). (1975). *Therapeutic process movement as integration*. Columbia: ADTA Pub.

Lewis-Bernstein, P., & Singer, D. (Eds.). (1982). *The choreography of object relations*. Keene: Antioch University.

Lewis, P. (1986). *Theoretical approaches in dance-movement therapy, Vol. I.* Dubuque: W.C. Brown-Kendall/Hunt Pub.

Lewis, P. (1987). *Theoretical approaches in dance-movement therapy, Vol. II.* Dubuque: W.C. Brown-Kendall/Hunt Pub Co.
Lewis, P., & Loman, S. (Eds.). (1990). *The Kestenberg movement profile: Its past, present and future applications.* Keene: Antioch University.
Lewis, P. (1993). *Creative transformation: The healing power of the expressive arts.* Willmette, IL: Chiron Publishing.
Lewis, P. (1994). *The clinical interpretation of the Kestenberg movement profile.* Keene: Antioch New England Provost Fund.
Lewis, P. (1999). *Schopfennshe prozesse. Kunst in der therapeutis chen praxis.* Zurich/Dusseldorf: Verlag Pub.

Articles and Chapters

Lewis-Bernstein, P., & Cafarelli, E. (1972). An electromyographical validation of the effort system of notation. *Writings on body movement and communication. Vol. II.* Columbia: ADTA Pub.
Lewis-Bernstein, P. (1972). Range of response as seen through a developmental progression. *What is dance therapy really?* Barbara Govine, (Ed.). Columbia: ADTA Pub.
Lewis-Bernstein, P., & Bernstein, L. (1973–1974). A conceptualization of group dance-movement therapy as a ritual process. *Writings on body movement and communication. Vol. III.* Columbia: ADTA Pub.
Lewis-Bernstein, P., & Garson, B. (1975). Pilot study in the use of tension flow system of movement notation in an ongoing study of infants at risk for schizophrenic disorders. *Dance therapy–Depth and dimension.* Delores Plunk (Ed.). Columbia: ADTA Pub.
Lewis-Bernstein, P. (1975). Tension flow rhythms: As a developmental diagnostic tool within the theory of the recapitulation of ontogeny. *Dance therapy–Depth and dimension.* Columbia: ADTA.
Lewis-Bernstein, P., Rubin, J., & Irwin, E. (1975). Play, parenting, and the arts. *Therapeutic process movement as integration.* Penny Lewis Bernstein, (Ed.). Columbia: ADTA.
Lewis-Bernstein, P. (1980). Dance-movement therapy. *Psychotherapy handbook.* Richard Herink (Ed.). New York: The New American Library Press.
Lewis-Bernstein, P. (1980). A mythic quest: Jungian movement therapy with the psychosomatic client. *American journal of dance therapy.* Spring, vol. 3, no. 2, pp. 44–55.
Lewis-Bernstein, P. (1980). The union of the gestalt concept of experiment and jungian active imagination within a woman's mythic quest. *The Gestalt Journal,* Fall, vol. 3, no. 2, pp. 36–46.
Lewis-Bernstein, P. (1981). Moon goddess, medium, and earth mother: A phenomenological study of the guiding archetypes of the dance movement therapist. *Research as creative process.* Columbia: ADTA Pub.
Lewis-Bernstein, P. (1982). Authentic movement as active imagination. *The compendium of psychotherapeutic techniques.* Jusuf Hariman, (Ed.). Springfield, IL: Charles C Thomas.
Lewis Bernstein, P. (1986). Embodied transformational images in dance-movement therapy. *Journal of Mental Imagery,* vol. 9, no. 4, pp. 1–9.
Lewis, P. (1987). The expressive therapies in the choreography of object relations. *The Arts in Psychotherapy Journal,* vol. 14, no. 4, pp. 321–332.
Lewis, P. (1987). The unconscious as choreographer: the use of tension flow rhythms in the transference relationship. *A.D.T.A. conference monograph.* Columbia: ADTA Pub.
Lewis, P. (1988). The transformative process within the imaginal realm. *The Arts in Psychotherapy,* vol. 15, no. 3, Fall, pp. 309–316.
Lewis, P. (1988). The dance between the conscious and unconscious: Transformation in the embodied imaginal realm. *The moving dialogue.* Columbia: ADTA Pub.
Lewis, P. (1988). The marriage of our art with science: The Kestenberg profile and the choreography of object relations. *Monograph 5,* Columbia: ADTA Pub.
Lewis, P. (1990). The Kestenberg movement profile in the psychotherapeutic process with borderline disorder. *The KMP: Its past, present application and future directions.* Lewis & Loman (Eds.). Keene: Antioch University Pub.
Lewis, P., and Brownell, A. (1990). The Kestenberg movement profile in assessment of vocalization. *The KMP: Its past, present application and future directions.* Lewis & Loman (Eds.). Keene: Antioch University Pub.

Lewis, P. (1991). Creative transformation: The alchemy of healing, individuation and spiritual consciousness. *Shadow and light: Moving toward wholeness.* Columbia: ADTA Pub.

Lewis, P. (1993). The use of reflection, reciprocity, rhythmic body action, and the imaginal in the depth dance therapy process of recovery, healing and spiritual consciousness. *Marian Chace. her papers, 2nd edition,* Sandel, S., Chaiklin, S., & Lohn, A. (Eds.). Columbia: ADTA Pub.

Lewis, P. (1993). Michael jackson, analysiert mit hilfe des kestenberg-bewegungsprofils in tanztherapie. Hormann, K. (Ed.). *The application of the Kestenberg movement profile and its concepts.* Zurich: Beitrage zur Augewandten Hogrefe.

Lewis, P. (1992). The creative arts in transference-countertransference relationships. *Arts in Psychotherapy,* vol. 19, no. 5, pp. 317–324.

Lewis, P. (1993). Kestenberg movement profile interpretation: clinical, cultural and organizational application. In *American dance therapy association proceedings.* Columbia: ADTA Pub.

Lewis, P. (1993). Following our dreams: Dance therapy as transformation. In *American dance association proceedings.* Columbia: ADTA Pub.

Lewis, P. (1994). Die tiefenpsychologisch orientierte tanztherapie. In *Sprache der bewegung,* Berlin: Nervenklinik Spandau Publication.

Lewis, P. (1996). Depth psychotherapy and dance-movement therapy. In *American Journal of Dance Therapy,* vol. 18, no. 2.

Lewis, P. (1996). Authentic sound movement and drama: An interview with Penny Lewis. Annie Geissinger interviewer. In *A Moving Journal.* Providence, vol. 3, no. 1.

Lewis, P. (1996). The gestalt movement therapy approach" In Tsung-Chin, Lee, (Ed.). *Dance Therapy.* Taipei, Taiwan: Publisher identified in Chinese Characters.

Lewis, P. (1996). Authentic sound, movement, and drama: An interactional approach. In Robbins, M. Ed. *Body oriented psychotherapy, Vol. I.* Somerville, MA: Inter. Scientific Community for Psycho-Corporal Therapies Pub.

Lewis, P. (1996). The Kestenberg movement profile. In Robbins, M. (Ed.), *Body oriented psychotherapy, Vol. I.* Somerville, MA: Inter. Scientific Community for Psycho-Corporal Therapies Pub.

Lewis, P. (1997). Multiculturalism and globalism in the arts in psychotherapy. In *The Arts in Psychotherapy,* vol. 24, no. 2, pp. 123–128.

Lewis, P. (1997). Appreciating diversity,commonality, and the transcendent. In *Arts in Psychotherapy,* vol. 24, no. 3.

Lewis, P. (1997). Transpersonal arts psychotherapy: Toward an ecumenical world view. In *Arts in Psychotherapy,* vol. 24, no. 3.

Lewis, P. (In process). An embodied relational model: The use of the somatic countertransference and inter subjectivity within the affective-imaginal realm. In Robbins, M. *Body oriented psychotherapy, Vol. II.* Somerville: Inter-Scientific Community for Psycho-Corporal Therapies.

Lewis, P. (1999). Healing early child abuse: The application of the Kestenberg movement profile. In Amaghi, J., Loman, S., Lewis, P., et al. *The meaning of movement: Developmental and clinical perspectives of the Kestenberg movement profile.* Newark: Gordon & Breach Pub.

Lewis, P. (1999). The embodied feminine: Dance and drama therapy in women's holistic health. In Olshansky, E. (Ed.), *Woman's holistic health care.* Gaithersburg, MD: Aspen Publishers, Inc.

FURTHER TRAINING

Alternate Route Certificate Program in Transpersonal Drama Therapy

Penny Lewis, Ph.D., LMHC, NCC, ADTR, RDT-BCT and Saphira Linden, MA, RDT-BCT co-direct this one to two-year 40 credit graduate level program that is individually tailored to meet each student's needs. If applicants have already fulfilled the requirements for some of the courses, they will be exempt from having to retake them. Additionally, work experience may also count for other NADT course requirements.

Class scheduling is suited to working and distance students as courses are given on weekends and intensives. The program is appropriate for individuals who are currently enrolled in graduate programs or who have completed a psychology/counseling, drama or arts therapy-based graduate program. The certificate program meets the NADT academic requirements for Alternate Training for (RDT) Registered Drama Therapist credentialing and continuing education credits for licensure.

The program is jointly located at the Institute for Healing and Wellness, Inc. in Amesbury and Omega Theater, Inc. in Jamaica Plains near Boston. The program has relationships with Antioch-New England Graduate School, Emerson and Lesley Colleges.

Curriculum

The curriculum utilizes the two stage transpersonal theoretical approach. It is sequentially designed to introduce the student to basic premises and gradually increase their knowledge and sophistication in various techniques. The Institute for Healing and Wellness and Omega Theater honor the students' inner vision of the embodied arts therapies and the discovery and expansion of their own gifts through the program so that each individual's unique potential may be realized.

The curriculum includes: Core courses in psychology; individual and group drama therapy recovery theory and techniques; individual, group, and community transpersonal drama therapy theory and techniques as well as supervised internships in drama therapy.

Scheduled Courses

Current scheduled courses can be found on the Internet at www.dramatherapy.com and www.omegatheater.org or by contacting:

Dr. Penny Lewis
27 Merrill Street
Amesbury, MA 01913

Phone: 978-388-3035 Fax: 978-388-5757
Email: drplewis@seacoast.com

Chapter 14

PLAYBACK THEATRE: A FRAME FOR HEALING

JO SALAS

GENESIS

PLAYBACK THEATRE BEGAN IN 1975 with Jonathan Fox's vision of a theatre in which ordinary people acted out the stories of their community. His vision combined aspects of tribal ritual–people whose lives are intertwined in everyday life coming together to celebrate or explore or heal through ceremonial and artistic action–and storytelling, an oral tradition in which wisdom and truth are embedded in stories told aloud. Jonathan was also inspired by Moreno's psychodrama, a specifically therapeutic approach that draws its strength from the body-and-soul involvement not only of the protagonist but of the group.

Jonathan and others, including myself, spent several years developing a viable form for this vision. The idea eventually spread internationally: there are currently 80 registered groups in over 30 countries, doing Playback in many different settings. To this day Playback Theatre challenges the customary divisions of our society. It is theatre with the power and intention to heal and transform individuals and social groups. Playback's attention to process, to inclusivity, to the well-being of the performers as well as the audience distinguishes it from more familiar forms of theatre in which the artistic success of the production is the only thing that matters. On the other hand, its commitment to aesthetics places it firmly in the realm of art.

So Playback Theatre is not primarily a therapy, but a versatile theatrical form that is equally at home in public theatres, in schools, hospitals, and institutions, corporate settings and conferences, and in forums for social change–on the streets of southern India with Dalit people telling stories about police brutality, or at an outdoor community event exploring diversity in a small American town.

At the same time, since Playback's early years, drama therapists and psychodramatists have recognized Playback Theatre's potential as a therapeutic approach. There has been a rich cross-fertilization between Playback Theatre and therapy: many Playback practitioners are also trained as therapists, usually drama therapists, psychodramatists, or creative arts therapists. They use Playback in their clinical work with trauma survivors, couples and families, adolescents, people in recovery from addictions, and other populations.

My own experience using Playback Theatre therapeutically has been with severely emotionally disturbed children ages 5 to 14, and it is this application that I will be describing in this essay. Working as a music therapist at a residential treatment facility, I trained a group of staff members in Playback Theatre. We formed an in-house company, performing every month or two for groups of children. Later, hoping to give children the additional therapeutic benefits of acting as well as telling stories, I co-led (with a member of the staff Playback group) Playback Theatre therapy groups, with groups of four or five children meeting weekly for six sessions.

PLAYBACK FRAME OF REFERENCE

Therapeutic Process

In a cleared space–a stage, or one end of a large room–two chairs are set up on the side, facing the empty space. The chair nearest the audience is for the conductor, Playback's onstage director or emcee. Across the back of the stage area, four or five actors sit on crates, boxes, or chairs. A musician with instruments at the ready is positioned further to the side, opposite the conductor. Upstage, there is a collection of large fabric pieces for the actors to use as elemental costumes or props.

The conductor invites someone from the audience to come and tell a story. Seated beside the teller, the conductor asks questions to find out what happened, who was there, how did it end–all from the teller's point of view. The conductor asks her to choose actors to play the key roles, starting with the teller herself. The actors stand up as they are chosen, not acting yet but preparing inwardly as they listen to the rest of the story.

The interview ends and the conductor hands the story over to the actors with an injunction: "Let's watch!" As music plays, the actors silently position themselves for the opening of the scene. There is no discussion. The actors act out the story as accurately and creatively as they can. The teller and conductor watch from the side. When the scene is over, the actors pause in place, looking toward the teller. The conductor invites the teller to comment, or perhaps just to pause before returning to the audience.

If the enactment was not true enough to the essence of the story to satisfy the teller, the conductor may ask the actors to redo some or all of it, incorporating the teller's corrections. Occasionally, with a story that has been accurately portrayed but has left the teller troubled, the conductor may invite him to imagine a new outcome, which the actors bring to life–a "transformation," as it is termed in Playback Theatre.

Another teller comes to the chair, and the process continues.

This is how Playback would look in a performance context, with a trained company of performers and a defined audience. In my work with children in residential treatment, it was "performance Playback" that we began with–the children were audience and tellers, not actors. But Playback Theatre may also follow a workshop model in which one or two experienced Playback leaders guide participants in enacting stories for each other: everyone has the chance to become an actor. The basic format remains the same, but without the emphasis on artistic competence that is required for public performance.

"Workshop-model" Playback is most often used in therapy. The therapy groups at my institution followed this model, with the children taking turns acting for each other as well as telling stories. (In both models, Playback also includes a variety of "short forms"–briefer structures for responding to a teller's experience or feeling.)

Basic Concepts

Playback Theatre is based on a constellation of beliefs and values. Practitioners generally share the following convictions:

- The characteristics of both a fully-realized human being and of an ideal culture include the capacity for connection with others, compassion, and creativity.
- People need stories in order to know who we are as individuals and as a society. The stories we tell of ourselves and our world crystallize and communicate social and personal self-knowledge.
- Personal stories hold wisdom and beauty for others, including strangers.
- Witnessing each others' stories fosters understanding and empathy.
- All human experience, including extreme suffering, finds meaning when it is communicated in aesthetic form.
- The connection that arises from sharing personal stories is a counterforce to increasing isolation and alienation.
- Given the right context, all people have the innate capacity and spontaneity to respond with empathic creativity to another person's story.

Healing Effects

These convictions have clear implications for Playback as a broadly healing experience in both performance and nonperformance settings. It is my observation that taking part in a Playback Theatre event creates movement toward wholeness for individuals and groups as they tell, hear, and watch stories about what is significant in their own and others' lives.[1] This movement is apparent in the comments of tellers about the lasting meaning and change that came from telling their stories; in the visibly empathic response of audience members as they watch and listen; and in the common Playback phenomenon of audience members–strangers two hours before–lingering to talk to each other and to the performers after a show.

In addition, there are a number of further specific effects for the storytellers: the profound affirmation and validation of having your story enacted according to your subjective perception; the certainty that you have been fully heard by performers and audience; the relief from aloneness that comes with bearing witness in a public or semipublic setting; the sense of distance or mastery in relation to a difficult past experience; new perspective or insight into a life situation; the catharsis of laughter or tears.

For the people who enact the stories, whether they are members of a company or a group doing workshop-model Playback, Playback's intrinsic healing effects go further. Taking active part as an actor helps to develop spontaneity (in the Morenean sense of having full access to all one's resources). It also promotes expressiveness, receptiveness to others, self-confidence, self-esteem, creativity, teamwork, playfulness, and the capacity for aesthetic mastery and pleasure.

Two further healing aspects of Playback are profound and pervasive: one is the atmosphere of respect and acceptance that is fundamental to any Playback event. The other is the presence of ritual, by which I mean the establishment of a ceremonial frame in space (the simple but formal arrangement of the stage), time (the protocols of eliciting and enacting a story), and demeanor (the attentiveness of the actors, the inspired leadership of the conductor), in which the stories of ordinary people are told and remembered.

Playback as a Drama Therapy Method

It is a natural step to go from the inherent healing effects in Playback Theatre to the use of Playback in clinical contexts. Most mental

[1] See Folma Hoesch, "The Red Thread," in Gathering Voices: Essays on Playback Theatre. Tusitala Publishing, 1999.

health clients are people who can clearly benefit from Playback's capacities to affirm subjective perception and experience, to strengthen identity, to increase awareness and compassion, to express emotion, and to respond creatively to the expressions of others.

A therapist integrating Playback into clinical practice will make choices about which particular aspects are most helpful and suitable for her clients. She may also need to modify or simplify Playback's structures according to client needs and capacities, as well as practical considerations such as limitations of time and space, and the availability of co-leaders.

When I first decided to bring Playback Theatre into the Neville home,[2] my intention was to give the children a chance to tell their stories–to provide Playback's accessible stage as a forum where they could speak and be heard. I knew that they had remarkable stories to tell, that they were full of lively responses to the world around them, and that in the rough-and-tumble of institutional life there were few opportunities for them to be heard other than in one-on-one therapy sessions. I thought that the ritual of Playback might prove a strong enough frame–even in this environment–for the children to bear witness in front of their peers.

After I had taught the staff group enough of the basics of Playback, we began with after-school performances in the gym for groups of about 15 children, the maximum number we thought we could manage successfully. Soon, teachers in the Neville's school invited us to do shows in their small classrooms. Although our performances followed the traditional Playback format, we learned quickly which aspects needed adapting or emphasizing. We found that the children responded better to enactments that were literal and concrete rather than metaphorical. The Playback form called Pairs, in which actors portray the struggle between two feelings at the same time, proved to require so much explanation that we stopped using it, realizing that its demand for emotional self-awareness was beyond the reach of most of the children. Special attention to openings and endings was needed: we sang with the children at the beginning to settle them into receptiveness and keep them occupied as latecomers straggled in. As the show ended we allowed time for verbal sharing, more singing, or art activities. More children wanted to be tellers than we had time for, and our closing activities gave the disappointed ones a chance to express a small part of the story they had not told.

In spite of occasional frustration at not telling their stories, the performances brought joy to the children–a healing effect in itself. They were happy to come to the shows and thought of them as a pleasurable activity whether after school or during the school day.

Examples

In one classroom performance, six-year-old Courtney told a nightmare about a witch who came to her while she was asleep and put horrible stuff on her nails and pricked her skin.

"What was the scariest thing, Courtney?"

"I'm scared I'll be like the witch."

During the enactment she yelled at the witch–"I'm over here!" I reminded her that Diane, the actor she had chosen, was being Courtney in the story, that she herself was just watching. She was very excited. I held her closely on my knee. When it was over, I asked her if she would like to make up a different ending for her story. It was at first hard for her to understand the possibility I was

[2] The names of the institution, staff, and children are fictional.

offering. Then she got it. Her eyes lit up. "I want to kill the witch, and I want my mom to hug me and say 'Good girl.'" With satisfaction she watched this amended scenario acted out.

Gary, who had been full of scathing complaints earlier, wanted to be the next teller. But when he came to the chair, he did not have a story. It was not unusual for children to long for the experience of being a teller while being not at all clear about what they wanted to tell. It was our job to find a story, however minimal, in whatever elements they could offer.

"Who's someone who might be in your story?" I asked Gary.

"My grandma," he responded immediately. I had heard that Gary's grandmother had died recently after a long illness. Soon a story emerged about the time she had entrusted him and his brother to go to the store for her. "She wasn't sick, she just too busy. We got everything and we gave her some change and she was real pleased."

We acted out the story, Gary calling out additional details from the side as he remembered them. "She wanted *soup!*" he yelled. Without missing a beat, the teller's actor added soup to the grocery items he was putting in his imaginary basket.

"Thank you for telling us about your grandma, Gary," I said when the scene was over.

"Thank you for acting my story," he said, peaceful and gracious.

In another school experience, we met in the staff library to do a show for Leah's class. They were all about eight or nine years old, though, like most of the Neville kids, they seemed far younger than their chronological age. The library, used less for reading than for staff meetings or occasional events for the children, was a cozy book-lined room with a long and massive table occupying most of the floor space. We moved things around as best we could to clear a stage area at one end of the room.

Ernestine's hand shot up as soon as I asked for a story, but I passed over her to Omar, whose hand was up as well. I was remembering an earlier time when Ernestine had been the teller. An angular little girl with darting eyes, she was one of the children who sailed close to psychosis. Her story a couple of months ago had been chaotic and without discernible relationship to reality. After Omar's story was over, Ernestine's hand was in the air again, waving urgently. Inwardly crossing my fingers, I invited her to the teller's chair.

"What's your story about, Ernestine?"

"It's about how I became an artist." she said. She was emphatic and clear. I listened, moved. She went on to tell, with perfect cogency, how she had started on the artist's path when she was five, thanks to a helpful teacher. "And I've been an artist ever since," she finished triumphantly.

Ernestine watched the scene intently. "Yes, that's right," she said turning to me when it was over. She was smiling broadly, delighted to share this sense of herself with all of us in the room.

For Courtney, Gary, and Ernestine, there were somewhat different healing outcomes from telling and seeing their stories. For Courtney, it was a way to gain mastery over a troubling dream, first by seeing it externalized and physically separate from herself, and then by the opportunity to reimagine the scenario. (In Playback, this "transformation" is always generated by the teller, in response to the conductor's invitation after the scene is first played as it happened. If a child needs help understanding such a profoundly creative possibility, the conductor may offer a "for example" or two. But it is only the teller's imagined scene that is acted out.) For Gary, telling a story about his recently-deceased grandmother was a chance to remember her as she was in life; it was his choice not to focus on her illness or death. In the company of witnesses, he honored her and his relationship with her–a primary function of any mourning ritual. Ernestine's story claimed the part of her that was creative and functioning. It was also an articulation of inner life unlikely to take place in any other context at the Neville.

Like all Playback audiences, the children told stories about things that were important to them. Sometimes a story revealed an aspect of the grievous history that had brought the child to the Neville–stories about a drug-addicted mother, an abusive stepfather, or violence on the streets or home. It was clear that telling and watching such a story helped in comprehending a painful reality; and letting others know about it lightened the burden of carrying such pain alone. But we neither encouraged nor discouraged the children from telling such stories. We conveyed our openness to whatever they wished to tell. We felt certain that there was a different and equally important healing taking place when the story was about a reward trip to get pizza or about being chosen as someone's friend. Such a story was an affirmation to the child herself and to the people in her world that she was a person with success and happiness in her life as well as trouble.

Whatever the content of the stories, the most therapeutic effect of all was the experience of being heard, fully, respectfully, and without analysis or judgment. Interpretation in the psychological sense[3] is not constructive in Playback Theatre, even in clinical applications. Playback Theatre works like art or dream, presenting images, patterns, associations, and allusions that are best comprehended on their own terms. Playback speaks the language of story, a right-brain language that holds potent meaning for the subconscious. It would have actually diminished the healing effectiveness of Courtney's story, for instance, to try to make explicit the relationship between her dream and her history. A relationship undoubtedly existed; but allowing it to remain embedded in the events and symbology of the dream gave Courtney's emotional processing far more power than any discussion of feelings or facts could have had.

Older tellers often spontaneously express cognitive insights after seeing their stories; but it is still important that such insights come from the teller and not from the conductor or actors.

Playback Therapy Groups

The children were eager to act as well as tell, and sometimes we invited one or two of them to join us onstage in a minor role. But in general we knew it was too risky to give these very volatile children the responsibility of enacting the stories–at least in a performance context. On the other hand, I was aware of the potential therapeutic benefits to be gained from the experience of acting as well as telling in Playback: the chance to develop expressiveness, empathy, connection to others, a sense of teamwork and belonging. I organized therapy groups of four or five children in which they took part in workshop-model Playback Theatre, learning how to enact stories as well as telling them. Over the period of a year and a half, I and a co-leader led eight different groups, each one meeting for six 45-minute sessions.

I knew from the outset that I needed someone to lead with me, for logistics–escorting children in different directions before and after sessions; for occasional crisis management–a reasonable likelihood with the Neville's population; and, most importantly, to support and guide the children's acting while I conducted. In the early phases

[3] Artistic interpretation, on the other hand, is legitimate and essential especially in performance Playback: the actor interprets the story the way a pianist interprets a Bach prelude, enriching it with her or his artistic vision.

of each group, Lisa, the co-leader, played whichever role required the most delicate handling, usually that of the teller. Later, as the groups gained cohesion and confidence, I invited the teller to choose freely from any of the actors. We made other adaptations as well, aimed at maximizing the children's success. We omitted music during the scenes since it was too difficult for them to create sensitive improvised music, and not practical to bring in another staff member. We also stopped using the fabric props when we saw that they were more distracting than helpful. As the conductor I gave far more direction to the actors than I did for adults, including, sometimes, a brief narration to begin the story, to move it along in the middle if it got stuck, or to cue an ending. We routinely debriefed with sharing after stories so that actors as well as tellers could speak about their experience during the enactment.

Each session followed a similar sequence, creating a predictable container for the creativity and openness that we were invoking. The quality of ritual in the structure of each session echoed the framing of the enactments themselves. We began with a song of greeting as we sat on the circle of pillows, sometimes followed by another "fill-in" song in which each child contributed a line expressing a feeling, an experience, or a wish. The warm-up phase often included one or two carefully-chosen drama games designed to develop expressiveness and connection. Such activities were structured to make them as accessible and enjoyable as possible. For example, in a game that required partners, we paired the children with Lisa and me until they were ready to work successfully with each other.

When it was time for stories, we set up our stage with plastic milk crates positioned along one wall for the actors, the piano bench on one side for teller and conductor, and the pillows moved back for the audience. The children readily learned the simple Playback procedure of the enactment itself: the telling of the story, the standing of the actors as they are chosen, the "Let's watch!" injunction of the conductor to signal the beginning of the action, the pause at the end when the teller is acknowledged by the actors, and the conductor's invitation to the teller to make a final comment.

After one, sometimes two stories, we returned to the circle of pillows for several minutes of sharing–how was it for the teller, for the actors, for the children watching if there were any. As in the psychodramatic practice of sharing, the emphasis was on expressing any feelings or memories that had been stirred, not offering analysis or counsel. (Sharing was another adaptation–in nonclinical Playback Theatre, we do not pause to share after enactments, instead trusting in the natural dialogue between stories and in the capacity of performers and audience members to cope with their individual responses.) We ended with another song to acknowledge each child and say good-bye until next time.

This routine, of course, was liable to change shape as each session evolved. Sometimes a warm-up activity expanded to take up most of the session (as with the role-playing activity I describe in the illustration below). At moments of particular intensity we sometimes paused and returned to the pillows for a song to help everyone express, contain, and integrate emotion. Singing became such a key element in these groups that the children sometimes initiated improvised songs, individually or as a group, as another way to tell their stories.

The Success of the Groups

Group therapy of any kind at the Neville was rare because of the children's instability. We were prepared for our experiment to fail as many others had. But it did not. The children relished the opportunity to tell stories in a more intimate setting. As in the performances, their stories often spoke of normality and humor, hope and love. But the intimacy and continuity of the group also allowed them to tell more tender stories, stories of loss or vulnerability that could be told only to trusted listeners–though still avoiding the stories of their worst traumas, sensing that even the relative safety of these groups was not enough to hold the extreme disclosures that many of them could have made. Their enactments were generally without artistic polish, but they were fully able to replay a story with enough accuracy and sensitivity to satisfy the teller.

They responded gleefully to the acting games and songs, often using them to express feelings in somewhat oblique and therefore unthreatening form. There was also a subtle change in their sense of themselves as people, citizens of the Neville. Day and night the message of their environment was that they were burdens, misfits, the cause of trouble for everyone around them–"emotionally disturbed." As actors in each other's stories they found an unfamiliar and precious opportunity to be the agents of comfort and learning for each other: helpers, not problem-causers. Their tolerance and understanding toward each other grew with their willingness to take on roles that crossed racial and gender divides.

Perhaps most significant of all was the growth of empathy. As they acted in or witnessed each others' stories, they found themselves stepping into another person's feelings in a way that they had seldom done before. A tough, violent boy watched a girl's story about being terrorized by a stepfather when she was two years old. "I felt bad for Sharelle. I wish her mom had come and helped her," he said afterwards, a rare expression of pity and identification. A black boy balked at playing a white grandmother in another boy's story, then did it with such effectiveness that the teller was moved. "How did you know what she's like?" asked the teller. "Just thought about my own grandma," was the answer. Taking roles in each other's stories, witnessing and reflecting each other's experiences, engendered a compassionate fellow-feeling that was generally absent from the interactions of children who had had little chance to learn about empathy from the adults in their lives.

In spite of numerous chaotic moments and occasional crises, the groups more than met our expectations as well as those of the children. Many expressed a wish to continue longer than the six weeks limit placed on us by the school authorities, understandably concerned as they were about the children missing too much of their academic studies.

I believe that to a large degree it was the ritualistic structure, both the protocol of enacting a Playback scene, and the design of each session itself, that accounted for the success of these groups. We organized time and space so that the children felt not only safe, generally, but invited and honored. They instinctively recognized the age-old presence of ritual, of a frame in which their personal experiences were communicated and held. Our circle of pillows on the floor, where we sat to greet each other and sing, embodied this framing of our time together, as did the creation each session of the "stage."

Playback Theatre is above all built around this sense of ceremony, the deliberate creation of an artistic and truth-telling space that is distinct from ordinary life. It is the element of ritual that accounts for Playback's power in any circumstance. The Neville children recognized and responded to it, telling their important stories to each other and enacting them with compassion, creativity, and respect.

Limitations and Growing Edges

We of course encountered difficulties as well as successes. The most challenging aspect was the lack of integration with the rest of the Neville program. It seemed difficult to gain a general acceptance from the staff, both for the performances and the groups. A number of them did appreciate its therapeutic value and were enthusiastic supporters. The attitude of these staff members–teachers, therapists, childcare workers–greatly enhanced the effectiveness of what we were doing. They took Playback seriously and made themselves available to follow up where needed, for instance after a story that exposed a vulnerable experience. They sat with the children during performances, keeping them company, helping them to stay focused and involved, modeling the kind of respectful attention we were asking from the children. But other staff considered Playback Theatre to be at best an entertainment and at worst a subversive encouragement for the children to believe their own faulty versions of reality. It had been, in part, to improve this situation that I initiated the therapy groups. My hope was that by inviting staff members to refer children, and by providing ongoing progress reports on what transpired, there would be an increased and synergistic understanding of the Playback approach. Although there was indeed some improvement, I remained unsatisfied with the place of Playback Theatre within the program as a whole.

The other challenge was the precariousness of the children's interactions. The atmosphere at the Neville was often fraught with violence. Many children were prone to losing control, at risk of hurting themselves, each other, or staff members. Although the ritual structure of Playback itself and of our sessions created a context of safety to a surprising degree, there were also occasions when one or more children had to be removed to avert conflict. We had to resort to a physical restraint once, when a girl became hysterically giggly as she acted out a story and could not regain control, spiraling rapidly toward violence.

We learned that for children to succeed in Playback Theatre therapy they needed enough ego strength to step into another role without losing the awareness of their own identity: some of the younger children, especially, could not cope with acting out even brief moments or feelings told by other group members. The Playback groups were also not suitable for the few near-psychotic children at the Neville. For someone who is unsure of the boundaries of reality, it is not safe to venture into the zone of "as if." However, with careful clinical framing, such fragile children could and did tell their stories in performances.

From my experience, as well as that of other therapists whose work I know of, Playback Theatre has proved itself as an effective therapeutic approach–when in the hands of people who have thorough training in both Playback and clinical practice. Playback Theatre's apparent simplicity is deceptive. It is a method of considerable power and subtlety. There are dangers to using it without adequate training, just as there are dangers in using Playback in clinical contexts without clinical training.

On the other hand, with a team of fully-prepared leaders, there are exciting potentials still to be fulfilled. One day there may be other places like the Elsinore Children and Youth Center in Denmark, where most of the staff is trained in Playback Theatre, allowing a synergistic relationship between the Playback work and every other aspect of the program–to the great benefit of the young clients.

CASE EXAMPLES

The Story of a Playback Group: Excerpts from Six Sessions

It was the first time. Like a pair of Pied Pipers, Lisa and I collected children from their various classrooms, our string growing as we progressed toward the Space Room, the small recreation room where the group was to meet. The children came in, curious and a little shy, and sat down on the circle of pillows. From staff referrals we had chosen two girls and three boys: tall, quiet Elizabeth, pixie-ish Kiki, Malcolm, calm and mature-seeming, with a habit of ducking his head to avoid eye contact; Albert with red hair and a touch of rakish glamour about him, and Ronnie, small and messy with shirt hanging out and glasses held together with Scotch tape. Malcolm and Kiki were African-American, the others white. All were 12 or 13 except Kiki, a precocious 9-year-old. Ronnie looked and behaved much younger than his actual years.

Sitting on the pillows, we sang a song of greeting. The kids joined in, briefly self-conscious then relaxing into enjoyment.

> Here we are, it's another day,
> Just one thing that I would like to say,
> Oh Kiki, and Albert, hello to you.

We sang around the circle, naming everyone.

I explained to them that in this group everyone was going to have a chance to tell stories and to act them out for each other. "And when you're not being an actor you can be a witness," I said. They looked at each other, confused.

"A witness?" asked Kiki. "You mean like in court?"

I realized this was the wrong term for children who were all too familiar with courtroom lingo. "I mean, you can be the audience. It's good to have someone to watch." They nodded.

"Is this therapy?" asked Elizabeth.

"Yes," said Lisa. "We want it to be helpful to you. We want it to be fun too." They nodded again, accepting.

Malcolm volunteered to tell the first story, after we had played a couple of warm-up games.

"When I was home last time," he began, "me and my cousin got into trouble because we took eggs from his mother's refrigerator and we threw them at kids in the street. So she got mad–she gets really mad sometimes but she don't hit us–and she made us go to the store and get some more eggs for her, with our own money. When we were in there, this kid, he was an older kid that my cousin knew, he told us to give him the eggs, but we wouldn't. So he waited for us outside the store, and he had a gun. So we gave him the eggs."

I asked Lisa to play Malcolm and invited him to choose actors for the other parts. As the teller's actor, Lisa helped keep the story on track.

They acted it out, Malcolm and I watching from the side. The kids surprised me by how well they remembered what their characters said and did. Albert was the bully with the gun. He managed to rein in his restless energy until the right moment, when he stepped into the scene with a menacing swagger. Malcolm was riveted.

"Yeah, that's what it was like," he said, shaking his head. "Man!" He was quiet for a moment. "Then later on, my other cousin, John, he really did get shot a couple of blocks from there. They killed him."

The other kids stared at him. Lisa and I waited. Malcolm's eyes were far away.

"Malcolm?" I said after a minute. "Do you want to tell us more about that?"

He turned to me, back in the room again. "Nope."

We came back to the circle of cushions for the last ten minutes of the session. I invited the kids to tell us what Malcolm's story might have reminded them of in their own lives. "Or you could tell us what it felt like being an actor."

"My grandma was shot in the stomach," said Ronnie. He seemed more proud than upset.

"I got shot in the arm. Look." Albert pulled up his sleeve to show a scar. "My brother's friends were fooling around. They were trying to scare me and they sure did."

I was taken aback. I could not get used to the dreadful familiarity so many of the children had with guns.

I asked Albert what it was like to play the threatening teenager in Malcolm's story.

"I felt bad! That guy was ugly." I thanked him for doing it. I told them that it was a kind of a gift they could give each other, to play the tough roles in each other's stories.

"I got something to say," said Malcolm, who had been listening without comment. "I hate guns. I hate people who use guns. They spoil everything for everyone. It's not fair." Malcolm was passionate. "My aunt, she belongs to Mothers Against Guns, and I think they're really cool. They want to make things safe again. They're sick of kids being killed."

It was time to go back to class. "Our plan is to meet every week for six weeks," I reminded them. "But it's your choice now. What do you think? Do you want to keep going?"

"Yes!" they all chorused. Lisa and I looked at each other, pleased.

When we met again, the children wanted to talk about Malcolm's story.

"It was a sad story," said Kiki, wrinkling her nose. "I don't really like sad stories."

"It wasn't so sad, though," said Elizabeth. "At least Malcolm didn't get shot."

"What I think is, if something bad happens, it's better to tell people about it. At least they get to know about it," said Albert.

"Yeah," said Malcolm. "Anyway my story wasn't that bad, not as bad as what happened to my other cousin." They were silent.

Later in the session Kiki had a story to tell. "I thought about this yesterday, that I would like to tell it when I came to the group. It's about when I was seven, and I was living with my mother and my little brother, Mason. He was four." Kiki, sweet and smart, had been removed from the dangerous care of her mother when she was eight. "My mom, she used drugs all the time, and her boyfriend too, and he used to beat her up when they got high." Once again I found myself trying to listen attentively while sickened inside by what I was hearing. "I was playing with my little brother in our room and I could hear them hunting everywhere for that thing that you use–you know, Malcolm, what's it called?" She mimed with her hands.

"You mean the cooker?"

"Yeah, that's it. Anyway, I was very scared because I had thrown it out the window. I knew they'd both beat me up if they found out. But then my mom told me to take Mason to the store. I sure was glad to get out of there."

The actors, Lisa as Kiki, acted it out. Kiki snuggled in as close to me as she possibly could, gripping my arm tightly. "Yeah, that really did feel like my story," she said, letting her breath out at last when it was over.

The others talked about what it was like for them to play it. "Sad," was the comment of most of them. "I felt sad for Kiki," said Elizabeth.

"Kiki, did you think it was a sad story?" I asked her, remembering her comment about Malcolm's story.

"Yes, it was, but I'm still glad I told it."

We talked, and sang, and acted out one more story. But they were still stirred up. I showed them how to take deep breaths and let their bodies relax as they exhaled.

It was time to end. Kiki turned and hugged me. "Anyone else want a hug?" I asked. They all did.

Albert arrived to the next session in a strange mood, disheveled and hollow-eyed. "I'm on special alert," he announced to everyone. "I got restrained five times today. I'm not allowed to go home for more than three days over vacation." The 10-day Easter break was coming up. I had not heard what the special alert was about, but it was usually the result of suicide threats. I knew that the anguish in his family was more than enough to make a child question the value of living. Albert and his three siblings had been raped for years by both their father and uncle Now in puberty, he was in trouble himself for sexually victimizing his younger brothers. The father had recently died of AIDS. The children and their mother lived with the knowledge that they might be infected, though tests so far were negative.

I watched Albert for signs of depression, and to see if he wanted to use this chance to explore what was on his mind. He did not, instead sabotaging the other children's attempts to express anything serious.

"I was thinking about something this week..." began Elizabeth.

"Hoo-wee! Elizabeth knows how to think!" interrupted Albert. "Make a note of that, will ya, Ronnie?" Ronnie was always ready to play along with Albert's clown, but their comedy act had never been as disruptive as it was today.

"Let's everybody take some deep breaths," suggested Malcolm at one point when tempers were rising. It helped, but only briefly. Lisa and I finally gave Albert an ultimatum: settle down or go back to class. Albert saw that we meant it. His demeanor changed. "OK, I'll calm down. Don't send me back." He tried hard for the rest of the session, lapsing sometimes but then catching himself. Ronnie followed his cues precisely.

We asked the kids, one at a time, to enter the room in the role of someone they knew well–"Think of someone who really likes you" was my instruction. Elizabeth went first.

"I'm Mrs Tait, Elizabeth's mom," she announced, sitting down in a chair.

"Welcome to the Space Room, Mrs Tait. Please tell us about your daughter Elizabeth."

"Well, I think she's wonderful," said Elizabeth as her mother. She told us about Elizabeth's ambition to become a schoolteacher. "And she'd be a good teacher. She really likes little kids."

We thanked "Mrs Tait" and said goodbye. Malcolm went next. He came into the room with a ghetto walk and sat down in the chair with his arms folded and his legs splayed out.

"I'm Malcolm's cousin Leroy. Malcolm told you about me. We almost got shot when this kid wanted our eggs, remember?"

"Hi, Leroy. What can you tell us about Malcolm?"

"He's OK. We do everything together. We're like this." Malcolm held up his fingers firmly linked together. "I look out for him, he looks out for me."

"What do you like best about Malcolm?" asked Lisa.

"Leroy" was suddenly bashful. "Well, it's like, it's just that he's my best friend, and my cousin too." He paused. "All I can say is, we stick together, and if one of us gets in trouble, we both get in trouble."

"So maybe you could help each other stay out of trouble, Leroy, what do you think?"

"Yeah, I guess."

We had time for one story. Ronnie told about getting sent to the crisis room during school the day before. For the first time in this group, I invited him to choose any actors he wanted. He chose Malcolm to play himself, Lisa for the teacher, Albert for the easygoing crisis room supervisor who played cards with him. Malcolm did a fine job.

In the next session, we played the Lying Game, a favorite in which each person tells something that may be true or a lie. Ronnie said: "Me and Albert are brothers." Everyone except Albert held up two crossed fingers to show they did not believe it. Ronnie and Albert protested in unison. "It's true!" For once they were not clowning.

"He's lived next door to me all my life," explained Albert. "We *are* like brothers."

"Yeah," said Ronnie. I had never seen him so intense and serious.

We had discovered too that there was another connection that Lisa and I had been unaware of when we chose children for this group: Kiki and Elizabeth had also known each other before coming to the Neville.

These long-established friendships accounted, at least to some extent, for some of the unusual cohesion of the group.

Albert was eager to continue the "interviews." I had heard meanwhile from his therapist that he had suggested this activity in their session. In the role of his friend Thomas, he had talked about how upset Albert was about the fighting that went on at home, with four wild children and a helpless mother. The next day he had written a note to the therapist–"Thank you for helping me express my feelings." She was astonished and moved.

In the Space Room, Albert decided to be his older brother Gary. His voice deepened and his body seemed to grow bigger.

"So what do you and Albert like to do together?" Malcolm asked him.

"Rough-housing, that's what I like. He squeals a lot but I don't care." Albert had told us before how he hated his brother's rough play.

"What do you think Albert wants more than anything?" I asked.

"Gary" looked thoughtful. "He wants to come home in the summer. He wants everything to be OK by then." When his turn was over, Albert had trouble letting go of the role, cuffing and teasing the others in a way that seemed unlike himself. We had to remind him two or three times–"Albert, you're Albert, remember? You're not Gary any more."

Ronnie surprised me by being able to take on another role consistently. "Hi, I'm Nicky," he said in a high voice. "I'm Ronnie's brother and I'm only three and a half." He looked convincingly like a small boy, swinging his legs under the chair and chewing on his hand.

"Do you and Ronnie get along?" asked Elizabeth.

"Well, he's always beating me up."

"How come he beats you up?"

"Because I always punch him."

"What does your mom do?"

"Sometimes she hits Ronnie and then he cries, then he beats me up again."

Kiki was last. She left the room and came back in smiling and dignified. "Hello, everyone. My name is Annabel and I'm Kiki's big sister. I'm nineteen. My job is managing a supermarket."

"Hi, Annabel. Tell us about Kiki."

"She's my favorite sister, she's very funny and I miss her. A lot. She's very smart, too. She wants to be a lawyer when she grows up." I was touched. I had no doubt that Kiki was bright enough to become a lawyer–but how was she going to get there from here? She was black, female, poor, the child of a drug addict, institutionalized for emotional disturbance at the age of nine. She would need more luck than seemed likely to come her way.

It was time to end. The role-playing exercise had taken the place of stories this session: another way to act out personal truth. Malcolm, who had a gift for sensing what the group needed, suggested a song. "How about 'We shall overcome'?" he said. All the kids knew it. They added their own words, prompted by the invitation that was in the air, to dream about the future:

"We'll have lots of money," sang Ronnie.

"We will all go home," sang Elizabeth.

"We'll grow up and be happy," sang Kiki.

"We will have nice families," sang Albert.

"There will be peace in the world," sang Malcolm, a little embarrassed but determined to say it. When the song was over he shook everyone's hand.

By the next group, Albert was in trouble again in school. When Lisa and I came to pick him up, his teacher was reluctant to let him go. "Albert, I just don't think you can handle it," she said.

"I can! I'll be all right! I really want to go, *please,* Carmen." At length she agreed. But as soon as he was in the Space Room he reverted to being giggly and rude. As usual, Ronnie caught his mood, and even Malcolm was affected. The girls were exasperated. Elizabeth wanted to tell us about her grandfather's death during the week. She had gone home for the funeral. Albert tittered as she spoke and tossed a pen from his pocket across the circle to Ronnie.

"Catch!"

Ronnie caught it and tossed it back. I grabbed the pen.

"Stop!" There was silence. "Everybody breathe." They did. I waited before going on. "Albert, do you want to listen to Elizabeth? Or do you want to go back to class?"

His tension released a little by the deep breathing, Albert's hysteria was subsiding. "It's OK, I can listen. Sorry, Elizabeth. I'm sorry about your grandfather."

"It's hard to think about death," I said. "But it happens in all our families."

They all nodded. "I got something to say," said Malcolm. He paused, looking down. "I'm thinking about my cousin. The other one. John." His voice was very quiet. "He was 28 and he had three little kids, and now he's dead. I'm scared about living in the city again. My mom wants us to move somewhere safer when I go home in June."

I wanted him out of that war zone. Malcolm was a remarkable boy. The world needed the adult that he would become, if he survived.

"My grandmother died, too," said Ronnie. "I was sad, *and* I was glad, because she wasn't in pain any more and also I got to see all my relatives." He was direct, sincere; so different from the Ronnie of a few weeks ago.

"When my dad died I laughed," said Albert, hunched over his knees. "My mom told me I should cry. I didn't know what to do, because he'd been real mean to us. I'm not sorry he's dead."

I was ready for this somber theme to continue when we did a story. But Elizabeth told about a good time with her brother and cousin and friends, all of them having an uproarious waterfight in the park. All of four of the other kids acted, expressive and imaginative in their assigned roles. They were a team, cohesive, disciplined, creative.

It was our last session. Elizabeth was missing, kept in class by an unrelenting teacher. Carol listened with pursed lips to our pleas–this is the last of six sessions, we think this group has been very significant for all of the children, our closure together is important–and shook her head. "You can take Ronnie, but Elizabeth's not going." It was a familiar dilemma. We wanted Elizabeth to come, for her own and everyone's sake. But forcing Carol to let her go might backfire on us later. We needed the teachers' goodwill and cooperation. Promising Elizabeth that we would find her after school, we took Ronnie and left her sighing over the schoolwork she had refused to do earlier in the day.

The others were disappointed not to see her. They were troubled that the group was ending and showed it by being distracted and giggly. It took them a while to settle down. We had brought art materials for a final activity: each of them was to make a card like a book cover bearing the title of her or his life story. Inside, the rest of us would write goodbye messages.

The Space Room was quiet as the children worked, decorating their book covers with drawings and symbols. Kiki's title was *The Girl Who Wanted to be a Lawyer.* Albert wrote *Albert's History.* Ronnie, glancing over Albert's shoulder, called his book *Ronnie's Humor.* Malcolm's was *Malcolm's Adventures in Life.* They passed their books around. "You are a kind and good person. I will always remember your two cousins." wrote Kiki in Malcolm's. "Thanks for letting me show my feelings," wrote Albert in Kiki's. "I had fun with you and everyone," wrote Ronnie. "When we're grown up and you're a lawyer, you can help me," wrote Malcolm to Kiki. "Now I know that we have stories in our lives," he wrote to Albert.

A few weeks later I tape-recorded individual interviews with Albert, Elizabeth, and Kiki about the experience of being in the group. One of my questions was about its duration–how did they feel about meeting for six sessions?

"It was too short," said Albert emphatically.

"*Way* too short!" said Kiki.

"I wish it was longer," said Elizabeth. "I wanted to keep coming."

"How long would you have liked it to be?" I asked them.

"A year," said Kiki.

"Maybe four months or six months," said Elizabeth.

"How long? *I* think, every single week," said Albert. "Yup, every single week, that would be better."

CONCLUSION

Although Playback Theatre is not primarily a therapy, it embodies significant therapeutic effects for people who participate as tellers, audiences, and performers, effects that can be applied and developed in clinical contexts. Performance Playback with institutionalized emotionally disturbed children gave them opportunities for the building of identity; mastery over difficult experience; expression of concerns, perceptions, and feelings; and the relief of realizing that one's story may be shared by others. When the children took part in ongoing therapy groups as actors as well as tellers, they gained additional benefits from belonging to an intimate group and acting out each others' stories, developing further expressiveness, confidence, a changed self-concept, and empathy.

The source of Playback Theatre's potency as a healing force is its basis in ritual and the language of story. The success of Playback in therapy depends on these qualities being fully recognized both by Playback-trained clinicians and by the institutions in which they practice.

REFERENCES

Fox, J. (1994). *Acts of service: spontaneity, commitment, tradition in the nonscripted theatre.* New Paltz: Tusitala Publishing.

Fox, J., & Dauber, H. (Eds.). (1999). *Gathering voices: Essays on playback theatre.* New Paltz: Tusitala Publishing.

Salas, J. (1993). *Improvising real life: Personal story in playback theatre.* New Paltz: Tusitala Publishing.

Salas, J. (1994). Playback theatre: Children find their stories. Chapter in *Handbook for treatment of trauma-attachment problems in children,* Beverly James (Ed.). New York: Lexington Books.

Salas, J. (In Process). *The Space Room: A story of children, madness, and the arts.*

FURTHER TRAINING

For training in Playback Theatre, contact:

School of Playback Theatre
www.playbacknet.org/school

Phone: 914-255-8163

For information about the International Playback Theatre Network contact IPTN, 1134 Linganore Place, Charlotte, NC 28203.

Chapter 15

CREATING NEW CULTURES: USING DRAMA THERAPY TO BUILD THERAPEUTIC COMMUNITIES IN PRISONS

JOHN BERGMAN

PRISON CULTURES CAN BE very dangerous. The anger that is part of prison life can become a deep and corrosive force stifling staff and prisoner alike. Geese Theatre Company USA has been involved with institutional change since 1980. It is our experience that one of the most effective challenges to institutional cultures are modified or total therapeutic communities inside the institution.

Geese Company has been involved in creating, running and training staff to work in total and modified therapeutic communities since 1988. We are finally beginning to create a practical set of principles for transforming staff and prison cultures so that they can run effective therapeutic communities. These principles are not yet set. Many of these praxis processes are self-evident to anyone who has worked in the field of therapeutic communities. Although there has been some evaluation of our work especially the effectiveness of one of the communities discussed here in Australia (Cook, Semmens, & Grimswade, 1999), we cannot yet be predictive and say that these principles will always lead to an effective community. There has been a great deal of very conclusive evaluation of both the use of therapeutic communities as well as the use of the cognitive-behavioral change principles with violent and juvenile offenders which we have incorporated into our drama therapy praxis for prisons. We believe that using drama therapy is a critical factor for these work practices to be effective.

This chapter reviews the issues that we faced and the processes that we used in two therapeutic communities in Australia and Romania. The issues were similar in both countries in that we were forced to deal with varying degrees of dense, angry resistance to change. In both sites we were attempting to challenge the cultures of the prisons. This meant understanding staff beliefs about prisoners, justice and punishment and making it possible for these deep-rooted beliefs to change.

It has been our experience that it is the intensity of staff beliefs that reduces the environmental support for inmate change. But therapeutic communities are environments for offenders to challenge and change their behaviors. Everyone involved in a therapeutic community must either believe or be able to maintain the belief that offenders can change. The staff in a therapeutic community are change agents, no matter what their rank or function.

In this chapter we hope to make clear that it IS possible to make profound changes in institutional behavior. We are clear after all this time that certain mechanisms in the institution must be present for change to occur and we have tried to document them through the account of the processes at the two sites. We hope to also make clear that drama therapists who engage in this work must be prepared to endure countertransferential affect and allow much time for staff to change. The success of the work is measured in the creation of an environment that supports change. It is individual belief that must do this. It is also important to be cognizant of the fact that this type of work has ramifications inside prison cultures that can be reflected for instance in hiring and firing, disciplinary reports, and even economic priorities. We hope to illustrate these ideas in this chapter.

It is our belief that drama therapy and cognitive-behavioral restructuring modified with drama therapy, embedded in the principles of a therapeutic community, create the intense fuel necessary for old beliefs to be changed sufficiently to challenge dangerous prison cultures.

GENESIS

Geese Theatre Company, USA was founded in 1980 by John Bergman, an ex-patriot from England. Geese Company's mission is to use the arts to make change in criminal justice settings, especially penitentiaries. Since its inception the company has performed original interactive productions to over half a million offenders in 43 states, received awards for its work from organizations like the American Correctional Association, established therapeutic communities in prisons, trained corrections staff in 6 countries, and helped train innumerable users of drama therapy in every aspect of criminal justice.

Currently there is a Geese training/drama therapy component in the United States, also in Romania in alliance with TRANSCAENA Company, and a very strong touring company and treatment component in the franchised Geese Theatre Company, United Kingdom.

Much of the work in the United States has focused on the use of drama therapy in prisons with violent and sexual offenders. Geese also trains all types of criminal justice staff to use elements of drama therapy onsite. In addition, Geese Company makes a cohesive fit between dominant therapeutic correctional modalities like cognitive restructuring and drama therapeutic principles (see Pin Point, Bergman & Hewish, 1996).

The work done with Transcaena, which is a new amalgamation of Geese Theatre Company USA and Grado, a human rights organization in Romania, has helped implement new emphases in the work. We are now working with Romanian staff to create from scratch some of the conditions for ethical work with police, children, prisoners and prison staff. This has led us into areas such as public policy and the retraining of staff away from older and more dangerous practices. More importantly it has also meant creating and managing acute cultural change in the prison setting. All of this new work has in turn forced a shift in our use of the drama therapy tools to use experiential means of introducing rapid behavioral change into the facilities.

One of Geese Company's basic premises is that prisons develop institutional thinking, metaphors, responses, and actions that are peculiar to them and to no one else. During its inception in 1980, Geese Company focused on how to acquire and convert prisoner images and metaphors (Violent Illusion, Bergman & Hewish, 1996) to drama-based techniques. Many of our philosophic work practices are based on understanding the metaphors peculiar to special populations. We believe that the drama therapy worker is a skilled listener with a set of "action" tools that can convert what she/he hears into systemic growth. The drama therapist allows the practical work/life metaphors of the institution to be seen and worked with in a different way.

One of our examples of this type of "listening" is our long-term use of masks with prisoners and correctional staff. During the first year of our work in prisons we decided to create an interactive performance about prisoners maintaining family relationships while being incarcerated. We spent quite some time with offenders asking them about their family issues. During one session at Joliet Correctional facility in Illinois, we were intrigued and somewhat shocked to hear that offenders consciously "put on masks" as they themselves said, to deceive their family members during visits. This led to creating masks that represented many types of resistance, deception, and affective control. The development of these masks was continuously cross-referenced with the offender's own perceptions. When the offenders saw these masks in performance many of them spontaneously called out for the actors to "take the masks off and tell the truth!"

DRAMA THERAPY FRAME OF REFERENCE

Basic Concepts

Interactive Performance Theatre and the Therapeutic Community

The success of some of our work is based in part on the fact that our metaphors, treatment processes and interactive psychoeducational performances have all been co-created through extensive listening and conversion of offender and officer perceptions into theatre-based modalities.

The strategies of work with staff in therapeutic communities that are outlined in this chapter therefore follow our two basic precepts:

- Work with what you really hear, not what you would like the client to say or be,
- All people can change if they get the opportunity to CONSCIOUSLY do so.

Theatre can and does actively teach people more about who they are. Drama therapy does this by:

a. Providing participants with a temporary mechanism to enact significantly alternative versions of their job or life behavior.
b. Providing a dynamic learning experience that also acts as a potent memory or mnemonic device especially for participants who respond poorly to paper and pencil lectures.
c. Giving a tool for creating new organizing principles for institutions.
d. Making powerful connections between self, therapeutic insight and action. We use drama therapy to highlight every aspect of cognitive restructuring–affective memories in offender cycle work; experiential enactment of cognitive-based changes, and the real-time testing of skills in high-risk situations.

Drama therapy mimics situations in a way that is safe but sufficiently real that participants can experience or create changes that have powerful meanings both at that time and for the future. Our training increases awareness of how offenders and staff think. It draws from newer psychological practices (attachment disorder, narrative therapy,

Arnold Mindell's process-oriented physical work) and is connected to well-known game and drama work, as well as criminal justice specific theatre-based strategies to stimulate affective responses. We can therefore attack the profound resistance of prison cultures using a very wide variety of institution-specific tools.

Systemic Dysfunction

Systemic Dysfunction: Officer versus Offender

Thirty years ago the then university lecturer Dr. Zimbardo (1973) used the basement of a college campus building to set up a make believe prison. Using the first students who signed up he arbitrarily assigned roles for jailer and jailed. Hours later he was forced to stop the experiment before things went too far. The students played their roles too intensely–the jailers/students became cruel and arbitrary, the jailed/students became secretive and defiant. The very metaexperience of prison produced antagonistic, insensitive and affectively dangerous interactions. Simply–a prison without specific psychological modification is an unsafe environment for human relationships. It makes its own rules for human behavior that are inimical to creative and safe living. The irony is that it is these types of institutions that we build to house people who have explosive issues with trust, difficulties with dealing intimately with others whether in authority or not, and who have deficits in attention, attachment and basic social skills.

Prisons, whether for adults or children, exacerbate everyone's problems, including the jailers. The beliefs and myths about prisons and prisoners, supported by officers' potent beliefs about justice and punishment, can clash dangerously with the basic considerations of institutional safety and ethical relationships. The overriding concerns of security staff and their often unacknowledged states of anxiety create hostility towards prisoners even without the periodic acts of violence done by prisoners.

It is our experience that the more acutely the clients are feared the more intensely the physical environment is monitored, and stripped of any material especially the sensory material to make personal change. A prison of fear gradually becomes merely bare walls, bars and the combat of competing control. The inmate's limited sense of self is more completely suppressed. This mimics his own past violence. He rebels. He is further monitored and suppressed. This combat may lead to an attempt to suppress all normative affect. At its worst this battle leads to violence.

The more the environment is affectively degraded the less it becomes a place for safe relationships that can promote habilitation. In many prisons the officer's fear is intensified by cultural components–racism, or local attitudes about working with sex offenders. Sometimes the officer's hatred is maintained on-site through unofficial or official museums of illegal weapons made from pens, paper, soap, plastic or whatever is available to clients in prison. These weapons prove the untrustworthiness and dangerousness of the prisoners. These violent artifacts are the circular proof to officers and administrators that offenders cannot be trusted, that they must live in a "THINGLESS, sterile world" constantly monitored, constantly checked, constantly mistrusted, constantly denied. The Zimbardo experiment points out the roles created by the very nature of prison. Fear and affective starvation potentiates the violence of these roles.

Highly sensitive incarcerated men and children, who experience even the mildest of put-downs as threatening, live by an internal code that demands extreme retribution. If they do not get revenge for a sleight, the offender may experience the sensation that he will be wiped off the map of life. He feels that he must respond in kind to the arbitrary imposition of any authority. Cruelty, or perceived unfairness, re-enforces his notion that ALL authority is unfair. He feels that the only recourse that is honorable is resistance that may include violent resistance. The staff interpret this as rebelliousness and as yet more signs of dangerousness.

In a recent article in the New York Times, there was a lengthy investigative article on current correctional practices on Riker's Island. The terms and actions have a war feel to them such as "cell extraction" for getting a prisoner to come out of his room, the common use of pepper spray for offender control, and the use of electric devices to give offenders massive electric shocks (50,000 volts) for control.

Fear reduces the available human surfaces for connection. Fear makes the other an enemy. Fear and fearful staff find ways to support institutional administrative bureaucracies that are conservative, cautious, reactive and maintain the status quo: the we/they of the Zimbardo prison roles. Correctional facilities then spiral down into using more and more specialized facilities for the dangerous. In the Texas Department of Corrections offenders can be sent to administrative segregation for endangering an officer. Administrative segregation can include being locked up for 20 hours or more a day for up to two years–alone. Endangering an officer may mean only talking back to him. It is not uncommon for staff in some institutions to have an unofficial goon squad that takes violent care of men that are perceived to be too mouthy, too dangerous.

This fear, in our experience, has a complex etiology. It is a fear that when you hear it close up has the raw edge of anger, of righteousness, of past injustices made into a way of thinking. Many male staff, in our experience, have survived dangerous family experiences as children. It is not uncommon in our trainings for male staff to talk about the use of violent punishment by their parents or siblings. Many have, we believe, learned that bad behavior must be punished swiftly. They have learned that aggressive punishment means good control, and good behavior. From their own behavior, it seems that these staff have never experienced or learned tolerance.

In practice the power of dangerous beliefs about justice and punishment can translate into demeaning, harsh, derisive and cruel ways of communicating with the incarcerated. Beliefs alone can lead to lowering the bar of humane relationships with in-house punishments that are arbitrary, unjust, clearly favoring some rather than others, and applied differently from shift to shift.

The offender in this environment is pitted every moment against the officer and the administration–the officer who is certain that the offender is out to kill him, the inmate certain that the officer is waiting to take his very life spirit from him.

In this culture, the worst that a prison can produce, there is no possibility of change. It is not what we mean by justice, unless we really think that the convicted should experience hell as a just punishment for his/her crime. It is not a place of trust. These types of institutional settings are not conducive to change.

Melbourne Juvenile Justice Centre had never really reached such a nadir. But it had an atmosphere of distrust, secret punishments and private beliefs about working with children. All of this was challenged by the CEO, a powerful steering committee, and the proposed culture change of the therapeutic community. Romania's prison system includes to this day some of the problems of institutional fear: lock-ins, disrespect, cruelty, torture, dangerous punishments and worse. But it too has a potent commandant and a will to change that has fueled the community called DESCATUSAREA.

Systemic Dysfunction: How an Administration can Make it Even Worse

Drama therapy is an invaluable tool for the institutional setting. The thinking drama therapist with a good handle on the language, mores, ins and outs of an institution, can achieve extraordinary successes. But institutional politics, administrative regulations and warring hierarchies can sabotage and block realistic work. The problem is complex since it is often not merely the administration versus change, but administrative staff versus line staff versus offenders versus change.

Prisons in particular are often run as paramilitary, top-down hierarchies. This applies in particular to Romania. Individual thinking, human rights, and ethical interventions are often ransomed to power relationships and allegiances that spell temporary safety for lower ranked staff. Life in the administrative section of a prison or prison system is Macchiavellian. New programs, or new thinking can become pawns in a game of influence and power. There are few steady loyalties. Without TOTAL support from the top no initiative has a chance.

But even with support from the top, it is still common for new ideas to be forced through/over staff. Institutions work through repetition, imitation, and obedience to plans that support variations of suppression in the name of safety. These plans are rarely democratically created. They are generally enforced, either benignly or in some cases with emotional force. The Zimbardo effect influences everyone. Perceived or imagined resistance is overcome by more rules or more force.

Sometimes, new ways of doing things are often put in place through "fake" democracy–lectures with a "you must" message, fiats by e-mail or on notice boards at the officer's muster. This is met by resistance and disbelief from all.

Even administrators themselves feel helpless and frustrated since they may introduce new ideas that are rarely implemented or superceded by fiats from above or in central office. Sometimes staff who have made their allegiance to a program are told overnight that their program no longer exists. Staff from all ranks lose any sense of purpose. The resistance mounts. The difficulty of maintaining standards makes it possible for recalcitrant staff to hide in the crannies and crevices of the institution. No one is accountable, there are no firings, the staff run the institution in whatever way they interpret the rules.

Clearly this chaos trickles down the hierarchy to the offenders. As their fear mounts, the pressure to defy mounts. The offender survives through temporary links with other offenders, through intimidation and imitation and detached momentary relationships with institutional staff. The administration feels hopeless.

In Romania the infrastructure is very new, but the old administrative strata are still secretly in power. When they are not in power, staff still believe that they are. This makes Romanian staff very pessimistic. This in turn makes change even harder to create. Since the country also has no deep resources, change is triply difficult. In Romania there was always the perceived problem of trying to work out people's loyalties. A question made in public to the administration is simply met by silence. As we found many times, it is still dangerous to speak. It is still not easy to understand the layers of the prison administration. There is, we believe, much more to unfold.

In Australia, many of the administrative problems had been breached by a very potent steering committee. But there was still a very significant resistance from "the good old boys" about the work. In short order the work was labeled as Spice World, Wobbies World, etc. One of the major goals early on was to try to persuade male administrators that the culture change was real, necessary and safe. The old culture had great strength and pull.

The Fundamental Task

A prison or a juvenile facility is a tapestry of connections, counterconnections, loyalties, counterloyalties, relatives, outcasts, tryers, destroyers, saboteurs, worriers, people sticking their heads in the sand, get by-ers, do my time-ers, nasty ones–and everyone is as Camus said-*innocent:* "We are all special cases. We all want to appeal against something! Everyone insists on his innocence, at all costs, even if it means accusing the rest of the human race and heaven" (The Fall, Camus, 1956).

This is critical. Neither those who make the institution survive from day to day nor those who make it fail see themselves as anything other than on the side of the angels. Unmindful of why they do what they do, many staff are simply people operating in accordance with what is congruent to their beliefs. No matter what the new or old mission statements really are, or how eloquent/elegant they are, staff often at heart find the pretty phrases irrational, ego dystonic, not congruent with the realities *as they see them.* The mission statements neither salve the edge of the Zimbardo nightmare, redress the endless resentment of perceived random pronouncements from the hierarchy, nor seem attuned to the reality of privately held beliefs. Mission statements do not solve the ethical issues of problems on the job.

A crucial thread in the work of any drama therapist must always be understanding how staff or clients construct their realities. We have to find out what things mean in a prison before we can change or consider changing its meaning. Why is a belt a powerful resonant object in the mind of some staff or clients? Why do the words *good, safe, wrong,* or *bad* produce such a huge response? Why do so many correctional staff have such a mammoth response to the word *fair?*

Each staff member has a map of meaning that he accommodates to what he believes the institutional map is all about. All those behaviors that we call digging in one's heels, sabotage, slowdowns, blue flus, including coming to staff meetings late, or coming to staff meetings and saying hunh, caballing, or threatening–are attributable to the difficulty of resolving differences between conflicting sets of values and beliefs. The problem is to link the map of meaning of the institution and the map of meaning of each staff member together. If I have grown up believing that all people are essentially good and that people will change if given the opportunity, there is every likelihood that I will clash with an officer who believes that all people in a prison are essentially bad, cannot change and should be punished for every infraction of the rules no matter what size.

We will go to war for the most extraordinary of things even though they are as abstract as a belief or as small as a nickel. A prisoner once told Geese USA how he had killed a man because he stole his last match. He actually said "If you let someone get away with something like that, they'll never stop. They'll take everything you have. You'll end up with nothing. You have to teach people lessons. Get what you can, before they get you." His beliefs supported his homicide.

Therapeutic Process

Surfacing the Beliefs

Part of the task of cultural change is surfacing beliefs and changing them. You cannot change what you do not know. You cannot compare what you believe with what a new therapeutic community might need to believe if you do not even know your own beliefs.

Most people in institutions are simply not aware of the power of their beliefs over their actions–and this is one of the most cherished tenets of cognitive behavioral change.

We create many exercises to surface the power of staff beliefs. In Romania, for example, there are two very famous football teams called Dinamo and Steua. In my first meeting with all of the officers in the Bucharest-based prison called Rahova, where we were due to open a therapeutic community, we asked the officers who supported which teams. After a show of hands we asked the 150 officers what they thought about their own teams and then about their rivals. Fortunately the differences were enormous–one is a team that represents the military and one a team that was the team of the justice department. In the old days that had included the feared Securitate, or special police force. Obviously when we asked staff about their teams, we also tapped into deep beliefs about the past, the state of the country and so on. Their responses were very lively for so early in the morning.

Then we asked the officers how much it would take to become an *ardent* supporter of the rival team. In a country where the average salary is $50–75 per month, one officer finally said a million dollars, and a white Rolls Royce. He then rebutted himself and said that actually he would still really be lying and that *nothing* could ever make him change teams.

An absurd exercise? Football teams are not justice, beliefs about punishment or the small thoughts that make up the support for action. But those football teams are metaphors for complex beliefs. Administrations ask staff in institutional settings to change their "teams" *on demand.* At worst they neither bargain with them, nor help them adjust to the new beliefs. In Australia and Romania we asked the staff to go from custody roles to therapeutic relationships. It is not uncommon for trainers and administrators to present the "new team" and its philosophy overnight "in a three-day training" with an unwritten implication that if you go along you will be accepted and if you do not you will be ostracized. But the Dinamo supporter would not change to the Steua team because of what he believed, and asking staff to change from fear and control to supportive connection with offenders is as intense a demand.

The drama therapist must use the art to create the gateway for either a profound change of beliefs or for an acclimation to beliefs that are uncomfortable. Many staff have never been on the other side of an argument, have never thought of what an offender experiences or has experienced. Some staff have never considered what it is like to be worried about whether your family will visit, or whether another adolescent might lose control and hurt you. Some staff view these problems as merely a question of getting good moral fibre and self control. Or believe that once a criminal always a criminal. Fear makes intolerance.

Changing Dysfunctional Beliefs

Drama therapy helps people see into the other side. It strips long-held beliefs of their validity for a short time. It makes it possible to think that the enemy is human.

The drama therapist's job is to help staff adjust the beliefs that they have, beliefs based on their own life experiences, so that they can deal compassionately with adults and children whose behaviors they naturally deal with in a judgmental or revengeful way.

One of the reasons that we also use cognitive behavioral change, is that this therapeutic tool helps people to become conscious of how they think very quickly. Becoming conscious of every thought, feeling, physical sensation, picture and belief is the heart of cognitive behavioral change and therefore an invaluable addition to drama therapy. In cognitive self-change for offenders one challenges beliefs that lead to old injurious behaviors. I am most grateful for the time that Dr. John Bush took while we worked together in Vermont, to teach me how to get staff and offenders to document their minds in the very simplest way possible. Perceived conscious thought, plus conscious feelings plus the awareness of the power of a belief is the meat of action. If one is to be successful in changing and training staff and prisons they must become conscious of the power of their own thoughts and feelings.

To make change for anyone especially in a prison, there must be a challenge and to change in the beliefs of the officers that drive interactions with offenders. There must also be a place in the institution where change is possible. That is the therapeutic community. There must be a mechanism that can drive personal and group change, and that can stimulate a dramatic desire to do so. That is the task of drama therapy. The staff must enter into a "what if" so that they can rehearse the consequences of new thought, new beliefs and feel safe about doing so. The new place has to be rehearsed so that staff can try out the new actions to see and experience "other." This is the task of the drama therapist creating cultural change in a prison.

The Therapeutic Community

"The American TC movement is influenced by a number of models including the AA model of Charles Dederich. Drug-focused TCs focus on the immaturity of the addict (Wexler)" (Yokley, 1999).

Incarcerated clients can be resistant, defiant, dependent, antiauthoritarian, victims of violence, suffer from intrusive memories, be deeply conservative, active thrill-seekers, obsessive, secretive, hostile, aggressive, determined, curious, courageous, emotionally unattached, and very afraid. Violent clients will not let you close. They fear to let people close and believe that the world is out to hurt them. These same clients paradoxically often have good humor, enormous insight into others, and a great argumentative tenacity in defending their own beliefs.

Typically incarcerated violent clients need to learn to control their aggression, deal with feelings of being overwhelmed by their emotions, practice intervening in their sexual impulsivity and handle safely feelings of hopelessness or overpowering rage. Often incarcerated clients have significant basic skill deficits, such as negotiating with others when they feel threatened, coping with disappointment without violent blaming or self-harm, being able to express safely what they feel, and resisting antisocial pressures. Loaded down with violent feelings, poor coping skills and avoidant behaviors, these men and children seek approval from others for what they believe and experience. It is easier to get approval for violently impulsive acts from those who feel similarly than from people who seek a peaceful life.

Prisons are often violent. Certainly prisons are filled with violent men with violent thoughts and beliefs. In antisocial environments aggressively defensive adults and children adapt by competing against feeling overwhelmed. They use coping skills like rage, intimidation and deception to deal with violent environments that they consider a threat to their own safety. Bad prisons make prisoners emotionally and psychosocially worse. Adult and adolescent incarcerated clients need at a minimum carefully crafted environments in which they can learn and practice alternative ways of responding.They need environments that challenge their thinking, engage them to try alternatives to the conservative responses and life-styles they engage in, and can be confronted by their own peers over their consistent irresponsibility.

"The therapeutic community movement implicitly adopts the view that deviant behavior, much of which is deemed criminal, represents a breakdown of the relationship between the individual and the structured society of which he is . . . a member" (Roberts, 1997). Strong therapeutic communities create whole societies with strong prosocial values against which offenders can measure their current new behaviors. In these types of environments nothing is overlooked. All behaviors are subject to scrutiny. Any one action can be seen as symptomatic of the entire behavioral outlook. In 1991, during a visit to the Missouri State penitentiary therapeutic community, a young prisoner told us of how he came to break out of his old behaviors. He had been in the community kitchen and had failed to wash his cup–the older peers in the TC simply confronted him until he saw how this represented his longstanding unwillingness to be responsible and respectful. "Successful socialization gives an ability to empathize with and place a value on other beings" (Roberts, 1997).

Therapeutic communities are high tariff environments. They are emotionally hot, intensive, and confronting. These environments do not give offenders their traditional means of escaping either responsibility or the emotions that they find so threatening. Thus TCs force offenders to interact with others, potentiating the long march towards empathy.

"TC learning experiences consist of a combination of natural and logical consequences which can be viewed as behavior therapy or social learning within the context of a positive peer culture and experiential framework" (Yokley, 1999).

In the Romanian and Australian TCs we insisted that staff look at punishment in a new way. For offenders to change they must be made to be conscious of their actions in an environment that actively mimics the real world but highlights positive reenforcing value behavior. TCs cannot work in an atmosphere of distrust, violence, changing standards and arbitrary pictures of punishment. It was paramount in Australia that we break the old culture of using enforced isolation to change behavior *alone.* Changed behavior must be practiced, supported, encouraged and made the norm.

"Extensive research has been done on TC treatment–significant decreases in criminal involvement after treatment has been demonstrated for both adults and adolescents in the community setting (DeLeon, 1984, 1987; Pompi, 1994) and for inmates in the correctional setting (Wexler & Love, 1994; Yokley, 1999).

The therapeutic community serves many purposes. It is a place where unlike any other unit in an institution, the focus is self-change and growth rather than mere incapacitation. It is a place where all people are expected to take on far more responsibilities than they do in a regular setting and even than in the real world.

It is an environment in which people are encouraged/expected to respond to things in a nonviolent way. It is an environment in which the new, the unexpected, the direct, the honest, the caring, the crying, the feeling, the hurting, the attempting, the getting there way of life is supported and created.

TCs are famous and notorious for being vital, creative, intense and hugely rewarding environments to work in. They put staff in diametrically new relationships with clients. The demands of a real therapeutic community are so intense that they automatically raise the caring standards of the workers in the unit. Thus this type of configuration is a remarkable strategy for creating a powerful example of a new culture in a facility.

The Institution's Role

Beginnings are critical. Drama therapists, like any visitor making changes, should pay attention to what the institution, or system, or central office leader actually sets in place. The institution must take on part of the task of supporting, alerting, and informing the system that there is going to be a huge cultural change from the outset.

For big changes you will need:

a. A management team that is organized, aware of the issues, has cleared, booked, found people, arranged for backfill and personnel support. This team may become some of your closest friends during the work. They must maintain their enthusiasm during the dark days when the new ideology is attacked.
b. Total support from the top of the system. I cannot stress this enough. If you are attempting to combat an entrenched prison culture and your authority is dependent on whims, favors, power plays your process will be at risk. The top person must be prepared to stand and deliver, to PUBLICLY support the work that you do.
c. Real funding that will cover a therapeutic community AFTER you have gone. Nothing will get staff attention more than the knowledge that there is a budget for your return and for the materials that they will need.
d. Real time to do the work–a measure of the seriousness of the institution or correctional system is their willingness to bend the rules, adequately ensure that staff have a real grounding in the work through lengthy training. Three-day trainings rarely accomplish much.
e. A high-placed person in the process to maintain the integrity and real meaning of the work hour to hour on the ground in the unit. Our success in Australia is in great part due to Di Garner, a youth worker administrator who remained committed to the process, maintained connection with us and dealt at every turn with vital issues of personnel, and client distress. Such a person is still being sought in Romania.
f. Staff who are prepared in some ways to create a new culture. This is of such importance. One of the key components of a resistant culture is the ongoing resentment of many staff at feeling forced to do yet another initiative that they have neither chosen nor debated. Staff and offenders must be polled, challenged, informed. They must have free will or they will not fight for the new culture and will crumble when the old guard fights back.
g. Someone who will manage the staff during your training. That is–staff can be very rude, antagonistic, even insulting. There must be a staff supervisor who will effectively discipline the trainee. I had to ask an officer in the Romanian training to leave when he insisted that "there is nothing good about inmates." I explained to him that I had to ask him to leave since the therapeutic community simply would use different values and beliefs from his own and that it looked as if it might be too hard to align them.

CASE EXAMPLES

The Romanian and Australian facilities in which we put these modified therapeutic communities seem on the surface enormously different. The maximum-security penitentiary in Bucharest where we created the TC is situated in a suburb of Bucharest called Rahova. It is a 1500 bed, soon to be 2000 bed prison for adult prisoners who have committed everything from theft to murder. On average, the men are serving five to ten years, and have either been sent directly to the prison or sent from other older prisons.

The prison is less than two years old. It is run by Dr. Florian Gheorghe who was both a high ranking member of the older prison system after Ceaucescu and is also a clinical psychologist. Dr. Gheorghe is a personable man in his forties with a deep passion about this work. He has written about the psychology of prisoners and was entrusted with the running of this prison as soon as it was conceived. He unfortunately inherited its less than useable design. He also inherited many of the staff, some of whom have come from prisons such as Gelava, a prison that has a notorious and dangerous reputation.

During his tenure as commandant he has seen a number of system bosses, but the current head of the prison services named the Direction General Penitenciar or D.G.P. is a former magistrate called Mr. Marian Eftimescu. He is the current General Director of the entire Romanian prison system. He is a warm and genuinely caring man who speaks openly about the problems that present-day Romania has inherited from the Ceaucescu days. This in itself is an act of great courage since there still exists a culture that represses open talk about anything that could be conceived of as controversial. One quickly learns, or believes, that it is normal to have spies working with you while you teach or train, reporting what one does to whoever thinks they need to know. It is normal for the staff to believe that there is always some type of Macchiavellian plot going on. Suspicion deeply permeates any work and relationships, and engenders cynicism and hopelessness. It is quite common in Romania for people to tell one as a trainer that there is not much point in doing any work. "It will only be sabotaged and destroyed."

Dr. Florian Gheorghe and I had begun discussions together in 1997. At that time his major concern was how to create a new, caring and humane cadre of officers and sub-officers. As we continued the discussions I spoke about the first unit for violent men that I had co-created and run with Jack Bush in the Vermont Department of Corrections in 1988. This unit was run by correctional officers as well as Jack and myself. It was our shared belief that correctional officers could make creditable prison group leaders using cognitive restructuring strategies and high risk role work. These are fundamental strategies for working with men convicted of violence.

This appealed strongly to Dr. Gheorghe and the objectives were to train five psychologists and 12 correctional staff to work together to run a therapeutic unit of 30 incarcerated men. There were also long-term comprehensive goals. We determined that the unit was to become a training centre for best practices and to be an experiential center for other staff from other penitentiaries. Dr. Florian was very concerned with how officers can do the right thing after many years of not doing so. He has taught some of his new staff to listen to the inmates concerns, a revolution in its own right in Romania.

The beginning was not auspicious. Many of the Romanian staff were completely unprepared for the work. The officers chose themselves at muster on the very day that we began. Money, always a crucial issue, had not been allocated for translators, nor was there money for supplies. We simply bought what we needed on the first days.

Dr. Florian was unavoidably on holiday for one of the weeks that we worked. It is sometimes critical that the boss be present when large changes are happening. Of much greater gravity very early on in the work, three officers put on hoods and beat an inmate very badly. We had no idea if this was a threat or a violent coincidence. But it cast a shadow over the work.

The impact of the commandant's absence was quite large, even though there was little that he could have done about this. One shift for example, seemed very proactive, ushering us politely through daily checks. Another held us up, asked for papers, kept other staff waiting. Senior officers did not always come to training. When it came to getting special packages for offender participants in the proposed new community the discussions became quite murky, especially without having the commandant to work with us. Paperwork, constructive meetings, equal discussions, feedback, constructive criticism, and reviews were almost nonexistent. To the credit of the Romanian team who worked with us, whatever we suggested they tried to do or get.

Many staff were unable to believe that change was possible and harbored deep angry beliefs about the prisoners. The language difference was sometimes too huge. But we were reassured by our meetings with General Director Marian Eftimescu. It was he who told us that inmates who participated in the therapeutic community would get packages and visits. In doing this he told us that the work would be supported.

The beginning of a project for lasting change brings out everything that the human and social organism can find to fight change. So when beginning be sure that your allies are really strong. As theatre therapy workers we face many temptations to break this rule–sometimes we simply must work to live. If you have worked inside institutions for any length of time you may have already found yourselves trapped too many times inside the political aspirations of someone from the criminal justice system who is delighted to be your mentor but in the final moment cannot or will not come through. Your top allies must support the real changes that we make when we do things like create therapeutic communities.

In Australia, this support was clear from the outset and became very crucial when the resistance to change became very ugly. The initial preparation for the work at the facility had been impeccable. Melbourne Juvenile Justice Centre is a prison for adolescents–it classifies, detains, imprisons and releases. The CEO, Diana Batzias, had gradually transformed the institution from a hard core imitation of an adult prison, contained a staff riot, let older youth workers go, supported a steering committee and its recommendations for change.

When we began our work there, as Diana Batzias said, the situation was RIPE. There was a significant core of administrative staff, and members of the chaplaincy and senior staff, overwhelmingly women, who wanted change. The pump had been primed by Patrick Tidmarsh a noted sex offender therapist in Australia who had worked in the 80s with Geese UK. We gave an introductory workshop on-site with the senior staff who then made recommendations that Melbourne Juvenile Justice Centre (MJJC) should create a new therapeutic unit.

In the case of MJJC, there were plenty of problems to deal with–entrenched notions of what the children could really do (or not do), a lack of trust in the children's ability to self govern, real ignorance about newer methods of working with defiant and oppositional behaviors, and in some cases a sense that the children were on a revolving door journey and that therefore nothing could work. Some staff felt that there was no point in doing anything, that it would be better to "lock 'em up since its the only thing they understand." In a few cases there was also a culture of restrained and unrestrained violence towards the children, the arbitrary use of the "slot"–isolation for children who were considered too defiant. In a few cases the violence and threats to the children were a permanent way of mind.

Each adolescent housing unit has anywhere from 7 to 15 children, ages roughly 13 to 18. The crimes committed by the adolescents, range from murder and rape to theft and repeated arrests for drug and alcohol use. The sentences in American terms are very low–2 years served for murder, generally serving no more real time than a year. In South Bank, one of the housing units at MJJC, the average time served by the children was under three months.

We found the basic ideologies and philosophies of understanding and working with children at MJJC confused and flawed. The most common that we first encountered was a notion of benign neglect that said "these children have suffered too much already, so they must be looked after and then returned to the community with as little interference from us as possible." Post Martinson, the architect of the notion that "nothing works, " suggests this had even been the law. The downside of this benign approach is that the heroin in Melbourne is cheap and powerful. Too many children were leaving the facility without self-restraint skills, or any conscious strategies for self-change and either reoffending or dying of overdoses. Many of the adolescents had simply not had a chance to try out any alternative behavioral responses to any stimuli. A tattoo of death was one of the images that my one-day initial workshop had uncovered for me.

We also took into account what we could fathom about the overall culture before we finalized a set of training and design principles. Patrick Tidmarsh had told us that the facility had some core staff who were very negative. We expected that there would be resistance, and the lack of male administrators at the one-day teaser training confirmed this. When we finally wrote to Di Garner who became one of the administrators most central to the success of the therapeutic community, we said the following:

The Premise:

1. Security and treatment are complementary.
2. Punishment alone is ineffective as a mode of change.
3. Treatment is not an alternative to taking responsibility for dangerous actions.
4. Treatment and security are part of a three-cornered hat that includes the children.
5. Security is the application of rules in a way that makes children understand their relationship with authority and encourages them to make change through treatment and behavioral experiment.
6. Children are smart enough to make their own choice to change.
7. Children must change their relationship with authority, which requires treatment to help with their thoughts and feelings, and behavioral practice, which is created in their relationships with the youth workers and the treatment community.

The Aims of This Training are:

1. To teach the methods of behavioral change using the security/treatment principles.
2. To teach youth workers how to apply these principles with youth in a treatment community.
3. To teach children how to reflect on their dangerous beliefs about authority and begin the process of seeing and taking responsibility for their relationships with authority.
4. To teach treatment staff their role in this model.

Institutions must know that change is coming. MJJC took a huge responsibility for making the ground as fertile as it could. The working drama therapist must make sure that he/she does the work that she/he is really responsible for. The institution must let the entire facility know what is going on, mobilize support all the way to the top, inform and educate.

Melbourne Juvenile Justice Centre was a full experiment in shifting the culture so that the whole institution could move on. Rahova on the other hand, was a great juggling improvisation to make one corner of the prison map a decent place.

How Did It Happen?

The creation of change in both the Australian and Romanian systems was similar in one way because time for both was so limited–ten days, eight hours a day, to train staff, and five days to get the system up and running with the clients. We had to start quickly.

In both countries, the central issue was to break through staff disbelief and resistance as quickly as possible. In Australia, part of the change was accomplished before we even started.

All the staff were alerted, no secrets were kept, a steering team kept the ball rolling and there were people who were accountable for introducing the entire process to the facility. The centre was put on notice in a clear and professional way that change was coming in 6 months–a reasonable amount of time for any forewarning of change. For our purposes as the change agents, we had a clear picture of what was happening, what we had to do and the knowledge that there would be people left on the ground who would make it their responsibility to create and maintain the work after we left. Di Garner was point person, the communicator, had a good line of authority to the CEO, and therefore enough authority to make the work happen. This is critical. We strongly recommend that drama therapists trying to take on an entire institutional culture, look clear-eyed at whether they have any of the above processes and people in place. Changing institutional beliefs will raise resentment and defiance. Without the determined support of the type we received from Di Garner and the CEO Diana Batzias, when you leave your work will become corrupted and marginalized.

The Process

The management team made sure that they knew what the work was and also wrestled with the issues. It was the management team that came to a one-day intensive that we did and fully participated in the experiential training. It was they who wrestled with the interviews and what "good" practice might really mean.

Many of the staff in Romania and Australia were nervous from the very beginning. At both sites some of them walked into training on the first day, and looked at our masks and dolls and toys with a mixture of fear and scorn. It is the norm for corrections. Our first task was to listen to the officers and administrators, empower them by recognizing their real knowledge, hear them out and make them feel as safe as possible.

Romanian staff were harder to read in the beginning and the language issues played against us. In the first days the novelty of the situation seemed to overwhelm the Romanian staff. Discussions were harder to maintain and the staff were more anxious to be led, to take notes. The drama games were a relief, but not a way to deal with truth. The trust issues were significantly greater and there was a greater sense of opacity of the staff. Romanian staff were poorly prepared in terms of information, the why and the what of the training. They had more to catch up with though this was balanced by the newness of some of them. They simply had not had time to create hard and fast beliefs and those who had we challenged. Of the basic training principles the most crucial was that they had at least volunteered, rather than being volunteered.

Check In

We always begin trainings by asking people what they want from the sessions, what they actually do at the institution and what they think the real issues are. We do this whether it is a conference, a training, or a three-hour workshop. It is democratic and it is a powerful moment for some of the staff. It sets a tone and in Romania signifies democracy. We believe that once people have been doing their prison job for a while they have something important to say. They are at least more expert about the stress and problems of their respective jobs than the outsider who comes to teach and visit. It is a hallmark for trainers working in criminal justice that 65 percent of the success of any training is getting the trust of the staff. They have to believe that you have been there, that you can take it, have confronted the violence and made it through. It is an unspoken challenge. When the staff share, or smile or confront each other in the presence of the trainer then you have begun to win.

Warm-Up Theater Games

Once the "check-in" is done we go straight to theatre games. Theatre games change atmospheres, loosen attitudes, affect and cognitions. Games are not nonthreatening to everyone. In prisons, play means letting down one's guard and so it is unusual and dangerous. Games mean losing face, appearing silly and out of control. In Australia, staff were far more sensitive about looking stupid and seemed strongly influenced by the "tall poppy syndrome," a culturally shared idea that people do not try to stand above or be different from each other.

Romanian staff, on the other hand, took to theatre games with gusto and great invention. They seemed to find the exercises an immediate relief from discussions about the prison. There is a greater fear of discussion in Romania, of naming truths. But Romanian staff were also considerably more comfortable in using metaphors, talking about masks. It is safer in Australia to talk, though discussions about institutional violence were never honestly dealt with. But the real point of the games was the start of the assault on dangerous institutional beliefs. Even to "play" is the start of giving some staff a key to other types of thinking–kinetic, visual, aural.

The choice of theatre exercises was crucial. Officers in our experience seem to key in strongly to action exercises. They are in "action" work. They are strongly responsive to running and chasing games. So the first exercises in both countries included:

1. Calling out five things to be touched in seven seconds, then shortening the time to five seconds and so on.
2. A blind conga line with a sighted leader who took the followers out of the space altogether and in Australia out into the street. This helped to foster the idea of safely breaking rules and that there would not be too much sitting down and being lectured to. The game also sent a message of excitement, and that there was less to fear than people expected.
3. Walks leading to jumps, touching backs, sudden turns, freezes. In other words kinetic action that focused staff on listening, responding quickly and giving up some of their control to us. Trust without saying the words.
4. Red light /Green light, an exercise that encourages silent kinetic control. We played a version of this exercise where the entire group had to work together to get a large set of keys back to the "beginning" without being seen by the one who is "it." This game is also a way to break up cliques, and set people to work with each other who are not accustomed to doing so. It was the first exercise where the staff had to figure out a problem together. There would be hundreds more.

As we taught we let staff know what the pattern of work every day would be–physical games and exercises first, then more intensive work, then more drama work then theory and so on. We did not do any large scale trust work on the first day because we did not know who people could not trust. In Romania in particular we were still very uncertain who the participants were and felt that it was our responsibility to not put the participants in jeopardy.

Much of the early days was action exercises followed by discussions. We challenged the staff to think about what the TC would be, how it would operate with the clients. We used sculpts to start the ball rolling into the dangerous territory of perceiving the clients in new ways. Rather than use discussions that might make staff feel like they had to defend an institutional way of doing things, we wanted the ball in our dramatic court, away from thoughts of resistance about theories of correctional change, and tired discussions of punishment. Using theatre exercises allows for discovering new ways for people to think about problems. Physical sculpts invariably give all staff a way to express the sense of a thing, and that allows for that thing to be seen anew. It makes the old facility suddenly exciting again. It is this excitement that we knew we had to generate in order to make an affective and experiential platform that would support change.

We used standard sculpts that we began from an exercise where groups had to first get specific numbers of feet and hands on the ground while leaning on each other, and then a smaller number of feet and hands and so on. This *physically* connected staff and gave them another problem to solve, while masking the fears of creativity and the sculpts to come. Once the staff were used to being kinetically connected we transformed the exercise into creating sculpts about Tower Bridge, broken bridges, blocked dreams, and finally shared pictures of the old unit as it had been and the perceived blocks to change this. We gave the staff very little time to talk to each other. We wanted to avoid their blocks about the work and to continue the idea of brainstorming in small groups, trusting the first best idea and acting on it. This work seemed to excite the staff in both countries and gave them an acute sense of solving problems.

Deepening the Process

It was at this point that we asked the groups to create sculpts about clients' issues. We focused the groups on creating sculpts with affectively intense titles such "Outcast," "I hate you," "Unwanted." Each sculpt was interpreted by the staff with as little comment from us to give everyone the sense that they could create in their groups without interference. When staff asked what a title referred to we said, "Whatever comes to mind is correct. There is no right or wrong answer."

From the outset we had watched some staff, especially those we suspected had more issues with violence in the unit is, trying to gauge how other staff were responding to the work. In Australia and to some extent in Romania the more defended staff repeatedly sent fearful or questioning looks to each other or rolled their eyes looking for an answering nod. Some for a short while,–two to three days,–hovered on resisting doing the work altogether. The great efforts of the steering committee really panned out for us here. The breaks were filled with fast-talking cliques some of whom looked very angry and gave us cold looks.

Working With Resistance

This is a pattern of response that we have seen repeated many times in Australia. Fearful staff, especially staff who hate offenders, think them dirty or dangerous, act their fear in disrespectful ways. They can gradually get ruder to the trainers, and challenge our ethical stances about offenders in very aggressive ways–"You can't do these things with "crims." "They just won't change"–is often the starting point. They back away from the exercises, or openly attempt to sabotage a game or role play. Staff who are working their way through years of personal hatred and discomfort act with blithe disregard for time and place. They are too afraid and angry. As a trainer, you have few choices. You must face this resistance directly, call the bluff, name the action, keep working and maintain focus with those who are trying hard to overcome their anxiety or fear. At the worst, you may have to ask for a staff member to be put out of the training as we did in Romania and nearly did in Australia. It is why getting the staff to "audition" for the training and the unit was so crucial to it is success. People who have competed to be in a training /unit will work far harder to challenge themselves. Where staff were coerced from another unit the results of the training were very poor and the therapeutic community will not work.

Exploring New Beliefs

We now asked each group to present their sculpt work to the others. This is a very dangerous moment especially for prison officers. It is the first time that staff can look at each other's drama work, dramatic ideas, new ideas, and comment. It is the first time that some staff are outside the collective identity of the prison. It is the first time that staff can show other identities. The rapport created from the work of making the sculpts can be easily jarred. The attack is through stupid comments, or the tired old private language of the institution that connotes hierarchy, defended self, and an acute anxiety about being out of control. In Australia we heard the phrase "comfort zone" used time and again. It was used as a wall against any experience that challenged the known. As the work progressed the phrase disappeared from the collective.

The intensity of the sculpt titles also gave us our first opportunity to see what staff thought when they heard these words, how they saw the prisoners, how they saw themselves. We used these exercises to start the work of getting staff to understand how people make decisions in their lives. It was a way to start the discussions about "other," about the realities of working with violence, about the fears that any reasonable person would have and what our vision and experience of violent people was. The "outcast" sculpt represented some of the staff who could not tell friends about their vocation, or the agony of the adopted and forgotten child/adolescent offender, or pictures of the worker versus the administration. But these sculpts helped set the tone–cruelty out, respect and connection in. The debate got hotter.

In Romania we had each staff member describe something good about the prisoners. One of them said there was nothing. At the break I asked him to leave. We talked about the fact that his values and those of the new community conflicted, and that there was no blame here. I cannot condemn a man for his beliefs, but I can challenge them in fair debate or ask someone to leave when they are antithetical to our work practices. In this new environment we demanded that people use an attitude of respect for the offenders. It meant finding something that one can believe about all mankind.

The other staff were shocked that I had got rid of the man. They glowered. But there was no turning back. We reiterated the basic beliefs and foundation principles. We focused over and over on respect. We reviewed the idea that an offender is a man who amongst things has broken the rules. But he is also a man like anyone else. He feels, responds, has dreams.

Foundation Principles for the Therapeutic Community

The work on sculpts, on understanding the dynamics of the outcast leads easily to the next phase–to get staff to work on the foundation principles for their therapeutic community. The foundation principles are a high-toned way into the concepts of therapeutic change and of modeling new beliefs and attitudes. The principles are like a United Nations charter of beliefs. They are the spine for any new community. They also release staff from the feeling that they are being led. The creation of the principles is small group work, high energy, intense.

Therapeutic communities take a huge amount of energy, and a lot of personality. All staff have to take on a lot of visible responsibility. Therapeutic communities are not places for "shrinking violets" and because they are environments in which the offenders have much more overt responsibility for the gist and running of the experience, staff must be more quickly engaged and present. They must have a set of principles to guide the new environment. We push the staff to work on the ideas for the TC.

We encouraged the staff to create these principles in the simplest language they could. We broke down the use of the mission-statement-type language of Australia and the patriotic language of Romania so that the language could be something that children could cope with and prisoners trust. We prepared the ground by asking the staff to do the Island exercise.

Each staff member first draws everything that he/she would want on their own island. Then they write the rules of their islands and what happens if anyone breaks the rules. Then we asked the the staff to pair up and share islands. This was hard. Some people had peaceful open islands without rules or punishment. Some staff had intensely private islands with rules for everything and a long list of punishments for breaking the rules. The parallels with the staff's lives are very obvious. In this "game" the staff had to negotiate beliefs and values and punishment with each other. Staff who hardly knew each other cautiously bared themselves through a *game* that had *real* meaning. We reminded them–*it is just a game,* and then contradicted this by reenforcing the need to work the problems out as if they were actually *real* problems. In small groups the staff discussed and challenged their own isolation.

These early days were jammed with break-off groups, action assignments and homework. The walls of the training space were covered with group thoughts, questions, new ideas for working with clients. This modeled the environment that we hoped the staff would create. We continued to monitor the resistance and resentment. The sculpts had opened the door to the beliefs about the clients. The foundation principles were too high-minded to allow ordinary prison-based resentment to occur. But we knew the rage would come.

This was the base work for the making of the foundation principles. From the Island exercise we asked people to create the most decent bases for co-existence in the TC. The principles are the drawing board for the functions of the TC. They are demanding, romantic and utopian. They are simple and nonbureaucratic. Some of the principles created for Eastern Hill in Australia and the Descatus area in Romania were remarkably similar and simply breathtaking. For instance:

"Anyone from anywhere is the same as anyone else."

"All life is sacred."

"In this place all people must be safe."

"Change is possible for every person."

The romance of these principles, the work of creating these principles together and of experiencing difference without violence created a growing sense that all things were possible, and a growing sense of fear and resentment. On the third day the Australian staff openly questioned our assertion that whatever we all created in this off-campus space would be the map for the work in the therapeutic community. It was as Australians say a "full on" confrontation. It was a mixed message challenge. It was a veiled way to sabotage the work and it was a way for some to say this is really stupid, nobody believes this work you are doing. It was a critical moment. It meant that some of the staff, especially the most anxious, were feeling too threatened and too far away from the institutional norms. This is a classic moment in the confronting of prison culture, and the creation of these types of communities. (The Romanian version of this moment was far more muted.)

Fortunately and by design the CEO was present. Diana Batzias got to her feet and in front of all the staff reaffirmed that she would support whatever we did in this preparation (rehearsal) stage. This affirmation is of huge importance. One simply cannot be successful without it. Without these public and private affirmations of the work staff are too likely to believe that this is all a game that will just go away, or that they are again merely being manipulated by "them." I believe that this was one of the Australian TC turning points. The angry staff got the point, felt the weight of the authority. Staff must get the message that this work is for real and *supportive* to the authority vested in the institution. This empowers us. The toys and the masks we use may have meaning, but in institutional cultures our drama therapeutic sense of meaning is fragile. The masks may work in principle, but the stamp of authority makes the masks and toys safe.

For the CEO this moment was a complete leap of faith. If the experiment had gone wrong she would have been badly hurt by the failure. So the drama therapists who take on these tests MUST be able to deliver. We bear a huge burden of responsibility. One should not do this work if one does not have the confidence or the knowledge or the ability to withstand the pressure and continue on with some degree of grace.

Changing Belief Crises

Throughout the next days all staff went through crises of belief, resistance and distancing. It is our way to name this, ask staff to share it. We overtly sympathize with this resistance but we try to keep working, answer and send the issues back, minimizing the analysis. We let the staff think about things without our interpretation, saying instead, "What does this mean to you?" We encourage respectful honesty. We try to model that it is all right to disagree, that kids and adult offenders will disagree and that this is human, not a sign of a rebellion to be crushed. We model listening, trying to get staff to tell us what they mean in what they say, sometimes playing back what we hear and so sending the message that what people say and think and believe is of critical importance to us. When it is safe I name the resistant thoughts that might be inside staffs' minds, so that they feel safe to defy. We repeat our philosophy over and over–your values may be different from ours–but how can you change what you believe, or moderate it to do this work. We did not compromise our beliefs no matter what exceptions the staff came up with. People are won and lost sometimes in these daily testings and debates. There is no place for relation for the trainers.

Lateral thinking is a vital part of the work of providing a base for beliefs to change. The drama exercises incite the staff to learn to use their innate creativity, use and create metaphors and venture into the world of the impossible and illogical. This is a critical need in order to cope with the multiple demands of a TC. The usual prison environment encourages staff to be too concrete. Fear causes staff to attribute negative reasons to any activity and reduce the number of possibilities that can exist in the institutional environment. Concrete thinking supports resistance to change and "institutionalized" answers. That is, staff rely on the well-worn paths of the institutional hierarchy and the reasoning associated with the status quo. Training must address this. We work very hard to introduce alternative thinking at every stage of the work, whether through using dolls and getting staff to create dialogue, humor, drawings and the constant use of improvisations, role play and the sense of sudden change. The idea is always to keep the staff a little unbalanced.

The Development of Creative Thinking

If the staff are to create very emotive environments, find thinking alternatives for clients about violent beliefs, and even challenge their own beliefs about offenders and punishment, they must have the skill of making quick lateral idea changes. A staff member in a TC cannot rely on "this is the rule so you do it like this or else." He/She has to be able to say, "Have you tried thinking about it in another way, what if . . ."

But lateral thinking is a safe "what if" way to experiment with the shock of new beliefs. We got the staff into the habit of free associating from games, setting up word plays without the idea that there was an expected answer. We began a session from a single sentence–"my horse has just eaten? . . . what?" and ask the staff to act or fill in the blanks. We played many variations of "Why are taxis painted yellow?" over the training period, pushing them to come up with more and more outlandish answers to these types of questions until they got used to "jumping off" the logic of the previous idea.

The effect of this work was cumulative. At first these lateral devices supported the staff in mocking, making jokes, playing safely in front of each other and therefore making the work less threatening. As we continued these processes, the staff creativity grew, and they began to make suggestions like bringing paints, paper, books, photographs into the proposed unit where once this material had been considered a security issue. The lateral devices created a "theatre of all possibilities." On the final day of the work one of the staff members came to see me. An adolescent in the unit had defaced a book. I expected her to say that he needed to be punished. Instead she said, " You know this will make a great group discussion with all the unit."

The drama therapy exercises deepened the focus of the training experience and the ability of staff to tap into their affect consciously, safely and PUBLICLY. The whole focus of the training is to challenge and change the unspoken or unacknowledged and dangerous assumptions, especially about prisoners, punishment and anger. Every tool the drama therapist uses must be for this conscious goal.

Cognitive Exercises and Homework

We also worked in part through nondramatic means, through the use of cognitive exercises. In the earliest days of the training we had taught the basic tools of cognitive behavioral change–close attention to one's interior conversations and sensations–thought, feeling and action, and then record this data without censoring anything. This we buttressed with focused homework assignments consisting of phenomenological cognitive reports of real life events.

These written homework assignments were handled in a workaday way, as process rather than therapy. The process begins by first splitting staff into pairs and asking them to create role plays based on conflicts that they have experienced within the last two weeks. We made one stipulation–no conflicts from home or from work. Each pair then enacted two role plays–some of which were quite emotionally hot. The themes of the situations in both sites were quite similar–conflicts with storekeepers, telephone operators, drivers, bus conductors, etc. But we knew that any focus on conflict gave us access to beliefs and thoughts that are relatively similar to the way in which staff dealt with any conflicts including with offenders. The assignment is to write down all the thoughts, feelings, sensations and beliefs that they remember having at the peak moment of the conflict. These were then objectively discussed in class.

This "thinking report" is a tool that we teach staff to teach to the clients. It is used as a major strategy to make prisoners mindful of their own thoughts. Publicly discussing the thoughts and actions of conflict is a very intimate act. It is a way for all the participants to see into the thoughts and feelings of their work friends. It is an unvarnished look at the beliefs that support anger, revenge, and even small acts of violence.

It is also the first time for many of the staff that someone else has listened to them think with total attention. All the group listen. We teach how to listen without critiquing, without pretending to be therapists. They are not in therapy. They are just officers and youth workers. We do not do analysis with the thinking reports. We do not interpret. They note their own meaning of their own thoughts. They note how their beliefs affect them. They see their hot thoughts, the interventions that they sometimes have not used. We all make *no* comments. We return to the foundation principles.

Staff are mesmerized by the simplicity of cognitive work. We teach the message of change like this–"What I think, feel, believe affects what I do–If I change what I think I can change what I do." It is elegant and it is surprisingly persuasive. Staff cannot change others if they do not have this tool. We cannot turn them into drama therapists, but we can teach them to use cognitive behavioral change tools because of their great simplicity. It makes staff feel like they have a powerful weapon. Cognitive change directly feeds our notions of fair consequences versus aversive punishment. It is the ideological reenforcer of the training.

Staff are very intensely affected by the thinking reports. We often found that this was the first time that most staff have ever stopped to listen to what they really think in their heads. Some of the staff came back the day after they had done a thinking report in training and talked about how they had stayed up all night, how they had been thinking and remembering, how they realized that they had bad tempers. Some staff talked to us privately about their difficulties with their own children at home and their fear about whether they were good parents.

Punishment

The cognitive tools raised the issue of punishment. People do what they do, in part, because of what they think and believe. Arbitrary punishment will not change people's acts because the beliefs that fuel the acts are so potent. This is central to what we teach. But we also teach that offenders must be given logical consequences for persistent rule breaking. The offenders must find a way to mute, mutate or change their thoughts and beliefs. Only by holding firm can we give the offenders a stationery target of change.

This is the hottest area of changing a prison culture. Some staff are so conflicted about using punishment and about how to use it. In many cases the guidelines in the prison are too flexible, unclear or subject to peer pressure. Some staff fear that without their old arsenal of control and punishment that they will be naked and vulnerable. They are conflicted by the power of the experience with seeing their own thoughts and beliefs and the intense institutional experiences using raw power to control and punish.

At this point we had intense disagreements with some staff in both sites about how to deal with inmate violence, verbal aggression and angry outbursts. Although we did not concentrate at this point on how to change beliefs with offenders, we discussed interventions, how to stop violence, how to create respectful environments without resorting to the punishment "slot." We focused repeatedly in Romania on the idea of respect, and in Australia on making connection with children who are radically unattached.

To make the point we used a psychodramatic exercise that reenacted old embarrassing experiences with violent teachers at school. When staff once again experienced the old humiliation of teenage school days, it was not hard to turn the debate to connection and respect. The experience of once again having those shamed, angry thoughts poignantly skewered those who held out for punishment versus controlling consequences. We used the same exercise many years earlier with high ranking central and south American policemen, and it worked to remind them of the hell they endured before they become powerful.

Role Play

Then we deepened the challenge. Building on role plays we asked the staff to begin to experience the beliefs of the clients. We split the staff into pairs giving them each single phrases like I want you to stay/ I want you to leave, or there's something I want to tell you/I do not want to hear it. We asked each pair to speak using only the assigned sentence. These are obviously the phrases of rejection and abandonment and anger. But we used the exercises as a way to start a practical discussion of what to do for children who have gone through violent experiences and how to counter their global beliefs, thoughts and feelings towards anyone who is an enemy. All staff now began to see what their clients were doing on a daily basis, rather than just attributing their actions to being bad, or morally flawed. They used lateral thinking skills to imagine the thinking behind many of the offenders actions. It was as if they were all in on the game of imagining.

Deepening Empathy

After much discussion amongst our selves we decided that it was time for the staff to deepen their empathy toward the clients. We had stressed that children cannot change without connection. We insisted that punishment was an ineffective tool to counter resistance. We repeated the need for consistent consequences as a way to focus children's thoughts. We created pictures of the children's fearful lives using full masks and mimed scenes of family violence.

We wanted to intensify the staff's understanding of the fragility and strength of the connection they needed to make in the therapeutic community. We created a mass improvisation in which half the staff, seated and with eyes shut, first created a safe place to be in their minds. Then they were slowly led to connect to the hand of someone else using only their fingers. When the connection was established, on cue the standing staff suddenly withdrew their hands. It was shocking. Some of the seated staff cried, some tried to follow the hand, some withdrew entirely. We reconnected the seated staff with their own personal place of safety through their visualization. Once the seated staff had been calmed everyone processed together. They talked for a long time.

We had needed to give staff a radical experience that gave them a picture of those clients whose lives have been so bitterly ripped apart. We no longer experienced the antagonism of any of the staff. Intriguingly it was decided that the Romanian staff were simply too fragile to do this exercise. The long history of the fear and reality of people being snatched, taken, seized and never coming back is just too close to the surface. There are many anomalies in Romania. Many of the work issues we faced pointed back to Ceaucescu. For instance, asking each group to come up with one best answer for the group seems to mimic the old Ceaucescu demand of sublimation to the group and an enforced loss of autonomy. We had the experience of being confronted for using this group strategy and told that we were communists.

We had to win the trust of the staff. In Romania one of the turning points in the training was our willingness to go out on limbs of responsibility, to go to General Director Eftimescu and to get promises for the offenders, to get writing materials, to entrust the youngest officers with intellectually challenging tasks, to practice democracy and not champion a hierarchical world. We had to actually PROVE that we were safe fathers.

Romanian culture in the main still sees the father as the dominant figure. Thinking otherwise has very limited roots. An example of this was the issue of the "chef de camera." Some staff were wed to the old way of having in each "camera" or cell block a "chef de camera" who "organizes" the inmates for the staff. As even they said, this leads to the "formal" " informal" "chef de camera." We had to challenge this strong father idea even though the new rule put in place by Dr Gheorghe was that the "chef de camera" was illegal. It took not just our insistence that this old kapo system was outmoded, dangerous and illogical but the dawning belief that we were going to get this community to work without it. The work created mantras. In Romania our mantra was that respect led to keeping the channels of communication wide enough to change and that without respect prisoners would simply not even believe. As of this date in November 1999, Descatusarea is working and experiencing significant growing pains over basic issues such as dealing with the concept of boss, or no boss, or who will have information, or who is controlling information. The experiment that is Descatusarea is a meta strategy for the ongoing battles for change in the Rahova/DGP culture.

As Mihaela Sasarman, a famous Romanian prison theatre specialist and drama therapist who co-works extensively with us in our shared company Transcaena said: "There is no history at the moment of making community. The sense of community created by the experience was very new for this staff. They know brutality from the hands of bosses and that at any time anything can change. It is hard to fight, because there is so much hopelessness. The training gave them a sense of life. But life is so dark for us. You can see that we do not have much, and that we cannot say. When I work with puppets and masks and ask the officers to speak, then they can do this. They can speak. We live in symbols and we are trapped by them. You make them speak aloud. It is dangerous. It is the way. Your work is full of hope. Hope is dangerous. But everyone is fighting to do it, to learn something, and to succeed. To build the new experience we fight to win this new way. We are very excited."

Working with the Offenders

At some point the staff at both sites became like gladiators. It was time to work with the offenders. This meant for some the reigniting of their fear and anxiety and for us the test.

In Romania we carefully orchestrated the respectful meeting of the offenders and the newly trained staff. Working with the mantra of respect we interviewed each prisoner in the presence of all the trainee staff. The offenders were as unsure as the staff. We openly modeled listening, not analyzing, assenting, asking if what we had heard was like what they thought they said, explaining the ideology of the community and it is voluntary basis. And respect! The prisoners responded with as much surprise and wonder and suspicion as the officers.

Gradually we handed the interviews over to the staff after we modeled and discussed what we were doing. Like a giant role play staff learned how to play the atmosphere, look for the "yes" opening, keep the ball in the air and not let the interaction with the offenders go flat. The staff were enormously excited. Two days of interviewing and explaining confirmed the simple idea that respect worked, that respect can keep the door open. For both staff and offenders this was the first time that they had met in this way. It was the cap to the attack on old beliefs. The proof was there. They believed. Descatusarea means "Break the chains." A few chains broke.

In Australia it was equally dramatic but in another way. On the very first day of the new unit, before we the trainers even got there, the staff sat down with the children and ate a huge breakfast together. They had already connected, and broken the old belief-based actions. The children were as amazed as anyone.

The staff watched closely as we went through the new ideas with the children. They watched as we coped without violence with the young offenders' fear, intransigence and anger at the new notions. We modeled that this could work even when the children rebelled. When one staff member went back to the old ways we took over. But the staff connected with the children–played, talked, listened, and asked. In fact their real skills simply took over from ours. Many of the staff know these young adolescents very well. They knew their parents, their homes, their lives. They taught me how not to scapegoat, something I do when I'm afraid. They reveled in the new and they looked proud. I have never seen anything quite like that moment of watching the staff play, talk, work to break through. It is the hallmark of Eastern Hill 22 months later.

Evaluation

Eastern Hill, the Australian therapeutic community at Melbourne Juvenile Justice Centre was evaluated by Latrobe University for one year using both qualitative and quantitative research methods. In addition, the researchers from LaTrobe University and the University of Melbourne-Cook, Semmens and Grimswade used the Moos Correctional Institution Environment Scale. Data was collected pretraining, during training and at the conclusion of the work, roughly from March 1998 to December 1998.

The evaluation's focus was to assess the impact on clients, staff, management and the environment. Information was analyzed from various sources including:

a. Incident reports before and after the work
b. Staff absences before and after the work
c. Taped interviews
d. The Moos scale
e. Observations by the researchers.

The Moos scale developed by Rudolph Moos in 1975 is a measure of institutional climate. Moos defines this as the way that the "organizational context of correctional institutions may shape individual behavior." (Cook, Semmens, & Grimswade, p. 73, 1999) Simmons and Cook refer to Moos' reference to Stern who defines "climate" as "the private percept that each person has of the events in which he takes part." Simmons and Cook also go on to say:

> Moos' definition is intended to include not only each individual's private world but also the point at which this private world merges with

> that of others to form a common interpretation of events in which they participate. Such common interpretations may differ from those of a detached observer because the ongoing interaction of the participants and their perceptions develops a dominant culture within the institution, and this is the prevailing institutional climate. (Cook, Semmens, & Grimswade, p. 73, 1999)

In Geese Company, we were particularly excited at this use of the Moos because it pointed to our beliefs about the need to change institutional beliefs in order to change culture. In addition, the subscales of the Moos includes measures of institutional relationships, treatment programs and system maintenance.

A modified Moos was given to the staff, clients and administration. In all cases the Moos notes the following–during the changeover to the new system of the therapeutic community the climate dips and then recovers and finally overtakes the original preprogram scores. In terms of administrative satisfaction the change is startling from a minus 10 to plus 26. For the clients the change is a nearly 50 percent change in satisfaction. The staff after 8 months show a smaller increase in their satisfaction in the climate.

Prison life is measured in part by trouble, or lack of trouble. When we were asked by the interviewers we predicted that the frequency of incidents would increase in the new system first especially as staff changed over their old disciplines and clients tested the new regime. We also predicted that over time the frequency of incidents would decline. (There is some issue as to whether reporting prior to the training was accurate or whether incidents were underreported. Certainly staff hinted that this might have been so.) But the statistics show that there was a high point of violent incidents immediately following the first training, and that after the second training this gradually tailed off.

Similarly we made predictions that there would be a drastic reduction in the use of the isolation cell as punishment.

> Prior to the training . . . 86% of incidents resulted in isolation being used. This figure reduced over a period of 8 months and after the next training to 46%. (Cook, Semmens, & Grimswade, pp. 76–77, 1999)
>
> Furthermore when isolation was used it was often in tandem with other disciplinary strategies such as counseling, group meetings, thinking reports, management reports, consequences and/or debriefing. In fact isolation was rarely used on it is own to a reported incident in the first 6 months after the initial training (3.8%) and was not used at all as a singular response during the second training session and after. (Cook, Semmens, & Grimswade, p. 77, 1999)

There are also significant statistics to show that verbal altercations eventually decreased quite dramatically. The statistics show a similar trend throughout–after the first training there was a highly complex and anxious turnaround, which showed in increased aggression and dissatisfaction which was resolved some few months after the second training when staff actually received further training and a manual of community therapeutic activities.

CONCLUSIONS

Changes in prison culture must be driven by powerful modalities since there is so much resistance to change. Drama therapy has a built-in advantage over many strategies in that it intensifies the affect necessary to challenge beliefs, and gives staff a rehearsal of new ways of relating that is safer than those that can be learned in pen and paper lectures.

Therapeutic communities have intensive demands. Because many clients respond well to the learning principles and opportunities of the therapeutic community, it is a good rehabilitative environment. The demands are such that staff must learn to operate at much more intensive levels of participation and creativity. The action methods of drama enhance responses so that staff can become acquainted and comfortable with rapid change and being in focus all the time.

Drama therapy accommodates prison staff well by being a way to blend theory and action. Prison staff respond well to action-based work. Changing prison cultures takes using a format that is unexpected, challenging and relentlessly honest. Drama therapy is driven by people in relationship with each other. It is meta alive. It is not an ideology but a praxis.

For cultural change in prison to be effective there must be a real democracy, a freedom of choice. Drama therapy operates by accepting all choices, seeing what happens when everything is tried. For the drama therapist to be effective there must be at the minimum a courageous leader with real power, access to the entire system and a person on the ground who will help drive the changes. We therefore acknowledge strongly General Eftimescu, Dr Florian Gheorghe, Mihaela Sasarman, Diana Batzias, Johan Top, Di Garner and Patrick Tidmarsh. Ultimately people make systems change.

REFERENCES

Bergman, J., & Hewish, S. (1996). The violent illusion in Liebmann, M. (Ed.). *Arts approaches to conflict*. London: Jessica Kingsley Publishers.

Bergman, J., & Hewish, S. (1996). Pin point–The precise fit of drama therapy and cognitive restructuring. In creative therapies and programs in corrections. *Correctional issues*. American Correctional Association, Maryland.

Camus, A. (1991). The fall trans by O'Brien J. Edited by McDonald, E. re-issue edition, Vintage Books.

Cook, S., Semmens, R., & Grimswade, C. (1999). Evaluation of Melbourne Juvenile Justice Centre Behavioural Program. LaTrobe University and University of Melbourne, unpublished. Melbourne: Australia.

Roberts, J. (1997). History of the therapeutic community. In Cullen, E., Jones, L., & Woodward, R. (Eds.). *Therapeutic communities for offenders*. Chichester: John Wiley.

Yokley, J.M. (1999). The application of therapeutic community learning experiences to adult abusers. In Schwartz B.K., & Cellini. H.R. (Eds.), *The sex offender*. Kingston, NJ: Civic Research Institute.

Zimbardo, P.G. (1973). On the ethics of intervention in human psychological research: With special reference to the Stanford prison experience. *Cognition, 2,* pp. 243–256.

FURTHER READING

Bergman, J., & Hewish, S. (1996). The violent illusion. In Liebmann, M. (Ed.), *Arts approaches to conflict*. London: Jessica Kingsley Publishers.

Bergman, J. (1995). Life, the life event and theater–A personal narrative in the use of drama therapy with sex offenders. In B.K. Schwartz & H.R. Cellini (Eds.), *The sex offender: Corrections, treatment and legal practice*. Kingston, NJ: Civic Research Institute.

Bergman, J., & Hewish, S. (1996). Pin point–The precise fit of drama therapy and cognitive restructuring, in creative therapies and programs in corrections. *Correctional Issues*. American Correctional Association, Maryland.

Boal, A. (1992). *Games for actors and non-actors*. London: Routledge.

Courtney, R. (1985). The dramatic metaphor and learning. In J. Kase-Polisini (Ed.), *Creative drama in a developmental context*. University Press of America, Lanham.

Cullen, E., Jones, L., & Woodward, R. (Eds.). (1997). *Therapeutic communities for offenders*. Chichester: John Wiley.

Goffman, E. (1959). *The presentation of self in everyday life*. New York: Doubleday.

Huizinga, J. (1955). *Homo ludens,* Boston: Beacon Press.

Piaget, J. (1962). *Play dreams and imitation in childhood.* New York: Norton.

Yokley, J.M. (1999). The Application of Therapeutic Community Learning Experiences to Adult Abusers. In Schwartz, B.K. & Cellini. H.R. (Eds.), *The sex offender.* Kingston, NJ: Civic Research Institute.

Yokley, M. (1999). Using therapeutic community learning experiences with youth sex offenders. In Schwartz, B.K. & Cellinin. H.R. (Eds.), *The sex offender.* Kingston, NJ: Civic Research Institute.

Chapter 16

UNWINDING RESISTANCE AND EXTERNALIZING THE UNSPOKEN: THE ENACT METHOD IN THE SCHOOLS

DIANA FELDMAN AND FARA SUSSMAN JONES

GENESIS

I CAME TO THIS WORK as many of us do: through a process of personal growth and development. When I was twenty-one, a dramatic life event forced me to take immediate action into my own healing process. I had just graduated from college, and was in the back seat of a friend's car returning home from a party. On the long ride, I had drifted off to sleep. I had a dream that our car was in a terrible accident and that we were all hurt. I heard sirens and people's voices, and as I drowsily opened my eyes I realized I was partially conscious, sitting on the floor, twisted and broken. The car had been hit by a drunk driver and was crushed like a can of tuna fish. While everyone else got out of the car, I was unable to move.

This accident led me to an epiphany that stays with me to this very day, and has led me to the work I am currently doing in drama therapy. While sitting in that car, though actually in shock, I thought I was paralyzed. Yet, suddenly I had a comforting thought: I decided that if I could not move, at least I could sing. It may not sound like much consolation, but it wasn't the *act* of singing I was focused on. It was the *creative energy* behind it. I experienced a new and inexplicable sensation–a most freeing, expansive experience that somehow gave me the peace of mind that everything would be all right.

During a year of rehabilitation, mending two broken legs and learning to walk again, I experienced a number of setbacks. Ultimately, however, I was fortunate to be working with movement therapists who empowered me to heal both physically and emotionally. Through my healing process, I had the unusual opportunity to relearn some early lessons such as simple motor skills and coordination. By working developmentally–at a level and speed that felt comfortable and organic to me–I discovered firsthand the significance of respecting and working in conjunction with an individual's developmental process. This, to me, seemed to be a most effective method of learning and healing.

I also learned how to address the problem of resistance, an issue I encounter so often in teenagers, by dealing with resistance of my own. A skilled body worker helped me to release deep holding patterns that were stuck in my body since the moment of impact with the car. She enlisted my body's physical resistance into the healing process. Although ultimately she wanted me to move my leg in the other direction, she gently encouraged me to move my leg in the direction that felt most natural. Holding my leg inward, she let it rest in that position and asked me how I felt. I immediately started releasing feelings and memories from the accident that had been repressed for so long. We worked together over the next year through what I came to understand was somato-emotional release and "unwinding," a term coined by John Upledger D.O. in his book, *Somato Emotional Release and Beyond* (1996). Eventually, as the trauma was released, my body found new opportunities to come into alignment and strengthen.

Because of experiences like these, as I reentered my life I was inspired to explore ways to help others tap into their own creative energy as a source for transformation and healing. Thus, my next 12 years were spent working with individuals of all ages and abilities towards opening up creative potential for the purposes of healing. I also employed a developmental approach to teaching new skills and facilitating the process of growth. Ultimately I created ENACT, a company that uses drama therapy techniques to work in the public schools. As of this writing, in 1999, ENACT has served 20,000 students and teachers in the New York City Public School System.

The Developmental Approach and Therapeutic Alliances

When I first began teaching in the New York City School system, I was asked to work in special education classes within a regular school setting. The classes were small and contained, and were run by both a teacher and an assistant teacher or "paraprofessional." This setting proved to be quite conducive to drama therapy work. I worked with students labeled "developmentally delayed," with difficulties ranging from autism to mild retardation. Additionally, I encountered students who were severely physically and emotionally challenged. Working consistently with these young people, I had the opportunity to learn how to connect with them. I endeavored to tune into their needs in an authentic way. As a result, the students began to guide me, through their responses, to the level at which they could learn and I should teach.

It was through this experience that I learned about and began to implement a "developmental approach" to teaching. As I worked to "join" students (i.e., meeting them where they were at emotionally and physically), to connect authentically with their ongoing needs, and to move at the pace developmentally appropriate for them, profound improvements in social and emotional functioning began to occur. My experience with these students also made clear the significance of creating a "therapeutic alliance." This dynamic has been described by family therapist, Salvador Minuchin, as the partnership/relationship formed between therapist and client whereby common goals are articulated and pursued and the client feels the therapist is working with and for him. In fact, it has been asserted that without the establishment of such a relationship, growth and change are less than likely to occur (Minuchin, 1981).

As time went on, the ENACT approach that I developed included creating alliances and working developmentally. The two foci became essential in my work with individuals of all ages and abilities. Today, we who are trained in this methodology continue to utilize and teach them as necessary foundations for facilitating growth and/or change with any population.

Creating a Safe Environment: The Container

Over the years as my work continued in the schools and we grew, so did the needs and challenges of the public school system. We at ENACT began to receive an increasing number of calls asking for assistance in managing students labeled "at risk" in both special and regular education classes. The Board of Education uses this term to mean at risk of dropping out of school (students labeled "at-risk" often exhibit extreme acting-out or withdrawn behavior). Meanwhile, teachers were reporting frustration with the growing chaos in classrooms as class sizes began to swell to 20 and 30 students. Larger classes meant less individual attention from teachers and increasingly disruptive behaviors from students. Changes in class size and student composition became increasingly challenging to our work. As a result, we endeavored to create an approach to our own work that created an opportunity for successful growth learning to occur.

We began to focus our attention on reaching the students labeled "at-risk" and creating a safe and structured environment that also allowed for creativity and self-expression. Based on our earlier work, we knew that successful learning was more likely to occur within such a contained setting. We found this type of environment to be more conducive to a developmental approach to teaching. We began to place a new emphasis on the "container"–the space within the larger setting of the classroom that allows for creativity and spontaneity to occur within a set of clearly defined boundaries and rules. The container was established either concretely (chairs or desks in a circle), or metaphorically (a collectively determined "playspace"). Working with the students, we established rules generally based upon those of the preexisting classroom as well as ENACT directives such as "Freeze" and "Focus." In some cases, contracts were negotiated between students and ENACT instructors whereby group rules were listed alongside the consequences of breaking those rules. The collective effort in the establishment of such contracts proved effective as students became as invested in following the rules as they were in co-creating them.

Once a safe and supportive container was established, we found that students were more willing and able to participate appropriately, both individually and collectively. Most important, we found students were more likely to express themselves and take risks. The results of these findings revealed yet another advantage of the container: the establishment of group cohesion and trust. Today, we continue to utilize and emphasize the importance of the container as a crucial element in our work. As a basis for establishing safety, creativity, and trust, we have found this type of environment to be optimal for promoting learning, growth, and change.

The Importance of Empathy

As students involved with ENACT continued to experience success in the classroom, teachers became increasingly interested in our work. They wondered how we were able to effect such meaningful changes in behavior, and expressed a desire to learn tools they could use for themselves to better reach their students on a day-to-day basis. In response to the growing needs of teachers and educators in the public school system, we began to explore ways to address their concerns in a meaningful way. What we found was that while it was not appropriate to teach classroom teachers the direct application of our dramatic and therapeutic techniques, we could teach our basic philosophy and methodology (see: *Basic Concepts: Philosophy and Methodology*). We believed in the effectiveness of the specific ENACT approach (see: *Workshop Format*), but realized that it was the underpinnings of our work that had so successfully created the openings for learning and behavioral change. Thus, we endeavored to find ways to teach our methodology in such a way that it would be applicable to teachers and educators in a variety of classroom settings. In 1997, we implemented teacher workshops in the schools, and the ENACT Training Institute, for teachers and teaching artists, was born.

Before we could thoughtfully teach our methodology, however, we felt the need to explore more closely why it was that students were responding to our work in such a meaningful way. While we had already identified and named some key concepts such as the developmental approach, creating alliances, and the container, further analysis of our work led us to the importance of empathy.

Empathy has been described as "the capacity to think and feel oneself into the inner life of another person" (Kohut, 1984). The therapist/teacher must be open and receptive to the thoughts, feelings, and needs of the client/student. As a crucial element of the therapeutic alliance, empathy validates the other's experiences and forges a connection with another human being. It is this empathetic connection we found to be yet another essential element in our work. In fact, it is that connection that led us to the discovery of one of our key techniques that we use with individuals of various ages and abilities. I discovered its profound impact while working with characteristically "unreachable" nonverbal autistic children, as described in the scenario that follows.

Working with Autistic Children: A Visit to the Moon Man

A group of about 12 severely autistic nonverbal children were wandering around the classroom when an ENACT instructor and I entered the room. The children did not seem disturbed by our presence because they continued wandering around the room, spinning in circles and playing with toys. Despite their teacher's efforts to get their attention, they continued what they were doing. Finally, the three of us were able to guide the students into a circle by having them hold hands to keep from wandering away. We began by moving together. Some children made little sounds, others just swayed back and forth. We moved together in the circle round and round in slow motion, and did various other simple exercises and techniques, using sound and movement, to assess their level of functioning and to see how we might connect with them.

We did connect to some extent, but I wanted to connect in a deeper way. I was picking up on the feelings of isolation that these children seemed to be experiencing, and I wanted to "join" them, to let them know that I understood. I brainstormed with my partner about the best way to do this, and we came up with the following day's main activity.

We were going on a journey to outer space to visit a man in the moon who was very sad because no one understood him and he could not speak their language. I was the pilot, my partner took up the back, and the teacher stood in the middle, helping with the task of getting on the ship. We stopped and started several times, and the students moved their bodies back and forth until we reached our destination. Maintaining our line, we journeyed out of the spaceship onto the moon in slow motion and looked for the moon man.

Suddenly we heard sounds coming from behind a large rock (the desk). It was the moon man (my partner under a flowing purple piece of material) making soft longing sounds. I asked the students if they heard it. I said he was very shy and that they would have to be gentle with him. He cautiously came around and stood in front of the rock and continued to make calling sounds. I asked one of the more outgoing students if he wanted to come up and greet the man in the moon.

Excited, the student came forward and gently touched the moon man, who jumped back in fear. The student seemed very concerned for the creature. I suggested to the student (knowing that he could make sounds) that maybe if he repeated back what the moon man said, he might feel more comfortable. The moon man said "aah," and the student repeated the sound. The moon man laughed and jumped up and down. The student was very happy. I encouraged another student to come forward and greet the moon man. He presented the moon man with an imaginary gift, and the moon man jumped with joy. The student smiled. One by one on their own, other students stepped forward. They each presented the moon man with a gift and the moon man responded with joy. Finally, I encouraged another student who made sounds to repeat the sounds of the moon man and see what would happen.

The moon man said "ooo"; the student said "OOO." The moon man said "hello"; the student (who normally only makes sounds and not words) said "hello." The moon man jumped in joy. I explained to the students how happy the moon man was because someone on earth was communicating with him. It was very moving to watch. After this communication with the students, it was time to go back to earth. The moon man said good-bye, and in unison, all of the students said good-bye. He disappeared behind the rock and we journeyed down back to earth.

Although as a class we could not really talk about what happened, there was an understanding and a true connection in the room. My partner came out from behind the desk and removed the material, showing the students that the moon man was not real. They each got under the purple cover and made believe they were the man in the moon, moving and making sounds.

Based upon experiential research, such as our experience with the "moon man," we concluded that students were responding to the ENACT work in a meaningful way because we were using empathy to connect with them on an emotional level. We were externalizing their feelings of isolation, which they were unable to express verbally. This joining technique helped them feel more validated and understood, which led to their willingness to learn to communicate.

DRAMA THERAPY FRAME OF REFERENCE

Basic Concepts and Premises

ENACT is an arts-in-education company that utilizes creative drama and drama therapy techniques to improve social and emotional learning in children and adolescents. Through creative drama techniques including role play and participatory theater games, students are offered alternatives and choices in learning new life skills. Presently, ENACT joins the ongoing work of the various arts-in-education companies in New York City. There are a few organizations that teach conflict resolution through the creative/dramatic application of various behavioral and cognitive approaches and techniques. While ENACT utilizes similar tools, it is the underlying methodology and drama therapeutic approach that makes ENACT unique and so successful in New York City schools.

Humanistic Developmental Approach

The ENACT methodology is based upon a humanistic approach to personality. We place an emphasis on self-awareness as an essential element of social and emotional functioning. We also stress a respect for individual differences in developmental (or growth) processes. We assert that all individuals have unlimited potential, are creative and unique, and are positively motivated towards growth and self-actualization. ENACT recognizes the source of individual potential as emanating from within. Therefore, we strive to empower students to tap into their own creativity and potential in service of building self-awareness. We believe that as a strong sense of self develops, communication improves, and conflicts can move towards resolution. Accordingly, ENACT's core teachings focus on "recognition of self" such as learning to identify and name feelings, managing emotions and behaviors, and taking ownership of action. Furthermore, since we view the developmental process as continuous, fluid, and specific to each individual, we work diligently to meet students where they are at and move with them respectively towards growth and change.

Dysfunction

Unfortunately, when the path to awareness and creativity is blocked, individuals are less likely to experience healthy social and emotional functioning. Consequences of the inability to recognize one's own thoughts and feelings (as well as the inability to act spontaneously and appropriately in any given situation) include inner conflict and anxiety. According to psychoanalytic theory, individuals will employ any number of *defense mechanisms* to protect themselves against such anxiety-provoking feelings (Wenar, 1994). One of the most frequently used defenses among the adolescents we have encountered is *resistance*. Resistance has been described as "the organized attempt at opposing the processes of becoming aware of the emergence of unconscious forces" (Emunah, 1994). This and other defenses can manifest themselves in a wide spectrum of behaviors ranging from withdrawal to acting out, and are often encountered in therapeutic situations. Since it is ENACT's goal to bring about conscious awareness of perception, feelings, and needs for emotional integration (with the ultimate goal of behavioral change), we endeavor to find ways to work through such obstacles and blocks.

Adolescence and Defenses

Normal adolescence is a period of rapid change and turmoil. Since individuals at this developmental life stage generally have not mastered the expression of their inner turmoil, they often display defensive behaviors that are destructive and/or counterproductive. In fact, many of the artfully creative defenses employed by adolescents not only serve to block out strong unwanted feelings (such as anger and fear), but keep students locked into unhealthy behavioral patterns. It should also be noted that adolescents with particularly difficult and traumatic life challenges tend to exhibit even more extreme degrees of defensive behaviors. Many of the adolescents ENACT works with come from inner cities and consequently are exposed to higher-than-average levels of crime, violence, and drug use. They are also more likely to come from broken homes, foster families, and/or crowded living conditions. As a result, these adolescents tend to display behaviors that are inappropriate not only because they have not mastered the expression of their inner turmoil, but also because environmental conditions are not conducive to healthy and adaptive functioning.

Since some defense mechanisms are necessary for survival, the challenge for anyone who works with this population is to find ways to work through those defenses while providing alternative tools for emotional protection. As we have observed time and again, defenses such as resistance most readily appear with students during any therapeutic processes aimed at increased self-knowledge and awareness. Resistance in adolescents during this type of work can manifest itself in any number of ways, including a refusal to participate, defensive body language, irritability, and even sabotage.

At ENACT, we believe that the first rule in dealing with resistance is to treat it with respect. We believe that in order to work through resistance, the therapist must join with it and enlist it into the therapeutic process. Thus, we employ various methods and techniques to "unwind" resistance in a playful, creative, and supportive way as we did in the situation that follows. In addition, we strive to create awareness of these defenses in the students who use them.

Overcoming Resistance: The Story of Tina

When I first met Tina, she would not say hello or acknowledge me at all. She appeared quite angry and distrustful, though highly intelligent. Tina was in a special education class because of her behavior. She was very resistant to learning and acted out often. Also, English was her second language and this added to her frustration. Each day when I entered the room, I said hello and Tina made it a point to turn her back and ignore me. Her body language was her armor. Her arms were always crossed, and her lips clenched tight. "Don't mess with me" was what I got. So I did not. I respected Tina's boundaries, because there are very real reasons for students to act the way they do (though I still did not appreciate it). Every day, I invited Tina to participate and every day she declined.

One day during the scene work, I created a character in a classroom who was extremely defensive to her teacher (this reflected many students, so it did not put Tina on the spot). With exaggerated body language (crossed arms and shutdown emotions), the character refused to do what the teacher asked. Following the scene, I asked the class if they knew why this character was acting this way on the outside and how she was feeling on the inside. Tina's arm went up. She said that the character did not trust anybody, that she had the right to be that way, that we did not know what she had been through, and that we should not expect her to do whatever the teacher asks. I agreed with Tina. I validated her feelings.

Over the next few days we did a lot of scenes about trust. One day Tina volunteered to come up. She wanted to do a scene about a group home. She played the Counselor. In the discussion that followed she revealed that she had been moved from group home to group home and was now at home taking care of her elderly father. She had come to the U.S. from another country and never really had a solid living situation. As she discussed her situation, her body language became more open. Her defenses melted away as she was able to verbalize her feelings. That year we did an Off-Broadway show. We asked Tina if she would like the topic of group homes in the show because we realized that it might heighten awareness for some people. We asked if we could use the scene that she created. She was delighted. Tina stood up and talked about the difficulties of group home living and parent care to an audience of 200 adults. She had found her voice. At the end of the year, Tina said to me,

"Thank you, this was the best thing that ever happened in my life!"

"Unwinding" Resistance

ENACT uses aesthetic reflective techniques and distance to unwind resistance via theater games and/or scene work. One such method incorporates specific activities highlighting defensive behaviors. For example, in a simple theater game students are asked to exaggerate their body language by showing the biggest "attitude" they can. They are then guided to bring their bodies back to a centered, grounded and relaxed position. In this way, highly defended students can become self-aware of their body language in a playful and safe way. Another method is to develop and implement games and activities that uncover the underlying motivations behind defenses. For example, the creation of tableaux can be used to symbolize resistance creatively by encouraging students to build group and/or individual statues that represent emotions such as anger, sadness, or fear. Once created, the therapist/leader then works with students to find ways to uncover possible thoughts, needs, and other feelings that might lie beneath their images. (For example, allowing students to interview members of the tableau.) In this way, students learn not only to identify and name their own feelings, but become aware of the concurrent and multidimensional feelings of others.

In addition, the therapist uses him/herself as an "empathetic container" (a term I use to describe the therapist acting as a vehicle to express what the group is feeling) to reflect back what he/she is picking up from the group through the use of metaphor, games, and reflective scene work. For example, if the leader senses resistance in the room, he or she may do a call-and-response exercise that externalizes the unspoken feelings of the group. In an exaggerated (distanced) way the leader feeds back what they are picking up. For example, the leader says, "I don't want to be here, it is so nice outside." The group repeats it. "I'm tired and hungry." The group repeats it. "I can't wait for lunch," and so on. As the leader senses the group's resistance moving aside, he may turn it around with something like, "Well, I'm here anyway so I might as well have fun." The group repeats it. The participants have had their feelings expressed and validated and are now ready to proceed with the activities.

ENACT reflective scene work is another creative way to help participants move past resistance. Carefully designed scenes are demonstrated by the therapist and co-leader to bring about conscious awareness of thoughts and feelings. We have found this particularly effective in working toward behavior change. By enacting familiar situations featuring resistant (i.e., aggressive or withdrawn) characters, participants can safely see themselves, and are often even able to laugh at their own behavior. In addition, the leader verbalizes underlying thoughts and feelings for the group such as " I am afraid I'll get in trouble," or "I am really angry." The underlying material is externalized (taken out of their defense system) and placed in a safe and validating space. It becomes less scary for them to see and hear what they are defending against. We have found these techniques and others to be successful in unwinding resistance, an essential step in working towards growth and change.

The Therapeutic Process

The basic ENACT format is similar to that of many creative arts programs. It has a warm-up, a main activity, and a closure. The warm-up introduces the theme for the day (which usually grew out of the day before) using theater games, metaphor, sound, and movement. The main activity is a scene demonstrated by the therapist and a co-leader that portrays an issue that is relevant to the group as a whole. A facilitated discussion and replay follows. The closure is an integration of the day's work and brings the day to an end.

The Warm-up

For adolescents and especially those with behavioral problems, the warm-up is essential. It sets up a safe creative space, which develops and builds a group dynamic. It creates community and introduces and enforces humanistic values. It is a container, an environment that promotes personal expression and the development of interpersonal skills while allowing individuals to express their own particular needs. In many cases, especially with larger number of individuals, a great deal of time is spent creating the container. Mutual responsibility and respect are essential in this process, and are reinforced on a regular basis.

The next step is to develop interpersonal skills, which can be challenging depending on the population. At ENACT we are often asked to work with highly acting-out populations who have poor impulse control. Without structure they often lose control and break all kinds of boundaries. The therapist must carefully design games that begin with high structure and "loosen the reins" as group safety and trust develop. In many cases the application and management of the games is the most challenging part for the therapist, who must be persistent, strong, and patient. Without a container it is almost impossible to move forward in any kind of productive way. With many groups that we work with, especially those that include students labeled "at risk," a contract of agreement is created and negotiated throughout the process to help reinforce commitment and responsibility in support of the work.

Since adolescents are afraid of looking or feeling infantile, especially in front of their peers, they often demonstrate a high degree of resistance. As explained earlier, ENACT games are designed to safely enlist and redirect resistance. Once resistance seems to have moved aside, the leader can continue to build interpersonal skills, which include individual expression and/or containment. It is essential for adolescents to feel a sense of their progress and accomplishment, and the therapist must artfully design games that both challenge and allow for achievement. If the therapist implements games that are not developmentally appropriate, however, student may increase their defenses and their behavior becomes more problematic.

In many ways the warm-up becomes an opportunity to enlist students in building a new kind of community, one they might not have experienced at home or in school. It is a chance to build a supportive, responsible atmosphere that encourages creative expression and self-worth.

ENACT Warm-up

- Creates a safe structured container
- Builds interpersonal and individual skills
- Addresses resistance
- Allows for success

Main Activity: Scene Work

Specialized scene work and facilitation are the main activity in ENACT workshops. This activity is the longest segment of the workshop (30 minutes) and usually includes a short reflective role play and facilitated discussion (a consciousness-raising phase).

The scene work is a springboard that creates an opening for self-reflection and awareness, essential for conscious change. The therapist and co-leader conduct a real-life scene that is relevant to the group. The context is designed to resonate with group experience. In our case, since we work in city schools, it usually demonstrates issues and conflicts around typical urban issues such as peer pressure, violence, and teacher-student interaction, and we usually survey teachers ahead of time about common concerns in the classroom or school and community.

The scenes are developed around specific issues that emerge from the group itself. The scene is brief–less than two minutes–and the therapist enlists the class in creating a container by asking them to say "quiet on the set," making them responsible for their own behavior. Carefully designed character work portrays the inner (needs and feelings) and outer behavior (defenses) of the characters. It is a powerful projective device that is engaging, reflective, and affirming. An example of the power of scene work is clear in the story of Sara in the case study section. Depending on the content that is to be dealt with (and later brought into conscious awareness by the group), the scene is appropriately distanced by exaggerated character work, or creating parallel characters and/or circumstances.

To assure that the therapist is on target and in alignment with the group, he may ask if what the students saw was realistic and if not, to explain what really occurs. This is the beginning of setting up trust, dialogue, and self-reflection. If this discussion is handled well, students feel seen, heard, understood, and respected. It is an initial way to meet them where they are at, to bring about self-awareness as thoughts, images, and feeling emerge.

ENACT Scene work

- Evokes memory and emotion
- Externalizes underlying realities
- Sets up an opportunity for self-reflection
- Creates a sense of commonality and bonding (very important to adolescents)
- Creates an opening for change by joining and validating students

The Facilitation Phase

The main goal of this phase is to use discussion to bring about conscious awareness of behaviors, needs, and feelings. The therapist is often aware of one or two specific students he or she wants to reach, but works with the entire group as part of a group consciousness. After presenting a scene, through question and answer, the therapist in gentle stages moves the participants from a connection with the material in the scene to a connection with themselves. Ping-ponging back and forth creates safety through distance with the ultimate goal of connection. The therapist moves from generalized to more specific questions like, "Does this kind of thing happen? Why?" "Can you give examples of a similar situation?" and so on. Students are given the opportunity to connect with their own experiences and feelings at their own pace and readiness level. Sometimes, as students give examples, they experience catharsis. By focusing on the feelings more than the student's story, the therapist can validate the student in front of his peers without breaking boundaries or doing one-on-one therapy.

To ensure safety once connection is made, the leader directs the student back to the character in the scene, encouraging the student and others to give the character suggestions. They are actually working on personal problem-solving since the character is a projection of themselves. Thinking through solutions brings the intellect, and not just the feelings, into the equation. This is very important for students who have behavior and impulse control problems. It encourages them to think before they act and helps avoid immediate regression, which can happen when students get lost in themselves, overwhelmed with feeling. The students have now moved from a state of preconsciousness to conscious awareness, which is our goal. The therapist elicits ideas from the students about how the character in the scene might have handled the scene's situation more effectively. The therapist then narrows down these ideas, reframes them, and writes them on the blackboard. The students are now ready to replay the scene with newfound information and tools.

The Facilitation Process

- Brings preconscious material to conscious awareness
- Validates thoughts, feelings, and needs
- Creates an opening for transformation of behavior
- Allows for supportive witnessing

The Replay

The goal of the replay is for students to integrate their newfound information into their bodies and minds. After the leader and students brainstorm, one or more students are usually willing to replace the actor who was the focus of the discussion. The scene is now replayed with the actor-student. The student is set up to win because suggestions for a successful outcome have been written on the board and discussed.

As the scene is replayed, the student practices naming feelings instead of acting out. Here, in this safe environment, he is able to practice making statements such as "I feel angry" instead of hitting, for example. In some circumstances when the therapist is aware that the student has poor impulse control, the therapist may stand behind the student as a coach, monitoring affect and control. The therapist may also decide to employ other drama therapy techniques, such as role-reversal or doubling. This is the time when, if appropriate, the therapist can actually do one-on-one processing. It is amazing to watch behavior transformation here. The most resistant and defensive students, when offered the opportunity to name their feelings, enlist with bravery and pride. Often their extreme body language is replaced with a statement of empowerment. The therapist also coaches students in other coping strategies such as proper breathing and other relaxation techniques to help students with self-expression. A round of applause is always generated from the group.

The Replay

- Allows for integration of social-emotional skills
- Promotes articulation of feelings and needs
- Demonstrates outcome of transformed resistance
- Allows for a new sense of empowerment

The Closure

The purpose of the closure is to bring the session to an end, assuring that participants feel a sense of completion. It gathers the emotional energy that was in the room and ritualizes it through theater games or affirmations, inviting students to use their minds and bodies to pull in and ground what they have just learned. The closure recreates the group bond and leaves them with a sense of accomplishment and excitement.

Special Concerns for the Therapist/Leader

Resistance is a common obstacle that presents itself as a defense mechanism and must be seriously taken into consideration when doing drama therapy, especially when dealing with youth. Young people are often especially creative in demonstrating resistance and the therapist must see the signs by honoring its purpose. It is all too easy to push on, and before the client knows it s/he suddenly feels manipulated or duped into a process that they were not ready for. Moving too quickly with feelings and ignoring resistance can backfire. Young people may act out even more, feeling tricked or made fun of. If they do not have the ego strength they can regress too easily. Resistance is a sign that should be an attention-getter for the drama therapist who much be prepared to deal with it through distance, unwinding, and various other techniques. The creative arts therapies can be all too engaging and empowering and can easily draw participants out of themselves. This is the powerful aspect of our work and must be handled with a great deal of care and sensitivity.

There are problems that the therapist may encounter in a classroom setting. Just as the students want their peers to like them, the therapist may fall into a parallel feeling, wanting to be liked as well. While the therapist is an ally to the students, he is not their friend and should not pretend to be. Because of the nature of the aesthetic projective work, boundaries can get shady, and it is crucial for the leader to keep his own boundaries. In addition, as in any therapeutic situation, countertransference can also occur. Many of the students the therapist may work with are skilled at pushing buttons, and he will have to be careful not to personalize and be reactive.

In addition, the precarious situation of just being an adolescent can remind the therapist of his own past. The therapist was that age, too. Just being back in a classroom, with its forgotten sights, sounds, and especially its smells, often creates flashbacks and memories. The therapist may have been teased or picked on, or maybe he was the bully. It is even more difficult when the therapist sees students whom he suspects may have been abused or neglected. This can bring out the therapist's own fear and rage, driving him to want to be the student's "savior." He must remember that as a therapist, he is only a guide, helping participants to help themselves to transform blocks and obstacles that get in the way of authentic expression. He cannot always create miracles. However, I believe that in doing this work, we are supporters of creative potential and the divinity that we each possess. Through drama therapy we are able to help others, and in many ways, this allows us to tap into our own potential.

Challenges

As drama therapists we are faced with many challenges. One such challenge lies in the settings in which we do our work. Sometimes we have to ask ourselves: Do we want to work only in settings that are optimal for drama therapy, or do we want to bring the work where it is desperately needed despite the potential challenges therein? If we are willing to work in environments that are not entirely conducive to our work, what are the steps we must take in order to be effective?

At ENACT, we have found that while the public school system is not always the optimal setting for drama therapy work, it is an establishment that can and does benefit greatly from the application of drama therapy methods and techniques. One of our challenges, then, has been to continually modify our approaches and techniques to meet the growing needs and challenges of the school system at large. Furthermore, we are faced with many of the challenges classroom teachers are faced with on a daily basis. Small classrooms, large student enrollment, and administrative issues such as scheduling conflicts and a lack of administrative support all present obstacles to our work. For example, large numbers of students and highly chaotic classrooms pose a challenge to the establishment of group safety and trust while restricting the ability for individual attention and focus. As a result, much of our energy and time is often focused on issues of creating and redesigning a safe container within the classroom that is conducive to the work. We often spend time on classroom management and coping with behavior difficulties before we can help individual students deal with their deeper social and emotional concerns and needs. Furthermore, we must consider that therapeutic solutions that might seem appropriate in the classroom setting may not always be viable options in the daily lives of the multicultural and diverse socioeconomic student populations with whom we work. While the public school system, with its focus on academia and its high degree of chaos, is certainly not always the best setting for drama therapy work, it is an excellent place to implement drama therapy techniques and to teach a variety of social and emotional skills.

The school system is changing rapidly in response to the growing needs of our children. Rises in school violence are an outcry of our youth. Adolescents need attention in areas other than academics, and schools are desperately looking for solutions. In addition, students in underprivileged areas are often the ones most in need of the work. Without the resources and support they deserve, many students "fall through the cracks" and deal in silence with neglect, abuse, and emotional disturbance. School years are a critical time for students to receive preventative attention if they are to mature into healthy and responsible adults, and it is just this sort of attention that drama therapists can provide.

CASE STUDIES

Creating a "Container" for Safety and Growth: The Story of John

In 1991, we were working in a public high school's special education department with at-risk youth known mostly for "acting out." We were asked to work with a class once a week for a double period. As this was to be a full-year program, we felt that we needed to work toward a culminating project and planned to develop a performance piece that expressed the needs and concerns of the students.

Day 1 was not much of a challenge. Although students had a difficult time focusing their attention on the exercises for more than a few minutes, they seemed motivated by the process and excited about the goals. We explained that in order to meet the program's goals we had to set up agreements. We had been told that there was a big problem with absenteeism, so we decided to include regular attendance as one of the criteria for participating in the final production that was to take place at an Off-Broadway theater.

On Day 2, John entered the room late, armed with a Walkman®, a comb, and a lollipop in each hand. He was a very large teenager with an awkward walk and a focus that continually jumped from one thing to the next. Since John had missed Day 1, he did not know about our class agreements (which he had already broken by arriving late). He continually interrupted and seemed hyperactive, unable to stand in one place for more than a minute. He was highly reactive. John had a way of upsetting everyone, including me.

As the days progressed, he continued to push the limits of the class. Each day was a struggle. John had a difficult time relating to the other students and broke every rule set by the group. At the same time he was a wonderful actor and had much to say. How could I get him to continue using his exceptional acting ability that contributed a great deal to the class, and teach him to contain his behavior at the same time? A great deal of time was concentrated on redirecting and channeling his creative energy into the work but he was still not willing to be a team player.

One day when John was late, one of the students suggested we kick him out. I knew that John really liked the acting process and felt this would be unfair without discussing it with him first. Just then John entered the room. We discussed our concerns with him and told him we wanted him to be in the show but could not continue to work with him this way. "What was going on?" we asked. John honestly explained that he had a really hard time controlling himself and that he would try. He pleaded with us to let him stay. We decided to set up a contract and hung it on the wall. It included rules about not hitting, not cursing, being respectful, and being on time.

John agreed that after three warnings he, and anyone else who was disruptive, had to sit out of the acting circle until he was ready to participate productively with the group. If he continued to disrupt the class he would be asked to leave. John did mess up a few times, but caught his own behavior and even stepped out of the circle before he was asked. He often apologized to the group and worked diligently on his lack of control. He was learning to take responsibility for his actions and began to see how these actions affected other people. He showed up every day and worked hard on improving his behavior. We continued to acknowledge him by reinforcing his positive attempts and successes. The work with John had a meaningful effect on the entire group as John's negative behavior was something to which each member could relate.

The night of the show John stood backstage holding hands with everyone. He had become an integral part of the group, and was saying a prayer for them all. For his work in the show he got rounds of applause, and in the audience discussion that followed, he was remarkable. One woman asked how everyone had worked so well as a group, and John volunteered a response, admitting, "At first it wasn't easy, but we all really tried." The group laughed. He had come through with shining colors, empowered and with new understanding about his behavior.

This case history demonstrates how important a contained environment that allowed for choice, expression, and creativity helped a student labeled "at-risk" gain personal awareness and social skills.

Empathy in the "At-Risk" Classroom: The Story of Sara

Sara was a 16-year-old girl placed in a school day-treatment center at a hospital in New York City because of severe emotional problems. I was told she almost never spoke. In fact, even when she worked with her psychiatrist, Sara used puppets to communicate. She always came to our workshops but sat in the back, not saying a word. She held her head down low, her body was turned into herself and her eyes shot back and forth very quickly. I rarely saw her smile but when she did, her entire face lit up. Though she was invited to work with us just like any member, she strongly refused, although she took responsibility for her behavior by saying the agreed-upon word, "pass," to indicate that she did not want to participate. She then sat quietly in her chair, observing the activities cautiously. Though my partner and I always invited Sara to participate, we respected her decision not to work. We assumed that when she was ready she would join us. Little by little, Sara participated in the group theater games and a smile broke out as she became a part of the whole. She never participated in the scene work, though she watched intently.

One day, after speaking to their teacher about the students' needs, we agreed to do a lesson that dealt with abuse; several of the girls were in abusive relationships. I had to carefully design a distanced scene that allowed them to connect at their own pace and level of safety. My partner and I presented a scene about two old friends. They were going out to the movies, a date they had been planning for a long time because it had repeatedly been called off. Amy's boyfriend was very possessive and demanded that she be with him every Saturday night. This Saturday, Amy decided to spend the night with Lisa, because she needed to feel more independent from her boyfriend.

Just as the two friends were about to leave, the phone rang and it was Jimmy. He insisted Amy drop her plans immediately and go directly to his house. Once again Amy was swayed, afraid Jimmy would leave her, and began to run out of the house. Lisa became furious, saying "Why do you drop our plans over him? You don't care about me. He doesn't respect you anyway–he hits you. Why do you keep doing this?" The quarrel built to a point of no resolution and the scene was frozen.

During the next part of the lesson we had a question-and-answer session aimed at guiding the students to focus on feelings about dependency and relationships. Though the scene was developed to initially focus on the friends' relationship, the students quickly chose to tune in on the issue of abuse. They were anxious to name what was going on as they made connections with the characters.

I continued the discussion by asking what the friend who was being abandoned by Amy should do. Suddenly and unexpectedly, Sara murmured from her chair, "I know, it happened to me." I could barely hear her. "What?" I said. "I know," she announced, in a much louder voice, "it happened to me!"

To continue to create a safe distance for her, we brought the discussion immediately to the characters in the scene. I asked Sara if she wanted to come up and role-play the friend in a scene. She jumped up immediately and said to Amy (in a voice that I had never heard from her), "Don't ever let anyone hit you. Do whatever you have to do, run away, call a hotline but don't ever let anyone hit you!" Sara's entire body language had changed as she spoke in an empowered voice. Everyone in the group was surprised and moved, and applauded as Sara broke into a big smile. Students came up and hugged her. Her teacher could not believe it, Sara seemed like a different person. The school counselor was notified and continued to work with Sara.

When doing scene work, in cases like this one with Sara, the therapist must carefully observe student behavior such as resistance and acting out, and artfully employ distance as they reflect it back so that students see themselves without feeling mocked.

REFERENCES

Caissy, G.A. (1994). *Early adolescence.* New York: Plenum Books.

Emunah, R. (1994). *Acting for real.* New York: Brunner/Mazel Publishers.

Feldman, D. (1997). *ENACT Workbook.* New York: ENACT Institute.

Jennings, S. (Ed.). (1995). *Dramatherapy with children and adolescents.* London: Routledge.

Upledger, J. (1996). *Somatoemotional release and beyond.* Palm Beach Gardens: UI Publishing, Inc.

Wenar, C. (1994). *Developmental psychopathology.* New York: McGraw-Hill, Inc.

FURTHER TRAINING

ENACT offers training through our Institute in New York. Contact ENACT at 212-741-6591 or enact@interport.net. Or visit our website at www.enact.org.

Chapter 17

OMEGA TRANSPERSONAL DRAMA THERAPY: A TRANSFORMATIONAL THEATER APPROACH

SAPHIRA BARBARA LINDEN

GENESIS

IN THIS CHAPTER, parallel histories of the formation of an experimental theater and work with clinical populations are woven together, for they served as the foundation for this model of transpersonal drama therapy. What follows is a selection of experiments, productions, and processes, which illustrate, each in a particular way, how the vision evolved and became more multidimensional.

The avant-garde theater of the 1960s shook people up. Theater pieces were designed to hit people over the head with everything that was wrong. People needed to be shaken out of their complacency, their indifference to the incredible number of injustices around them. Just talking about what was wrong was no longer effective; and so the age of nonverbal expression was born, the world of environmental theater, which forced actors and audience into a more intense intimate relationship. Theater Workshop Boston, Inc. was created to develop original plays about timely important issues and create new forms of audience/actor relationships within the 'environmental theater' genre. We felt well aligned with the work of The Living Theater and The Open Theater in New York. A couple of years later, the three theaters all received grants from the new experimental theater division of The National Endowment of the Arts.

Drama Therapy with Institutionalized Special Needs Children and Adolescents

In the late sixties, I took a job teaching inpatient schizophrenic and retarded adolescents in Boston State Hospital, through the Boston School system. Since the Boston Public schools at the time had no "Special Education or Special needs" division, Boston State Hospital's program was run under an inept elderly female supervisor in the "physically handicapped" department. There were no books, no supplies, no curriculum, nor assistance of any kind. In this hospital's adolescent unit, there were two classrooms, both composed of long-term institutionalized schizophrenic patients. One of the classes had relatively normal-intelligence learners, while the other had a range of retarded learners from severely autistic to learning disabled.

I was told, "They need to be prepared with the basic academic skills as well as practical life skills to make it in the world if they ever leave the hospital."

Ignorance and apathy and a defeatist attitude prevailed; the program was very poorly administered by both the school system and the hospital. Who really cares about these young people? I wondered. All I had to work with in the way of learning materials were fundamentally my students and myself, period! In certain ways, I was probably well served by my lack of knowledge and experience. For example, I did not know that a student with a certain I.Q. score was supposed to be able to learn only up to a certain level. Using the tools of what we now call drama therapy processes, many of these patients well exceeded their expected learning capacities.

Later, at Kennedy Memorial Hospital for handicapped and emotionally challenged students an what would now be called a drama therapy program was created: the use of role playing, theater games, and in particular, the use of puppets to reach these young people. In this experience, I discovered the power of puppets to gain the trust of these students, who had lost their trust in adults, and to engage them in depth emotional dialogues about their illnesses.

Environmental Participatory Theater with Children

What I knew best was theater. I had been exposed to Grotowski's *Towards a Poor Theatre,* which encourages the use of the actor for everything including sets and props, and also Viola Spolin's *Improvisation for the Theater,* which similarly demonstrates how actors can create images of people, places, and things using themselves. Spolin's work introduced me to theater games and inspired me to teach cognitive material in that modality.

In Theater Workshop Boston's first play, RIOT (Portman & Rollins, 1968), a total environment was created in a church basement in which the audience had the experience of being in the center of an actual riot, of being trapped, of being unable to get out. There was no audience/stage separation. Rather than just watching a riot, they became part of one reproduced through sound, movement and light.

Inspired by the power of creating a theater environment where the boundaries between actors and audience were designed to catalyze intimate actor–audience relationships, I wanted to take our theater experiment one step further with young people. Since children had fewer expectations about what theater should be, it felt inspiring to experiment with an even more intimate form. I wanted to create a meaningful educational experience and environmental form where the young audience members would be active participants throughout a well-crafted and structured play. While adults needed to be shaken out of their complacency, children needed to become more aware of what was really happening in the world.

Example of Participatory Theater

In TRIBE (Linden), children in the audience became active spectators. As soon as they entered the theater, they were immediately initiated into one of three tribes of Native Americans. In this way, they first experienced directly the beauty and the joy of these cultures; then they were led to feel the injustice of being pushed off their land. In theatrical terms, they were forced to leave beautiful, spacious, colorful environments, in which they experienced interesting, creative rituals, and then to travel in a dark, cold, empty space, ending up being shoved together onto a crowded dark gray platform, which represented the reservation. The adults who brought the children in the audience to the theater were seated as elders of these tribes and experienced being left behind.

Making learning fun through the use of creating a "special engaging environment" and simple theater games became a key to working with my challenged hospital students. A sterile state mental hospital classroom was transformed into a magical theater store. Every shelf had produce and products that utilized different levels of math and reading skills. These disturbed and retarded adolescents learned basic math skills at their own level without embarrassment. They were either working in the produce department (with simple arithmetic) or the canned goods section (with algebra), while enjoying taking on the roles of shopkeepers, clerks, or consumers in the food section that corresponded to their level of learning. Thus, I was initiated very early into the connection between theater, therapy and education. Using the environmental theater model we were evolving in the theater and integrating it with the education and therapy work happening in the hospital, we had discovered a new classroom process. We called it:

E.T. Theater

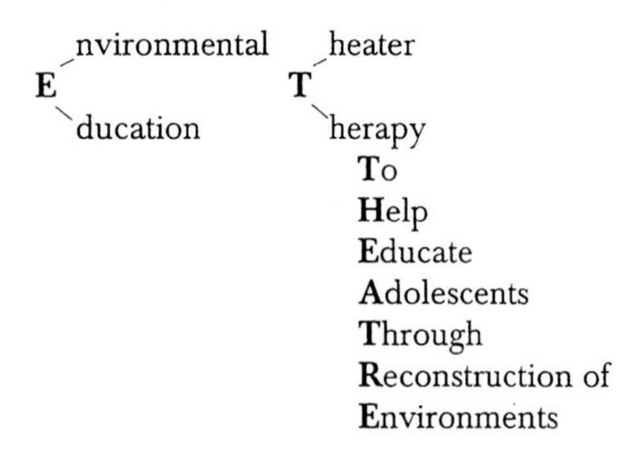

Drama Therapy in Educational and Ssocio-Political Theater

Out of several successful theater educational experiments, a Teaching Company within our then blossoming Theater Workshop Boston was formed. We had asked to work with the most disturbed, disabled and challenged students both on elementary and high school levels. The Teaching Company was invited into several different school systems. A primary goal was to help students develop self-esteem and self-confidence, the basic foundation of successful learning. Thus, we worked with their often long built-up learning blocks by creating a noncompetitive, creative and enjoyable process. The curriculum that we developed was also based on the principle that people learn more effectively when all of their senses and whole body are involved in the learning experience.

The next experiment in our Theater Workshop Boston's playwriting process was to create a play about pollution for adults and children and to integrate the use of different environments for both adults and children in the same performing space. In CREATION, (Linden & Rosenberg), adults were seated in a harried city environment exemplifying polluted values and the children physically became part of a country world of new values and natural living. There was also a third environment, in between the city and country environments, consisting of a factory run by a bureaucrat who represented the voice of selfish capitalism. Children and adults rather than simply watching a land being destroyed by the insensitivity of polluters, directly experienced their environments being taken over by a river filled with waste. Theatrically, an ever-expanding, ugly plastic form with long arms was periodically inflated and expanded more and more after each bureaucrat scene, forcing the audience to keep moving back for protection. The children were driven back to the city to take responsibility to work for change. They begged the adult audience to look at the dying world around them and listen to their pleas for action.

All of these sociopolitical plays were created out of one theater but reflected an attitude prevalent among many experimental theater artists: people are blind to what is going on around them–hit them over the head, demonstrate passionately what is wrong. We began to realize, however, that a theater wishing to help its audience open to the possibility of change must create a safe and warm environment where its actors place themselves on the line, become vulnerable, take risks, and invite people to share the experience with them.

Example of Family Participatory Theater

Toward the one, a Family Board Game (Linden & Dym) was a participatory theater piece for families that created a safe, fun environment in which family members made new discoveries about each other and became exposed and vulnerable through improvisational play. Using many art forms within a theatrical setting, a people-sized board game was created. Each family formed their bodies into some kind of vehicle to move between experiences. A family therapist took the role of Game-Guide and was assisted by actor-facilitators. We utilized many different expressive arts therapies within the context of a family theater experience.

Drama Therapy in Organizational Development: Drama Therapy in the Corporate World

The earlier sociopolitical theater of the 60s rejected government, big business and corporate America, as though it were all one entity to be scorned and destroyed at all costs. At some point we realized that in order for significant change to happen, it was necessary to recognize our collective responsibility in the government we have and in the capitalistic system that we have created. Working with people in positions of power could foster significant change. We realized that there is no "them" and "us." It's a rationalization of our mind. The sacredness of life is about realizing our essential connection to all of life's creation.

When the President of our theater's Board of Directors, George Litwin, an experienced leader in the Management Training field, strongly encouraged us to bring our skills and extensive teaching and facilitating experience into the corporate world, we welcomed the opportunity. He was a master at what he did and was a personal guide to many top executives in large Fortune 500 companies. He had experienced much of our work personally and assured us that we had much to offer these organizations. Over a period of several years, he invited me into select client jobs with him and together we co-created what we called transformational learning experiences. I found that I had a personal mentor par excellence. We wrote a paper together on *Visioning: A Transformational Process.* The essence of it was about left-brain strategic planning coming out of right brain visioning processes with the goal of building a world class company–thinking out of the box. Drama therapy processes were interwoven into these training programs as our theater company was learning to do in a variety of other venues in which we were working.

For over two decades within the corporate world, we have worked with many of the same educational principles and values in designing creative transformational learning programs in leadership training, visioning, creative problem solving, goal setting (examining the company's goals in the context of one's life ideals and goals), corporate culture change, communication, conflict resolution, stress management, team building and company review processes.

Examples of Drama Therapy in Corporate Systems

The following is an example of an innovative corporate format: I brought my core theater company, who were also trained facilitators and teachers, into one of the largest banking organizations in the world. They observed a meeting of corporate managers. The actors (unknown to the managers) were each assigned one manager to observe. At a certain point, I stopped the meeting and invited the actors to take the seats of the managers. The actors then assumed the role of the manager they had observed. They role played the subtext of the perceived feelings and thoughts that were not being expressed. The managers were totally astounded at the accuracy of the portrayals. This helped motivate them to try to engage in much deeper and more honest communication. We then worked with the managers in a workshop in which the personal dynamics and communication that surfaced in the role plays were explored and worked through.

In that same corporation, my mentor, George Litwin, had created a bank-wide training program called "Managing People." We were charged with the task of creating a videodrama for the Vice President's Annual Meeting. Many of the Vice Presidents had 5,000 people working under them. In one case, a very bright, charismatic V.P. had just gone through a corporate disaster. In the process of creating a mass change, converting all of his clerk level jobs to technology-based systems, he had neglected to attend to the people issues that arose in the process. People were burned out, felt devalued, and as a result, a host of other things happened that produced chaos and a major financial failure. We identified the principles behind what happened and created a script with a different situation and characters that made the point about how important it was to be conscious of the people resources and their feelings and needs. The video production was created as a major learning vehicle that demonstrated that bottom line success necessitates a real consciousness about our human resources, i.e., people sensitivity is good business.

In another very large old Fortune 500 company, I was called in to do team building. First, I interviewed some old-timers, some of whom had been in the same jobs for 40 years and in some cases had never left the small town in which they lived and worked. I asked them to fantasize about an ideal job, without considering the salary or training for such a job. What would they do, if they could do anything, that would really inspire them and make them feel that they were being well used? They visualized it and then told the story of what it would be like. I did this to help them stretch out of their limited self-concept about their work. Then, during the weekend training, I did a number of exercises to help these managers connect with deeper parts of themselves in order to be more effective on the job. We worked on relating to others better and being more honest about what they were feeling. We did psychodramatic role plays to help them in this process. Finally, we helped them integrate their goals and encouraged them to take risks, be more creative and do things that expanded their thinking and possibilities in their current jobs. We also encouraged them to do the same with the people who report to them.

On another occasion, a marketing consultant for a large food corporation client elicited my services to help design a training program for their marketing staff on "Empathy." The idea was to give them an experience of empathy personally with themselves, their families and co-workers in order to develop empathy for their consumers. Several drama therapy exercises were created to accomplish this, culminating in the creation of scenes, playing the roles of the consumers (children, men, women, athletes, etc.) of their different food products. Out of this work, new marketing strategies were developed.

Another application of drama therapy in business was the development of a vision. In a small high-tech start-up company, the two founders were about to have a strategic planning meeting with the new CEO who had just joined the company. I suggested creating a shared vision first, out of which the strategic planning could more clearly evolve. They agreed and so I designed for them a right-brained visioning process. Listening to soothing music, they closed their eyes and were taken through a relaxation and guided visualization process that culminated in their each drawing an image that crystallized the essence of their visioning process, accompanied by writing a poem or a succinct piece of prose that expressed their vision. They shared their drawings and writing with each other and then tried to distill the best from each and integrate their collective images into one vision that felt good to all of them. Finally, at a company-wide off-site meeting, all of the employees were introduced to the collective vision of the three executives and invited to participate in the same process. This time, after drawing the vision, people were instructed to gather in small groups in which they were to collaborate in creating a dramatic skit that reflected their group's shared vision. All of the skits were performed. Out of the richness of their collective creativity, a mission statement was created along with some guiding principles that included much of the company-wide input. This process allowed everyone to take some ownership of the vision, mission and guiding principles of the organization, which served to motivate people and ameliorate the particular challenges that face a start-up company, who work long hours under a lot of pressure.

Moving Into the Transpersonal Dimension

Psychodrama Origins

Earlier, in the second year of my job at the state hospital, another teacher was hired. My colleague, Ildri Ginn, and I decided to train with Jacob Moreno, the founder of Psychodrama, to help us in this challenging clinical/education situation. With his inspiration we began to experiment in our clinical setting with the psychodrama techniques we were learning. We were experimenting with the same techniques to explore highly charged emotional issues in our personal lives.

Working with traditional Psychodrama and cathartic experience alone was often insufficient to get the needed insight or perspective. In one such psychodrama, I connected with the light in a lamp in the room. I began to identify with the light and internalize it. I closed my eyes and essentially role played, becoming the voice of that light, or as I understand it now, the voice of my soul or higher self that is always pure. In this way I was able to view the world and my life more clearly from a mountaintop perspective. For several sessions, after working with a current conflict and entering into intense emotional states, I stopped, became quiet and still, internalized this physical light and spoke from that consciousness to the part of me in conflict. Each time I did this, I was able to gain insight and clarity in a way that astounded me. This became the beginning of my understanding and work in developing methods of accessing and identifying the parts of my being that have the answers, that know what is best, and that can offer specific advice to the part of me who is in emotional turmoil and confusion. I had wanted to explore meditation and metaphysical experiences within the context of Psychodrama techniques. The development of our therapeutic approach includes many ways of accessing the soul essence or source of one's strength and clarity beyond the client/patient's limited view of him/herself, which has become the foundation of the Omega Process.

Therapeutic Theater and Sufi Origins

The therapeutic disciplines in our actor, teacher and manager training allowed our students, clients and audiences to be more honest and direct about their feelings and to find solutions to their immediate concerns. At the same time we were gaining insight about how the childhood experiences of our clients (and of ours too) have affected everyone's adult lives. Through this work, our actors and teachers became more aware of their bodies, and learned to discover where fears and tensions were stored up. In this way, we all became more comfortable with ourselves and were able to confront feelings of alienation in ourselves and towards others and the larger society. We noticed that as the psychological work deepened and intensified, the focus on a self-centered ego perspective tended to prevail. We felt a need to expand our consciousness and our awareness of who we really are. We turned to meditation.

Many of us were attracted to the Sufi path, known as the "path of the Heart." This tradition has a long history of integrating spiritual perspectives with expression through the arts: poetry, music, dance, architecture, and the visual arts. Maybe that is why it is also known as the path of the metaphysics of ecstasy. Today, the path of the heart has captivated readers and audiences all over America. In fact, Jelaludin Rumi, a 16th Century Sufi Poet, has in recent years been recognized as the most widely-read poet in the world. These are some of the Sufi themes that appealed to us in our work: the search for truth through experience of the inner nature of reality; consciousness of a larger reality beyond our immediate selves; and unity within the diversity of creation. The teachings and practices evolved from the mystical branches of many ancient traditions (including the early mystery schools), provide an energy source for opening individuals and communities to the potential for dynamic change. The emphasis is on practicing inner discipline while working in the world, with the goal of experiencing states of increased joy, strength and peace. The work includes meditative practices based on breath, light and sound vibrations (mantram or wazifa), sacred dance and walks.

For the next two summers after beginning to work with these teachings, our Sufi teacher, Pir Vilayat Inayat Khan invited me to assist him in creating and producing a pageant at the summer Sufi Camps in California based on The Holy Grail legend. It was to be a spiritual practice for everyone in the camp. There would be no audience; everyone would participate. In telling the story of Parsival and his journey to find The Holy Grail, Pir Vilayat cast everyone into roles according to the nature of their souls. The role itself was to become a spiritual practice, an inner concentration physicalized into a character in the myth, an angelic being (representing a particular state of higher consciousness), or a certain energy field, or musical expression of the celestial spheres. It was my job to help people translate these inner states and qualities into outer expressions in performance.

I remember when we did our first camp pageant, Allaudin Mathieu (an accomplished and gifted musician and choir director), and I were working together on the pageant as we were to do many times in the future. I had also brought members of my professional theater company to the camp. Something happened in an atmosphere where everyone was doing deep inner work by holding an inner concentration while performing an outer drama and music that was magical and very inspiring. It had a life of its own. Participants went through transformational experiences before our eyes. In fact, we witnessed one of the most powerful pieces of theater that any of us had ever experienced as theater pros or as audience.

The Omega Process

I had been introduced to the powerful role of archetypes in transformation and healing and what can happen when people truly identify with an archetype that is resonant with who they are in their essence. Viewing the soul, pure in itself, as the "I" clothed in the personality, my company and I began to understand how people become trapped in a limited perspective or a negative self-image by a mistaken identification. Since we already viewed healing as one of the main purposes of our theater, the Sufi teachings we had experienced helped expand our perspective. We learned that the healing process involves awakening to the eternal qualities of the soul rather than identifying with the limitations of the personality. We wanted to create in theater, with our students, clients and audiences, an experience of the total human condition in which emotional, social, political and spiritual goals unite in a new vision of what is possible.

Processes within transformational theater work and individual work with clients evolved to help people identify with the cosmic view. From this vantage point one is able to view more clearly the soul's essence or what might be called true nature, beyond their limited view of who they take themselves to be. We called this the Omega process, taken from a phrase of the Christian Mystic, Teilhard de Chardin's: Omega consciousness, moving from Alpha, which is the cause, one's history to Omega, which views the larger purpose toward which we are heading. As the Sufi Mystic, Hazrat Inayat Khan, says, "The purpose is like the horizon. The closer we get to it, the more it recedes." One's purpose is continually evolving.

Examples of Transformational Theater

The Cosmic Celebration, originally called *The Cosmic Mass* (Khan & Linden) is a large scale pageant that moves far in the direction of embodying a cosmic perspective-recollection by the collective memory of the cosmic drama which sets the pace of earthly events. *The Cosmic Celebration* is an extraordinary gift that was given to us, that seems to transcend any personal ownership of the work. This mythic pageant, celebrating the unity of the human family, was produced for 11 years in several cities in the United States and Europe. As many as 350 people in each production were cast into roles that reflected and helped to develop some aspect of their essential nature. Everyone was given an inner concentration of a soul quality (through a meditation practice) that helped develop the archetypal character of the prophet or angelic being that they were to portray for the audience. The rehearsal process was designed to help people embody, sing, dance and dramatize the character from the consciousness of the inner concentration. The influence of higher states of consciousness is woven into the drama of history as depicted in the parallel events and rituals of the five major religions of the world. It is a celebration of the unity of all religious paths and of the whole human family. This large pageant form reflected ancient Greek Theater, where the plays served as healing and educational celebrations for the entire community. In our audition process, members from the larger spiritual community, including the full range of religious and spiritual paths, were drawn together, some to participate in a play, others in a spiritual ritual, others in a happening; all felt a sense of something larger than any single person, beyond a project, reaching beyond the ordinary world of events. Most participants were not trained actors; the rehearsal process became for all a sadhana, a spiritual practice, a surrendering to a larger purpose manifesting through us. All participants, even those working on publicity, set and costume design, technical support, fund raising and other aspects of production, were given inner concentrations or sacred phrases to maintain through the work. Through these practices, the inspiration came for manifesting the original concept in form and movement. The inner concentrations were also meant to transmit to a general audience the vibrations of the corresponding inner states creating a sacred atmosphere supported by a fabric of dramatic musical and visual imagery.

We then worked on designing a full-scale therapeutic theater piece for our special needs students in the Boston Public Schools. ***Sunsong: A people puppet pageant for children of all ages*** is a participatory children's play for children that combines both psychological and spiritual disciplines in a healing experience, but without any religious or esoteric language. The play integrates a family systems therapy model with a Sufi Healing practice, based on the healing energies of earth, water, fire and air, as an underlying framework for change. In a delightful musical piece, the whole audience become members of one of four element groups and participates in creative warm-up exercises, dancing and singing. By identifying with the qualities of one of the four elements (earth, water, fire and air) and the healing power of those energies operating inside them, children begin to discover new potential to heal others and in the process themselves. They work together to develop creative healing rituals for one of the two puppet children, in the form of songs, dances, improvisations and rituals. The audience children enact roles of one of these elements of nature in the earth, water, fire or air groups and become the healers of the people puppet family. The two puppet children receive the creative gifts of healing and learn that they can be empowered to change their family's dynamics, by making healing changes in themselves. The concept of a systems theory of family dynamics (the underpinnings for most family therapy today) is the basis for the psychological changes taking place in the troubled puppet family. This approach helps children realize that change is possible and that change in one family member (in this case a child) can help growth happen in the whole family. The relationships of the puppet family are conceived as a microcosm of everyday situations and also of the interplay of cosmic forces. Initially, the family of people puppets is a humorous presentation of classic family dynamics demonstrating how our higher selves become distorted or unbalanced in the acting out of our personalities in daily life. Without trying to magically "cure all" the puppet family sings "though all our problems are not worked out, that's what life is all about and we can laugh to help us make it through."

We wanted next to use all the tools of our theater experiences to create real characterizations based on our essential beings or true nature, which we learn to recognize through concentrations on divine attributes (in Sufism these are archetypes that represent our cosmic dimension). Over a two-year period, our company of actors worked on themselves in depth, beginning by participating in a Sufi alchemical meditation retreat. During this process, each discovered essential qualities of their own souls in the context of their life challenges. The actors worked with the discoveries from the retreat and improvised characters that represented their archetypal beings. Working with the playwright and director, their improvised characters and stories were fully crafted into a script. The outcome was a play called ***Awakening.*** Five archetypal characters are trapped overnight in the observatory tower of a Boston skyscraper. A janitor-shaman who thinks he is going to die is the instrument of their liberation. The audience is taken through the transformation process leading to awakening to the higher self and a larger view of life as each character breaks down and gains new insights into his/her true self. Each character's realization corresponds to a different stage in the alchemical transformation process.

Educational Outreach: We felt the need to bring our work into schools, nursing homes, hospitals, churches, synagogues and other centers. We found opportunities to reach a variety of populations all within the same communities. We developed a series of programs for the Boston Public Schools (elementary and secondary) and elsewhere, especially focusing on students with special needs. We designed and performed in a language arts public television series entitled *How Can I Tell You,* based on the five senses, to teach Language Arts for grades 1–6. We also created a statewide teacher-training program to help teachers use the programs and our improvisational theater approach to teaching language arts.

We received a grant to be in residence in the Berkshires. We designed and implemented workshops including performance segments for elementary schools, high schools, a vocational school and a nursing home in three different towns. We trained teachers in theater techniques (as they related to their curricula) and designed theater workshops to deal with concerns of women's groups, men's groups and families.

Drama Therapy in Diversity Training, Community Healing and World Issues

In our community we have worked to heal racial and multicultural tensions toward developing ethnic unity through community drama therapy. Working with Boston's Court Mandate to the Boston School Committee to integrate the schools, we developed programs that brought together urban and suburban high school students to work with their concerns, issues and dreams for their future. We worked with drug, alcohol and food abusers to help them tell their stories. One of the high school programs that we did several times was *American Roots,* which attempted to translate parts of our Omega Process within an educational setting. While busy exploring their ethnic roots, students brought together from a suburban and an inner city school discovered something about who they were—their feelings, their creative ideas, their talents. They worked together as a group on an original dramatic demonstration of the ten-week process, learning about cooperation, responsibility, and basic group attunement. They also shared experiences that built feelings of unity, of rising above differences and distinctions, which they have also been seeing in an affirming, appreciative light.

We also were given an opportunity to work in a school hard hit by urban blight. Through a pairing with Harvard as part of the regular academic curriculum, students created an original theater piece reflecting the realities of street life, e.g., drugs and violence. By probing underneath their attitudes toward these themes they discovered positive feelings about themselves which were expressed in the development of the play.

Examples of Transformational Theater Events

Coming Home

We created and produced the opening participatory theater event for our community's new art center, entitled *Coming Home.*

Using three floors of performing, studio and classroom space, we created a participatory multi-arts theater event that told the history and dramatized the common Native American ancestry of the community. Experiencing different ethnic artistic experiences with multicultural and racial artists from the community, families theatrically journeyed on one of the transit lines through the arts center to experience different arts experiences.

The First Earth Run for Peace

In the larger Boston Community, we created the city wide arts event to receive the runners from The First Earth Run. A global torch relay in commemoration of the United Nations International Year of Peace, beginning at the United Nations, was organized to move around the world. *The vision:* To create an event of such magnitude that we are compelled by the image it generates: A great thread of light passed around the world by tens of thousands of people, linking us and showing us that we are together, igniting a global sense of hope for the future. *The goals:* To inspire individuals, communities and countries to believe in the power of cooperation. To recognize and honor community projects around the theme of cooperation. We produced the arts event that welcomed the runners to the first city of the global run. Within the ceremony-event, well-known athletes, religious leaders, transformational performing artists from different ethnic backgrounds and transformational visual artists lent their talents in the service of this vision. For example, the memory of Irish singers performing harmoniously in Faneuil Hall Market Place, next to Afro-Caribbean musicians in that time of angry hostility between those two ethnic groups in Boston made a very powerful statement in itself.

Ethnic Diversity: A Festival of Light

A *Festival of Light,* a high school healing arts event celebrating the ethnic diversity of the school community was a unique multicultural healing celebration created for an ethnically diverse high school community. It resulted in a student performance with singing, poetry reading, storytelling, dancing, art and drama. Most of the student body, their families, the faculty and staff were involved in the festival. At the time of year when seasonal darkness is at its peak, many cultural and religious traditions celebrate the return of the light. The event, entitled The Festival of Light, unfolded as a many-leveled symbolic process. Candles placed upon altars are often symbolic of remembering the sacred light. "To see the light" means to see the fundamental truth and, after serving a year on the Parent Diversity Committee, it occurred to me that there was real value in giving the students an opportunity to appreciate some of the fundamental truths of diversity and commonality. The capacity to see the light and its many meanings frequently comes about through an experience of the Light, and the arts have been used throughout time for this very purpose.

The power of the inclusion of the transpersonal helped to create a uniquely powerful event, which, during the last week, seemed to have a life and spirit beyond what the community could have anticipated. Those directly involved experienced how a creative process and performance that honors a range of ethnic, religious and racial differences fosters a genuine appreciation of the commonality among differing world views. Although difficult to describe, many experienced the ways in which the transpersonal draws individuals together through manifesting a conscious intention that had the power to transform all who participated. It is felt that the creation of a sacred dimension in a project such as this can augment the power of the arts to move and influence not only the artists but the audience as well. In this way, the adults, who may have more deeply rooted prejudices, can be influenced by the capacity of a community of diverse youth to experience communal healing. The third annual Festival of Light is being produced, having become a tradition in this school.

World Symposium On Humanity

We learned that a World Symposium on Humanity dealing with serious discourse on the future of humanity was being produced in three countries hooked up by satellite to facilitate communication between them. Leading thinkers in the fields of science, education, public health, politics, and religion were to come together for this momentous happening. I had occasion to meet the organizers and I asked whether the valuable role that artists could play in such an event had been considered. Next thing I knew, we had accepted the position of organizing Arts Festivals in Toronto, Los Angeles and London. The brochure said the following:

> The Arts Festivals of the World Symposium on Humanity form a tapestry, weaving together the strands of each artist's unique offering. There will be performances, classes, workshops, art galleries, creation circles, and media cathedrals. Workshops will provide opportunities for artists to share ideas and explore a specific art form together. Space will be set aside for 'creation circles' where musicians, dancers, actors and poets can gather to attune, improvise and harmonize. There will be two media cathedral events, transmitted by satellite, which will bring all participants together in celebrations, sacred rituals of our time to stand as symbols of our unity and commitment to action.
>
> As coordinators of the Arts Festivals, we see an unprecedented opportunity to bring together artists from around the world who are exploring new dimensions of consciousness. We view the Festivals as a major step toward creating a network of artist-healers which would provide periodic exchange of work and ideas, mutual support through information and inspiration, and opportunities for collaboration.

The Omega Arts Network

In the process of creating the guidelines for what kind of visionary and transformational artists and artistic work the arts festivals would present, we discovered isolated artists from all over the world who were working with a consciousness and intention to create transformational art, and in many cases, believed they were unique in this regard. We also realized that artists, as a rule, do not network like politicians and people in other fields. Many artists told us how valuable it would be to do that. Using the database of the participating artists as well as others who emerged in the process, we created The Omega Arts Network of Artist-Healers who saw themselves as vehicles for transformation and healing.

Since its inception in 1979, groups of artist-healers have been organized throughout world. Our vision was for artists all over the world to collectively create a vision of a better world for the general public to experience. *"To unite artists of all cultures who are consciously working toward creating a vision of a better world with works that are healing, transforming and uplifting for the spirit."*

This is another application of transpersonal drama therapy. It takes the principles of transpersonal drama therapy and creates a structure within which artist-healers everywhere share a common script of ideals and play it out on a global stage with the potential of reaching a much wider audience. Collectively, we have the intention of using our artistic and therapeutic skills to reach and heal a wider community.

In each of the Transformational Theater events we do or encourage others to do, we try to help people tune in to the possibilities for transforming suffering into joy, viewing their pain as energy that can be channeled into hope and faith that people can work together toward a revolution of consciousness in humanity.

Revisioning a New World: SEJECHO: Voice of the Earth

Through The Omega Arts Network, we encouraged artist–healers in all art forms, to reenvision "a new world" during the 1992, 500th anniversary of Columbus' journey. We created a weekend event that included a multiethnic concert/theater evening, a juried exhibition of contemporary transformational art called "Visions of a New World," and an original participatory sacred musical theater event for planetary unity for people of all ages. *The Finding Place: A Ceremonial Journey,* is an original play that began with three Sejecho Mother Earth Goddess-Crones, initiating each audience participant through chanting and an eye contact ritual into one of the elemental-animal groups. Each group had an animal representative, who guided a creative warm-up for their participating audience group. They included: Eagle/Air, Buffalo/Earth, Coyote/Fire, Whale/Water, corresponding to the four directions of the Native American medicine wheel. The *Sejecho* festival celebrated the 500th anniversary of the official founding of this country, mourned how we have raped and disrespected the earth, and honored our Native American heritage. We were celebrating the need to honor the rainbow of races in our culture, the beauty and gifts of all animals, and Mother Earth's elements: earth, water, fire and air, appreciating the interconnectedness of all living beings.

The seeds for this event were planted in a series of group meditations beginning on the winter solstice of 1990 with a circle of visionary women. Their work together, to listen to the cry of Mother Earth and explore the emergence of a new myth, resulted in visions of multicultural rituals to evoke planetary harmony. (This solstice process continues ten years later.) These visions were the inspiration of the Sejecho (a word from the Native American Bri Bri language that means Voice of the Earth) celebration. The program stated: "This is a time of great change upon the Earth. According to certain Native American traditions, this weekend is a pivotal turning point in the ancient calendar system. Part of our purpose here is to help call forth a new myth and a positive vision for a new world." All generations were invited to experience these artistic–healing events together.

Women's Issues: Eartheart

Eartheart is an original theater piece about the stories of two Jewish women as children, adolescents and adults that reflect the larger story of the earth. The play evolved over a three-year period, in which parts of it were shared as a work in progress. Both the creators were very interested in catalyzing the audiences, young and old, to explore their own spiritual roots and experience.

As women, we wanted to share our perspective of the feminine voice, needing to be heard at this time. From the brochure that describes *Eartheart:* "Through a series of interconnected vignettes and stories with Jewish themes and universal and timely messages, *Eartheart* offers a 'soulful' experience in which each audience member is invited to uncover his/her own spiritual roots. A revealing, humorous and meaningful drama unfolds that examines the impact of our early experiences upon our psychological and spiritual development. It is an interactive theater experience, for parents and children to experience together, for women's groups, for religious education faculty and students and parents to use as an educational instrument and as a vehicle through which the wider community can heal, grow and be inspired."

DRAMA THERAPY FRAME OF REFERENCE

Originally called Transformational Theater, the Omega Process describes the stages and methods that are used. With the later evolution of drama therapy as a field, the approach is now identified as Omega Transpersonal drama therapy with Transformational Theater as one of the central ways of working within a broader landscape of methods. The core goal in this healing model is to help clients and audiences to learn to identify with their essential nature or higher self while they work through their limited self images from early and later conditioning. In order to go more deeply into healing the traumas and challenges of one's life, if the client/student is taught to identify with his/her source of strength, that quality that h/she can always rely on. When this occurs, the person is usually able to be far less defended and blocked in looking at what is difficult. Those qualities are identified as soul qualities, i.e., one's essence, which transcend any limitation of one's being.

Using the methods of ancient esoteric and spiritual traditions, participants/clients learn the tools taught in other cultures, much like the ABC's are taught in ours, to access and identify with this essential self.

Basic Concepts

Transpersonal Psychology

The transpersonal approach begins with an assumption of a human being's fundamental health and wholeness, rather than pathology first. Whatever are the problems and challenges in one's life, they can be viewed within the context of a larger identity individually and within the greater consciousness of humanity.

The following is a definition from John F. Kennedy University's Graduate School for the Study of Human Consciousness:

> Transpersonal Psychology includes the developing wisdom and methodology of psychoanalytic, behavioral and humanistic psychology and expands beyond these approaches to incorporate an understanding of the spiritual aspects of human experience. It addresses attention to experiences in which one's sense of self extends "trans-," meaning beyond and through, the personal or social identity of the individual to connect with a greater whole. This state of being which lies beyond the encultured personality–call it Consciousness, Spirit, Higher Self–is of special interest to transpersonal psychologists.

Spiritual Principles Derived from Sufism in the Transpersonal Model

LOVE. Embracing the totality of the heart's experience is the Sufi path–the path of the Heart. It is said that all emotions have love as their base. The therapeutic work is about helping clients (and audiences) accept and love themselves more and more–as artist-healer practitioners learn to do the same. By honoring all emotional life, including fear, anger and frustration, as a natural part of the human life journey, the authentic experience of love can begin to be experienced.

ARCHETYPES AND THE SOUL'S ESSENCE. By learning to identify with soul's essence, also known as higher self, individuals can overcome personal limitation and low self-esteem. With this source of strength, then they are more able to look at the painful and wounded parts of themselves, without being as defended. From this soul connection, access to the divine qualities discussed in Sufism and the archetypes of world mythology, (gods/goddesses, heroes, heroines, masters, saints and prophets), as well as the archetypal elements in nature, earth, water, fire and air is possible. The Omega Transpersonal Drama Therapist holds an inner concentration and identity to four archetypal roles: artist, healer, educator and shaman or high priest or priestess.

SACRED SPACE AND BEAUTY. The sense of the sacred and beauty is cultivated in both the training and therapy settings as well as in the theater environment. The creating of a temenos or sacred container allows a person's deepest self to surface and be experienced. In order to access one's total being, it is important to enter a sacred space, where one can reconnect to his/her essential self, or soul essence (referred to above), which is never tarnished from the abuses and traumas of life. Beauty in the work/performing environment helps to transmute the ugliness of emotional trauma. The atmosphere can become like a beautiful rose holding each person in her warm embrace and lovely fragrance. Whether it is working with an individual client, a therapy group, a training group for artist healers or a large general audience coming to a Transformational Theater performance, it is important that a sacred atmosphere be created to inspire people to connect with their deeper fuller selves. This allows the possibility for each participant, in the sacred space, to experience a meaningful step in his/her own transformational growth and healing process.

ONENESS AND UNITY. Experiencing the interconnection and interdependence between all living beings (humans as well as other life forms) is created by breaking down the distinctions and differences that divide people from people and people from their environment. Much of the work is about entering the consciousness of those with whom one is in conflict, and working toward embracing their emotional experience and points of view. Exercises in nature that are designed to receive the healing power of Mother Earth are created with improvisations, meditations and exercises that relate a person's own experience (including challenges and future possibilities) to the experience of the earth.

MASTERY/SELF DISCIPLINE. The development of personal capacity to manifest one's greatest potential, depends on consciousness in both thought and action. Discipline and focus lead toward the realization of the Self.

BALANCE. The Sufi masters teach that the essence of the Sufi message is balance: balance of receptive and expressive energies, yin and yang, activity and repose, inner masculine and feminine, spirit and matter, transcendence and immanence.

LIFE AS ART. The culmination of this work is the application of creativity in everyday life; then lives can become works of art.

Techniques

Psychodrama

Psychodrama is one of the methods that is integrated into the approach. Psychodrama is a group therapy process with a specific set of techniques and forms through which the protagonist (client) works through challenging issues and relationships in his or her life. There is a warm-up procedure, the enacted drama and a process by which the group share issues in their lives, catalyzed by the protagonist's drama. In an early book *Theater of Spontaneity* Moreno includes many transpersonal concepts. Transpersonal dimensions of psychodrama include: the protagonist conversing with people who have already died, with angelic presences, with one's own higher self (as mentioned previously), or with a divine quality that someone role plays like a spirit of compassion, joy, forgiveness, inspiration or clarity.

Transformational Theater

Transformation is not about changing people to become something else, but rather about releasing their limited self from early conditioning to remember who they really are in their true nature. Using a variety of techniques from theater arts and the intuitive arts, therapy processes were developed. As this drama therapy process evolved, it has served individual and group client populations in a variety of clinical, educational and other community settings. It also serves those individuals and professionals interested in using theater as a healing art for themselves and others. There are a number of ways that this can happen. One is by using these methods therapeutically to access one's own life material, and learning techniques to be able to craft and effectively communicate this material to an invited audience, with whom the group can be vulnerable with their intimate material. The second is to create biographical theatrical works for larger audiences with healing and transformation as a goal. This can be done either as a one-person performance or as part of a larger ensemble work. The third is in the creation of large community healing events, in which the intention is for the whole process as well as performance to be therapeutic and transformational.

Storytelling

Dr. Carl Gustav Jung said that the mental health of a society is based on people's abilities to tell their stories. The proliferation of the 12 step recovery groups, and the expansion of the storytelling field as an art form, are indications of the broad-based need for people to access and communicate their life stories. The Transformational Theater process is a development of this naturally occurring impulse in our culture at this time. Adding the dimension and support of accessing one's source of strength or personal soul essence, people are more able to access and communicate their trauma history. This makes it possible to transform these earlier wounded patterns into the creation of a new story. The new story evolves about how they wish to live unencumbered by their limited sense of self, based on their earlier "tapes," which all of us have, about how we are not good enough and in what way we feel inadequate. One exercise entails the selection of an object on one's person that is meaningful (a piece of clothing or jewelry, glasses, etc.). People then create the object character and tell the story of one's deeper inner life through the lens of the object character.

Music and Sound Healing

Music has been called the universal language of the soul that transcends individual religious, racial, ethnic bias or identities. One of the most effective way of creating an attunement within a therapy or training group or within a public theater environment, is by consciously working with vibrational resonance. Weaving beautiful sound and music textures that open hearts creates a safe and nurturing chalice to contain our sacred stories. This helps participants feel safe about opening themselves to attune to the deeper dimensions of their life experience.

My colleague, Sarah Benson, helps a participant find his/her voice by singing one's soul song. These songs are created spontaneously as an expression of the person's emotional state and transformational edge through pure sound expression. Often the client/trainee is sung to by the group as part of the process. Many times people are encouraged to move in relation to the sound, in order to fully embody the experience. In Sarah's words:

> There's no place to hide in the sound of our voice. It carries the vibration of the truth of the

moment, of the life. Our fear, anger, guilt and shame–our love, joy, and delight are reflected in the sound of our voice. As we learn to release the fear, anger, guilt and shame through releasing the voice, blockages, both physical and emotional, are released and the energy begins to flow with greater ease. In the release of our emotions, we have more space to experience love, joy and soul integration, which can also be sounded by the voice. Songs of anger, songs of love, walk hand in hand as we explore mysterious regions in the forest of the self.

As we experience the retelling of our story, we open to another level of expression when we let our story become our song. Or after a particularly strong cathartic release, to then translate the emotion into sound and allow the energy of the emotion to ride the current of music and movement.

When we are in nature, or in sacred space, allowing the energy of the place, the rock, the flower, the ocean, the mountain, the ancestors, to have expression through our song is another facet of the crystalline voice. Stand or sit in the space, declare your intention to be an instrument for the highest good, breathe the light and the energy of the place or object, feel the merging, the "becoming one with," and let the song be born from the breath, the beauty or the pain from the coming together of your being with the spirit of nature, the spirit of the place.

Connecting with our soul and the Beloved, the sacred marriage, the eternal light living within, and expressing that union, wholeness and deep peace is the next step in the process of sound healing and drama therapy. Experiencing the light of the soul sounding through the body voice is for some, ecstatic. Singing to the other, becoming one with their essence and allowing that energy to sing and express the beauty of the other can be a profound and sometimes, healing experience.

The voice is an extension of the breath and the breath is the extension of light. If we speak with the awareness and intention that we are carrying divine light love sound vibration through our body voice, healing may happen for ourselves and others. The human being is an amazing instrument for the music and dance of prana, chi, spirit, life force, light and love. This energy is as close as our breath, our voice, our true story/song, the sound of the sacred and the song of our soul. (Brochure)

SOUL SONGS. The group member is asked what name they would like to hear and a color with which they resonate. The person sits or stands in the middle of the circle. The group sings his/her name three times on the steps of an ascending major chord with harmonies. As the sound of the name rises, the arms rise with the sound. Group members are instructed to visualize the release of whatever that person does not need. As the arms come down, the group visualizes healing golden light flowing in and around that person. The person receives the energy and vibration that is mirrored to him/her. Then the person is encouraged to make sound from the energy they received and develop it into a soul song, in whatever way naturally evolves. There is no pressure to "sing a song" in tune or anything like that. Each person's song evolves organically. Often the song moves naturally into a soul dance as well.

Archetypal Exercises for Healing

IDEAL MENTOR EXERCISE. First, people are guided into a relaxed, meditative state. Second, they are guided to journey to a mountaintop or other peaceful setting where s/he finds him/herself sitting opposite an ideal mentor. It cannot be anyone that a person knows in real life, but may embody the qualities of several beings that one knows or has heard of. Third, participants are invited to visualize first the physical attributes of this being: age, sex and actual physical appearance. Then they are asked to visualize the qualities that are positive, since they represent the ideal. Examples may include: intuitive, intelligent, calm, compassionate, friendly, good sense of humor, or majestic. Then, they visualize the more subtle presence of this being. Next, they are invited to draw the being as they perceive him or her. The final step in the exercise is to physicalize this being and create a sound and movement language for him or her. People learn that what they created was a picture of their own soul qualities, essence or source of strength.

Sufi Purification Breath Practice and Improvisation Exercise

This breathing practice works with the healing magnetism of the earth, water, fire and air. (See Sunsong, p.354, the play that evolved out of the healing energies of working with this practice.) Each of the elements has a corresponding breath practice. Each is done five times:

EARTH BREATH. (yellow), Filtering the impurities–Breathe in through the nose and out through the nose five times. Breathe in through the soles of the feet, up to the base of the spine, on up the spine to just above the crown center. As you inhale, feel the magnetic field of your body replenishing itself with the earth's fresh magnetism. As the energy rises upwards through your body, feel the filtering effect on the different chakras. Exhale down the spine and into the earth. As you exhale, feel the magnetic field of the earth draw the magnetic field of your body towards it, drawing off the denser, stale magnetism.

WATER BREATH. (green), Washing the impurities–Breathe in through the nose and out through the mouth five times. Inhale through the soles of the feet and the crown center simultaneously. Feel the fluid magnetism that is continually circulating in the atmosphere, washing you clear, cleansing you of all impurities. Exhale down the spine. Stand on your tiptoes, letting your hands hang in the air. Feel the magnetism dripping from your fingertips, like water from a shower.

FIRE BREATH. (red), Consuming the impurities–Breathe in through the mouth and out through the nose five times. Breathe into the fire in the solar plexus, consuming the impurities. Breathe out radiating light from the heart center, through the shoulder blades. Inhale fire, exhale light. Become light.

AIR BREATH. (light blue), Dissolving the impurities–Breathe in through the mouth and out through the mouth five times. Inhale through the pores of the skin with palms facing out. Imagine you are porous. Expand into the vastness of space. Let the wind blow through the spaces between the cells of your body, dissolving the impurities.

Once people are familiar with the breathing practices, they are guided to embody these energies through walks in a circle that are practiced as an extension of each breathing practice, accompanied by the corresponding drum beat to maintain the correct rhythm. Out of the structured walk practices developed by Sufi Master Samuel Lewis people are invited to create free movement and sound. This evolves organically into the creation of improvisational archetypal characters and qualities that represent these energies. Some examples: Earth–Educator: protective, responsible, majestic, characters: farmer, Native American Medicine Man/Woman, ground hog (or other earth animals); Water–Healer: compassionate, loving, friendly, characters: mermaid, dancer, dolphin (or other sea creature); Fire–Artist: inspiring, ecstatic, energetic; characters: knight, genius inventor, the sun; Air–Priest(ess): visionary, intelligent, intuitive, characters: clergyman/woman, eagle (or other bird), oracle. After invoking the pure elemental energies, the characters evolve from the unconscious and often become shadow or hidden energies that manifest in a variety of forms.

Mirrors: Body, Heart and Soul

BODY. In partners, One person is A, the other B. Partners are instructed to establish eye contact accompanied by dance music;

person A leads a movement piece, person B mirrors the movement. Later the facilitator says, "leaderless," and the dance evolves without one person taking the lead.

The process then moves to the transpersonal level.

HEART. In the same pairs, both people either standing or sitting maintain eye contact as they chant *Ya Rahman (Divine Compassion)* vibrating the heart center with three AH sounds. Movement in the mirroring form evolves from the chant, still with eye contact.

SOUL: In pairs, sitting partners reestablish eye contact and mirror the same synchronized breath rhythm. The exercise becomes subtler and quite still. Here the people focus more intently on the eyes as windows to the soul.

The Healer and the Wounded

This exercise is an adaptation of a classical mime exercise. Organize several pairs of people into A & B members. Instruct all the A's of each pair to line up facing the wall and their B partners across from them, facing the opposite wall. The A's are the healers. They will chant Ya Quddus, the Holy Spirit. The B Group goes into a contracted movement and sound that represents their wounded, most limited self that is in need of healing. Both sides get into their concentration and turn to face their partner, establish eye contact, and never lose it throughout the exercise.

The goal of the exercise is for the wounded one to receive the healing from the healer, to the extent that they are authentically able to make contact. They move toward each other as the wounded one is able to slowly let go of his/her stuck place. The exercise is complete when they are able to make physical contact.

People reverse roles and do the exercise again.

Archetypal Enactment

Working with the archetypes of gods, goddesses, heroes, heroines, power animals, people create masks that reflect the archetypes. They then create characters, and dramatic scenarios unfold using these masks. In another exercise people are invited to select something from nature with which he/she identifies in its pure form. They can then physicalize, move, sound, and poeticize it.

Videography

Finally, I was introduced to the power of video technology in transformational theater work by Ellen Burstyn, a wonderful friend and theater Mentor. Placing a monitor next to the camera, the participant is invited to look at the image of him/herself on the screen, while being guided step-by-step from the physical to the soul level of awareness.

These are a few examples of techniques and exercises that have been developed to access a transpersonal identity that can be a source of strength in working with trauma, abuse, low self-esteem and limitation on any level.

CASE EXAMPLES

Ray Concord's Transformational Theater and Transpersonal Drama Therapy Journey: Freeing Our True Self From the Bonds of Addiction

Many different modalities within our work in drama therapy have evolved with serious addiction and abuse cases. This case study is an example of a healing process in the challenges and triumphs of overcoming a 20-year, two and a half pack a day, nicotine addiction. I will use excerpts from Ray's own writing from his journal to attempt to describe our approach in The Omega transpersonal drama therapy work within our Transformational Theater and Sound Healing groups, as well as in my private therapy sessions, which often work hand in hand for an individual student/client. The brief summary will demonstrate how the integration of some transpersonal psychology approaches and disciplines into the therapeutic work with a serious addiction can make a significant difference in the treatment process. This approach not only facilitates the recovery process, but helps to foster the emergence of one's true identity. This new identity is the core essence of the person, which is uncovered, gently and creatively, from beneath the dark clouds of self-denigration, trauma and despair.

What follows is Ray's own description about this therapeutic process:

"Omega Theater was a new experience. Just move around, make sounds . . . this was so simple, almost child-like.

"It *was* like being a child. Liberating. I was taking deep breaths, relaxing, and then someone began to speak about breathing: there were four ways a body could breathe, and each way was tied to an element: earth, water, fire, air; and to an archetype: teacher, healer, artist, spiritual guide.

"We were moving in a circle, practicing one of the breaths, the Fire breath, breathing in through the mouth and out of the nose, when my spine became warm, a rippling warmth up and down my spine, an emotional warmth to everyone in the room, wanting to love them, invite them into my heart; my heart opening to everyone in the room, unafraid. I was asked if I wanted to 'sound' what I was feeling, to create a soul song. I stood in the center of the circle and opened my mouth and my body began to move in a dance, the sounds shaping into a song, a tone poem expressing a deep love for everyone around me. I had overcome one of my greatest fears: being in front of people without having anything 'prepared.' The pure sounding created a vibrational resonance in me that opened my heart and made me unafraid. I did not care. I started to play with the sounds, modulating them, feel the vibrations in the chambers of my heart, soul and body.

"I continued the weekly classes. It wasn't so much what we did but the safe and sacred space that was created to do it in. Stuff inside me kept loosening, floating up to my consciousness, taking shape in stories, poems. My next experience came during a meditation exercise. We were meditating on the chakras and when we came to the (third eye) chakra, I saw in my mind's eye this loving eye looking back at me. It was so conscious and loving. I was overcome with tenderness. There was a trust that was growing inside me for the process I was going through and where it was leading."

Core Unresolved Issues

Where it was leading was not to a place, outside, but to a space, inside. My center, my core. I was terrified. Unresolved issues with my father floated up.

My father–a good provider, loving and faithful, a good Christian example,
A decent, kind, peaceable human being. It's been 22 years since my 21st birthday.
Why am I writing to him for the first time in my life to express my true feelings?

I did not know where to begin, how to deal with this pain, anxiety. I had not the courage to deal with this, i.e., confront my father with these feelings: and even if I did, they were raw emotions, inexpressible.

This has to do with my relationship to you . . .
This has to do with being catholic . . .
The role models you held up to me were St. Augustine and Thomas Merton . . .
Did you hope and pray I would become a priest?

During a private session, I was asked to imagine my father seated beside me. To tell him everything in my heart. I start, slow at first–this is hard!–but words, tears begin to flow. When I hit an impasse, to my astonishment, I am asked to reverse roles: be my father answering me. Then reverse roles again; and again until I (as my father) say "I'm so confused!" I am completely purged, relieved. This is followed by an assignment. Write a letter (which you may or may not mail) to your father. I start it that night and come up with seven pages! The words flowing freely. This letter became the ground, the raw material from which I shaped a dramatic presentation called "My Father."

The disciplines I was learning in drama therapy and transformational theater were preparing me for one of my greatest challenges in my adult life: giving up an addiction–nicotine. For most of 20 years I had smoked two packs of cigarettes a day. I tried everything from sheer willpower to acupuncture to hypnosis, as well as various eastern and western medicines and nothing took hold.

The art of role playing and writing exercises (letter, diary and journal) provided a safe space for me to explore my terrors and fears about addiction. Not only did this give me confidence in confronting past traumas and resolving old wounds but it had the net result of embodying me in the present. It felt as if moral strength and courage had been added to my core/center where fear had resided.

Such Sufi concepts as befriending your pain, transforming your inner pain into a work of art and offering it back as healing to the community, the Sufi breath disciplines (which the act of smoking was a counterfeit of), visualization techniques of principal archetypes–Teacher, Healer, Artist, Priest/Priestess; group dynamics where other participants could role play different aspects of your self; storytelling and the creation and performance of a theater piece as a concrete goal and, most of all, the safe and sacred space to birth this in–all these disciplines were tools and weapons I used, with one hand, creating a work of art out of my withdrawal process, and the other, fighting off the inner and outer demons that would pull me back.

The Cigarette Papers

I began a journal called The Cigarette Papers. I set aside a specific time each day when I would not smoke. The gap would be long enough for the need of the drug to kick in. When the pain came forth from its hiding place, screaming for release, a threshold would be crossed and

I began to yield to the pain
let it seep into me
up from my center to my chest and head
down to my loins my legs my feet
the pain becomes sweet, but it hurts so . . .
but it is sweet and I marvel at this.

I would return to my studio to write, as accurately as I could, what was going on inside me. The discipline of journal-keeping and dialoguing with the pain provided me with a container to put the "withdrawal" in, transforming itself into cosmic and tragic poetic monologues which in turn would be acted out before the group and shaped into theater pieces.

Now into my third year with Omega Theater and working with Saphira, I am beginning to realize the fruit of all I have learned and will continue to learn. I came to Omega Theater knowing a poet is not a person who only writes poems. Through the work there, I was reminded that a poet educates, heals, teaches, and shares the wisdom of life's path. This was confirmed through my experience in the training. I had the desire and the fire. What was lacking was the container to hold the fire, the disciplines to focus the flame and harness the energy into light and warmth.

I was reading a book of poems by Denise Levertov, *To Stay Alive*. I came across these words:

Make a place for yourself
in the darkness
and wait there. Be there.
Go down into your well,
it's your well
go deep into it
into your own depth as into a poem.

How do you make a container for a hole? What do you surround it with to make visible the space, to contain it, examine what is in it?

It was in one of the group sessions, helping one of the members go through a particularly dark place in her past that began to open up the door in me to explore the same. Maybe it was seeing another make it through that gave me the courage; or the group functioning as a container, a net holding and helping her through the process; watching her come out the other side. During that session I felt something–a shadow rising in the back of my mind–some fear, terror reminding me of things/barriers I was unable to overcome in my past: about my family, my father, being catholic–shadowy stuff about guilt, sex, I wasn't able to break through; receded from the barrier only to pop up years later.

One worry that comes to mind: if I am healed of this dark place, this "hole," will it take away from the energy/catalyst that is part of my creative process? Part of me worries, fears to upset whatever internal balance I have–the dance I do with the dark and the light that enables me to midwife, bring to birth the poems I've created thus far.

During this time, dream journaling opens other doors. I recall all the times in childhood I "froze" when performing: in a play in second grade, little league baseball. Interesting that this comes up as I am thinking of the letter I am writing to my father.

Exploring The Hole

11/24

I begin to explore the relationship between intimacy and addiction. During a private session poems come up about nicotine/liquor/food. I explore the "feel" of the hole inside me that I keep stuffing with abuses. I explore the geography of the Hole/Whole. Intimacy related to my father–need unfulfilled–and trying other things–liquor, cigarettes, coffee–to fill it. My problems are in (negative space). My father's sins were sins of omission. They are harder for me to locate and define. Finger–in the gaps, cracks, what fell through the holes, fell into the dark places.

What is a hole? Empty space. Gaps. Cracks. Hole. A vacuum–sucking light and healing, negating its effects. I went to a healer to be delivered of dependence on cigarettes. The "hole" in me was so powerful, it sucked in the healing powers!

But a hole can also mean something else. A dark place, the womb, the earth–the birthing process–out of a dark place, near death/shadow of death: the woman giving birth. The seed that must die in order to sprout. Maybe the hole in me isn't bad. Maybe I should stop seeding, penetrating it with abuses. Maybe I should let the Spirit, the Life/Creative force make love to that place in me, let the seed be planted, to give birth to poems, stories and give birth to a changed, new man, leaving behind my former self. It is the old self that hinders intimacy with all beings and things (relating to them only as objects). It is as if an intimate dialogue is a prerequisite for that being/thing to feel comfortable, trust you with its essence: you bring to the intimacy honor and respect so the being feels safe and trusting to share with you its essence, allows you to "reveal" it, give voice to it, say, in a poem or work of art. St. Francis comes to mind. And the native peoples of the Americas. The reason they are so eloquent, so "poetic" is that they dwell in harmony with creation, and creation feels safe to share its "Speaking" through them as vessels.

So this hole is a sacred space that should be tended, nourished and respected. But this space inside me is in so much pain. Why do I numb it with substances? Who wants pain! Yet I am reminded of what I am beginning to learn in transformational theater, what the Sufis say: Start a dialogue with your pain. Embrace it as a friend. Let it speak, give it voice. It is a natural part of creation. Don't try to run away from it, numb it.

Now I am thinking of my letter to my father. This is what parents should be doing. Nourishing this space in the child. Being masks of the Creator until the child matures and can tend this space on their own. The soul spot. And this spot seems to be the most neglected. So what happens? Everything–good and bad–jumps in, a cacophony of mixed messages, static and general confusions running around inside.

Now my father tried to put God/the church into that space inside me but it wasn't the living spirit of Christ, only the form. This is why it did not take hold and grow in me. Saphira suggests that the letter to my father/dialogue with the hole would be a good basis for a performance piece for the workshop.

11/25

I wake up with an old Beatles tune running through me:

I'm fixing a hole where the rain gets in to stop my mind
from wandering where it will go . . . I'm filling the cracks that
ran through the floor . . . I'm taking time for a number of
things that were not important yesterday . . .

Holes. Holes. My mind is on holes. A good sign I am dealing with this.

Had a great feature at the White Whale in Beverly. I did very well in the space (gaps, holes) between the poems where I must relate to the audience. Good dialogue, goofing, joking with them. It's becoming easier to communicate–not just my poems, but me, who I am–to the audience.

Recording dreams, another tool used in transformational theater, helped me connect (again, a gap) the space between waking and sleeping states. What was too traumatic/dramatic to work out in the workshop was risked in my dreams: In one dream, I am performing one of my poems and all of a sudden, dance out on one of the lines right into conversation with the audience, then back to the text of the poem, then back out into improvisation. I began to lose the creative tension of the poem and the connection to the audience, but I kept at it and finish the poem. What was most important was that I did not freak out, freeze or get filled with stage fright. I just rolled with it. The weekly workshops where I must improv pieces two or three times during the course of the evening has been good training. This involved working with a partner in a "performance piece" that required spontaneous dialogue. On the stage this discipline is transforming itself into conversing with the audience as I am performing the poem. This is like squaring the power. I am beginning to enjoy this.

The weekly workshop was also a way of keeping the internal dialogues out on the table, in the group. It is difficult to share my story with the group. I am nervous, embarrassed but their support gives me courage. I am asked to:

Take the resistance (the present momentary struggle) and use it,
its energy to create with. Step inside of it and relax and it will help
transform, become the art. Trust your instinct. Jump into the piece.
The words and the art are waiting for you to shape them.

I try this with one of the members of the workshop, but spend most of my time running away, avoiding getting into my "Hole" where all the grief is. I resist doing an improv, but my partner is there to encourage me, so I give it a try. What happens is that I start off OK in centering myself in the "Hole" and the mood is serious and I am in character, experiencing the grief and somehow transmuting it to the audience, but at a certain point a split happens in me: I continue to verbally describe the "Hole" and my feelings, but my tone, mood and movement, facial expressions become radically altered. I shift into my playful/trickster mode with (as my partner describes) a smile on my face and begin to do hopscotch movements acting out the completely contrary emotion of grief. Up to the point of the "split" I am speaking and acting in a calm, slow, deliberate manner in words and movement. Then I become hyper, speak quickly and move in a jerky, mimed fashion like a clown or a circus mime. I use the joyful face of the clown/elf/trickster to deal with (numb) the pain and sorrow in me, displacing it rather than dealing with it. The feedback is invaluable, enabling me to see into the mirror of my actual actions that are contrary to the emotions I am attempting to convey.

The inner self becomes a battleground now: the place in me fighting the healer who is approaching the "Hole." I just want to dance, skate over the emotions, just going through the motions until I am safe on the other side. I sure do not want to sink into the Pain!

O Lord, please help me with this. I know you want me to deal with this.
Help me to acknowledge my pain, get to know it, accept it, experience it.
Grant me Grace to find the courage to endure the pain long enough to learn what it has to teach me.

I explain to a friend how frustrating it is, fighting myself, wrestling the angel to the edge of the Hole only to run away again. He says what I am really doing is wearing down a good path each time I try, making each successive time easier because I know the path. This will enable me to tolerate staying there longer and longer, to get to know the pain.

Conclusion

What is this Core? It seems to have to do with Fear–fear of failure, rejection. The burden as a poet of not knowing each day if you're going to create, or the continual agony of holding within yourself the creative process, like grains of sand in an oyster, midwifing the poems to birth and then when you do, fearing it won't be good or strong enough. Perhaps this is Life. This is the everyday reality of the artist. To accept it, to get to know it, dialogue with it, learn to love it. It keeps coming back to the Sufi maxims I've been learning: Get to know and embrace your pain. This tells you your heart is alive. How these truths are beginning to resonate in me!

In my private therapy sessions I talk about fusing the apparent polarities in my life that keep running off in opposite directions–the monk and the lover, the poetry and the business, the need to live wild and free and the demand of Life to grow and mature, to nourish the Child within and the maturing Adult at the same time. How many artists have stumbled trying to do this, defaulted in areas of their life, failing to incorporate the entire vision.

There is a hunger in me to unite all these different parts and aspects of my life and experiences–the personal and political, the romantic and spiritual, the metaphysical and philosophical, the holy and profane, the chaos and the order, the wild and the sober–a passion to unite, meld, fuse all of this into a vision that will span my entire life, and the art I create along the way, a deep, rich, broad tapestry with many hues and colors that is as wide as it is high as it is deep–a life's work with all its many scenes and motifs, however individual and disparate from each other, but each one, each poem having within it the intimations, harmonies, and sympathetic vibrations of the whole.

Ray has been nicotine-free now for six years. He developed *The Cigarette Papers* into a full one-man performance piece and went on tour with it, inspiring others with the possibility that they, too, could overcome a long ingrained addiction. As he "wrestled with his demons," and opened more and more to his essential nature, his compassion, faith, inspiration and free spirit became more manifest. He truly embodied the artist as healer, educator and shaman through the vehicle of sharing his story with many audiences. He has told me that the stronger those identities became the more motivation he had to resist the temptation of returning to smoking cigarettes. He continues to be aware of this desire, from time to time, but how could this poet/priest/teacher/healer not "walk his talk" as he realizes part of his larger purpose is to be this messenger of an important story of faith, healing and transformation.

Aiko: The Recovery Process of a Japanese/Korean-American Woman

Aiko's Background

Aiko entered the Transformational Theater: Drama Therapy and Sound Healing program, with great interest, but also with some reticence. She had grown up in a privileged Japanese class. Her early life was characterized by an appreciation for the beauty of Japan's countryside, the wisdom of her beloved grandparents, the intelligence, strength, rigidity and severe wounding of her mother. Her mother lived daily with the unacceptable situation of her husband's six concubines and her father's total preoccupation with his very successful business life, and financial position. Over a period of hundreds of years, Aiko's paternal ancestors were forcefully brought from Korea to Japan as slaves. Gradually, over generations, they were able to climb the social ladder and build wealth and position, managing to erase their Korean heritage. But her father never lost the ancestral stigma of having been subjugated. Because of this, he identified with the abuser. It was an accepted practice among Japan's social elite for the men to have concubines, whom they fully support financially. In this way, he became the "slave owner" and projected his "dominator" mentality onto these women. Aiko had been sent away by her mother to Canada to study music at the age of nine. She also studied dance, as she had done in Japan from an early age. One of the first things she shared in the group was how uprooted and split she always felt, in having been cast out of her homeland.

To work with Aiko therapeutically, it was important to understand the traditional Japanese values and norms with which she grew up. It was not within her cultural norms to share intimate feelings, especially about dark family issues. Euro-American values for healing, therapy goals and processes are frequently contradictory to Asian, particularly female gender-based values. Lee and Richardson in their book, *Multicultural Issues in Counseling: New Approaches to Diversity* (1991), state that much of traditional Japanese culture can be traced to the philosophical precepts of life that were dictated by Buddhism. Within this cultural system, the individual is superseded by the family, specific hierarchical roles are established for all family members, and rules of behavior and conduct are formalized. An individual's adherence to this code of conduct is a reflection not only on the immediate family, but on the extended kinship network as well.

The father is the leader and decision-maker of the nuclear family. His authority is unquestioned. The welfare of the family rests squarely on the father's shoulders. He enforces family roles and is the primary disciplinarian. The traditional role of the mother is that of the nurturing caretaker of both her husband and children. The mother is clearly the emotionally devoted, nurturing parental figure. The stronger emotional attachments, therefore, tend to be with the mother.

In Aiko's case, the father was able to maintain his life-style despite great protests by his wife and uncomfortable, unexpressed feelings by his daughters. Aiko's mother, unlike the cultural norm, was not the emotionally devoted, nurturing parental figure, but was cold, angry and fearful. Aiko feels this was due, in part, to her unhappy marriage.

Highly developed feelings of obligation govern much of the personal relationships of Japanese Americans. The often unspoken obligatory reciprocity within relationships is a serious consideration in the life of a Japanese American. The individual is expected to express affection and gratitude as well as respect and obedience to parents and others in authority positions.

In a social structure where interdependence is so highly valued, the fear of losing face can be a powerful motivating force for conforming. The withdrawal of confidence and support by the family, community or society, and the exposure of an individual's wrong actions for all to see, is a profound shaming experience to be avoided at all costs. When Aiko began this work, she was able to express to the group her discomfort with sharing her family secrets as well as her own issues. This made it possible for everyone, both leaders and members, to actively encourage and support her in her current emotional dilemma. She soon was able to appreciate the opportunity to come to terms with and work through several significant issues.

Beginning With Psychodrama

In the first session, one of the group members enacted a psychodrama, which focused on that woman's relationship with her mother. Aiko role-played this woman's mother in the psychodrama. Then, after the main drama, when everyone shares something of his or her own story that was catalyzed by the 'protagonist's' drama, Aiko made a connection with her own mother. It was then suggested that everyone remember a moving moment with their mother and give expression to that moment by allowing a spontaneous song to emerge. By doing this, the participants created a positive container in which the more difficult object relations issues could be addressed.

Aiko referred to her mother in her first journal entry:

> October 2 "I wanted to remember only beautiful images of her today, and moments when she was in her elements, moments when she was joyful and vigorous. I remember her in her

sunflower garden laughing in the sun. I remembered her in the Zen Village of Niigata (on the Northwest province of Japan, facing the Sea of Japan). I remembered her bicycling, running around, laughing again. Why did I want to remember mainly good and warm memories of her? Because I now see also the tragedy of her life, marrying someone too complicated for her to comprehend. Her family was all heart feeling. My father's family was almost all mind thinking, conniving and calculating how to survive. From joy to coldness and to madness. It was too much for her. In the end, she entered into the coldness and went mad. In this mad-childlike state for a year, she took her own life.

Introducing The Transpersonal

From the time our work together began, it appeared that it would be most effective to relate to Aiko through a transpersonal/spiritual orientation. This was familiar to her from her Buddhist roots, which was naturally integrated into her early daily life. Zen Buddhism in its essence is the art of seeing into the true nature of one's being. It points the way from fear and desire to freedom from suffering. The goal of Zen Buddhism is to achieve Satori or enlightenment through zazen (emptying the mind) and Koan practices. The Zen Buddhist aesthetic of unselfconscious artfulness provides the basis of classical Japanese culture. Aiko told of Buddhist Monks coming often to homes in the community for different life events, to sit together with an awareness of their breath, and to meditate and chant. Since the transpersonal approach that is included in our work was especially helpful to Aiko, optimal opportunities were created to work on that level when it seemed appropriate. It was clear that every exercise and reference to spiritual language and experience opened Aiko to more easily face what was difficult for her, in her complex emotional history. It was natural for this Japanese woman to sit still, work with meditations and a variety of exercises that begin with an awareness of the breath including visualizations, voice and movement exercises, and the validation of transpersonal dimensions of consciousness. Reference to the purity of her soul's essence deeply resonated with her. It soon became clear that this approach did help to create the bridge from her reticence to build her trust and open her to deep, less familiar, emotional work. The transpersonal dimension can be significant in anyone's therapeutic process, but with Aiko, because of her cultural heritage, this became the "key" in opening to her buried pain.

Dreams have been discovered to be a powerful gateway to the unconscious. Marion Woodman, well-known Jungian Analyst, writer, and an expert with dream work, offers her perspective after many years of working with people in analysis as well as in large conferences and workshops. She considers the relationship of working with the transpersonal level of the soul vital in dealing with early emotional issues. "When you work on the rotten foundations, which is what we do in therapy, you have to recognize your own rot. In order to get rid of rot, you've got to dig it up. At the same time, you're finding this magnificent soul that's buried beneath it." (See bibliography.)

Interviewer: Did psychologists always recognize the soul?

Marion: Psyche means soul. Psychology is knowledge of the soul. Jung recognized soul. He recognized the spiritual dimension of dream images that connects a person to what he called the Self. The Self is the God-image within, like the golden ball within fairy tales. That golden ball takes you where you need to be led in order to find all the parts of yourself.

I do think a lot of people start out in therapy thinking they will find the blocks, that they will take the energy that's blocked in negative mother and negative father, for example, and release it from those complexes in order to make it available to the ego. But the journey becomes so fascinating that they tend to stay

> with it. The blossoming ego begins to relate to its own creativity, to the creation within. That process ultimately leads to surrendering to transpersonal energy, what Jung calls the Self. (Marion Woodman, 1989)

In Aiko's Transformational Theater/ drama therapy group, participants were invited to remember two dreams, one from early childhood and a meaningful recent dream. The dreamer then selects group members to enact each of the dream images from both of their dreams. The dreams come back to life before the dreamer's eyes, triggering memories of parts of the dream that were forgotten, often resurfacing emotional states from that time. At other times, new feelings surface as insights and connections are made, catalyzed by watching the dream images enacted. The dreamer is helped to see the inevitable relationship between both dreams in terms of core emotional issues and ongoing life challenges. A transpersonal dimension helps people to identify what are called soul qualities or essential parts of the human psyche that are our source of strength. Examples of these positive qualities are: clarity, magnanimity, sacredness, sense of humor, purity, majesty, creativity, peace, love, intuition. At least one and often more qualities can be seen in both dreams. The soul qualities can be identified as that place that we are able to turn to in ourselves that can never be tarnished from any abuse or life trauma. Helping people shift their identity from their sense of limitation, low self-esteem, shame, and feelings of inadequacy to these positive, essential parts of themselves is perhaps at the core of the healing process.

Participants are also helped to expand their identity to embrace the archetypes of Artist, Healer, Educator, Shaman or Spiritual Guide. Integrating these archetypes into their professional identities as well as into their general view of themselves, becomes another source of strength and tool for transformation for group members. According to Jung, "The experience of the archetype is frequently guarded as the closest personal secret, because it is felt to strike into the very core of one's being" (Jung, 1966). When that archetypal shift in one's own identity genuinely begins to happen, then a person's whole way of viewing him/herself shifts, influencing all aspects of the person's life.

Integrating The Cultural Elements

To create the accommodation for this to happen for Aiko, a basic Japanese value needed to be understood and addressed in subtle ways. For example, in many non-Western cultures, identity is not seen apart from the group orientation. The personal pronoun "I" does not exist in the Japanese language (Sue & Sue, 1990).

There were several things that happened in Aiko's therapy process that honored her cultural orientation. First, she was a part of a group process, where the group became very bonded as a kind of extended family. By enacting other peoples' dreams, for example, and participating in other group exercises, Aiko became increasingly more comfortable in honoring and dealing with her own individual issues. Secondly, many process approaches were framed in spiritual language and values, so that if there was any sense of loss of one spiritual goal, in this case the valuing of the individual's privacy, other spiritual goals were honored and expressed. Thirdly, because this Japanese woman is naturally very creative with a distinct clarity of mind (perhaps reinforced through her meditation experience), she was fascinated by the depth of dream work and what was to be discovered in the rich terrain of the unconscious, as insights were revealed.

> October 9 Dreams have power–my first discovery. Interpreting dreams have real power. Connecting two of my dreams, from childhood and adulthood was a surprise. Father image/

male image certainly occupies me. My father certainly did and does have profound effect on my life. All life revolved around him, when I was a child and even now. Saphira said, "Honor the pain. In our society, we numb the pain by drinking, eating, drugs and working, among other things. Do not avoid the pain. Pain will naturally occur in life. When it does, simply embrace it and honor it. If we do not avoid the darkness, then one can also see the light." If not, then it's often more difficult to see the light. She also said, "Breath means inspiration. From breath, inspiration springs."

Participants are encouraged to identify, and to honor and dramatize shadow elements, in their psyches, within this work. In trying to make the unconscious conscious, people discover that there are many hidden things buried deep within. These things are not always negative and when they reach the light of our conscious self a power is unleashed in our healing and creative processes (Jung, 1958).

October 16 My Truth: I do not digest my food well. Same with life issues– There is a black despair about everything I touch.–So many unresolved issues I carry in my constipated life–Running away literally from difficult issues has been my constant state.

Delving Into the Shadow

A number of theater/therapy exercises were presented to help people discover their shadow characters and create them. These characters became an expression of hidden parts of themselves. For Asian people, overcoming the strong value of not sharing the dark side is often more of an obstacle than for Americans, as was mentioned earlier. In the safe, creative atmosphere that was created, it seemed to flow quite easily, even for Aiko. Everyone sounded, sang, and danced their shadow. Questions helped the process: Who are you? Where do you come from? How do you move and sound? Why have you stayed hidden? They told their story, sang and danced and often cried. Further expression and more developed characters were encouraged to evolve.

Aiko learned from an early age to escape–escape from the bonds of her patriarchal, oppressive family and cultural roots. In so doing, she discovered that she was also escaping from the potential joys of her current life and the possibilities of deeper intimacy in her personal relationships.

November 6 Shadows are dark! My darkness was a hollow hole. Try as I previously did to fill it with harsh discipline of long hours of work, it did not fulfill this emptiness. I needed a power greater than my human effort and sweat could provide. I needed to tap into source power. Grandmother was one who guided me into this power. In this power there flowed a steady, sustaining light. My grandmother was smiling as she led me to this river of quiet energy. "River" is one of the names given to me by a Burmese Monk. When I was totally stuck in my life, frozen and broken, he gave me this name so that I may defreeze. I discovered today, that when I release from my unconscious, away from my head (which is quick and overactive), amazing things happen. Perhaps in my unconscious is hidden my real self.

At this stage in the process, Aiko was able to receive a great deal of solace in connecting to her strong sense of peace and purity (soul qualities), which she experienced in nature, surrounding her aunt's country house, in which she spent her early childhood. However, images of her experience of men as violent, warlike, and powerful, symbolizing the oppressive patriarchal roots of her culture, presented itself in both of her dreams. These images suggest that owning her own female shadow and inner male (animus, in Jungian terms) is a key in her own healing process. Carl Jung also said, that if we do not face our shadow, it will become our fate (Jung, 1977). If we do not own our own rage or violence, we will play it out.

Aiko shared with the group that she has had an abortion, without her husband's knowledge, which devastated him when he later learned of it. She described the process as being driven to do that by her own destructive impulse, without even thinking about all the pros and cons. She had told no one about what she had done until working with the group.

Through a life incident improvisational exercise, in which participants recall significant incidents as a child, an adolescent and a young adult, another woman in the group revealed and dealt with the intense emotions around sexual abuse. This woman dramatized a powerful scene with her older brother, who had molested her. This triggered other sexual abuse memories in the group, many of which had been repressed and some of which had never been shared before. Through the other woman's drama, which the group helped to enact, Aiko got in touch with two traumatic events in her own life. One was an incident with her father, who took her away with him on a trip and tried to molest her as a young girl. The second situation was the abortion, which she first shared at this time.

Aiko's next two journal entries reflect her discoveries and experience with her sources of strength, the light and the dark, transpersonal dimensions and the nature of the healing process that she was experiencing at this time.

> February 12. Sources of strength–what a wonderful phrase and they are all already inside ourselves, waiting for us to tap into them. What are my sources of strength? My kind and merciful God, forest and animals surrounding our cabin, who constantly surprise and delight me with their resourcefulness. Thousand stars and the moon, who descend so close to me every night. My patient husband, who truly has embraced me with all my faults. Rekindling what I feel in my innermost being when I move. Transformational theater where we bring our darkness into light and make friends with them.

> February 19. Life challenge dissolved by source of strength. Darkness dissolved by light. Seriousness dissolved by play. Shutting down dissolved by love. Tonight I really felt the power of love. When P. [group member] put her hands on my heart and sang, her love breathed into my soul and body and her intent of goodness towards me confirmed for me that life was good. Also, when we felt each other's aura emanating heat and whatever else, we confirmed for each other that we were creatures, not only of this earth but of places beyond.

Since overt expression of angry feelings are discouraged in the Asian culture, many Japanese people somatize these feelings and are encouraged to present an appearance of peace and joy even when they are in conflict and pain. The combination of enacting one of the roles in another woman's drama, to help her, and then, from within the role, observing and identifying with the victim position, Aiko had a total, full bodied, emotional experience. This is a striking example of the therapeutic value of drama therapy.

Final Performance

People were helped to create final performance pieces. They were to present their challenging life material as well as their transformational possibility, including their source of strength. They were encouraged to speak their truth. The final pieces were created by each individual and they could have other group members play the different roles in their drama, enacting people, environments, sound textures, as individuals or as an ensemble. People write their story as dramatic monologues, scenes, in prose, poetry, song, naturalistic or stylized, or a combination of the above. They can choreograph movement pieces within it. They can incorporate music in whatever way they choose. They can build in costumes, props, masks, set pieces or whatever helps them tell their story more authentically. The group invites family and friends to be their audience. The process of objectifying the issues, after working through them in part, creating an artistic form to express them and then giving it away to the audience as a gift offering, has proven to be a very effective therapeutic tool. The process of creating the pieces takes everyone through struggle and creative tension, proving in the end, almost always, to be a very cathartic, healing and satisfying process for the participants. This was certainly the case for Aiko.

She chose to dress in a traditional Japanese costume and white face. She created her piece within a movement/dance structure. Aiko had not danced for some time, but had studied dance when she was younger, so it became important to her to work in that form. She also chose to insert phrases in Japanese at specific dramatic moments in her piece.

Final Performance Piece

1. When I was born, I was immediately taken away from the warm breath of my mother. [movement]
2. She had already decided to leave my father. He had six concubines. (In Japanese, my mother speaking): How filthy! How disgustingly dirty! How long do you think you can continue to lie to me!!
3. Yes, the blood of incest and misguided sexual energy runs in my family. [movement]
4. When I was twelve, my father took me on a little trip, just the two of us. In the middle of the night, I felt Father's big hand descend on me. (In Japanese): What are you doing, Dad?! What are you doing?! [movement]
5. Today, I no longer feel, [movement) breathe, [movement] or play [movement].
6. (The group gathering around me.) Chieko-chan asobo, chieko chan asobo, little chieko, come and play! [movement]
7. Yes, sexual impurity appeared in me, too. I aborted my first child, my only child. I willed her death. [scream, movement]
8. (In Japanese) Please forgive me, please forgive me! [movement] I love you, I love you very much!
9. [As if holding the baby, sing lullaby in Japanese]
10. [With music accompaniment, dance improvisation]
11. [Bringing the cloth and the group across the stage, start the transformational dance-song] (The whole group rocking), Licking our wound, licking our wound.

Burning in the fire, burning in the fire.
Honoring our pain, honoring our pain
Breathing dearly, breathing dearly.
Looking into our darkness, looking into our darkness.
Loving our soul, loving our soul
Trusting our impulses, trusting our impulses.
Forgiving ourselves, forgiving ourselves.
Loving the God in us, loving the God in us!
[Grab the cloth in the center and start the dervish whirl as light fades.]

Aiko expressed her feelings that with the new understanding she had gained, and through the surfacing and purging of so much pain and suffering, she now could forgive her parents. Our assessment was that she had done a significant piece of emotional work and that most likely she would discover that the depth forgiveness will take more time. Furthermore, in many sexual abuse cases, after the initial anger is expressed with the perpetrator father, the often-deeper feelings of abandonment by the mother surface: Where was she when I needed her and why did she not protect me? Aiko's feeling that she unconsciously blamed her mother needs to be further explored and those feelings validated, rather than dismissed.

Concluding reflections written by Aiko, in her evaluation of her process:

1. Externalization of my trauma enabled me to defreeze my trauma and start to move it and to be objective about it.

2. Defreezing of my trauma enabled me to go deep into my darkness which subsequently allowed me to go into my light.

A specific group exercise that was particularly transformative was the exercise in which I dramatized my family, by becoming my father one moment, my mother the next moment, and myself the next moment. This experience revealed to me how the whole world changes when one is in another's shoes. It allowed me to sympathize.

As a group, we became very close and caring for each other. In order to really help each other, our individual faculties as the artist, healer, educator, and Shaman were demanded to be polished to the highest degree.

My sympathies went to all members of the group who were struggling with their families. I was profoundly shocked and assured, at the same time, of our common human struggles on this earth. During this process, my patience with other peoples' struggles (outside the group) became larger.

Freedom to be who we each are
In the dance of searching, exploring
Laughing and crying
Up and down
Sideways and backwards

Can we be safe enough to not have the answers
While fully embracing the questions
Moving a single step closer
To a new becoming
Free to be our essential selves.

REFERENCES

Bentov, M. (1973). *Improvisation in the classroom.* Roxbury, MA: Rice Printing.

Jung C.G. (1977). *Psychology and religion: West and east, Vol. 11, Collected works.* Princeton: University Press.

Khan, H.I. (1973). *The Sufi message of Hazrat Inayat Khan, Vol. II: The mysticism of sound.* London: Barrie and Jenkins Ltd.

Lee, C., & Richardson, B. (Ed.). (1991). Traditional Japanese values and norms. *Multicultural issues in counseling: New approaches to diversity.* Virginia: American Counseling Association.

Moreno, J.L. (1947). *The theater of spontaneity.* Beacon, New York: Beacon House.

Portman, J., & Rollins, B. (1967). *Riot Play.*

Sue, D.W., & Sue, D. (1990). *Counseling the culturally different, theory and practice.* New York: John Wiley & Sons.

Woodman, M. (1989). The conscious feminine. Interview with Barbara Goodrich. *Common boundary,* vol. 7, no. 2 (Mar./Apr., 1989).

BIBLIOGRAPHY

Linden, S. (1997–1998). Creative healing methods in the Sufi alchemical retreat, A dialogue between Retreat Guide and Retreatant, with Hayra Prull, Fall, Winter.

Linden, S. (1997). A festival of light: A high school healing arts event celebrating the ethnic diversity of the school community. *The Arts in Psychotherapy,* vol. 24, number 3.

Linden, S. (1997). Aiko: drama therapy in the recovery process of a Japanese/Korean-American Woman. *The Arts in Psychotherapy, vol. 24,* number 2.

Linden, S. (1996–1997). An Interview with Marion Woodman, written with Taj Inayat Glantz, *Heart and Wings Newsletter.* Sufi Order, Seattle, WA, Winter.

Linden, S. (1986–1993). *The Omega Arts Network News, Editor* (six issues). Boston: Omega Theater.

Linden, S. (1991). *Studies, reflections, reports from the chrysalis connection: The feminine council of the Sufi order.* Ed. with Sophia Moore and Xvarnah Tune, Boston, MA.

Linden, S. (1989–1990). Creating gaia and ourselves as works of art, *Emergence: Journal for Evolving Consciousness, Vol. 3,* Number 1, Colorado, Winter.

Linden, S. (1988). *Visioning as a transformational process,* with Dr. George H. Litwin, Boston, MA.

Linden, S. (1983). *The cosmic celebration.* Video tape production (with slides from 2 productions and a sound track), with Nader Ardalan and Henry Xvarnah Terk.

Linden, S. (1981). Free to create. *New Age Journal,* Boston, MA; September.

Linden, S. (1979). The nature of inspiration. Interview in *East West Journal.* June.

Linden, S. (1978). Women in the world. *The crystal chalice: Spiritual themes for women.* Taj Inayat, The Abode Press .

Linden, S. (1978). *Managing people.* Citibank, produced by Theater Workshop Boston for Forum Corporation, George Litwin, V.P. with The Video Picture Company, Inc.

Linden, S. (1977). Theater Workshop Boston: An anniversary review, *Forum for correspondence and contact,* International Center for Integrative Studies, vol. 8:3.

Linden, S. (1972). Selecting and developing actors. Participatory theater for young audiences: *A handbook for directors,* edited by Pat Hale.

Theater & TV Productions

Awakening. Linden, Dir. Hanna, Playwrite, OM Company. (1978).

Barbara Linden: Artist in America. WGBH/PBS. Hauser Productions. (1971).

Coming home. Linden, Dir. & Omega Theater Co. (1987).

Cosmic celebration. (aka *The cosmic mass*). Pir Vilayat Inayat Khan, Linden, Dir., Mathieu, Musical Dir., & OM Company. (1973–1983).

Creation. Linden & Rosenbert. New Plays, Inc. (1970).

Eartheart. Linden & Nisenbaum-Becker. (1995–present).

How can I tell you? Linden, Tribal Players & Sarson Productions. (1970).

Sunsong: A people puppet pageant for children of all ages. Linden, Dir. & Playwrite, Sonneborn, Musical Dir., OM Company. (1976).

The finding place. A ceremonial journey. Linden, Dir., Sejecho Arts Festival. (1992).

The first earth run. Linden, Omega Theater, Earth Ambassadors, Rosenthal, & Tyler. (1986).

Toward the one: A family board game. Linden, Dym, & Hallowell. (1974).

Tribe. Linden & Tribal Players. New Plays, Inc. (1969).

FURTHER TRAINING

Transpersonal drama therapy
Certificate Program
A sequentially based, individually tailored
alternate route training program
Saphira Linden, MA, RDT-BCT, and
Penny Lewis PHD, RDT-BCT Co-directors

Transformational Theater and
Sound Healing
Saphira Linden, MA RDT-BCT,
Sarah Benson, MA, and
Nat Warren-White, MA

Please see our webpage:
www.omegatheater.org
Omega Theater
P.O.B. 1227
Jamaica Plain, MA 02130

Phone: 617 522-8300

Chapter 18

FAMILY DYNAMIC PLAY

Steve Harvey

As a family of four walk through a city square, the two young boys began to chase the pigeons that were eating bread crumbs. Several of the onlookers watched the boys aged three and five as they laughed and were clearly caught up in their game of running after the birds who flew away as the boys approach only to land a few feet away. The boys followed these quick bursts of flight that led them in every direction. The rise and fall of their enthusiasm was contagious to many of the adults also visiting the city. A group of foreign tourists became delighted with the boys and began taking pictures and laughing with enjoyment. The two parents watched the boys and the tourists. They begin to talk about the possibility of moving to another country. The mother and father had been discussing such a move for several months often with sharply different and opposite views. The foreign onlookers were from the country; the father had been offered a job. As the parents both relaxed by watching the scene unfold, the mother said that she could see how such a move could be possible watching how positively the tourists were viewing her children. Occasionally the father joined the boys both to keep them from running out into the street and to lift the younger son in a playful effort to give him a better chance to touch the birds. During these times the mother took some pictures. Later that evening, the mother and father had a more elaborated and empathic conversation with each other about their current living situation.

Such episodes of play with the accompanying shifts in mood and discussion occur naturally throughout family life. The play both reflects and generates a general atmosphere. This improvisation functions to help family members experience mutual emotional changes, as well as recreate intimacy and security that follow the tension of disagreements, transitions, and conflict. If the above example can be seen as a drama/dance for a moment and the activities extended into a metaphor, connections between the flight of the birds, the boys running, the tourist's interest, the mother's picture-taking, the father's joining and limit setting, as well as the accompanying mood shifts can take on extra meaning in light of the consideration of a family move. The conversation and relaxed time together can also help to transform the tension such a major move can produce. While such an event may not lead to a direct decision about whether to move or not, the playful afternoon of bird chasing can become one of many events influencing the emotional life of this family. Times like this afternoon walk in the square can become forgotten, however such moments influence and contribute to an emotional history. Such improvisation can be used in family interventions to help families identify their naturally occurring creativity in their everyday life to solve their relationship challenges.

Dynamic family play is an intervention style in which artistic, dance/movement, dramatic, storytelling, and video expression are used in an integrated fashion among families to address problems. The goal of these activities is to help a family bring more of their naturally occurring creativity into their day-to-day activities as well as develop metaphors that give meaning, emotional significance, and contribute to transformation of conflict. A central premise of this intervention style is that creativity is a naturally occurring ability that influences the quality, form, and meaning of interpersonal interaction, especially among family members. Both the process and content of the stream of interaction are seen as being created in ongoing fashion by family members. This is especially seen in the process of nonverbal communications. Much of this process is unconscious. In dynamic family play, family interactive patterns, themes, and metaphors are identified through expressive play activities. Families are then coached to elaborate and extend the meaning of their metaphors as well as to change their ongoing, day-to-day conflicts. As families begin to engage in more mutual creativity together, a more positive and hopeful emotional atmosphere develops. With the experience of this mood change, families can develop play that is significant to them.

Elements from the family visit to the square presented above can be extended in an office or in the home using Dynamic Play to facilitate the complicated decision of whether to move or not. The family could be helped to use the movement elements of the boys' bird chasing in making dances about leaving, using the associated feelings or other freely associated images the family might generate to make connections between the dancing and moving. The mother's picture-taking could lead to art or storytelling about her feelings of the boys and family security/insecurity related to change. The inclusion of the tourists might lead to various role playing about the family's future life in the other country. Various parts of the activities could be videoed for later viewing to identify particularly significant moments and interactions as well as to extend creative metaphor development through "movie making." The resulting process could then be used to develop strategies for making the straightforward decision of whether to move or not. Additionally the resulting net of connections of images and emotions could be collected into metaphors to explore the deeper emotional significance of a family transition when challenged by the general basic elements of separation and change. Importantly such activity would include all family members. As most families are usually not aware of the creative potential in such everyday episodes such use of active metaphor-making from and about their life can be quite enriching. Families are often not able to generate such play in any consistent way due to the severity of their problems, and such play can help family members develop intimacy. The techniques of Dynamic Play are designed to generate family playful interaction and then facilitate its creative development both in the home and in office activities. These approaches can be flexibly applied to many family situations.

A nine-year-old girl was referred following the stabbing murder of a classmate. Despite a generally successful community crisis intervention shortly after the event, the girl continued to be aggressive to her peers to the point of being asked to leave an after-school day-care program. She also had difficulty sleeping. The girl's single mother brought her to treatment with some thought that the girl's behavior might be related to the murder. During the initial interviews, the girl reported that she had thought of stabbing herself a year ago due to her sadness and difficulties with her peers. The classmate's stabbing had awakened her thoughts. This experience was very frightening for her. Her disclosure was the first time her mother had known of these thoughts. After making sure the girl was not actively at risk for self-harm, the mother and girl were asked to develop a story about a family using several large stuffed animals, pillows, and colorful scarves. The girl mostly took the lead having her mother close her eyes while she hid all the animals, identifying them as being very dangerous. When the mother opened her eyes, the girl and mother did not know what to do. The therapist asked the girl to introduce her mother to her animal world. As the two were finding the dangerous animals, the mother asked the girl what they might do together. They then built a zoo in which the animals could be safe and admired from a distance. After some conversation, they began to connect how the girl's secret thoughts about the knives were like the hidden dangerous animals the mother was not able to see. Further, the girl's disclosure was like showing her mother the animals' hiding places. The mutual activity of placing the animals in a safe zoo then led to a more truthful, secure, and intimate relationship. They then drew various versions of danger in the home including the mother's kitchen knives and found ways to distance or place them in the "zoo." Not only did the initial problem of aggression become more manageable through active family problem solving, but the mother and child became emotionally closer to each other than they had been in many years. The girl's thoughts about the knives disappeared. While this example is from a brief crisis-related intervention, dynamic family play can be used with families with more severe long-term problems as well.

GENESIS

Dynamic Play was developed from the author's experience in the performing arts, creative arts therapy, and clinical psychology over the last 30 years. The journey began with time spent doing experimental drama and dance in the late 1960s and early 1970s, and was extended through training in creative arts therapy some time later. Later, formal study of attachment, family therapy, and creativity led to the application of such ideas to clinical settings involving foster, adoptive, and birth families with troubled children. Such applications involved adapting concepts and techniques of drama and dance improvisation in a family play therapy approach.

Dance and Drama Influences

Dramatists became quite interested in physical play as well as in the emerging styles of group psychotherapy as ways to enhance actor training and theatrical performance in the late 1960s. The central thrust of this movement was an attempt to make performance more emotionally honest. Jerzy Grotowski (1968) developed a performing method in which the central focus of the action was placed on the physical and vocal expression of the actors. The use of costuming, elaborate sets and props was reduced if not eliminated altogether to highlight and intensify the direct emotional expression of the performer. In the United States, Richard Schechner (1970) extended some of these concepts to a performance piece of the Bacchi in which encounter group techniques, physical expression, and ritual were used to form a dramatic piece.

The current author used several of these ideas to develop a company who together developed several pieces in a story theater format. The main training/rehearsal technique involved the actors developing improvised sound/movement phrases starting with simple physical activities such as stretching, swinging limbs, and isolation of joints while producing sounds in coordination with their physical action. Words and more meaningful dialogue were introduced as the actors got a physical "feel" for their lines. The most interesting action came as the actors began improvising sound and movement action together in dyads and small groups. Such episodes were developed as coordinated activity emerged among the actors and dissolved as the activity lost its momentum on its own. Such scenes did not have any preset or meaningful goal, however very interesting dramatic activity developed. Some of these scenes were later refined in performance such as physical fights being staged by actors who were pushing each other in a back-to-back way or the dancing and striking of blows and bodily response across the distance of 40 feet coming together in a kinetic fit. In one very moving scene, a male actor verbally improvised a dance of his father's heart attack while the audience members and other cast held and squeezed each others' hands in a rhythm of a heartbeat. While the intended purpose of this activity was to help train performers to have more range of movement and vocal expression, the result led to a dramatic action in which actors produced characters and interactions based on the dynamic physical feel of their mutual activity. Productions were then staged using techniques to best show this physical feel among the performers.

Contact Improvisation

Some time later, the current author became involved with contact improvisation (Banes, 1980). This movement form involves a small group of dancers who join together usually in a dyad to produce improvised dance action using touch and the exchange of their weight. The resulting movement can resemble action such as martial arts, wrestling, or the lifts from classical or modern dance except that all the mutual movement is totally improvised in the moment. There are lifts and falls that evolve organically out of a continuous process of finding and losing balance. Social roles of who is the lifter and who is the lifted or who is active, who is passive, likewise change in a flexible manner to meet the need of the mutual movement. The form resists more formal definition and rules while maintaining the central theme that the participants develop and keep a kinetic exchange with each other. Nancy Stark Smith, one of the central teachers and performers of the form, described how she kept discovering that as she or others tried to define a rule of what made contact improvisation, that rule changed. "First we thought that the dancers always had to be in constant contact with each other, and then that there could only be two dancers, later we attempted to keep the dancing very smooth. Each time we found out that we could break these rules and new and exciting dances could develop" (1982). Not only was the central activity of contact improvisation being generated by the movers in the moment, but the basic form proved to be very plastic as well. What "contact" became to be understood as being was the basic kinetic feel between partners as they shared attention with each other during mutual activity. Though certain kinds of activity seemed to reoccur during improvised episodes such as mutual exchange of touch and weight, a certain relaxed physical and mental state of participants, a relatively few number of dancers in any one dance; no specific requirement of activity or type of personal behavior was always demanded. The resulting dances seemed to have a kind of "naturalness" to the interaction and physical playfulness among the participants.

Later the author used freely associated verbalized images in connection with contact improvisation to make use of a natural tendency for watchers to project meaningful narrative on the fluid interactive movement contact can produce. This led to a form in which the audience was asked for true life stories which were later danced using a more structured form of contact improvisation (Harvey & Kelly, 1991, 1992, 1993).

Expressive Therapy Influences

Expressive arts therapies refers to psychotherapy techniques that utilize expressive action. Expression refers to art, dance/movement, drama, music, storytelling, and video making. While some applications make use of a single discipline such as art or dance only, some practitioners have developed approaches in which various expressions are integrated. Such techniques have been applied to several populations from a variety of theoretical backgrounds. However, these techniques are different from the respective art forms in that the expressive process is emphasized over the production of an end-product (Levy, 1988). Likewise the expressive art therapies differ from psychotherapy in that the creativity of expression is a central part in therapeutic change (Robbins, 1986). This emphasis on a shared personal creative process has provided a main influence in the development of dynamic family play.

Psychodrama

The current author participated in an ongoing psychodrama community for many years as a participant, double, and later as a leader. Within this community, psychodramatically-oriented groups were held weekly with additional day-long groups held over the weekend monthly. Psychodrama (see Garcia, this volume for a review) proceeds as an individual is directed to present a situation from his or her life, others are chosen to take roles in this situation, and then the individual and these group members improvise an enactment. Through a series of role reversals this enactment follows the individual's emotional reactions. Often such dramatic action leads to other conflicts from the person's life as an emotional logic is followed. Often in the experience of the long-term group, a person begins an enactment of a relatively minor present day event only to have this scene transform into an enactment of past traumatic events usually involving the family of origin. As the scene develops over a period of several months, typically only certain elements of the beginning scene remain apparent in later transformations. Interestingly, many times the same actors from the current scene are chosen to portray the more emotionally relevant characters from the main person's earlier life. Also the transformation from present situation to past enactment proceeds through a series of steps that are not altogether logical or rational but rather conform to the emotional and/or bodily-felt events of the enactment itself.

It was not unusual for a person to begin a scene stating that though they felt they needed to express themselves, they had no words to use. An initial enactment would be set up between the person in a role of not being able to talk, confronting an actor who would not allow him not to talk. Through a series of role reversals and scene transformations usually taking place over several months, the same person enacted a scene from their past involving their family of origin in which they were confused and unable to verbally express any thoughts in the face of a very tragic family event. Often the same actors from the first enactment were again chosen to play the significant family members. The person then expressed very strong emotion in a genuine way. This movement from present day and more commonplace irritation to strong emotion and catharsis was only apparent by the end of a series of scene transformations.

Another interesting part of this experience from the long-term work was that several general scenarios emerged as offering good dramatic staging for certain types of scenes. These usually involved general kinds of physical activity. For example, a scene involving a death of a family member or loved one was staged with the person playing the dead person laying down as if speaking from the grave and finding a moment to hold onto the living survivor. A physical struggle then usually emerged as the survivor attempted to leave the grave to "return to his life." This physical struggle often mirrored the inner conflict of separation from an attachment figure and helped facilitate a grieving process.

Dance Therapy

The current author received training in creative arts therapy with a major in dance therapy. He also spent several years leading creative art therapy groups with both groups of psychiatric inpatients as well as young children with significant developmental and emotional disabilities in which dance was the central expressive modality. While dance therapy consists of a variety of techniques, the central focus is for the therapist to facilitate movement in which basic physical expression is extended into a form to communicate inner experience that is difficult to verbalize. One of the primary techniques (Chace Technique, see Chaklin, 1975) involves the therapist developing dances using a person's own movement responses. The Chace Technique can be applied in a group as well as individual setting. Usually such dances incorporate both unison movement as well as individual variation. As individual variations occur, the therapist then facilitates movement changes to incorporate such new expression using a moment-to-moment creativity. Such facilitation works as a therapist observes the movement of others, carefully noticing both the quality of muscular tension and release as well as body shape of such movement. Therapist also attempts to extend the potential of a patient's expression by developing a feel or kinesthetic empathy for the movement from an awareness of their own body (Lewis, 1984).

As themes emerge, the therapist then focuses on movement that can have psychological relevance for the participants. The therapist can then help patients verbalize their experience and begin to use words with movement phrases to give meaning. Examples include helping a patient develop a full pushing movement while using verbalization related to psychologically "pushing" something away or setting a psychological boundary. These themes can then be extended using art techniques to develop the metaphor.

Applications to Children and Families

During the late 1970s, the current author began working with children who had particular difficulty with verbal expression including young children in the foster/adoptive system. Several of these children had experienced significant physical and sexual abuse as well as multiple separations from their adult caretakers. Some had parents who were mentally ill themselves (see Harvey, 1991, 1993, 1994, and 1995 for case presentations). These children's anxiety-related problems as well as their behavioral difficulties were especially resistant to change with individual expressive sessions. The adult caretakers were asked to join the sessions, with much better results. Sometimes as foster children were moved from one home to another both caretakers were included in a transition ritual. Specific problems associated with abuse and adoptions were addressed with family-related expressive activities. A broad understanding of the general applications of family play therapy emerged. This work was influenced by the theoretical concepts of attachment and creativity to help explain what parents and children were experiencing as they began to play with each other.

DRAMA THERAPY FRAME OF REFERENCE

Basic Concepts

Attachment

A general theme that has emerged from the experiences in the performing arts, expressive arts therapy, and clinical application to families described above is the importance of a mutually physically-felt relationship in the quality of shared expression. Perhaps the most profound influences of how such physical relationship is experienced comes from the development of initial attachments. Attachment refers to the basic relationship that develops between a parent and child. Attachment in dynamic family play also refers to the net of attachment relationships within the immediate family. After many years of careful observation, John Bowlby (1972, 1973, 1982) observed how important and long lasting the attachment between parents and children can be. Parents who consistently match their emotional responses to their young children's nonverbal communication of distress generate feelings of security within the family. However, parents and children may also form insecure attachments characterized by avoidance, ambivalence, and disorganization in their ongoing nonverbal communication with each other, especially in strong emotional situations. The outcome of secure attachment is the development of an emotional, bodily felt sense of trust between parents and children. Parents and their children with insecure attachments tend to experience an overriding physical sense of mistrust and fear.

According to Bowlby, an additional concept related to secure attachment is that of a secure base for exploration. This idea is based on the notion that there is a direct relationship between the amount of security and the amount of effective clear exploration a child engages in as he or she grows. Conversely, insecure children's exploration is negatively affected. These concepts can be applied to the family situation in which the entire system of a family contributes to a secure base (Byng-Hall, 1991). However, if this sense of security is negatively impacted, as in the case of divorce, loss, or trauma, exploration and mastery of emotional conflict are likewise negatively impacted. Exploration occurs in mutual play activities. So in this way play can both reflect the kind of family attachment and help to produce more security.

Bowlby points out children develop a strategy or preferred way to achieve security or insecurity. During infancy or toddler years, these strategies are expressed in direct physical interactive behavior. Secure one-year-olds will predictably approach their mothers directly when they are distressed. Such physical action shows clear movement and vocal intention. When the distressed child gets close, both mother and child mold their bodies to each other and the child achieves a calm and oriented state. Insecure children show various strategies of avoidance, ambivalence, or disorganization as seen in such physical actions as a child's moving away from the adult, being unable to regain a calm state while close to the caretaker's body, or showing odd interactive behavior such as unnatural stillness or falls while approaching the caretaking adult. As children mature, such physical interactive behavior strategies also become expressed in imaginative play. A secure preschooler's stories or dramatic play contain themes of positive reunions and rescues following high intensity emotionality, conflict or danger. Similar play themes from insecure children however contain only danger and/or isolation. Adult parent's verbal stories of their early family life show similar strategies in how they describe their early emotional experiences.

Likewise a family's attachment experience becomes generalized in the patterns and strategies of their everyday expression, both verbal and nonverbal. The dramatic staging and choreography of nonverbal posturing and patterns of gestures involved in such simple activities as having dinner together or taking a walk show familiar themes that lead to a characteristic emotional atmosphere. A family's experiences with loss and trauma can influence such patterns in strong ways. Such emotional history becomes present in the ongoing communication qualities of the family's daily life such that a new visitor to the family can begin to physically experience variations of security and insecurity, which lead to an overall emotional "feel" merely by participating in a hour-long picnic.

Creativity and Play

A greater or lesser amount of spontaneous creativity is present both within individual members and among family group expression. The quality of such creativity is directly related to the characteristic emotional atmospheres that result from the sum of the network of attachments. Torrence (1974) describes creativity as the ability to sense "gaps" in what is previously known and produce something new that can be communicated and understood. Getzel and Csikszentmihaly (1976) describe the process of creativity as a problem finding/solving activity in which the result is not known at the beginning. It is only when someone becomes involved and develops a focused "flow" of activity that a problem even emerges which can then easily be solved. Such solutions involve novel combination or recombination of ideas. Often such combinations involve elements that were only incidental to the initial starting place.

Play

Play, especially for children, is the laboratory for spontaneous experimentation. Creative acts can be seen in child's play from the earliest moments of life. Such play is intrinsically motivating and captivates the players completely. Whether in the dramatic play of preschoolers or the more physical games of younger children's peek-a-boo, creative combinations of new elements are constantly being produced.

One of the central aspects of family relationships utilized by dynamic family play is the spontaneous, flexible, and mutual play between parents and children. One of the most striking elements of such parent/child play is its naturalness and ease; such episodes can emerge at seemingly any time. Play can be thought of as the activity that generates attachment or at least the motivation to engage in positive mutual emotional experience. Those researchers and clinicians (Harvey, 1994c; Stern, 1985, 1990; Tortera, 1994) interested in infant-parent play clearly observe how such playful exchanges develop a natural dance or choreography involving eye contact, smiling, and responsiveness in mutual, nonverbal exchanges. As the child grows, such games become more elaborate, using sound and face making, verbal exchanges and the larger sensory-motor play involving running, jumping, and tumbling often with the aid of and in relationship with parents. In the preschool years, mothers, fathers, and their young children engage in an extended range of dramatic role playing in addition to a wider variety of physical exchanges. A visit to a playground or park where young children and their parents are playing reveals a wide variety of such family exchanges. Such play develops into more verbal and humorous exchanges as a family matures. In observing this play, one is struck by the spontaneity and naturalness of the participants and how such play generates a spirited and emotional joining. It is characterized by an attunement or responsiveness and by the ability of parents and children to resolve conflicts with flexibility.

In these episodes, themes tend to repeat, and emotional issues become quite evident. Examples of such themes include a young toddler who has just been injured casting his willing mother or father into the role of doctor to "cure" him; a young infant who is frightened by separation-initiating nonverbal communication to cue her parent's secure embrace, physical holding, and visual attention through face games; a preschooler's playful exploration with a role in which he magically transforms himself into an all-powerful hero problem-solver under his mother's watchful eye and sometimes active participation. Even a teenager's sense of humor while in conflict with his parent can be quite soothing and help to regain a sense of family. Clearly in the best of circumstances, families' mutual play produces a healing process in which their mutual creativity and imagination transforms such themes in a way that the players experience affiliation, intimacy, attachment, and affirmation. Schaefer (1993) has identified several curative powers of such play. These powers appear to be generic to the experience of mutual play itself.

The positive experience with play clearly contributes to a family's emotional growth. However, for those who have observed families with children who have experienced abuse or trauma, or are in the midst of loss or divorce, are quick to see how difficult and painful such mutual play and engagement can be. From these observations it is clear that the task for the play therapist is to help families who experience difficulties discover for the first time or rediscover their own natural play and creativity that can address emotional conflict and pain, thereby rebuilding intimacy

Dynamic Play and Family Play

The central concepts of dynamic play grew from an interaction of influences from physical drama, contact improvisation, expressive arts therapies, clinical applications of attachment theory, creativity, and play. This intervention style draws on the dramatic improvisations that arise from physical interactions. In such improvisation the use of role playing and the narrative development of scene and story interweave with interactions in which actors pay attention to and use the qualities of their physical expression in fluid ways. The shared "story" emerges from verbal content or character in one moment and a shared spontaneous dance in another. While such expression can produce an atmosphere of "anything goes," the actor/dancers can make use of their own kinetic feel of the situation to guide their spontaneity so that the development of relationships with their partners is forwarded. The general experience of contact improvisation highlights what this "feel" consists of more clearly. In this form, movers join each other's flow of movement using actual weight sharing and touch, or the past experience of such concrete sensation, to playfully explore their contact in the present moment. Interactions that result are remarkable for the freedom enjoyed as individuals' make use of their own internally felt sensation to produce movement with their partners. Even rules and preset verbal expectations give way to the present physicality of the moment. Results can resemble a kind of joint-free association of their relationship guided by the bodily perception of each other or the "contact point."

When such drama and movement interactions are used to explore emotional experience as with psychodrama or dance therapy, it is remarkable how everyday events and simple gestures or bodily postures are related to significant personal events. As an individual's drama unfolds through role playing or a group's dance emerges using variations of simple movement, strong emotional themes can emerge. When families engage in such expressive activity, such themes relate to experience with attachment, loss and trauma. Family play is a naturally occurring improvisational resource in which such themes are addressed with creativity and have a restorative manner in everyday life. A toddler's chase games with her mother that express separation and union simultaneously are like a family dance therapy or contact improvisation. The dramatic play of a five year old while he feels the loss during his father's absence for work is like his psychodrama or physical theater only with a more fluid manner of expression. Such play is naturally adapted to developmental needs such that a parent's and infant's face play may lead some 14 years later to the teenager's humorous role playing of his parent's comments. However these episodes are based on the similar theme of following the emotional "contact point" of their attachments. Such play ability is seen in the quality and process of a family's communication during everyday events as well in a more pronounced form during actual play episodes that naturally spring out of ongoing family life. This basic improvisational activity can be isolated through a focus in the therapy room and encouraged to be generalized to the home setting to help families generate a more positive and supportive emotional atmosphere.

The following general concepts form the theoretical base of Dynamic Play:

- Families play together naturally. Such play both reflects and helps to produce their emotional life together. It also helps to reestablish intimacy following moments of conflict and isolation. Play episodes also offer a way for a family to experience catharsis in times of emotional difficulty.
- Such play is strongly influenced by a family's history with attachment, loss, and trauma.
- Observations of the flow of a family's play and the breaks in such flow provide an understanding of their underlying emotional life.
- Intervention attempts to help families rediscover or experience for the first time their play potential by helping to review relationships that have become stalled in conflictual interactive expressive patterns. Such interventions make use of the intimacy that occurs with mutual play.

How Health and Dysfunction are Viewed

In a normal situation families play together and such play helps to forward their positive relationship with each other. In a concrete way, such play is characterized by a spontaneity and natural flow. Creativity occurs through moment to moment interactions in small ways as well as in full play episodes. Both verbal and nonverbal play activity function to produce positive emotional states such as shared attunement and intimacy between the players. However, families who are confronting problems do not engage in such play with any regularity, if at all. When such mutual play does occur, it is characterized by breaks in play flow. This play style produces alienation, isolation, and a negative emotional mood among the players.

Harvey and Kelly (1993) observed a girl's interactive play with her birth mother as well as her foster mother. The observations occurred when the girl was 18 months and later at 36 months. The girl had been physically abused by her birth mother and removed from her care in infancy. She had developed a secure attachment with her foster parents who later adopted her. The observations of the girl and her foster parents in comparison with her birth mother were striking for the differences in play. It was as if there were two different girls. Interactions between the girl and her birth mother were characterized by little face to face or actual physical contact. The girl tended to play quite a distance from her mother and when her mother got closer, the girl's play activity consisted of repetitive motions showing little of the spontaneity, enjoyment, and metaphor making that is usually associated with play. Importantly, the girl consistently introduced activities that would stop any nonverbal sharing of expressive rhythms or attunement (Stern, 1985). The girl avoided her mother by turning her back and distancing herself when her mother came into the room or even when the mother came close. The girl was the opposite with her foster mother, using closeness, touch and positive physical interactions such as chase and throwing the ball. Metaphorical puppet play with themes of emotional closeness emerged spontaneously. The flow of moment-to-moment interactions were characterized by almost continuous matching of expressive rhythms (attunement). No breaks in this flow were apparent. Additionally the girl warmly greeted her foster mother with a hug and immediately included her in play activity upon a reunion after a brief separation.

The same style of play was observed when the girl was both 18 as well as 36 months. Interestingly, the girl introduced a play theme in which a large frightening character with " spiders in her stomach" intruded into her home when she was engaged in play therapy to address fear-related symptoms such as nightmares following her adoption some nine months after the last observation. When the now adoptive mother was able to join the girl's play around this theme by chasing the imposing figure out of the home in a spirited and spontaneous way, the girl's fears diminished significantly. These observations led to the conclusion that the characteristics of play flow, expressive attunement, and breaks introduced in such play by the players led to an important understanding of the emotional atmosphere shared by family members.

Harvey and Soderquist (1995) observed several families who had a history in which at least one child had experienced incest some years earlier as well as a similar number of families who were well functioning. All families were asked to engage in physical and dramatic activities such as free play, follow-the-leader, make up a story about a family using large stuffed stuffed animals, and complete an obstacle course of large pillows while tied together with stretchy bands. Videos of interactions were later rated as showing attuned or nonattuned play. Attuned play was characterized by a continuous and spontaneous matching of both nonverbal as well as verbal expression and lead to clear positive feeling among the family members. Attuned families were able to coordinate their mutual physical activities together in an enjoyable manner, and resolve any disturbing or threatening dramatic imagery introduced throughout the play with safety and mastery. Monsters were chased away together and homes were built together. Nonattuned play consisted of activity that lacked such mutuality and led to an emotional isolation. Disturbing imagery when introduced was not resolved and joint physical activity was brief and not enjoyable.

Using such concepts, families with a history of trauma were reliably distinguished from those without such a history. In general, the normal families completed the activities easily with such enjoyment that they transformed their play far beyond the initial game rules into their own versions in order to further the positive experience with each other. One family, for example, added an improvised scene in which the youngest, an eight-year-old was applauded and singled out for an award for completing a cartwheel during her turn at leadership during the game of follow-the-leader. Such creative additions were typical and tended to give the impression that such interactions could go on without the families coming to an end voluntarily. In contrast, interaction among the families who had experienced trauma tended to be much shorter and lacked sustained intrinsic motivation to continue mutual play. Play, when it did occur, tended to be completion of the minimum requirements and were concrete representations of the required tasks. Little or no creative elaborations were spontaneously added. Family members declined to participate in such activities, or had problems choosing who would introduce the initial ideas. In one telling example, a young girl, who had been sexually assaulted by her mother's boyfriend some years before, and her mother sat together giggling nervously for over ten minutes unable to generate any play together when given the opportunity. The same girl was unable to take a leadership role in a follow-the-leader game. In general the disturbing dramatic imagery when it was introduced by such families was not recognized or resolved. Nonverbal exchanges lacked a sharing of face to face, gesture, or full body enjoyment. Family members appeared to be relieved when they reached the end of their play period together. In general, the most striking difference was that the intrinsic enjoyment and creative absorption that typically accompanies play seemed to be missing from the more troubled families.

It is important to note that families who did participate with a history of a traumatic family event had received the appropriate social service interventions required to insure child protection such as removing the perpetuators of abuse from the home and had also received some verbally-oriented family therapy. However, as James (1995) has pointed out, the experience of trauma negatively impacts a family's sense of attachment and physically felt sense of security. This occurs even if the origin of the trauma originates outside of the family and the family had developed a secure style of interacting prior to the traumatic event. While secure attachments can certainly help a family recover from loss and traumatic events, strong emotional events can overwhelm a family's ability to cope and affect their relationships with each other in ways that are unconscious to them. In such a way, events such as loss, separations, and trauma can have long-lasting influences particularly on the intimacy and basic creative resourcefulness of family members. Play reflects such changes and can offer a concrete way to engage families in intervention.

The problems addressed in dynamic play are conceptualized as any expression within the system of family relationships that detracts from the sense of overall bodily-felt security experienced by family members which continues for a long enough time to detract from the family's ability to develop intimacy in a spontaneous way. In short, they lose their ability to play with each other in a developmentally appropriate manner. Clearly Bowlby's ideas concerning a parent's, child's, or family's collective experience of unresolved separation and loss and a parent's history with intimacy, attachment and trauma serve as the underlying contributors to the amount of security in a family's emotional life. In turn, insecurity in a family's attachments affects their natural play together. As in the above examples, the parents as well as children who experienced a traumatic event were unable to find a sense of security, and their play was likewise impacted by disorganization, avoidance, and ambivalence. This general sense of disruption of security can be extended to several specific situations such as divorce, loss of a child or older relative through death, alcoholism, or individual psychopathology of a family member.

Given a family situation in which defensive communication replaces intimacy and family play becomes eroded, problems requiring intervention can easily develop. In this state, the more spontaneous expressions between family members become quite painful, producing more problems and emotional tension than can be resolved. The sense of free expression and playful exploration become limited. Individual family members typically introduce expressions designed to protect their own self-esteem and fragile feelings of closeness. Personal differences are not tolerated. Typically such strategies are designed to control others, avoid intimacy, and withdraw basic affections. Daily exchanges develop characteristic rigid patterns that are easily recognizable. Argumentative contrariness and/or withdrawal dominate all expression. Play becomes likewise patterned if it develops at all.

Goals of Treatment

The goal of treatment is to guide families in improvising their mutual play. When the connection between play and basic core attachments is considered and the idea that mutual play which reflects and generates such intimacy and emotional security is a largely unconscious process, change in play behavior becomes more complex. Overall the main treatment goal of intervention is to help a family experience a greater sense of security with each other. Secondarily, using the exploration that secure play can produce, emotional issues such as loss, trauma and interactive behavior can be addressed. The therapist needs to use both verbal as well as experiential expressive play sessions to accomplish these goals.

Therapeutic Process

Unlike other forms of family therapy, evaluation of problems is very closely connected to intervention efforts. How families perform in their initial sessions usually provides a good estimate of functioning. The accomplishment of this progression follows from a (1) basic evaluation period in which presenting problems are identified both verbally and in play, (2) followed by a phase in which the therapist is directed to focus on specific issues, coach and organize more flexible play interactions, (3) a phase involving the crystallization of a "core scene" in which a family's specific emotional issue with the accompanying characteristic pattern of expressions becomes defined and addressed, and (4) finally, a period in which the family becomes able to generate their own play which more consciously addresses their problems with spontaneity and intrinsic motivation.

Phase I: Evaluation Period

Specific types of play activities are used in each of these phases with accompanying therapeutic strategies of verbalization. The role of the therapist is also different in each of these stages. In general, evaluation activities are preset by the therapist to observe an individual family's style across several different expressive media. A verbal interview is conducted to review presenting emotional and behavioral concerns as well as obtain a clinical history of attachment, loss, separation and emotional trauma.

The main task during these initial sessions is to then help the family make connections between the content and style of their play and the emotional-behavioral theme they present. Therapy goals are then defined in both play as well as verbal terms. The therapist is more of an observer in such sessions. Verbalizations are reflective and offer information as well as questions to better define problems and relevant history. For example, a depressed mother and her preschooler who have had difficulty playing a follow-the-leader game can be helped to see that their inability to initiate turn taking and extend their game is a play equivalent of their problematic emotional interaction. The therapist can then help the child and mother to spontaneously take turns as a way to address the depression and withdrawal of affection.

Phase 2: Development of Mutual Parent-Child Improvisation

During the next phase, some initial activities are introduced by the therapist to help family members begin to use the various play materials in a more organized yet improvised fashion. Here the therapist incorporates the family's break of play into new improvisations to facilitate a growth of mutual curiosity and shared intrinsic experience of positive feeling with each other. A main aim of this phase is to help parents and children begin to enjoy more organized improvisations together and generate "expressive momentum." The metaphor making possibilities of the various play modalities are also explored. Verbal strategies here consist of labeling emotional states and connecting such states to expressive activities. The therapist becomes a participant/observer of the play, sometimes modeling positive play expression, sometimes suggesting variations, and always observing mutual expression and the emotional states that are generated.

The inability of the depressed mother to match her preschooler's initiatives from the example mentioned above might be addressed by asking the mother to continue a follow-the-leader game. As the game breaks down, the therapist can help label feelings of helplessness the mother might be experiencing as well as the wildness and abandonment the child might feel. At the same time, the therapist can change the physical game of follow-the-leader to an art activity in which the mother and daughter can chase each other's scribbles on paper to extend the general theme of mutual play in another media. The therapist can join the art activity as a way to model how such mark making can be accomplished with high energy and enjoyment. The therapist might also add a spontaneous story about a mother and baby animal to the scribble "chase," using each stroke of the markers as a way to extend the narrative. In this way, the therapist can help the mark activity become a metaphor about the mother/child relationship. The therapist can also use props, such as stretchy bands of material to help the mother hold onto the child to coordinate physical activity to develop more attunement. Verbal comments about the material as being a mother's "holding" are used to help facilitate mutual, metaphor-making. The therapist can also then extend this idea of metaphor making into the joint expression through the use of telling a story about the moment-to-moment activity the mother and child are engaged in. The therapist is observant of how the parent/child interaction can be coached with actual suggestions of different activities, can introduce different expressive media, and can use spontaneous metaphor making to facilitate more organized and motivated mutual play.

Phase 3: Identification of Core Theme, Conflict, or Interactive Process

During the next phase of treatment, the therapy goal is to identify what basic theme, conflict, or interactive process as well as emotional content appears to be underlying family interactions. Usually such themes are related directly to the main emotional events of the family's history. If the mother and preschooler from the previous example had experienced a loss such as divorce, their difficulties in matching each other's expression would be related to this event. The therapist would then facilitate some play activities, rituals, as well as encouragement of new life options to both the mother and her child. A ritual developed with art, drama, and video in which the mother and child said good-bye to the previous pre loss family might be one such step in addressing this core scene. Symbolic expressions developed from office sessions could extend to the home environment. The therapist takes a less active role in the play activities during this stage, spending more time helping to plan new activities with family members.

Phase 4: Family Members Generate Their Own Positive Corrective Play

Finally, the family is helped to develop their own free play in the final part of intervention. Interventions here are meant to help facilitate positive and present moment emotional exchange between them as well as with the therapist in the play. Termination is dealt with during this phase as well.

Techniques

Common aspects of the techniques such as play materials, room set-up, integration of different expressive media, and methods of observation will be presented. Such aspects are used throughout all phases of treatment.

Using these ideas, strategies for organizing observations and interventions of specific family play activities have been devised. Certain simple structured movement, drama, and art tasks have proven to be quite useful due to their wide applicability and ease of completion during each stage of treatment. Episodes of family free play are also useful in viewing how a family can organize themselves together in a relatively ambiguous situation that invites their open creative expression. Difficulties with developing organized play given varying kinds and amounts of structure provides indications of problems in the home setting. While no formal rating system has been developed for clinical application, certain principles guide observations of such activities into workable units.

The Play Room, Creative Materials and Projective Props

The most advantageous playroom for Dynamic Play is one in which a variety of expressive and imaginative activities are encouraged. It is best if such play is conducted in a relatively large open space where family members can use whole body movements. There should be potential for activity such as chase games, tug of wars, and hide and seek. Stuffed animals of varying sizes help suggest imagined dramatic play scenarios with families. Large soft pillows can be used to make physical play safe as well as in making houses or imagined walls. Colorful scarves and elastic ropes are easily employed in simple physical play and as props for large dramatic activity. Large sized newsprint paper along with varying types of markers, crayons, pencils, and clay should also be available. In general, the play material is relatively nonspecific and designed to help the family members use their physical, dramatic and artistic imagination to turn these materials into what their play demands in the moment and then to easily transform it into something else a few moments later. A large pillow might be used by a mother and preschooler as a safe place to fall into together as an ending of a chase game only to be used as a wall for an imaginary house filled with stuffed animals signifying both parents and children a few minutes later. It is very helpful to have a video camera and monitor in the room so that action episodes can be videoed and reviewed shortly after the performance.

Observational and Intervention Strategies

Qualitative impressions of performances can be organized through a series of more focused categories. Such categories are purposefully general to help the observer gain a view of the whole family atmosphere no matter how many individuals are involved. Using these observational strategies, an overall impression can be generated for a mother-child dyad as well as for a larger family of two parents and five children. The purpose of the categories is to develop a better understanding of how the mechanics of the family's play behaviors function. The family's play behaviors may contribute in a variety of ways: (1) to encourage a positive emotional atmosphere, (2) to engage in an intrinsic motivation to connect with each other, (3) to produce a sense of alienation and withdrawal from intimacy, or (4) to decrease the desire to solve problems in a mutual way. These categories help to clarify how expressive activities can be changed with intervention.

Attuned Play

Attunement in play refers to activity in which two or more players (usually parent and child) join together in the same event with a similar intent. Usually in attuned play the participants are using similar physical expressive rhythms within a close time and place proximity. For example, as a child begins a rapid circular walking movement during a follow-the-leader game, his parent matches his quickness and approximate path in attuned play. The parent slows and stops when the child does. Importantly, both family members exhibit similar affective states. Play interactions can have (1) no attuned events, (2) islands of attuned events separated by time, or (3) can have long periods of highly matched and attuned play in which the players co-create their play expressions together. When nonattuned play is observed, the therapist can extend the play parameters to allow for such mismatching to occur with the activity. For example if a parent and child separate themselves with a large distance in the playroom, the therapist can use storytelling to frame the separation as a "journey away or toward home." The family member can be asked to draw "feeling letters" and send them to each other. Expressive media can be changed as well.

Expressive Momentum

Expressive momentum is generated as parents and children share enough spontaneous attunement with each other that their play activity becomes more elaborated and includes new ideas, more shared movement, more imaginative metaphors, and more creative engagement over time. It is what is used to unite separate play events and players. Often as players share expressive momentum with each other the resulting play goes in unexpected directions. Such play often offers solutions to previous interactive difficulties. During this process, parents and children become intimate, flexible, and are open to each other. A great deal of pleasure is generated and experienced by all the family members. When little or no expressive momentum is present, interventions provide opportunities for family members to generate positive expression with each other. Such techniques include using props that connect the players physically such as stretch bands so that member can pull each other, balls or balloons that can be tossed, and scarves that can be thrown at each other. Setting these interactions within some kind of mutual simple competitive task such as keeping the balloons off the floor or seeing how many times a ball can be caught and not dropped, can also increase engagement in ongoing activity. Participants can then be encouraged to add their imagery to the activity such as identifying feelings with the scarves as they are throwing them at each other.

Flow/Break

This is the major observational and intervention tool in Dynamic Play. The observer watches when the players use expressive momentum and attuned play in which one event leads easily to the next over time and when such flow is broken or interrupted. This tool is meant to help the observer focus on the play process rather than on the actual content of what is being played out. Here it is more important to identify how, by whom, and when the mutual play is continued or stopped. Flow is the activity that occurs when the players are jointly playing together. Breaks are those events that function to stop the flow. Examples of breaks include: one partner changing the rules of an activity while another continues, strong shifts in emotional states, small injuries, very unexpected and surprising play expressions, and harsh verbalizations. After such variations in play expression are noticed, the task of the therapist is to incorporate such expression into a new play structure in an improvised way. The breaks are conceptualized as representing the family's basic insecurity and resulting core emotional conflict intruding into the flow of intimate play. Such breaks are how core emotional conflict arises in improvised play. The new rearranged play expression that can emerge from the incorporation of these breaks is thought to represent the emerging of therapeutic change. It is this mutual experience of a creative state shared together that is thought to foster new emotional intimacy even if such breaks are small and the newly improvised play form varies only slightly from the more rigid play originally introduced.

Form and Energy Balance

A functional balance between form and energy needs to occur for an improvised flow of family play to proceed. In this context, form is the ability to establish boundaries, definition, and focus for expressive activity. Energy refers to the more improvised and freely generated expressions. Form is usually accomplished with the use of rules, verbalizations, and planning and redirecting activities. Energy is generated by impulsive expression that is quite often physical and has intrinsic or internal motivation. When play has too much form, alienation can occur. When it has too much energy, expression can be random, scattered, and lose a shared focus. As play improvisation stops, the form and energy lose balance. If activity becomes too disorganized, interventions such as slowing down the action, adding rules, switching media, or involving less people are used to add more form. If action loses expressive interest and becomes overly rigid, interventions to add more energy are used such as suggesting that individuals extend what they are already doing further, involving physical activity, or carrying out dramatic action to its end through imaginative leaps. If, for example, a follow-the-leader game has degenerated into the children running throughout the room, form can be added by turning the activity into a slow motion game in which one partner calls, "slow," and another, "fast" with such rules determining the speed at which the family moves. This activity can be videoed and how the rules were followed can be discussed after a short game episode. If, on the other hand a follow-the-leader game has become overly rule-bound and some individuals are losing interest, energy can added by turning the game into chase with no bases.

Play Metaphors and Imagery

It is important for the therapist to make note of dramatic and/or verbal images which are (1) repeated throughout the assessment, (2) suggestive of strong emotional themes such as nurturance, aggression, and victimization, (3) are expressed while in isolated play, and (4) are not addressed or resolved in family expression. Usually such imagery contains themes that are relevant to the family's functioning and difficulties. It is important to understand how such imagery functions within the context of the created play episode. Such imagery is placed within the categories of attuned play, expressive momentum, or flow/break to help develop such a contextual understanding of this imagery.

If a child introduces play breaks by physically distancing himself from his parents when nurturant themes are introduced in dramatic play, for example, the therapist might bring up the question of how nurturance is experienced by the parents and child. Similarly, if a parent and child are able to generate expressive momentum when they introduce themes of leading and following, a possible positive aspect of power sharing might be present in the parent/child relationship. Such salient imagery and play themes are very useful for the therapist to help the families connect emotional meaning to their play. Scenes that extend this imagery become a very effective way to heighten core emotional experience that has not been consciously expressed within family communication. The distancing behavior in the presence of nurturant themes can turn into a story of running away with a parental search to further a theme of separation.

Parent/Child Roles

Dynamic play can be a very flexible expressive experience. However, parents are mostly in the role of facilitator/player while the children are more in the role of a player only. While styles can vary widely, parents who have secure relationships with their children usually move a little slower, use more levels, produce less images, and respond to, elaborate with, and organize their children's more spontaneous play impulses. Parents certainly can and do introduce and initiate spontaneous ideas of their own but it is usually accomplished with the flexibility to return to a supportive role when needed. The main model of parent play is to respond to the child's initiation and then to help elaborate and extend these child impulses into a more organized whole. Observation of parent/child functioning in the family play can help the therapist better understand what may be happening between them in a more general way. When such parent or child roles are not functioning in this way, interventions can be set up realign the interactions. For example when a follow-the-leader game breaks down with either an overly rigid parental leadership or overly active child response, a new game can be introduced in which the parent is the "Big Leader," or the one who decides when to change leadership. Parents can then be coached to recognize child initiatives and to elaborate and organize such initiatives by how and when they choose the child to begin and stop being leader.

Techniques for Stage One: Evaluation Activities

Treatment begins with an initial interview in which the therapist meets with the family. In this session the family is asked to describe their current problems and give a history of events in their life which are relevant to development of these problems as well as how discipline and play occur. A family is also asked to describe any major experiences with trauma, emotional loss or separations. The parents are then asked about how they were parented and about their experiences with the birth and early life of their various children. In the next session, families are observed completing a series of expressive play activities that are designed to highlight particular aspects of their interactions.

Observations should be carried out with activities involving movement games, art, and drama to view interactions across a variety of expressive modalities. Free play in which families generate expression of their own choosing when given access to all the play materials also provides useful information as to how activity is improvised and structured and what media are preferred. General interactive themes that repeat in the various forms of expression are significant. Some families show particular strengths with one medium while being unable to generate useful play in the other areas. To accomplish this multimodal evaluation, observations of activities focus on three types of expression, (1) primarily physical–tasks in which full bodily expression is central such as tug of wars, chase, or an improvised soccer match; (2) primarily dramatic–tasks involving mutual role taking, storytelling and the use of verbal imagination such as becoming an animal; and/or (3) primarily artistic–tasks that involve mutual drawing such as mural making. Free play is accomplished by having the family come into the playroom with no preset directions except to invite them to play as they wish. The therapist chooses the number of activities needed in order to get to know the family. This series of activities usually includes one dramatic, graphic, and movement activity from the list below.

Activities are then performed by the family to their completion with little or no comment by the therapist. Such episodes can be videoed for later review. Each family's unique communicative style influences both the process and the content of their play performance. The therapist then helps the family make connections between the play and their problematic behavior and past psychological history. Then the family including the children are asked to design how their play might be like if their problems were resolved. Therapy goals are then set using both play images as well as verbal statements. Evaluation activities include:

FOLLOW THE LEADER WITH EVERYONE GETTING A CHANCE TO BE LEADER. This activity pulls for how power is shared in the family. Successful families usually allow all members no matter how young to be a leader with other members in the following role. Such games usually turn into spontaneous play improvisations which loosely keep the leadership structure but change to allow for all members to express their enthusiasm. Problem families have trouble allowing such leadership as one member dominates the others in some way. Such domination significantly interferes with the contribution of others.

SWING YOUR CHILD INTO A PILE OF PILLOWS/CALM YOUR CHILD DOWN. This activity samples general parent/child attunement. Successful families use positive body contact and are able to coordinate their swing in such a way that positive feelings are shared. This game usually ends with the children asking for "more!" Children are calmed down with a physical activity usually led by the parents with is slower and involves slower breathing and calm verbalizations. Problematic families usually show a great deal of physical discomfort and are unable both to generate positive feeling in the swing and are not able to calm down when asked.

SHOW A STORY ABOUT A FAMILY OF ANIMALS/PARENTS AND CHILDREN TOGETHER AND CHILDREN ALONE. In successful families, disturbing themes and imagery are resolved and play activities and themes are relatively continuous from scenes in which parents are present through scenes in which children are playing by themselves. Problematic families introduce distressing themes and imagery without resolution. Such themes usually do not make much dramatic sense in the stories being created and tend to repeat in intrusive ways. Play is very different with parents and children together and when the parents leave children alone to play by themselves. Often in families in which secrets are an issue, children will introduce themes around the secret during their solo play and change their play completely when their parents return to rejoin them. If a parent/child relationship is insecure, interactive play with that parent is less developed. Likewise if abandonment or loss is affecting the family, children's solo play is then also affected often to the point that they are not able to play at all even if they are beyond their early preschool years.

MUTUAL DRAWINGS. Families with children old enough to begin mark making can be observed drawing with their parents. Parents are asked to draw with these toddlers or young preschoolers and then move away to the other side of the room while their child continues. The parents are then asked to rejoin. The resulting series of pictures can reflect the children's feelings concerning attachment and separation. Older children (4–5) and their parents are asked to independently draw a house and themselves coming out of this house to join each other in some activity. More normal families can accomplish this and usually draw themselves together doing something. Problematic families are not able to create such mutuality. Families with children over six are also asked to each independently draw their house on a sheet of paper. Then each member is asked to take a series of turns creating a series of roads and a town on a large single paper. After several rounds of adding some part to the town and system of roads, each family member is then asked to draw themselves coming out of their house and meeting the other people. Usually some mutual story develops using both sketch mark making and storytelling. The idea behind this activity is for the family first to mutually make a "game" of interaction, the town with a series or houses and roads, and then to play with it by coming out and interacting with each other. Again, problematic families find this quite difficult while more successful families can use both drawing and imaginative storytelling to create several interactive scenes. Another drawing activity includes having the family draw themselves doing something together.

PARENT TELLING THE CHILD THE STORY OF HIS/HER BIRTH, LEAVING FOR A BRIEF TIME, AND THEN RETURNING AND TELLING THE CHILD HIS/HER FUTURE. These series of activities were adaptive from the Marasack Interaction Method (Marasack, 1960). In the MIM, these activities are considered as separate and are completed while one parent and child dyad are seated with each other at a table. In Dynamic Play, these activities occur together to sample the family representation of feelings concerning attachment and future. Whole families can complete this series. Families are asked to complete the activities in the playroom and have full access to all the materials so different forms of movement and dramatic enactment are possible. Usually the pillows are used to help assist parents and children in sitting together in ways that can be very intimate and comfortable to them. Observations of the dramatic and physical presentation along with the verbal narrative of these events are used to identify a family's metaphorical "story" as well as observe the kind of physically felt security they generate among themselves. As with other activities, problematic families show difficulty generating emotional security and the stories of birth and future have little continuity. Separations produce little additional play activity and are generally full of distress for the children. For successful families, this series of activities are performed with shared enjoyment.

PARENT TEACHES THE CHILD SOMETHING. This activity is another adaptation from the MIM. In the dynamic play version, a parent is asked to teach their children something. The family has access to all the play and art materials and the whole room. This activity samples the parent's ability to offer both structure and challenge in a learning task to their child/children as well as sampling a child's ability to orient to the environment and use play to learn something new. Again successful families are able to teach their children something and usually with some imaginative techniques. Problematic families are not able to accomplish this task and both parents and children become disinterested or distractible quickly.

FACE GAMES. Parents and children are asked to look at each other and make faces. This activity pulls for ability for families to experience intimacy. Intimate families can maintain eye contact in an enjoyable way and play with each other by making several faces while experiencing positive feelings between them. Problematic families have particular difficulty gaining and maintaining eye contact. Their face play is characterized by avoidance and discomfort. Even if they do make faces at each other, very little time is spent looking at the partner such that the faces seem somewhat unresponsive and wooden.

COMPLETE AN OBSTACLE COURSE WHILE TIED TOGETHER. This activity pulls for a family's ability to be physically intimate as well as engage in cooperative problem solving. The therapist sets up various obstacles throughout the room using the pillows and other props. The family members are then connected with the stretchy ropes and asked to go from one part of the room to another. Successful families engage in physical cooperation to get over and through the piles of props while the problematic families often avoid the obstacles all together or even become argumentative as to how to proceed.

TECHNIQUES FOR STAGE TWO: INITIAL GAMES. Following the evaluation process and the development of therapy goals in both play and verbal terms, the therapist and family begin a series of activities designed to help the family begin to organize their play improvisations with both more focus on emotional issues as well as encouraging positive feelings with each other. A main goal for the play is for the family to experience some expressive momentum and positive feelings that come with such play. Often these activities take on a game-like format, with rules to organize give and take, turn taking, and mutual participation and a competitive element to help generate more motivation, challenge, and expressive momentum between the family members. A by-product of such competition is that parents and children actually begin to play together for longer periods of time in an engaged way. These games are therapist directed at first. An initial starting place for improvisation is set up. This starting place has a simple interactive task with basic rules.

The format of these initial games usually offers a solution to the surface problem presented by the family such that if the game can be completed with some imagination and enjoyment, the problem will likely be reduced at home. However, due to the attachment and trust-related difficulties, it is expected that such initial structures will take on a life of their own as the family introduces breaks and various disorganizing communications. By using these breaks and allowing the games to become more individualized, a more emotionally relevant interactive scene is thought to emerge.

During this stage, various sub-groupings of the family are seen together. Children and parents can even be seen in solo sessions with the understanding that they will come back together and involve each other in play activities they develop by themselves. Parent sessions may also involve verbal sessions to address their parenting and behavioral management issues. Some expressive activity is expected to come out of these sessions as well. Usually the initial games are conducted with one or both parents and the most problematic child. Then after some success in developing more spontaneous play, these games are extended to other siblings.

It is expected that the family's emotional difficulties will then introduce breaks into this initial format especially when they begin to experience positive mutual emotion. The therapist notices these breaks and helps the family change their game to better incorporate these breaks into the improvisations. This changes the original game into something more emotionally relevant. These second order or third order games are usually not something the family would do using their more defensive play style. But as the therapist coaches creative play, more options are introduced. An example of using play breaks to change mutual play occurred with a mother and her recently adopted six-year-old daughter. The girl had been taken from an abusive family situation some years before and had been in several foster families prior to placement with her adoptive family. She had difficulty trusting adults. The adoptive mother reported that the girl was misbehaving at home despite the positive redirection she had offered. The therapist directed the two to sit close together and play face games with each other. This was immediately difficult for the girl and she kept avoiding the adoptive mother's eyes. The therapist used this as the opportunity to define the play problem as the inability to maintain eye contact in a playful way.

He then introduced an initial game of having each draw the other's face. The girl refused to complete the drawing and kept looking behind her to the back of the room. The therapist used this break in the activity to introduce a new direction. He asked the girl to go to where she was looking. She then went to the back of the room and crawled into the pillows. She was asked to make the pillows into a house. As she did, she began to look at her mother in a game-like way. The therapist used this as a cue to begin a game in which the girl tried to look at her mother without being seen while her mother tried to see her as well. As the game progressed the girl tried to look quickly at her in an engaged way, and the mother picked up on the game, trying to catch the quick glimpse as well. They became caught up in the game together and the play became more naturally attuned. The girl became quite involved in trying to outwit her mother by looking without being seen.

The therapist at this time asked the girl if she could imagine herself as an animal. She replied that she was a squirrel. The therapist then improvised a story about a young squirrel and her mother squirrel, having the story match their looking actions. The story proceeded into the next session. Finally the girl asked her mother squirrel to come up into her home. At this point, the therapist suggested the squirrel had found her mother and was able to discuss what accepting a new mother was like for the girl.

The process of developing an interactive metaphor that had relevance to this adoptive mother and girl from a simple game of making faces developed in a straightforward and rapid way. Usually such metaphors occur over many sessions and takes several games which lead in different directions before something as clearly relevant is co-created in such as spontaneous way. However, this example points to the general flow of using an initial activity to start interactive play which the therapist guides using the physical breaks in interaction as cues to develop an entirely new game format. The combination of using the avoidance of eye contact, and the challenge of not being seen to develop some expressive momentum in the girl's expression toward her adoptive mother, and the additional expressive media of storytelling helped this parent and child experience co-creating a metaphor together that had relevance to their family life. This play experience helped them find intimacy together in a relatively natural way.

The following are some initial games that have proven quite useful as a general play activity that leads to breaks which in turn can be developed into intrinsic improvisations around common family problems. Some general paths the breaks can lead into will be presented for the first game "monster." Other games will be presented to address several presenting problems. This list is not exhaustive however. As each game and resulting improvisation is responsive to the moment-to-moment play of each family, these examples are thought of as good starting places only.

Monster

This initial structure is very useful for children who have experienced trauma after they have became comfortable with using the different media to express themselves. In this game, the therapist uses a stuffed animal to approach the child and parent with the instruction to tell the monster to "go away." As the monster approaches, the therapist watches how both the parent and child react and then uses that reaction as the cue to chase the monster away. If the child becomes very frightened and is unable to verbalize, the therapist uses the strongest physical reaction as the way to chase the monster away. So if the child's foot begins to move, the therapist encourages the child and parent to kick the monster away. If the child begins to blink his/her eyes, then blinking the eyes becomes the way to send the monster away and the animal takes one step back with each blink of the eye.

The game is played using the parents and child's physical cues this way to encourage more engaged physical "chasing." Several times as the child elaborates this game, he/she may pretend to die. One way this death can be extended to facilitate security in a family is for a parent to be coached to come over the "dead" child's body and wait until the child initiates some small movement. The parent is then encouraged to make dances using touch and small movements of their own with the child's moving part, usually fingers or toes, as a way to bring the child back to life. Other play surprises can be extended in a similar way to produce a unique dramatic scene of dealing with this fearful image. The following are some other helpful starting places:

Volcano

This initial game is useful to help with anger. In this activity, a child is asked to lie down and pillows are piled up over him/her. The child is then asked to kick the pillows off while the therapist and parents try to throw them back on. A game develops where the child attempts to keep the pillows off while the adults throw them back. The child is then asked to draw a picture of the volcano and asked to identify what feelings are in the volcano in his/her body.

The Trouble Pit

This activity is used when a child has been unable to stop their misbehavior both at home and at school. The parents and child are directed to use all the props to make a large pile called the trouble pit. The child is told to get into the pit and the parent given the task of getting the child out by any means including physically pulling them out.

Goodland and Badland

In this activity, the child and a parent divide the room into a good part to represent acceptable home behavior and a bad part to represent misbehavior. The parent is asked to start off trying to get the child to come into Goodland without crossing over into Badland. Often the parent uses the stretch rope to lasso the child and pull him/her out, while the child tries to run and hide under pillows. Roles can be reversed.

The Stealing Game

This activity is used with families who have a child who steals. The room is again divided between the parent's side and the child's side. All of the play props are on the parent's side and the child is told to try to "steal" the parent-controlled props by moving them to his/her side. The parent tries to keep this from happening. As the child gets one prop, he/she can tell the parent to immobilize one body part such as "close your eyes." As more props are taken, the child is able to have the parent immobilize more parts such as putting an arm behind the back. This continues one for each item taken to the child's side until there is nothing left to "steal." The roles can be reversed several times. Often in this role reversal, the game breaks down and offers several new types of game opportunities such as with the adult trying to "find" a child who is "hiding" or has disappeared in the props.

The Telling Ball or Scarf

This activity is used when a family member, usually the child, has a secret or is very constricted in their expression of feelings. This activity is not used when active ongoing abuse is occurring. It is a good activity when a child is in a safe home. The child is asked to make "safe lands" of pillows and then go between these areas. The parent or therapist then throws a soft Nurf® ball or scarf to touch the child. If the child is touched, then he or she has to tell one "part" of the secret or feeling. So if a scarf touches an ankle, the child tells an "ankle's worth" assuming that the whole body is the secret. An alternative is to have the child show a dance of the secret using the touched part and not use words at all. So if an ankle is touched, the child makes a spontaneous dance using the ankle to show the feeling.

The Scarf Story

This activity is used with very impulsive children and/or who also have difficulty expressing their feelings. In this activity, the parents and the therapist move a scarf or parachute up and down at varying speeds. A child is underneath and moves in a dance while the material is raised and stops when the material is brought down. The therapist helps the parents tell a story about the child using the child's movement. The verbal comments initially describe the child's movement and then feelings are attributed. Finally a story line can be developed.

Scribble Drawings

This activity is used when family members have a conflict and are unable to change it.

Usually this is best done with just two individuals. Large paper is used. The two members are instructed to choose a single color and try to place more scribbles on the paper than their partner. One person is instructed to start the contest with a "go" while the other stops the contest with "stop." When the contest is over a winner is chosen. As this is usually impossible, another contest usually occurs. The family members are then asked to use their imagination to find a character or animal in the resulting scribble. The therapist then leads a conversation between these two figures. Stories and enactment can follow. The resulting imaginative conversation usually has metaphorical significance for the individuals. Often this is a more painful emotional issue that the constant conflict is not allowing into open family communication.

Another version of the scribble drawing can occur with preschool-aged children and their parents. As a child begins to scribble, the parent is encouraged to match or follow the child's marks. The therapist then begins to tell a story about the little girl (boy) scribble and the mommy (daddy) scribble using a combination of the mark-making activity and what the emotional issues are at hand. Comments like "the little girl scribble ran away while the mommy scribble kept trying to help her find a home" could easily occur in such a story. Such stories are used to reinforce the positive aspects of the attachment between the parent and child.

Maps and Obstacle Courses

These activities are used with children who are somewhat older (over eight) and after understanding of the presenting problems in the home has been achieved. The instruction is to identify a starting and ending place either in the room or on paper. The starting place is defined as the current state and the ending place a time when the problems have been solved. The individual child or child with parent are then asked to design all the obstacles and emotional trials that must be confronted before the end place can be reached. The map is drawn and the course is completed both with and without parents present. Older boys in particular have become very engaged in using a high wall of pillows to represent the problems to be overcome in therapy. Such a wall becomes a place to be high jumped over and and/or run through. It is when parents are included in these activities that breaks often appear.

Movie Making

Older latency-aged boys in particular become very engaged in movie making using the video equipment. Movies can also be used to address reoccurring conflicts within a family. Such videos are made in the office and then taken home to be viewed and extended using imaginative devices. One way to start movie making with children is to have them close their eyes and have a parent or therapist design a scene around them using the stuffed animals, pillows, scarves and other props. When the child opens his/her eyes the scene is described as a dream or an underwater event. The child's resulting enactment is filmed and reviewed for updates and extensions. Families or a parent/child dyad who have an ongoing conflict are asked to imagine this conflict as a recent popular movie and use the movie name as a label. The family is then asked to make a brief episode of this movie together using the play materials. This episode is then filmed. The result is taken home for viewing at prescribed times, either before or after their actual home argument.

Techniques for Stage Three: The Core Scene

As the family members are able to generate more organized and self-sustaining play interactions without the coaching of the therapist, treatment enters the stage of using their play to address their main emotional concerns. Some families reach this stage relatively quickly, however other families whose attachments are less secure will take many more sessions of guidance. The therapist is able to use the family's ability to generate enjoyable interactive play together using a free play format with few initial games or other therapist-coached intervention as an indicator of readiness. At this time, the therapist then will begin to bring up the important events surrounding trauma, separations, and loss as possibilities to be included in the expressive activity more consciously. Even the possibility of change can represent conflict. Often the emotionality of such events has presented itself in the dramatic themes and imagery from the extended initial games or from free play. The therapist can encourage the family to use such themes with more awareness in the play. As such past events are usually quite painful, rituals can be used as well. The family usually needs several sessions to address these core issues in a creative manner to help them achieve some emotional resolution and acceptance. Such play rituals are planned and prepared. The whole family is brought back together for such events.

The therapist's role during this stage is more of an observer and facilitator than an active participant. The following are rituals that can be adapted for use at this stage of treatment. The family and therapist can develop other rituals as well.

The Emotional Courtroom

Many children have experienced major life changes or been influenced by legal decisions. Often they have not been present and almost universally they experience feelings of helplessness and not having their experience considered. Even if they have been legally well represented, the courtroom is not an avenue for the expression and resolution of emotions surrounding trauma from abuse or attachment and loss. Many children who are abused have the experience that the people who have abused them are not punished and certainly have no concept of their experience. Such feelings can impact their family life. The following ritual drama was designed to address this issue in a family setting.

This scene has been adapted for adoption (particularly for the adoption of children beyond infancy) as well as for abuse victims. In this drama, the therapist usually plays the judge and the child and parents present the evidence using art work, videos from past therapy, and direct verbal statements concerning their feelings about the past events. The adoption scene is a more dramatic adaptation of a ritual described by Imber-Black (1989). In the dynamic play adoption scene, the therapist/ judge questions the adoptive parents on their intention about keeping their child and their ability to unconditionally love and accept the child even if misbehavior and conflict occurs. The questions are adapted to what has occurred throughout the course of therapy. The child then hears this evidence and decides if the parents will be adopted. As this scene has been prepared for several weeks by the family, the outcome is known in advance. However the ritual of courtroom helps with the final resolution. A document is prepared of the child's adoption of the family using art materials to end this ritual.

The emotional courtroom is also used for victims of physical and sexual violence. In such scenes, the therapist again plays the judge, and the parents are the child's attorneys. An image of the perpetrator is created through art work or casting an animal into the role. The therapist asks questions about how the violence has changes the victim's life and especially about their emotional reactions. Questions of punishment to "even the score" are discussed by all and an emotional punishment is issued.

Loss

Rituals for the death for a family member are designed, prepared for and enacted in this stage of therapy as well. Divorce can be thought of as the death of the previous family and a ritual can be performed by the members of the original family. The form of these events is similar. Art and other representations of the past are made together and then buried in the playroom or some other place chosen by the family.

Holidays and Birthdays

Major holiday events, birthdays, and changes in residences can also be addressed with ritual. Birthdays are celebrated by having parents and children design a place for the younger age and a place for the new age. A method of physical transport between the ages is then designed. Dances are encouraged. Speeches and art works are prepared to announce all the changes the child and family has gone through. This ritual is also used to prepare for the end of therapy. At Christmas time, parents and children are asked to use the pillows and scarves to wrap up the child as a present for the parent. The parent then approaches the present and opens the package. This event is filmed to be viewed when the family opens presents at this holiday. This ritual of having the child be the parent's present is usually quite positive and generates a significant amount of strong feelings for the parent. Often such feelings are addressed in individual sessions prior to the ritual.

An example of how such a ritual event helped resolve a core emotional event developed from this Christmas present event. A ten-year-old girl had come to live with her father after having been separated from him through a divorce when she was an infant. The girl's mother was unable to care for her, and the girl had been sexually and physically assaulted throughout her life. She had been removed from her mother's care and the father had resumed caring for her in his new family. She initially was very withdrawn and irritable and showed significant problems learning. After she and her father had successfully completed several initial games and were able to play freely together the therapist suggested that they complete the present ritual. When the father opened the present box of pillows and scarves containing his daughter, she immediately leaped into his arms to the surprise and emotional relief of them both. The girl and father repeated the opening of the present several times. This was very moving and helped establish an attachment that no amount of verbal reassurance had been able to secure. Though this father and daughter still had to talk about the specifics of her past, the present ritual provided the emotional resolution between them.

Techniques for Stage Four: Free Play and Termination

The final stage of therapy consists of allowing the family to engage in free play together with each other in a natural way. The therapist assumes the role of observer at this time reflecting themes and feelings as well as pointing out changes in the play style. Positive moments that occur spontaneously are particularly important to notice and reinforce. Comparisons of original play style and themes are made with current expressions and play themes. Termination of therapy is addressed by reviewing the play episodes and art material. As the end date gets closer, the therapist and family prepare drawings of what they remember. A final session is planned and a ritual is developed. The family is encouraged to discuss their newfound capacity to play at home.

Populations Served

Dynamic Family Play is a very flexible form and can be used with populations of any age. However, the basics of the techniques presented here are best used with families whose children are preteen and under. Family therapy with teenage children is best done with primarily drama techniques not presented here. Also creative art therapy approaches for adults are likewise presented more fully in other chapters of this volume. Developmentally appropriate adaptations for interventions with toddlers are discussed more fully in the author's work elsewhere (Harvey, 1994c). Within the population of families with young children, dynamic family play has been used with families who have significant problems due to attachment difficulties and trauma. Specific case material and techniques dealing with adoption (Harvey, 1992), with sexual abuse and adoption (Harvey, 1994), with ritual abuse (Harvey, 1993), and with physical abuse and divorce (Harvey, 1997) have been presented elsewhere.

Limitations, Challenges, and Growing Edge

Recently dynamic play has been used in a brief therapy format to meet the current demand for short-term services. There seems to be a potential for the development of focused action-oriented and solution-oriented approaches in short-term treatment. Because of the emphasis on positive family interaction and the use of play metaphors to concretely define therapy goals, dynamic family play appears to offer techniques that can be adapted for brief therapy. This is particularly true for families whose problems are with adjustment-related events rather than more profound attachment and trauma conflicts. Currently the author is using the evaluation techniques as a way to define problems and map out strategies for problem solution in play terms so as to involve the children in such interventions. This area offers an area of new development.

CASE EXAMPLE

Mary was referred for treatment by her adoptive mother when she was ten years old due to her increasing inability to maintain relations with her peers, emotional withdrawal in the home and her increasing sadness. Mary had been removed from her home at the age of two and a half due to significant neglect. The social services agency had also confirmed that she had been sexually assaulted by her mother and father. She had received a long-term intervention when she had been originally adopted which had been very successful in helping her make an adequate family adjustment. However, as is often the case with children who have experienced trauma at young ages, her adoptive mother stated that she again needed treatment.

After a brief interview in which the therapist reviewed Mary's history with her and her adoptive mother, the therapist asked Mary and mother to make up a story with the animals. The story was about a family completing a series of normal daily events. Then Mary's mother was asked to leave. Mary stopped almost all activity, and described falling into a long dark cave. She lay motionless while this was occurring. When the mother returned, Mary had seated herself and was not able to play with her mother in any activity. The therapist reviewed this with Mary and her mother and set a therapy goal of having the mother be able to go into the cave with Mary as a way to understand her fears which were likely a recurrent theme from her past.

The therapist set up an initial game of volcano to focus on Mary being able to express whatever she might be experiencing in the cave metaphor. Mary's mother was present and was about to take a turn with her daughter under the pillows in the volcano. However, Mary changed the game and crawled out of the pillows as a new character in an angry role. As Mary was told that she should be kicking the pillows, her coming out in a dramatic role was a clear break in the game. The therapist then changed the activity to accommodate this meeting of a girl who had survived a volcano. An interview with the character followed. The character was named Victoria by Mary. Victoria was clearly quite powerful and full of rage. As this change in activity was clearly more dramatic rather than movement-oriented, the therapist encouraged Mary to become several other characters. She then taught these personalities to the therapist and the mother and several scenes developed. One of these characters was very nice and polite and another was quite withdrawn.

Mary became very interested in younger toddler-aged children at this time. She brought a picture of herself with her birth mother at this time at the therapist's urging. During one of the dramas in which the characters were meeting, the polite girl wanted to play being a mother to one of her dolls. The other characters, Victoria in particular, would have none of it. Several scenes were set up with the polite girl in which she attempted to take care of the baby doll. These scenes were prepared for by having Mary pick out lullaby music, sing it to her baby, and even make a lullaby dance using the soothing rhythms from her chosen music. However every time in the scene in which Mary approached the doll she could not hold the doll. This inability to involve her body was noticed and pointed out as a break by the therapist. The mother was asked if she could hold Mary. Mary was verbally agreeable to this but was unable to relax in a way in which she could calm down in her mother's arms.

Mary then reported feeling wild when her teacher called her "sweet." The therapist used these physical events as well as the reaction of being "wild" as cues to set up another series of games. Over the next series of sessions, Mary was asked to divide up the room into a calm side and a wild side to physicalize the feelings she was verbalizing. There was a clear dividing line. Music was chosen for each side to help her make a wild or calm dance. The calm music was again the lullaby music from the earlier scenes and the wild music was a piece of contemporary rock and roll. Mary chose her mother to be on the calming side along with several very soft large pillows. The therapist was chosen to be on the wild side. Scarves were selected to help make a "wild dance." A great deal of time was devoted to making a machine out of pillows which would transform Mary from calm to wild and back again. Clearly Mary was showing a great deal of expressive momentum in this project. In the session when the dances and switching were to occur, Mary was only able to dance on the "wild" side for a very brief time and returned to the calm side. Even on this side she was quite dazed and did not relax or respond to her mother's touch and holding.

During the next session, the therapist mentioned the break of the emotional shift from excitement to the unexpected fearful response to the wild dance. He suggested that Mary and her mother use art work for a few sessions. They chose to draw events from Mary's past. When they were drawing a picture of a family, Mary brought up her birth parents and how angry she was at them for leaving and sexually abusing her. The therapist suggested that she might go back into a dramatic activity to put them on trial. The intervention then entered the stage of addressing the core scene. Mary, her adoptive mother, and therapist then planned how to set up the emotional courtroom. The therapist played the judge and the prosecutor, the adoptive mother played Mary's attorney, and the large stuffed animal was the birth parents. Mary got her chance to give her emotional evidence and offer a sentence. During the scene, Mary was unable to complete her testimony. The therapist then suggested that the character of Victoria could be brought in to help testify. Mary then changed into this character and was able to express a great deal of anger at the figures representing her birth parents. Though she considered it, "Victoria" was unable to pronounce a death sentence on the parents. A conference was then held between Victoria, the other characters Mary had identified, the therapist and the adoptive mother and it was decided that the parents would always be without the love of a child and the social services agency would again be notified to ensure that no other children would again be so misused. A meeting with the social service worker was set up.

This trial lasted several sessions and was improvised easily by all involved without requiring any coaching by the therapist. The scenes themselves were quite emotionally cathartic for Mary and her adoptive mother. Mary and her adoptive mother were able to connect their expressive momentum to a very emotionally relevant event in their life in a way that balanced both the form and energy of play improvisation. The meaning of the play metaphor was also very clear to all the participants. The development of this core scene was not known by anyone prior to the beginning of treatment and unfolded in a seemingly natural way as the therapist helped Mary and her adoptive mother to incorporate various breaks in the play flow utilizing several expressive media.

After the series of trials, Mary and her adoptive mother designed and enacted several free play sessions. In one of these Mary wanted her mother to join her in making a volcano and throwing and kicking pillows and stuffed animals out of a large area she called home. She was able to do this using her body in a very forceful way. She also stated that she enjoyed the activity very much. Termination included a review of the events and watching old films of the various parts of treatment. A good-bye ritual was planned in which the adoptive mother, Mary, and therapist ate together. A real picnic was planned for and occurred some weeks later. Mary's depressive and agitated behavior had lessened significantly over the year of treatment and she had formed a friendship with another girl her age. Mary, her adoptive mother and therapist considered treatment a success.

REFERENCES

Banes, S. (1980). *Terpsichore in sneakers: Post modern dance.* Boston: Houghton Mifflin.

Bowlby, J. (1972). *Attachment and loss: Vol. I, Attachment.* London: Hograth Press.

Bowlby, J. (1973). *Attachment and loss: Vol. II, Separation.* New York: Basic Books.

Bowlby, J. (1980). *Attachment and loss: Vol. III, Loss.* New York: Basic Books.

Byng-Hall, J. (1991). The use of attachment in understanding and treatment in family therapy. In C.M Parks, J. Stevenson-Hynde, & P. Marks (Eds.), *Attachment across the life cycle.* London: Tavistock-Rutledge.

Chaikin, H. (Ed.). (1975). *Marian Chace: Her papers.* Columbia, MD: American Dance Therapy Association.

Getzels, J.W., & Csikzentmihalyi, M. (1976). *The creative vision: A longitudinal study of problem finding in art.*

Grotowski, J. (1968). *Towards a poor theatre.* New York: Simon and Schuster.

Harvey, S.A. (1990). Dynamic play therapy: An integrated expressive arts approach to the family therapy of young children. *The Arts in Psychotherapy, 17* (3), 239–246.

Harvey, S.A. (1991). Creating a family: An integrated expressive arts approach to adoption. *The Arts in Psychotherapy, 18* (3), 213–222.

Harvey, S.A. (1993). Ann: Dynamic play therapy with ritual abuse. In T. Kottman & C. Schaefer (Eds.), *Play therapy in action: A case book for practitioners.* New Jersey: Jason Aronson, Inc.

Harvey, S.A., & Kelly, E.C. (1993). The influence of the quality of early interactions on a three years play narratives. *The Arts in Psychotherapy, 20,* 387–395.

Harvey, S.A. (1994a). Dynamic play therapy: Expressive play intervention with families. In K. O'Connor & C. Schaefer (Eds.), *Handbook of play therapy: Volume two, advances and innovations.* New York: John Wiley & Sons.

Harvey, S.A. (1994b). Dynamic play therapy: creating attachments. In B. James *Handbook for treatment of attachment-trauma problems in children.* New York: Lexington Books.

Harvey, S.A. (1994c). Dynamic play therapy: A integrated expressive arts approach to family treatment of infants and toddlers. *Zero to Three. 15,* 11–17.

Harvey, S.A. (1995). Sandra: The case of an adopted sexually abused child. In F. Levy (Ed.), *Dance and other expressive arts therapies: When words are not enough.* New York: Routledge.

Harvey, S., & Soderquist, M. (1995). Results of the Malmo project. Conference presentation at the twenty-eighth annual conference of the American Dance Therapy Conference. Rye, New York.

Harvey, S.A. (1997). Dynamic play therapy: A creative arts approach. In K. O'Connor & L. Braverman (Eds.), *Play therapy theory and practice: A comparative presentation.* New York: John Wiley & Sons.

Imber-Black, E., Roberts, J., & Whiting, R. (Eds.). *Rituals in families and family therapy.* New York: Norton.

James, B. (1994). *Handbook for treatment of attachment-trauma problems in children.* New York: Lexington.

Lewis, P. (1984). *Theoretical approaches in dance movement therapy. Vol. II.* Dubuque, IA: Kendall/Hunt.

Marschak, M. (1960). A method for evaluating parent-child interactions under controlled conditions. *Journal of Genetic Psychology. 97,* 3–22.

Robbins, A. (1986). *Expressive therapy: A creative arts approach to depth-oriented treatment.* New York: Human Sciences Press.

Schaefer, C., & Carey, L. (1994). *Family play therapy.* New Jersey: Jason Aronson Inc.

Schaefer. C. (1993). *The therapeutic powers of play.* Palo Alto: Science and Behavior Books.

Schechner, R. (1970). *Dionysus in 69: The performance group.* New York: Farrar, Stratus, and Giroux.

Smith, N.S. (1982). *Personal communication.* Boulder, CO.

Stern, D. (1985). *The interpersonal world of the infant: A view from psychoanalysis and developmental psychology.* New York: Basic Books.

Stern, D. (1990). *The diary of a baby.* New York: Basic Books.

Torrence, E.P. (1974). *Torrence test of creative thinking.* Lexington, MA: Ginn.

Tortera, S. (1994). Join my dance: The unique movement style of each infant and toddler can invite communication, expression, and intervention. *Zero to Three. 15,* 1–10.

FURTHER TRAINING AND STUDY

At present, training in dynamic play is offered only by the author. Such training is advertised by the International Association of Play Therapy and the National Association of Drama Therapy. Several case studies and applications of these techniques are included in the references at the end of this chapter.

Section III

COMPARATIVE ANALYSIS

Chapter 19

METHOD OF COMPARISON AND RESEARCH PROCESS

PENNY LEWIS

WITH THE FORMATION of the National Association for Drama Therapy in 1979, a group of independent innovative therapists employing the "intentional use of drama and or theater process to achieve the therapeutic goal of symptom relief, emotional and physical integration and personal growth" came together. Twenty years later members of the executive board and invited board certified master teacher trainers (RDT-BCT) discussed the need for an integrated body of knowledge in the field of drama therapy. During these past two decades many approaches in addition to psychodrama and sociodrama have been developed, employed in various settings, published, and taught to trainees in drama therapy. With much richness in the field, it was clear that the time had come to begin to formulate an integrated, inclusive, implicit, and conceptually grounded body of knowledge.

THE INQUIRY AND PURPOSE OF THE STUDY

The purpose of this research is to uncover a unifying theory of drama therapy. This theory is termed implicit in that it represents fundamental conceptual constructs in common among the most widely used frames of reference in drama therapy in the United States and Canada. It is hoped that this integrated frame of reference will provide an ever expanding foundation or trunk upon which the various approaches or branches can be supported, feel a connection to the whole, and be able to draw from the strength that comes from a sense of commonality. The achievement of this goal is based on the understanding and integration of the meaning of the major frames of reference in drama therapy in the United States and Canada through the use of phenomenological qualitative research. Through a process of theoretical sampling, 16 key approaches in drama therapy were discriminantly sampled. Either the founder or the key proponent of the approach in drama therapy was selected to respond to various questions designed to reveal the theoretical frame of reference. This editor/ researcher then analyzed the data through a phenomenological coding process based upon the responses to the predetermined questions as well as allowing the data to elucidate new categories of conceptual formulations (Lewis, 1978, 1986; McMillan & Schumacher, 1997; Straus & Corbin, 1998).

REVIEW OF LITERATURE

This research design and methodology has been utilized in the elucidation of a body of knowledge in a creative arts therapy field. In 1978, a phenomenological research study was conducted in dance therapy utilizing key proponents of the most widely employed approaches. The subject/author/therapists responded to conceptual questions regarding their theoretical base entailing (1) the view of the individual, the health dysfunction continuum and dance movement therapy, (2) the method of identification and evaluation of the health dysfunction continuum, and (3) the therapeutic process. Responses to these questions were extrapolated from the protocols in the form of natural meaning units. The situated concepts were cleared of any language that couched them in the specific idiom related to the approach. The unsituated themes were then organized and synthesized to produce a fundamental body of knowledge in the field of dance therapy (Lewis, 1978, 1986).

No such research has been carried out in the field of drama therapy; however, Landy (1994) discussed the conceptual basis of drama therapy, citing the following sources:

- Play and play therapy
- Ritual, magic, and shamanism
- Psychodrama and sociodrama
- Psychoanalysis
- Developmental psychology
- Sociological theory: symbolic interactionalism
- Performance theory
- Theater history, and
- Educational drama and theater.

Additionally, Landy cited derivative concepts found to be essentially dramatic in nature and crucial to his formulation of drama therapy. They are: role, representation, distancing, spontaneity, and the unconscious.

Jones (1996), a British dramatherapist, has discussed nine core processes in an attempt to define how drama therapy is effective. They are:

- *Dramatic projection* of aspects of themselves into the dramatic process or external materials for the purpose of perspective, exploration and insight
- *Therapeutic performance* for the use of dramatic access and expression
- *Drama therapeutic empathy and distancing* which encourages identification and perspective respectively
- *Personification and impersonation* for the purpose of distancing, representation, exploration of meaning, focus, perspective and the capacity to transform within the imaginal realm
- *Interactive audience and witnessing* for the purpose of perspective and interactive support
- *Embodiment* for the purpose of a here now encounter in order to deepen the experience, explore, and transform
- *Playing within the play space* for the purpose of increased expression, creativity and development of mentally-based healing and progression
- *Life drama connection* for the purpose of exploring a real relationship, a specific life event or for the reenactment of mythic material or the creation of a new story, and
- *Transformation* for the purpose of healing and exploring new possibilities of expression, feeling and encounter. (pp. 99–121)

All of these concepts are either explicitly or implicitly embedded in the integrated body of knowledge elucidated from the 16 key approaches in drama therapy in the United States and Canada. This would suggest an international commonality among drama therapists worthy of further exploration and research. However, the list is somewhat problematic. Though immensely helpful in directing our attention to a potential vocabulary that all drama therapists can share, Jones' list mixes concepts at different levels of abstraction and across different arenas of experience. Nevertheless, Jones' pursuit of the identification of commonalties is commendable and has continued the dialogue between integrators and specialists.

METHODOLOGY

A phenomenological methodology of qualitative research is utilized to select subjects through the process of discriminate sampling of theoretical frames of references, the identification of research questions and the development of an organizing system. This system requires data analysis through a coding process based upon the responses to the predetermined questions as well as allowing the data to elucidate new categories of conceptual formulations. Additionally, analysis requires the reorganizing, reduction and synthesis through constant comparison toward an integrated body of knowledge agreed upon by the subjects.

Selection of Subjects

The subjects were selected based on their capacity to represent directly or indirectly the most widely utilized frames of reference in drama therapy. Direct representation is by virtue of the fact that they formulated and created the approach. This category includes those proponents that have applied an existing theoretical psychotherapy frame in drama therapy. Indirect representation is by virtue of their being viewed by the field as a key proponent of the approach. Of the 16 author/subjects, 14 are considered the founders or co-founders of the approach presented. The exceptions are sociodrama and psychodrama created by the late J.L. Moreno. All subjects have practiced these approaches with appropriate populations and have taught the approach to those seeking training in drama therapy. Three quarters of the proponents have created and/or taught in graduate programs in universities and institutes and have achieved board certified status in drama therapy. The judgment regarding the selection of the subjects was also made based on their sphere of influence through both a contribution to drama therapy literature and in the numbers of students now professional drama therapists that they have trained.

Design

The qualitative research analyzed the written statements presented in this text as chapters written by drama therapists in response to a delineated outline of questions designed to clarify the major theoretical constructs and populations served by the approach. The drama therapists have a further opportunity of locating their experience of the concepts or hypotheses they used both historically in terms of their personal and theoretical evolution in a "Genesis Section" and by example through a demonstration via a "Case Study Section."

Based on an understanding of conceptual constructs, frame of reference and theory building in the fields of the embodied creative arts therapies (Lewis, 1978, 1979, 1984, 1986) as well as discussions generated at the pivotal April, 1999 meeting of members of the executive board of the National Association for Drama Therapy and Board Certified Master Teacher/Trainers in Drama Therapy, the following questions were asked the subject/author/drama therapist and their written protocols or chapters:

- What is the definition of your drama therapy approach?
- What are the basic concepts of your drama therapy approach?
- What is your conceptual experience of health?
- What is your conceptual experience of dysfunction?
- What is your conceptual experience of the methods of identifying and evaluating health and dysfunction?
- What is your conceptual experience of your therapeutic process?
- What is your conceptual experience of the key drama therapy techniques your approach utilizes?
- What is your conceptual experience of the role of the therapist in your approach?
- What populations does your approach serve?

Comparative Analysis

Phenomenological data analysis integrates the operations of organizing, analyzing, and interpreting the data. The following represents the steps in this qualitative research process:

Step 1: Each protocol or chapter was read first to get a sense of the whole in a process of immersion that requires both objectivity and sensitivity. "Objectivity is necessary to arrive at an impartial and accurate interpretation of events. Sensitivity is required to perceive the subtle nuances and meanings in data and to organize the connections between concepts" (Strauss & Corbin, 1998, pp. 42–43).

Step 2: Conceptual constructs situated in the language of the particular approach are then arranged according to the predetermined research questions in a 3–5 page frame of reference summary for each of the 16 approaches. Because theoretical sampling is cumulative, each theoretical approach chapter builds from and adds to the previous protocol and analysis. In the initial stating of concepts from the first chapters, it was important to generate as many concepts as possible as it was unclear which constructs would be germane to a large proportion of the 16 approaches researched.

Steps 3 and 4: The conceptual constructs from the three to 5 page frame of reference summaries are then unsituated, that is, cleared of any language which couched them in the specific idiom related to the approach and placed on a large grid in which all 16 approaches could be cataloged as either agreeing or not agreeing to the particular conceptual construct. The unique concepts and postulates revealed within each approach are not lost however, but appear in the Glossary Addendum.

Step 5: The theoretical concepts on the grid are then further reduced and densified. During the process, sub-categories began to reveal themselves as the conceptual meaning units group themselves around topic areas such as those found in the sections on "basic concepts" and "therapeutic process."

Steps 6 and 7: In the final stage of the grid, concepts that had under 3 proponents agreeing with them were removed. The grid was then sent out to all 16 proponents to insure accuracy of conceptual formulation and agreement. The subject authors were requested to cross out any "X's" corresponding to a theoretical construct not a part of their frame of reference and add any "X's" in relationship to any additional constructs that they did agree with as being foundational to their theoretical approach.

Steps 8 and 9: The return grids were then consolidated. See Table 1. The concepts were then retransposed back into prose to provide the summary description of the implicit theoretical body of knowledge in drama therapy in the United States and Canada. This description can be found in the final chapter, "Toward a Body of Knowledge in Drama Therapy."

REFERENCES

Jones, P. (1996). *Drama as Therapy.* London: Routledge.

Landy, R. (1994). *Drama therapy concepts, Theories and practices.* Springfield, IL: Charles C Thomas.

Lewis Bernstein, P. (1978). *Toward an implicit theory of dance movement therapy.* Dissertation. San Francisco: Saybrook Institute.

Lewis Bernstein, P. (1979). *Eight theoretical approaches in dance-movement therapy.* Dubuque, IA: Kendall/Hunt Pub.

Lewis, P. (1986). *Theoretical approaches in dance-movement therapy Vol. I.* Dubuque, IA: Kendall/Hunt Pub.

Lewis, P. (1984). *Theoretical approaches in dance-movement therapy Vol. II.* Dubuque, IA: Kendall/Hunt Pub.

McMillan, J., & Schumacher, S. (1997). *Research in education.* New York: Addison Wesley Longman, Inc.

Moustakas, C. (1990). *Heuristic research.* Thousand Oaks, CA: Sage Publications, Inc.

Strauss, A., & Corbin, J. (1998). *Basics of qualitative Research.* Thousand Oaks, CA: Sage Publications, Inc.

Body of Knowledge in Drama Therapy	Role Theory	Integ Phases	Dev'tal Trans.	Narra drama	Dev'tal Themes	Socio Drama	Psych Drama	Play Back	Stop Gap	Ritual Drama	Psycho-Anal.	RecoOv Individ	Thera. Comm	Enact	Omega Trans	Family Play
1.Definition of Drama Therapy Model Drama Therapy is an action method in which drama therapist, actors or participants engage in an enactment of relevant community and larger social or emotional issues for the purpose of stimulating discussions, greater understanding, transpersonal growth, exploring new options, or role training in aspects about which they may feel uncomfortable.	X	X				X	X		X				X	X	X	
Drama therapy is a performance-based approach that utilizes the enactment of actual personal stories, the transformation of core themes and roles, or the evocation and enactment of archetypes in the construction of a theater piece for the purpose of affirmation, healing and transformation of individuals and/or social groups.		X						X		X					X	
Drama Therapy is a deep action method which employs engagement in improvisational play or enactment of habitual scenes or roles from clients' lives, dreams or fantasies in an effort to heighten awareness, connect with themselves, others and/or transpersonally in an embodied manner, gain new insights and understandings, and practice new and more satisfying roles and stories intrapsychically and in social situations.	X	X	X	X	X		X		X		X	X			X	X
Drama therapy is a depth developmental approach which utilizes the arts, the unconscious and, in some approaches, the transference and countertransference relationship while entering into the dramatic fantasy realm of the client to construct an understandable story about the events of the client's or family's life, remove resistances, and promote healthy development, attachment and creative coping skills.	X	X	X		X		X				X				X	X

Table 1. The Conceptual Constructs of Drama Therapy.

Body of Knowledge in Drama Therapy	Role Theory	Iinteg Phases	Dev'tal Trans.	Narra drama	Dev'tal Themes	Socio Drama	Psych Drama	Play Back	Stop Gap	Ritual Drama	Psycho-Anal.	RecoOv Individ	Thera. Comm	Enact	Omega Trans	Family Play
1. Basic concepts: General Truth is socially determined and negotiated.	X			X		X	X					X	X			
Spontaneity is the moment to moment readiness for creative action in service to an adequate response to a new situation or a new response to an old situation.	X	X		X		X	X	X				X			X	
Peak spontaneity or universal consciousness is the point at which the ego disappears and there is a sense of connection and flow with the universe.		X	X			X	X					X			X	
Memory is stored in the body and can be recovered through embodied enacted experience.		X	X		X		X					X	X		X	
Shamanic healing rituals are found in the origins of theater and the basic healing structures of drama therapy.		X								X		X			X	
Archetypes are universal symbols and energy engendering forces emerging from the collective unconscious in dreams, delusions, fantasies, and the imagination and are at the core of complexes.	X					X	X			X					X	
Numinosum is that phenomenon which emerges from the archetypal stores and has the power to heal and transform those who experience it within the liminal realm.	X	X				X	X			X					X	
Resistance is any defensive mental process or behavior that interferes with the task of understanding or an individual's spontaneous and adaptive response to life.	X	X			X	X	X		X		X	X	X	X	X	
The unconscious lies in the body, operates out of awareness and connects present reality to past reality.	X	X			X	X	X				X	X		X	X	
Consciousness is the capacity to be fully present, involved in the bigger picture, and either spiritually be in relationship to the Universal Source and /or mystically to feel at one with the All.			X		X	X	X					X			X	
Emotions are stored in the body due to emotional or physical trauma and can be released through embodied enactment.	X		X			X	X			X		X	X		X	

Body of Knowledge in Drama Therapy	Role Theory	Integ Phases	Dev'tal Trans.	Narra drama	Dev'tal Themes	Socio Drama	Psych Drama	Play Back	Stop Gap	Ritual Drama	Psycho-Anal	RecoOv Individ	Thera. Comm	Enact	Omega Trans	Family Play
Empathy is the capacity to think and feel oneself into the inner life of another person	X	X			X	X	X	X	X			X	X	X	X	
Self actualization is a process through which an individual unfolds and grows from the inside out		X			X	X	X		X			X	X	X	X	
A humanistic approach places emphasis on self awareness and respect for differences		X			X	X		X	X			X	X	X	X	
A psychodynamic approach utilizes concepts such as ego adaptation, self formation, and internalization of the primary care giver with a goal of bringing unconscious material into conscious ego mediation.		X			X		X				X	X			X	
A cognitive approach upholds that thought constructs reality and influences behavior and emotions and works to solve problems through behavioral changes.	X	X		X		X	X					X	X			
A transpersonal approach acknowledges and utilizes a spiritual and/or mystical frame and works toward a client's relationship to the above.		X			X	X	X			X		X			X	

Table 1. The Conceptual Constructs of Drama Therapy (Continued).

Body of Knowledge in Drama Therapy	Role Theory	Iinteg Phases	Dev'tal Trans.	Narra drama	Dev'tal Themes	Socio Drama	Psych Drama	Play Back	Stop Gap	Ritual Drama	Psycho-Anal.	RecoOv Individ	Thera. Comm	Enact	Omega Trans	Family Play
Basic Concepts: Individual &Societal worldview																
Source or soul is a formless presence located at the center of the desiring self.		X	X	X	X							X			X	
Human Development: An infant develops from state of oneness to a capacity to discriminate me from not me.		X	X		X	X	X			X		X	X		X	X
Attachment refers to the basic relationship that develops between a parent and child. Infants need to be doubled or be mirrored when they are newborns. Infants need the presence of others or auxiliaries to help them develop roles through interaction.		X	X		X		X					X	X			X
Boundaries such as the ego, body, and personal space boundaries serve to protect the individual and aid in discriminating what is conscious from unconscious, real from not real, and what is the domain of the individual from that of others.	X	X	X		X		X					X	X		X	
Basic concepts: Creativity & Imagination																
Imagination or the imaginal realm is a right brain, dreamlike, symbolic language that can be accessed through the arts in service to healing, growth, and development.	X	X			X	X		X		X		X	X		X	
Creativity is the ability to think beyond our own personal limitations, be fully present in the moment, capable of spontaneously seeing and responding to the world in a new way.	X	X		X	X	X	X	X				X	X		X	X
Basic Concepts: Regarding Role																
Role is the actual tangible form that the self takes. It is a discrete pattern of changeable behavior that suggests a particular way of thinking, feeling or acting. Role is a unit of behavior that reflects	X	X				X	X		X			X	X	X	X	

Body of Knowledge in Drama Therapy	Role Theory	linteg Phases	Dev'tal Trans.	Narra drama	Dev'tal Themes	Socio Drama	Psych Drama	Play Back	Stop Gap	Ritual Drama	Psycho-Anal.	RecoOv Individ	Thera. Comm	Enact	Omega Trans	Family Play
socially agreed upon boundaries. A role has both collective and private components.																
Role playing occurs when a person enacts a role with some freedom and comfort from the rigidity of society's definition.	X	X	X	X	X	X	X					X	X	X	X	
Role taking is the ability to imagine oneself as another. It occurs when someone follows the parameters of the role exactly as the culture or	X	X				X	X	X					X		X	
person has established them.	X	X					X						X			
Role training is a rehearsal for life situations that are to come through practicing a variety of behaviors to meet any given situation for the desired behavior or action one chooses.	X	X		X	X	X	X		X	X			X	X	X	
De-roling occurs when an individual no longer enacts a specified role in a drama therapy process.	X	X		X	X	X	X					X	X		X	
Protagonist is defined as the client whose is the focus of the therapeutic enactment..	X	X				X	X								X	
Role reversal is the switching of roles with another during a drama therapy process.	X	X		X	X	X	X					X	X		X	
Audience are those individuals witnessing the dramatic experience. Their role is to give support and reassurance, participate in the dramatic action, and provide feedback and sharing.	X	X				X	X	X	X	X		X		X	X	
Auxiliary egos are the other group members who play roles for the protagonist in the psychodrama							X					X			X	
Transference occurs when the patient re-enacts a role of the past by transferring a prior relationship onto the therapist.	X	X			X		X				X		X		X	
Countertransference occurs when the therapist consciously or unconsciously acts upon the role material received by the transference in relation to the client.	X	X			X		X				X		X		X	
Childhood survival mechanisms are those role defining behaviors and thoughts developed in childhood in order to survive when healthy boundaries have not been developed.	X	X			X		X					X	X			

Table 1. The Conceptual Constructs of Drama Therapy (Continued).

Body of Knowledge in Drama Therapy	Role Theory	Iinteg Phases	Dev'tal Trans.	Narra drama	Dev'tal Themes	Socio Drama	Psych Drama	Play Back	Stop Gap	Ritual Drama	Psycho-Anal.	RecoOv Individ	Thera. Comm	Enact	Omega Trans	Family Play
The therapeutic alliance is a partnership relationship formed between the therapist and client whereby common goals are articulated and pursued and the client feels the therapist is working with and for him/her.	X	X	X		X	X	X				X	X	X	X	X	

Body of Knowledge in Drama Therapy	Role Theory	Integ Phases	Dev'tal Trans.	Narra drama	Dev'tal Themes	Socio Drama	Psych Drama	Play Back	Stop Gap	Ritual Drama	Psycho-Anal.	RecoOv Individ	Thera. Comm	Enact	Omega Trans	Family Play
Basic concepts: Theme or story																
Developmental theme is the story along with its associated roles and settings which is required for an individual to successfully integrate all that is necessary at a particular life stage.	X	X			**X**		X				X	X		X	X	
Self- story or self-narrative are the stories persons have about their lives that shape, constitute, and influence current behavior.	X	X		**X**	**X**	X	X	**X**				X	X		X	
Circular patterns occur in dominant stories in which actions and self-descriptions are problem-saturated resulting in the client being unable to move forward and be effective.		X		**X**	**X**							X	X			X

Table 1. The Conceptual Constructs of Drama Therapy (Continued).

Body of Knowledge in Drama Therapy	Role Theory	Iinteg Phases	Dev'tal Trans.	Narra drama	Dev'tal Themes	Socio Drama	Psych Drama	Play Back	Stop Gap	Ritual Drama	Psycho-Anal.	RecoDv Individ	Thera. Comm	Enact	Omega Trans	Family Play
Basic concepts: Setting																
Sacred space is the deliberate creation of a ritual-like artistic and truth telling space that is distinct from ordinary life for the purpose of healing and growth.		X			**X**		**X**	**X**		X		X	X		X	
Ritual is the establishment of a ceremonial frame, space, time and demeanor for transformative purposes.		X		**X**	**X**	X	**X**	**X**				X	X	X	X	
Ritual community is a group-based enactment to celebrate or explore or heal through ceremonial and artistic action.		X				X	**X**	**X**				X	X		X	
Bi- personal field or the creative playspace is the container for the improvisational embodied encounter between the therapist and client or within a group.		X	**X**		**X**				X			X			X	
A transitional space is created where clients can be constructed and reconstruct themselves.		X			**X**					X		X	X		X	
Ritualization in liminal time and space helps gives repetitive structure and a sense of security.		X						**X**		X		X			X	
The container is the playspace within a larger setting that allows for creativity and spontaneity to occur within a set of clearly defined boundaries and rules.		X			**X**			**X**	X	X				X	X	

Body of Knowledge in Drama Therapy	Role Theory	Integ Phases	Dev'tal Trans.	Narra drama	Dev'tal Themes	Socio Drama	Psych Drama	Play Back	Stop Gap	Ritual Drama	Psycho-Anal.	RecoOv Individ	Thera. Comm	Enact	Omega Trans	Family Play
Basic Concepts: Dynamic Dramatic Elements																
Catharsis is the spontaneous full expression and release of pent-up emotions.		X			**X**	X	X						X		X	
The transformative process is the process through which immature patterns of behavior are cleared and replaced with age appropriate adaptive behavior and/or expanded consciousness through the use of drama within the imaginal realm.		X			**X**	X	X				X	X			X	
Play is seen as dramatic improvisation with oneself, between two individuals or among a group that can be used as a tool for continued transformation.	X	X	**X**		X	X	X	X		X		X	X		X	X
Play reflects unconscious thoughts, habitual patterns and trauma through free associational symbolic material		X	**X**		X				**X**			X	X		X	X
Improvisational drama allows for spontaneous and open dialogue	X	X	**X**	X	X	X			**X**		X	X	X		X	X
Interactive Theater entails the involvement of the audience in the drama, scripting, or processing of the performance.		X				X		X	**X**				X	X	X	
Transformation of the psyche occurs within the imaginal realm of the enactment or authentic drama experience.		X	**X**		X	X	X	X		X	X	X			X	X
2. Goals of Drama Therapy																
To facilitate catharsis or abreaction serving integration, insight and role training.	**X**	X			X	**X**	X		**X**			X			X	
To increase client's role repertoire through exploring existing roles and experimenting with new or problematic roles intrapsychically and in social situations.	X	X		**X**	X	X	X		**X**			X		X	X	
To increase the capacity to play, be flexible, spontaneous and creative.	X	X	X	**X**		X	X	X		X			X		X	X

Table 1. The Conceptual Constructs of Drama Therapy (Continued).

Body of Knowledge in Drama Therapy	Role Theory	Integ Phases	Dev'tal Trans.	Narra drama	Dev'tal Themes	Socio Drama	Psych Drama	Play Back	Stop Gap	Ritual Drama	Psycho-Anal.	RecoOv Individ	Thera. Comm	Enact	Omega Trans	Family Play
To crystallize and communicate social and personal self-knowledge.	X	X				X	X	X						X	X	
To foster understanding, respect, insight, trust, compassion, acceptance, empathy, and creative spontaneous communication among people.	X	X	X	X	X	X	X	X	X			X	X	X	X	X
To create movement toward wholeness for individuals and groups.	X				X	X	X	X				X	X		X	
To promote identity, self-confidence, dignity, security, and self-esteem.	X	X			X	X	X	X	X	X	X	X	X		X	X
To support an individual ego functioning at an age appropriate level and to support their moving through the various life stages to come.	X	X			X	X	X	X	X			X	X		X	
To facilitate a renewed flow, connection, attachment, and or intimacy between the self, others, and/or the transpersonal.	X	X	X		X	X	X			X	X	X			X	X
To become consciously present and embrace continuous change from moment to moment.	X	X	X		X	X	X					X	X		X	
To re-create the past, and correct the scene, changing history so that the block is disintegrated and the individual moves more freely in his /her present life.	X	X			X		X	X	X		X	X	X		X	
To abstain and recover from addictions	X	X		X	X	X		X	X			X	X		X	
3. Health Health is the capacity for spontaneous and creative engagement in the playing of life roles in relation to both self and others in an affectively and cognitively balanced manner.	X	X				X	X		X			X	X	X	X	X

Body of Knowledge in Drama Therapy	Role Theory	Integ Phases	Dev'tal Trans.	Narra drama	Dev'tal Themes	Socio Drama	Psych Drama	Play Back	Stop Gap	Ritual Drama	Psycho-Anal.	RecoOv Individ	Thera. Comm	Enact	Omega Trans	Family Play
Health is the capacity to utilize play, creativity, spontanitey, imagination, resourcefulness, and hope in the present and future.	X	X	X	X		X	X	X		X		X	X	X	X	X
Health is the continuous capacity to evolve and adapt throughout the lifespan as one constructs one's life and identities relationally, maturely and with judgment.	X	X		X	X		X					X	X		X	
Health is exhibited in a positive empathic compassionate respect and acceptance of oneself.	X	X	X		X	X	X	X	X			X	X	X	X	
Health is exhibited in a fully realized human being who has the capacity for attuned empathic, compassionate respect, acceptance and connection with others.	X	X			X	X	X	X	X				X	X	X	X
Health is the successful integration of all previous developmental stages and the capacity to utilize what one has experienced in an adaptive manner.		X			X	X	X		X			X			X	X
Health is the capacity to expand a repertoire of roles and new alternative stories with flexibility .	X	X		X	X	X	X		X	X		X	X	X	X	
Health is the capacity for a transpersonal connection and expanded consciousness.	X	X			X	X	X			X		X		X	X	
Health is the capacity for intimacy, attachment and full encounter with another.	X	X	X		X	X	X		X			X	X		X	X
Health is the capacity to be fully embodied.	X	X	X		X			X	X			X			X	
Health is the capacity be fully present in -the – moment, improvising from moment to moment making it up as one goes along.	X	X	X		X	X	X	X				X	X		X	

Table 1. The Conceptual Constructs of Drama Therapy (Continued).

Body of Knowledge in Drama Therapy	Role Theory	Integ Phases	Dev'tal Trans.	Narra drama	Dev'tal Themes	Socio Drama	Psych Drama	Play Back	Stop Gap	Ritual Drama	Psycho-Anal.	RecoOv Individ	Thera. Comm	Enact	Omega Trans	Family Play
Health is seen in a realistic sense of self and other.	X	X	X		X	X	X	X	X		X	X	X	X	X	
Health is seen in ego strength that is the ability to recognize feelings, handle problems, have adaptive coping styles and to deal with the realities of the inner and outer world appropriately.	X	X	X		X	X	X				X	X	X	X	X	
4. Dysfunction Dysfunction is exhibited by a lack of spontaneity, creativity, playfulness and the capacity to engage in a variety of life roles adaptively.	X	X	X	X	X	X	X	X				X	X		X	X
Dysfunction is seen in isolation, insecurity and disconnection from oneself, others, and the Source.	X	X	X		X	X	X	X		X		X	X	X	X	X
Dysfunction is exhibited by an undeveloped or negative sense of self.		X			X		X	X	X	X	X	X	X	X	X	
Dysfunction occurs when healthy development is arrested due to trauma within the family system or externally or the inability of the primary care givers to create the required ontogenetic setting and associated role relationship.	X	X			X							X	X		X	X
Dysfunction is seen in unavailable, poorly developed, or inappropriately intrapsychically or interpersonally aligned roles.	X	X				X	X		X			X	X		X	
Dysfunction is seen in an individual who is unable to see alternatives to a solution because their creativity and imagination seems overshadowed by a problematic habitual story.	X	X		X	X	X	X	X		X		X	X		X	
Dysfunction is a dominant story, habitual desire,	X	X		X	X		X					X	X	X	X	

Body of Knowledge in Drama Therapy	Role Theory	Iinteg Phases	Dev'tal Trans.	Narra drama	Dev'tal Themes	Socio Drama	Psych Drama	Play Back	Stop Gap	Ritual Drama	Psycho-Anal.	RecoOv Individ	Thera. Comm	Enact	Omega Trans	Family Play
thought, or image restricting spontaneity of an individual through blocking or filtering out experiences that do not fit with the existing story.																
Dysfunction is seen in the client's experience of themselves as defeated, devalued and victimized.	X	X			X				X	X		X	X		X	
Dysfunction is seen in an undeveloped and/or unrealistic ego, sense of self and other.	X	X			X						X	X	X	X	X	
Dysfunction is seen in fragmented or split off parts of the self, faulty boundaries and attachments, and habitual childhood survival mechanisms limiting the capacity of the individual to make appropriate meaning of internal and external reality.	X	X			X		X				X	X	X	X	X	X
Dysfunction is seen in the presence of addictions.	X	X			X	X	X		X			X	X	X	X	
Dysfunction is seen in an inability to play or breaks in the flow of mutual play or dramatic improvisation.			X				X	X					X		X	X
5. Method of identification and evaluation of health or dysfunction The method first entails the identification of the various roles individuals play intrapsychically and interpersonally.	X	X				X						X	X		X	
Assessment is based on the identification of key themes, dominant stories, scripts or narratives through interviews or observation during warm up.	X	X		X	X	X	X			X			X	X	X	
Initial assessment interviews that take a social and developmental history are made.		X	X		X	X					X	X	X		X	

Table 1. The Conceptual Constructs of Drama Therapy (Continued).

Body of Knowledge in Drama Therapy	Role Theory	Integ Phases	Dev'tal Trans.	Narra drama	Dev'tal Themes	Socio Drama	Psych Drama	Play Back	Stop Gap	Ritual Drama	Psycho-Anal.	RecoOv Individ	Thera. Comm	Enact	Omega Trans	Family Play
Through the use of projective techniques such as art and sand play and drama techniques and assessment tools an evaluation is made.	X	X		X	X	X	X			X	X	X	X		X	X
Through the observation and participation of a client's dramatic play.	X	X	X		X		X	X			X	X			X	X
Through the observation of developmentally-based interactional themes.		X			X	X	X				X				X	X
6. Therapeutic process: Step I: Warm-up The first stage of the therapeutic process is to define a thematic problem members would like to solve: this problem may address being better able to deal with a situation, to gain greater understanding, to be able to make a decision, or to train them in certain role aspects about which they may feel uncomfortable.		X				X	X		X			X	X	X	X	
A warm-up dramatic play phase entails improvisation, drama, theater games and mask exploration designed to develop expressiveness, trust, a connection to oneself and/or the transpersonal.	X	X				X	X	X		X			X	X	X	
Verbal interviews occur in order for the client to inform the therapist of their problems, personal history, previous therapies, and goals.	X	X	X		X		X					X	X	X		X
The drama therapist facilitates interactive exercises and play designed to facilitate the emergence of group trust and/ or issues of importance to group members.	X	X	X	X		X	X	X		X		X	X	X	X	X

Body of Knowledge in Drama Therapy	Role Theory	Iinteg Phases	Dev'tal Trans.	Narra drama	Dev'tal Themes	Socio Drama	Psych Drama	Play Back	Stop Gap	Ritual Drama	Psycho-Anal.	RecoOv Individ	Thera. Comm	Enact	Omega Trans	Family Play
Therapeutic Process: Step II: Role defining & Assignment The stage is set up, the participants volunteer or are assigned roles by the director. The director readies participants to play their roles by interviewing them in role or through the technique of walk and talk. The enactors are warmed up to the specific situation of the drama they spontaneously interact.						X	X					X			X	
The protagonist or individual who will engage in personal work is selected either by the drama therapist, the group, the system, or self selection.	X	X		X			X	X				X			X	
Role training is given to the auxiliary egos, actor or participants in an individual's drama through physiological descriptions, personality characteristics, and interviewing.		X		X			X	X	X			X	X		X	
The development of a relationship and spontaneous play roles occur by entering into the dramatic play.	X	X			X	X	X		X		X	X	X		X	X
Key issues are revealed and then more related scenework is developed.	X	X		X	X	X	X		X		X	X	X	X	X	X
Therapeutic Process: Step III: Dramatic Enactment or Action Phase During the enactment the director utilizes various techniques to assist the group in accomplishing its goals.	X	X			X	X	X	X				X	X	X	X	
In the action phase, roles and thematic narratives are enacted, worked through, and alternatives explored by the client and/or group members with the therapist facilitating as a bridge between the two.	X	X		X	X	X	X		X			X	X	X	X	X

Table 1. The Conceptual Constructs of Drama Therapy (Continued).

Body of Knowledge in Drama Therapy	Role Theory	Iinteg Phases	Dev'tal Trans.	Narra drama	Dev'tal Themes	Socio Drama	Psych Drama	Play Back	Stop Gap	Ritual Drama	Psycho-Anal.	RecoOv Individ	Thera. Comm	Enact	Omega Trans	Family Play
The client's improvisational enactment is facilitated to help the client work through a dilemma with the capacity to both think and feel effectively and adaptively apply the roles intrapsychically and in social situations.	X	X			X	X	X		X			X	X		X	
The dramatic process entails improvisational embodied encounter in the playspace between the therapist or parent and client or individually improvised by the client and observed by the therapist responding symbolically where appropriate.	X	X	X		X						X	X				X
Scenes are created that become a collective experience for the group to explore issues and feelings the whole group can identify with, relate to and contribute to.	X	X	X			X			X			X	X	X	X	
<u>Experiential enactments</u> of cognitive interventions and <u>Role rehearsing</u> new skills can occur.	X	X		X		X	X		X			X	X	X	X	
An <u>interactive psycho educational performance</u> regarding systemic or personal issues are employed						X			X				X	X	X	
<u>Theater/drama performance</u> based on predetermined goals or story.				X				X	X	X			X	X	X	
<u>Reflective scene work</u> are carefully designed real-life scenes demonstrated by the therapist and co-leader to bring about conscious awareness of thoughts and feelings toward behavioral change from the audience. Responding individuals from the audience can be asked to enter into the reflective scene work and bring about purposeful change in behavior.		X				X			X			X	X	X	X	

Body of Knowledge in Drama Therapy	Role Theory	Iinteg Phases	Dev'tal Trans.	Narra drama	Dev'tal Themes	Socio Drama	Psych Drama	Play Back	Stop Gap	Ritual Drama	Psycho-Anal.	RecoOv Individ	Thera. Comm	Enact	Omega Trans	Family Play
During the facilitation phase a discussion brings about conscious awareness of behaviors, needs and feelings by shifting the participants from a connection with the material in the scene to a connection with themselves for the purpose of personal problem-solving and transformation of behavior.	X	X							**X**			X	X		X	
Therapeutic Process: Step IV: De-roling, Sharing, & Processing																
A cooling down segment called sharing allows for feedback processing and/or personal expression from group members. In this stage enactors express what they are feeling in the role and/or what they learned from playing the role and any audience responds personally.	X	X				X	X	X				X	X	X	X	
The enactors de-role and integrate back into the group.	X	X			X	X	X	X				X	X	X	X	
Closure occurs through rituals, theater games and /or affirmations, for the individual or the group as participant(s) integrate what they have learned.	X	X		X			X	X		X			X	X	X	X
7. Drama therapy techniques Role reversal entails the enactor switching places and exchanging roles in order to imagine and express what the other feels like in any given situation for the purpose of the development of empathy, understanding, insight, perspective, and spontaneity. It is also employed to help the enactor see himself or herself as others see them or to facilitate cool down if the enactor is overheated in	X	X		X	X	X	X					X	X		X	X

Table 1. The Conceptual Constructs of Drama Therapy (Continued).

Body of Knowledge in Drama Therapy	Role Theory	Iinteg Phases	Dev'tal Trans.	Narra drama	Dev'tal Themes	Socio Drama	Psych Drama	Play Back	Stop Gap	Ritual Drama	Psycho-Anal.	RecoOv Individ	Thera. Comm	Enact	Omega Trans	Family Play
role.																
The double is an enactor who portrays the inner voice or role of an enactor. The double expresses unexpressed thoughts and feelings of an enactor in order to maximize the feelings expressed by the enactor, to verbalize nonverbal gestures, movements, and sounds, to make self observations, to help the enactor question themselves, or to offer support.		X			X	X	X					X	X		X	
The aside is utilized when the enactor does not want to say directly to the other person in the enactment what he wants to acknowledge verbally to himself and the audience by turning his head to the side.		X			X	X	X	X				X			X	
The soliloquy is a monologue in which enactors speak aloud his/her thoughts and feelings at some length.	X	X			X	X	X	X				X			X	
Walk and talk entails the director walking around the stage with enactors discussing with them the parameters of the role they are to play. It is also used during sociodramas when directors ask audience members to make suggestions for handling the problem in the scene or in conflict situations in which enactors are getting overheated.	X	X				X	X					X			X	
Empty chair occurs when a chair is put before the group or an enactor and they are encouraged to imagine that someone or some quality is in the chair and dialogue with it.	X	X			X	X	X					X	X		X	
Playback Theatre entails the enactment of another person's personal story.					X			X				X	X		X	

Body of Knowledge in Drama Therapy	Role Theory	Iinteg Phases	Dev'tal Trans.	Narra drama	Dev'tal Themes	Socio Drama	Psych Drama	Play Back	Stop Gap	Ritual Drama	Psycho-Anal.	RecoOv Individ	Thera. Comm	Enact	Omega Trans	Family Play
Sand play or World Technique is a technique in which an individual moves or shapes sand in a box or arranges small symbolic figures in the sand. These figures are then personified, interviewed and possibly rearranged in order to experience their meaning and any possible transformation.	X	X		X	X						X	X				
Ritual drama is the creation of sacred dramatic rites of passage which can help honor and support the transition from one developmental stage to another, or the use of ceremonies, archetypes and mythology in service to the balancing and healing of the patient's.	X	X			X		X			X		X			X	X
Projective techniques are the placement of roles onto objects such as puppets, sand play (world technique), and masks for the purpose of identification, distancing and externalization.	X	X		X	X		X			X	X	X	X		X	X
Role enactment is the playing of either a collective, presentational or a personal role with some measure of improvisation.	X	X	X	X	X	X	X	X	X	X	X	X	X	X	X	X
Role retraining or role rehearsal occurs when a client reconstructs a problem scene by replaying it in a preferred way.		X		X	X	X	X	X	X			X	X	X	X	
Distancing through style changes and externalization is a way to move a client closer or further away from the role in order to discover balance.	X	X		X	X	X	X		X	X		X	X	X	X	
Repetition within and/or of a scene allows for clients to obtain greater awareness and clarity of emergent elements.	X	X	X		X	X	X				X	X	X			

Table 1. The Conceptual Constructs of Drama Therapy (Continued).

Body of Knowledge in Drama Therapy	Role Theory	Integ Phases	Dev'tal Trans	Narra drama	Dev'tal Themes	Socio Drama	Psych Drama	Play Back	Stop Gap	Ritual Drama	Psycho-Anal.	RecoOv Individ	Thera Comm	Enact	Omega Trans	Family Play
Mirror occurs when the protagonist steps out of the scene and chooses someone to take his role.	X	X			X	X	X		X			X	X		X	
Pause is a technique in which the drama therapist stops the action of the improvisation and engages the clients in the dialogue about the feelings of the characters and asks for input as to what the options for a particular character might be.	X	X		X	X	X	X					X	X	X	X	
Therapeutic theater. Performative drama therapy utilizes the evocation of key themes and roles in the construction and enactment of various kinds of performances for the purpose of providing a container for healing, transformation and/or learning for the client /actors and the audience.		X			X				X	X		X	X		X	
Improvisational play and drama as a form of free association is employed.	X	X	X		X						X	X	X		X	X
Theater games are used to change the atmosphere by loosening attitudes, affects and cognitions. The participants are then able to free associate from the games and address the real issues of the task.		X		X		X	X						X	X	X	X
An interactive psycho-educational performance regarding systemic issues are performed with audience participation.						X				X			X	X	X	
Theatrical scenework is the improvising of developed roles and characters to facilitate expression and role- expansion.		X		X			X		X			X	X	X	X	
Theme, role or exercise based dramatic/play improvisation is suggested by the therapist.	X	X		X	X	X	X		X	X		X	X	X	X	X

Body of Knowledge in Drama Therapy	Role Theory	Integ Phases	Dev'tal Trans.	Narra drama	Dev'tal Themes	Socio Drama	Psych Drama	Play Back	Stop Gap	Ritual Drama	Psycho-Anal.	RecoOv Individ	Thera. Comm	Enact	Omega Trans	Family Play
8. Role of the drama therapist The role of the therapist is to direct the drama session. He/she creates a comfortable non-judgmental environment and upholds the contract of the group. The therapist facilitates the action segment of this session and assists the group in the process of integration of learned material after the drama has ended.	X	X				X	X	X	X			X	X	X	X	
The drama therapist needs to be adept at identifying developmental life themes. The drama therapist participates within the bi-personal field of the imaginal realm and enacts developmentally based roles, which help support the individual's integration of the life stage. The therapist is relationally genuinely caring and capable of relating dramatically within the imaginal realm to individuals from infants to the aged.	X				X		X				X	X			X	X
The drama therapist facilitates the client's play in order to help the client discover a balance of affect and cognition, inner and outer, or unconscious and conscious experience so that the client may be able to work through a dilemma while remaining intact.	X	X			X	X	X			X	X	X	X			X
The therapist holds to a non- expert, non-directive and client-centered position and invites the process of collaboration with the client. The client, family or group are considered the primary authors of alternative stories.	X	X	X	X			X		X						X	
The therapist stays fully present and follows the process from moment to moment.	X	X	X			X	X	X	X		X	X	X		X	X
The therapist creates a free, supported, dramatic play environment that encourages the client's	X	X	X			X	X		X		X	X	X			X

Table 1. The Conceptual Constructs of Drama Therapy (Continued).

Body of Knowledge in Drama Therapy	Role Theory	Iinteg Phases	Dev'tal Trans.	Narra drama	Dev'tal Themes	Socio Drama	Psych Drama	Play Back	Stop Gap	Ritual Drama	Psycho-Anal.	RecoOv Individ	Thera Comm	Enact	Omega Trans	Family Play
creativity in transforming the problem situation through drama.																
The role of the therapist is to demonstrate the containing power of the playspace through interweaving the dramatic scenes with the client's personal material, here and now processing, and previously unimagined possibilities.	X	X	X		X				X		X	X				X
The role of the therapist is to attend to the client and to become their playobject within the play space in order to reveal the client.	X		X		X						X					
The role of the therapist entails entering into the imaginal realm of the client.	X	X	X		X	X	X			X	X	X	X		X	X
The therapist creates a safe environment for the client(s) that encourages and supports self-exploration, dignity, respect and personal empowerment in a non-invasive manner.	X	X	X	X	X	X	X	X	X	X	X	X	X	X		X
The therapist insures that all roles are appropriate for the physical, psychological and emotional needs of the clients involved.	X	X		X	X	X	X	X	X	X		X	X	X	X	X
The role of the therapist is to be relationally and emphatically real.	X		X		X	X	X		X			X			X	
The role of the therapist is to clarify feelings, aid in the integration of a sense of self and other, healthy attachment, and encourage spontaneity and an expanded role repertoire.	X	X			X	X	X	X	X		X	X	X		X	X
The therapist is to be in service to the transpersonal process.		X			X	X	X			X		X			X	

Body of Knowledge in Drama Therapy	Role Theory	Integ Phases	Dev'tal Trans.	Narra drama	Dev'tal Themes	Socio Drama	Psych Drama	Play Back	Stop Gap	Ritual Drama	Psycho-Anal.	RecoOv Individ	Thera. Comm	Enact	Omega Trans	Family Play
9. Population served																
Types Group	X	X	X	X	X	X	X	X	X	X	X	X	X	X	X	
Individual	X	X	X	X	X	X	X				X	X			X	X
Couples	X	X	X	X	X	X	X					X			X	
Families	X	X		X	X	X	X					X			X	X
Organizations, schools, prisons and other systems within the community	X	X		X		X	X	X	X			X	X	X	X	
Age Geriatric		X	X	X		X	X	X	X	X		X			X	
Adults	X	X	X	X	X	X	X	X	X	X		X	X		X	X
Children	X	X	X	X	X	X	X	X	X		X	X	X	X	X	X
Adolescents	X	X	X	X	X	X	X	X	X		X	X	X	X	X	
Clinical populations																
Developmentally disabled		X	X	X	X	X	X			X			X	X	X	
Physical disabilities	X	X	X	X		X	X	X	X		X	X			X	
Drug and alcohol abuse	X	X	X	X	X	X	X	X	X			X	X		X	
Psychotic population	X	X	X		X	X	X			X					X	
Anxiety and/or affective disorders	X	X	X		X	X	X	X	X		X	X	X		X	X
Personality disorders	X	X	X		X	X	X				X	X	X		X	

Table 1. The Conceptual Constructs of Drama Therapy (Continued).

Body of Knowledge in Drama Therapy	Role Theory	linteg Phases	Dev'tal Trans.	Narra drama	Dev'tal Themes	Socio Drama	Psych Drama	Play Back	Stop Gap	Ritual Drama	Psycho-Anal.	Reco0v Individ	Thera. Comm	Enact	Omega Trans	Family Play
PTSD	X	X	X	X	X	X	X	X	X		X	X			X	X
Neurological impairments		X		X		X	X	X			X	X	X			
Attachment disorders	X	X	X		X		X				X	X			X	X
Societal & Developmental Issues																
Life Stage Transition	X	X	X	X	X	X	X	X	X			X			X	
Prison populations	X	X	X	X		X	X		X			X	X			
Homeless		X	X	X		X	X	X	X			X	X			
Catastrophic Illness	X	X	X	X	X	X	X		X	X		X			X	
At risk Youth	X	X	X	X	X	X	X	X	X		X	X	X	X	X	
Teachers	X	X	X	X	X	X	X	X				X		X	X	

Chapter 20

TOWARD A BODY OF KNOWLEDGE IN DRAMA THERAPY

PENNY LEWIS

THE FOLLOWING REPRESENTS the fundamental conceptual structure of the major frames of reference employed in the training, clinical and psychoeducational work of drama therapists. Important to know here is that this is a comparative analysis and is not meant to be exhaustive in its identifying the themes of drama therapy theory. Rather it intends to begin the task of revealing and delineating the body of knowledge that is consensual to the field of drama therapy. It is toward this journey that this analysis has addressed itself.

Additionally, no attempt is made to evaluate the approaches; that is left to the reader. Some frames of reference have sophisticated complex theories with many techniques servicing a variety of populations; while others, address a particular approach, technique, or population. Based upon the researched results of the body of knowledge phenomenological reduction grid sent out to all 16 creators or proponents, the following concepts, constructs, and propositions can be said to be foundational to the field of drama therapy.

DEFINITION OF DRAMA THERAPY

Drama therapy is a profession and an action method which is utilized clinically and psychoeducationally:

Clinical Drama Therapy is an embodied action method in which a client, the drama therapist(s), and/or group members engage in improvisational play or the enactment of habitual scenes or roles from an individual's life, dreams or fantasies. This is done in an effort to heightened awareness and connection with oneself, others and/or transpersonally; gain new insights and understandings; and practice new and more satisfying roles and stories intrapsychically and in social situations. For many, clinical drama therapy is a depth approach that utilizes the unconscious and in some cases the transference and countertransference relationships while entering into the realm of imagination of the client. These depth approaches often utilize an understanding of normal and pathological human development. Drawing upon ego psychology, object relations theory, attachment theory, self psychology, and others; they attend and are sensitive to an understanding of habitual childhood behavior. These approaches address the removal of resistance and the promotion of healthy development and more adaptive coping skills through embodied transformational processes. At times puppets, masks, sand play, or other objects or props are utilized for the purpose of dramatic projection and distancing. Individuals can then personify and impersonate for the purpose of transforming, differentiating or reintegrating.

Clinical drama therapy can also be performance-based, utilizing the enactment of the actual personal story by the individual or others, the transformation of core themes and roles, or the evocation and enactment of archetypes in the construction of a theater piece. The performance is carried out for the purpose of affirmation, healing and transformation of individuals. Therapeutic performance often addresses a need to express oneself and be affirmed through the witnessing process of the audience. The audience in turn, may identify and gain insight and/or experience catharsis and healing through the safety of empathic distancing. Transformation can occur through the role taking, rehearsing as well as the performance. In some cases interactional–theater is utilized. The client may either be part of the audience, one of the enactors, or play various roles in the piece.

Psychoeducational and Societal/Systems-Oriented Drama Therapy is an action method in which drama therapist, actors or participants engage in enactments of a relevant community or larger social or emotional issues for the purpose of stimulating discussions, greater understanding, transpersonal growth, exploring new options, or role training in aspects about which they may feel uncomfortable. This approach is frequently performance-oriented and often entails interactive theater.

Clinically Oriented:
Psychanalytic
Role Theory
Five Stage
Developmental Transformations
Narradrama
Developmental Themes
Recovery and Individuation
Psychodrama
Family Play
Ritual Theater
Playback

Psychoeducationally Oriented:
Sociodrama
ENACT
STOP GAP

Societal/Systems Oriented:
Omega Transformational Theater
Geese Theater: Therapeutic Community

FOUNDATIONAL CONCEPTS

Imagination, Spontaneity, and Creativity

Foundationally core in drama therapy is the engagement of imagination. Sometimes called the imaginal realm, the liminal realm, or the *mundus imaginalis,* utilization of this right-brain, dream-like, symbolic language, movement, and images is the *sine qua non* of any art form. From this source comes the creative process. Creativity is seen as the ability to think beyond one's own personal limitations, be fully present in the moment, capable of spontaneously seeing and responding to the world in a new way. Spontaneity is the moment-to-moment readiness for this creative action in service to a unique response to an old situation or in adaptive response to a new situation. Without experience of imagination through play, improvisation, projectives, witnessing or other avenues, creativity and spontaneity cannot be accessed. Without the capacity for and experience with creativity and spontaneity, no healing, transformation, integration, expansion or change in beliefs can have a lasting effect. Imagination, creativity and spontaneity are the very life force of possibility.

For many drama therapists, the capacity for spontaneous creativity is an indicator of a self-actualizing individual capable of unfolding and growing from the inside out and experiencing peak spontaneity or universal consciousness. This capacity can also indicate an individual's level of Consciousness, which is viewed as the capacity for presence and involvement in the bigger picture of society, nature, and/or the transpersonal.

Human Development and Personality

Individuals develop in an organized sequential matter shifting from the state of oneness to a capacity to experience uniqueness and independent thought and action. Many clinically-oriented drama therapy approaches uphold the distinction between the conscious and the unconscious. Many feel that the unconscious lies in the body along with associated stored emotions due to physical or emotional trauma and can be released through embodied dramatic enactment. Most of these approaches adhere to the concept of resistance. Resistance is viewed as any defensive mental process or behavior that interferes with the task of understanding or an individual's spontaneous and adaptive response to life. Various clinically-oriented drama therapy processes are utilized to draw awareness to and work through blocks, habitual stories or roles or outmoded childhood survival behaviors that would inhibit creativity and spontaneity.

KEY DRAMATIC CONCEPTS

Role

Role is a discrete pattern of changeable behavior that suggests a particular way of thinking, feeling or acting. It is seen as a unit of behavior that reflects socially agreed upon boundaries. A role has both collective and private components. Role playing is a fundamental part of most all drama therapy approaches. Role enactments occurs when a person plays out either a collective, presentational, or a personal role with some measure of improvisation. Role training is a rehearsal for live situations that are to come through practicing a variety of behaviors to meet any given situation in order to have access to a chosen desired behavior or action.

Role training is based on the premise that one learns best through the experience of something rather than through the talking about it. If, in fact, the goal reflects some form of behavioral change, than it certainly makes sense that the approach, whether therapeutic or psychoeducational, actually entails embodied behavioral experience. This premise is obvious to all drama therapists. What is surprising is that it can elude others.

Those who participate as the audience whether it be the drama therapist, members of a group, or those witnessing a performance, also provide a role. Their role is to give support and reassurance, participate in the dramatic action, and /or provide feedback and sharing.

There is a myriad of possibilities for roles. Some drama therapy approaches focus on the various roles both intrapsychically and/or interpersonally that their clients and those around them take and need to integrate. Expansion of role repertoire is a fundamental goal of the majority of drama therapy approaches. This is carried out through the exploring of existing roles and in the experimenting with new or problematic intrapsychic and/ or interpersonal roles.

Theme or Story

Central to drama is the script or story that is played out. Self-stories or self-narratives are the stories that persons have about their lives that shape, constitute, and influence current behavior. Many of these plots can be seen to have originated in the individual's past and have become habitualized. These actions and self-descriptions are problem-saturated resulting in the client being unable to move forward and be effective. Many stories are associated with particular developmental phases. Developmentally-based themes can be identified and utilized in dramatic processes to promote healing and growth. In psychoeducationally-oriented drama therapy beliefs systems affect stories not only regarding oneself but others as well. These dominant stories keep being reenacted in the present thereby inhibiting creativity and a capacity to be fully present spontaneously creating and improvising the stories as they unfold in the moment.

Setting

The setting is the imagined or real space in which the drama processes occurs. Transitional space is the imagined space created by the clients within which the clients can construct and reconstruct themselves. The bipersonal field or creative *playspace* is the container for the improvisationally embedded encounter between the therapist and client or within a group. This container within a larger setting allows for creativity and spontaneity to occur within a set of clearly defined boundaries and rules.

For many drama therapy approaches, the setting for the work is considered *sacred space.* There is a deliberate creation of a ritual-like artistic and truth-telling space that is distinct from ordinary life. The creation of this Temenos is for the purpose of healing and growth. The root of this concept can be found in the idea of ritual or the establishment of a ceremonial frame, space, time and demeanor for transformative purposes. Historically community rituals were group-based enactments for the purpose of celebration, rights of passage, healing, communion with nature or the sacred through artistic action. Ritualization in liminal time and space helps give repetitive structure and a sense of security to the participants.

Dynamic Dramatic and Theater Elements

Improvisation, the spontaneous flow of dramatic process, is present in most drama therapy approaches. *Play* is seen as dramatic improvisation with oneself, between two individuals or among a group that can be used as a tool for continued transformation. For many approaches play reflects unconscious thoughts, habitual patterns and trauma through free association of symbolic material. Dramatic improvisation and play are also seen as the vehicles within which healing, transformation and growth can occur. This postulate is based on the assumption that since habitual patterns, trauma, and all of what one can be lies within the imagination, that it is only through entering into the imaginal realm through such avenues as improvisation and play that one can call forth and change what needs to be addressed.

Another important element, *catharsis* is frequently viewed as the spontaneous full expression and release of pent-up emotions. Others, however, appreciate that this process may also be subtle without losing its potential for creativity. Catharsis may be both part of the enactors' and the audience's experience. Catharsis in and of itself is felt to be transformative. In many drama therapy approaches it is but one dynamic process in a myriad of others.

Distancing through style changes and externalization is a way to move the client closer or further away from the role in order to discover balance and gain just the right relationship to the material to facilitate the goals of the drama therapy process. Distancing is created through a variety of drama therapy techniques. These may include projection such as sand play, mask work and puppets; the client witnessing the dramatic process, or through the generalization of the problem so that the client does not feel singled out.

Therapeutic theater utilizes the evocation of key themes and roles in the construction and enactment of various kinds of performances for the purpose of providing a container for healing, transformation and/or learning for the client/actors and the audience. The performance may entail *interactive theater* in which the audience is involved in the drama, scripting, or processing of the performance. *Psychoeducational theater,* utilized in prevention, intervention, the changing of belief systems and the expansion of conscious awareness, may also entail interactive theater.

GOALS OF DRAMA THERAPY

Connection

Most goal setting is done interactively between the drama therapist and the clients or participants. In some instances, however, the goals are contracted between the drama therapist and the hiring system such as a school, correctional facility, or organization. The following goals will be discussed in the order of their agreement among the approaches presented in this book. Nearly all approaches seek to promote identity, self-confidence, dignity, security, and self-esteem. This connection to and realistic appreciation of the self appears to be a *sine qua non* of depth approaches in the field. Of equal importance is the fostering of understanding, respect, insight, trust, compassion, acceptance, empathy, and the capacity for creative spontaneous communication with others. In addition to the capacity for a renewed flow and connection with oneself and others, a relationship to the transpersonal is also felt by most to be an important goal of the work.

Expansion

The ability to increase the capacity to be playful, flexible, spontaneous and creative appears also to be foundational to the field. Fundamental as well is the ability to increase one's role repertoire through exploring existing roles and experimenting with new or problematic intrapsychic and interpersonal roles. The expansion of consciousness and the capacity to be fully present in the moment creatively responding to what presents itself is also key.

Change, Transformation, Integration and Growth

The capacity to overcome habitual roles and stories can entail catharsis, abreaction, the communication of personal self-knowledge as well as the abstinence from addictions and addictive beliefs along with the working through of resistances. Many depth clinical approaches explore the recreation of the past and the transformation of historical themes so that the blocks are disintegrated or altered allowing the individual to move more freely in his or her present life. In doing so, individuals are supported to function at age-appropriate level and to continue to move toward wholeness throughout their life span.

CONCEPTS OF HEALTH AND DYSFUNCTION

Creativity, Spontaneity and Presence

Health is seen as the capacity to utilize play, creativity, spontaneity, imagination, resourcefulness, and hope in the present and the future. This entails the creative engagement in the playing out of life roles in relationship to both one's intrapsychic self and others in an effective and cognitively balanced matter. Additionally, an individual needs ego strength in order to be able to not only recognize feelings and handle problems but also to have the capacity for creative adaptive coping styles required to deal with the realities of the inner and outer world appropriately. In order to respond with creative spontaneity an individual must have the capacity to be fully present in the moment in an embodied encounter with life, improvising from moment-to-moment making up as one goes along.

Dysfunction is exhibited by a lack of spontaneity, creativity, and playfulness. This may be seen in an inability to play or in breaks in the flow of mutual play or dramatic improvisation. Generally it is seen in behavior which restricts the spontaneity of an individual through blocking or filtering out of experiences that do not fit with existing dominant or habitual stories or roles and inhibiting their capacity to seek alternatives to a situation.

Connection and Acceptance

Health is seen in a realistic sense of self and other. This is exhibited in a positive empathic compassionate respect and acceptance of oneself and others. This entails the capacity for intimacy, attachment and full encounter with another. Some approaches adhere to the premise that health also reflects the capacity for a transpersonal connection and expanded Consciousness.

Dysfunction is seen in an undeveloped and/or unrealistic ego, sense of self and other. The client may have a negative sense of self and experience themselves as defeated, devalued and/or victimized. Dysfunction is seen in isolation, insecurity and disconnection from oneself, others, and the source. This may be due to fragmented or split-off parts of the self, faulty boundaries and attachments, and resistances such as addictions and habitual childhood survival mechanisms limiting the capacity of the individual to make appropriate meaning of internal and external reality.

Expansion and Growth

Health is seen as the capacity to continuously respond and adapt throughout one's life span, expanding one's repertoire of roles and new alternative stories with flexibility.

Dysfunction is seen in unavailable, poorly developed, or intrapsychically or interpersonally inappropriately aligned roles. When healthy development is arrested due to trauma within family systems or externally, an individual can be seen to repeat habitual roles, stories, and themes.

METHODS OF IDENTIFICATION OF DYSFUNCTION AND HEALTH

Identification of various roles individuals play intrapsychically and interpersonally, key themes, dominant stories, scripts or narratives occurs through initial assessment interviews, the use of projective and dramatic techniques, and/or the observation and participation in the client's improvisational dramatic play.

THERAPEUTIC PROCESS

Phase I : Warm up

The first stage of the work varies depending upon whether the approach is clinical work with individuals or groups, performance-oriented and/or psychoeducational in nature. With the more classic psychotherapy approaches the drama therapist begins with a verbal interview in order for the client to inform the therapist of their concerns, personal history, previous therapies, and goals. With group drama therapy typically a warm-up dramatic play phase occurs entailing improvisation, drama and theater games and use of props and projectives designed to develop personal and group expressiveness, trust, and connection. From this process and awareness of key issues, roles and stories develop.

In psychoeducational drama therapy, the first stage of the therapeutic process is to define a thematic problem members would like to solve. This problem may address being better able to deal with a situation, to gain greater understanding, to be able to make a decision, or to train them in certain role aspects about which they may feel uncomfortable.

Phase II: Role Defining and Assignment

In the second phase, key issues are revealed and more related scene work and roles are developed. This can be carried out through spontaneous play roles occurring in improvisational dramatic play or actual role identification and assignment. In a clinical group approach, the protagonist or individual who will engage in personal work is selected either by the drama therapist, the group, the system, or self-selected. The drama therapist or director facilitates role training of group member participants engaging in an individual's drama through psychological descriptions, personality characteristics, interviewing or through the technique of walk and talk. When the enactors are warmed up to the specific situation of the drama, they spontaneously interact. This type of role training also occurs in psychoeducational groups as well.

Phase III: Enactment or Action

In the action phase of most approaches, the therapist facilitates the enactment of roles and dramatic narrative, the working through process, and the exploration of alternatives by the client and/or group members. With some this is a two-phase process: The first or facilitation phase entails a discussion which brings about conscious awareness of behaviors, needs and feelings by shifting the participants from a connection with the material in the scene to a connection with themselves for the purpose of personal problem solving and transformation of behavior. The second phase or reflective scene work entails carefully designed real-life scenes demonstrated by the therapist/leader to bring about the audience's conscious awareness of thoughts and feelings toward behavioral change.

Responding individuals from the audience can be asked to enter into the reflective scene work and bring about purposeful change in behavior. Most approaches however engage the client in improvisational enactments facilitated to help the client work through a dilemma and adaptively apply roles intrapsychically and in social situations. Although many employ therapist intervention techniques entailing experiential enactment, role rehearsing, therapeutic theater, and/or interactive performances; some approaches adhere to a pure improvisational embodied encounter. The latter occurs with the client alone, between the client and therapist, parent and child, couples, and/or among groups.

In psychoeducational or societal systems group scenes and theatrical performances are created that become a collective experience for the group to explore issues and feelings with which the whole group can identify, relate and contribute. This includes both the enactors and audience.

Phase IV: De-Roling, Sharing and Processing

All enactors de-role and returned to their normal identities. Typically a cooling down segment called sharing allows for feedback, processing and/or personal expression from individuals or group members. In this stage actors express what they were feeling in the role and or what they learned from playing the role and the audience responds personally. In many approaches closure occurs through rituals, theater games, and or affirmations. Individuals and group members integrate what they have learned.

Approaches that adhere to a pure improvisational play frame do not go through a processing or sharing experience. Rather, they leave the experience within the imaginal realm to continue to transform.

DRAMA THERAPY TECHNIQUES

Numerous techniques are unique to the particular drama therapy models presented in this book. The following represent techniques that are present in several of the approaches and therefore are considered to be more a part of the consensual body of knowledge in the field of drama therapy.

Role-Related Techniques

Role improvisation is at the core of drama therapy process. One of the most widely used role enactment technique is *role reversal.* It entails the enactors switching places and exchanging roles in order to imagine and express what the other feels like in any given situation. This is carried out for the purpose of the development of empathy, understanding, insight, perspective, and spontaneity. It is also employed to help the enactor see himself or herself as others see them or to facilitate cool down if the enactor is overheated in the role.

Another role-related technique created by Moreno is the double. *The double* is an enactor who portrays the inner voice or role of an enactor. The double expresses unexpressed thoughts and feelings in order to maximize the feelings expressed by the enactor, to verbalize nonverbal gestures, movements, and sounds, to make self-observations, to help the enactor self-question or to offer support.

The *soliloquy* is a monologue in which an enactor speak aloud his or her thoughts and feelings at some length. *The aside* is utilized when the enactor does not want to say directly to the other person in the enactment what he or she wants to acknowledge verbally to his or herself and the audience. The technique commences by the enactor turning his or her head to the side. *The mirror* technique occurs when the enactor steps out of the scene and chooses someone to take his or her role.

Walked and talk entails the director walking around the stage with the enactor discussing with him or her the parameters of the role they are to play. It is also occurs when the director asks the audience members to make suggestions for handling a problem in the scene or in conflict situations in which enactors are getting overheated. The *empty chair* technique occurs when chairs are put before the group or an enactor and s/he is encouraged to imagine that someone or some quality is in the chair and dialogue with it.

Theatrical scenework is the improvising of developed roles and characters to facilitate expression and role expansion.

Improvisational Techniques

Dramatic improvisation, in which stories emerge spontaneously, is foundational in drama therapy. Drama therapists utilize a variety of techniques to support this process. *Pause* is a technique in which the drama therapist stops the action of the improvisation and engages the client in a dialogue about the feelings of the characters and asks for input as to what options there might be for the participants. Drama therapists also enter into the improvisational story and utilize the technique of *interviewing* to further clarify the enactments. Additionally, drama therapists can make interventions within the symbolic realm of the improvisational process.

Projective Techniques

Projective techniques are the placement of roles onto objects such as *puppets* and *masks* for the purpose of identification, distancing and externalization. *Sand play* or *world technique* is a technique in which an individual moves or shapes sand in a box or arranges small symbolic figures in the sand. These figures are then personified, interviewed and possibly rearranged in order to experience their meaning and any possible transformation.

Games and Structured Exercises

Theater games are used to change the atmosphere by loosening attitudes, affects and cognitions. The participants are then able to free associate from the games and address the real issues of the task.

Theater or Performance-Based Techniques

Playback theatre entails the enactment of another person's personal story by actors or group participants while the person witnesses the scene.

Ritual drama is the creation of sacred dramatic rites of passage and ceremonies that can help honor and support the transition from one developmental stage to another or the use of archetypes and mythology in service to the balancing and healing of the clients.

ROLE OF THE DRAMA THERAPIST

The therapist creates a safe environment for the client that encourages and supports self-exploration, dignity, respect and personal empowerment in a noninvasive manner. The therapist ensures that all roles are appropriate for the physical, psychological and emotional needs of the clients involved. In most approaches it is the role of the therapist to direct the drama session. He or she creates a comfortable nonjudgmental environment and upholds the contract of the group or with the individual. The therapist facilitates the action segment of the session and assists the group or individual in the process of integration of learned material after the drama has ended.

In clinical drama therapy, the therapist stays fully present and follows the process from moment-to-moment facilitating the client's play. This is done in order to help the client discover a balance of affects and cognitions, inner and outer, or unconscious and conscious experience so that the client may be able to work through a dilemma while remaining intact. In more purely improvisational-oriented approaches the drama therapist may enter into the imaginal realm of the client intervening within the symbolic realm or becoming a play object for the client. The therapist demonstrates the containing power of the playspace through interweaving the dramatic scenes with the clients personal material, here now processing and previously unimagined possibilities.

The role of the therapist ranges from being the director actively intervening in the dramatic process to that of a nonexpert, nondirective and client-centered position that invites the process of collaboration with the client. Role modeling relationally genuine empathic caring is key in these approaches.

POPULATIONS SERVED

Types

All approaches with the exception of family play employ group drama therapy. With the exception of some performance-based approaches, all drama therapy frames also employed individual drama therapy. Several engage in couples and family work and many work with systems and organizations such as schools, prisons and businesses.

Age Range

All approaches, with the exception of specifically child drama therapy, utilized drama therapy with adults. And all approaches with the exception of ritual drama include work with children and adolescents. Most include the geriatric age group as well.

Clinical Populations

Of those drama therapy approaches which work with clinical populations most all work with those with anxiety and/or affects disorders, post-dramatic stress and drug and alcohol abuse. Many work with those with personality and attachment disorders. Others work with those with physical disabilities, catastrophic illness and neurological impairments, and roughly half the approaches are applicable to psychotic populations.

Societal and Developmental Issues

Both clinically and psychoeducationally-oriented drama therapy approaches address life stage transitions, at-risk youth, teachers and those marginalized by society through incarceration and homelessness.

FINAL CONSIDERATIONS

It is hoped that this consensually-based research will be a beginning step in the creation of an integrated body of knowledge in the professional field of Drama Therapy.

And just as drama therapists know that transformation cannot occur through the "talking about" issues, these approaches cannot be truly understood by "the reading" of them. Both require embodied experience. The editors and contributing authors invite the readers to experience for themselves the power of drama therapy in all its richness and variety that these approaches represent.

GLOSSARY

Acting circle is the container of the playspace, safeguarded by agreed-upon rules within which participants engage in improvisational drama and/or play.

Act hunger is the urge or desire for expression, understanding, and mastery in a situation.

Action phase is the middle stage of drama therapeutic process in which the clinical therapist facilitates the enactment of roles and dramatic narrative, the working through process, and the exploration of alternatives by the client and/or group members. In psychoeducational or societal systems, group scenes and theatrical performances are created that become a collective experience for the group to explore issues and feelings with which the whole group can identify, relate and contribute.

Active listening entails the clarifying and reflecting of the client's feelings by the therapist.

Ambiguity is the degree to which the therapist has not determined the spatial configuration, tasks, or roles.

Anima/ae represents the inner feminine aspects of a man's psyche. Within each intrapsychic complex is an archetypal core.

Animus/i represents the inner masculine aspects of a woman's psyche. Within each intrapsychic complex is an archetypal core.

Antagonist is the counter role to the role an individual plays.

Archetypes are universal symbolic images, sounds, actions, themes and energy engendering forces which emerge from the collective unconscious and are core to intrapsychic complexes.

Aside is a technique which occurs when the enactor does not want to say directly to the other person in the enactment what he wants to acknowledge verbally to himself and the audience. The enactor does this by turning to the audience when s/he speaks. The other person in the enactment supposedly does not hear what is being said.

Attachment refers to the basic relationship that develops between a parent and child. Infants need to be doubled or be mirrored when they are newborns. They need the presence of others or auxiliaries to help them develop roles through interaction.

Attuned play is an activity in which two or more players use similar physical expressive patterns through an unconscious to unconscious connection. Where one participant is a caregiver or therapist, s/he empathically attends to the other by reflection of affect and needs through movement, tone, and vocal content.

Audience are those individuals witnessing the dramatic experience. Their role can be to give support and reassurance, participate in the dramatic action, provide feedback and sharing, and/or experience catharsis.

Authentic sound, movement, and drama is an active imagination technique which entails an individual or group engaging in improvisational sound, movement, and/or drama; the technique encourages the interaction between therapist and individual when it supports relationally-oriented developmentally-based growth and advocates group interaction in which individuals can co-participate through projection and transference in each other's imaginal realm.

Auxiliary egos are group members who play roles for the protagonist in the psychodrama.

Bi-personal field is the container within the imaginal realm or transitional space for embodied encounter between the therapist and client or within a group.

Biographical theater is a transformational theater piece scripted, director and acted by the client.

Boundaries, such as the ego, body, and personal space boundaries, serve to protect the individual and aid in discriminating what is conscious from unconscious, real from unreal, what is the domain of the individual from that of others and in the creation of an adaptable safe private space surrounding the individual.

Call and response is an exercise which entails the therapist expressing a feeling and the group repeating it for the purpose of externalizing unspoken feelings of the group.

Catharsis is the spontaneous full expression and release of pent-up emotions.

Childhood survival mechanisms are those role-defining behaviors and thoughts developed by the individual to survive childhood when healthy boundaries have not been developed.

Circular patterns are based upon repetitive closed systemic thinking and occur in dominant stories in which actions and self-descriptions are problem saturated resulting in the client being unable to move forward and be affective.

Closing ritual is present in the final phase of the drama therapeutic process and assists in integration, celebration and the departure from the playspace.

Collective role addresses the common denominator of the role that is similar to all who play it.

Complexity is the degree to which the space, task, and roll structures include multiple elements.

Concretization is the manifestation of intrapsychic and interpersonal habitual behavior by providing a visual enacted symbol of patterns that restrain persons.

Consciousness is the capacity to be fully present, involved in the bigger picture, and either spiritually be in relationship to the Universal Source and/or mystically feel at one with the All.

Consumer role play is a technique in organizational development work used to develop empathy for fellow staff and consumers for the purpose of developing new marketing strategies.

Container is the playspace within a larger setting which allows for creativity and spontaneity to occur within a set of clearly defined boundaries and rules.

Contracts are the rules and consequences that are negotiated between students and clients and drama therapist in order to have a safe constant container.

Core scene is a family's specific emotional issue with the accompanying characteristic pattern of expression that becomes defined and addressed. This can manifest through improvisation, spontaneous mutual play, or through more structured drama therapy exercises and techniques.

Counter role is the shadow side of the conscious role being played or the figure that works on the other side of a role that may be denied, avoided, or board.

Countertransference occurs when the therapist consciously or unconsciously acts upon the material received from the transference or projection consciously or unconsciously sent by the client.

Create a movie set is a creative technique used with preadolescents and adolescents for assessment purposes.

Creative playspace (also known as the **bi-personal field**) is the container for the improvisational embodied encounter between the therapist and client or within a group.

Creative void is the experience of being fully present in the moment capable of spontaneously responding to life.

Creativity is the ability to think beyond personal limitations and see the world in a new way. It is the spark from whence the novel emerges.

Culminating scenes are authentic emergent enactments manifesting the transformed proficiency of the client.

Cultural conserve is any finished product of the creative process which preserves the values of its creators whether they be individuals, groups or cultures. These routines and habitual behaviors can be institutionalized and repress spontaneity.

Cut to the chase refers to the use of shortcuts to explain what the client already knows about the situation being role played.

Deep play is a phenomenon which occurs when both client and therapist experience being fully present in the moment.

Depth psychotherapy is a rite of passage that takes one into the unconscious and then out again.

De-roling occurs when an individual no longer acts a specified role in a drama therapy process.

Developmental theme is the story along with its associated roles and settings which is required for an individual to successfully integrate all that is necessary at a particular life stage.

Developmental theme-based improvisational drama is a spontaneous enactment within the imaginal realm which addresses the repetition or transformation of a particular story or process which is related to a developmental stage.

Developmental themes approach is a drama therapy approach which identifies the life span-related themes along with their associated roles and settings which are not age appropriate; then helps the client clear any immature behavior from unconscious habituation and redramatize healthy development toward an age-appropriate expanded behavioral repertoire. Additionally, the approach supports further life stage development by supplying the needed settings, roles, and themes for their integration through dramatic enactment.

Developmental transformations utilizes an improvisational embodied encounter in the playspace between the therapist and client in order to treat disorders of embodiment, encounter, and play.

Director is the group leader, producer, analyst and therapist of the psychodrama.

Distancing is a way to move a client closer or further away from the role in order to discover balance and aid in healing, growth, and role expansion through style changes and externalization.

Diverting is the use of emergent elements in the dramatic play used to shift attention in order to help the client pay attention to what they are experiencing in the moment.

Double is the one who portrays the inner voice or role of an enactor. The double expresses unexpressed thoughts and feelings of an enactor in order to maximize the feelings expressed by the enactor, through verbal and nonverbal gestures. S/he uses movements and sounds to make the self-observations to help the enactor question him/herself, or to offer support.

Double descriptions is a technique which utilizes enactment to compare the effect of problem stories with the effects of alternative stories.

Dramatic improvisation is the spontaneous creation of a role, setting, and/or story from the individual's imagination.

Dreamwork as theater is reentering the dream space and dramatically interviewing and/or enacting the various characters and symbols in the dream for the purpose of the dreamer coming to understand the meaning of the dream through the experience of it.

Dynamic family play is an intervention style in which art, dance-movement, dramatic storytelling, and video expression are used in mutual play with families to transform conflict and insecure attachments and promote mutual creativity.

Embodied or enacted archetype is a theme-based improvisational drama technique utilizing interview, soliloquy and the embodied psyche technique in an engagement in which an intrapsychic relationship to the various universal aspects of the inner masculine and inner feminine is ascertained.

Embodied psyche technique is a drama therapy process in which intrapsychic complexes are personified, interviewed, and enacted to ascertain and transform psychic energy distribution and their placement and power within the personality.

Empathy is the capacity to think and feel oneself into the inner life of another person.

Empty chair is a psychodrama technique in which a chair is put before the group or an enactor. They are then encouraged to imagine that someone or some quality is in the chair and dialogue with it.

Enact is an arts in education company which utilizes creative drama and drama therapy techniques to improve social and emotional learning in children and adolescents.

E.T. t.h.e.a.t.e.r. is a theater in education drama therapy process which entails the use of performance to help educate adolescence through the reconstruction of environments.

Expression is the degree to which the action and/or imagery is personal and embodied.

Externalizing conversation is an account of how a problem has been affecting a person's life and their relationships in a way that allows for the person to dis-identify or separate from the problem–thus disempowering and objectifying the problem.

Externalizing language is a technique that asks the clients their relationship to the problem or an aspect of the problem rather than suggesting they enact the problem.

Facilitation phase is the part of a drama therapeutic process in which a discussion brings about conscious awareness of behaviors, needs and feelings by shifting the participants from a connection with the material in the scene to a connection with themselves for the purpose of personal problem solving and transformation of behavior.

False mothers are addictions who falsely cajole the addict into believing that they are taking care of the adult ego and/or core self or inner child.

Family therapy assessment games are activities which are utilized for the evaluation of attachment and systemic problems; such as, follow the leader, swing your child into a pile of pillows and calm the child down, show a story about a family of animal parents and children together and children alone, mutual drawings, parent telling the child the story of his/her birth, leave for a brief time and then return and tell the child his/her future, parent teaches the child something based upon games, and complete an obstacle course while tied together.

Five-stage model entails a course of drama therapy treatment which begins with (1) dramatic play to develop a therapeutic relationship and a sense of trust in the therapist and group; (2) scene work entailing structured nonpersonal dramatic scenes to begin to explore new roles; (3) role play of dramatic themes based on real-life situations of the clients to try out new options; (4) culminating enactment through psychodrama entailing the exploration of developmental origins to develop empathy and externalize and transform recurrent themes and roles through culminating scenes, and (5) Ritual closure.

Focus on feelings is the creation of improvisational scenes that focus on characters that either mask or distort their feelings or behave ineffectively or inappropriately which enables the clients to recognize their own feelings and gain insight into the feelings of others.

Free play is an improvisational activity without cues or suggestions given by the therapist.

Future projection is the dramatization of the scene from the future.

Geese Theatre Company is an interactive criminal justice specific theater company which integrates the use of drama therapy and cognitive behavioral restructuring to create complete therapeutic communities in institutional settings.

Guide is a transitional figure that stands between the role and the counter role and is used by either one as a bridge to the other. The guide serves integration and can be moral, amoral or immoral.

Guided shamanic journeys are visualizations of descents and ascents for the purpose of encountering spiritual beings for spontaneous dialoguing about the concerns of the individual.

Humanistic approach is a psychotherapy approach which places an emphasis on self awareness, the possibility of growth and respect for differences.

Ideal mentor exercise is an organizational development technique utilizing a guided visualization for the location and creation of an inner guide.

Imaginal realm is a right-brain dreamlike symbolic language that can be accessed through the arts in service to assessment, healing, growth, and development.

Imagination (see ***Imaginal realm***).

Improvisational drama is the spontaneous creation of story utilizing the imagination.

Improvisational play is a free associational use of spontaneous creation of role, setting, and/or stories from the imagination.

Improvisational family play therapy helps family members experience mutual emotional changes and the recreation of intimacy and security through spontaneous creations of stories, settings and roles from the imagination.

Improvisational role playing are creative enactments that open the space for clients to understand each other and to discover new possibilities in the group at a given moment.

Individuation is that process of therapy which entails an individual becoming more fully who s/he is, connecting to his/her personal path or quest, and expanding his/her consciousness and relationship to the transpersonal.

Infra-reality is an individual's subjective experience of the world.

Inner child recovery is a process which entails the embodied location, rescue, and continuous care and relationship with the core self through the use of role enactment within the imaginal realm.

Inner child(ren) is (are) the inner feelings and desirings of the core self (selves).

Intensification is used within improvisational play to explore or extend the play.

Interactive psychoeducational performance is a theater-based forum in which the actors engage the audience in the dramatic process utilized for the understanding and transformation of systemic and societal issues.

Interactive theater entails the involvement of the audience in the drama, scripting or processing of the drama.

Interpersonal demand is the level of interaction required among members of a group, as well as whether the roles are inanimate, animal, or human form.

Interpretation is a technique which entails the therapist translating and making meaning of unconscious dramatic material to the client.

Intimate play occurs when the client improvisationally plays out thoughts and feelings about the therapist.

Kinetic action is an improvisational process in which the participant focuses on listening, responding quickly and giving up some control.

Media of expression is seen in action being expressed along a developmental continuum of movement, sounds, image, role, or word.

Meglomania Normalis is a term Moreno gave for that human state of wanting to be at the center of the universe.

Mirror is a technique in which the protagonist steps out of the scene and chooses someone to take his role. The protagonist then observes his mirror enact the scene.

Mutual creativity is the interpersonal use of play toward a greater sense of intimacy and affiliation.

Mutual play is the interpersonal use of creative expression toward the creation of a more positive emotional atmosphere and capacity to resolve conflict.

Mythelogems are universal archetypal life themes and plots frequently found in culture's externalizations through myths, fairy tales, religious ritual, and stories of gods and goddesses.

Narradrama is a narrative drama therapy approach which first determines what a person's preferred way of living and interacting with themselves and others is and then assists persons to step more into those preferred stories through the deconstruction of problem saturated dominant stories and the reconstruction of alternative stories along with an expanded repertoire of roles.

Narrative is the self-story that determines which aspects of our lived experience get expressed.

Narrative story enactment is a technique that entails the taking on of roles within stories from the client's life in order to elucidate the meaning and usefulness of the story.

Numinosum is that transpersonal phenomenon which emerges from archetypal stories, big dreams, ritual, and spiritual practice and presence which has the power to heal, transform, and bring grace to those who experience it.

Object relations is the mother/child drama which results in the formation of the sense of self and the internalization of the mother within the infant/toddler.

Open tension systems are the unresolved issues either intrapsychic or interpersonal within which individuals have act hungers.

Pathological creativity is a compulsive drive for creativity that becomes so great that the quest for the new overwhelms the need for adequacy and constancy.

Pairs is a form of playback theater in which the actors portray the struggle between two feelings at the same time.

Pause is a technique in which the drama therapist stops the action of the improvisation and engages the clients in the dialogue about the feelings of the characters at this point and asks for input as to what the options for a particular character might be.

Peak spontaneity is the point at which the ego disappears and there is a sense of connection and flow with the entire universe.

Persona (also known as ***private role***) addresses an individual's personality or identity in their portrayal of various roles.

Persona play is the improvisational process which occurs when the client and therapist play out various interpersonal and intrapersonal roles.

Personal agency mask (also know as ***spirit guide mask***) a projective technique which assists the client to discover personal resources through mask work.

Person-centered therapy is Rogers' client-centered approach which values the subjective experience of the client and seeks to explore the client's perception and work from within it.

Photo problem sculpture (also known as ***sculpt***) is the technique that allows the clients to show their relationship to a problem by placing themselves in a physical position in relationship to the problem. Through this externalization technique open space is created for persons to join in protest against the problem.

Physical task games are embodied exercises such as tugs of war, chase, or a soccer match are used to assess an individual's interpersonal functioning.

Physicalization is embodied experience which allows persons to communicate through their bodies and open themselves to new meanings.

Play is seen as dramatic improvisation with oneself, between two individuals, or among a group which can be used as a tool for continued transformation. It is the laboratory for spontaneous experimentation within the transitional space of the imagination.

Playspace is the mutual agreement among play participants that what is occurring is pretend; it functions as the container of the imaginal realm.

Playback Theater is a drama therapy approach which reenacts personal subjectively told stories of the participants for the purpose of affirmation, healing, transformation, and the validation and connection to oneself and others, and social groups.

Preferred problem relationship sculpture is a technique in which clients place themselves in a preferred physical position in relationship to the problem.

Private role (see ***Persona***).

Projective technique is the placement of roles onto objects such as puppets, sand play (world technique), and masks for the purpose of identification, distancing and externalization.

Protagonist is defined as one of the client's roles that s/he plays in life. In psychodrama, the protagonist is the person who is the focus of the psychodrama.

Psychic determinism is the linking of mental processes by unconscious activity.

Psychoanalytically-oriented drama therapy utilizes clarification, interpretation, and understanding of unconscious material and the transference and countertransference relationship while entering into the fantasy realm of the client to construct and maintain an understandable story about the events of the client's life in order to remove resistances, and promote healthy adaptation and coping skills.

Psychodrama is a deep action method in which people enact scenes from their lives, dreams or fantasies in an effort to express unexpressed feelings, gain new insights and understandings, and practice new and more satisfying behaviors.

Psychodrama a deux is a technique in which there are many empty chairs as there are auxiliaries in the drama and the protagonist enacts the various roles by sitting in the chairs with the director serving as double and interviewer.

Psychodramatic role is a role that is enacted intrapsychically within the imaginal process of the individual.

Psychodymanically-oriented play reflects unconscious thoughts, resistances, transference and countertransference through free associational symbolic improvisation.

Psychosomatic role is a role which manifests physically.

Reality is the group or collective's view of what is.

Reauthoring is the process by which individuals take over the stories about the lives and relationships of other people and make them their own.

Recovery is that therapeutic process which clears past trauma and inhibiting survival patterns and addictions, reconnects the individual to his/her core self, creates healthy boundaries and a capacity for intimacy with others, the Higher Power and the ability to be fully present.

Redramatization of object relations is a technique that entails thematically-based developmental enactments of the mother/child embodied relationship by the client and therapist within the bi-personal field of the imaginal realm for the purpose of self-formation and object internalization.

Reflective scene work are carefully designed real-life scenes demonstrated by the therapist and co-leader to bring about conscious awareness of thoughts and feelings toward behavioral change from the audience. Responding individuals from the audience can be asked to enter into the reflective scene work and bring about purposeful change in behavior.

Repetition is a technique which allows for the emergent elements in a scene to be repeated to help clients pay attention to what they are feeling from moment-to-moment.

Replay is a technique in which the student–actor, participant practices healthier behavior, expression of feelings and needs, and transforms resistance based upon the newfound information from the facilitation process.

Resistance is any defensive mental process or behavior that interferes with the task of understanding and an individual's spontaneously and adaptively responding to life.

Ritual is the establishment of a ceremonial frame, space, time and demeanor for transformative purposes.

Ritual/theater/therapy is a performance drama therapy approach which utilizes the evocation and enactment of archetypes in the construction of a theater piece for the purpose of providing a ritual container of healing for the client/actors.

Ritual community are group-based enactments to celebrate, explore, or heal through ceremonial and artistic action.

Ritual drama is the creation of sacred dramatic rites of passage and ceremonies which can help honor and support the transition from one developmental stage to another or through the employed use of archetypes and mythology, can be in service to the balancing and healing of the client.

Ritualization is repetition of a structure or exercise utilized to provide a sense of security and containing within liminal time and space.

Role is a discrete pattern of changeable behavior that suggests a particular way of thinking, feeling or acting. Role is a unit of behavior that reflects socially agreed upon boundaries and has both collective and private components.

Role creating occurs when the enactor adds something new to the role or creates a totally different vision which may entail the development of novel solutions to phenomena within the role.

Role diagram is an inventory of the roles a person plays which can be used to assess role partnerships and relationships.

Role enactment is the playing of a collective, presentational, or a personal role with some measure of improvisation.

Role playing is a person's enactment of a role with some freedom, flexibility, spontaneity, and comfort from the rigidity of society's definition.

Role profile test is an assessment in which the subject is asked to rate a list of roles to assess the quantity and quality of roles taken and played.

Role rehearsal or ***Role retraining*** occurs when a client reconstructs a problem scene by replaying it in a preferred way or practices an unfamiliar role in order to learn new behaviors and expand his/her role repertoire.

Role repertoire consists of all the roles an individual plays in life.

Role reversal is a drama therapy technique which entails the enactor switching places and exchanging roles in order to imagine and express what the other feels like in any given situation for the purpose of the development of empathy and understanding, insight, perspective, and spontaneity. It is also employed to help enactors see themselves as others see them or to facilitate cool down if the enactor is overheated in role.

Role system is the totality of conscious and subconscious roles intrapsychically available at any one moment in an individual's personality.

Role taking is the ability to imagine oneself as another. This occurs when someone follows the parameters of the role exactly as the culture or person has established them. In psychodrama, role taking refers to an enactment of a role in a routinized, somewhat stilted way.

Role theory and methods in drama therapy utilizes an understanding of a taxonomy of roles in service to the identification and dramatic facilitation of an individual's role system for the purpose of the client's conscious awareness and connection with the various roles, counter roles, and guide and his/her capacity to competently and adaptively enact them both intrapsychically and in social situations.

Role training is a rehearsal for life situations that are to come through practicing a variety of behaviors to meet any given situation for the desired behavior or action one chooses.

Role types are repeated character types that seem to transcend time, genre and culture that serve a specific function. They are either presentational, a more abstract cognitive form, or representational, a more reality-based affective form.

Sacred space is the deliberate creation of a spiritual, ceremonial or ritual-like artistic and truth telling space that is distinct from ordinary life for the purpose of healing and growth.

Sand play (also known as ***world technique***) is a technique in which an individual moves or shapes sand in a box or arranges small symbolic figures in the sand. These figures are then personified, interviewed and possibly rearranged in order to experience their meaning and any possible transformation.

Scene work entails structured dramatic and developed roles that are not part of the person's behavior and role repertoire.

Scenes is a technique in which dramas are created based on personal experience without being the actual experience of a particular client.

Sculpt (see ***Photo problem sculpture***) is an externalization technique that allows the clients to show their relationship to a problem by placing themselves in a physical position in relationship to the problem.

Self actualization is the process in which an individual unfolds and grows from the inside out.

Self-narratives are the stories a person has about their life that shape, constitute, and embrace our lives.

Shadow are intrapsychic complexes which represent same sex aspects of an individual psyche which are seeking to be integrated by the ego. Within each shadow aspect is an archetypal core.

Shamanic healing rituals are archetypal indigenous sacred ceremonies found in the origins of theater and basic to healing structures of drama therapy.

Sharing is the final phase of most drama therapy processes in which all participants including the audience express their response to the enactment on a personal level including what they have learned.

Social atom explores all the relationships real or fantasy, dead or alive, that a person brings with them into the room in order to gather information, assess functioning level, set treatment goals, and make interventions. They consist of all those who are significant to the individual at any given time.

Social barometer (see ***Spectrogram***) reflects how a person feels in relation to activities and social issues. It is based on a continuum between 0 and 100%.

Social roles are reciprocal roles that are reenacted in relation to other people within a person's familial or social sphere.

Sociodrama is an action method in which individuals enact an agreed upon social situation spontaneously for the purpose of defining a problem that members would like to solve, gaining greater understanding, clarifying a decision which they would like to be able to make or for training themselves in certain role aspects about which they may feel uncomfortable.

Sociogram is a graphic representation of the social choices a group has made and the connection that people have with one another based upon a particular criteria.

Sociometry is the measurement of social choices and a set of intervention tools designed to facilitate social change. It is also the invisible and visible connections among group members.

Soliloquy is a monologue in which an enactor speaks aloud his thoughts and feelings at some length.

Somatic countertransference is a technique in which unconscious feelings, sensations, thoughts, and/or images are received from the client's unconscious into the body unconscious of the therapist and is held, transformed, and/or sent back to the client's unconscious or conscious awareness for the purpose of integration and healing.

Somato-emotional release is the expression of emotions that have been stored in the body due to emotional or physical trauma.

Soul songs are songs created spontaneously as an expression of the person's emotional states and transformational edge through pure sound expression

Spectrogram (also known as a ***social barometer***) reflects how a person feels in relation to activities and social issues. It is based on a continuum between 0 and 100%.

Spirit guide mask (see ***Personal agency mask***).

Spontaneity is the moment-to-moment readiness for creative action in service to an adequate response to a new situation or a new response to an old situation.

Spontaneity theory and training is based upon the premise that humans are "fallen gods" longing to experience the First Universe of the boundarylessness of infancy. Psychodramatic spontaneity training is utilized as rehearsals for life by decreasing the anxiety caused from the experience of the separation from the other and by increasing the capacity to live in the here and now.

Spontaneous mutual play is the moment-to-moment improvisational use of creative expression between two people toward healthy encounter and adaptivity.

Stop-gap is an interactive improvisational theater approach in which a team, consisting of two professional actors and the drama therapist, utilizes enactment to stimulate dialogue about relevant issues to particular populations, the clarification of feelings, and the exploration of options.

Storytelling is an oral tradition in which a society's world view and history is conveyed to its people. As a drama therapy technique it may be used by the therapist to assist in the integration of unconscious material. In transformational theater it is the process of telling one's own story through enactment.

Surface play is the improvising with the social stereotypes and issues at the level of body as other between client and therapist.

Surplus reality incorporates the perspective beyond group and individual experiences of reality and is used in the psychodramatic process

Swing the pendulum is a technique in which the actors take opposing positions to get a strong response not only from the other character in the scene but also from the clients.

Tableaux are frozen human sculptures that symbolize feelings or behaviors.

Tele is a deep, accurate knowing and acceptance of the self and the other.

Tell-a-story technique occurs when the therapist instructs the client to tell a story. Miniature objects or puppets may be used. The client is asked to specify the characters in the story and answer questions reporting the qualities, function, style, and the theme of the story. The technique assesses the individual's ability to invoke a role, counter role, and guide and to move toward some integration among the roles.

Theater games are dramatic exercises used to change the atmosphere, loosening attitudes, affect and cognitions. The participants are then able to free associate from the games and address the real issues of the task.

Theater performance as a drama therapy technique is co-created through extensive listening in conversation with the participants and is a faithful rendering of their experience.

Theatrical scene work is a drama therapy technique in which developed roles and characters are improvised to facilitate expression and role expansion.

Theme-based movement/drama improvisation is a movement/drama therapy technique in which the client is given a story or theme from dream material, projectives, sand play or life to amplify through embodied creative expression.

Therapeutic alliance is a partnership relationship formed between the therapist and client whereby common goals are articulated and pursued and the client feels the therapist is working with and for him/her.

Therapeutic theater is a performance-based approach which encourages the awareness, healing and/or growth from the actors and audience. In ritual theater it is a performative drama therapy process which utilizes the evocation and embodiment of archetypes or key themes in the construction and enactment of various kinds of performances for the purpose of providing a container for the healing of the client/actors or changing behavior.

Thinking report homework assignments are cognitive-based journaling of all thoughts, feelings, sensations and beliefs remembered before, during and after a conflict, particular behavior, or dysfunctional thought process.

Toward the One is a people-sized board game participatory theater piece for families in which family members could make new discoveries about each other and become vulnerable through improvisational play .

Tracking is the noting from moment-to-moment what gets the individual's attention.

Transference is the psychodynamic relational construct which occurs when the patient reenacts the past by transferring a prior relationship onto the therapist.

Transformation of the psyche is the process of personality change which occurs within the imaginal realm when a client integrates, brings into conscious engagement, and/or shifts the position or psychic energy distribution of a complex.

Transformation to the Here and Now is the changing the scene into reality by the therapist or client in order to help clients move toward fully experiencing the moment.

Transformative process is the process through which immature patterns of behavior are cleared and replaced with age-appropriate adaptive behavior through the use of drama within the imaginal realm.

Transformational theater utilizes spiritually-based theater pieces in which the playing of the roles themselves become a spiritual practice. Participants do the inner work by holding an inner concentration while performing in the outer drama. Thus, both the actors and the theater piece itself are transformed.

Transitional space is a liminal imaginal playspace created where clients can construct and reconstruct themselves, heal, transform, and grow.

Two-stage model in drama therapy first focuses upon the use of dramatic roles in the recovery from past abuse and addictions toward being fully present and able to connect with themselves, others and transpersonally. Secondly, dramatic roles· and themes are utilized to support clients' individuation process undergoing adult life stages transitions, deepening their meaning of life, and expanding their spiritual consciousness.

Unique outcomes story is an alternative story enactment, a photo sculpture, improvisation, or mime vignette which opens the space for more awareness and options.

Unwinding is a technique which reduces resistance through playful creative dramatic processes and theater games.

Video drama is a technique employed in organizational development which, from interviews of staff, identifies the underlying problems and creates a script and a dramatic production which demonstrates an alternative way of interacting within the organizational system using the familiar "training film" style.

Videoing is used to identify significant moments and interactions for further awareness, assessment, as well as to extend the creative metaphor through *movie making*.

Walk and talk is a technique which entails the director walking around the stage with the enactor discussing with them the parameters of the role they are to play. It is also used during this sociodrama when directors ask audience members to make suggestions for handling the problem in the scene or in conflict situations in which enactors are getting overheated.

Warm-up is the first phase of the drama therapy therapeutic process in which the participants are prepared for the drama therapy process to come through dramatic play phase designed to develop personal and group expressiveness, trust, and connection and/or the delineation of a thematic problem members would like to solve.

Who-what-where cards are cards which allow clients to identify characters and situations occurring between them from their life experience that they would like to see role played. The elements are defined as: Who: the client may indicate any two characters; What: the client describes briefly what's going on between the two characters; Where: the client describes the setting.

Witnessing circle is a small circular carpet, utilized by the therapist when s/he witnesses the client's play within the playspace.

World technique (see ***Sand play***).

BIBLIOGRAPHY

DRAMA THERAPY BIBLIOGRAPHY BY COMPETENCY AREAS

BOOKS ON DRAMA THERAPY: INTRODUCTION AND ADVANCED COMPETENCIES AND DRAMA THERAPY WITH SPECIAL POPULATIONS

Astell-Burt, C. (1981). *Puppetry for mentally handicapped people.* Cambridge, MA: Brookline Books.

Ayalon, O., & Flasher, A. (1993). *Children and divorce: Chain reaction.* London: Jessica Kingsley Publisher.

Bailey, S. (1993). *Wings to fly: Bringing theatre arts to students with special needs.* Bethesda, MD: Woodbine House (currently available through author at 1102 Merwood Drive; Takoma Park, MD 20912).

Bannister, A. (1997). *The healing drama: Psychodrama and dramatherapy with abused children.* New York: Free Association Books.

Behr, M.W., Snyder, A.B., & Clopton, A.S. (1979). *Drama integrates basic skills: Lesson plans for the learning disabled.* Springfield, IL: Charles C Thomas.

Boal, A. (1995). *The rainbow of desire: The Boal method of theatre and therapy.* New York: Routledge.

Casdagli, P. (1998). *Trust and power: Taking care of ourselves through drama.* London: Jessica Kingsley Publisher.

Cattanach, A. (1997). *Children's stories in play therapy.* London: Jessica Kingsley Publisher.

Cattanach, A. (1992). *Drama for people with special needs.* New York, Drama Book Publishers.

Cattanach, A. (1993). *Play therapy with abused children.* London, Jessica Kingsley Publisher.

Cattanach, A. (1994). *Play therapy: Where the sky meets the underworld,* London: Jessica Kingsley Publisher.

Chesner, A. (1995). *Dramatherapy for people with learning disabilities: A world of difference.* London: Jessica Kingsley Publisher.

Cohen, H. (1995). *Dramatically able: Making drama accessible to participants with disabilities.* Ann Arbor, MI: Wild Swan Theatre.

Cossa, M., Fleischmann, E.S.S., Grover, L., & Hazelwood, J.L. (1996). *Acting out: The workbook.* Washington, DC: Taylor & Francis.

Courtney, R., & Schattner, G. (Eds.). (1981). *Drama in therapy.* New York: Drama Book Specialists.

Courtney, R. (1990). *Drama and Intelligence.* Montreal, Canada: McGill-Queen's University Press.

Crimmins, P. (1997). *Storymaking and creative groupwork with older people.* London: Jessica Kingsley Publisher.

Dayton, T. (1990). *Drama games: Techniques for self development.* Pompano Beach, FL: Health Communications, Inc.

Dayton, T. (1994). *The Drama Within: Psychodrama and Experiential Therapy.* Deerfield Beach, FL: Health Communications, Inc.

Duggan, M., & Grainger, R. (1997). *Imagination, identification and catharsis in theatre and therapy.* London: Jessica Kingsley Publisher.

Dunne, P.B. (1988). *Media in drama therapy: An exercise handbook.* Los Angeles: Drama Therapy Institute of Los Angeles.

Dunne, P.B. (1990). *The creative therapeutic thinker* (2nd Ed.). Los Angeles: Drama Therapy Institute of Los Angeles.

Dunne, P.B. (1992). *The narrative therapist and the arts: Expanding possibilities through drama, movement, puppets, masks, and drawings.* Los Angeles, CA: Drama Therapy Institute of Los Angeles.

Dunne, P.B. (1995). *Creative journal.* Los Angeles, CA: Drama Therapy Institute of Los Angeles.

Dunne, P.B. (1993). *Drama therapy activities with parents and children: An exercise handbook* (Revised Ed.). Los Angeles, CA: Drama Therapy Institute of Los Angeles.

Dunne, P.B. (1997). *Double stick tape: Poetry, drama, and narratives as therapy for adolescents.* Los Angeles: Drama Therapy Institute of Los Angeles.

Emunah, R. (1994). *Acting for real: Drama therapy: Process, technique, and performance.* New York: Brunner/Mazel.

Gersie, A. (Ed.). (1996). *Dramatic Approaches to Brief Therapy.* London: Jessica Kingsley Publisher.

Gersie, A. (1997). *Reflections on therapeutic storymaking: The use of stories in groups.* London: Jessica Kingsley Publisher.

Gersie, A. (1992). *Storymaking in bereavement: Dragons in flight in the meadow.* London: Jessica Kingsley Publisher.

Gersie, A., & King, N. (1990). *Storymaking in education and therapy.* London: Jessica Kingsley Publisher.

Gold, M. (1991). *The fictional family: In drama, education, and groupwork.* Springfield, IL: Charles C Thomas.

Grainger, R. (1990). *Drama and healing: The roots of drama therapy.* London: Jessica Kingsley Publisher.

Grainger, R. (1995). *The glass of heaven: The faith of the dramatherapist.* London: Jessica Kingsley Publisher.

Hoey, B. (1997). *Who calls the tune? A psychodramatic approach to child therapy.* New York: Routledge.

Jenkins, M. (1996). *The play's the thing: Exploring text in drama and therapy.* New York: Routledge.

Jennings, S. (1974). *Remedial Drama.* New York: Theatre Arts Books.

Jennings, S. (1987). *Drama therapy: Theory and practice for teachers and clinicians.* Cambridge, MA: Brookline Books.

Jennings, S. (1990). *Dramatherapy with families, groups, and individuals: Waiting in the wings.* London, Jessica Kingsley Publishers.

Jennings, S. (1995). *Theatre, ritual, and transformation: The senoi temiars.* New York: Routledge.

Jennings, S. (1997). *Introduction to dramatherapy: Theatre and healing: Ariadne's ball of thread.* London: Jessica Kingsley Publishers.

Jennings, S. (Ed.). (1995). *Dramatherapy with children and adolescents.* New York: Routledge.

Jennings, S. (Ed.). (1990). *Dramatherapy theory and practice 1,* New York: Routledge.

Jennings, S. (Ed.). (1992). *Dramatherapy theory and practice 2,* New York: Routledge.

Jennings, S. (Ed.). (1996). *Dramatherapy Theory and Practice 3,* New York: Routledge.

Jennings, S., Cattanach, A., Mitchell, S., Chesner, A., & Brenda, M. (1994). *The handbook of dramatherapy.* London: Routledge.

Jennings, S., & Minde, A. (1992). *Art therapy and dramatherapy: Masks of the soul.* London: Jessica Kingsley Publishers.

Johnson, D.R. et al. (1992). *Collected papers on the developmental method and transformations.*

New Haven, CT: New Haven Drama Therapy Institute.

Johnson, D.R., & Sandel, S.L. (1987). *Waiting at the gate: Creativity and hope in the nursing home.* New York: Haworth Press.

Jones, P. (1996). *Drama as therapy: Theatre as living.* New York: Routledge.

Landy, R. (1994). *Drama therapy: Concepts, theories, and practices* (2nd Ed.), Springfield, IL: Charles C Thomas.

Landy, R. (1993). *Personna and performance: The meaning of role in drama, therapy, and everyday life.* New York: Guilford Press.

Landy, R. (1996). *Essays in drama therapy: The double life.* London: Jessica Kingsley Publisher.

Langley, D. (1983). *Dramatherapy and psychiatry.* London: Croom Helm.

Lewis, P. (1993). *Creative transformation: The healing power of the arts.* Wilmette, IL: Chiron Publications.

Lindkvist, M.R. (1997). *Bring white beads when you call on the healer.* New Orleans: Rivendell House.

Link, A. (1992). *Mirrors from the heart: Emotional identity and expression through drama.* Ontario, Canada: Snailworks.

MacDougall & Yoder, P.S. (Eds.). (1998). *Contaminating theatre: Intersections of theatre, therapy, and public health.* Evanston, IL: Northwestern University Press.

Mitchell, S. (1995). *Dramatherapy: Clinical studies.* London: Jessica Kingsley Publisher.

Pearson, J. (Ed.). (1996). *Discovering the self through drama and movement: The Sesame approach.* London: Jessica Kingsley Publisher.

Peter, M. (1994). *Drama for all: Developing drama in the curriculum with pupils with special education needs.* London: David Fulton Publishers.

Piggins, C., & Thurman, A. (1996). *Drama activities with older adults: A handbook for leaders.* Binghamton, NY: Haworth Press.

Salas, J. (1993). *Improvising real life: Personal story in playback theatre.* Dubuque, IA: Kendall/Hunt Publishing.

Schattner, G., & Courtney, R. (Eds.). (1981). *Drama in therapy: Volume one: children.* New York: Drama Book Specialists.

Schattner, G., & Courtney, R. (Eds.). (1981). *Drama in therapy: Volume two: Adults.* New York, Drama Book Specialists.

Schechner, R. (1994). *Environmental theatre.* New York: Applause.

Schutzman, M., & Cohen-Cruz, J. (1994). *Playing boal: Theatre, therapy and activism.* New York: Routledge.

Shaw, A., & Stevens, C. (Eds.). (1979). *Drama theater and the handicapped.* Washington, DC: American Theater Association.

Slade, P. (1959). *Dramatherapy as an aid to becoming a person.* London: Guild of Pastoral Psychology.

Telander, M., Quinlan, F., & Verson, K. (1982). *Acting up!: An innovative approach to creative drama for older adults.* Chicago, Coach House Press.

Thompson, J. (Ed.). (1998). *Prison theatre: Practices and perspectives,* London: Jessica Kingsley Publisher.

Tomlinson, R. (1989). *Disability, theatre, and education.* Bloomington, IN: Indiana University Press, 1982. with Disabled People, Ontario, Canada: Captus Press.

Way, B. (1972). *Development through drama.* New York: Humanities Press.

Weisberg, N., & Wilder, R. (Eds.). (1988). *Creative arts with older adults: A sourcebook.* New York: Human Sciences Press.

Wethered, A.G. (1997). *Movement and drama in therapy: A holistic approach,* 2nd ed. London: Jessica Kingsley Publisher.

Wiener, D.J. (1994). *Rehearsals for growth: Theatre improvisation for psychotherapists.* New York: W.W. Norton.

Wilder, R. (1986). *A space where anything can happen: Creative drama in the middle school.* VA: New Plays-Books, Inc.

Winn, L. (1994). *Post traumatic stress disorder and dramatherapy: Treatment and risk reduction.* London: Jessica Kingsley Publisher.

INTERDISCIPLINARY BOOKS ON CREATIVE ARTS THERAPY WHICH INCLUDE DRAMA THERAPY

Anderson, W. (Ed.). (1977). *Therapy and the arts: Tools of consciousness.* New York: Harper Colophon Books.

Fryear, J., & Fleshman, B. (1981). *The arts in therapy.* Nelson-Hall.

Hillman, G., & Gaffney, K. *Artists in the community: Training artists to work in alternative settings.* New York: Americans for the Arts' Institute for Community Development and the Arts.

Hornyak, L.M., & Baker, E.K. (1989). *Experiential therapies for eating disorders.* New York: Guildford Press.

Kaye, C., & Blee, T. (1996). *The arts in health care: A palette of possibilities.* London: Jessica Kingsley Publisher.

Levine, S.K., & Levine, E.G. (1998). *Foundations of expressive arts therapies: Theoretical and clinical perspectives.* London: Jessica Kingsley Publisher.

Liebmann, M. (Ed.). (1996). *Arts approaches to conflict.* London: Jessica Kingsley Publisher.

McNiff, S. (1998). *Art-based research.* London: Jessica Kingsley Publisher.

Rogers, N. (1993). *The creative connection: Expressive arts as healing.* Palo Alto, CA: Science & Behavior Books.

Warren, B. (Ed.). (1994). *Using the creative arts in therapy: A practical introduction (2nd Ed.).* New York: Routledge.

Weiss, J.C. (1984). *Expressive therapy with elders and the disabled: Touching the heart of life.* Binghamton, NY: Haworth Press.

PSYCHODRAMA AND SOCIODRAMA

Blatner, H.A. (1973). *Acting in: Practical applications of psychodramatic methods.* New York: Springer Pub. Co.

Blatner, A., & Blatner, A. (1988). *Foundations of psychodrama: History theory and practice.* New York: Springer Pub.

Fuhlrodt, R.L. (Ed.). (1989). *Psychodrama: Its application to ACOA and substance abuse treatment.* East Rutherford, NJ: Thomas W. Perrin.

Farmer, C. (1995). *Psychodrama and systemic therapy.* London: Karnac Books.

Fox, J. (Ed.). (1987). *The essential Moreno: Writings on psychodrama, group method, and spontaneity.* New York: Springer.

Gendron, J. (1980). *Moreno: The roots and branches; and bibliography of psychodrama 1972–1980.* Beacon: Beacon House.

Greenberg, I.A. (Ed.). (1974). *Psychodrama: Theory and therapy.* New York: Behavioral Pub.

Goldman, E.F., & Morrison, D.S. (1984). *Psychodrama: Experience and process.* Phoenix: Eldemar Corp.

Haas, R.B. (1961). *Psychodrama and sociodrama in American education.* Beacon: Beacon House.

Hale, A.E. (1981). *Conducting clinical sociometric explorations: A manual for psychodramatists and sociometrists.* Roanoke: Royal Pub.

Haskell, M.R. (1975). *Socioanalysis: Self direction via sociometry and psychodrama.* Long Beach, CA: Role Training Associates of California.

Heisey, M.J. (1982). *Clinical case studies in psychodrama.* Washington DC: University Press of America.

Holmes, P. (1992). *The inner world outside: Object relations theory and psychodrama.*

Holmes, P., & Karp, M. (Eds.). (1991). *Psychodrama: Inspiration and technique.* New York: Routledge.

Holmes, P., Karp, M., & Tauvon, K.B. (1994). *The handbook of psychodrama.* New York: Routledge.

Holmes, P. et al. (1994). Psychodrama since Moreno: Innovations in theory and practice. *Journal of Group Psychotherapy, Psychodrama and Sociometry.* Washington, DC: Heldref Pub.

Kellerman, P. (1992). *Focus on psychodrama: The therapeutic aspects of psychodrama.* London: Jessica Kingsley Publisher.

Leveton, E. (1992). *A clinician's guide to psychodrama* (2nd ed.). New York: Springer Publishing Company.

Moreno, J.L. (1994). *Psychodrama, 4th ed.,* Volumes I, II, and III. McLean, VA: ASGPP.

Moreno, J.L. (1993). *Who shall survive? Foundations of sociometry, group psychotherapy, and sociodrama.* McLean, VA: ASGPP.

Moreno, J.L. (1975). *The theatre of spontaneity, Volume 1.* New York: Beacon Press.

Roine, E. (1997). *Psychodrama: Group psychotherapy as experimental theatre.* London: Jessica Kingsley Publisher.

Smilansky, S. (1968). *The effects of sociodramatic play on disadvantaged children.* New York: John Wiley.

Starr, A. (1979). *Psychodrama: Rehearsal for living.* Chicago: Nelson-Hall.

Sternberg, P. (1998). *Theatre for conflict resolution in the classroom and beyond.* Portsmouth, NH: Heinemann.

Sternberg, P., & Garcia, A. (1994). *Sociodrama: Who's in your shoes?* Westport, CT: Prager.

Torrance, E.P., Murdock, & Fletcher, D. (1988). *Sociodrama: Creative problem solving in action.* Buffalo: Bearly Limited.

Wiener, R. (1997). *Creative training: Sociodrama and team-building.* London: Jessica Kingsley Publisher.

Williams, A. (1989). *The passionate technique: Strategic psychodrama with individuals, families, and groups.*

Yablonsky, L. (1992). *Psychodrama: Resolving emotional problems through role-playing.* New York: Brunner/Mazel.

IMPROVISATION, THEATER AND THEATER GAMES

Blatner, A., & Blatner, A. (1988). *The art of play: An adult's guide to reclaiming imagination and spontaneity.* New York: Human Sciences Press.

Boal, A. (1992). *Games for actors and non-actors.* London:Routledge.

Boal, A. (1979). *Theatre of the oppressed.* New York: Theatre Communications Group.

Brook, P. (1968). *The empty space.* New York: Avon.

Frost, A., & Yarrow, R. (1990). *Improvisation in drama.* London: MacMillan.

Johnstone, K. (1979). *Improv: Improvisation and the theatre.* New York: Theater Arts Books.

Pasolli, R. (1970). *A book on open theater.* New York: Avon.

Schechner, R., & Schuman, M. (Eds.). (1976). *Ritual, play, and performance: Readings in the social sciences/theatre.* New York: The Seabury Press.

Spolin, V. (1969). *Improvisation for the theatre.* Evanston, IL: Northwestern University Press.

Stanislavsky, K. (1961). *Creating a role.* New York: Theatre Arts Books.

Stanislavsky, K. (1972). *Building a character.* New York: Theatre Arts Books.

Stanislavsky, K. (1989). *An actor prepares.* New York: Theatre Arts Books.

Stanislavsky, K. (1970). *An actor's handbook.* New York: Theatre Arts Books.

Turner, V. (1982). *From ritual to theater.* New York: Performing Arts Journal Press.

CREATIVE DRAMA AND THEATER IN EDUCATION

Bolton, G.M. (1984). *Drama as education.* Harlow: Longman.

Bolton, G.M. (1979). *Towards a theory of drama in education.* Harlow: Longman.

Courtney, R. (1974). *Play, drama, and thought.* New York: Drama Book Specialists.

Courtney, R. (1982). *Replay: Studies of drama in education.* Toronto, Ontario: Institute for Studies in Education.

Hermann, A., & Clifford, S. (1998). *Making a leap–Theatre for empowerment: A practical handbook for creative drama work with young people.* London: Jessica Kingsley Publisher.

Hornbrook, D. (1989). *Education and dramatic art.* Oxford: Blackwell.

Jennings, S. (1987). *Creative drama in groupwork.* London: Winslow Press.

Landy, R. (1982). *Handbook of educational drama and theater.* New York: Greenwood.

McCaslin, N. (1994). *Creative drama in the classroom and beyond.* New York: Longman.

Slade, P. (1995). *Child play: It's importance for human development.* London: Jessica Kingsley Publisher.

Slade, P. (1954). *Child drama.* London: University of London Press.

CHAPTERS AND JOURNAL ARTICLES ON DRAMA THERAPY

Aach, Susan. Drama: A means of self-expression for the visually-impaired child. *New Outlook for the Blind,* 1976, Vol. 70 (7), pp. 282–285.

Allan, John A. The use of creative drama with acting-out sixth and seventh grade boys and girls. *Canadian Counsellor,* 1977, Vol. 11 (3), pp. 135–143.

Antinori, Deborah & Moore, Penelope. The controlled approach exercise in cultural diversity training with clinicians. *The Arts in Psychotherapy,* 1997, Vol. 24 (2), pp. 173–182.

Bailey, Sally D. Drama: A powerful tool for social skill development. *Disability Solutions,* 1997, Vol. 2 (1), pp. 1–5.

Barsky, Marilyn & Mozenter, Gerry. The use of creative drama in a children's group. *International Journal of Group Psychotherapy,* 1976, Vol. 26 (1), pp. 105–114.

Barratt, Gill & Segal, Barbara. Rivalry, competition and transference in a children's group. *Group Analysis,* 1996, Vol. 29 (1), pp. 23–35.

Bielanska, Anna, Cechnicki, Andrzej, & Budzyna-Dawidowski, Prezemyslaw. Dramatherapy as a means of rehabilitation for schizophrenic patients: Our impressions. *American Journal of Psychotherapy,* 1991, Vol. 45 (4), pp. 566–575.

Brand, David. In Massachusetts: Theater therapy. *Time,* November 9, 1987, pp. 12–16.

Bromfield, Richard. The use of puppets in play therapy. *Child and Adolescent Social Work Journal,* 1995, Vol. 12 (6), pp. 435–444.

Buchanan, Dale Richard. Moreno's social atom: A diagnostic and treatment tool for exploring interpersonal relationships. *The Arts in Psychotherapy,* 1984, Vol. 11, pp. 155–164.

Burton, Caroline. Peekaboo to "all the all the outs in free": Hide-and-seek as a creative structure in drama therapy. *The Arts in Psychotherapy,* 1986, Vol. 13 (2), pp. 129–136.

Bush, Catharine S. Creative drama and language experiences: Effective clinical techniques. *Language, Speech and Hearing Services in the Schools,* 1978, Vol. 9 (4), pp. 254–258.

Casson, John. Archetypal splitting: Drama therapy and psychodrama. *The Arts in Psychotherapy,* 1996, Vol. 23 (4), pp. 307–309.

Cattanach, Ann. Drama and play therapy with young children. *The Arts in Psychotherapy,* 1995, Vol. 22 (3), pp. 223–228.

Cohen, Hilary U. Conflicting values in creating theatre with the developmentally disabled: A study of Theatre Unlimited. *The Arts in Psychotherapy,* 1985, Vol. 12, pp. 3–10.

Cossa, Mario. Acting Out: A pilot project in drama therapy with adolescents. *The Arts in Psychotherapy,* 1992, Vol. 19 (1), pp. 53–55.

Couroucli-Robertson, Katerina. Cultural differences and similarities in drama therapy. *The Arts in Psychotherapy,* 1992, Vol. 19 (2), pp. 117–121.

Davies, Darlene G. Utilization of creative drama with hearing-impaired youth. *Volta Review,* 1984, Vol. 86 (2), pp. 106–113.

Davis, Barbara W. The impact of creative drama training on psychological states of older adults: An exploratory study. *Gerontologist,* 1985, Vol. 25 (3), pp. 315–321.

Davis, Barbara W. Some roots and relatives of creative drama as an enrichment activity for older adults. *Educational Gerontology,* 1987, Vol. 13 (4), pp. 297–306.

Dunne, Pam Barragar. Drama therapy techniques in one-on-one treatment with disturbed children and adolescents. *The Arts in Psychotherapy,* 1988, Vol. 15 (2), pp. 139–149.

DuPont, Sherry. The effectiveness of creative drama as an instructional strategy to enhance the reading comprehension skills of fifth grade remedial readers. *Reading Research and Instruction,* 1992, Vol. 31 (3), pp. 41–52.

Eberle, Bob. Does creative dramatics really square with research evidence? *Journal of Creative Behavior,* 1974, Vol. 8 (3), pp. 177–182.

Eliaz, Eliran. The concept of dramatic transference. *The Arts in Psychotherapy,* 1992, Vol. 19 (5), pp. 333–346.

Eliaz, Eliran & Flashman, Alan. Road signs: Elements of transference in drama therapy: Case study. *The Arts in Psychotherapy,* 1994, Vol. 21 (1), pp. 59–73.

Emunah, Renee. Drama therapy with adult psychiatric patients. *The Arts in Psychotherapy,* 1983, Vol. 10 (2), pp. 77–84.

Emunah, Renee. Drama therapy and adolescent resistance. *The Arts in Psychotherapy,* 1985, Vol. 12 (2), pp. 71–79.

Emunah, Renee. The use of dramatic enactment in the training of drama therapists. *The Arts in Psychotherapy,* 1989, Vol. 16 (1), pp. 29–36.

Emunah, Renee. Expression and expansion in adolescence: The significance of creative arts therapy. *The Arts in Psychotherapy,* 1990, Vol. 17 (2), pp. 101–107.

Emunah, Renee & Johnson, David Read. The impact of theatrical performance on the self-images of psychiatric patients. *The Arts in Psychotherapy,* 1983, Vol. 10, pp. 233–239.

Fink, Siobhan O. Approaches to emotion in psychotherapy and theatre: Implications for drama therapy. *The Arts in Psychotherapy,* 1990, Vol. 17 (1), pp. 5–18.

Finneran, Lanell R., Unruh, David, & Bartscher, Beverly. The therapeutic classroom: A cooperative effort between Lawrence Public Schools and Bert Nash Community Mental Health Center. *Continuum: The Journal of the Association for Ambulatory Behavioral Healthcare,* 1997, Vol. 4 (2), pp. 153–174.

Fontana, David & Valente, Lucilia. Drama therapy and the theory of psychological reversals. *The Arts in Psychotherapy,* 1993, Vol. 20 (2), pp. 133–142.

Furman, Lou. Theatre as therapy: The distancing effect applied to audience. *The Arts in Psychotherapy,* 1988, Vol. 15 (3), pp. 245–249.

Ghiaci, Golshad & Richardson, John T. The affects of dramatic play upon cognitive structure and development. *Journal of Genetic Psychology,* 1980, Vol. 136 (1), pp. 77–83.

Gomes, Ralph C. & Count Van Manen, Gloria. Family Life Laboratory: The uses of creative dramatic processes in university social sciences settings. *Journal of Mental Imagery,* 1984, Vol. 8 (1), pp. 109–115.

Goodrich, Janet & Goodrich, Wells. Drama therapy with a learning disabled, personality disordered adolescent. *The Arts in Psychotherapy,* 1986, Vol. 13 (4), pp. 285–291.

Gray, Bronwen. This is the story of Wicked: Community drama theatre with at-risk Aboriginal Australian youth. *The Arts in Psychotherapy,* 1997, Vol. 24 (3), pp. 275–279.

Hackney, Patty W. Education of the visually handicapped gifted: A program description. *Education of the Visually Handicapped,* 1986, Vol. 18 (2), pp. 85–95.

Harvey, Steve. Dynamic play therapy: An integrative expressive arts approach to the family therapy of young children. *The Arts in Psychotherapy,* 1990, Vol. 17, pp. 239–246.

Harvey, Steve. Creating a family: An integrated expressive approach to adoption. *The Arts in Psychotherapy,* 1991, Vol. 18, pp. 213–222.

Harvey, Steve & Kelly, E. Connor. Evaluation of the quality of parent-child relationships: A longitudinal case study. *The Arts in Psychotherapy,* 1993, Vol. 20 (5), pp. 387–395.

Herman, Lisa. Good enough fairy tales for resolving sexual abuse trauma. *The Arts in Psychotherapy,* 1997, Vol. 24 (5), pp. 439–445.

Hiltunen, Sirkku S. Initial therapeutic applications of Noh Theatre in drama therapy. *Journal of Transpersonal Psychology,* 1988, Vol. 20 (1), pp. 71–79.

Huddleston, Roz. Drama with elderly people. *British Journal of Occupational Therapy,* 1989, Vol. 52 (8), pp. 298–300.

Irwin, Eleanor C. Play, fantasy, and symbols: Drama with emotionally disturbed children. *American Journal of Psychotherapy,* 1977, Vol. 31 (3), pp. 426–436.

Irwin, Eleanor, C. Externalizing and improvising imagery through drama therapy: A psychoanalytic view. *Journal of Mental Imagery,* 1985, Vol. 9 (4), pp. 33–42.

Irwin, Eleanor C. On being and becoming a therapist. *The Arts in Psychotherapy,* 1986, Vol. 13, pp. 191–195.

Irwin, Eleanor C. Drama therapy in diagnosis and treatment. *Child Welfare,* 1986, Vol. 65 (4), pp. 347–357.

Irwin, Eleanor C. Drama: the play's the thing. *Elementary School Guidance and Counseling,* 1987, Vol. 21 (4), pp. 247–283.

Irwin, Eleanor C., Levy, Paul, & Shapiro, Marvin I. Assessment of drama therapy in a child guidance setting. *Group Psychotherapy and Psychodrama,* 1972, Vol. 25 (3), pp. 105–116.

Irwin, Eleanor C. & Rubin, Judith A. Art and drama interviews: Decoding symbolic messages. *The Arts in Psychotherapy,* Vol. 3, pp. 169–175.

Irwin, Eleanor C., Rubin, Judith A., & Shapiro, Marvin I. Art and drama: Partners in therapy. *American Journal of Psychotherapy,* 1975, Vol. 29 (1), pp. 107–116.

James, Miller & Johnson, David Read. Drama therapy in the treatment of combat-related post-traumatic stress disorder. *The Arts in Psychotherapy,* 1997, Vol. 23 (5), pp. 383–395.

Johnson, David Read. Effects of a theatre experience on hospitalized psychiatric patients. *The Arts in Psychotherapy,* 1980, Vol. 7, pp. 265–272.

Johnson, David Read. Principles and techniques of drama therapy. *The Arts in Psychotherapy,* 1982, Vol. 9 (2) 83–90.

Johnson, David Read. Developmental approaches in drama therapy. *The Arts In Psychotherapy,* 1982, Vol. 9 (3), pp. 183–189.

Johnson, David Read. Establishing the creative arts therapies as an independent profession. *The Arts in Psychotherapy,* 1984, Vol. 11, pp. 209–212.

Johnson, David Read. The field of drama therapy. *Journal of Mental Imagery,* 1984, Vol. 8 (1), pp. 105–109.

Johnson, David Read. Representation of the internal world in catatonic schizophrenia. *Psychiatry,* 1984, Vol. 47 (4), pp. 299–314.

Johnson, David Read. Expressive group psychotherapy with the elderly: A drama therapy approach. *International Journal of Group Psychotherapy,* 1985, Vol. 35 (1), pp. 109–127.

Johnson, David Read. The developmental method in drama therapy: Group treatment with the elderly. *The Arts in Psychotherapy,* 1986, Vol. 13 (1), pp. 17–33.

Johnson, David Read. The role of the creative arts therapies in the diagnosis and treatment of psychological trauma. *The Arts in Psychotherapy,* 1987, Vol. 14, pp. 7–13.

Johnson, David Read. The diagnostic role-playing test. *The Arts in Psychotherapy,* 1988, Vol. 15, pp. 23–36.

Johnson, David Read. The theory and technique of transformations in drama therapy. *The Arts in Psychotherapy,* 1991, Vol. 18 (4), pp. 285–300.

Johnson, David Read & Eicher, Virginia. The use of dramatic activities to facilitate dance therapy with adolescents. *The Arts in Psychotherapy,* 1990, Vol. 17, pp. 157–164.

Johnson, David Read, Forrester, Alice, Dintino, Cecelia, Miller, James, & Schnee, Greta. Towards a poor drama therapy. *The Arts in Psychotherapy,* 1996, Vol. 23 (4), pp. 293–306.

Johnson, David Read & Lubin, Hadar. Healing ceremonies. *Family Therapy Networker,* 1998, Vol. 22 (5), pp. 38–39, 64–67.

Johnson, David Read & Ryan, Edward R. Freedom and discovery within the therapeutic bond. *The Arts in Psychotherapy,* 1983, Vol. 10, pp. 3–7.

Johnston, Janis C., Healy, Kathryn N., & Tracey-Magid, Dolores. Drama and interpersonal problem solving: A dynamic interplay for adolescent groups. *Child Care Quarterly,* 1985, Vol. 14 (4), pp. 238–247.

Jones, Carrye B. Creative dramatics: A way to modify aggressive behavior. *Early Childhood Development and Care,* 1991, Vol. 73, pp. 43–52.

Kedem-Tahar, Efrat & Kellerman, Peter Felix. Psychodrama and drama therapy: A comparison. *The Arts in Psychotherapy,* 1996, Vol. 23 (1), pp. 27–36.

Kellerman, Peter Felix. Concretization in psychodrama with somatization disorder. *The Arts in Psychotherapy,* 1996, Vol. 23 (2), pp. 149–152.

Landy, Robert. Training the drama therapist–A four-part model. *The Arts in Psychotherapy,* 1982, Vol. 9, pp. 91–99.

Landy, Robert. The use of distancing in drama therapy. *The Arts in Psychotherapy,* 1983, Vol. 10 (3), pp. 175–185.

Landy, Robert. Conceptual and methodological issues of research in drama therapy. *The Arts in Psychotherapy,* 1984, Vol. 11 (2), pp. 89–100.

Landy, Robert. Puppets, dolls, objects, masks, and make-up. *Journal of Mental Imagery,* 1984, Vol. 8 (1), pp. 79–89.

Landy, Robert. The image of the mask: Implications for theatre and therapy. *Journal of Mental Imagery,* 1985, Vol. 9 (4), pp. 43–56.

Landy, Robert. The concept of role in drama therapy. *The Arts in Psychotherapy,* 1990, Vol. 17 (3), pp. 223–230.

Landy, Robert. The dramatic basis of role theory. *The Arts in Psychotherapy,* 1991, Vol. 18 (1), pp. 29–41.

Landy, Robert. A taxonomy of roles: A blueprint for the possibilities of being. *The Arts in Psychotherapy,* 1991, Vol. 18 (5), pp. 419–431.

Landy, Robert. The case of Hansel and Gretel. *The Arts in Psychotherapy,* 1992, Vol. 19 (4), 231–241.

Landy, Robert. The child, the dreamer, the artist and the fool: In search of understanding the meaning of expressive therapy. *The Arts in Psychotherapy,* 1993, Vol. 20 (5), pp. 359–370.

Landy, Robert. Three scenarios for the future of drama therapy. *The Arts in Psychotherapy,* 1994, Vol. 21 (3), pp. 179–184.

Landy, Robert. Isolation and collaboration in the creative arts therapies: The implications of crossing borders. *The Arts in Psychotherapy,* 1995, Vol. 22 (2), pp. 83–86.

Landy, Robert. Drama therapy–The state of the art. *The Arts in Psychotherapy,* 1997, Vol. 24 (1), pp. 5–15.

Landy, Robert. Drama therapy in Taiwan. *The Arts in Psychotherapy,* 1997, Vol. 24 (2), pp. 159–172.

Leveton, Eva. The use of doubling to counter resistance in family and individual treatment. *The Arts in Psychotherapy,* 1991, Vol. 18, pp. 241–249.

Lewis-Bernstein, Penny, Rubin, J., & Irwin, E. (1975). Play, parenting, and the arts. *Therapeutic process movement as integration.* Penny Lewis Bernstein, Ed. Columbia: ADTA.

Lewis-Bernstein, Penny. The union of the Gestalt concept of experiment and Jungian active imagination within a woman's mythic quest. *The Gestalt Journal,* 1980. Fall, Vol. 3 (2), pp. 36–46.

Lewis, Penny. (1984). Expressive arts assessment profile. *Theoretical Approaches in Dance-Movement Therapy,* Vol. II, Lewis. Dubuque: Kendall-Hunt Pub.

Lewis, Penny. The expressive therapies in the choreography of object relations. *The Arts in Psychotherapy,* 1987. Vol. 14 (4), pp. 321–332.

Lewis, Penny. (1987). The unconscious as choreographer: The use of tension flow rhythms in the transference relationship. *A.D.T.A. conference monograph.* Columbia: ADTA Pub.

Lewis, Penny. The transformative process within the imaginal realm. *The Arts in Psychotherapy,* 1988. Vol. 15, No. 3, Fall, pp. 309–316.

Lewis, Penny. (1988). The Dance between the conscious and unconscious: Transformation in the embodied imaginal realm. *The moving dialogue.* Columbia: ADTA Pub.

Lewis, Penny. (1988). The marriage of our art with science: The Kestenberg profile and the choreography of object relations. *Monograph 5,* Columbia: ADTA Pub.

Lewis, Penny. (1990). The Kestenberg movement profile in the psychotherapeutic process with borderline disorder. *The KMP: Its past, present application and future directions,* Lewis and Loman, Eds. Keene: Antioch University Pub.

Lewis, Penny. (1991). Creative transformation: The alchemy of healing, individuation and spiritual consciousness. *Shadow and light: Moving toward wholeness.* Columbia: ADTA Pub.

Lewis, Penny. The Creative Arts in Transference-Countertransference Relationships. *Arts in Psychotherapy,* 1992, Vol. 19, No. 5, pp. 317–324.

Lewis, Penny. Authentic sound movement and drama: An interview with Penny Lewis. Annie Geissinger interviewer. In *A Moving Journal.* Providence, 1996, Vol. 3 No. 1.

Lewis, Penny. (1996). Authentic sound, movement, and drama: An interactional approach. In Robbins, M. Ed. *Body oriented psychotherapy,* Vol. I. Somerville, MA: Inter. Scientific Community for Psycho-Corporal Therapies Pub.

Lewis, Penny. (1996). The Kestenberg movement profile. In Robbins, M. Ed. *Body oriented psychotherapy,* Vol. I. Somerville, MA: Inter. Scientific Community for Psycho-Corporal Therapies Pub.

Lewis, Penny. Multiculturalism and globalism in the arts in psychotherapy. In *The Arts in Psychotherapy,* 1997, Vol. 24, no. 2, pp. 123–128.

Lewis, Penny. Appreciating Diversity, Commonality, and the Transcendent. In *Arts in Psychotherapy,* 1997, Vol. 24, no. 3.

Lewis, Penny. Transpersonal arts psychotherapy: Toward an ecumenical worldview. In *The Arts in Psychotherapy,* 1997, Vol. 24, no. 3.

Lewis, Penny. (1999). Healing early child abuse: The application of the Kestenberg movement profile. In Amaghi, J., Loman, S., Lewis, P., et al. *The meaning of movement:*

Developmental and clinical perspectives as seen through the Kestenberg movement profile. Newark: Gordon & Breach Pub.

Lewis, Penny. (1999). The embodied feminine: Dance and drama therapy in women's holistic health. In Olshansky, E. *Woman's holistic health.* Gaithersburg, MD: Aspen Pub.

Lewis, Penny, & Brownell, Ann. (1990). The Kestenberg movement profile in assessment of vocalization. *The KMP: Its past, present application and future directions,* Lewis & Loman (Eds.). Keene: Antioch University Pub.

Lewis, Sheila. Creative drama in the treatment of emotionally disturbed children from six years of age to pre-adolescence. *Australian Occupational Therapy Journal,* 1974, Vol. 21 (1), pp. 8–22.

Linden, Saphira. Aiko: Drama therapy in the recovery process of a Japanese/Korean-American woman. *The Arts in Psychotherapy,* 1997, Vol. 24 (2), pp. 193–203.

Lippe, Wendy A. Stanislavski's affective memory as a therapeutic tool. *Journal of Group Psychotherapy, Psychodrama, and Sociometry,* 1992, Vol. 45 (3), pp. 102–111.

Lowenstein, L.F. The treatment of extreme shyness in maladjusted children by implosive, counselling and conditioning approaches. *Acta Psychaitria Scandanavia,* 1982, Vol. 66, pp. 173–189.

MacKay, Barbara. Uncovering buried roles through face painting and storytelling. *The Arts in Psychotherapy,* 1987, Vol. 14 (3), pp. 201–208.

MacKay, Barbara. Drama therapy with female victims of assault. *The Arts in Psychotherapy,* 1989, Vol. 16 (4), pp. 293–300.

MacKay, Barbara, Gold, Muriel, & Gold, Erica. A pilot study in drama therapy with adolescent girls who have been sexually abused. *The Arts in Psychotherapy,* 1987, Vol. 14 (1), pp. 77–84.

Mazor, Rickey. Drama therapy for the elderly in a day care center. *Hospital and Community Psychiatry,* 1982, Vol. 33 (7), pp. 577–579.

McClure, Bud A., Miller, Geri A., Russo, & Thomas, J. Conflict within a children's group: Suggestions for facilitating its expression and resolution strategies. *School Counselor,* 1992, Vol. 39 (4), pp. 268–272.

Moffett, Louis A., & Bruto, Liliana. Therapeutic theatre with personality disordered substance abusers: Characters in search of different characters. *The Arts in Psychotherapy,* 1990, Vol. 17 (4), pp. 339–348.

Morgan, Vicky, & Pearson, Simon. Social skills training in a junior high setting. *Educational Psychology in Practice,* 1994, Vol. 10 (2), pp. 99–103.

Mosely, Jenny. An evaluative account of the working of a dramatherapy peer support group within a comprehensive school. *Support for Learning,* 1991, Vol. 6 (4), pp. 154–164.

Newman, Geoffrey W. & Collie, Kelsey E. Drama therapy training and practice: An overview. *Journal of Mental Imagery,* 1984, Vol. 8 (1), pp. 119–125.

Noble, Grant, Egan, Paul, & McDowell, Sandra. Changing the self-concepts of seven-year-old deprived urban children by creative drama or videofeedback. *Social Behavior and Personality,* 1977, Vol. 5 (1), pp. 55–64.

O'Doherty, Susan. Play and drama therapy with the Down's Syndrome child. *The Arts in Psychotherapy,* 1989, Vol. 16 (3), pp. 171–178.

Pendzik, Susana. Drama therapy as a form of modern shamanism. *Journal of Transpersonal Psychology,* 1988, Vol. 20 (1), pp. 81–92.

Pendzik, Susana. The theatre stage and the sacred space: A comparison. *The Arts in Psychotherapy,* 1994, Vol. 21, (1), pp. 25–35.

Petitti, Gregory J. Video as an externalizing object in drama therapy. *The Arts in Psychotherapy,* 1989, Vol. 16 (2), pp. 121–125.

Petitti, Gregory J. The operational components of drama therapy. *Journal of Group*

Psychotherapy, Psychodrama, and Sociometry, 1992, Vol. 45 (1), pp. 40–44.

Phillips, Mary Ellen. Looking back: The use of drama and puppetry in occupational therapy during the 1920s and 1930s. *American Journal of Occupational Therapy,* 1996, Vol. 50 (3), pp. 229–233.

Rosenberg, Helane, S. & Pinciotti, Patricia. Imagery in creative drama. *Imagination, Cognition, and Personality,* 1983–1984, Vol. 3 (1), pp. 69–76.

Schnee, Greta. Drama therapy in the treatment of the homeless mentally ill: Treating interpersonal disengagement. *The Arts in Psychotherapy,* 1996, Vol. 23 (1), pp. 53–60.

Seligman, Zivya. Trauma and drama: A lesson from the concentration camp. *The Arts in Psychotherapy,* 1995, Vol. 22 (2), pp. 119–132.

Smith, Joan Dianne, Walsh, Richard T., & Richardson, Mary Ann. The clown club: A structured fantasy approach to group therapy with the latency-age child. *International Journal of Group Psychotherapy,* 1985, Vol. 35 (1), pp. 49–64.

Snow, Stephen. Fruit of the same tree: A response to Kedem-Tahar and Kellerman's comparison of psychodrama and drama therapy. *The Arts in Psychotherapy,* 1996, Vol. 23 (3), pp. 199–205.

Steinhardt, Lenore. Creating the autonomous image through puppet theatre and art therapy. *The Arts in Psychotherapy,* 1994, Vol. 21 (3), pp. 205–218.

Stevens, Sally. A multidisciplinary day unit for the treatment of substance abuse. *British Journal of Occupational Therapy,* 1984, Vol. 47 (4), pp. 117–120.

Stirtzinger, Ruth, & Robson, Bonnie. Videodrama and the observing ego. *Small Group Behavior,* 1985, Vol. 16 (4), pp. 539–548.

Strongylou, Nina, & Woodard, Victoria. Exploring images of the Greek-Cypriot woman through drama therapy. *The Arts in Psychotherapy,* 1993, Vol. 20 (2), pp. 161–165.

Stuart-Smith, Sue. Reaction to Hill End Adolescent Unit: Interviews with 20 ex-patients. *Journal of Adolescence,* 1994, Vol. 17 (5), pp. 483–489.

Trafford, Bill, & Perks, Alison. Drama therapy in a child and family psychiatry unit. *British Journal of Occupational Therapy,* 1987, Vol. 50 (3), pp. 94–96.

Valente, Lucilia, & Fontana, David. Drama therapist and client: An examination of good practice and outcomes. *The Arts in Psychotherapy,* 1994, Vol. 21 (1), pp. 3–10.

Vorenberg, Bonnie, L. Drama in a supportive environment: It's more than just a play. *Activities, Adaptation and Aging,* 1985, Vol. 7 (2), pp. 45–48.

Waite, Lesley M. Drama therapy in small groups with the developmentally disabled. *Social Work with Groups,* 1993, Vol. 16 (4), pp. 95–108.

Walsh, Richard T., Kosidoy, Myra, & Swanson, Lynn. Promoting social-emotional development through creative drama for students with special needs. *Canadian Journal of Community Mental Health,* 1991, Vol. 10 (1), pp. 153–166.

Walsh, Richard T., Richardson, Mary Ann, & Cardey, Raymond M. Structured fantasy approaches to children's group therapy. *Social Work with Groups,* 1991, Vol. 14 (1), pp. 57–73.

Walsh-Bowers, Richard T. A creative drama prevention program for easing early adolescent adjustment to school transitions. *Journal of Primary Prevention,* 1992, Vol. 13 (2), pp. 131–147.

Warger, Cynthia L. Creative drama for autistic adolescents: Expanding leisure and recreational options. *Journal of Child and Adolescent Psychotherapy,* 1984, Vol. 1 (1), pp. 15–19.

Warger, Cynthia L., & Kleman, Diana. Developing positive self-concepts in institutionalized children with severe behavior disorders. *Child Welfare,* 1986, Vol. 65 (2), pp. 165–176.

CREATIVE ARTS THERAPIES

Alvin, J. (1978). *Music Therapy.* London: Hutchinson.

Amaghi, J., Lewis, P., Loman, S., & Sossin, M. (1999). *The meaning of movement: Developmental and clinical perspectives as seen through the Kestenberg Movement Profile.* Newark, NJ: Gordon & Breach Pub.

The American Journal of Art Therapy. Washington, DC: AATA.

American Journal of Dance Therapy. Columbia, MD: ADTA.

Anderson, W. (Ed.). (1977). *Therapy and the arts: Tools of consciousness.* New York: Harper Colophon Books.

The Arts in Psychotherapy Journal. New York: Pergamon Press.

Bettelheim, B. (1976). *The uses of enchantment: The meaning and importance of fairytales.* New York: Random House.

Blanton, S. (1960). *The healing power of poetry.* New York: Crowel.

Brand, A.G. (1980). *Therapy in writing.* Lexington: Lexington Books.

Fryear, J., & Fleshman, B. (1981). *The arts in therapy,* Nelson-Hall.

Harrower, M. (1972). *The therapy of poetry.* Springfield: Charles C Thomas.

Hornyak, L.M., & Baker, E.K. (1989). *Experiential therapies for eating disorders.* New York: Guildford Press.

Hynes, A.M., & Hynes-Berry, M. (1986). *Biblio/poetry therapy: The interactive process.* Boulder, CO: Westview.

Johnson, D. (1999). *Essays on the creative arts therapies.* Springfield, IL: Charles C Thomas.

Journal of Music Therapy. Washington DC: NAMT.

Journal of Poetry Therapy. New York: Human Sciences Press.

Kaye, C. & Blee, T. (1996). *The arts in health care: A palette of possibilities.* London: Jessica Kingsley Publisher.

Kalff, D. (1981). *Sandplay: A psychotherapeutic approach to the psyche.* Boston: Sigo.

Krauss, D. & Fryear, J. (Eds.). (1983). *Phototherapy in mental health.* Springfield, IL: Charles C Thomas.

Leedy, J.J. (Ed.). (1969). *Poetry therapy: The use of poetry in the treatment of emotional disorders.* Philadelphia: JB Lippincott.

Leedy, J.J. (Ed.). (1973). *Poetry the healer.* Philadelphia: JB Lippincott.

Levine, S.K., & Levine, E.G. (1998). *Foundations of expressive arts therapies: Theoretical and clinical perspectives.* London: Jessica Kingsley Publisher.

Lewis-Bernstein, P., & Singer, D. (Eds.). (1982). *The choreography of object relations.* Keene: Antioch University.

Lewis, P. (1986). *Theoretical approaches in dance-movement therapy, Vol. I.* Dubuque, IA: W.C. Brown-Kendall/Hunt Pub.

Lewis, P. (1987). *Theoretical approaches in dance-movement therapy, Vol. II.* Dubuque, IA: W.C. Brown-Kendall/Hunt Pub Co.

Lewis, P., & Loman, S. (Eds.). (1990). *The Kestenberg Movement Profile: Its past, present and future applications.* Keene: Antioch University.

Liebmann, M. (Ed.). (1996). *Arts approaches to conflict.* London: Jessica Kingsley Publisher.

McNiff, S. (1998). *Art-based research.* London: Jessica Kingsley Publisher.

Morrison, M.R. (Ed.). (1987). *Poetry as therapy.* New York: Human Sciences Press.

Rogers, N. (1993). *The creative connection: Expressive arts as healing.* Palo Alto, CA: Science & Behavior Books.

Rubin, J. (1984). *The art of art therapy.* New York: Brunner/Mazel.

Rubin, R.J. (Ed.). (1978). *Bibliotherapy sourcebook.* Phoenix: Oryx Press.

Sandel, S., & Johnson, D. (1987). *Waiting at the gate: Creativity and hope in the nursing home.* New York: Haworth Press.

Ulman, E., & Dachinger, P. (Eds.). (1976). *Art therapy in theory and practice.* New York: Scholken.

Warren, B. (Ed.). (1994). *Using the creative arts in therapy: A practical introduction* (2nd Ed.). New York: Routledge.

Weiss, J.C. (1984). *Expressive therapy with elders and the disabled: Touching the heart of life.* Binghamton, NY: Haworth Press.

INDEX

H

I

J

K

L

M

T

U

V

W

Z